# Environmental Risk Management — A Desk Reference

Edited by
Eric B. Rothenberg
and Dean Jeffery Telego

RTM Communications, Inc.
Alexandria, Virginia
1991

## Publisher's Note

This Publication is crafted to provide accurate and authoritative information and technical data relative to the topics and materials covered. This book is sold with the understanding that this publisher is not engaged in providing legal or financial professional services. If such services are needed or required, a professional should be retained; most of our authors provide such professional services if you choose to contact them directly.

The publication of this book does not designate that the contents accurately reflect the views, beliefs or policies of RTM Communications, Inc.

---

First Edition

Published by
RTM Communications, Inc.
1020 N. Fairfax Street
Suite 201
Alexandria, VA 22314
U.S.A.
(703) 549-0977

Printed and bound in the United States of America

# Acknowledgements

The Managing Editors wish to thank and acknowledge all those who labored with them to produce this desk reference. As we recall those who helped us during the year of planning, assembly and production, we must start with the authors of each chapter, without whom the book would be impossible. Environmental risk management is an evolving field and not known completely. What is true and timely today can change by tomorrow — as we discovered in October as we prepared to go to press and Congress passed a new Clean Air Act and reauthorized Superfund. Our authors are our peers, our co-workers, our friends and our competition upon whom we rely for the best information available in their fields of expertise. Each of them has labored with patience and cooperated unceasingly to prepare their part of this book.

Then there are those whose names do not appear elsewhere: the assistants, secretaries, computer experts, typists, typesetters and graphic artists who worked with us or in spite of us. We want to thank by name Betsy Thraves, Dorothy Attwood, Stephanie Fischer, Elizabeth Fischer Jones, Ken Ratkiewicz, and Marie LeBlanc for their assistance and advice and attention to detail. Our special thanks goes to Laurie Gagnon who did cover art.

We especially want to acknowledge the work of our Executive Editor, Grammarian, Thesaurus, Dictionary, Word Processor, Proofreader, Punctuation Artist, Bookkeeper, Marketing Expert, Deadline Enforcer, Publicist and Patient Co-Worker. We are fortunate to have had all these skills in Tacy Cook Telego, APR, who worked long and hard to assure a book of which we could be proud to be Managing Editors.

Our profound thanks to these and others who ably assisted us throughout the year 1990.

## Table of Contents

# List of Tables and Figures, By Chapter

# Foreword

Environmental risk management has become an integral part of corporate life. Modern business transactions, from the corporate acquisition or financing to the initial public offering, increasingly turn on the balancing and apportionment of environmental liabilities. Business audits take cognizance not only of environmental infractions, but also conduct that may result in the imposition of criminal sanctions on officer and board members.

This volume provides a comprehensive guide to the environmental risk management process. It illuminates the web of environmental regulation confronting business in the United States and abroad. Seasoned environmental specialists provide protocols for evaluating and quantifying environmental risk across the full spectrum of regulatory programs. Perhaps most unique in these pages, is an account of insurance and risk management enterprises that are increasingly available to assist in the management and containment of environmental exposures identified by the risk manager.

*Environmental Risk Management* should make a fine companion for environmental professionals in the full range of legal, engineering and business disciplines. As a planning tool, the book tells us much about environmental liabilities in the 1990s.

*Environmental Risk Management* provides the tools for corporate management to measure, control, retain or transfer past and present pollution risk.

*John Quarles, Partner*
*Morgan, Lewis & Bockius and*
*Former Acting Administrator, Deputy Administrator and*
*General Counsel,*
*United States Environmental Protection Agency*

# Introduction to Environmental Risk Management

*Eric Rothenberg, Partner*
*Morgan, Lewis & Bockius*
*New York, New York*
*and Dean Jeffery Telego, President*
*Risk Management Technologies, Inc.*
*Washington, D.C.*

The expense of environmental pollution touches all segments of our society. State legislatures are spawning billion dollar environmental initiatives financed by taxpayers. Business and financial establishments struggle to quantify compliance and environmental remediation costs in pre-acquisition due diligence and ongoing management of investments.

The cost of pollution control has skyrocketed from $27 billion spent in 1972 to over $100 billion today. The private sector is expected to spend between $750 billion to $1 trillion over the next 50 years in cleaning up sites contaminated with hazardous substances.

The new Clean Air Act amendments, signed on November 15, 1990, are estimated to cost between $25 and $30 billion per year to implement. Those who are unable to absorb or transfer these staggering compliance costs will face expensive and time-consuming enforcement proceedings.

How can such enormous liabilities be prevented or contained? The solution lies in the comparatively new science of pro-active environmental risk management. Examples of integrated risk management can be found in a number of widely publicized experimental company and industry association programs: Dow Chemical's "Waste Reduction Always Pays," 3-M Corporation's "Pollution Prevention Pays," and the Chemical Manufacturers Association's "Responsible Care, Waste and Release Reduction Code of Management Practices" are good examples. These programs seek to instate pollution prevention and waste minimization management systems driven by top management and integrated (by means of incentives and penalties) throughout the corporate structure.

This book will, we hope, fill the need for a systematic, step-by-step reference on environmental risk management. We have brought together some of the finest and most creative environmental specialists available to provide the tools for five basic steps of environmental risk management--risk identification, risk evaluation, risk prevention and loss control, risk financing, and effective monitoring of developing risk trends.

In preparing this book, it has become clear to us that cost-containment is not the only factor that should motivate an environmental risk management program. First, and most obvious, civil and criminal enforcement of the environmental laws define norms of business conduct that must be observed at all levels of management. Second, either directly through the form of public hearings or indirectly through the Freedom of Information process, environmental laws increasingly give the public an important and sometimes decisive role in the process of environmental risk management which needs to be recognized, accepted and integrated into the planning process. Third, throughout the United States, the Pacific Rim and the European community, emerging initiatives require business to engage in meaningful conservation and protection of our natural resources. Foremost among these initiatives are those oriented towards environmental auditing, waste prevention, recycling and reuse.

The book is organized under the five rubrics of environmental risk management described above. The first 13 chapters set the stage for identifying environmental risk and working within the legal framework. The reader will be introduced to recent developments under the major U.S. and international regulatory programs including such topics as the new Clean Air Act amendments. Increasingly stringent limitations on the generation and handling of waste under the Resource Conservation and Recovery Act toxicity characteristic rule are discussed as well as land ban restrictions and corrective action requirements for existing waste management facilities. The Occupational Safety and Health Administration's proposed rule on process safety management of highly hazardous chemicals is succinctly evaluated from industry's perspective. Our Superfund chapter provides a guide to the recent case law, an overview of the enforcement and settlement process, a commentary on recent enforcement trends, and a tabularized reference to the ever-growing number of State Superfund programs.

The second section of our book is dedicated to the risk evaluation and quantification process. Here our authors discuss tools and techniques for quantifying potential environmental loss exposures and costs, not only in the area of environmental compliance, but also in the realm of auditing for effective waste reduction and minimization. We have also included a discussion of a proposed environmental due diligence protocol developed by the American Society for Testing and Materials (ASTM) for use in business and real estate transactions.

In section three, our authors describe how a program of risk prevention may be developed in order to effectively manage wastes, communicate environmental risk and plan against catastrophes. The authors in this section share their insights on such topics as pollution prevention, risk communication and crisis management.

The fourth section of our book focuses on risk financing techniques. This includes an evaluation of an array of risk transfer and risk retention methods for safeguarding corporate income and assets through commercial insurance, risk retention groups and captive insurance companies.

Our final section describes future environmental trends and issues in the 1990s. Here, we have focused on expansion of environmental regulation in the energy field, judicial trends and availability of insurance coverage for pollution claims, and recent development in both criminal and civil enforcement and environmental, occupational and safety health law.

As we go to press with *Environmental Risk Management — A Desk Reference*, we contemplate a revised and expanded text in the coming year. We hope that you, our readers, will assist us in this process by providing us with your thoughts, comments and criticism.

*Your Managing Editors,*
*Eric B. Rothenberg and*
*Dean Jeffery Telego*

**Introduction to Environmental**
**Risk Management**

4

**Environmental
Risk Management**

# II

# Clean Air Act — Separating the Old and New Versions

*Frank H. Hackmann\**
*Partner*
*Sonnenschein, Nath & Rosenthal*
*St. Louis, Missouri*

Before discussing the Clean Air Act Amendments of 1990, it is necessary to review briefly how the Nation came to where it was under the 1977 Clean Air Act. This is very important to understanding the difficulties faced by Congress, and the different points of view expressed on Clean Air Act reauthorization as the Clean Air Act Amendments of 1990 were debated and signed on November 15, 1990, and enacted into law.

While there was federal air pollution control legislation as far back as 1955, it is generally considered that the 1977 Clean Air Act had its genesis in the Clean Air Amendments of 1970 to the 1967 Clean Air Act. The most significant amendments to the Act since 1970 were the Clean Air Act Amendments of 1977 which added a number of significant new provisions to the Act. The amended Act remained essentially intact from 1977 until 1990. Because the most significant deadlines of the 1977 Amendments were written on a 5 to 10 year planning time frame, the time seemed ripe for another Clean Air Act revision well before 1990. Why this did not occur sooner, what we can expect from the new Amendments, and the critical issues yet remaining will be the focus of this chapter. The emphasis is principally on industrial stationary sources and regulated community control issues. Auto emissions and acid rain will be discussed briefly, but not in depth. Each title to the new amendments is summarized in Table One. The noted goal of the Clean Air Act still remains the attainment of the National Ambient Air Quality Standards.

* © 1990 by Frank H. Hackmann and RTM Communications, Inc.

## Executive Summary

### The Clean Air Act Amendments of 1990

A. Basic Structure of the Existing Act
1. Ambient Air Standards
2. Emission Inventories
3. Source Registrations
4. State Implementation Plans/Revisions
5. PSD/Nonattainment
6. Definition of "Nonattainment"
7. NSPS/NESHAP
8. Motor Vehicles
9. California car/U.S. Car
B. Key Features of the 1990 Amendments
1. Basic Structure Retained — 1970, 1977
2. Significant Revisions Added in 1990:
    a. Auto Related
       (1) Tighter Auto Standards
       (2) Longer Warranties
       (3) Reformulated Gasoline
       (4) Oxygenated Fuels
       (5) Fleet Requirements
       (6) "California Car"/"Rest of U.S. Car"
       (7) Federal Preemption on Auto Standards
    b. Smog/Ozone Related
       (1) 96 Urban Nonattainment Areas
       (2) Classified by Degree/Severity
       (3) Varying Compliance Dates
       (4) 3% per Year Actual VOC Reductions
       (5) Major Sources are 100 Tons per Year (or less)
       (6) Regulated Sources Down to 10 Tons per Year (L.A.)
       (7) Additional Rules for "High Smog" Areas
       (8) Special Rules for Smaller "Area" Sources
       (9) More Detailed Information and Modeling Required
    c. Air Toxics
       (1) Named Source Categories
       (2) About 200 Chemicals

## Environmental
## Risk Management

    (3) Coverage at 10 to 25 Tons/Year Emissions
    (4) Same Rules — Old/New Sources
    (5) Technology/Risk Driven
    (6) Maximum Available Control Technology
    (7) Case by Case Risk Assessment — Further Reductions
    (8) No Buffer Zones
d. Acid Rain Provisions
    (1) Ten Million Ton per Year $SO_2$ Reduction
    (2) Two Step Reduction
    (3) Electric Power Plant Specific
    (4) National $SO_2$ Cap
    (5) Emission Trading
    (6) Innovative Technology
    (7) NOx Reduction
e. Ozone Reduction
    (1) Phase out CFC, Chloroform, Methyl Chloride
    (2) Appliance Servicing/Disposal
f. Operating Permits
    (1) Nationwide Operating Permits
    (2) Includes All Covered "Sources/Stacks"
    (3) Detailed Application Forms
    (4) Signed by "Responsible Corporate Official"
    (5) Schedule of Compliance
    (6) Affected/Adjoining States Can Comment
g. Enforcement/Penalties
    (1) Broader Penalties/Felonies
    (2) "Field" Citations by EPA
    (3) Citizen Suits
    (4) Self Reporting/Compliance Certification
    (5) Recordkeeping and Permit Application
    (6) Emission/Technology Violations

**The Clean Air Act — Separating the Old and New Versions**

## Economic Impact Areas

| | |
|---|---|
| **Electricity Costs** | Scrubbers, Low Sulfur Coal, Coal Miners |
| **Auto Costs** | New Controls, Onboard Computers, On Board Vapor Controls, Warranties, Mileage Extensions |
| **Industry Costs** | Restrictions On New Growth, Expansion, Substitute Materials, Consumer Products, Technology Costs, Permit Costs, etc. |
| **Government Costs** | Costs To Implement and Comply, Growth Impacts, Program Costs |
| **Small Business Costs** | Large Impacts on Small Businesses Historically Unregulated by EPA |
| **State Initiatives** | States are Free to Adapt Tighter Standards on Everything Except Cars |

## Planning for the Future

- Assess Clean Air Act Impact on New Business Ventures, New Products, Raw Materials, etc.
- Anticipate Where Rules are Headed.  Participate in Rulemaking Process.
- Review Filings from Managerial, Technical, Legal Perspectives.

# Basic Goals of the 1977 Clean Air Act and the Clean Air Act Amendments of 1990

The Clean Air Act as amended in 1977,[1] represents what several courts have referred to as one of the most bafflingly complex pieces of legislation enacted by Congress.  Although the details of the 1977 Clean Air Act are admittedly extraordinarily complex, its basic purposes as stated by Congress are clear and straightforward and remain unchanged in the 1990 Amendments.  They bear repeating prior to any extensive discussion of the Clean Air Act Amendments of 1990.

**Environmental
Risk Management**

The purposes of the Act are:
- To protect and enhance the quality of the nation's air resources so as to promote the public health and welfare and the productive capacity of its population;
- To initiate and accelerate a national research and development program to achieve the prevention and control of air pollution;
- To provide technical and financial assistance to state and local governments in connection with the development and execution of the Air Pollution Prevention and Control Programs; and
- To encourage and assist the development and operation of regional air pollution control programs.

These are Congress' stated goals under the Clean Air Act. Without exception, they are sound public policy goals and represent, in the abstract at least, a workable blueprint to which various legislative proposals can be compared. As noted, the stated basic goals of the Clean Air Act Amendments of 1990 remain unchanged from those of the 1977 Act.

Congress also made certain findings in adopting the Clean Air Act Amendments of 1977. The findings still hold true today, and no significant change was made in the Clean Air Act Amendments of 1990. The key Congressional findings are:
- That the predominant part of the nation's population is located in its rapidly expanding metropolitan and other urban areas, which generally cross the boundary lines of local jurisdictions and often extend into two or more states;
- That the growth and the amount and complexity of air pollution brought about urbanization, industrial development, and an increasing use of motor vehicles, has resulted in mounting dangers to the public health and welfare including injury to agricultural crops and livestock, damage to and deterioration of property, and hazards to air and ground transportation;
- That the prevention and control of air pollution at its source is the primary responsibility of state and local government; and
- That federal financial assistance and leadership is essential for the development of cooperative federal, state, regional and local programs to prevent and control air pollution.

Translating these Congressional findings, and the basic goals of the Clean Air Act, into workable public policy that is capable of being read and understood by the regulated community, that meets the political requirements of the various affected constituencies, and that strikes an appropriate balance between the many competing interests affected by Clean Air Act legislation is a Herculean task. The difficulty of accomplishing this task is the principal reason that there was not a revision and reauthorization of the Clean Air Act between 1977 and 1990.

## Basic Regulatory Structure of the 1977 Act

The basic regulatory structure of the 1977 Clean Air Act was:

- Ambient air quality standards are set for specific types of pollutants based on scientific and technical criteria documents. Primary standards are designed to protect health with an adequate margin of safety. Secondary standards are designed to protect welfare. Prevention of significant deterioration increments apply in "Attainment" areas and are designed to protect clean air areas from excessive pollutant increases. Specific emission reduction requirements are set for "nonattainment areas" where current air quality fails to meet the ambient standards.
- All geographic areas of the United States are broadly classified on a pollutant by pollutant basis as "attainment" or "nonattainment". Any single geographic area may be in one classification for one pollutant and another classification for another pollutant. For example, attainment for nitrogen oxides, nonattainment for particulates, nonattainment for ozone, and so forth.
- States establish implementation plans. These state implementation plans (SIPs) are requirements for regulating existing sources, which, when combined with state and federal new source performance and/or review standards, will cause any necessary emission reductions and achievement of the ambient standards within the specified time frame.
- Certain types of sources, notably specific new stationary sources and automobiles, have minimum federal standards which must be met regardless of geographic location. Also,

there are provisions for federal control of hazardous air pollutants from new and existing sources. Cars made for the California market must meet tighter standards.

- Various types of permitting rules are set up. These permits, whether issued by the local, state or federal government, represent a key element in tracking future emissions and recording current status. Numerous recordkeeping requirements are also established. The 1977 Act did not require local agencies to issue operating permits, however.
- Various enforcement methods, including citizen suits and state and federal enforcement suits are authorized, as well as substantial civil and criminal penalties, including civil penalties designed to remove any economic advantage achieved by noncompliance.
- Provision is made for periodic revision of the state implementation plans as facts warrant. The Clean Air Act Amendments of 1977 required the submittal of revised SIPs with the hope that by 1987 most, if not all, areas of the United States could be brought into compliance with the ambient air quality standards.

It is this last step that brought things to where the Administration proposed its new Clean Air Act in July, 1989. Pollution control in the United States was becoming more and more a "zero sum game." The easy control methods and readily available offsets had been used. Further, the 1977 Act remained strongly biased toward a "command and control" type of approach in which the EPA specified what types of control should be applied to what type of source. This approach led to inflexible, and even absurd, results in some cases. The Act also made very significant regulatory distinctions between types of sources, particularly "old" sources versus "new" sources, and "major" sources versus "minor" sources. This tended to encourage two types of expansion — small additions to large existing facilities or new, smaller "tea kettle" plants. Finally, the Act imposed extraordinarily complex regulatory "pathways" in its permitting procedures for major projects. The 1977 act neither encouraged, nor provided for, any significant level of "market forces" to encourage air pollution trading in connection with new plant locations or existing plant expansions.

As would be expected with any law that imposes very large costs on some segments of the economy, and very small costs on others, as well as one that distributes the relative benefits disproportionately among affected interest groups, there was intense debate on these issues reflecting differing views of what type of world we wish to live in, how we will do so, and who will pay the costs and the burdens of our choices and efforts. This debate has continued to the present time.

## Critical Perspectives — Recent Developments

There are several different perspectives affecting federal developments under the Clean Air Act in the past year. Accordingly, we will discuss the legislative outlook, principally focusing on the Clean Air Act Amendments of 1990; the regulatory outlook, principally focusing on EPA's current and anticipated rulemaking; the judicial outlook, examining some recent cases; and the public policy outlook, focusing on key issues likely to remain with the principal interest groups active in the Clean Air Act process. Each of these different perspectives has played a significant role in the developments under the federal Clean Air Act to date, and will continue to do so in the years ahead.

In any event, it is important to understand the Clean Air Act Amendments of 1990 represent only a point in time. They do not represent a final resolution of the ongoing challenge of developing a consensus program on air pollution control that passed the Congress, been signed by the President, and enacted into law, and hopefully accepted by the public at large, the regulated community, and various other interest and advocacy groups.

## Federal Legislative Developments

### Clean Air Act Amendments of 1990

The 1990 Clean Air Act Amendments of 1990 contain a number of extraordinarily significant features effecting the regulated industrial community. Any attempt at summarizing necessarily risks simplification beyond what is desirable in any specific application. Therefore, the reader is urged to examine the exact text of the 1990 Act as

## Environmental Risk Management

enacted and applicable regulations, and to consult with competent professionals, before making any site specific decisions regarding operations potentially subject to the Act. The information summarized in this chapter is based on the 1990 Act as passed and enacted and signed by President George Bush on November 15, 1990. Other key versions of the new law include the Administration proposed Clean Air Act dated July 21, 1989, the Senate-passed Clean Air Act of April 3, 1990 and the House-passed Clean Air Act of May 23, 1990. Other sources of background information include materials released by the White House Office of Public Liaison, the *Congressional Record*, Congress, and related private and public sources active in the reauthorization process.

The Clean Air Act Amendments of 1990 build upon the 1977 Act framework. However, many provisions were added making the new Amendments more stringent and more complex in many ways, especially as applied to both stationary sources and smaller "area sources." Therefore, the principal focus of this Chapter will be on identifying what provisions of particular interest to the regulated community will be significantly more stringent under the Clean Air Act Amendments of 1990, what entirely new provisions have been added, and what provisions were otherwise altered in a significant way. Also, there are certain provisions in the new Amendments which make major policy shifts from the 1977 Act. These will also be summarized.

The Clean Air Act Amendments of 1990 as passed contains Eleven Titles:

| | |
|---|---|
| Title I | Provisions for Attainment and Maintenance of National Ambient Air Quality Standards |
| Title II | Provisions Related to Mobile Sources |
| Title III | Hazardous Air Pollutants ("Air Toxics") |
| Title IV | Acid Deposition Control |
| Title V | Permits |
| Title VI | Stratospheric Ozone Protection |
| Title VII | Provisions Related to Enforcement |
| Title VIII | Miscellaneous Provisions |
| Title IX | Clean Air Research |
| Title X | Disadvantaged Business Concerns |
| Title XI | Clean Air Employment Transition Assistance |

Each of the titles will be discussed separately.

### Title I — Nonattainment Provisions

Perhaps the most significant feature of the 1990 Act is the recognition that the 1977 Act, which divided all of the United States into areas treated as "attainment" or "nonattainment" for purposes of application of the various emission control strategies, failed to take into account the wide range of levels of nonattainment which could be present in specific geographic areas, especially on ozone. For example, the 1977 Act and regulations defined nonattainment for ozone as any area of the United States that experienced an average of more than one day of violation of the 1 hour ozone standard per year for the preceding 3 years. However, specific individual cities had days of nonattainment ranging from 5 or fewer to almost 150 in Los Angeles. Further, such classification could be based on a single monitoring location in a large geographic area which made the entire area "nonattainment" for the day in question. Clearly, public policy considerations and pragmatic recognition of the magnitude of the problem require different strategies in areas with such vastly different nonattainment situations. The 1990 Amendments address this by separating approximately 100 ozone nonattainment areas into five categories: extreme, severe, serious, moderate, and marginal. The Table below illustrates the specific basis on which each area will be classified, and the revised date by which the area will have to meet the ambient air standard for ozone. The "design value" is used by EPA to assess the "target" ozone concentration for future SIP Planning. Generally, it represents the fourth highest observed data point in the last four years, since one "exceedance" per year is allowed before an area is considered "nonattainment".

## Table 1

### Ozone Nonattainment Area Classification Summary
### Based on Ozone "Design Value"
### taken from Ambient Air Monitoring

TIME EXTENSION AFTER ENACTMENT

| | Type Of Area | To Meet Ambient Standard |
|---|---|---|
| "Design Value" Ozone | | |
| | Attainment Areas | None |
| | Nonattainment Areas | .12PPM or below |
| Marginal | 3 years | .121 up to .138PPM |
| (39 metropolitan areas) | | |
| Moderate | 6 years | .138 up to .160PPM |
| (32 metropolitan areas) | | |
| Serious | 9 years | .160 up to .180PPM |
| (16 metropolitan areas) | | |
| Severe | 17 years for 2 | .180 up 50 .280PPM |
| (8 metropolitan areas) | areas, 15 for others | |
| Extreme | 20 years | .280 and above |
| (Los Angeles) | | |

All Attainment Areas, the rest of United States, must remain in compliance in the future and maintain ozone levels at or below .12PPM. Non attainment areas with design values within 5% of the next "worst" or "better" category may seek to be "reclassified" within 90 days of the initial classification of all areas by the Administrator.

---

Carbon monoxide nonattainment areas are broken into two categories. Moderate areas, 9.1-16A, PPM design value have until 1995 to comply. Serious areas, 16.5 and above, PPM design values have until the year 2000.

A second major area of the nonattainment provisions, particularly for ozone, and to a lesser extent for carbon monoxide emissions, is the provision for firmly keying all future conduct subject to the Act to existing baseline emissions. While this concept was present in the 1977 Act, the 1990 Amendments make it far more explicit and generally much less susceptible to state or local agency flexibility and implementation. States will be given approximately three years to develop updated and revised emissions inventories and new state implementation plans. Basically, all existing actual emissions during calendar year 1990 will form the future baseline for emissions subject to the Act, including most importantly, for most stationary sources, volatile organic compound (VOC) emissions. The baseline emissions for the Acid Rain provisions, aimed principally at electric utilities, are beyond the scope of this chapter. Essentially, 1990 actual utility $SO_2$ emissions are used on a plant by plant basis to determine the emission baseline, with certain adjustments allowed. Computations of initial allowables will generally be based on 1985-1987 emissions multiplied by a 2.5 LB/MMBTU $SO_2$ emission, unless adjusted.

In addition to establishing a new baseline, the ozone nonattainment provisions related to volatile organic compound control also establish a requirement that, in the more heavily polluted areas, there be continued future reductions from the overall baseline emission. In general, this reduction in actual emissions is expected to be three percent per year on an annual average, after the initial 15 percent (for all but marginal areas) over the next six years. Clearly, some sources will be subject to greater reductions because other sources will not be able to reduce three percent or more per year. Further, many items will not "count" toward this three percent reduction. In essence, the three percent overall reduction will be in **addition** to other requirements of the Act, such as Reasonably Available Control Technology (RACT), gasoline vapor pressure reduction, Stage II vapor recovery and auto emission reductions. Thus the three percent overall reduction will be on a "base" much smaller than all emission sources in an area. Required offset notices will vary by area, from 1.20 to 1.50 in serious, severe and extreme areas.

A certain level of flexibility will be given to state and local air pollution control agencies to require additional reductions either from subclasses of stationary sources or by implementation of additional transportation control related measures. States will be required to furnish far more detailed emission inventories by 1993, but, as a practical matter, will probably commence the effort much sooner as part of the SIP update process and the process to issue the newly required operating permits.

As noted, the Act will mandate the use of Reasonably Available Control Technology, adherence to any control technology guidelines, and require further reductions on top of those standards equal to an approximate average of three percent actual reductions per year in total emissions for most nonattainment areas until the area meets the standard. It cannot be overemphasized that the focus will be almost exclusively on actual emissions rather than emission potential with respect to these reductions. Therefore, manufacturing operations that are not currently operating at their normal capacity levels may find themselves significantly impeded in forward production planning due to the selection of a nonrepresentative baseline. While there is some limited ability to deal with this under the Act, it will be more difficult than in the past to obtain production capacity increases, or changes with accompanying emission increases, in nonattainment areas regardless of their willingness to invest in pollution control equipment. This will be especially true for sources which already employ relatively efficient control technologies.

### Title II — Mobile Sources

The new Amendments make a number of significant changes in mobile source requirements. The major changes are the extensions of the warranty on major emission devices, the requirement for future "on board computers" to diagnose emission control system malfunctions, new (and much tighter) standards for tailpipe emissions on cars, trucks and buses.

The new car (and light truck and van) tailpipe standards will ultimately require a 35 percent reduction in hydrocarbons and a 60 percent reduction in nitrogen oxides on a phased in schedule by 1998, with 40 percent of the new vehicles to achieve the standards in 1994.

EPA may require an additional 50 percent emission cut after 2003 based on a study it will complete in the mid-1990's. The Amendments continue federal preemption of new car emission standards by allowing only two types of cars — the "California" car and the "rest of U.S. car". States may elect to require the "California" car in their own states to reduce emissions, but testing and certification must be in conformance with California practice. As in the past, the "California" car will have much tighter standards. Further, the California Air Resources Board is already working on a new integrated system of more closely matching "clean fuels and low emissions vehicles" as an overall design objective. If ultimately adopted, these standards will be tighter than those in the amendments and may be applied by other states in the future.

The new Amendments also mandate reformulated gasoline by 1995 in the nine cities with the worst ozone problems. The reformulated gasoline would be designed to achieve 15 percent lower VOC emissions by 1995, along with additional reductions by the year 2000. These standards would also require the use of more oxygenated fuels, lower benzene levels and reduced aromatic levels. A target oxygen level of 2.7 percent is set for 41 cities with carbon monoxide starting in 1992.

Complex certification and emission credits among fuel types in designated geographic areas will be established as will EPA fuel certification programs.

Standards will also be set for car fleets and heavy duty fleets. The fleet program applies in all severe, serious and extreme nonattainment areas. A *fleet* is 10 or more vehicles capable of being centrally fueled but excludes vehicles normally garaged nightly at personal residences.

### Title III — Hazardous Air Pollutants ("Air Toxics")

The next major change the 1990 Act will present versus the 1977 Act is the regulation of "toxic air emissions" from industrial sources.[2] This program is a significant departure from EPA's historical effort of setting such air pollutant standards on a case-by-case basis for specific air pollutants. Instead of the case-by-case designation of a hazardous air pollutant followed by the designation of a particular air emission control technology, the 1990 Amendments list 189 specific chemicals (and their isomers/mixtures/compounds) which are presumptively considered "toxic" and therefore subject to specific regulation under the Act. (The final version of the 1990 Act signed into law deleted ammonia and hydrogen sulfide). These are listed in Table 2.

## Table 2

| Cas No. | Chemical Name | Cas No. | Chemical Name |
|---|---|---|---|
| 75070 | Acetaldehyde | 334883 | Diazomethane |
| 60355 | Acetamide | 132649 | Dibenzofurens |
| 75058 | Acetonitrile | 96128 | 1,2-Dibromo-3-chloropropane |
| 98862 | Acetophenone | 84742 | Dibutylphthalate |
| 539632 | Acetylaminofluorine | 106467 | 1,4-Dichlorobenzene (p) |
| 107028 | Acrolein | 91941 | 3,3-Dichlorobebzidene |
| 79061 | Acrylamide | 111444 | Dichloroethyl ether (Bis (2- |
| 79107 | Acrylic Acid | | chloroethyl) ether) |
| 107131 | Acrylonitrile | 542756 | 1,3-Dichloropropene |
| 107051 | Allyl chloride | 62737 | Dichlorvos |
| 926714 | Aminobiphenyl | 111422 | Diethanolamine |
| 7664417 | Ammonia (deleted in final bill) | 121697 | N,N-Diethyl aniline (N, N- |
| 62533 | Aniline | | Dimethylaniline) |
| 90040 | o-Anisidine | 64675 | Diethyl sulfate |
| 1332214 | Asbestos | 119904 | 3,3'-Dimethoxybenzidine |
| 71432 | Benzene(including benzene from gas-oline) | 60117 | Dimethyl aminoazobenzene |
| | | 119937 | 3,3'-Dimethyl benzidine |
| 92875 | Benzidine | 79447 | Dimethyl carbamoyl chloride |
| 98077 | Benzotrichloride | 68122 | Dimethyl formamide |
| 100447 | Benzyl chloride | 57147 | 1,1-Dimethyl hydrazine |
| 92524 | Biphenyl | 131113 | Dimethyl phthalate |
| 117817 | Bis (2-ethylhexyl) phthalate (DEHP) | 77781 | Dimethyl sulfate |
| 542881 | Bis (chloromethyl) ether | 534521 | 4,6-Dinitro-o-cresol, and salts |
| 75252 | Bromoform | 51285 | 2,4-Dinitrophenol |
| 106990 | 1,3-Butadiene | 121142 | 2,4-Dinotrotoluene |
| 156627 | Calcium cyanamide | 123911 | 1,4-Dioxane (1, 4- |
| 105602 | Caprolactam | | Diethyleneoxide) |
| 133062 | Captan | 122667 | 1,2-Diphenylhydrazine |
| 63252 | Carbaryl | 106898 | Epichlorohydrin (1-Chloro-2,3- |
| 75150 | Carbon disulfide | | epoxypropane) |
| 56235 | Carbon tetrachloride | 106887 | 1,2-Epoxybutane |
| 463581 | Carbonyl sulfide | 140885 | Ethyl acrylate |
| 120809 | Catechol | 100414 | Ethyl benzene |
| 133904 | Chloramben | 51796 | Ethyl carbamate (Urethane) |
| 57749 | Chlordane | 75003 | Ethyl chloride (Chloroethane) |
| 7782505 | Chlorine | 106934 | Ethylene dibromide (Dibromoe-thane) |
| 79118 | Chloroacetic acid | | |
| 532274 | 2-Chloroacetophenone | 107062 | Ethylene dichloride (1,2- |
| 108907 | Chlorobenzene | | Dichloroethane) |
| 510156 | Chlorobenzilite | 107211 | Ethylene glycol |
| 67663 | Chloroform | 151564 | Ethylene imine (Aziridine) |
| 107302 | Chloromethyl methyl ether | 75218 | Ethylene oxide |
| 126998 | Chloroprene | 96457 | Ethylene thiourea |
| 1319773 | Cresols/Cresylic acid (isomers and mixture) | 75343 | Ethylidene dichloride (1,1-Dichloroethane) |
| 95487 | Cresols/Cresylic acid (isomers and mixture) | 50000 | Formaldehyde |
| | | 76448 | Heptachlor |
| 108394 | Cresols/Cresylic acid (isomers and mixture) | 118741 | Hexachlorobenzene |
| | | 87683 | Hexachlorobutadiene |
| 106445 | Cresols/Cresylic acid (isomers and mixture) | 77474 | Hexachlorocyclopentadiene |
| | | 67721 | Hexachloroethane |
| 98828 | Cumene | 822060 | Hexamethylene-1,6-diisocyanate |
| 94757 | 2,4-D, salts and esters | 680319 | Hexamethylphosphoramide |
| 3547044 | DDE | 110543 | Hexane |

**The Clean Air Act — Separating the Old and New Versions**

## Table 2 (cont.)

| Cas No. | Chemical Name | Cas No. | Chemical Name |
|---------|---------------|---------|---------------|
| 302012 | Hydrazine | 78875 | Propylene dichloride (1,2- |
| 7647010 | Hydrochloric acid | | Dichloropropane) |
| 7664393 | Hydrogen fluoride (Hydrofluoric | 75569 | Propylene oxide |
| | acid) | 75558 | 1,2-Propylenimine (2-Methyl |
| 7783064 | Hydrogen sulfide (deleted in final | | aziridine) |
| | bill) | 91255 | Quinoline |
| 123319 | Hydroquinone | 106514 | Quinone |
| 78591 | Isophorone | 100425 | Styrene |
| 58899 | Lindane (all isomers) | 96093 | Styrene oxide |
| 108316 | Maleic anhydride | 1746016 | 2,3,7,8-Tetrachlorodibenzo-p- |
| 67561 | Menthanol | | dioxin |
| 72435 | Methoxychlor | 79345 | 1,1,2,2-Tetrachloroethane |
| 74839 | Methyl bromide (Bromomethane) | 127184 | Tetrachloroethylene (Perchloroe- |
| 74873 | Methyl chloride (Chloromethane) | | thylene) |
| 71556 | Methyl chloroform (1,1,1- | 7550450 | Titanium tetrachloride |
| | Trichloroethane) | 108883 | Toluene |
| 78933 | Methyl ethyl ketone (2-Butanone) | 95807 | 2,4-Toluene diamine |
| 60344 | Methyl Hydrazine | 584849 | 2,4-Toluene diisocyanate |
| 74884 | Methyl iodide (Iodomethane) | 95534 | o-Toluidine |
| 108101 | Methyl isobutyl ketone (Hexone) | 8001352 | Toxaphene (chlorinated cam- |
| 624839 | Methyl isocyanate | | phene) |
| 80626 | Methyl methacrylate | 120821 | 1,2,4-Trichlorobenzene |
| 1634044 | Methyl tert butyl ether | 79005 | 1,1,2-Trichloroethane |
| 101144 | 4,4-Methylene chloride bis (2- | 79016 | Trichloroethylene |
| | chloroaniline) | 95954 | 2,4,5-Trichlorophenol |
| 75092 | Methylene chloride (Dichlorome- | 88062 | 2,4,6-Trichlorophenol |
| | thane) | 121448 | Triethylamine |
| 101688 | Methylene diphenyl diisocyanate | 1582098 | Trifluralin |
| | (MDI) | 540841 | 2,2,4-Trimethylpentane |
| 101779 | 4,4'-Methylenedianiline | 108054 | Vinyl Acetate |
| 91203 | Naphthalene | 593602 | Vinyl bromide |
| 98953 | Nitrobenzene | 75014 | Vinyl chloride |
| 92933 | 4-Nitrobiphenyl | 75354 | Vinylidene chloride (1,1- |
| 100027 | 4-Nitrophenol | | Dichloroethylene) |
| 79469 | 2-Nitropropane | 1330207 | Xylenes (isomers and mixture) |
| 684935 | N-Nitroso-N-methylurea | 95476 | Xylenes (isomers and mixture) |
| 62759 | N-Nitrosodimethylamine | 108383 | Xylenes (isomers and mixture) |
| 59892 | N-Nitrosomorpholine | 106423 | Xylenes (isomers and mixture) |
| 56382 | Parathion | 0 | Antimony Compounds |
| 82688 | Pentachloronitrobenzene (Quintoben- | 0 | Arsenic Compounds (inorganic |
| | zene) | | including arsine) |
| 87865 | Pentachlorophenol | 0 | Beryllium Compounds |
| 108952 | Phenol | 0 | Cadmium Compounds |
| 106503 | p-Phenylenediamine | 0 | Chromium Compounds |
| 75445 | Phosgene | 0 | Cobalt Compounds |
| 7803512 | Phosphine | 0 | Coke Oven Emissions |
| 7723140 | Phosphorus | 0 | Cyanide Compounds*FN+X CN |
| 85449 | Phthalic anhydride | | where X = H or any other group |
| 1336363 | Polychlorinated biphenylis (Aroclors) | | where a formal dissociation may |
| 1120714 | 1,3-Propane sultone | | occur. For example KCN or CA |
| 57578 | beta-Propiolactone | | (CN).+ |
| 123386 | Propionaldehyde | | |
| 114261 | Propoxur (Baygon) | | |

**Table 2 (cont.)**

| Cas No. | Chemical Name | Cas No. | Chemical Name |
|---|---|---|---|
| 0 | Glycol ethers*FN+includes mono- and di- ethers of ethylene glycol, diethylene gylcol, and triethylene glycol R-(OCH$_2$CH$_2$)n-OR' where n = 1, 2, or 3 R = alkyl or aryl groups R' = R, H, or groups which, when removed, yield glycol ethers with the structure: R -(O CH$_2$ CH)nOH Polymers are excluded from the glycol category plus | 0 | Mineral fibers*FN+includes glass microfibers, glass wool fibers, and slag wool fibers, each characterized as "respirable" (fiber diameter less than 3.5 micrometers) and possessing an aspect ratio (fiber length divided by fiber diameter) greater than 3. plus |
| | | 0 | Nickel Compounds |
| | | 0 | Polycylic Organic Matter*FN+includes organic compounds with more than one benzene ring, and which have a boiling point greater than or equal to 100 C plus |
| 0 | Lead Compounds | | |
| 0 | Manganese Compounds | | |
| 0 | Mercury Compounds | 0 | Radionuclides (including radon)*FN+a type of atom which spontaneously undergoes radioactive decay plus |
| | | 0 | Selenium Compounds |

NOTE:    For all listings above which contain the word "compounds" and for glycol ethers, the following applies: Unless otherwise specified, these listings are defined as including any unique chemical substance that contains the named chemical (i.e., antimony, arsenic, etc.) as part of that chemical's infrastructure.

---

The EPA will have a specific time frame in which to select specific classes and categories of sources which represent declining percentages of these aggregate emissions approximately 250 source categories will be subject to regulation. Provisions exist for EPA to revise the list.

The standards will apply to sources in the various categories and generally require the use of Maximum Available Control Technology (MACT), which is generally the best available control technology, taking cost into account. Standards are to be set for approximately 40 categories within two years and set for all 250 source categories within 10 years. Existing sources must meet MACT within three years after promulgation, with a possible one year extension. The actual goal will be to reduce such emissions by about 90 percent and to establish acceptable risk levels (residual and risk levels), including cancer risk levels, for affected populations. EPA is also to consider impacts on the environment as well as human health effects in listing pollutants and setting standards.

The basic concept will be that a single technology should be used by both new and existing sources, although differences may be permitted in specific cases, especially on the resulting control levels. The standard will permit the use of substitute materials, changes in work practices or formulations, and other related changes as a substitute for end of pipe control so long as equivalent reductions are achieved. The overall umbrella goals are designed to achieve substantial reductions in air toxic emissions within the next 10 years. Sources making voluntary reductions of 90 percent from the 1987 emission levels reserve a six year extension on the MACT compliance date.

For covered sources in general, the 1990 Amendments recognize that in certain cases, the use of MACT may not provide adequate "residual risk" protection. If, after installing MACT, an unacceptable residual risk remains, EPA must tighten the standards eight years after the initial MACT promulgations. The appropriate risk standard expected to be used is an additional 1 in 1,000,000 risk of cancer for the person in the general population theoretically exposed at or beyond the fence line of a facility and "an ample margin of safety to protect public health, unless a more stringent standard is necessary to protect the environment." The Amendments recognize that such a standard may mandate the closure of certain industrial facilities. Coke ovens may, under certain conditions, receive extensions of the "residual risk" standard until the year 2020. Maximum Available Control Technology will generally represent what is being achieved by the 10 percent best controlling sources in a particular source category.

In addition to control on the traditional types of stationary sources, the "Air Toxics" provisions of the 1990 Amendments will impact "area source categories" such as dry cleaners, gas stations, woodstoves, small combustion units, etc. EPA can regulate such sources with MACT control. EPA must also list sufficient source categories to assure that 90 percent of the emissions of the 30 most serious area source provisions are regulated.

EPA must also propose a national urban air toxics strategy to reduce cancer risks associated with urban air toxics by 75 percent. The study is due five years after enactment of the Amendments with progress reports by EPA due in eight and ten year intervals.

In addition to these provisions, a number of items dealing with accidental releases have been added. They set forth a risk manage-

accidental releases have been added. They set forth a risk management approach and general duty for an owner or operator handling "extremely hazardous substances" to operate safely. EPA is to publish a list of about 100 such chemicals, two years or less from enactment. The Amendments list 20 such "extremely hazardous substances" specifically. The list is printed in Table 3.

### Table 3
### "Extremely Hazardous Substances
### — Accidental Release Protection"

| | |
|---|---|
| Chlorine | Anhydrous Ammonia |
| Methyl Chloride | Ethylene Oxide |
| Vinyl Chloride | Methyl Isocyanate |
| Hydrogen Cyanide | Ammonia |
| Hydrogen Sulfide | Toluene Diisocyanate |
| Phosgene | Bromine |
| Anhydrous Hydrogen Chloride | Hydrogen Fluoride |
| Anhydrous Sulfur Dioxide | Sulfur Trioxide |

The administrator shall promulgate a list of 100 substances not later than 24 months after enactment of the Clean Air Act Amendments of 1990. The substances listed above shall be included. The administrator shall use, but is not limited to, the list of extremely hazardous substances published under SARA Title III. The initial list shall include at least 100 substances. Regulations establishing the list shall include an explanation of the basis for establishing the list. The test may be revised from time to time. It is expected that the complete list will come from the SARA Title III list.

Operating permits will be required for covered sources emitting ten tons per year of any one listed chemical or twenty-five tons of total tested chemicals. These permits may be issued by local authorities under the general air/permits program of the 1990 Act. A more detailed summary of the new operating permit program is in Appendix A.

Utility emissions of air toxics would be regulated only if EPA studies the issue and finds regulation is warranted. Finally, new standards will be set for municipal hospital, commercial and industrial incinerators.

### Title IV — Acid Deposition Control

Another major item of interest to industrial sources in the 1990 Clean Air Act are the provisions related to Acid Rain controls, aimed at reducing Sulfur Dioxide ($SO_2$) and Nitrogen Dioxide ($NO_x$) emissions. The major impact on other industry will be two-fold. Certain sources that generate large amounts of on-site power or otherwise burn large amounts of fuel may be potentially subject in their own right to state efforts to reduce $SO_2$ and $NO_x$ as part of state programs to achieve overall $SO_2$ reductions. Secondly, stationary source operations typically are significant users of electricity. Any increase in electrical generating costs for the electric utilities will be passed on to their customer base, including their industrial customers. Under the 1990 Amendments most of the economic impact of the acid rain controls will fall on Midwestern coal fired utilities and their customers, although there will be a significant impact on localized areas elsewhere in the country. Also, there are provisions for limited nationwide cost sharing, under Title IX, of the adverse impact of the acid rain control requirements on some high sulfur coal miners who experience job losses. There is no comparable provisions to share costs among utilities. The provisions related to "emission trading" and "emission allowances" between utilities, as well as the specific mechanics, are beyond the scope of this chapter. Overall, however, the 1990 Act will require a 10,000,000 ton $SO_2$ reduction and a 2,000,000 ton reduction on $NO_x$ over the next ten years. The Act also established an "emission cap" such that once the reduction is achieved, total emissions will not increase. As noted, the general baseline for reductions is calendar 1980, unless adjusted.

The $SO_2$ emissions by utilities must be cut 3,500,000 tons per year by 1995 and an additional 5,400,000 tons per year by the year 2000. The 1995 deadline may be extended two years for utilities ordering scrubbers that allow burning high sulfur coal. The year 2000 deadline may be extended to 2004 if alternate clean coal technology is installed.

### Title V — Air Operating Permits

A second major provision of the new Act when compared to the 1977 Act is the significantly broadened requirements for obtaining operating permits for affected sources. While a permitting provision has always been present in the Clean Air Act, it was aimed at certain types of large construction or modification projects or projects requiring a "Prevention of Significant Deterioration" review. Operating permits were implemented on an as needed basis by the state or local agency. It was not mandated by the EPA for all geographic areas or for nonattainment areas. Historically, permits for existing sources were not required from the Federal EPA, except for certain types of registration related to the hazardous air pollutant emission program, PSD permits, or permits related to construction or modification of major sources. However, the new Act will require detailed applications and permits, similar to the National Pollutant Discharge Elimination Systems (NPDES) required under the Clean Water Act, for all covered sources. In extreme nonattainment areas (Los Angeles), covered sources can be as small as those emitting 10 tons a year of volatile organic compounds. In serious and severe areas it will be 25 tons. In marginal and moderate areas, it will be 50 tons per year. Attainment areas will remain at 100 tons per year. This size cutoff will encompass a number of very small sources not currently subject to significant restrictions under the 1977 Act. In addition to this provision of the permit program, there will also be requirements that there be no construction or modifications of sources requiring permits until EPA, or a delegated authority, has issued any required permits. EPA will have a veto authority over state issued permits. It is likely that the permitting process will be relatively complex and may be slow because of the huge number of applications (estimated 50,000 plus sources will require permits), which will need to be processed, although provisions are made to try and phase in the issuance of permits over a three year time frame. Provisions for validating data on permit applications may, in some cases, necessitate extremely expensive source testing or mathematical modeling to qualify emissions from more complex source facilities. The modeling processes available, such as the Urban Airshed Photochemical Grid Model, will allow much closer correlations to be made between emissions and Ambient Air Concentrations at specific geographic locations. It is hoped this will enable the EPA to more accurately target further controls to positive impacts in the desired portion of the nonattainment area. Provisions are included for permit application fees as well.

With regard to guidance for the typical stationary source owner/ operator, the most important factor is to know the emissions and the emission sources as accurately as possible. The importance of accurate baseline data cannot be overemphasized. The initial baseline selected will drive the process for determining future allowable increases (if any) and required reductions. It will also affect capacity and product planning, as well as product formulations.

In general, it is recommended that the appropriate Air Pollution Agency with principal authority over a specific facility be contacted to determine what emission inventory numbers are now being used for the operation. This contact should also verify the regulations that affect the sources in question. While historically it has been possible to change and update these emission numbers if errors are made, this will probably become much more difficult in the future. Accordingly, the prompt verification of existing baseline emission inventory data is extremely critical. Second, all key chemicals or materials which may be subject to regulation under the 1990 Act, whether as criteria pollutants, hazardous materials, toxic air pollutants, or otherwise, should be identified in an overall summary of what materials are used in the facility, where the air emissions associated with their use go, and other related factors, such as control equipment, control efficiency, etc. Careful attention should also be paid to making the best estimates possible of any fugitive emissions which may occur. Once all this information is assembled it will be possible to make some initial estimates of to what extent, if any, a particular source will be subject to the various specific control requirements of the Act as a function of the attainment or nonattainment level in the jurisdiction where the source or sources are located. The EPA AP-42 Air Pollutant Emission Factors can be used as an initial guide in making emission estimates.

The 1990 Amendments require that permit applications be signed by responsible corporate officials. There are significant potential penalties (both civil and criminal) for errors in submitted data or failure to meet permit terms and conditions. Therefore, it is recommended that such applications and related correspondence be carefully reviewed by managerial, technical and legal representatives before being filed with the permit-issuing authority. This will reduce the potential for unexpected or unanticipated difficulties with the final permit.

In summary terms, the 1990 Amendments will add to the existing Act the codification of the reasonable extra efforts program for selected nonattainment areas, will require additional technology to be used, will set new standards for different industries, will establish percent reductions against actual baseline emissions as a target for future reductions, will make future growth from existing sources or the construction of new sources much more problematic, and will, in large measure, create a situation where the newly issued operating permits will effectively replace the SIP itself as the principle document governing the sources emissions and defining its technology level. Finally, the 1990 Amendments clearly state that state or local agencies are free to improve.

## Title VI — Stratospheric Ozone Protection

As noted previously, the Amendments provide for the essential phase out of CFC's, halons, carbon tetrachlorides, and methyl chloroform on a designated phase out schedule the most immediate imports will be requirements recapture, recycling and safe disposal commencing on a phase in schedule on January 1, 1992 and prohibitions on atmospheric venting during appliance servicing, repair and disposal beginning July 1, 1992, and a requirement to recycle emissions from automobile air conditioner servicing by January 1, 1992. Other requirements include labeling and a variety of other specific methods, along with studies on sources and control options for methane emissions, including methane emissions associated with agriculture.

## Title VII — Provisions Related to Enforcement

The language of the 1990 Amendments contains very significant enforcement revisions including increased civil penalties, provisions for EPA issued penalties, including Field Citations and criminal enforcement provisions that are of particular concern to the regulated community. Enforcement sanctions exist not only for the substantive emission limit and technology standards, but also potentially for various errors or omissions in the permit application itself and the various standard conditions in any issued permits. Citizen suit and direct Federal enforcement authority is broadened.

The 1990 Amendments contain significantly stronger civil and criminal penalties than did the 1977 Act. The new Amendments significantly broaden the number and type of events for which such penalties may be asserted as well. Finally, the 1990 Act gives EPA significantly greater enforcement flexibility, including the ability to collect administrative penalties up to $200,000 and the authority to issue field citations with penalties up to $5,000. EPA does not have explicit authority to use contractors to do inspections. EPA will also have authority to issue administrative subpoenas for compliance data. EPA will also be able to issue compliance orders with schedules for compliance of one year or less. The 1990 Amendments also create, for the first time under the Clean Air Act, the separate crimes of "negligent endangerment," and "knowing endangerment." Civil penalties are provided as well. In general, the criminal provisions are aimed at persons other than those who are a "stationary engineer or technician responsible for the operations, maintenance, repair or maintaining of equipment and facilities." Specific language is included related to responsible management personnel or a corporate officer or official, in discussing who will and will not be potentially liable. Knowing and willful violations are not within the protection generally approved "lower level" employees.

Finally, the conference noted: "Nothing in subsections 113(c) is intended to discourage owners or operators of sources subject to this act from conducting self-evaluations or self-audits and acting to correct any problems identified."

Owners and operators of sources are in the best position to identify deficiencies and correct them, and should be encouraged to adopt procedures where internal compliance audits are performed and management is informed. Such internal audits will improve the owner and operators ability to identify and correct problems before rather than after government inspections and other enforcement actions are needed.

The criminal penalties available under subsection 113(c) should not be applied in a situation where a person, acting in good faith, promptly reports the results of an audit and promptly acts to correct any deviation. Knowledge gained by an individual solely in conducting an audit or while attempting to correct any deficiencies identified in the audit or the audit report itself should not ordinarily form the basis of the intent which results in criminal penalties.

### Title VIII — Miscellaneous Provisions

A new program will be established to deal with air pollution associated with drilling on the Outer Continental Shelf. EPA will control efforts to study and evaluate sources of visibility improvement. Both

EPA and GAO will make comprehensive analysis of the costs and benefits of the various requirements of the new Amendments. The law also establishes a council of independent experts to predict the future costs and benefits of various future Clean Air Act regulations and/or control programs. The law also establishes a program to collect data on $CO_2$ emissions on an annual basis. This information is to be based on emissions monitors or other comparably precise measures, but is not intended to require continuous monitoring.

### Title IX — Clean Air Research

A variety of research programs are established or expanded under the new Amendments. These include continuation of the National Atmospheric Precipitation Assessment Program (NAPAP) coupled with a task force review of program results to date, and procedures to recommend future work.

Work will be expanded at the Liquified Gaseous Fuels Spill Test Facility in Nevada to develop improved models for atmospheric disbursion of chemicals and to evaluate hazard and emergency response.

Provisions are included for EPA to conduct environmental health research on the short-term and long-term effects of air pollution. In addition, EPA is directed to conduct a basic engineering research program to develop and demonstrate non regulatory strategies for air pollution prevention and to assess the risks and benefits to human health and the environment related to the use of conventional gasoline and diesel fuels. Finally, EPA is directed to do more coordination of its research with other federal agencies and to assess pollution control technologies from some other industrial countries.

### Title X — Disadvantaged Business Concerns

The new Amendments set forth a variety of factors related to disadvantaged business concerns, including requirements, to the extent practicable, that 10 percent of total federal finding for Clean Air research be available to disadvantaged business concerns.

### Title XI — Job Displacement Provision

The Amendments encourage the Department of Labor to give technical assistance on preparing grant applications. Unemployment compensation benefits will be extended based on need and will be provided keyed to current family income in relation to the "lower living standard income levels". Coal miners displaced from mines currently supplying the approximately one hundred and ten (110) coal fired utility power plants subject to Title IV will be presumed to have lost their jobs due to the Amendments and thus be able to qualify under Title XI for the needs-based, extended payments.

# Recent Developments in the Courts

The United States Supreme Court issued a decision in June 1990 stating that EPA's failure to act on a SIP provision within the four month period was not a bar to enforcement of the existing SIP, even when a revision was pending which would result in compliance.[3]

There are several Federal Implementation Plan (FIP) cases still pending, none of which are expected to be completely eliminated by provisions of the 1990 Amendments. However, the savings clause preserves all existing items to the extent they are not "otherwise inconsistent with" the new Amendment. So far as can be determined, the 1990 Act will preserve any existing FIP litigation through to conclusion although the parties can be expected to be influenced by Congress' new requirements in the Clean Air Act. The FIP proposal for the Chicago area was issued on June 29, 1990[4] as a Notice of Final Rulemaking. This publication has several exceedingly significant concepts including the use of computed annual maximum theoretical emissions **without** considering control equipment or permit restrictions in determining the technical cutoffs for coverage on VOC emissions, the use of the photochemical reactive grid model to assess air quality impact, and numerous industry specific control requirements. Several significant FIP cases are also pending in California. It is premature at this point to predict the nature and extent the new Amendments will influence existing FIP litigation.

With respect to new source performance standard litigation, there were no major opinions in the most recent time period with the exception of the *Wisconsin Electric* case[5] holding that significant replacement of key parts of a coal fired boiler, coupled with the potential for significant emission increases, is sufficient modification or reconstruction to trigger applicable new source performance standards having the net effect of requiring substantially greater control on the source. The 1990 Act attempts to reduce some of the impact of this decision by defining what types of activities will trigger NSPS coverage and encourages EPA to resolve the underlying issues in future rulemakings dealing with "modifications" of otherwise potentially covered sources.

There are a number of other recent federal Clean Air Act cases summarized in Appendix B, which the reader is invited to pursue further.

## Regulatory Developments — Recent Rulemaking

The most significant regulatory developments in the last year have centered on the issuance of the small boiler New Source Performance Standards (NSPS), SIP revisions to protect visibility, withdrawal of the protection of stratospheric ozone due to Congressional action related to additional limits on the use of chlorofluorocarbons (CFC's), the adoption of new source review requirements for surface coal mining and fugitive emissions,[6] the withdrawal of new source performance standards for organic solvent degreasing and items related to regulating various other air pollutants. Also, EPA issued significant new rules on fuel volatility control and control of excess evaporative losses and new diesel fuel quality standards.

The Agency adopted final national emissions standards for hazardous air pollutant (NESHAP) standards for chromium emissions associated with comfort cooling towers,[7] and also adopted standards for radio nucliides.[8] The benzene litigation continued, with final action taken in March.[9] Additional requirements related to benzene are part of the 1990 Amendments because benzene, including benzene from gasoline, is listed as a "hazardous air pollutant". Finally, there were changes in the procedures related to auto emissions; test procedures for trap equipped diesel vehicles and engines were withdrawn. The NESHAP on cadmium was withdrawn as well, but cadmium is on the hazardous air pollutant list.

## The Clean Air Act — Separating the Old and New Versions

### Regulatory Agenda — Future Rulemaking and Emerging Issues

The Clean Air Act related items from EPA's semi-annual regulatory agenda[10] are summarized in Appendix C. While space does not permit an in depth review, the reader is encouraged to refer to the Agenda itself as published by the EPA, and any updates. It provides an excellent illustration of the scope, complexity and potential impact of EPA's current and planned rulemaking efforts. Several of the issues are sufficiently important to briefly reiterate, however. These include the various reviews of the National Ambient Air Quality Standards, guidance for risk based alternate emissions, new hazardous air pollutant standards, regulations on designating nonattainment areas by degree of severity, chromium from industrial cooling towers, dry cleaning and degreasing standards, fossil fueled stream generator standards revisions, and the continuing debates regarding indirect methods of $SO_2$ emission control such as moving to a shorter time period standard, restricting stack heights, etc.

EPA estimates that at least approximately 30 major new rulemaking efforts (and many more "subsets") will have to be initiated within twelve months of passage of the new 1990 Amendments, and more thereafter. Most of these are in addition to rulemaking now underway.

## Future Trends in Public Policy

The debate over the 1990 Amendments, and Clean Air Act issues in general, often represents not a debate at all, but different points of view talking past one another. For example, according to recent EPA data, most areas officially classified as nonattainment had only a few days of violation per year. Many others had fewer than 5 or 6 days per year. Los Angeles had 154. The different areas of the country represent different facts and circumstances regarding ozone levels which may at first appear essentially identical when described simply as nonattainment. As noted earlier, this difference is being addressed in the new Amendments. Moreover, it is apparent that tremendous progress has been made in reducing the number and severity of exceedances of the ambient standards in some parts of the nation, while other types of nonattainment have proven far more intractable.

An article in *The Amicus Journal*,[11] profiled "L.A. Air," and discussed the far reaching programs James Lents, the Executive Director of the South Coast Air Quality Management District, predicted may be necessary in that area. Mr. Lents outlined his thoughts on how the area can cope with the projected population increase from 20 million to 40 million people state-wide by the early 21st Century. According to the article, he sees a need for more carpool lanes, restrictions on where future industry and business can locate, and a need to encourage industrial growth in areas close to affordable housing for potential employees. A major benefit of such a program would be avoiding $100 billion of additional highway construction.

Lents is also encouraging alternate fuel and alternate technology vehicles to reduce dependence on gasoline powered vehicles. Many of these changes are part of the proposed revisions to the South Coast Air Quality Management Districts air pollution regulations now under consideration. In large measure, they foreshadowed some of the probable provisions of the 1990 Amendments.

Finally, changes in people's habits and lifestyles would be encouraged, if not compelled. For example, the use of staggered working hours, changes in highway use limits for trucks, and related changes would all be considered for implementation, as would electric cars and even lower auto emission standards. Whether all of these requirements came about or not, the fact they are being suggested in California as possible responses to the area's air quality problems is extremely significant as the regulated community, state and local officials and the public at large attempts to plan its future under the new Clean Air Act. Therefore, continued close attention should be paid to the evolving status of air pollution control and regulations in California.

The public policy debate about the Clean Air Act appears likely to continue, with no lasting resolution in sight. Even with the 1990 revisions, many of the most significant developments under the Clean Air Act, which impact stationary sources, state and local officials and the public at large will continue to be debated and discussed in the years ahead.

## About the Author

Frank H. Hackmann is a Partner with the law firm of Sonnenschein, Nath & Rosenthal in St. Louis, Missouri. Mr. Hackmann provides legal advice on a wide variety of environmental topics. He is a frequent speaker and author on a wide variety of environmental and regulatory topics, including the Clean Air Act. Mr. Hackmann received his B.S. degree in Chemical Engineering from the University of Illinois and his J.D. degree from St. Louis University Law School. He previously worked at Ralston Purina Company in various environmental law positions and at Monsanto Company as an engineer in a chemical manufacturing plant. He is currently the chairman of the St. Louis Regional Commerce and Growth Association Energy and Environment Clean Air Subcommittee.

Source Definitions - (§ 501(1) and (2))
    "Source" generally continues to have a dual definition as either an individual unit, operation or process, or an entire plant. The coverage of "source" is generally 100 tons per year of emissions, but can be lower in certain cases. In VOC nonattainment areas, the source "cut off" can go as low as 10 tons per year in extreme areas. The "Air Toxics" source definitions is 10/25 tons per year of emissions. All covered sources will require permits, as will electrical generating plants not otherwise exempt. Area sources or other stationery sources may be subject to permits by future EPA rules.

Schedule of Compliance - (§ 501(3))
    Means a schedule of remedial measures, including an enforceable sequence of actions or operations, leading to compliance with an applicable implementation plan, emission standard, limitation or prohibition.

Permit Program Violations - (§ 502(a))
    After the effective date of any permit program approved or promulgated, it shall be unlawful to:
        One — violate any permit requirement
        Two — operate affected sources, major sources, or other sources (including areas sources)
        or — operate any other stationery source in a category designated by the EPA
        Except when in compliance with a permit

    Permit requirements for construction or modification remain in place. The EPA may exempt one or more source categories from operating permits if compliance is "impractical, infeasible, or unnecessarily burdensome". Major sources may not be exempted. Violations are subject to both civil and criminal penalties.

Permit Program Regulations (§ 502(b))
    — EPA shall, within 12 months, promulgate minimum elements of a state/local permit program, including:
        — a standard permit application form
        — criteria for determining completeness

— monitoring and reporting information
— annual fees (or periodic fees) to cover all reasonable direct and indirect permit program costs including: reviewing and acting upon the application; implementing and enforcing terms and conditions; conducting emissions and ambient monitoring; preparing general regulations or guidance; conducting modeling, analysis and demonstrations; preparing inventories and tracking emissions. (Numerous details on fee collection and expenditure are also in the law.)
— requirements for adequate personnel and funding
— authority to issue permits and assure compliance
— permits may not exceed 5 year terms
— incorporate new limits or other SIP requirements upon renewal
— terminate, modify, revoke and re-issue permits
— enforce permits and permit fee requirements and requirement to secure permits (Civil/Criminal penalties are provided)
— EPA may object to permit issuance
— adequate procedures to determine application completeness and provide for public comment/judicial review
— provisions to allow judicial review if there is unreasonable delay in acting on a permit or permit renewal
— provisions to make permit applications, compliance plans, permits, and monitoring and compliance reports publicly available
— Provisions to incorporate new standards in existing permits for major source permits within 18 months of EPA issuing such new standards
— Limited ability to change operations without a permit revision if not a "modification" and no increase in "allowable emissions". EPA must still be advised seven days in advance.

Single permit (§ 502(c))
Single permits may be issued for an entire facility.

Plan Submission and Approval (§ 502(d)):
— Plans, including adequate legal authority, must be submitted within three years. EPA must approve or disapprove the plan, in whole or in part, within one year. Necessary revisions shall be submitted in 180 days.

— If a plan is not approved 18 months after the initial due
date, sanctions may be imposed.
— Additional sanction apply to nonattainment areas.
— EPA may also promulgate, administer and enforce a plan
after a two-year delay by the State.

Suspension (§ 502(e))
— Once a state program is approved, the EPA shall suspend
issuing federally issued permits
— The EPA may enforce all State issued permits

Prohibition (§ 502(f))
No partial permit program may be approved by EPA
unless it meets specified minimum conditions including all
requirements applicable to "affected sources", "major
sources", "new sources" and other "sources" requiring
permits.

Interim Approval (§ 502(g))
EPA may grant interim approval for up to two years.

Effective Date (§ 502(h))
Programs are effective when approved or promulgated by
EPA.

Administration and Enforcement (§ 502(i))
The EPA may impose sanctions if the State or local permit
program, or portion thereof, is not being adequately
administered and enforced.

Permit Applications — Applicable Date (§ 503(a))
Sources requiring permits must have them by the latter of the
effective date of a permit program (or interim program) or the
date the source becomes subject to § 502(a).

Permit Applications — Compliance Plan (§ 503(b)
— Applicant shall include a compliance plan.
— Progress reports are due every 6 months.
— Annual certification of compliance is required.
— Self reporting of deviations is required.

Permit Applications — Deadline (§ 503(c))
— Permit applications, including a compliance plan, are due
12 months after a source is subject to the permit program
(or earlier if so required by permit authority).

— Applications must be signed by a responsible official who certifies the accuracy of the information submitted.
— Permits are to be issued or denied in 18 months.
— A phase in schedule exists for issuing permits.
— About one-third of the permits annually for three years will be issued.
— The permit issuing Authority may set priorities for construction or modification permits.

Permit Applications — Timely and Complete (§ 503(d))
— If a timely application is filed, failure to be granted a permit is not a violation **unless** due to the applicants' failure to submit information requested or required.
— This provision does **not** apply to construction or modification permits.
— No violation exists until a source is required to file a permit application.

Permit Applications — Copies; Availability (§ 503(e))
— A copy of each permit application, compliance plan (including schedule of compliance), emissions or monitoring report, and certification shall be available to the public.
— Trade secret protection is provided under § 114(c).
— The permit **itself** is publicly available even under § 114(c) trade secrets provisions.

Permits Requirements and Conditions (§ 504(a))
— Each permit shall contain:
— enforceable emission limitations and standards;
— a schedule of compliance;
— a requirement that the permittee submit, at least every 6 months, results of required monitoring;
— such other conditions as are necessary;
— any other requirements of the applicable SIP.

Permit Requirements and Conditions — Monitoring and Analysis (§ 504(b))
— EPA by rule will determine permissible procedures and methods for determining compliance and for monitoring and analysis.
— Continuous emission monitoring need not be required if alternate methods give sufficiently reliable and timely compliance data.
— No preemption of other monitoring requirements.

Permit Requirements and Conditions — Inspection, Entry, Monitoring, Certification and Regulating (§ 504(c))
— Each permit issued shall set forth inspection, entry, monitoring, compliance certification and reporting requirements to assure compliance with permit terms and conditions.
— Such monitoring and reporting requirements are to be consistent with § 504(b).
— Any reports to be submitted under a permit issued to a corporation shall be signed by a responsible corporate official who shall certify its accuracy.

Permit Requirements and Conditions — General Permits (§ 504(d))
— General permits, after notice and opportunity for hearing, may be issued for numerous similar sources.
— Such sources must still file applications under § 503.

Permit Requirements and Conditions — Temporary Sources (§ 504(e))
— Single permits may authorize emissions from similar operations at multiple temporary locations.
— Compliance is required with all other requirements of the Act.
— Advance notice required of location changes.
— Separate fees may be required.

Permit Requirements and Conditions — Compliance (§ 504(f))
— Compliance with a permit is compliance with § 502.
— Except as otherwise provided by EPA rule, the permit may be deemed compliance with other provisions of the Act if:
— the permit includes such applicable requirements; or
— the permitting authority determines such provisions are NOT applicable (such determinations must be included in the permit).

Notification to Administration and Contiguous States (§ 505) Transmission and Notice (§ 505(a))
— All applications, and compliance plans, shall be sent by the permitting authority to the EPA, if EPA so requires.
— All proposed and final permits shall be sent to EPA.
— Contiguous states whose air quality may be affected are to be notified of proposed permits.

— States within 50 miles of the source are to be notified of proposed permits.
— Affected states can comment.
— The issuing authority must notify the commenting state and EPA in writing of any decision not to accept comments and the reasons.

Objections by EPA (§ 505(b))
— EPA shall object to permits not in compliance with the Act.
— EPA must object within 45 days and state reasons in writing.
— A copy of the EPA objections and statement of reasons shall be provided to the permit applicant.
— Within 60 days, after the 45 days, any person may petition the EPA to object to a permit issuance.
— Such objections may be based only on comments previously raised (except for good cause shown).
— The EPA Administrator shall grant or deny petitions and may not delegate these requirements.
— Petition denials shall be subject to judicial review under § 307.
— If the Administrator objects, the permitting authority may not issue a permit unless it is revised, revoked or modified.

Issuance or Denial (§ 505(c))
— The permit issuing authority must, within 90 days of EPA objections, submit a revised acceptable permit,
or
— The Administrator shall issue or deny the permit. There is no judicial review until the Administrator takes final action to issue or deny a permit.

Waiver of Requirements (§ 505(d))
— EPA may waive § 505(a) and (b) for any category, except major sources.
— EPA may by regulation exempt categories of sources to which § 505(a) and (b) do not apply, except major sources.
— EPA may exclude from waiver notice to other states under 505(a)(2).

Refusal of Permitting Authority to Terminate, Modify, or Revoke
and Reissue (§ 505(e))
>    — EPA may require a permitting authority to terminate,
>      modify, or revoke and re-issue a permit.
>    — Action to be taken within 90 days of the EPA
>      notifications, unless extended.
>    — Provisions exist to resolve objections to permit terms.
>    — Final authority is with EPA.

Other Authorities (§ 506)
>    — States, or interstate permitting authorities, may establish
>      additional permitting requirements not inconsistent with
>      the Act.
>    — The permit provisions apply to acid rain requirements
>      unless modified by that title.

Small Business Stationery Source Technical and Environmental
Compliance Assistance Program (§ 507)
>    — Provisions adopted for certain types of small business
>      sources to receive assistance in obtaining permits.

## Appendix B
## Summary — Recent Key Federal Court Decisions
## Clean Air Act Related

### Supreme Court

*General Motors Corporations v. United States (6/14/90) 31 ERC 1441* —
EPA had no duty to approve or disapprove proposed SIP revision
within four month period. Therefore, EPA may take enforcement action against a company alleging violation of existing SIP even if
agency unreasonably delayed review of proposed SIP because the
only "applicable SIP" was the existing one and not the proposed revision. (Opinion below 29ERC 1689)

### Circuit Court Of Appeals

*Wisconsin Electric Power Company v. EPA (CA7 1/19/90) 30 ERC 1889*
— Replacement of certain component parts of a coal fired power
plant, coupled with increase in emissions triggered coverage by EPA
new source standards for coal fired power plants. Interpretation
based on requirement for construction or modification subject to
new source performance standards. EPA's comparison of baseline
1987 actual emissions to maximum plant capacity after renovation
was impermissible. EPA's contention that the modification would
also be subject to PSD requirements was impermissible due to the
agency methodology selected.

*U.S. v. Alcan Foil Products (CA6 11/21/89) 30 ERC 1641* — EPA's failure to approve a SIP revision within the four month time limit did
not require dismissal of enforcement case. District court should have
considered EPA's delay in assessing any appropriate penalty.

*NRDC v. EPA (CA2 9/18/89) 30 ERC 1513* —There is no statutory
duty imposed upon the EPA under the existing Clean Air Act which
requires the Agency to list known hazardous air pollutants, or probable human carcinogens as pollutants.

*Puerto Rico Cement Company v. EPA (CA1 10/31/89) 30 ERC 1650* — Jurisdiction is properly before a federal appeals court on the issue of
applicability of PSD review procedures to cement company conver-

sion of two old cement kilns to newer, more efficient kilns. EPA has not objected to company appeal even though the PSD review procedure was not complete at time of appeal. EPA's authority to restrict prior baseline use for purposes of emissions credit is upheld because source reductions for which credit was sought occurred more than five years previously.

*Farmers Union Central Exchange, Inc. v. EPA (CA9 8/4/89) 30 ERC 1504* — While EPA's discretionary authority to approve the sale of banked lead credits is not moot even though lead credit programs lapsed in 1987, EPA was under no duty to approve such credit transfers.

*Coal Industries, Inc. v. U.S. (CAFC 7/24/89) 30 ERC 1179* — Penalties paid to the EPA for violation of air water pollution control laws are not deductible for income tax purposes.

*Greater Cincinnati Chamber of Commerce v. EPA (CA6 7/17/89) 30 ERC 1265* — The EPA's notice to Ohio of SIP deficiencies is not itself final agency action subject to judicial review.

*Delaney v. EPA (CA9 3/1/90) 30 ERC 1001* — EPA improperly determined that attainment plans for CO in certain Arizona counties contained adequate control measures because the plan failed to include all measures listed in the Clean Air Act as reasonably available.

*EDF v. EPA (CADC 3/13/90) 31 ERC 1167* — EPA improperly adopted certain standards for nitrogen oxide emissions when setting allowable increments in PSD areas.

*NRDC v. EPA (CADC 4/27/90) 31 ERC 1233* — Appellate court has jurisdiction to review claim that EPA acted improperly in failing to set secondary standard for fine particulates to protect against an acidic deposition. EPA ordered to supplement record to provide reasons for failing to set a standard to date.

*U.S. v. Gardner (CA5 2/6/90) 31 ERC 1036* — Automobile salesman committed criminal fraud when importing vehicles using names not belonging to actual owners and his acts concealed relevant facts from the EPA.

**The Clean Air Act — Separating the Old and New Versions**

### Court Of Appeals

*National Tank Truck Carriers, Inc. v. EPA, (CADC 6/26/90) 31 ERC 1521* — EPA acted arbitrarily and capriciously in establishing an affirmative defense to fuel volatility regulations that presume transporters who deliver nonconforming fuel are liable for violations.

### District Courts

*U.S. v. Zimmer Paper Products, Inc. (DCSIND 12/5/89) 30 ERC 2093* — EPA improperly altered methods for determining VOC emission compliance without proper opportunity for notice and comment. District Court has jurisdiction over counterclaim related to Clean Air Act enforcement action based on challenge of interpretive memo issued in violation of EPA.

*U.S. v. Coastal Refining, Inc. (DC Southern Texas 6/7/89) 30 ERC 1359* — Mandatory penalty provisions under Act for violating lead banking requirements violate U.S. Constitution by denying court power to modify penalty and denying defendant equitable defenses.

*U.S. v. Unitank Terminal Service (DC Eastern Pa. 10/31/89) 30 ERC 1904* — Benzene emission hazardous air pollutant regulations applied to bulk liquid storage terminal handling liquid benzene.

*U.S. v. R.E.A.G. (DC Connecticut 8/2/89) 30 ERC 1638* — U.S. may sue on EPA's behalf in enforcing asbestos hazardous air pollutant regulations against demolition contractor. Contractor is liable for violations occurring during removal of asbestos from Navy facility because contractor was owner/operator and contractor failed to respond in timely fashion to EPA's request for information and failed to comply with applicable standards.

*U.S. v. Schaeffer Muffler Shops, Inc. (DC S. Texas 2/28/89) 30 ERC 1658* — Muffler shop owner was properly fined for Clean Air Act violations for removing emission control device from automobile.

*U.S. v. Pilot Petroleum Associates, Inc. (DC ENY 5/30/89) 30 ERC 1073* — Gasoline distributors are liable for violations for lead standards involving gasoline which they redistribute. Total assessed penalty was $610,000.00. Gasoline distributors were presumed liable for violations.

*Bunker Hill Mining and Smelter Complex (DC Idaho 1/11/90) 30 ERC 2070* — EPA administrative warrant to obtain certain documents was limited by court to those relevant to compliance with EPA regulations. Owner, not EPA, is proper person to search files for responsive documents because inspection warrant is similar to subpoena which limits EPA authority to review records directly.

*U.S. v. Moore American Graphics, Inc. (DC N. Illinois 10/13/89) 30 ERC 1663* — Court will reconsider $250,000.00 fine levied against printing company for failure to comply with consent decree because certain events of noncompliance may have been unavoidable. Prior opinion asserting full penalty issued 7/6/89. (30 ERC 1347).

*Citizens for a Better Environment v. California (DC N. CA. 3/9/90) 31 ERC 1213* — California agencies are liable under Act for failure to adopt and implement certain air pollution control measures for stationary source categories in the San Francisco Bay area as required by earlier SIP.

*U.S. v. Ford Motor Company (DC W. MO 4/23/90) 31 ERC 1286* — EPA may not enforce certain emission limits in SIP after state approved alternative compliance plan dealing with emissions.

*U.S. v. Solar Turbins (DC MPA. 11/28/89) 31 ERC 1396* — EPA may not sue company for allegedly constructing facility without proper approval when state permit was issued and company relied thereon and there was no violation of objective performance standards.

*U.S. v. Tennessee Air Pollution Control Board (DC M. Tennessee 1/17/90, 3/2/90, 4/10/90) 31 ERC 1492, 1500, 1503* — United States Army is liable for illegal asbestos removal at structures in military base in Tennessee because Congress waived sovereign immunity for civil penalties under the Clean Air Act. The State of Tennessee may assert civil penalties against the Army facility for violation of the Act.

### District Courts

*Citizens for a Better Environment v. California (DC N. CALIF) 5/7/90) 31 ERC 1545* — In a citizen suit to enforce a previously adapted SIP, the Metropolitan Transport Commission was held liable on summary judgment for failure to conform to the SIP in assessing the air quality impacts of road construction. Imposition of a remedy was delayed pending additional information.

*U.S. v. MPM Contractors, Inc. (DC Kau 5/30/90) 31 ERC 1550* — Both plaintiff's and defendant's motions for summary judgment in a civil asbestos NESHAP action were denied because there were material issues of fact.

*Note. This listing is not intended to reflect all recently decided clean air cases. It includes those judged to be of significant broad based interest to the regulated community. All citations and summaries are from the Bureau of National Affairs Environment Reporter Cases, Volumes 30 and 31.*

**Prerule Stage**

| _Item_ | Date _Fed. Reg. Cite_ | _Action_ |
|---|---|---|
| Guidance for Risk-Based Alternative Emissions | Undetermined | Undetermined |
| NAAQS: Carbon Monoxide (Review) | 12/00/90 | Advisory Commission Review |
| NAAQA: Nitrogen Dioxide (Review) | 06/00/92 | Complete Review of Criteria Document and Staff Paper |
| NSPS: Asphalt Processing and Asphalt Roofing Manufacturing Plants (Review) | 08/00/86 12/00/91 | Begin Review End Review |
| Development of a List of Source Categories for Hazardous Air Pollutants Subject to Section 112 of the Clean Air Act | Dates to be determined by Clean Air Act Amendments of 1990, Title III | Undetermined |
| Regulations Governing Exemptions from Standards for Hazardous Air Pollutants Due to Early, Voluntary Emission Reduction | Undetermined | Undetermined |

| | | |
|---|---|---|
| Statement of Policy Regarding Petitions under Section 112 of Title II of the Clean Air Act Amendments of 1990 | Undetermined | Undetermined |
| Emissions Control System Defect Warranty Regulations | 00/00/00 | ANPRM |

## Proposed Rule Stage

| *Item* | Date *Fed. Reg. Cite* | *Action* |
|---|---|---|
| Volatility Regulations for Gasoline and Alcohol Blends Sold in Texas in Calendar Year 1991 | 10/00/90 | NPRM |
| Nonconformance Penalties or 1994 Model Year Emission Standards for Heavy-Duty Vehicles and Engines | 06/00/91 | NPRM |
| Revisions of Gasoline Volatility Enforcement Procedures | 11/00/90 | NPRM |
| Alternative Fuel Corporate Average Fuel Economy Labeling Requirements | 12/00/90 00/00/00 | NPRM Final Action |
| Protection of Stratospheric Ozone (Recycling) | 05/01/90 (55 FR 18256) 00/00/00 | ANPRM NPRM |
| Protection of Stratospheric Ozone (Phase-Out) | 11/15/90 08/15/91 | NPRM Final Action |

| | | |
|---|---|---|
| NAAQS: Lead (Review) | 01/11/90 | CASAC Closure |
| | 00/00/00 | NPRM |
| NAAQS: Ozone (Review) | 00/00/00 | NPRM |
| NAAQS: Fine Particulate Matter | 07/01/87 (52 FR 24670) | ANPRM |
| | 00/00/00 | NPRM |
| New Source Review Requirements-CMA Exhibit B | 00/00/00 | NPRM |
| | 00/00/00 | Final Action |
| Approval and Promulgation of Implementation Plans: Revision of the Visibility FIP for Arizona | 02/01/91 | NPRM |
| | 10/16/91 | Final Action |
| NSPS: Municipal Landfills | 10/00/90 | NPRM |
| | | 01/00/92 Final |
| NSPS: Medical Waste Incineration | 03/00/92 | NPRM |
| | 09/00/93 | Final Action |
| NESHAP: Coke Oven Emissions from Coke Oven Charging, Door Leaks, and Topside Leaks on Wet-Coal-Charged Batteries | 04/23/87 (52 FR 13586) | NPRM |
| | 12/30/88 (53 FR 53014) | NPRM (Supplimental) |
| | 10/00/91 | NPRM (Revised) |
| NESHAP: Asbestos-Comprehensive Revisions | 09/00/91 | NPRM |
| | 12/00/92 | Final Action |
| NESHAP: Chromium - Industrial Cooling Towers | 03/00/92 | NPRM |
| | 06/00/93 | Final Action |
| NESHAP: Chromium - Electroplating | 06/00/91 | NPRM |
| | 07/00/92 | Final Action |
| NESHAP: Hazardous Organics (SOCMI) | 08/00/91 | NPRM |

| | | |
|---|---|---|
| NESHAP: Perchloroethylene Dry Cleaning | 12/26/85 (50 FR 52880) | NOTICE-Intent to List |
| | 04/00/91 | NPRM |
| | 04/00/92 | Final Action |
| NESHAP: Ethylene Oxide from Commercial Sterilization | 07/00/91 | NPRM |
| | 07/00/92 | Final Action |
| NESHAP: Organic Solvent Degreasing | 08/17/87 | NOTICE: (Solicitation of Public Participation) |
| | (52 FR 29548) | |
| | 02/00/92 | NPRM |
| | 02/00/93 | Final Action |
| Guideline on Air Quality Models (Revision) | 01/00/91 | NPRM |
| | 06/00/92 | Final Action |
| On-Board Vehicle Based Diagnostic System Requirement | 03/00/91 | NPRM |
| | 00/00/00 | Final Action |
| Emission Standards for Light-Duty Trucks (Revision) | 09/08/86 (51 FR 32032) 00/00/0 | ANPRM NPRM |
| Revisions to Regulations for Gas Guzzler Tax | 03/00/91 | NPRM |
| | 00/00/00 | Final Action |
| Emissions Standards for New Motor Vehicles and Motor Vehicle Engines Fueled with Compressed Natural Gas or Liquified Petroleum Gas | 12/00/90 | NPRM |
| | 00/00/00 | Final Action |
| Amendments to Motor Vehicle Imports Regulations Pertaining to Canadian Vehicles | 06/00/91 | NPRM |

| | | |
|---|---|---|
| Revisions to the Stack Height Regulation | 00/00/00 | NPRM |
| Alternative Test Procedure for the Voluntary Aftermarket Part Certification Program | 08/08/89 (54 FR 32598) 02/00/91 | NPRM NPRM (Supplemental) |
| Fuel and Fuel Additives: Health and Emissions Effects Testing | 08/01/90 (55 FR 32218) 01/00/92 06/00/93 | ANPRM NPRM Final Action |
| General Requirements for Determination of Gasoline Metal Content | 12/04/89 (54 FR 49999) 09/00/91 | ANPRM NPRM |
| Fuel and Fuel Additives: Enforcement of Section 211(f)(4) Waivers | 00/00/00 | NPRM |
| Revisions to Regulations on Registration of Fuel and Fuel Additives | 00/00/00 | NPRM |
| Control of Air Toxics from Motor Vehicles | 00/00/00 | NPRM |
| Radon User Fees | 10/00/90 00/00/00 | NPRM Final Action |

Treatment, Storage, and Disposal Facility Area Source Air Emissions RCRA Standards

Phase I Leaks and Vents

| | | |
|---|---|---|
| | 02/05/87 (52 FR 3748) | NPRM |
| | 06/21/90 (55 FR 25454) | Final Action |

Phase II Tanks and Impoundments

| | | |
|---|---|---|
| | 10/00/90 | NPRM |
| | 10/00/91 | Final Action |

| Individual Constituents Standards-Phase III of RCRA Air Emission Standards | 00/00/00 | NPRM |
|---|---|---|

## Final Rule Stage

| Item | Date Fed. Reg. Cite | Action |
|---|---|---|
| Reorganization of 40 CFR Part 86, Subpart A | 11/00/90 | Direct Final |
| Revision of 40 CFR Part 80 to Delete Outdated Sections | 10/00/90 | Direct Final |
| State Implementation Plans: Attainment Status Designations | 06/06/88 (53 FR 20722) 08/05/88 (53 FR 20722) 00/00/00 | NPRM NPRM Comment Period End Final Action |
| NAAQS: Sulfur Oxides (Review) | 10/02/79 (44 FR 56730) 04/26/88 (53 FR 14926) 00/00/00 | ANPRM FPRM Final Action |
| NSPS: Polymer and Resin Manufacture | 09/30/87 (52 FR 36678) 10/00/90 | NPRM Final Action |
| NSPS: Automobile and Light-Duty Truck Coating Operations (Revision) | 07/29/82 (47 FR 32743) 00/00/00 | NPRM Final Action |
| NSPS: Fossil Fuel-Fired Stream Generators (Revision) | 10/21/83 (48 FR 48960) 00/00/00 | NPRM Final Action |

| | | |
|---|---|---|
| NSPS SOCMI Reactor Processes | 06/29/90 (55 FR 26953) | NPRM |
| | 09/00/91 | Final Action |
| State Implementation Plans: Policy on Post 1987 Ozone and Carbon Monoxide Plan Revisions for Areas Not Attaining the National Ambient Air Quality Standards | 11/24/87 (52 FR 45044) | NPRM |
| | 00/00/00 | Final Action |
| NSPS: Municipal Waste Combustors | 07/07/87 (52 FR 25399) | ANPRM |
| | 10/06/87 (52 FR 37335) | ANPRM-Comment Period End |
| | 12/20/89 (54 FR 52251) | NPRM |
| | 12/00/90 | Final Action |
| NSPS: Calciners and Dryers | 04/23/86 (51 FR 15438) | NPRM |
| | 00/00/00 | Final Action |
| Rural Fugitive Dust Policy for PM10 | 07/01/87 (51 FR 15438) | NPRM |
| | 00/00/00 | Final Action |
| NESHAP for Asbestos (Compliance Revisions) | 01/10/89 (54 FR 912) | NPRM |
| | 10/00/90 | Final Action |
| PSD Increments for PM10 | 10/05/89 (54 FR 41218) | NPRM |
| | 00/00/00 | Final Action |
| Motor Vehicle Test Procedures for Evaporative Hydrocarbons (Revision) | 01/19/90 (55 FR 1914) | NPRM |
| | 08/00/91 | Final Action |

| | | |
|---|---|---|
| Decision on Air Pollution Regulatory Strategies for the Gasoline Marketing Industry | 08/19/87 (52 FR 31162) 00/00/00 | NPRM Final Action |
| Interim Cold Ambient Air Temperature Carbon Monoxide Emission Standards | 09/17/90 (55 FR 38250) 00/00/00 | NPRM Final Action |
| Nonconformance Penalties for 1991 Through 1993 Model Year Emission Standards for Heavy-Duty Vehicles and Engines | 04/25/90 (55 FR 17532) 10/00/90 | NPRM Final Action |
| Motor Vehicle Emissions Performance Warranty Short Tests | 12/23/88 (53 FR 51956) 00/00/00 | NPRM Final Action |

## Completed Actions

| Item | Date Fed. Reg. Cite | Action |
|---|---|---|
| Fuel Volatility Control for 1989 and Beyond | 06/25/90 (52 FR 23658) | Final Action |
| NAAQS: Carbon Monoxide (Review) | RIN Changed to 07/23/90 Regulatory Program RIN 2060-AA63 (Listed under Prerule Stage) | |
| Federal Promulgation of State Implementation Plan to Protect Visibility | 06/13/90 (55 FR 24060) | Final Action |
| NSPS: SOCMI Air Oxidation Process | 06/29/90 (55 FR 26912) | Final Action |

**Environmental Risk Management**

| NSPS: SOCMI Distillation Operations | 06/29/90 (55 FR 26931) | Final Action |
|---|---|---|
| NSPS: Small Boilers | 09/12/90 (55 FR 37675) | Final Action |
| NSPS: Medical Waste Incineration | RIN Changed to 07/23/90 Regulatory Program RIN 2060-AC62 (Listed under Proposed Rule Stage) | |
| NESHAP: Cadmium | 07/31/90 | Withdrawn |
| Control of Excess Evaporative Emissions/Fuel Volatility | 06/11/90 (55 FR 23658) | Final Action (Additional Control) |
| Trading and Banking of Heavy-Duty Engine NOx and PM Emission Credits | 07/26/90 (55 FR 30584) | Final Action |
| Diesel Fuel Quality Standards | 08/21/90 (55 FR 34120) | Final Action |

# Endnotes

1. 42 U.S.C. § 7401 *et. seq.*

2. Covered sources emit 10 tons/year of any hazardous pollutant listed or 25 tons of any combination. In general, such sources will be subject to permit provisions and technology standards for approximately 250 source categories. EPA has initially identified 48 source categories that must have technology standards set within the next two years. The general goal is a 90 percent reduction. Some exceptions apply. Further, covered sources will be subject to residual risk analysis.

3. *General Motors Corp. v. United States*, 58 U.S.L.W. 4803 (6/14/90).

4. 55 *Fed. Reg.*. 26814.

5. *Wisconsin Electric Power Company v. Reilly*, CA 7 1/19/90 30 ERC 1889.

6. 55 *Fed. Reg.*. 48876, November 20, 1989.

7. 55 *Fed. Reg.* 222, January 3, 1990.

8. 54 *Fed. Reg.* 51654, December 15, 1989.

9. 55 *Fed. Reg.*. 8292, March 7, 1990.

10. 55 *Fed. Reg.* 45134, October 29, 1990.

11. *The Amicus Journal*, "L.A. Air," (Summer, 1988), published by the National Resources Defense Counsel.

#  Water Management Issues: Clean Water Act, Safe Drinking Water Act and Groundwater Protection

### J. Brian Molloy, Partner
### Piper & Marbury
### Washington, D.C.

In recent years, there have been a number of water management developments, most of which have grown out of the Water Quality Act of 1987 and the Safe Drinking Water Act Amendments of 1986. This chapter presents an overview of the Clean Water Act, followed by discussions of recent developments in regulating water discharges, including toxic hotspots, water quality standards for toxics, whole effluent toxicity testing, pretreatment, combined sewer overflows, storm water management, anti-backsliding, and enforcement. In addition, this chapter discusses regulation of wetlands, drinking water and ground water.

## Clean Water Act

### Statutory and Regulatory Background

With the enactment of the Federal Water Pollution Control Act Amendments of 1972, Congress charted a new course for federal regulation of water quality. Since then, Congress has fine-tuned its handiwork by amending the statute twelve times. Although most of the amendments were minor, major changes were made in 1977,

1980 and 1987. The 1972 Act, and its subsequent amendments have come to be commonly known as the "Clean Water Act" (CWA or the Act).

Set forth below are the basic provisions of the CWA, including discussions of the permit requirements, technology-based effluent limitations, water-quality-based effluent limitations, and enforcement.

### NPDES Permit System

As the centerpiece of the 1972 Act, Congress prohibited the discharge of pollutants into waters of the United States without a permit.[1] A nationwide program for implementing the permit requirement was established — the National Pollution Discharge Elimination System (NPDES).[2]

Under section 402(a) of the Act, authority to issue permits is vested in EPA. Section 402(b), however, directs EPA to allow qualified states to administer the NPDES permit program for discharges to waters within their state. To date, 39 states are authorized to issue NPDES permits.[3] For dischargers in states that do not qualify to issue permits, EPA remains the permitting authority. States authorized to issue NPDES permits must do so in accordance with federal regulations and guidelines.[4]

Water pollution is primarily controlled by imposing limits in each discharger's permit on the amount of pollutants that may be discharged. Such limits are known as "effluent limitations." The CWA and its regulations establish two types of effluent limitations: (1) technology-based effluent limitations, and (2) water-quality-based effluent limitations.

EPA supplements effluent limitations with best management practices for toxic and hazardous pollutants from ancillary manufacturing activities.[5] Best management practices are intended to control runoff, spills and leaks of toxic and hazardous materials that may reach waters of the United States.[6] Ancillary manufacturing operations include material storage areas; in-plant transfer, process and material handling areas; loading and unloading operations; plan site runoff; and sludge and waste disposal areas.[7]

In addition to effluent limitations, permits must include provisions regarding compliance and enforcement; mitigation of violations that adversely affect human health or the environment; proper operation and maintenance, inspection, monitoring and recordkeeping; reporting requirements; and upset and bypass conditions.[8] Generally, a discharger is not subject to a new state or federal requirement until the requirement is incorporated into its permit.[9]

### Technology-Based Effluent Limitations

Effluent limitations were conceived as a two-tier system of limitations based on technology and water quality. The first tier comprises limits established by EPA that are based upon use of different types of technology. This first tier was intended to provide a minimum nationwide level of pollution control.

Under section 301(b) of the CWA, EPA establishes technology-based effluent limitations on an industry-by-industry basis. Effluent limits have been established for approximately 50 industrial categories, most of which have many subcategories.[10]

All privately-owned point source dischargers existing at enactment were required to comply with effluent limits based on the "Best Practicable Control Technology Currently Available" or BPT.[11] Beyond BPT, the type of effluent limitation that applies depends upon the type of pollutant to be discharged. The CWA distinguishes among three types of pollutants: (1) conventional pollutants; (2) toxic pollutants; and (3) nonconventional pollutants (i.e., pollutants that are neither conventional nor toxic). For conventional pollutants (pH, fecal coliform, total suspended solids, biochemical oxygen demand, and oil and grease), Congress imposed limits based on "Best Conventional Pollutant Control Technology."[12] Existing sources of toxic and nonconventional pollutants must employ the "Best Available Technology Economically Achievable."[13]

Conventional, toxic and nonconventional pollutants were required to have achieved the prescribed treatment levels by no later than March 31, 1989.[14] New sources must meet limitations based on Best Available Demonstrated Technology within 90 days from the start of operations.[15]

Municipal sewage treatment plants or Publicly Owned Treatment Works (POTWs) were required to meet limitations based on "secondary treatment" by July 1, 1988.[16] *Secondary treatment* is defined by regulation to control biochemical oxygen demand (BOD), suspended solids, and pH.[17]

The CWA and its regulations provide for several variances from treatment standards. The most widely used variance allows relaxation of effluent limitations for individual facilities that show they are subject to "fundamentally different factors" from those considered by EPA in developing the category-by-category standards.[18] Few variances have been granted on this basis to date. Where EPA has not yet established nationally applicable technology-based effluent limits, section 402(a)(1)(B) of the CWA authorizes permit writers to establish technology-based limits on a case-by-case basis using the best professional judgment (BPJ) of the permit writer.[19]

### Water-Quality-Based Effluent Limits

As discussed above, technology-based effluent limits provide a national floor for water pollution control. The second tier of water pollution control applies when technology-based limits are not sufficiently stringent to provide for designated water uses in particular bodies of water. Unlike technology-based limits, which are set by EPA and are nationally uniform, water quality standards are generally set by states and vary throughout the country.[20]

Several steps are involved in establishing water quality based effluent limitations. First, a state must establish a "water quality standard." States are required to review and revise water quality standards every three years.[21] Water quality standards are composed of a "designated use" for the body of water (e.g., fishing, swimming) and a set of water quality "criteria."[22] Water quality criteria are the maximum level of pollutants that may be present in the water without harming the designated use of the water.

Once numerical water quality criteria have been adopted, a state then calculates the total maximum daily load of pollutants that all individual permittees together may cumulatively discharge into a portion of a water body without exceeding the water quality criteria in the receiving water.[23] The total waste load is then allocated among permittees. Finally, an individual waste load allocation is incorporated into the permit as an effluent limitation. In states that do not have permitting authority, EPA may establish water quality based effluent limitations to protect particular bodies of water.[24]

### Pretreatment

Facilities that discharge into a Publicly Owned Treatment Works rather than directly into waters of the United States are known as "indirect dischargers" or "industrial users" and are not subject to the

NPDES permitting requirements. Instead, indirect dischargers are subject to a parallel set of requirements, including the National Pretreatment Standards and POTW Pretreatment Programs.

The National Pretreatment Standards are composed of two elements: (1) the General Pretreatment Program,[25] and (2) the Categorical Pretreatment Standards.[26] EPA's General Pretreatment Program is applicable to all indirect dischargers. It includes a general prohibition against discharge of pollutants that either pass through POTWs or interfere with POTW pretreatment processes.[27] Interference includes not only disruption of POTW treatment operations, but also disruption of sludge processes, use or disposal.[28] The General Pretreatment Program also contains some broad prohibitions such as on discharges that create fire or explosion hazards.[29]

The Categorical Pretreatment Standards are discharge limits established by EPA for specific industry categories.[30] Users must comply with categorical standards no later than three years after their promulgation.[31] Variances from the Categorical Pretreatment Standards may be granted for individual facilities that show they are subject to "fundamentally different factors" than those considered by EPA in developing the categorical standard.[32]

Indirect dischargers also must comply with applicable POTW Pretreatment Programs. A POTW is required to develop a pretreatment program if the POTW has a design flow greater than 5 million gallons per day and receives pollutants that pass through or interfere with POTW operations.[33] As part of a POTW Pretreatment Program, the POTW must establish specific controls, known as "local limits" to implement the general and specific prohibitions of EPA's pretreatment regulations and the effluent limits which EPA has imposed upon the POTW.[34] Local limits are considered to be Pretreatment Standards established under section 307(d) of the CWA and are enforceable by EPA.[35]

POTWs control the discharges of industrial users through permits, orders or similar means.[36] As a result, when EPA imposes limits on POTWs, those limits are passed on to the industrial users.

### Enforcement

EPA has four mechanisms to enforce the requirements of the CWA or of permits issued under section 402.

(1) **Administrative Orders** — EPA may issue compliance orders specifying a time for compliance.[37] Issuance of a compli-

ance order does not preclude EPA from using other enforcement mechanisms. Along with orders, administrative penalties may be imposed by EPA under a two-tiered penalty system.[38] The tier under which penalties are sought is not affected by the type of violation; EPA may proceed in its discretion under either tier. The difference between the penalty tiers lies in the procedures that are used and the amount of the penalties that may be assessed. To assess Class I penalties, EPA must provide an opportunity for the defendant to request a hearing, but the hearing need **not** be a formal "on the record" hearing in accordance with the Administrative Procedures Act. Class II penalties, on the other hand, may be assessed only after a formal "on the record" hearing. Class I penalties may not exceed $10,000 per violation, with a maximum penalty of $25,000. Class II penalties may not exceed $10,000 per day for each day that the violation continues with a maximum of $125,000.

**(2) Civil Actions** — EPA may bring a civil action in federal court seeking an injunction or penalties up to $25,000 per day for each violation, or both.[39] The United States Supreme Court has held that the defendant has the right to a jury trial in an action for civil penalties.[40]

**(3) Criminal Prosecutions** — Any person who willfully or negligently violates most requirements of the CWA is subject to a fine of up to $25,000 per day.[41] If a person knows that the violation places another person in imminent danger, the actor is subject to the "knowing endangerment" provision.[42] For a first offense, an individual may be fined up to $250,000 and imprisoned for up to 15 years.[43] Fines for organizations are up to $1 million.[44] Penalties double for subsequent offenses.

**(4) Debarment** — Section 508 of the CWA prohibits federal agencies from entering into contracts with persons criminally convicted under section 309(c). Moreover, EPA maintains that it has authority to "blacklist" a facility whenever a civil action has been commenced or an administrative order has been violated.[45]

Independent of federal enforcement, states with NPDES permitting authority may bring civil and criminal actions under state law to enforce NPDES permit requirements.[46] Generally, states have enforcement mechanisms parallel to EPA's enforcement mechanisms.[47]

In addition to enforcement actions by EPA and states, any **citizen** may commence a civil action against any person (including the United States) alleged to be in violation of an effluent standard, limitation or order under the CWA.[48] Prior to filing suit, a plaintiff must give a 60-day notice to the alleged violator and the appropriate federal and state agencies.[49] A citizen suit may not be brought if either EPA or a state agency "has commenced and is diligently prosecuting a civil or criminal action."[50] The Supreme Court has held that citizen suits for "wholly past" violations are barred.[51] As a result, a citizen suit is generally barred if the alleged violator is in compliance when the citizen suit is filed. As a practical matter, most violators will try to come into compliance during the 60-day notice period, thus preventing the citizen suit from being brought. The "wholly past" violation rule, however, does not bar citizens from bringing suits for intermittent or continuous violations.[52]

## Recent Clean Water Act Developments

### Toxic Hotspots: CWA Section 304(l)

With the enactment of the Water Quality Act (WQA) of 1987, the focus of water pollution control has shifted from the first-tier technology-based approach to the second-tier water quality based approach. One of the major goals of the 1987 amendments was the control of toxics. To achieve this goal, Congress added section 304(l), the so-called "toxic hotspots" provision, to the Clean Water Act. States are required to develop three separate lists of waters impaired by toxic, as well as other, pollutants. Specifically, section 304(l) required each state to submit to EPA by February 4, 1989 the following lists:

(1) Those waters that, after application of technology-based effluent limits, cannot reasonably be anticipated to attain or maintain numeric water quality standards for toxic pollutants due to point or non-point sources (the "Mini-List");[53]

(2) All waters that, after application of technology-based effluent limits, cannot be reasonably anticipated due to point or non-point sources to attain or maintain water quality that

will protect public health, public water supplies and use of waters for agriculture, industry, aquatic life and recreation (the "Long List");[54]

(3)   Waters that, after application of technology-based effluent limits, the state does not expect will achieve applicable water quality standards due entirely or substantially to point source discharges of toxics (the "Short List").[55]

For the third list, states must determine the specific point sources that are discharging toxic pollutants impairing water quality and the amount of each toxic pollutant discharged by such sources.[56] States must then develop and submit an individual control strategy (ICS) for each of the point sources impairing waters on the Short List.[57]

ICSs must lead to reduced discharges of toxics so that the water quality standard will be met as soon as possible, but not later than three years after the establishment of the ICS.[58] If a state failed to make a timely submission of ICSs, or EPA does not approve the state's ICSs, EPA was supposed to have (in cooperation with the state and after notice and comment) developed the required lists and ICSs by June 4, 1990.[59]

On June 13, 1989, as a result of submittals by the states, EPA released a list of 879 facilities whose discharges are causing excessive levels of toxic substances in 595 receiving streams. Two hundred forty of the 879 facilities were municipal sewage treatment plants that receive toxics from industrial users.

The net result of section 304(l) is that many facilities will be forced to tighten severely their control of discharges of toxics. Indirect dischargers will be affected when POTWs pass on to them through the pretreatment process the more stringent requirements resulting from the 304(l) process.

### Development of Water Quality Standards for Toxics

Prior to the WQA of 1987, few states had developed numerical criteria for toxic pollutants. Instead, states employed narrative standards for toxics (e.g., "No toxics in toxic amounts"). Unhappy with the progress that had been made in controlling toxics, Congress in 1987 added section 303(c)(2)(B) to the Act, requiring states to develop numerical criteria for all toxics for which EPA had published numerical criteria under section 304(a).[60]

Although EPA published a compendium of recommended section 304(a) criteria (the "Gold Book") in 1986,[61] states have been slow to adopt numerical criteria for toxics. States have relied heavily on the Gold Book in developing criteria, but Gold Book criteria frequently have not been directly applicable. For example, when establishing a criterion for a carcinogen a state may wish to adopt a risk level other than the one used by EPA or the state may wish to establish a criterion based upon different species of aquatic life than EPA considered. Thus, although EPA's recommended criteria have been helpful to states, states must nonetheless address tough policy and technical issues before promulgating criteria.

## Whole Effluent Toxicity Testing

Setting chemical specific numerical water quality criteria is a complex task, often taking years to complete. As a result, recent legislative and regulatory developments have paved the way for increased use of biological techniques, known as bioassays or "whole effluent toxicity" (WET) testing, to set numerical criteria for toxics.

WET testing involves laboratory testing of various dilutions[62] of effluent on aquatic life to determine whether there are toxic effects. WET tests are generally used by EPA in two ways. First, they are used as a trigger for a toxicity reduction evaluation (TRE). If a WET test indicates toxicity, the permittee must conduct further testing to determine the particular chemical constituents that are causing the toxicity and then must take steps to reduce those constituents in the effluent.

Second, EPA may use whole effluent toxicity as an effluent limitation. EPA has explained that "[a] limit on whole effluent toxicity refers to a numeric effluent limitation expressed in such terms as toxic units, no observed effect level (NOEL), $LC_{50}$, or percent mortality." [63] Where effluent toxicity is used as an effluent limit, a violation of a WET test is a permit violation subject to the full range of federal and state penalties.[64]

Use of toxicity effluent limits is not new. EPA first authorized permit writers to set effluent limitations based on biological testing in 1979.[65] Then, in 1984, EPA issued a formal policy on use of toxicity testing.[66] Industry groups challenged EPA's use of toxicity as an effluent limitation. Industry argued that "toxicity" is not a "pollutant" and, therefore, that EPA lacks authority to regulate toxicity. The United States Court of Appeals for the District of Columbia Circuit disagreed, holding that "toxicity" is an attribute of pollutants which EPA may use to regulate pollutants.[67]

Only recently, however, has consideration of WET testing requirements become mandatory. Under section 303(c)(2)(B) of the WQA of 1987, Congress required states to establish water quality criteria based on biological monitoring when EPA has not published constituent specific numerical water quality criteria.[68] In 1989, EPA promulgated procedures for establishing water quality based effluent limitations in which permit writers are required to impose WET limits in a permit if the permit writer determines that the permittee's discharge has the "reasonable potential" to violate either a **narrative** criterion or a numeric criterion for whole effluent toxicity.[69]

In addition to being used as either a screening condition or an effluent limitation, WET tests are now required as part of the NPDES permit application for all POTWs larger than of one million gallons per day and all POTWs with approved pretreatment programs.[70] Other POTWs also may be required to submit WET tests based on consideration of (1) variability of pollutants; (2) dilution of the effluent in the receiving water; (3) existing controls on point or nonpoint sources; and (4) receiving stream characteristics.[71]

### Recent Pretreatment Developments

On July 24, 1990, EPA promulgated significant revisions to its pretreatment regulations.[72] One of these revisions, which was discussed in the last section, requires all POTWs with approved pretreatment programs to submit whole effluent toxicity test results as part of the application for an NPDES permit.[73] Other revisions affect (1) the General Pretreatment Prohibitions; (2) the POTW Pretreatment Program Requirements; and (3) reporting requirements for POTWs and Industrial Users. The revisions to each of these three latter requirements are discussed below.

Industrial users are now prohibited from discharging the following into POTWs:[74]

(1) petroleum oil, nonbiodegradable cutting oil or mineral oil products that will cause interference or passthrough;

(2) pollutants that result in toxic gases, vapors or fumes in the POTW; and

(3) any trucked or hauled pollutants except at discharge points designated by the POTW.

POTWs must control the user's discharges to the POTW through a permit, order or similar means. The revisions specify that for signifi- cant industrial users the control device must contain the following:

(1) a statement of duration (no more than five years);

(2) a limitation on transfer without, at a minimum, notification to the POTW;

(3) effluent limits based on the general pretreatment standards, categorical standards, local limits, and state and local law;

(4) self monitoring, sampling, reporting, notification, and recordkeeping requirements; and

(5) statement of civil and criminal penalties for pretreatment violations and any applicable compliance schedule.[75]

The revisions also specify that POTWs must develop and implement procedures to:

(1) randomly sample and analyze the effluent from industrial users and conduct surveillance activities in order to identify occasional and continuing noncompliance with pretreatment standards;

(2) inspect and sample effluent from each significant industrial user at least once every year; and

(3) evaluate at least every two years whether each significant industrial user needs a plan to control slug discharges, including discharges from accidental spills.[76]

The revisions call for annual publication in local newspapers of the names of facilities that are in significant noncompliance with applicable pretreatment requirements.[77]

The revisions require Significant Noncategorical Industrial Users to submit reports to EPA every six months describing the nature, concentration and flow of their pollutants.[78] Under the revisions, all Industrial Users must promptly notify the POTW of any substantial change in the volume or character of their discharge.[79] With some exceptions, Industrial Users must also notify the POTW, the EPA Regional Waste Management Division Director, and the state hazardous waste management authorities in writing of any discharge into a POTW of any substance, which, if otherwise disposed of, would be a hazardous waste.[80] This one-time notification must include the name of the hazardous waste, the EPA hazardous waste number, and the type of discharge (continuous, batch, or other).[81] In addition, if more than 100 kilograms per month is discharged by one user, the notification must also (1) identify the hazardous constituents in the wastes, (2) estimate the mass and concentration of the constituents discharged during the month, and (3) estimate the mass of constituents expected to be discharged during the following twelve months.[82] Notification must be made within 180 days of the effective date of the rule. For industrial users who commence discharging after the effective date of the rule, notification must be made within 180 days of discharge.[83]

An industrial user must notify the authorities only once **for each hazardous waste discharged.** The notification requirement does not apply to pollutants already reported under the self-monitoring requirements of the pretreatment regulations.

### Combined Sewer Overflows

Many municipal sewer systems are designed with collection systems that carry industrial and domestic wastewater as well as storm water to publicly-owned treatment works. Such systems are known as combined sewers. During snowmelts or heavy rainfalls, the combined flows may exceed the capacity of the treatment works, causing untreated wastes to overflow into the receiving water. EPA estimates that there are approximately 15,000 to 20,000 combined sewer overflow (CSO) points in the United States.

Because CSOs can significantly affect water quality, on August 10, 1989 EPA issued a strategy to control CSOs.[84] EPA has three objectives to its strategy:

(1) To ensure that CSO discharges only occur due to wet weather;
(2) To bring all CSO points into compliance with technology-based requirements and applicable state water quality standards; and
(3) To minimize the impacts from wet weather overflows.

The strategy specified that states should have submitted permitting strategies to EPA no later than January 15, 1990 and Regions should have approved strategies no later than March 31, 1990.

## Storm Water Management

The Water Quality Act of 1987 added section 402(p) to the Clean Water Act, allowing EPA and the states to issue storm water discharge permits for (1) storm water **associated with industrial activity**; or (2) storm water from medium or large municipal separate storm sewer systems.[85] With some exceptions, section 402(p) prohibits EPA from requiring permits for other storm water discharges until 1992.

Section 402(p) required EPA to promulgate regulations concerning permit applications by February 4, 1989. Under that section, industrial and **large** municipal dischargers were required to submit permit applications by February 4, 1990. For any permit applications submitted, EPA is required to approve or deny applications for permits by February 4, 1991. Compliance must occur as soon as possible, but no later than three years after issuance of the permit. For **medium** municipal storm water dischargers, EPA is required to establish permit requirements by February 4, 1991; permit applications for such dischargers are due by February 4, 1992. EPA must then issue or deny permits by February 4, 1993.

On December 7, 1988, EPA proposed permit application requirements for storm water discharges associated with industrial activity and discharges from **large** municipal separate storm sewer systems (the "1988 Proposal").[86] EPA missed the statutory deadline of February 4, 1989 for promulgating final regulations and a law suit was brought to require EPA to promulgate the regulation. EPA entered a court approved consent decree, agreeing to promulgate final storm water permit application regulations by July 20, 1990. EPA missed this deadline too, and recently, the U.S. District Court for Oregon ordered EPA to promulgate the regulations by October 31, 1990.

Although EPA failed to promulgate application requirements, EPA takes the position that industrial and large municipal dischargers were still required to comply with the February 4, 1990 deadline for submitting storm water permit applications.[87] To do so, dischargers would have had to submit information in accordance with EPA's generic NPDES permit application requirements.[88]

Because the 1988 Proposal, together with its preamble, spans more than 70 pages in the *Federal Register*, a complete description of the proposed storm water permit application regulations is obviously beyond the scope of this publication. Accordingly, the proposed permit application requirements are described below generally.

EPA's proposed regulation broadly defines "storm water discharge associated with industrial activity" as:

any 'point source'. . .which is used for collecting and conveying storm water and which is located at an industrial plant or directly related to manufacturing, processing or raw materials storage areas at an industrial plant.[89]

The term does **not** include "areas located on plant lands separate from the plant's industrial activities, such as office buildings and accompanying parking lots as long as the drainage from the excluded areas is not mixed with storm water drained from lands used for the plant's industrial activities."[90]

EPA has proposed two options for permit applications: (1) individual permit applications, and (2) group applications.[91] Under the proposed regulations, individual applications would be due within one year after publication of the final rules.[92] Group applications could be filed by groups of facilities that are either (1) part of the same effluent subcategory, or (2) are "sufficiently similar."[93]

Group Applications would be submitted in two parts. The first part is designed to enable EPA to determine whether a Group Application would be appropriate.[94] This would be due within four months of publication of final rules.[95] The second part of the application would be due within 18 months of publication of the final rule.[96]

Generally, facilities that discharge storm water associated with industrial activity would be exempt from storm water management regulations if they discharge into a municipal separate storm sewer system.[97] To receive this exemption, however, such systems must supply certain information to the municipality within six months after publication of the final regulations.[98]

Applications for medium and large municipal separate storm sewers would be due in two parts. The first part would provide information about the municipality's existing storm water management program.[99] The second part would include information on proposed storm water management programs and test results on discharges from a representative number of outfalls for the system.[100] For large municipal separate storm sewer systems, part one of the application would be due within one year after promulgation of the final rules; part two would be due within two years.[101] For medium separate storm sewers, part one of the application would be due by November 4, 1990; part two would be due by February 4, 1992.[102]

## Anti-Backsliding

In an effort to preserve progress toward improved water quality, the WQA of 1987 restricts the relaxation of effluent limits and water quality standards ("backsliding"), during permit renewal, reissuance, or modification.

Under section 402(o) of the CWA, a discharger with a permit based on best professional judgment (BPJ) may not obtain a less stringent technology-based permit limitation even if EPA promulgates a less stringent effluent limitation. Similarly, under section 303(d)(4) of the CWA, a discharger's water quality based effluent limitations may not be relaxed even if the state promulgates less stringent water quality standards.

For technology-based limits set by use of BPJ, section 402(o)(2) establishes six narrow exceptions to the prohibition on backsliding. Four of these six exceptions also apply to water quality based effluent limits. Importantly, section 402(o)(3) of the CWA provides that in no event may a revised BPJ or water quality based permit violate either applicable national technology-based guidelines or state water quality standards.

On January 4, 1989, EPA promulgated a regulation codifying the anti-backsliding provisions of section 402(o).[103] Previous to this codification, under 40 C.F.R. § 122.62(a)(15), EPA had allowed a BPJ permit to be modified due to excessive costs. This exception was eliminated in the codification amendment.

EPA is currently developing guidance on implementation of its anti-backsliding rules. Recently, it issued draft guidance entitled "Interim Guidance on Implementation of Section 402(o) Anti-Backsliding Rules for Water Quality-Based Permits." EPA expects to publish final guidance on anti-backsliding soon.

## Enforcement Developments

On April 17, 1990, EPA Administrator Reilly rendered a decision that could have a major impact on the use of compliance schedules. Reilly ruled that compliance schedules may not be used to delay compliance deadlines for water quality standards with mandatory deadlines.[104]

EPA has long used compliance schedules, putting dischargers on a timetable for compliance, when it has been clear that the dischargers could not meet statutory deadlines. Compliance schedules have been used as a negotiating tool in reliance on a 1978 memorandum by the Office of General Counsel (OGC).[105] In the 1978 memorandum, OGC noted that the CWA is silent on use of compliance schedules and concluded that EPA should be free to use compliance schedules as it sees fit. Reilly disagreed, however, ruling that compliance schedules may not be used unless authorized by state regulations.[106]

The issue of whether compliance schedules may be used is not settled. On August 13, 1990, in a highly unusual move, OGC filed a petition for modification of Reilly's decision. EPA sources believe that Reilly would reach a decision on OGC's petition early in 1991.

In a case that may have a major impact on federal enforcement actions, the court in *United States v. Winchester Municipal Utilities*, No. 84-289 (E.D. Ky. May 14, 1990), ordered the federal government to pay attorneys' fees incurred by a POTW in defending a CWA enforcement action. In that case, the Department of Justice, on behalf of EPA, sought up to $50 million in civil penalties from Winchester Municipal Utilities (WMU) for violations of the CWA. The violations resulted from defects in the wastewater treatment plant due to problems in engineering, construction and equipment provided by WMU's contractors.

Eventually EPA and WMU entered a consent agreement giving WMU a longer period to construct its plant than the government originally sought, relaxing certain interim effluent limitations, reducing the "stipulated penalties" for violations of those limitations and making other concessions to WMU. In return, WMU agreed to pay a civil penalty of $10,000.

WMU then sought attorneys fees and expenses under the Equal Access to Justice Act (EAJA).[107] The court awarded almost $200,000 in fees to WMU, ruling that WMU was the prevailing party because the terms of the final consent decree were closer to WMU's original settlement position than to the government's.

## Regulation of Wetlands

Wetlands are regulated under section 404 of the CWA, which prohibits the discharge of "dredged or fill" materials into "navigable waters" without a permit. Although wetlands often are not "navigable" within the common usage of that term, section 404 extends to wetlands because "navigable waters" is defined broadly by regulation to include "wetlands" and "adjacent wetlands."

For the most part, wetlands are regulated by the Army Corps of Engineers with oversight by EPA. Three recent developments have affected the interaction of these two agencies with respect to wetlands regulation. These developments, which concern (1) wetlands identification, (2) use of mitigation in wetlands regulation; and (3) enforcement of wetland violations, are discussed below. In addition, two recent court decisions which concern "takings" of wetlands are briefly discussed.

### Joint Wetlands Identification Manual

Three criteria are important in determining whether an area constitutes wetlands: (1) the presence of water; (2) the presence of certain types of vegetation; and (3) the presence of certain soil types.[108]

Until recently, the four federal agencies with wetland responsibilities — EPA, Fish and Wildlife Service, Army Corps of Engineers, and Soil Conservation Services — each had their own methods for identifying wetlands, each giving different emphasis to the three wetland criteria. As a result, the jurisdiction of these agencies was often confused. On January 10, 1989, these agencies put an end to the confusion by adopting a joint Federal Manual for identifying and delineating wetlands. Significantly, although all three wetlands criteria — water, vegetation and soils — must be present under the new joint wetlands manual, the manual allows one criterion to be presumed from the presence of another. This development has caused great concern among many landowners who fear that use of the new joint manual will result in a major increase in the amount of the land designated as "wetland". Because of these concerns, the Corps has accepted public comment on this manual.[109]

### Memorandum of Agreement on Use of Mitigation

On February 6, 1990, the Corps and EPA entered into a memorandum of agreement on the use of "mitigation" in the wetlands permitting process, thereby ending a longstanding dispute between the two agencies.

Under the Corps regulations, mitigation includes "avoiding, minimizing, rectifying, reducing, or compensating for losses." It typically includes setting aside valuable wetlands and creating new ones. The Corps' mitigation regulation further provides that "[l]osses will be avoided to the extent practicable. Compensation may occur on-site or at an off-site location."[110] Historically, the Corps has viewed mitigation as a basis for granting a permit that would otherwise be contrary to the public interest. In contrast, EPA took the position that mitigation should not be as a basis to make the permit decision, but should be used only to lessen the adverse impacts of a project that warrants a permit without consideration of mitigation.

The February 6, 1990 Memorandum of Agreement on the Use of Mitigation under the EPA 404(b)(1) Guidelines (the "Mitigation MOA") contains several important provisions. First, the Mitigation MOA incorporates the concept of "no net loss" to wetlands. The Mitigation MOA recognizes that "no net loss" is a goal that may not be achievable in each permit action. Second, the Mitigation MOA provides the following hierarchy for mitigating losses: (1) avoid impact to wetlands; (2) minimize impacts; and (3) compensate for losses.

Third, where there are unavoidable wetland losses the Mitigation MOA looks for compensation-to-loss ratio of at least 1:1. When establishing compensation-to-loss ratios, the likelihood of success of a created wetland must be considered. If the new wetland is unlikely to thrive, the Mitigation MOA provides that a greater amount should be created. The Mitigation MOA further provides that the respective values of the destroyed and created wetlands must be considered. If the wetlands to be destroyed are of low value, a lesser amount of high value created wetlands may be required.

Lastly, the Mitigation MOA approves of the idea of wetlands banking. Under this concept, a developer may create wetlands and later use them to set off wetland losses.

### Memorandum of Agreement on Enforcement

On January 19, 1989, EPA and the Corps signed a Memorandum of Agreement on Enforcement (the "Enforcement MOA"). In the past, EPA and the Corps each had some jurisdiction for prosecution of wetlands violations. The Corps would prosecute violations of Corps-issued permits, but EPA would prosecute discharge violations when no permit was issued. Under the Enforcement MOA, the Corps takes a greater role in enforcement. The Corps will conduct investigations and use its enforcement authorities to prosecute wetland violations. The Corps will act as lead agency for all violations of Corps-issued permits. Lastly, the Corps will enforce against unpermitted discharges, except in the following four cases in which EPA will enforce violations: (1) repeat violators; (2) flagrant violations; (3) EPA requests a class of cases or a particular case; or (4) the Corps recommends that an EPA administrative penalty may be warranted.

### Recent Court Decisions on "Takings" of Wetlands

The Fifth Amendment of the United States Constitution provides in part, "Nor shall private property be taken for public use, without just compensation." For the first time federal courts in two recent decisions have found that denial of wetlands permits constituted "takings" of private lands. Accordingly, the courts ordered the government to compensate the landowners.

In each of the cases, *Loveladies Harbor, Inc. v. United States*, No. 243-83L (Cl. Ct. July 23, 1990) (available on WESTLAW at 1990 WL 103691) and *Florida Rock Industries v. United States*, No. 266-82L (Cl. Ct. July 23, 1990) (available on WESTLAW at 1990 WL 103774), the U.S. Claims Court found that by denying wetland permits to the landowners, the Army Corps of Engineers had left the landowners without an economically viable use for their property. In the *Loveladies Harbor* case, the court awarded the landowners $2,685,000 as compensation for the taking. In *Florida Rock Industries*, the court awarded the landowners $1,029,000 as compensation.

## Regulation of Drinking Water

In 1986, Congress enacted significant amendments to the Safe Drinking Water Act.[111] Under the SDWA Amendments, EPA regulates public water systems that have at least fifteen service connections or serve at least 25 people.[112] The SDWA Amendments direct EPA to set Maximum Contaminant Level Goals (MCLGs) and National Primary Drinking Water Regulations (NPDWRs) for 83 specific contaminants.[113] EPA also must establish MCLGs and NPDWRs for any other contaminant in drinking water that "may have any adverse effect upon the health of persons and which is known or antici-pated to occur in public water systems."[114]

MCLGs are nonenforceable goals that must "be set at the level at which no known or anticipated adverse effects on the health of per-sons occur and which allows an adequate margin of safety."[115] NPDWRs may be either Maximum Contaminant Levels (MCLs) or treatment technique requirements.[116] MCLs must be set at a level "as close to maximum contaminant level goal as is feasible."[117] "Feasible" refers to "the use of the best technology, treatment techniques and other means, which the Administrator finds, after examination for ef-ficacy under field conditions, are available (taking cost into consider-ation)."[118] To date, EPA has promulgated MCLGs and NPDWRs for 34 contaminants.[119]

Under the SDWA Amendments, EPA was required by January 1, 1988 (and every three years thereafter) to publish a list of drinking water contaminants that may require regulation under the SDWA.[120] EPA must publish MCLGs, NPDWRs and monitoring requirements for at least 25 contaminants by January 1, 1991 and every three years thereafter.[121] On August 18, 1988, EPA proposed MCLs and MCLGs for lead and copper.[122] On May 22, 1989, EPA proposed MCLs and MCLGs for 30 synthetic organic chemicals and eight inorganic chem-icals.[123] On July 25, 1990, EPA proposed MCLs and MCLGs for an ad-ditional 18 synthetic organic chemicals and six inorganic chemi-cals.[124] EPA tentatively expects to promulgate a final rule for these contaminants by June 1991.

Under the SDWA, states have primary enforcement responsibility for public water systems when EPA determines that the state has met its approval criteria. Every state and territory has qualified to enforce the SDWA program except the District of Columbia, Indiana and Wyoming. As a result, EPA rarely brings enforcement actions under this act.

The SDWA has had an important impact on the RCRA and Super-fund programs, however. Under RCRA, the groundwater monitor-ing levels for 14 hazardous constituents are based on the MCLs.[125] Although the MCLs for these constituents have since been amended, the groundwater monitoring levels in the RCRA regulations contin-ue to be based on the original MCL levels.

Under EPA's recently proposed RCRA Corrective Action Rule for Solid Waste Management Units, EPA also has proposed using MCLs as action levels that would trigger a remedial investigation once the level of contamination in the groundwater exceeds the MCL.[126] In the preamble to the proposal, EPA notes that groundwater would probably be required to be cleaned up to the levels of MCLs if the groundwater could be used as a public drinking water supply. If it could not be used as a public drinking water supply, it might not have to be cleaned up to MCL levels.[127] (See Chapter V by Karl S. Bourdeau for a detailed analysis of corrective action.)

MCLs and MCLGs also are referenced in CERCLA. The Superfund Amendments and Reauthorization Act of 1986 provides that in a CERCLA cleanup MCLGs are binding where they are "relevant and appropriate."[128] The recently promulgated amendments to the National Contingency Plan provide that in a remedial action, MCLGs that are set above zero "shall be attained for ground or surface waters that are current or potential sources of drinking water, where the MCLGs are relevant and appropriate."[129] If an MCLG for a contaminant either is set at zero or is determined not to be relevant and appropriate, the MCL must be attained where it is relevant and appropriate.[130]

Thus, the SDWA has implications far beyond protection of public water supplies.

## Groundwater Protection

### Wellhead Protection Area Programs

To aid in the protection of groundwater, Congress enacted section 1428 of the SDWA, requiring states to develop wellhead protection area programs. "Wellhead protection areas" are those surface and subsurface areas surrounding a water well or wellfield through which contaminants are likely to move to reach the well or wellfield. Section 1428 required states to submit their wellhead protection area programs to EPA by June 19, 1989. As of the date of this writing, EPA's Office of Groundwater Protection had received 34 state submittals; only six programs had been approved.

Wellhead protection area programs must (1) specify the duties of state and local agencies and public water supply systems; (2) determine the wellhead protection area for each wellhead; (3) identify sources of contamination within each wellhead area; (4) describe a program containing technical and financial assistance, implementation of control measures, education, training and demonstration projects to protect the water supply; (5) include contingency plans to provide for alternate drinking water supply in the event of well contamination; and (6) require that all potential sources of contaminants within the wellhead area be considered.[131] EPA may reject a state's wellhead protection program if EPA judges that the program is inadequate to protect public water systems. The state must then modify its program based on the recommendations of EPA and resubmit it to EPA. States are required to implement their program within two years of submitting the program to the Administrator.

### Underground Injection Control

In another effort to protect underground sources of drinking water, SDWA required EPA to develop regulations for state programs concerning underground injection control (UIC).[132] Such regulations are required to contain minimum requirements for effective programs to prevent underground injection which endangers drinking water sources.[133] States that receive approval from EPA for their UIC programs will have primary enforcement responsibility for underground water sources.[134] For states that either do not develop a UIC program or fail to obtain EPA approval, EPA is authorized to create a UIC program for the state.[135] EPA may enforce UIC programs in states with primary enforcement authority only after giving the state 30-days notice.[136] In states that do not have primary enforcement authority, EPA is not required to notify the state before commencing an enforcement action.[137]

# Conclusion and Future Trends

EPA's national effluent guidelines program is substantially non-functioning at the moment. All of the effluent guidelines except those for organic chemicals were basically promulgated prior to 1983 and are already reflected in the permits. Permit writers, for the most part, are no longer attempting to develop more stringent, *ad hoc* best available technology economically achievable (BAT) limits for most facilities. Instead, the emphasis has clearly shifted to the water quality based approach and to more stringent limitations based on state water quality standards and the enforceable bioassay testing or whole effluent toxicity (WET) limits.

Finally, future trends in water management will include planning for meeting the permitting requirements for discharges of storm water from industrial facilities. About 100,000 industrial facilities are expected to be affected by this final rule, which will create a massive burden of permits to be managed by EPA. The November 16, 1990, *Federal Register* published EPA's final regulation implementing the storm water program, which was signed October 31, 1990, by Administrator Reilly. This rule will require a large number of industrial facilities to apply for and obtain NPDES permits covering their specified discharges. Operators of many construction areas may need to obtain NPDES permits for any onsite storm water discharges. Facilities like hazardous waste treatment, storage and disposal facilities operating under Subtitle C of RCRA, Subtitle D landfills, land application sites, recycling facilities, steam electric power generating facilities, transportation facilities, and other specific SIC industry segments also will be affected by this rule.

In the rule, EPA has adopted several innovative procedures for expediting the process. In addition to the individual application or participation in a group application, a final alternative for permit application consists of submitting a "notice of intent" that is to be covered by a "baseline general permit" promulgated by either EPA or an NPDES-delegated state. In early 1991, EPA is expected to develop additional baseline general permits covering large categories of industrial discharges in states where EPA runs the NPDES program.

In states that have received authority to administer their own NPDES programs, the EPA baseline general permits can be expected to serve as models. As the storm water program evolves, EPA can be expected to reduce the coverage of the baseline general permits.

The Clean Water Act comes up for reauthorization in the 102nd Congress and many of these issues may be clarified and/or redefined during the reauthorization process.

## About the Author

J. **Brian Molloy** is a partner in the law firm of Piper & Marbury in Washington, D.C. Previously, he was Director of the Enforcement Division of the U.S. Environmental Protection Agency, where he was responsible for the direction of EPA's national water pollution and hazardous waste enforcement and compliance monitoring programs. Prior to that position, he had been Assistant Director of the NPDES Permit Program. Mr. Molloy received a Bachelor of Civil Engineering degree from Manhattan College, a Master of Science degree in Civil Engineering from New York University and a J.D. degree from Georgetown University Law Center. He is a member of the bars of Virginia and the District of Columbia and is a Professional Engineer in the District of Columbia.

## Endnotes

1. CWA §§ 301, 402, 33 U.S.C. §§ 1311, 1342.

2. CWA § 402, 33 U.S.C. § 1342.

3. 53 *Fed. Reg.* 49416, 49438, col. 1 (Dec. 7, 1988). Note that the term "state" refers to both states and territories, including the District of Columbia, the Commonwealth of Puerto Rico, the Virgin Islands, Guam, American Samoa, the Commonwealth of the Northern Mariana Islands, and the Trust Territory of the Pacific Islands. CWA § 502 (3), 33 U.S.C. § 1362(3).

4. CWA § 402(c), 33 U.S.C. § 1342(c); 40 C.F.R. Part 123.

5. CWA § 304(e), 33 U.S.C. § 1314(e); 40 C.F.R. Part 125 Subpart K.

6. 40 C.F.R. § 125.102.

7. *Id.*

8. *See* 40 C.F.R. § 122.41.

9. CWA § 402(k), 33 U.S.C. § 1342(k).

10. *See* 40 C.F.R. Parts 405-71.

11. CWA § 301(b)(1)(A), 33 U.S.C. § 1311(b)(1)(A).

12. CWA § 301(b)(2)(E), 33 U.S.C. § 1311(b)(2)(E).

13. CWA §§ 301(b)(2)(F), 307(a), 33 U.S.C. §§ 1311(b)(2)(F), 1317(a).

14. CWA § 301(b)(2)(C)-(F), 33 U.S.C. § 1311(b)(2)(C)-(F).

15. CWA § 306, 33 U.S.C. § 1316.

16. CWA § 301(i), 33 U.S.C. § 1311(i).

17. 40 C.F.R. § 133.102.

18. CWA § 301(n), 33 U.S.C. § 1311(n); 40 C.F.R. § 122.21(m)(1).

19. *See* 40 C.F.R. § 125.3.

20. Although water quality standards are generally set by states, EPA has authority to establish water quality based effluent limitations in order to protect uses of specific segments of water bodies. CWA § 302, 33 U.S.C. § 1312.

21. CWA § 303(c), 33 U.S.C. § 1313(c).

22. *See* CWA § 303(c)(2)(A), 33 U.S.C. § 1313(c)(2)(A).

23. CWA § 303(d)(1)(C), 33 U.S.C. § 1313(d)(1)(C); 40 C.F.R. § 130.7.

24. *See* CWA § 302, 33 U.S.C. § 1312. NOTE: § 302 has never been used.

25. 40 C.F.R. § 403.5.

26. 40 C.F.R. § 403.6.

27. 40 C.F.R. § 403.5(a).

28. 40 C.F.R. § 403.3(i).

29. 40 C.F.R. § 403.5(b).

30. EPA has established more than 40 industrial categories that are subject to National Categorical Pretreatment Standards. 40 C.F.R. Part 403, App. C.

31. CWA § 307(b), 33 U.S.C. § 1317(b).

32. CWA § 301(n), 33 U.S.C. § 1311(n); 40 C.F.R. § 403.13.

33. 40 C.F.R. § 403.8.

34. 40 C.F.R. § 403.5(d).

35. 40 C.F.R. § 403.5(d); CWA § 307(d), 33 U.S.C. § 1317(d).

36. 40 C.F.R. § 403.8(f)(1).

37. CWA § 309(a), 33 U.S.C. § 1319(a).

38. CWA § 309(g), 33 U.S.C. § 1319(g).

39. CWA § 309(b), U.S.C. § 1319(b).

40. *Tull v. United States*, 481 U.S. 412 (1987).

41. CWA § 309(c), 33 U.S.C. § 1319(c).

42. CWA § 309(c)(3)(A), 33 U.S.C. § 1319(c)(3)(A).

43. *Id.*

44. *Id.*

45. *See* 40 C.F.R. Part 15.

46. A state may not obtain NPDES permitting authority unless the state has adequate authority to enforce permits and the permit program. CWA § 402(b)(7), 33 U.S.C. § 1342(b)(7).

47. *See, e.g.,* Virginia Code § 62.1-44.32 (civil penalty provision).

48. CWA § 505, 33 U.S.C. § 1365.

49. CWA § 505(b)(1), 33 U.S.C. § 1365(b)(1).

50. *Id.*

51. *Gwaltney of Smithfield v. Chesapeake Bay Foundation*, 484 U.S. 49 (1987).

52. *Id.*

53. CWA § 304(l)(1)(A)(i), 33 U.S.C. § 1314(l)(1)(A)(i); 54 *Fed. Reg.* 23868, 23869, col. 3 (June 2, 1989). *See* EPA Office of Water, *Final Guidance for Implementation of Requirements under section 304(l) of the Clean Water Act as Amended* 10-13 (March 1988).

54. CWA § 304(l)(1)(A)(ii), 33 U.S.C. § 1314(l)(1)(A)(ii); 54 *Fed. Reg.* 23869, col. 3 (June 2, 1989).

55. CWA § 304(l)(1)(B), 33 U.S.C. § 1314(l)(1)(B); 54 *Fed. Reg.* 23869, col. 3 (June 2, 1989).

56. CWA § 304(l)(1)(C), 33 U.S.C. § 1314(l)(1)(C).

57. CWA § 304(1)(1)(D), 33 U.S.C. § 1314(l)(1)(D).

58. *Id.*

59. 40 C.F.R. §§ 130.10(d)(9) and 123.46(b).

60. CWA § 303(c)(2)(B), 33 U.S.C. § 1313(c)(2)(B).

61. EPA has developed aquatic life criteria for 32 of the 126 priority pollutants. 55 *Fed. Reg.* 14350, col. 3 (April 17, 1990).

62. The word "whole" in the phrase "whole effluent toxicity" does **not** preclude dilution of the effluent. 54 *Fed. Reg.* 23868, 23871, col. 1 (June 2, 1989).

63. 54 *Fed. Reg.* 23868, 23871, col. 2 (June 2, 1989).

64. *Id.*

65. 44 *Fed. Reg.* 34396-97 (June 14, 1979).

66. "Development of Water Quality-Based Permit Limitations for Toxic Pollutants; National Policy," 49 *Fed. Reg.* 9016 (March 9, 1984).

67. *Natural Resources Defense Council v. EPA*, 859 F.2d 156, 189 (D.C. Cir. 1988).

68. CWA § 303(c)(2)(B), 33 U.S.C. § 1313(c)(2)(B).

69. 40 C.F.R. § 122.44(d).

70. 55 *Fed. Reg.* 30082, 30128, col. 2-3 (July 24, 1990) (to be codified at 40 C.F.R. § 122.21(j)(1)).

71. 55 *Fed. Reg.* at 30128, col. 3 (to be codified at 40 C.F.R. § 122.21(2)).

72. 55 *Fed. Reg.* 30082 (July 24, 1990).

73. 55 *Fed. Reg.* at 30128, col. 2-3 (to be codified at 40 C.F.R. § 122.21(j)(1)).

74. 55 *Fed. Reg.* at 30129, col. 2 (to be codified at 40 C.F.R. § 403.5(b)(1)).

75. 55 *Fed. Reg.* at 30129, col. 3 (to be codified at 40 C.F.R. § 403.8(f)(iii)).

76. 55 *Fed. Reg.* at 30130, col. 1 (to be codified at 40 C.F.R. § 403.8(f)(v)).

77. 55 *Fed. Reg.* at 30130, col. 2 (to be codified at 40 C.F.R. § 403.8(f)(vii)).

78. 55 *Fed. Reg.* at 30131 (to be codified at 40 C.F.R. § 403.12(h)).

79. 55 *Fed. Reg.* at 30131, col. 1 (to be codified at 40 C.F.R. § 403.12(j)).

80. 55 *Fed. Reg.* at 30131, col. 2-3 (to be codified at 40 C.F.R. § 403.12(p)); *see also* 55 *Fed. Reg.* at 30099-30105.

81. *Id.*

82. *Id.*

83. *Id.*

84. *See* 54 *Fed. Reg.* 37370 (Sept. 8, 1989) (announcing availability of National Combined Sewer Overflow Document).

85. "Large" municipal separate storm sewer systems serve more than 250,000 people; "medium" systems serve more than 100,000, but less than 250,000, people. 53 *Fed. Reg.*

49416, 49467 (Dec. 7, 1988) (Proposed 40 C.F.R. § 122.26(b)(4) & (7)).

86. *See* 53 *Fed. Reg.* 49416 (Dec. 7, 1988).

87. Memorandum from James R. Elder, Director of Office of Water Enforcement and Permits, to Water Management Division Directors, Regions I-X and NPDES State Directors re February 4, 1990 Deadline for Storm Water Permit Applications (Jan. 31, 1990).

88. *Id.; see* 40 C.F.R. § 122.21(f).

89. 53 *Fed. Reg.* at 49467-68 (Proposed 40 C.F.R. § 122.26(b)(13)).

90. *Id.*

91. 53 *Fed. Reg.* at 49468-69.

92. *Id.* at 49473.

93. *Id.* at 49469.

94. *Id.* at 49469-70.

95. *Id.* at 49473.

98. *Id.*

99. *Id.* at 49466.

100. *Id.*

101. 53 *Fed. Reg.* at 49470.

102. *Id.* at 49471.

103. *Id.* at 49473.

104. *Id.*

105. *See* 54 *Fed. Reg.* 246 (Jan. 4, 1989) (codified at 40 C.F.R. § 122.44(1)(2)).

106. *In the Matter of Star-Kist Caribe, Inc.,* NPDES Appeal No. 88-5 (April 17, 1990) (Order on Petition for Reconsideration).

107. Memorandum from James A. Rogers, Associate General Counsel, EPA Water and Solid Waste Division, to the Deputy Assistant Administrator for Water Enforcement (Dec. 28, 1978).

106. *In the Matter of Star-Kist Caribe, Inc.,* at 20-21.

107. 28 U.S.C. § 2412(d).

108. 40 C.F.R. § 232.2(r) provides:
Wetlands means those areas that are inundated or saturated by surface or ground water at a frequency and duration sufficient to support, and that under normal circumstances do support, a prevalence of vegetation typically adapted for life in saturated soil conditions. Wetlands generally include swamps, marshes, bogs, and similar areas.

109. *See* 55 *Fed. Reg.* 24138 (June 14, 1990) and 55 *Fed. Reg.* 33349 (Aug. 15, 1990).

110. 33 C.F.R. § 320.4(r).

111. Pub. L. No. 99-339, 100 Stat. 642 (1986).

112. SDWA § 1401(4); 42 U.S.C. § 300f(4).

113. 42 U.S.C. § 300g-1(b)(1) (referring to lists of contaminants published at 47 *Fed. Reg.* 9352 (March 4, 1982) and 48 *Fed. Reg.* 45502 (Oct. 5, 1983)).

114. SDWA § 1412(b)(3)(A), 42 U.S.C. § 300g-1(b)(3)(A).

115. SDWA § 1412(b)(4), 42 U.S.C. § 300g-1(b)(4) & (7)(A).

116. SDWA § 1412(b)(4) & (7)(A), 42 U.S.C. § 300g-1(b)(4).

117. SDWA § 1412(b)(4), 42 U.S.C. § 300g-1(b)(4).

118. SDWA § 1412(b)(5), 42 U.S.C. § 300g-1(b)(5).

119. 55 *Fed. Reg.* 30798, 30817, col. 1 (July 27, 1990); 40 C.F.R. Part 141, Subparts B, F & G.

120. SDWA § 1412(b)(3), 42 U.S.C. § 300g-1(b)(3).

121. *Id.*

122. 53 *Fed. Reg.* 31516 (Aug. 18, 1988).

123. 54 *Fed. Reg.* 22062 (May 22, 1989).

124. 55 *Fed. Reg.* 30370 (July 25, 1990).

125. 40 C.F.R. § 264.94.

126. 55 *Fed. Reg.* 30798, 30876 (July 27, 1990) (Proposed 40 C.F.R. § 264.521).

127. 55 *Fed. Reg.* at 30816-17.

128. CERCLA § 121(d)(2)(A), 42 U.S.C. § 9621(d)(2)(A).

129. 55 *Fed. Reg.* 8666, 8848 col. 2-3 (March 8, 1990) (to be codified at 40 C.F.R. § 300.430(e)(2)(i)(B)).

130. 55 *Fed. Reg.* at 8848, col. 2-3 (to be codified at 40 C.F.R. § 300.430(e)(2)(i)(B) and (C)).

131. SDWA § 1428, 42 U.S.C. § 300h-7.

132. SDWA § 1421, 42 U.S.C. § 300h.

133. *Id.*

134. SDWA § 1422, 42 U.S.C. § 300h-1.

135. SDWA § 1422(c), 42 U.S.C. § 300h-1(c).

136. SDWA § 1423(a), 42 U.S.C. § 300h-2(a).

137. SDWA § 1423(b), 42 U.S.C. § 300h-2(b).

# IV

# Recent Resource Conservation and Recovery Act Developments

*Mark C. Pennington, Esq.*
*Morgan, Lewis & Bockius*
*New York, New York*

In the past five years, EPA has churned out an unprecedented volume of regulations under the Resource Conservation and Recovery Act (RCRA).  Much of this regulatory activity is mandated by the 1984 Hazardous and Solid Waste Amendments (HSWA), in which an impatient and untrusting Congress set a series of tight deadlines (soft and hard hammers) for EPA action and legislated many of the technical fine points of a new hazardous waste program.  The highly detailed nature of the HSWA requirements has created extraordinary challenges for EPA, for the courts, and for the regulated community.  Meanwhile, refinements of the definition of solid waste and reevaluations of the regulatory status of mining and mineral processing wastes continue to affect the list of wastes subject to RCRA Subtitle C regulation.

This chapter discusses a number of significant regulatory and judicial developments relating to hazardous waste regulation in recent years, with special emphasis on the toxicity characteristic rule, rulemakings relating to mineral processing wastes, and EPA's land disposal restrictions program.  It closes with a summary of EPA's own reflections on the RCRA Subtitle C program and its future.

## Definition of Solid Waste

In *American Mining Congress v.* EPA (AMC),[1] the D.C. Circuit held that EPA lacked authority to regulate secondary materials that are recycled and reused in an ongoing manufacturing or industrial process.  The Court's opinion was grounded in the premise that EPA's authority under RCRA is limited to regulation of materials that are discarded in the ordinary meaning of that word. In response to the *AMC* decision, EPA proposed a revised definition of solid waste.[2] EPA's proposal has drawn fire from industry as an overexpansive assertion of regulatory authority based on a flawed reading of the AMC decision.

In *American Petroleum Institute v. U.S. Environmental Protection Agency*,[3] the D.C. Circuit addressed another aspect of the continuing debate over when materials destined for reclamation are subject to regulation as solid wastes, and therefore as hazardous wastes. Environmental groups and the commercial treatment industry had challenged EPA's decision not to set treatment standards for K061 residues under the land disposal restrictions program. The Court remanded the rule, rejecting EPA's contention that the *AMC* decision precluded EPA from establishing treatment standards for K061 treatment residues.

K061 waste is the emissions control dust or sludge generated in the production of steel in electric furnaces. In a rulemaking under the land disposal restrictions or "land ban" program, EPA selected high temperature metals recovery as the treatment standard for the high-zinc nonwastewater category of K061 wastes. The metal reclamation process required by EPA's treatment standard is a process separate and distinct from the steel production process that generates the waste, and typically occurs at off-site reclamation facilities. Ordinarily, the residues derived from treatment of a listed hazardous waste are themselves considered hazardous wastes which may not be land disposed unless they meet land ban treatment standards.[4] However, EPA declined to set treatment standards for the residual slag from the recovery process, reasoning that the K061 slag ceases to be a discarded material when it reaches a metal reclamation facility.[5] EPA further justified its decision by explaining that the secondary materials reclaimed in zinc smelters such as those required by EPA's K061 treatment standard are indigenous to the recovery of zinc, and thus beyond the scope of RCRA authority.[6]

The Court rejected EPA's position that the *AMC* decision precluded EPA regulation of K061 residues. "Unlike the materials in question in *AMC*," the Court observed, "K061 is indisputably 'discarded' **before** being subject to metals reclamation," and thus "appears to remain within the scope of the Agency's authority."[7] The Court's remand includes specific instructions for EPA to reconcile its rulemaking with the broader purposes of RCRA and the Agency's prior interpretations of RCRA.

The D.C. Circuit reaffirmed this reasoning in another more recent case captioned *American Mining Congress v. EPA*,[8] rejecting AMC's contention that sludges from metal smelting operations were not solid wastes because they might be reclaimed in the future. The court held that K064, K065, and K066 sludges stored in surface impoundments are solid wastes because they have been removed from the ongoing industrial process and placed in units where they may pose a threat to human health and the environment.[9]

## Definition of Hazardous Waste

### The Toxicity Characteristic Rule

On March 29, 1990, EPA issued a final rule changing the test method to be used for determining whether wastes are hazardous by virtue of their toxicity, and adding 25 organic chemicals to the existing list of regulated toxic chemicals.[10] EPA also set regulatory thresholds for the new organic chemicals based on the toxicity of each constituent (chronic, risk reference doses), and the expected fate of the constituent when released into the environment.

The final rule replaces the existing Extraction Procedure (EP) Toxicity test with the toxicity characteristic leaching procedure (TCLP) as a test for determining whether a waste is hazardous for toxicity. Under the EP toxicity test, hazardous constituents are extracted through contact with an acidic leaching medium designed to simulate conditions in a municipal landfill.[11] The resulting leachate is analyzed to determine whether it contains any of 14 toxic contaminants (eight metals, four insecticides, two herbicides) in concentrations exceeding drinking water standards or health-based concentration limits. The TCLP was first developed in the land disposal restrictions program as a test to determine whether certain wastes require treatment before land disposal and whether certain treated wastes comply with treatment standards.[12] EPA's toxicity characteristic rule adds several refinements to the TCLP for use in both the land disposal restrictions program and as a test for determining whether wastes are hazardous for the characteristic of toxicity.[13] The new TCLP test retains the 14 existing contaminants and

## Recent Resource Conservation
## and Recovery Act Developments

their respective thresholds, while adding 25 organics, including such solvents as benzene, trichloroethylene, vinyl chloride, and carbon tetrachloride.

The final regulatory levels for the new organic constituents are based on the toxicity of each constituent and its expected fate in the environment, expressed as a dilution/attenuation factor of 100, which when multiplied by the toxicity value, results in the regulatory level.[14] The dilution attenuation factor was developed using a subsurface fate and transport model based on mismanagement of wastes in a municipal landfill. Despite comments that the landfill mismanagement scenario was inappropriate for surface impoundments, EPA concluded that it was unnecessary to develop a separate mismanagement scenario for surface impoundments. EPA determined that the landfill model could be used to predict leachate concentrations resulting from wastes managed in surface impoundments because dilution attenuation factors for wastes managed in impoundments and landfills were roughly equivalent.[15]

The toxicity characteristic rule takes effect on September 25, 1990, for large quantity generators (generators of more than 1,000 kilograms/month), and on March 29, 1991, for small quantity generators (generators of less than 1,000 kilograms per month). Up to 17,000 facilities will be affected by the rule, as many as 15,000 of them falling subject to RCRA hazardous waste regulations for the first time.[16] The bulk of the wastes newly regulated under the rule are wastewaters.

On the appropriate dates, facilities must come into compliance with applicable RCRA Subtitle C regulations for units that actively manage wastes containing any of the newly regulated chemicals at or above the regulatory levels. Interim status facilities must submit amended permit applications for newly regulated units, and permitted facilities must modify their permits to include such units.

Existing wastewater treatment ponds containing the newly regulated organic contaminants at regulatory levels must be retrofitted by March 24, 1994, with liners and groundwater monitoring stations. Retrofitting requirements may apply earlier for restricted wastes managed in landfills and surface impoundments during a national capacity variance.[17] Because the cost of such retrofitting is likely to be prohibitive, many facilities are expected to replace treatment ponds with tanks subject to Clean Water Act requirements rather than RCRA requirements.

The major costs of compliance are retrofitting surface impoundments or converting from impoundments to tanks; or for those units unable to convert in time, the additional costs of RCRA Subtitle C closure for impoundments and the RCRA corrective action costs triggered by operating the facility under interim status until closure and conversion to tanks.

EPA has determined that the rule creates an annual compliance cost of between $130 million and $400 million, roughly half of which will be borne by the petroleum refining, wholesale petroleum marketing, and petroleum pipeline industries.[18] Other significantly affected industries include organic chemicals, synthetic rubber, synthetic fibers, pulp and paper, and pharmaceuticals.[19]

While the revised toxicity characteristic will not be used as a criterion for determining whether or not to undertake Superfund cleanup actions or RCRA corrective actions, soil and contaminated debris from such cleanups that exhibit the toxicity characteristic must be handled as hazardous waste.[20]

The Agency has temporarily deferred the application of the new toxicity characteristic to cleanups of petroleum-contaminated media from leaking underground storage tanks. Pending further rulemaking, petroleum-contaminated media and debris that exhibit the toxicity characteristic for any of the newly listed organic constituents and are subject to corrective action will not be considered hazardous wastes.[21] The Agency is conducting an evaluation of the potentially enormous impact the rule could have on the large numbers of such cleanups underway or anticipated in coming years. Options under consideration for managing the large number of cleanups include an exemption for petroleum-contaminated materials exhibiting the toxicity characteristic and a streamlining of the regulatory process for tank cleanups.

## Bevill Wastes

In 1980, Congress temporarily excluded from Subtitle C regulation all "solid wastes from the extraction, beneficiation and processing of ores and minerals"[22] pending further study as to the appropriate regulatory controls for these wastes. Subsequently, EPA has withdrawn the so-called "Bevill Exclusion" for a number of waste categories.

### Metal Smelting Wastes

In 1988, EPA relisted as hazardous wastes six metal smelting wastes that were conditionally exempted from Subtitle C regulation by the Bevill Amendment.[23] In *American Mining Congress v. EPA*,[24] a group of industry petitioners challenged the relisting on procedural and substantive grounds. The court found that EPA had satisfied notice and comment requirements when it first proposed the wastes for listing in 1980, and that the Agency was not obligated to reopen the rule for comment. However, the court held that EPA had failed to provide a reasoned bases for relisting five of the six smelting wastes (K064, K065, K066, K088, K090, and K091). In relisting these wastes, EPA relied only on the background documents from the original listings in 1980 and on summary conclusions about post-1980 studies. The court remanded the rule to EPA for a fuller explanation of these five relistings, and upheld the relisting of K088 as adequately supported.[25]

On September 1, 1989, EPA refined its definition of mineral processing wastes and established final "high-volume, low-hazard" criteria for determining which mineral processing wastes may remain eligible for the Bevill exclusion.[26] Under the rule, wastes must meet all the relevant criteria to retain their status as excluded wastes. "High-volume" is defined as a minimum of 45,000 metric tons per facility per year for solid wastes and a minimum of 1 million tons per facility per year for liquid wastes. Wastes qualify as "low-hazard" if they generate a leachate with a pH of 1 to 13.5 after being subjected to EPA Test Method 1312, a pH toxicity and mobility test designed to simulate the effects of leachate generated by acid rain.

Applying these criteria to 25 mineral processing wastes, EPA determined that five wastes[27] met the criteria and should remain within the scope of the exclusion pending a final regulatory determination in January 1991. EPA concluded that an additional 20 wastes should remain within the temporary exclusion pending collection of further data. Effective March 1, 1990, all previously excluded mineral processing wastes apart from these 25 are subject to the hazardous waste regulations (in unauthorized states) if they display one or more of the characteristics of hazardous waste.[28]

On January 23, 1990, EPA issued a final rule removing five of the 20 conditionally exempt wastes from the Bevill exclusion.[29] The wastes are: furnace off-gas solids from elemental phosphorus production, process wastewater from primary lead processing, air pollution control dust/sludge from lightweight aggregate production, sulfate waste acids from titanium dioxide production, and sulfate process waste solids from titanium dioxide production. Effective July 23, 1990, these wastes are subject to Subtitle C regulations (in unauthorized states) if they exhibit a hazardous characteristic (or are otherwise identified or listed by EPA as hazardous).

Consistent with its policy of not regulating under Subtitle C wastes that were disposed of prior to the effective date of regulations identifying those wastes as hazardous, EPA does not intend to regulate existing waste management units whose contents are deemed hazardous by virtue of the narrowing of the Bevill exclusion.[30] Thus, a unit that received Bevill wastes before they were "de-Bevilled" (including wastes now considered hazardous) may continue to receive non-hazardous wastes, provided that no non-Bevill wastes that display hazardous characteristics are managed in these units. However, active management of hazardous de-Bevilled wastes, such as physical disturbances of accumulated wastes or disposal of additional hazardous wastes, will subject such units to Subtitle C regulation.

## The Land Disposal Restrictions Program

On May 8, 1990, in the latest stage of a familiar drama, EPA Administrator William K. Reilly signed a final rule establishing land disposal restrictions for "Third Third scheduled wastes." Reilly's action effectively removed the last of a series of "hammers" that had hovered menacingly over the Agency since passage of the RCRA Hazardous and Solid Wastes Amendments in 1984 ("the 1984 Amendments" or HSWA).

The 1984 Amendments established a series of deadlines by which EPA was required to evaluate land disposal of specific groups of hazardous wastes and to promulgate appropriate regulations prohibiting land disposal of wastes that do not meet Agency-specified treatment standards. Failure to issue regulations for certain high-priority wastes by the statutory deadlines would have triggered the "hard hammer": wastes in these categories would have been automatically banned from all forms of land disposal unless it were demonstrated that they would not migrate from the disposal unit for as long as they remained hazardous.

EPA has labored intensely to meet its mandate, publishing rules on dioxin and solvent containing wastes on November 7, 1986; "California List" wastes on July 8, 1987; and the remaining hazardous wastes in successive "thirds," the First Third on August 17, 1988, the Second Third on June 23, 1989, and the Third Third on June 1, 1990.[31] The Agency has taken full advantage of the flexibility afforded by the statute, deferring action on certain wastes until after the statutory "soft hammer" deadlines, and transferring some categories of wastes to later Thirds.[32] The process continues as EPA develops treatment standards for newly identified wastes and refines the standards for prohibited wastes, some of which were established based on limited data in the press to meet the final deadlines.

In the intervening months, the D.C. Circuit Court has issued a series of decisions on industry and environmental group challenges to the land ban regulations. Some of the Court's earlier decisions have shaped the latest installations in the land ban framework, and will be the subject of continuing debate in future rulemakings and litigation.

### Summary of the Land Ban Regulatory Framework

The land disposal restrictions program prohibits land disposal of specified hazardous wastes after certain dates unless:
(1) the waste meets best demonstrated available technology treatment standards; (2) the operator of a disposal unit has demonstrated that there will be no migration of hazardous constituents from the disposal unit for as long as the waste remains hazardous; (3) the prohibition for a particular waste has been postponed due to a nationwide lack of alternative treatment capacity; or (4) an individual facility obtains a case-by-case extension based on inability to arrange for alternative treatment capacity by the effective date of the prohibition.[33] "Land disposal" includes "any placement of...hazardous waste in a landfill, surface impoundment, waste pile, injection well, land treatment facility, salt dome formation, salt bed formation, or underground mine or cave."[34]

The land disposal restrictions apply prospectively. Thus, "hazardous wastes land disposed after the applicable effective dates are subject to the restrictions, but wastes land disposed prior to the effective dates are not required to be removed or exhumed for treatment. If however, wastes subject to the land ban are actively managed after the restrictions take effect, (i.e., removed or treated), they are subject to the land ban and to land ban treatment standards."[35]

Treatment standards under the land disposal restrictions program are based on the performance of the best demonstrated available technology to treat the waste (BDAT). BDAT standards may be expressed either in terms of concentrations of hazardous constituents in the waste or an extract of the waste, or as a specified technology. When BDAT is expressed in concentrations, any technology may be used to meet the standard. When BDAT is expressed as a specified technology, only that technology may be used to meet the standard. The regulations include a variance process to account for variations in waste matrices that may prevent achievement of the standards.[36]

A successful "no migration" demonstration allows land disposal of untreated hazardous wastes for up to ten years at a time in interim status disposal units, and for the length of the RCRA permit in permitted units. EPA's regulations provide specialized requirements for no migration demonstrations for underground injection of hazardous wastes.[37] Petitioners must demonstrate either that injected wastes will be rendered non-hazardous within the injection zone, or that injected wastes will remain confined in the injection zone for at least 10,000 years.[38] To demonstrate no migration, petitions must also show that there will be no movement of hazardous constituents outside the injection zone by means of molecular diffusion.[39]

Normally, prohibitions are effective immediately upon promulgation. However, EPA has the authority to postpone the effective date of a prohibition for up to two years if there is insufficient nationwide capacity to treat, store or dispose of a restricted waste by other means.[40] In situations of shortfall, EPA compares available and projected alternative treatment capacity with the volumes of waste requiring treatment, and schedules prohibitions according to the earliest date that adequate capacity will become available.

Individual facilities can obtain a one year reprieve (renewable once) from a prohibition by showing that they have entered into a binding contractual commitment to construct or otherwise provide for alternative capacity, but due to reasons beyond their control, capacity cannot reasonably be made available by the effective date of the prohibition.[41]

# Land Ban Case Law

### Technology-Based Treatment Standards

In *Hazardous Waste Treatment Council v. U.S. EPA*,[42] the Court of Appeals for the D.C. Circuit upheld EPA's decision to base treatment standards for solvent and dioxin wastes on best demonstrated available technology rather than on risk-based "screening levels."[43] However, the Court remanded the rule to EPA to clarify why it had selected only technology-based treatment standards, as opposed to the risk-based standards also included in the proposal.[44]

Industry petitioners challenged EPA's best demonstrated available technology approach for its failure to "cap" treatment standards at levels below which further treatment is no longer necessary to minimize threats to human health and the environment. In the face of statutory language citing "uncertainties associated with land disposal," the Court rejected the notion that EPA was required to set treatment standards at levels at which "it is conclusively presumed that no threat to health or the environment exists."[45] While finding that the statute did not foreclose EPA's technology-based approach, the Court cautioned that EPA was not free to require treatment beyond the point at which such threats to human health and the environment no longer exist.[46]

The Court rejected industry's claim that EPA's land ban treatment standards were unreasonable because they required treatment to below established hazard levels in other regulatory programs, observing that wastes at concentrations below the cited thresholds could still pose threats to human health and the environment.[47]

In response to the Court's remand, EPA justified its approach by observing that RCRA does not mandate the use of risk-based standards, and that the legislative history in fact expresses a preference for use of best available technology.[48] EPA explained that it was not in a position to establish risk-based standards because of difficulties in setting threshold levels for hazardous wastes at which threats to human health and the environment are minimized.[49] Until such thresholds can be established, EPA believes that the technology-based approach satisfies Congressional intent by removing as much as possible the uncertainties associated with land disposal of hazardous waste. The Court accepted EPA's explanation and dismissed the litigation on March 15, 1990.

### Leachate and Contaminated Media

In *Chemical Waste Management, Inc. v. EPA,*[50] the D.C. Circuit upheld EPA's application of land ban treatment standards to leachate derived from wastes that were not regulated as hazardous wastes at the time they were disposed. The Court found that EPA's application of First Third treatment standards to leachate derived from pre-RCRA wastes was prospective rather than retroactive in effect in that it applies to active management of residues occurring after the effective date of the ban on the wastes from which they are derived. In the Court's view, collection of leachate from historic wastes is a form of active waste management sufficient to trigger Subtitle C regulations and land ban treatment standards.

On a related issue, the Court upheld EPA's interpretation that soil and debris contaminated with listed hazardous wastes are listed hazardous wastes subject to land ban treatment requirements. The Court accepted EPA's position as a logical extension of the "derived-from" and "mixture" rules and of the existing policy that wastes from leaks and spills of hazardous wastes must be managed as hazardous wastes.[51]

Chem Waste also had sought review of the so-called "waste code carry-through principle," under which leachate derived from multiple listed wastes ("multi-source leachate") is considered subject to treatment standards for each of the listed wastes from which the leachate derives. The Court's review was limited to the retroactivity and contaminated media issues because of the impending settlement under which all multi-source leachate was transferred to the Third Third rulemaking.

### Minimum Technology Requirements
### for National Capacity Variance Wastes

In *Mobil Oil Corporation v. EPA,*[52] the Court upheld EPA's determination that land disposal of First Third wastes subject to a national capacity variance is permitted only if the individual landfills or surface impoundments into which they are placed satisfy minimum technology requirements under RCRA subsection 3004(o) (leachate collection, double liners, and groundwater monitoring).

RCRA subsection 3004(h)(4) provides that wastes subject to a national capacity variance "may be disposed of in a landfill or surface impoundment only if such facility is in compliance with the requirements of subsection (o) of this section." In a prior rulemaking, EPA interpreted the term *facility* in this subsection to mean a collection of individual units at a waste management complex.[53] Since minimum technology requirements did not apply to existing units, EPA reasoned, a "facility" was in compliance with subsection 3004 (o) as long as new and expanded units at the complex were equipped with leachate collection, double liners, and groundwater monitoring systems. National capacity variance wastes could be disposed of in landfills and surface impoundments that did not meet those standards, provided that any new units at the facility satisfied them.

Upon re-evaluation of this issue in the First Third rulemaking, EPA determined that the term *facility* refers to the individual waste management unit.[54] Mobil challenged EPA's new reading as unreasonable and inconsistent with various prior Agency interpretations of the term *facility*. The Court found that EPA is entitled to construe the term to mean different things in different contexts, provided that the individual interpretations best satisfy the purposes of the statute.[55] By interpreting the statute narrowly to require safeguards for disposal of national capacity variance wastes, EPA acted consistently with congressional intent that untreated wastes be managed in a protective manner.

### Land Treatment

In *American Petroleum Institute v. U.S. Environmental Protection Agency*,[56] the petroleum industry sought review of EPA's determination that land treatment may not be considered best demonstrated available technology for petroleum refining wastes. Land treatment involves "the application of wastes to the soil surface or the incorporation of wastes into the upper layers of the soil in order to degrade, transform, or immobilize [their] hazardous constituents."[57] The Court upheld EPA's decision not to consider land treatment as BDAT, observing that Congress specifically designated land treatment as a form of land disposal, and that the 1984 Amendments require treatment **before** disposal.

## Underground Injection of Hazardous Waste

In *Natural Resources Defense Counsel v. EPA*,[58] the D.C. Circuit Court upheld EPA's regulatory framework for deep well injection against a challenge by industry and environmental group petitioners, but remanded the rule for further clarification of its applicability to salt domes.

## The Petition Process

Industry petitioners challenged EPA's exemption petition requirements[59] as unlawful on the ground that EPA prohibited deep well injection of hazardous wastes without first making the determination that such injection was not protective of human health and the environment. With respect to wastes listed under RCRA Subsection 3004(g), the Court concluded that HSWA does not require EPA to find that a land disposal method for such wastes is unprotective before prohibiting it; Congress had already "legislatively assumed" that land disposal was unsafe.[60] As for wastes listed under RCRA Subsection 3004(f), the Court found that EPA had properly determined that deep well injection "might not be protective of human health and the environment" unless it were controlled by the requirement for site-specific approval prior to injection.[61] Although Subsection 3004(f) does not explicitly require a demonstration of "no migration," it was within EPA's discretion to require a showing of "no migration" in order to demonstrate that deep well injection is protective of human health and the environment.[62]

## Molecular Diffusion

The Court also upheld EPA's decision to require "no migration" demonstrations to account for molecular diffusion. The Court found that EPA properly concluded that molecular diffusion could cause migration of hazardous constituents, and that "the statute forbids even a migration of only a few feet."[63] Similarly, the Court upheld the 10,000 year time frame for "no-migration" demonstrations as reasonable and consistent with the statutory purpose of preventing migration of hazardous constituents for as long as the wastes remain hazardous."[64]

## Migration of Hazardous Constituents

The Court rejected the environmental petitioners' claim that the "no migration" standard would be violated if a single molecule of a hazardous constituent migrated out of the injection zone at a time when waste remaining in the injection zone remained hazardous. Under RCRA Subsections 3004(d), (e) and (g), a particular method of land disposal may not be considered "protective of human health and the environment unless it has been demonstrated. . . to a reasonable degree of certainty that there will be no migration of hazardous constituents from the disposal unit or injection zone for as long as the wastes remain hazardous."[65] Reading the word "wastes" to refer to the wastes leaving the injection zone, EPA took the position that hazardous constituents may migrate from the injection zone as long as the migrating wastes do not contain such constituents in hazardous concentrations.[66] After a lengthy review of the legislative history, the Court concluded that there was "neither focus nor choice nor explanation nor clarity" in the evolution of the no migration language of Section 3004. In the absence of a challenge to the reasonableness of EPA's policy choice, the Court reluctantly affirmed it.[67]

## Salt Domes

In its regulatory preamble EPA indicated that the regulations governing underground injection of hazardous waste could constitute performance and permitting standards for salt domes,[68] but did not define the class of salt domes to which the regulations may apply. The Court remanded the rule to EPA to either withdraw its assertion that the regulations "could apply" or to specify what kinds of salt domes are covered and why.[69]

# The Third Third Rule

The Third Third rule establishes prohibitions and treatment standards for approximately 350 waste codes: all Third Third wastes, including characteristic wastes; all wastes previously subject to the "soft hammer" restrictions; wastes that were rescheduled to the Third Third (i.e., multi-source leachate, mixed hazardous/radioactive wastes), and five wastes that were listed after the enactment of the 1984 Amendments.

In addition, the rule establishes new interpretations relating to permissible and impermissible dilution of wastes, special tracking requirements for characteristic wastes, and new requirements governing waste analysis plans and waste testing. Citing the complexity of the rule and the difficulties faced by the regulated community in identifying and implementing appropriate compliance measures, EPA granted an across-the-board national capacity variance until November 8, 1990, for all wastes affected by the Third Third rule.[70] As justification of this unusual and controversial move, EPA explained that delays in achieving compliance were in effect the equivalent of a shortage of alternative capacity, "because part of the notion of available capacity is the ability to get wastes to the treatment capacity in a lawful manner."[71]

### Treatment Standards for Characteristic Wastes

In the final Third Third rule, EPA cites *Hazardous Waste Treatment Council* as support for setting treatment standards for certain characteristic wastes at levels below the threshold at which these wastes are considered hazardous by RCRA characteristic.[72]   At the same time, EPA cautiously observes that none of the proposed treatment standards were set at levels below which threats to human health and the environment were minimized.[73]

### Treatment Levels

Treatment standards for characteristic wastes in the Third Third rule take a variety of forms, ranging across the board from standards below the characteristic levels (e.g., for EP Toxic nonwastewaters), to standards requiring removal of the characteristic (most corrosive, ignitable, and reactive wastes), to standards at levels equal to or above the characteristic levels (for EP toxic metals). In addition, EPA has expressed treatment standards for some wastes as a specified treatment technology (i.e. incineration of high-TOC ignitible nonwastewaters and EP toxic pesticide wastewaters), observing that such standards in effect required treatment below the characteristic level.[74] The varying forms the standards derive from the specific nature of the wastes and the treatment data available to EPA.

EPA's choice of a treatment standard above the characteristic level for EP toxic metals was dictated by the diversity of waste matrices involved and by the matrix-dependent nature of vitrification or stabilization, the treatment technologies on which the standards are based.[75] By contrast, the standards for EP toxic wastewaters are expressed as incineration, a non-matrix dependent technology capable of reducing concentrations to well below the characteristic level.[76] For most corrosive, reactive, and ignitable wastes, EPA determined that the most appropriate treatment was simply to remove the characteristic for which these wastes were deemed hazardous. However, where wastes in these categories also displayed some form of toxicity (such as ignitable wastes with high total organic carbon content), EPA developed treatment standards to address the toxicity.

### Point of Generation and Dilution

Closely related to the issue of EPA's authority to set the treatment standards for wastes at below the characteristic level is the question of EPA's authority to prohibit land disposal at the point at which a waste is generated rather than at the point at which it is disposed. Characteristic wastes pose a special regulatory conundrum in that many wastes that exhibit a characteristic at the point of generation become nonhazardous at the point of disposal through aggregation with other wastestreams. EPA observes that if it were limited to imposing treatment requirements only upon wastes that exhibit the characteristic at the point of disposal, it would lack the ability to prevent dilution or to require full treatment of toxic constituents that are not removed by dilution.[77] Examples of EPA's decisions to regulate at the point of generation include (1) its choice of specified technologies as treatment standards for certain characteristic wastes (without regard for the concentrations of hazardous constituents these wastes may have displayed at the point of disposal), and (2) its implementation of the dilution rule with respect to characteristic wastes.[78]

Nonetheless, EPA's Third Third rule recognizes certain situations in which precluding dilution or imposing prohibitions at the point of generation would have created severe disruptions by subjecting large numbers of hazardous waste management units to Subtitle C regulation for the first time. Recognizing that certain categories of units were already subject to safeguards under other regulatory programs, EPA engaged in a balancing analysis to determine when it was appropriate to prohibit dilution or regulate at the point of generation.[79]

The final Third Third rule maintains the existing dilution prohibition set forward at 40 C.F.R. § 268.3, while establishing the following exceptions: (1) characteristic wastes managed in National Pollution Discharge Elimination System (NPDES) or pretreatment systems and subsequently discharged under Clean Water Act regulations are not subject to the dilution prohibition unless the treatment standard for these wastes is expressed as a specified technology; (2) the dilution prohibition does not apply to characteristic wastes disposed of in Class I injection wells; and (3) where a treatment standard for characteristic waste is expressed as a specified technology, that technology need not be used if the wastes are disposed of in a Class I injection well.[80]

### The Dilution Prohibition as Applied to Centralized Treatment

In the Third Third proposal, EPA proposed to clarify the dilution prohibition as applied to aggregation of wastes for centralized treatment by requiring that such aggregation must cause "some actual reduction in the toxicity or mobility of at least one BDAT constituent in each prohibited waste that is treated, to the extent that these constituents are present in initial concentrations that exceed the treatment standard for that prohibited waste."[81] In the final Third Third rule, EPA chose instead to offer limited additional guidance on what constitutes legitimate aggregation and to provide specific examples of the application of the rule in different situations. Dilution is an acceptable method of treatment for non-toxic characteristic wastes. For aggregations of listed waste streams or streams containing toxic characteristics, aggregation is permissible provided that the mixed wastes are amenable to the same form of treatment.[82] Dilution to remove a characteristic is permissible for non-toxic ignitable, reactive and corrosive wastes and in injection well systems and facilities whose discharges are regulated under the NPDES system. However, in all other situations, dilution may not be used to render a waste non-hazardous.[83]

### Tracking System for Characteristic Wastes

Existing regulations require generators, treatment facilities and disposal facilities to maintain certain records documenting whether the wastes they handle are restricted and the manner in which they are managed.[84] The Third Third rule specifies that such records must be kept for characteristic wastes even when the characteristic is removed prior to disposal or when the waste qualifies for an exclusion from the definition of solid or hazardous waste after the point of generation.[85] Generators and treatment facilities who treat characteristic wastes to meet the standard need not send tracking forms to non-hazardous waste facilities, but must send the forms to the appropriate regulatory authority.[86]

### Treatment Standards for Newly "De-Bevilled" Wastes

In final rules issued September 1, 1989, and January 23, 1990, EPA removed certain mineral processing wastes from the scope of the Bevill Exclusion, subjecting them to regulation as hazardous wastes.[87] In the Third Third final rule, EPA decided not to subject these newly "de-Bevilled" wastes to the newly promulgated treatment standards for characteristic wastes. EPA determined that these wastes are newly identified within the meaning of RCRA Section 3004(g)(4), despite the fact that they were not included as hazardous wastes by virtue of a new characteristic. RCRA Section 3004(g)(4)(c) requires EPA to promulgate treatment standards for "newly identified" wastes within 6 months of their identification as hazardous wastes. Lacking data to show whether the newly regulated mineral processing wastes could be treated to the levels specified for characteristic wastes, EPA will conduct further study to identify appropriate treatment standards for these wastes.

### New Treatment Standards for Toxicity Characteristic Wastes

EPA has determined that wastes that exhibit the toxicity characteristic by virtue of the TCLP are newly identified wastes, and intends to develop treatment standards for these wastes within 6 months of the final toxicity characteristic rule. Until such standards are established, wastes that are toxic by virtue of the TCLP but not the EPA are not prohibited, regardless whether the toxic constituent is also controlled by the EPA.[88]

## Treatment Standards for Multi-Source Leachate

EPA has established a separate treatability group for multi-source leachate, designated by a new RCRA waste code, F039. In addition, EPA has established a fixed set of wastewater and nonwastewater treatment standards for all multi-source leachate and residues derived from the treatment of such leachate. Leachate derived **solely** from F020-F023 and F026-F028 (dioxin) wastes must comply with the treatment standards for those wastes.[89] In order to cover the potential universe of listed wastes present in multi-source leachate, these standards contain concentration-based limits for almost the full range of BDAT list constituents. EPA did not establish separate treatment standards for characteristically hazardous multi-source leachate on the theory that all of the properties that define a characteristic waste will be addressed by treatment that satisfies the concentration-based levels for the full range of BDAT list constituents.[90]

## Waste Analysis and Testing

In the Third Third proposal, EPA expressed concern over an ambiguity in the existing requirements for waste analysis prior to treatment or disposal of restricted wastes. The ambiguity arose out of EPA's comment that off-site treatment or disposal facilities could rely on the generator to supply the necessary waste analysis information.[91] Apparently, commercial waste treatment facilities have interpreted this comment to mean that they can not be required to analyze the waste in situations where the generator has provided a waste analysis. Citing a need for corroborative testing by treatment and disposal facilities, EPA has now modified its waste analysis requirements to require such facilities to conduct periodic analysis of the waste streams they receive.[92] In addition, EPA has specified that this obligation is not superseded when the treatment or disposal facility receives information from a generator.[93]

## Case-By-Case Extensions

In the preamble to the Third Third rule, EPA states that the "binding contractual commitment" requirement of the case-by-case extension regulations can be met by a showing that EPA has proposed to grant a "no migration" petition or a treatability variance.[94] In prior rulemakings, EPA had indicated that the pendency of a no migration petition was not grounds for a case-by-case extension because it remained to be seen whether the no migration petition would in fact be granted.[95] Perhaps tempered by experience with the logistical hurdles of the petition process, EPA has now decided to provide a measure of flexibility to the process.

EPA reasons that once the Agency has proposed to grant a petition, the petitioner has done everything it can do to obtain adequate alternative treatment or disposal capacity. Moreover, a regulatory proposal carries EPA's partial imprimatur and suggests a substantial likelihood that the petition will be granted.[96] In any event, extensions granted in such situations may be withdrawn if the treatability variance or no migration petition is denied.[97]

## Future Direction of the Program

In the recent "RCRA Implementation Study," a thorough and candid review of the status and direction of the RCRA Subtitle C program, EPA's Office of Solid Waste and Emergency Response (OSWER) acknowledges that its efforts to ensure consistency between new and existing regulations have suffered during the rush to meet the HSWA hammer deadlines.[98]

The study aptly describes the RCRA rulemaking process in recent years with the words "too many, too fast,"[99] and recommends that existing regulations be corrected before new ones are added. Significantly, the study notes that the definitions of *solid waste* and *hazardous waste* and the recycling regulations are confusing and difficult to implement and enforce. OSW recommends revisiting these definitions, while recognizing that such changes "could reopen a whole web of regulations for possible legal challenges because they were in some part based on these definitions."[100] Other significant findings and recommendations of the study include the following:

- The RCRA program lacks an effective means of excluding from hazardous waste regulation wastes that do not require the restrictive controls of the Subtitle C program. EPA should continue its efforts to develop a *de minimis* rule that would exempt from Subtitle C regulation listed hazardous wastes that contain hazardous constituents at levels so low that they pose a negligible environmental risk;[101]

- The absence of self-testing and self-reporting requirements for generators have hindered EPA's enforcement efforts. EPA can improve enforcement by increasing funding for EPA sampling activity, by requiring generators to routinely sample their wastes, or by requiring generators to sample their wastes for hazardous characteristics when EPA has received information that the waste may be hazardous;
- The stringency of Subtitle C regulation creates a strong incentive for waste minimization. Additional regulatory incentives should be explored, including fees on waste generation, disposal tipping fees, and deposits on products;[102]

Pollution prevention has emerged as the ruling environmental principle for the 1990s, and the movement is in favor of source reduction and against end-of-pipe and disposal solutions. Pollution prevention and recycling policy sponsored by EPA should set goals that minimize waste generation and therefore reduce the extraordinary challenges of compliance for the regulated community.

Significant challenges lie ahead, for EPA in fine-tuning its regulations, for the regulated community in understanding and complying with them, and for the courts in reconciling EPA's regulatory decisions with EPA precedent and with congressional intent. In view of the interrelated nature of regulations in the RCRA "web," new refinements in the regulatory scheme are likely to be controversial. Favorable resolution of these controversies would result in a welcome streamlining of the RCRA regulatory scheme.

## About the Author

Mark C. Pennington is a graduate of Yale University (B.A. 1979) and the New York University School of Law (J.D. 1985). After a clerkship with U.S. District Judge Barbara B. Crabb (W.D. Wisconsin), he joined the law firm of Bryan, Cave, McPheeters & McRoberts in Washington, D.C., where he represented trade associations and individual clients in matters relating to EPA's land disposal restrictions program and regulations governing underground injection of hazardous waste. Mr. Pennington recently joined the New York office of Morgan, Lewis & Bockius, where he is active in a wide range of environmental matters, including litigation, regulatory counseling, and environmental due diligence in connection with real estate transactions, financings, and mergers and acquisitions.

## Endnotes

1. 824 F.2d 1177 (D.C. Cir. 1987).

2. 53 *Fed. Reg.* 519 (Jan. 8, 1987).

3. No. 88-1606, slip op., (D.C. Cir. June 26, 1990).

4. *See* 40 C.F.R. 261.32(c) 55 *Fed. Reg.* 22537 (June 1, 1990).

5. Slip op. at 26.

6. Slip op. at 14-15.

7. Slip op. at 28-29.

8. No. 88-1835 (D.C. Cir. July 10, 1990).

9. *American Mining Congress v. EPA,* No. 88-1835, slip op. at 14 (D.C. Cir. July 10, 1990).

10. 54 *Fed. Reg.* 11798 (March 29, 1990).

11. *See* 40 C.F.R. § 261, Appendix II (1989).

12. 54 *Fed. Reg.* 40,594-95 (Nov. 7, 1986).

13. 55 *Fed. Reg.* 11827 - 11828.

14. 55 *Fed. Reg.* at 11,843.

15. 55 *Fed. Reg.* at 11,807-08.

16. 55 *Fed. Reg.* 11855, 11856.

17. *See,* **Minimum Technology Requirements for National Capacity Variance Wastes,** *Infra.*

18. 55 *Fed. Reg.* 11850; Regulatory Impact Analysis at 3-12.

19. 55 *Fed. Reg.* 11855.

20. 55 *Fed. Reg.* 11834, 11837.

21. *See* 55 *Fed. Reg.* 11836; 40 C.F.R. § 261.4(b)(10)(as corrected at 55 Fed. Reg. 269865, 26987 (June 29, 1990).

22. RCRA Section 3001(b)(3)(A)(ii).

23. 53 *Fed. Reg.* 35,412 (Sept. 13, 1988).

24. *American Mining Congress v. EPA,* No. 88-1835 (D.C. Cir. July 10, 1990).

25. *Id.* at 16-22.

26. 54 *Fed. Reg* 36592 (Sept. 1, 1989).

27. Slag from primary copper smelting, slag from primary lead smelting, red and brown muds from bauxite refining, phosphogypsum from phosphoric acid production, and slag from elemental phosphorus production.

28. EPA's final rules removing certain mineral processing wastes from the scope of the Bevill Exclusion do not take effect immediately in states that have received authorization to administer their own RCRA program in lieu of U.S. EPA. In these states, newly "de-Bevilled" wastes will not be regulated as hazardous wastes until an amended state program including these wastes is authorized by U.S. EPA. In unauthorized states, "de-Bevilled" wastes fall subject to RCRA regulation on the effective dates of the rules that remove them from the exclusion.

29. 55 *Fed. Reg.* 2322 (Jan. 23, 1990).

30. 54 *Fed. Reg.* 36,597.

31. *See* 51 *Fed. Reg.* 40572 (Nov. 7, 1986)(solvents and dioxins); 52 *Fed. Reg.* 25760 (California List); 53 *Fed. Reg.* 31138 (Aug. 17, 1988)(First Third); 54 *Fed. Reg.* 26594 (June 23, 1989)(Second Third); and 55 *Fed. Reg.* 22520 (June 1, 1990)(Third Third).

32. RCRA 3004(g)(6) provides that if EPA fails to set treatment standards for scheduled wastes by the applicable deadline, those wastes may be disposed of only in landfills and surface impoundments that meet minimum technology requirements and upon a showing that such disposal is the only practical alternative available.

33. *See* 40 C.F.R. § 268.

34. RCRA Subsection 3004(k); 42 U.S.C. § 6924(k).

35. 53 *Fed. Reg.* 17580 (May 17, 1988).

36. *See* 40 C.F.R. § 268.44.

37. Underground injection involves the disposal of industrial wastewaters through "deep wells" into geologic formations thousands of feet below the earth's surface, isolated below low-permeability confining layers. Along with its regulatory framework for injected wastes, EPA promulgated prohibitions on deep well injection of solvent and dioxin wastes. 53 *Fed. Reg.* 28,118 (July 26, 1988). Subsequently EPA issued prohibitions and treatment standards for injected California List wastes and certain First Third wastes. 53 *Fed. Reg.* 30,908 (Aug. 16, 1988); and for additional First Third injected wastes, 54 *Fed. Reg.* 25,416 (June 14, 1986). Land ban regulations for injected Second and Third Third wastes were incorporated in the rulemakings governing all other land disposal facilities.

38. 53 *Fed. Reg.* 28,118 (July 26, 1988); 40 C.F.R. § 148.20.

39. 40 C.F.R. § 148.20(a).

40. RCRA subsection 3004(h)(2).

41. 40 C.F.R. § 268.5.

42. 886 F.2d 355 (D.C. Cir. 1989)("HWTC III").

43. 886 F.2d at 363.

44. 886 F.2d at 364 to 366.

45. 886 F.2d at 361.

46. 886 F.2d at 362.

47. *Id.*

48. 55 *Fed. Reg.* 6640 at 6642 (Feb. 26, 1990).

49. *Id.*

50. 869 F.2d 1526 (D.C. Cir. 1989).

51. 869 F.2d at 1539.

52. 871 F.2d 149 (D.C. Cir. 1989).

53. 51 *Fed. Reg.* 40,603-40,604 (Nov. 7, 1986).

54. 53 *Fed. Reg.* 31,186 (Aug. 17, 1988).

55. 871 F.2d at 153.

56. No. 88-1606, slip op., (D.C. Cir. June 26, 1990).

57.  51 *Fed. Reg.* 1702 (Jan. 14, 1986).

58.  No. 88-1657, slip op. (D.C. Cir. June 29, 1990).

59.  40 C.F.R. Part 148.

60.  Slip op. at 14.

61.  Slip op. at 16-19.

62.  Slip op. at 20.

63.  Slip op. at 23.

64.  Slip op. at 24.

65.  42 U.S.C. §§ 6924(d), (e) and (g).

66.  53 *Fed. Reg.* 28,122 (July 26, 1988).

67.  Slip op. at 32.

68.  53 *Fed. Reg.* at 28,131.

69.  Slip op. at 37.

70.  55 *Fed. Reg.* 22650.

71.  *Id.*

72.  55 *Fed. Reg.* 22652, n. 7.

73.  54 *Fed. Reg.* 44372, 48, 381 (Nov. 22, 1989).

74.  55 *Fed. Reg.* 22530 (June 1, 1990).

75.  55 *Fed. Reg.* 22655.

76.  *Id.*

77.  55 *Fed. Reg.* 22651.

78.  *See* Technology-Based Treatment Standards, *supra.*

79.  55 *Fed. Reg.* 22657-22659.

80.  55 *Fed. Reg.* 22530, 22657-22658.

81.  54 *Fed. Reg.* 48494 (Nov. 22, 1989).

82.  55 *Fed. Reg.* 22666.

83.  *Id.*

84. 40 C.F.R. § 268.7.

85. 55 *Fed. Reg.* 22662.

86. 55 *Fed. Reg.* 22662-22663.

87. *See* Bevill Wastes, *supra.*

88. 55 *Fed. Reg.* 22660.

89. 55 *Fed. Reg.* 22533.

90. 55 *Fed. Reg.* 22622.

91. 55 *Fed. Reg.* 22669.

92. 40 C.F.R. §§ 264.13 and 265.13.

93. Comment to 40 C.F.R. § 264.13(a)(2).

94. 55 *Fed. Reg.* 22647.

95. *See* 51 *Fed. Reg.* 40582 (Nov. 7, 1986); 53 *Fed. Reg.* 28124 (July 26, 1988).

96. 55 *Fed. Reg.* 22647.

97. *Id.*

98. USEPA, Office of Solid Waste and Emergency Response, The RCRA Implementation Study: The Nation's Hazardous Waste Management System at a Crossroads, July 1990.

99. *Id.* at 31.

100. *Id.* at 38.

101. *Id.* at 39.

102. *Id.* at 39-40.

# V

# Corrective Action Requirements Under The Resource Conservation and Recovery Act*

*Karl S. Bourdeau, Partner*
*Beveridge & Diamond*
*Washington, D.C.*

Prior to the enactment of the Hazardous and Solid Waste Amendments of 1984 (HSWA), the Resource Conservation and Recovery Act (RCRA) was essentially a prospective statute addressing current waste management practices. The federal Environmental Protection Agency was without substantial authority under RCRA, which HSWA amended, to require the remediation of historical contamination at facilities that currently manage hazardous wastes. EPA could only issue orders requiring testing and analysis of certain releases of hazardous wastes[1] and either issue orders or seek court orders requiring such action as may be necessary to abate imminent and substantial dangers posed by hazardous or solid wastes.[2]

The corrective action provisions of HSWA dramatically expanded the scope of EPA's RCRA program. The required cleanup of historical solid waste management units (SWMUs) envisioned by these authorities has given birth to one of the most expensive regulatory and remedial programs the industrial community has ever faced in the environmental area. Indeed, many experts believe that the magni-

---

* *Portions of this chapter are adopted from Bourdeau, K., "Corrective Action: Emerging Implementation of the Hazardous and Solid Waste Amendments of 1984," Business Publishers, Inc., (1988).*

tude and cost of HSWA corrective action will rival, if not exceed, that of the response action program under the Comprehensive Environmental Response, Compensation and Liability Act (CERCLA or Superfund).[3] (See Chapter IX, by E. B. Rothenberg.)

Although implementation by EPA of its HSWA corrective action authorities is only in its infancy, it is now clear that the Agency has taken an expansive view of the scope of those provisions. Several federal court decisions have upheld EPA's view that its corrective action authority under Section 3004(u) of RCRA extends to any area where solid waste has ever been managed within the property boundaries of any facility receiving any kind of RCRA hazardous waste management permit after November 8, 1984. Aided by this, the Agency has embarked upon a systematic regulatory initiative under that provision to remedy historical contamination created by, among others, virtually any facility with a land-based hazardous waste management unit which either received hazardous waste after July 26, 1982 or failed to certify closure by January 26, 1983. Moreover, EPA has taken the position that it has additional authority with few limits under Section 3008(h) of RCRA to issue administrative orders to any facility that ever treated, stored for more than 90 days, or disposed of hazardous wastes after November 19, 1980 to require that facility to address releases of hazardous constituents from anywhere within the facility. EPA has even interpreted these two provisions as extending to certain releases associated with manufacturing activities and, in some situations, to only potential releases.

Because these authorities extend to releases of hazardous constituents into any environmental medium, their impact will be far-reaching. The actual extent of that impact is likely to become more apparent once EPA resolves a number of fundamental issues associated with this program. These issues were addressed in a rulemaking that was proposed by EPA in July 1990 (hereinafter referred to as the Proposed Rule). That proposal is directed to, among other things, the "trigger" and "target" levels for site studies and cleanup actions; possible adjustment to, or waiver of, cleanup standards; the point of compliance for meeting cleanup standards; permissible use of "institutional," i.e., non-engineered, controls in lieu of active remedial measures; employment of "conditional" remedies that permit on-site corrective measures to be undertaken over time based on likelihood of exposure to hazardous constituents; and the role that cost considerations may play in cleanup activities. Until that rulemaking is finalized, EPA's implementation of this program will continue to proceed on the basis of an extensive set of unpublished guidance documents (as well, presumably, as the proposed rule) that have been issued to the Agency's regional offices.

Because cleanup standards under RCRA become potentially applicable or relevant and appropriate requirements (ARARs) governing the extent of cleanups under Superfund, EPA's forthcoming corrective action regulations will no doubt play an influential role in shaping response actions under the latter statute as well. Despite considerable debate over the relative merits of being subject to RCRA versus Superfund cleanup authorities for those facilities potentially subject to both, it is likely that EPA will seek to minimize distinctions between the two programs in an effort to reduce any advantage to be gained (or lost) by proceeding under one statute rather than the other. The extent to which EPA will be able — or will want — to accomplish this task remains unclear given inherent differences in the statutory schemes and a seeming willingness on the part of the Agency to date to recognize salient distinctions between typical RCRA and CERCLA facilities[4] and use those differences as a basis for adopting a less prescriptive study and cleanup approach under RCRA. Whatever the result, however, the Agency seems intent on handling contamination problems associated with SWMUs at active RCRA facilities under the RCRA rather than CERCLA program except in unusual circumstances.[5]

The discussion which follows provides first a brief description of the HSWA corrective action authorities and EPA's approach to date in implementing them. An analysis of the likely shape of the Agency's forthcoming Section 3004(u) regulatory program is then provided, together with a summary of various likely similarities and differences between the RCRA and CERCLA cleanup programs. Finally, certain issues relating to the scope of EPA's authority to issue administrative corrective action orders under Section 3008(h) of RCRA are addressed.

## The Corrective Action Provisions of HSWA

Unlike the extraordinarily prescriptive approach Congress has taken in shaping the CERCLA response program and other RCRA regulatory provisions, the sparse legislative language of HSWA's corrective action provisions arguably affords EPA considerable discretion in establishing the various elements of a program to remediate historical SWMUs at RCRA facilities. All of HSWA's corrective action provisions are written in general terms, and none provide detailed directives to EPA.

Section 3004(u) of RCRA requires every facility seeking a RCRA Section 3005 permit after November 8, 1984 to undertake corrective action for all releases of hazardous wastes,[6] or of hazardous constituents from non-hazardous solid wastes, from SWMUs at the facility, regardless of when the waste was placed in the unit involved. That provision also provides for schedules of compliance in RCRA permits for undertaking corrective action and requires financial responsibility assurances for completing such action. Section 3004(v) of RCRA requires that corrective action be undertaken beyond the facility's property boundary to address offsite contamination where necessary to protect human health and the environment, and where access from adjoining property owners can be secured. Section 3005(i) states that certain corrective action requirements are to be imposed upon designated hazardous waste management units that received hazardous waste after July 26, 1982. Finally, Section 3008(h) authorizes EPA to either issue administrative corrective action orders to those RCRA "interim status" facilities[7] which have released hazardous waste into the environment necessitating a response, or institute a civil judicial action for appropriate relief.[8]

Believing EPA's previous corrective action program for "regulated" ongoing hazardous waste management units[9] to be deficient in certain respects, Congress determined that the HSWA authorities for SWMUs should extend not only to releases to groundwater within the facility property boundaries (as under EPA's program for regulated units), but also to releases to all environmental media and to contamination beyond the facility boundary. (Because regulated units are also SWMUs, they too are now subject to these broader requirements.) However, unlike CERCLA, neither HSWA nor its accompanying legislative history explicitly addresses a number of fundamental issues, e.g., cleanup standards and the location at which such standards must be met. Congress left it to EPA and the courts to lend flesh to this bare-bones regulatory/remedial/enforcement structure.

Because Section 3004(u) and Section 3008(h) only apply to facilities that have obtained, or are required to obtain, a RCRA permit, generators, transporters, and those who store hazardous wastes for no more than 90 days are not subject to these authorities. These classes of parties must nonetheless exercise care with respect to their hazardous waste activities to ensure that they do not engage in actions that will unwittingly subject them to the fenceline-to-fenceline investigation of past waste management practices envisioned by HSWA's corrective action program. For example, a generator-only facility that employs a mobile treatment unit onsite for voluntary waste minimization, emergency response, or longer-term site remediation may trigger a RCRA hazardous waste permit requirement, thereby implicating HSWA corrective action for the entire facility.[10] Similarly, voluntary remediation of historical contamination predating RCRA (e.g., collection of leachate or groundwater, or excavation of contaminated soil) may involve the management of what is considered by EPA to be regulated hazardous waste (despite its generation and disposal prior to RCRA or its implementing regulations) fully subject to RCRA permit, and therefore, corrective action requirements.[11]

## Implementation of the Section 3004(u)
## Corrective Action Program to Date

Thus far, EPA has interpreted its Section 3004(u) corrective action authorities in an expansive manner that has been fully endorsed by the courts. Because the program is still in its formative stages, much of the current implementation has been on a case-by-case basis by EPA Regional Offices informed by a large number of unpublished internal Agency guidance documents (of which most of the regulated community has neither received formal notice nor had a meaningful opportunity for comment). Although the absence of a comprehensive regulatory structure has provided facilities an opportunity to negotiate with EPA Regions in individual cases, in many instances the Regions have predictably interpreted their mandate broadly.

In its First Codification Rule implementing HSWA authorities,[12] EPA codified certain of its corrective action authorities and related permit requirements. That rulemaking provided, among other things, EPA's broad definitions of *facility* (encompassing all land within the plant's contiguous property boundaries); *release* (covering virtually all ways in which a hazardous constituent may enter any

## Corrective Action Requirements
## Under RCRA

environmental medium, and without the CERCLA statutory exemptions from the definition of that term); and *SWMU* (extending to virtually any discernible area where solid wastes were ever managed and from which a hazardous constituent **might** migrate, but excluding transportation spills). The First Codification Rule also set forth EPA's interpretation that Section 3004(u) applies not only to facilities required to obtain operating permits, but also to facilities subject to RCRA "post-closure" permits and certain "permits-by-rule,"[13] to EPA's analysis of the intent of Section 3005(i)'s "rollback" provision, and to certain Agency legal interpretations of the scope of Section 3008(h) orders.[14]

In judicial challenges to that rulemaking, the United States Court of Appeals for the District of Columbia Circuit upheld the Agency's view that Section 3004(u) applies to: (1) Any facility obtaining merely a permit-by-rule for certain underground injection control (UIC) wells or a post-closure permit, and (2) All SWMUs anywhere within the property boundary of the plant, rather than merely those SWMUs within that portion of property currently used for hazardous waste management.[15]

In its Second Codification Rule,[16] EPA addressed, together with several other issues, permit application information requirements regarding releases from SWMUs; the nature of the obligation to undertake cleanup beyond the facility property boundary; in further detail and with some modifications, the applicability of the post-closure permit requirement and of Section 3004(u) to facilities that have ceased active management of hazardous wastes but nonetheless must obtain post-closure permits, or only manage UIC wells receiving permits-by-rule; and the applicability of Section 3004(u) to special study wastes identified under Section 3001(b) of RCRA (e.g., certain fossil fuel combustion wastes, mining wastes, cement kiln dust wastes, and oil and gas wastes).

In a judicial challenge to this rulemaking, the D.C. Circuit (1) Affirmed its earlier decision upholding the application of Section 3004 (u) to facilities required to obtain only UIC permits-by-rule or post-closure permits, and (2) Upheld EPA's decision to apply Section 3004(u) to SWMUs containing only special study wastes.[17] These rulings, together with those resulting from the challenge to the First Codification Rule, obviously increase significantly the scope of EPA's investigation into past waste management practices at RCRA-permitted facilities and the potential impacts and costs of this program's requirements.

In its only other final rulemaking to date implementing Section 3004(u), EPA authorized its Regions to accept feasibility studies and corrective action plans for regulated units after a final RCRA permit is issued so that releases from such units can be addressed at the same time as releases from other SWMUs under schedules of compliance authorized by HSWA.[18] In addition, EPA has proposed financial responsibility requirements for demonstrating financial assurance for the costs of corrective action.[19]

The above rulemakings, together with the numerous guidance documents drafted by EPA to date, demonstrate the Agency's intention to utilize corrective action authorities to address contamination resulting from a wide range of historical activities conducted by facilities subject to these provisions. Going even a step beyond its position that Section 3004(u) extends to all discernible areas from fenceline-to-fenceline where solid wastes of any kind have ever been managed,[20] EPA has also stated its view in Agency guidance that "leakage from product storage and other types of releases associated with production processes" will be considered SWMUs subject to Section 3004(u) if the releases are "routine, systematic and deliberate."[21] Despite its admission that one-time or episodic spills or releases from raw material or product storage areas, manufacturing processes, and transportation incidents are not subject to Section 3004(u) because they do not involve systematic human activity, EPA has stated that the limitation that covered releases be "deliberate" is not intended to require a showing that the release was knowingly caused. (However, the Agency has apparently had second thoughts on this issue since the "deliberate" concept has been dropped entirely in the Proposed Rule.)[22] Moreover, although the Agency has indicated that it does not intend to routinely examine a facility's production, handling, and storage areas during Section 3004(u) investigations, "coincidental" identification of possible releases from such areas during the course of an Agency inspection may result in the owner/operator being required to investigate further to verify releases and to address such releases under a RCRA permit or Section 3008(h) order.[23]

EPA has also taken the position that its corrective action authorities may be applied to situations involving only **potential** future releases (e.g., buried drums which, though not currently leaking, could leak in the future). The Agency apparently intends to limit its reach in such situations to circumstances "where there is reasonably strong evidence that such releases are likely during the term of the permit" and not act merely for the purpose of protecting against accidental releases.[24]

It would seem clear, then, that EPA has chosen as a policy matter to cast with a broad net in establishing regulations with respect to both the universe of facilities subject to corrective action authorities and those situations at such facilities that are within the embrace of these authorities. The nascent regulatory program EPA is currently formulating to address covered releases suggests that the procedural and substantive requirements embodying these authorities could be similarly expansive despite Agency efforts to account for the vast disparity of situations it is likely to encounter under the HSWA corrective action program.

# The Proposed Section 3004 (u) Omnibus Rulemaking

In July 1990, EPA Administrator Reilly signed a long-delayed proposed rulemaking that sets forth the structure of the Agency's intended approach to HSWA corrective action (the Proposed Rule). This rulemaking, which will create a new Subpart S of 40 C.F.R. Part 264,[25] will establish more clearly the applicability of Section 3004(u) requirements; priorities for, and timing of, corrective action responses at individual facilities; and the procedural and technical requirements for conducting SWMU investigations, evaluating remedial alternatives, and selecting and implementing remedies.

Although space constraints preclude an examination of many of the particulars of this proposed rulemaking, a number of its important aspects bear mentioning. First and foremost, because the CERCLA blueprint for responding to Superfund sites (which has been severely criticized as delaying actual cleanup efforts through overextensive and unnecessary analysis) is not mandated by RCRA, EPA possesses considerable discretion to craft a flexible, workable program reflecting the distinctions that often exist between RCRA and CERCLA sites.[26] While EPA understandably desires to preserve more than a semblance of similarity in its approach to implementing the two statutes, whose underlying direction to the Agency — "protection of public health and the environment" — is identical, the Agency appears poised to recognize that a sound basis exists for certain differences.

Consistent with this recognition, the Agency, in developing basic operating principles to guide its Section 3004(u) rulemaking, has enunciated five principles to govern the program:

- The highest priority should be placed on environmentally significant facilities and on the most significant problems at individual facilities. While prompt remedial action and interim measures may be required for offsite contamination, more flexibility in timing of response may be appropriate for less serious risks;

- The level of EPA management and oversight of corrective action should depend on the degree of risk posed by the site. For facilities with risks and complexity comparable to Superfund sites, a CERCLA-like approach entailing analysis of a wide range of remedies, including "permanent" treatment solutions, is warranted. For less risky or simpler sites, a single remedial approach might be readily apparent and selected, even though the cleanup goals would be the same. The emphasis should be on expeditious interim measures, followed by flexible, pragmatic approaches to final remedy decisions.

- Conditional remedies involving prompt action to reduce risks to levels acceptable for current uses may be appropriate in some cases, particularly where final cleanups to media protection standards are presently impracticable. Although ultimate cleanups would typically be to levels acceptable for all reasonably expected future uses, cleanups to levels consonant with current uses may be warranted for areas under the management control of the owner/operator. This approach might blend conditional remedies with institutional land use controls to prevent unacceptable exposure;

- Regulatory disincentives to independent voluntary cleanup activities by owner/operators should be minimized to the extent legally permissible and environmentally protective. Voluntary actions may be incorporated as interim measures in permits subject to RCRA permit modification procedures; and

- Facility investigations should be streamlined to focus on plausible concerns and likely remedies. Wise use of limited resources should be a goal, so that investigations proceed in a step-wise fashion and analyses are streamlined where the problem and approach are evident. (For example, release investigations would focus on a subset of hazardous constituents likely to have been released based on available information, unless the waste involved is unknown or multiple constituents are likely to have been released.)[27]

While these principles are plainly commendable, it remains to be seen whether they will be incorporated by the Agency in its final omnibus Section 3004(u) rulemaking and whether the specifics of EPA's final rule, and the approach of the Agency's regional offices in implementing it, will truly encourage their realization.

### Voluntary Cleanups

One significant issue addressed by the Proposed Rule is the ability of a facility owner/operator to undertake prompt, cost-effective cleanup of historical contamination outside the normal regulatory context in order to reduce potential cleanup costs and liability concerns. This issue can arise for facilities not otherwise subject to a RCRA permit (and Section 3004(u) obligations), as well as for facilities already subject to Section 3004(u) but desiring to expedite cleanup prior to a Section 3004(u) review by the relevant regulatory agency. In the former situation, the owner/operator must concern itself with taking action that could necessitate a RCRA permit to treat, store, or dispose of the contaminated material involved,[28] thereby subjecting itself to the parade of horribles posed by a facility-wide Section 3004(u) review. In the latter case, the owner/operator is faced with subsequent second-guessing by the regulatory agencies over whether the cleanup implemented was adequate.

For facilities not subject to a RCRA permit requirement, the Proposed Rule states that in order to avoid such a requirement the facility must either take response action that is exempt from permitting requirements (e.g., reliance on the 90-day rule for storage or treatment in containers or tanks),[29] or voluntarily submit to a consensual (or perhaps not so consensual) Section 7003 administrative order or consent decree,[30] in which case the Agency may be willing to waive the permit requirement for the actions involved. Neither of these options is necessarily appealing; the former restricts the type of activities that can be undertaken and the latter has self-evident disadvantages to anyone who has ever reviewed a Section 7003 order or decree. Moreover, this approach discourages the use of alternative treatment technologies that could potentially provide more permanent solutions to contamination problems.[31] The Agency has offered at least limited relief, however, by taking the position in the Proposed Rule that "emergency permits" granted to authorize immediate actions that involve treatment, storage, or disposal of hazardous waste necessary to protect human health and the environment in true emergency situations do not implicate Section 3004(u).[32]

For facilities already subject to a RCRA permit, EPA seems inclined toward an approach that would provide sufficient regulatory oversight for proactive owner/operator cleanup initiatives to prevent possible untoward environmental impacts without creating undue disincentives for those desiring to pursue such an approach. Under the Proposed Rule, owners/operators would need to notify EPA of their intended activities but would not need to obtain formal approval of them.[33] EPA would screen the proposal to ensure it comported with a final remedy and did not present unacceptable risks, but would not focus on whether the proposal comported with Subpart S as a whole. If the Agency agreed with the proposal, it could be implemented subject to further Agency review. Although this approach may encourage some "preemptory" activity on the part of owners/operators, the public participation requirements attendant to it, together with the likely insufficiency of Agency resources and natural disinclination to process such requests, make its benefits problematic.[34]

### Remedial Investigations

EPA will require facilities to conduct a RCRA Facility Investigation (RFI), akin in certain respects to a Remedial Investigation under CERCLA, if the initial RCRA Facility Assessment (RFA) performed by the Agency (or a state with an authorized corrective action program) indicates that a release of 40 C.F.R. Part 261, Appendix VIII or Part 264, Appendix IX hazardous constituents is occurring or has, or is likely to have, occurred.[35] The Agency expects that the nature and scope of these investigations will be tailored to specific conditions and circumstances at the facility involved and will be phased to eliminate unfounded concerns quickly. Despite these expectations, such investigations are likely to become time-consuming and costly at complex facilities given the numerous tasks the Agency contemplates will be undertaken to satisfy contamination characterization objectives.

EPA's "RCRA Facility Investigation Guidance," including its risk assessment methodologies, will apparently continue to be used by EPA Regions in determining the adequacy of remedy investigations proposed by facilities.[36] The extent of EPA's authority to require that this and other corrective action guidance documents be followed without a reasoned basis for doing so in individual circumstances is an issue which may receive considerable attention.[37]

### Corrective Measures Study

Under the Proposed Rule, a permittee could request a determination (subject to public comment) that no further action was required if the results of the RFI reveal that there are no continuing releases of hazardous constituents posing a threat to human health or the environment (based on a number of possible factors). Even if such a determination is made, EPA could require continued monitoring and/or a subsequent corrective action investigation of the SWMU involved.[38]

Absent a "no further action" determination, a Corrective Measures Study (CMS), analogous to a CERCLA Feasibility Study, will need to be undertaken to identify and evaluate cleanup alternatives. The trigger for a CMS would typically, but not necessarily, be the exceedance of an "action level" (a concept discussed below). Recognizing that the scope of and analytical approach to a CMS should depend upon the nature and extent of environmental contamination present at a facility, EPA has proposed that the level of effort required for a CMS be geared to the level of risk and complexity of cleanup posed by the contamination involved.[39] The principal difference in approach would relate to the range of remedial alternatives that would need to be evaluated. In this manner, EPA appears prepared to take a more flexible approach to remedial alternative analysis and selection under RCRA than it has under CERCLA (which emphasizes selection of a permanent remedy).

In light of the Agency's apparent intention to gear the scope of a CMS to the nature and extent of contamination at a RCRA facility, the advisability of early data gathering by such facilities for the purpose of characterizing SWMU releases must be seriously considered by facility owners/operators. The existence and reasoned interpretation of such data by owners/operators may influence considerably the direction and scope of both further investigatory and remedial alternatives analysis subject to Agency review and approval.

### Cleanup Goals and Standards: Trigger and Target Levels

Consistent with its approach under CERCLA, EPA believes that cleanup of environmental contamination must ultimately be to a level protective not only of current but of realistic future uses as well. Because this goal may necessitate source removal (or control) and waste treatment, the new Subpart S requirements will represent a shift of emphasis from the current "management of migration" approach characterizing groundwater cleanups for regulated units under 40 C.F.R. Part 264, Subpart F, which will be amended to provide similar source control authority for such units.

In sum, EPA's corrective action cleanup strategy, as set forth in the Proposed Rule, would generally require cleanup of releases to the SWMU boundary to concentration levels safe for lifetime human exposure. The timing for achieving these levels at these compliance points would vary depending upon a number of site-specific factors, such as the extent and nature of the contamination, exposure potential, availability of technologies, and other criteria.

EPA apparently will establish both trigger (or action) and target (or media cleanup standard) levels for RCRA corrective action. The former represent levels of hazardous constituents, that if found in any environmental medium, will typically trigger a CMS to identify necessary and appropriate remedial actions. The Agency will establish different concentration levels for each constituent depending upon whether it is found in groundwater, surface water, soil, or air. Although exceedances of "action levels" will constitute rebuttable presumptions that remedial action is warranted, facilities will be permitted to demonstrate, as under CERCLA, that "no action" is acceptable.[40]

EPA has seemingly decided to set action levels at health- and environmental-based concentrations derived from promulgated standards or, in their absence, from application of general decisional criteria to be set forth in the regulation.[41] These levels typically represent contaminant concentrations that are suitable for human consumption or exposure, even if such consumption or exposure is not in fact occurring at the time of assessment. Adoption of this approach would eschew alternative options basing such levels on background concentrations (which are difficult to determine and may be inappropriately low); detection limits (which are hard to define and not related to the "protectiveness" goal); or a range of levels (whereby higher concentrations would be permitted where no current or likely future exposure exists).

Of course, the location at which these concentration levels would have to be determined for purposes of triggering a CMS is a major issue. Because the Proposed Rule does not specify sampling locations for all environmental media, it is unclear whether EPA has made definitive determinations in this regard. Preliminary indications are that action levels for groundwater in aquifers would ordinarily be measured anywhere within the plume up to the SWMU boundary. Action levels for surface water (which would be set taking into account the use for which the body of water has been designated by the state involved) presumably would normally be measured at the assumed point of entry of a release. Levels for soil would apparently be measured on the surface anywhere outside the waste management unit boundary and would be set under a "reasonable worst case scenario" assuming a residential use pattern with long-term direct contact and soil ingestion by young children. Air action levels would not be measured at the location of the most exposed individual (i.e., where people spend a significant amount of their time on a regular or continuous basis rather than on a temporary or transient basis) but instead typically at the facility property boundary.[42] Thus, depending upon the medium involved, action levels would apparently be measured at what could be points of actual ongoing exposure (e.g., for surface water); at the facility property boundary (e.g., for air); or at points within the property boundary at which exposure is unlikely or could be controlled (e.g., soil and groundwater).

The Agency recognizes that this approach employs conservative assumptions in setting and analyzing for action levels but apparently believes it is appropriate to do so since these levels merely dictate further study without necessarily requiring actual cleanup activities (although, as indicated below, cleanup levels will often be identical to action levels). Given this conservatism and EPA's recognition that appropriate institutional controls at active RCRA facilities with ongoing management should adequately control exposure to environmental contamination, careful consideration should clearly be given by facilities to the specific locations at which action levels must be measured for purposes of setting a CMS in motion at any given time.

Cleanup levels, which are the media and contaminant specific concentration levels that must typically be attained for hazardous constituents as determined in the remedy selection process, may differ from action levels. EPA recognizes that a range of cleanup levels may be appropriate for different hazardous constituents in different environmental media under varying site-specific circumstances. Therefore, the Agency has not attempted to establish specific clean-up levels for different hazardous constituents in each medium; instead, those levels will be established as part of the remedy selection process on a case-by-case basis. For carcinogens, a $1 \times 10^{-4}$ to $1 \times 10^{-6}$ risk range would typically be employed, with remedies at the more protective end of this range normally preferred. For non-carcinogens, cleanup levels will probably be established at concentrations at which adverse effects are not expected to occur in the human population (including sensitive subgroups) for such "threshold" pollutants; these levels will typically be the same concentrations used for setting action levels.

The Agency has apparently opted in favor of establishing specific decisional criteria for selection of a risk level in individual cases, rather than adopting a more subjective, case-by-case analysis by the Regions.[43] These criteria include:

- Whether multiple contaminants are present in the medium;
- Exposure threats to sensitive environmental receptors;
- Other site-specific exposure to contaminated media; and
- The reliability, effectiveness, practicability, and other relevant features of the remedy.

The Agency has attempted to articulate its general cleanup level approach for various environmental media. Typically, groundwater cleanups would be to levels safe for drinking throughout the contaminated zone, regardless of whether the water is currently being consumed. These levels would normally be maximum contaminant levels (MCLs) established under the Safe Drinking Water Act.[44] Where no such levels have been established, concentrations within a protective risk range would be set. In certain situations where the water is not potable for reasons other than contamination by the facility in question (e.g., a Class III aquifer or areawide groundwater contamination from non-SWMU sources is involved), alternative levels safe for other uses would be established.

Soil cleanup levels would be set at concentrations consistent with plausible future uses, although the Agency is considering using different exposure assumptions based on current and projected land uses. Where access is unrestricted, levels appropriate for residential development assuming soil consumption by young children would be set. For industrial sites themselves, less stringent levels, together with appropriate institutional controls to ensure that land use patterns do not change, might be acceptable.

Surface water target levels would be consistent with potential uses. If the water could potentially be used for drinking water, potable concentrations would have to be achieved. Lower levels might even be required if necessary to protect aquatic organisms. In any event, the state-designated use of the receiving waters would play a prominent role in determining the use to which the water could potentially be put and, therefore, the appropriate cleanup concentrations.

Air cleanup levels, as with soil levels, would be based on plausible current or future use patterns focusing on continuous, rather than intermittent, exposure. Remedial measures for air releases would typically involve source control rather than media cleanup efforts.[45]

As a general matter, then, the primary consideration in setting cleanup standards in any given case will be "protectiveness of human health and the environment." Although EPA can be expected to start with the action level for the constituent/medium involved in making this determination, flexibility would exist to modify that level based on site-specific considerations relating to the extent of exposure to contaminants, the level of uncertainty associated with the situation or cleanup approach, and technical limitations attached to the remedial technologies involved. Likely specific considerations include whether multiple contaminants are involved (in which case a cumulative risk standard might be set where carcinogens are at issue);[46] sensitive environmental receptors (e.g., wetlands) are at risk; and other sources of contamination in the same or other media are contributing to the problem. The practicability, reliability, and effectiveness of the remedy selected would be other relevant factors in determining cleanup approaches and levels.

### Point of Compliance

The geographic location at which cleanup standards must be met will undoubtedly be the subject of much scrutiny. Neither RCRA nor CERCLA explicitly addresses the "point of compliance" issue.[47] For active RCRA units, EPA has established the downgradient waste management unit boundary as the compliance point for groundwater contamination, on the theory, at least in part, that it is more cost-effective to treat releases before they spread significantly.[48] That rationale does not pertain where the release has already migrated beyond the unit or property boundary, as with many CERCLA sites (where EPA has often set the compliance point at the site property boundary) or SWMUs.

Despite EPA's apparent willingness to use the property boundary as an acceptable point of compliance for groundwater contamination in at least some circumstances at Superfund sites, the Agency appears prepared to adopt a more stringent position for RCRA facilities. Although the Agency seemingly will evaluate actual exposures in establishing compliance points for air, the Agency would generally set the compliance point for soil and groundwater contamination at any place that exposure might conceivably occur, i.e., at any location where soil is contaminated on the surface and direct contact could occur and at every point throughout the contaminated groundwater.[49] This approach, if adopted, would seemingly require cleanup to protective levels throughout the environment regardless of the availability of enforceable land use controls to prevent exposure and, therefore, harm. The harshness of this result may be ameliorated if, as discussed below, the Agency and authorized states willingly accept "conditional" remedies incorporating institutional controls to prevent exposure during active management of RCRA facilities and/or establish alternative points of compliance where exposure is highly unlikely or several units located close together provide a common source of release. However, unless EPA is prepared to accept permanent controls restricting access to contaminated land, owners of RCRA facilities may not easily be able to cease operations and transfer properties for alternative uses without cleaning up all portions of these properties (including potentially the SWMUs themselves) to levels consistent with all plausible future uses.

### Waiver of Cleanup Standards and Conditional Remedies

Unlike CERCLA, which specifies those instances in which cleanup standards can be waived, RCRA does not address the acceptability of remedies which do not meet environmentally protective levels that would otherwise be sought. Although the Agency is seemingly of the view that RCRA remedies must ultimately be accomplished to levels that take into account all plausible future uses, the Agency also appears willing to accept the notion that those levels need not

**Corrective Action Requirements
Under RCRA**

necessarily be met during the time a facility is actively managed subject to a permit providing enforceable mechanisms to impose other conditions necessary to protect human health and the environment. As such, "conditional" interim remedies not meeting cleanup standards could be implemented provided that certain specified conditions were met.[50] In general, conditional remedies would allow existing contamination (perhaps at existing levels) to remain within the facility boundary if the conditions designated in a permit or order are met.[51]

This approach is intended to recognize that viable RCRA facility owners/operators subject to permit conditions can control and restrict facility access and that such facilities often pose significantly lower risks than typical Superfund sites. If seriously pursued by EPA regional offices, this policy should enable facilities to spread their corrective action costs out over time. However, because the Agency is likely to impose a heavy burden on facilities to demonstrate that further environmental degradation will not occur within the facility boundaries absent implementation of a final remedy, it may prove difficult to persuade EPA Regions of the acceptability of cost-effective conditional remedies. Consequently, owners/operators would be well-advised to attain a comprehensive understanding of site contamination and hydrogeological conditions in ample time to prepare such a demonstration.

The Agency also recognizes that there may exist situations in which no cleanup, or cleanup above target levels, would be acceptable. This result could pertain where no threat of exposure from SWMUs existed or cleanup would not result in significant risk reduction. A specific example would be where significant areawide contamination exists independent of the facility in question and contamination from the facility itself is trivial in comparison. In that event, EPA might use its CERCLA authorities to address the primary sources of contamination and subject the RCRA facility, for example, to merely a limited set of control measures.

Finally, the CERCLA concept of "technical impracticability"[52] is likely to find itself in the Section 3004(u) lexicon as well. While the scope of the concept is still somewhat unclear, remediation of releases to media protection standards would presumably not be required under Section 3004(u) where, for example, the nature of the hydrogeologic setting or limitations of available technologies would prevent attainment of those standards (e.g., where dense, immiscible contaminants in mature Karst formations or in highly fractured bedrock are involved). A critical issue in groundwater cleanups is whether EPA will seek, in such instances, to establish alternate cleanup standards which it believes can be met, or allow active corrective measures to cease once ample time has passed to demonstrate the inability to meet original target levels and the stabilization of contaminant concentrations (subject to imposing institutional controls and/or revisiting the situation if conditions change or new technologies develop). The former approach, if adopted in complex groundwater contamination situations, could subject facilities to tremendous burdens without yielding appreciable environmental benefits. A more reasonable approach would permit an analysis of alternative steps, including institutional controls and risk assessment principles, to ensure that public health and safety was being adequately protected. The preamble to the Proposed Rule suggests that the Agency is poised to adopt this latter stance.

### Selection and Timing of Remedy

All final corrective action remedies selected by EPA or an authorized state would have to satisfy the following four criteria:
- Be protective of human health and the environment;
- Attain cleanup standards determined appropriate for the site;
- Control the sources of releases so as to reduce or eliminate, to the extent practicable, further releases that may threaten human health or the environment (recognizing that a wide variety of remedial approaches, including containment options, that account for technical limitations in achieving effective source control are possible); and
- Comply with standards established by EPA for the management of corrective action wastes.

In selecting a remedy that meets these four criteria, five general factors would be taken into account:
- Long-term reliability and effectiveness;
- Short-term effectiveness;
- Reductions in toxicity, mobility, or volume of the waste involved;[53]
- Implementability; and
- Cost (including capital and operation and maintenance costs, as well as the costs of potential future remedial actions if the remedy fails).[54]

These factors are similar to those employed in selecting CERCLA remedies under the revised Superfund National Contingency Plan.[55] Two additional factors in choosing CERCLA remedies — state and community concerns — would not be evaluated in RCRA decisions due to the ability of states to assume responsibility for implementing the corrective action program if they so desire[56] and the opportunity for the public to comment during the RCRA permit process.

The weight to be given to each of these five factors would vary from facility to facility depending, in part, upon the risks posed. Although EPA clearly believes that cost is an important and relevant factor in deciding among remedial alternatives which offer an equivalent degree of protection in terms of the four basic criteria for RCRA remedies, as with privately implemented remedies under CERCLA the Agency does not intend to engage directly in cost-balancing, i.e., weighing the merits of less protective remedies merely because the costs of achieving them would be less.

EPA appears willing to take advantage of the flexibility afforded the Agency under RCRA with respect to the timing of Section 3004 (u) corrective action. As a general matter, EPA is likely to seek "aggressive yet realistic" schedules of compliance. A number of factors would be considered in evaluating when remedial activities would have to be commenced and completed in individual cases. These include:

- The extent and nature of the contamination;
- the practical capabilities of the remedial technologies employed;
- The availability of treatment and disposal capacity for wastes to be managed as part of the remedy;
- The desirability of using emerging technologies not yet widely available which offer significant advantages over those that currently are;
- The health and environmental risks resulting from delays in initiation or completion of corrective action; and
- Other relevant factors relating to the facility, wastes, and technologies involved (on a case-by-case basis).[57]

If the Superfund experience is any guide, the level of public interest and concern regarding the facility is also likely to be of paramount importance in influencing timing decisions.[58]

## Management of Corrective Action Wastes

Implementation of corrective action measures will typically result in the generation and management of additional solid waste, some of which may be characterized as hazardous by EPA. If deemed hazardous,[59] the waste would generally need to be managed as a hazardous waste subject to RCRA Subtitle C requirements, including land disposal ban restrictions (LDRs) and minimum technological requirements (MTRs).[60] If non-hazardous, the waste would typically be subject to Subtitle D requirements for such waste unless EPA determined that additional controls were necessary to protect human health and the environment. In either case, other applicable federal, state, and local requirements (including, unlike with CERCLA "onsite" response actions, permit requirements) could also be invoked to impose additional management controls. In the absence of a specific regulatory hook, EPA could use its omnibus regulatory authority under Section 3005(c)(3) (or general statutory authority under Section 3004(u)) to impose whatever additional protective requirements it found necessary under the circumstances.

Recognizing that strict adherence to potentially applicable regulatory requirements in all cases could hinder timely and effective corrective action, EPA may take a liberal view of the applicability of these requirements in certain circumstances. Certain "temporary" management units, for example, are unlikely to be subjected to the full panoply of hazardous waste management regulations.[61]

In addition, consistent with a developing approach to be taken at some Superfund sites, the Agency may deem broad areas of contamination to be a single waste management unit so that movement, consolidation, or treatment *in-situ* of waste materials within that so-called "corrective action management unit" (CAMU) will not necessarily trigger LDRs or MTRs.[62] On the other hand, where necessary to protect public health and the environment (e.g., where non-hazardous waste nonetheless contains high concentrations of hazardous constituents), EPA will apparently attempt to reserve and exercise authority to impose more stringent controls than would otherwise be required under applicable regulations.

### Closure Obligations

EPA intends to modify in certain respects the closure requirements imposed by 40 C.F.R. Parts 264 and 265 to accommodate the objectives of the corrective action program. Some of these changes would be aimed at preserving flexibility with respect to closure of active hazardous waste management units so that they could be used to manage corrective action wastes. For example, temporary suspension of receipt of hazardous wastes could occur at active units awaiting the arrival of corrective action waste without triggering the closure process. In addition, the timetable for completion of closure activities could be modified to account for corrective action activities.

One fundamental issue concerns the closure and, where wastes are left in place, post-closure obligations pertaining to SWMUs. Where corrective action remedies involve capping of or waste consolidation within SWMU(s), EPA apparently intends to analyze closure and post-closure obligations for such units on a case-by-case basis, and incorporate such permit conditions as may be necessary to protect human health and the environment under the circumstances. This site-specific approach, in lieu of reliance on the post-closure care obligations and period established by 40 C.F.R. Part 264, Subpart G for regulated units, has implications for the CERCLA program as well to the extent that SWMU requirements constitute relevant and appropriate requirements under Superfund. The appropriate time period for operation and maintenance of CERCLA remedies has been a contentious issue in Superfund settlement negotiations, with EPA often seeking "perpetual" care and responsible parties arguing in favor of an approach akin to that for regulated units in 40 C.F.R. § 264.117.

### Application of Corrective Action Authorities to Transferred Property

The applicability of Section 3004(u) requirements to those portions of a facility that are transferred to a new owner/operator is obviously of fundamental importance to both the new and former owners. Significantly, the preamble to the Proposed Rule states that "a transfer of property before permit issuance would probably not implicate § 3004(u) responsibilities. Transfers occurring after the permit is issued but before remedy implementation or interim measures have begun (e.g., some transfers during the RFI and CMS stages) should perhaps be subject to different rules than transfers occurring after remedial activities have begun."[63] Consequently, the timing of property transfers may impact dramatically the corrective action obligations of new and former owners of the parcel transferred.

EPA apparently intends that facilities have permits during the entire time that corrective action activities are being undertaken, and that if a property transfer occurs after initial permit issuance, that the new owner assume responsibility for any corrective action requirements under its own permit. The Agency currently intends to develop a comprehensive provision governing corrective action responsibilities upon property transfer in the final Subpart S rule.

### Dispute Resolution

The myriad of technical decisions that will need to be made with respect to SWMU investigation and remediation will undoubtedly engender numerous differences of opinion between EPA and/or state agencies on the one hand and the permittee on the other. The elaborate public participation requirements that EPA has proposed to enable citizen involvement in corrective action decisions are likely to heighten the intensity of these debates in many cases.[64] Therefore, although the Proposed Rule was clearly not intended to address comprehensively the procedural mechanisms by which disputes will be handled, the Agency has given some thought to the means by which such disputes will be resolved.

EPA is hopeful that many technical disputes can be resolved informally between the parties. Briefly put, in circumstances where they cannot, or where decisions need to be made which merit public input in EPA's judgment, the Agency would establish a two-tier system of review and approval to resolve the issue. More minor or "routine" modifications to corrective action requirements (e.g., amendment of certain monitoring requirements) would be addressed through a streamlined permit modification procedure, pursuant to which final Agency decisions would be immediately subject to judicial review without an intervening administrative appeal. For more complicated or otherwise significant issues (e.g., selection of a remedy), EPA's new permit procedures for major modifications[65] would be employed, resulting in the need to seek first an administrative appeal from adverse Agency decisions. Other factors (e.g., timing and public participation considerations) may also impact EPA's choice between these two types of permit modifications and, therefore, the appeal rights available to a permittee.

In situations where the need for the change in direction dictates prompt resolution of the issue involved, the Agency would preserve its option to exercise its statutory authorities to either undertake response action itself (e.g., under Section 104 of CERCLA), order that such action be taken (e.g., under Section 106 of CERCLA or Section 7003 of RCRA), or seek to enforce what it believes are the clear requirements of the permit (e.g., under Section 3008(a) of RCRA). Where no exigent circumstances exist, the Agency has raised the possibility of employing alternative dispute resolution techniques involving a neutral, third-party mediator in a time-limited, non-binding negotiation process.

The Superfund experience has taught that the vagaries of site investigation and remediation render the dispute resolution process a very significant factor in determining the parameters of a responsible party's remedial obligations. In light of the importance of this issue and the due process considerations attendant to RCRA permit obligations and appeals, EPA will need to give considerable additional thought to the specifics of dispute resolution mechanisms in various circumstances if the RCRA corrective action process is to proceed in both an equitable and progressive fashion.

## Future Trends With
## Corrective Action Orders

As broad as its interpretation of Section 3004(u) is, EPA has interpreted its authority to issue interim status corrective action orders (ISCAOs) under Section 3008(h) even more expansively. According to internal EPA guidance documents, Section 3008(h) extends beyond SWMUs to encompass non-routine releases from raw material or product storage or handling areas **anywhere** within the facility boundaries. As such, EPA believes it can issue an ISCAO for a non-SWMU release and in its discretion extend any corrective action requirements imposed under the order to permit conditions under Section 3004(u) by virtue of its Section 3005(c) omnibus authority.[66] Moreover, the Agency has taken the position that Section 3008(h) extends not only to facilities currently operating under interim status but also to any facility that ever operated pursuant to interim status requirements.[67]

It should be noted that unlike under Sections 7003 and 3013 of RCRA, Section 3008(h) orders are not conditioned upon a finding of an imminent and substantial endangerment or substantial hazard. In EPA's view, the Agency need only find a release into the environment of a hazardous constituent (although Section 3008(h), unlike Section 3004(u), speaks in terms of "hazardous wastes" rather than "hazardous constituents").[68] Upon such a finding, EPA believes it can require implementation of any response measure (whether specified in its hazardous waste regulations or not), provided that it can demonstrate that the measure is necessary to protect human health and the environment. The Section 3004(u) regulations will presumably provide a benchmark for, but will not necessarily limit the universe of, such measures.

The stringency of the ISCAOs that have been issued to date[69] dictate careful analysis of the advisability of proactive approaches on the part of owners/operators potentially subject to them who are aware of substantial environmental contamination problems at their facilities. Although strapped Agency resources would suggest that the number of such orders might be limited, EPA has increasingly turned to such orders as an effective remedial tool.[70] The difficulty of contesting these orders,[71] together with their far-reaching and detailed nature, warrant consideration of voluntary site investigation and remediation efforts similar to those contemplated by responsible parties facing possible Superfund liabilities. Despite the limits potentially placed on such cleanup activities by the aforementioned EPA interpretations of applicable permit and other regulatory requirements, timely efforts of this sort will at least enable facilities to marshall the facts, develop reasoned arguments regarding risk, take interim measures as appropriate, and evaluate strategic options, all of which are likely to stand the facility in good stead should the situation be serious and/or EPA or state authorities contemplate response or enforcement actions.

Although any facility that ever operated under interim status is **potentially** subject to an ISCAO, EPA has taken the position that every facility requiring most types of RCRA permits (or permit renewal) after November 8, 1984 can expect the eventual certainty of a Section 3004(u) review. As such, facilities that have merely stored or treated, but not land disposed, hazardous waste during interim status (and that can therefore avoid the imposition of a post-closure permit and Section 3004(u) corrective action) would do well to weigh the advantages of obtaining a RCRA permit for the right to continue such activities against the potential Pandora's box such a permit might deliver to their doorsteps.

EPA's implementation of its HSWA corrective action authorities carries with it an extraordinary potential to place onerous burdens on the regulated community. Despite the policy rationale favoring a consistent approach to responses to environmental contamination under RCRA and CERCLA, salient differences regarding the nature of the sites typically addressed under the two statutes provide a reasoned basis for certain distinctions between the programs. The wider range of potential health and environmental risks likely to be encountered at RCRA facilities, together with the ability of viable owners/operators to prevent or minimize exposure to such contamination within at least their property boundaries, warrants a more flexible and practical approach to RCRA corrective action. This approach arguably should focus on interim remedies necessary for protecting current uses and exposures, while recognizing the need to account, at some appropriate later point and in an environmentally protective fashion, for reasonably likely future uses and exposures. The discretion provided EPA by Congress in HSWA affords the Agency ample latitude to fashion such a measured program taking facility-specific considerations into account.

## About the Author

**Karl S. Bourdeau** is a partner in the Washington, D.C., office of Beveridge & Diamond, which specializes in the practice of environmental law. He graduated from Muhlenberg College (B.S., *summa cum laude*) and Harvard Law School (J.D., 1978), where he served as Federal Developments Editor of the Harvard Environmental Law Review. Mr. Bourdeau has practiced exclusively environmental law for twelve years, engaging principally in an administrative, legislative, and litigation practice relating to hazardous substance and hazardous waste issues. Recently, he has devoted much of his time to environmental liabilities associated with corporate and real estate transactions. Mr. Bourdeau has written and lectured extensively on liabilities associated with hazardous substance contamination and is on the Advisory Board of the *Environmental Claims Journal*.

1. Section 3013 of RCRA authorizes EPA to issue an administrative order requiring the owner or operator of any facility where the presence or release of hazardous waste may present a substantial hazard to human health or the environment to conduct monitoring, testing, analysis, and reporting reasonably necessary to determine the nature and extent of the hazard.

2. Section 7003 of RCRA, which was amended by HSWA in several respects, authorizes EPA to issue administrative orders or seek injunctive relief requiring any person contributing to the management of any solid or hazardous waste which may present an imminent and substantial endangerment to health or the environment to take such action as may be necessary to address the endangerment. Section 7003 is more far-reaching than Section 3013 in that it extends not only to investigative but to cleanup measures as well; pertains to non-hazardous, as well as hazardous, wastes; and includes within its ambit not only current and prior owners of the facility in question, but offsite generators and transporters of waste located at that facility as well.

3. 42 U.S.C. § 9601 *et. seq. See, e.g.,* "The Nation's Hazardous Waste Management Program at a Crossroads - The RCRA Implementation Study", EPA, July, 1990, pp. 76-77 (hereinafter the "RCRA Implementation Study"); "Corrective Action Cleanups Will Take Years to Complete," General Accounting Office, December 1987, pp. 20-25 (hereinafter the "GAO Report"). EPA has estimated that approximately 5,700 facilities, with as many as 80,000 SWMUs, are potentially subject to RCRA corrective action authorities (*See* 55 *Fed. Reg.* 30861 (July 27, 1990)), and that the number of facilities that will ultimately need corrective action may be three times the number of sites currently on the Superfund National Priorities List of most significantly contaminated sites to be addressed under the CERCLA program. RCRA Implementation Study, p. 76. Moreover, the Agency apparently believes that the costs of the corrective action program could approach or exceed that of the Superfund program (which some EPA estimates indicate will eventually clean up approximately 2,500 sites at a cost of approximately $22.7 billion), and that comprehensive remedies at RCRA facilities may not be largely in place until the year 2005. GAO Report, at 2.
Early EPA upper-bound estimates for duration and costs of Section 3004(u) actions indicated that the per facility expense and time period for completing necessary corrective action were likely to be considerable in many cases. *See* 50 *Fed. Reg.* 28738-39 (July 15, 1985); *see also* GAO Report, pp. 20-25. These cost figures were refined in the Regulatory Impact Analysis (RIA) accompanying EPA's July 1990 proposed omnibus corrective action rulemaking (discussed below). The results of that RIA (which will be further refined by EPA) revealed that 31 percent of facilities subject to the corrective action rule (1,700 facilities) are projected to require corrective action for releases to groundwater. (The costs of remediating releases to other media were not analyzed due to data and modeling limitations.) The average annualized per facility costs for non-Federal facilities are estimated to range from $0.4-1.8 million. The mean present value cost per non-Federal facility ranges from $6.3-26.9 million. The total present value national cost of the proposed HSWA corrective action program is likely to range between $7-42 billion for such facilities. The lower-bound cost estimates assume more flexibility in allowable corrective action remedies (*e.g.*, use of exposure controls where certain active remedial measures are technically infeasible or prohibitively expensive). According to EPA's RIA, almost one-half of facilities undertaking RCRA groundwater cleanups could be expected to require over 75 years to complete the cleanups.

4. Insofar as remediation of environmental contamination is concerned, RCRA facilities typically differ in two fundamental respects from CERCLA sites. First, unlike many Superfund sites, which are abandoned and pose problems of unrestricted or largely unrestricted access, RCRA facilities are typically operated by financially viable parties who have considerable incentives for a variety of reasons to control access to, and harmful exposure from, conditions at the facility. Second, unlike CERCLA, which is designed to address either true emergencies or sites that have been demonstrated through a systematic Hazard Ranking System scoring to pose significant long-term threats, SWMUs at RCRA sites are likely to present a greater range of health and environmental risks. At least in situations where controlled access and low risk levels exist at RCRA sites, a reasoned argument can be advanced that greater flexibility is warranted so that, for example, the worst SWMUs and more likely exposures are addressed first, and unnecessary study and analyses of relatively innocuous releases are avoided where the response (or lack of need for a response) is clear from the onset.

5. *See, e.g.,* 50 *Fed. Reg.* 47912 (Nov. 20, 1985); 54 *Fed. Reg.* 41004 (Oct. 4, 1989) (EPA policies for listing of RCRA facilities on the CERCLA National Priorities List of top priority sites).

6. 42 U.S.C. § 6924(u). The term "hazardous waste" is defined in Section 1004(5) of RCRA and in 40 C.F.R. Part 261 (1989). All subsequent references to the Code of Federal Regulations are to the 1989 version unless otherwise specified. For Section 3004 (u) purposes, the Agency intends to use the broader statutory definition. The term "hazardous constituents" refers to those constituents identified in 40 C.F.R. Part 261, Appendix VIII (*See* H.R. Rep. No. 198, 98th Cong., 2nd Sess., Part I, at 60, *reprinted in* 1984 *U.S. Code Cong. & Admin. News* 5576, 5619), although EPA intends to include 40 C.F.R. Part 264, Appendix IX constituents as well. The discussion of those terms in the preamble to the Proposed Rule should be referenced.

7. "Interim status" refers to the status conferred upon a hazardous waste management facility to authorize it to treat, store for more than 90 days, or dispose of hazardous waste until it receives a final RCRA permit. *See* RCRA, § 3005(e); 40 C.F.R. Part 270, Subpart G.

8. The statutory language and legislative history of these provisions raise a host of interpretative questions regarding their intended scope which have only begun to be addressed by EPA and the courts. Some, but certainly not all, of those statutory construction issues are addressed in this chapter.

9. *See* 40 C.F.R. Part 264, Subpart F (1984). Regulated units are surface impoundments, waste piles, land treatment units, and landfills which received hazardous waste after July 26, 1982. 40 C.F.R. § 264.90. Because regulated units represent a subset of the SWMU universe, EPA intends to amend its Subpart F regulatory approach for such units to make it consistent with that being adopted for other SWMUs.

10. In a proposed rule regarding permit requirements for mobile treatment units (MTUs), EPA took the position that the location-specific permit requirement for MTUs will trigger Section 3004(u) at facilities that would otherwise not be subject to a RCRA permit obligation. *See* 52 *Fed. Reg.* 20914, 20921-22 (June 3, 1987). However, EPA has not yet finalized its position on this issue, which remains the subject of intense debate given the need to encourage voluntary waste minimization and site remediation actions.

11. *See Chemical Waste Management, et al. v. EPA*, 869 F.2d 1526 (D.C. Cir. March 14, 1989) (EPA decision to apply RCRA hazardous waste listings "retroactively" to current active management of wastes disposed of prior to effective date of their listings, and to characterize as hazardous waste environmental media containing any concentration of a "listed" hazardous waste, upheld as a reasonable interpretation of the Agency's regulations). A substantial factual issue may often arise as to whether hazardous contaminants found in contaminated soil, groundwater, or leachate derived from historical disposal of wastes that would today be considered "listed" wastes.

12. 50 *Fed. Reg.* 28702 (July 15, 1985).

13. *See* 40 C.F.R. § 270.1(c). Post-closure permits must be obtained by certain hazardous waste management facilities that leave hazardous wastes or constituents in the ground after closure of a hazardous waste management unit. Permits-by-rule are granted to, among other entities, facilities that underground inject hazardous wastes subject to a permit issued under an approved Underground Injection Control Safe Drinking Water Act program.

14. *See also* EPA Memorandum, "Interpretation of Section 3008(h) of the Solid Waste Disposal Act" (Dec. 16, 1985).

15. *United Technologies Corporation, Pratt & Whitney Group, et al. v. Environmental Protection Agency*, 821 F.2d 714 (D.C. Cir. 1987). *See also American Iron and Steel Institute, et al. v. Environmental Protection Agency*, 886 F.2d 390 (D.C. Cir. 1989), *cert. denied sub nom. American Mining Congress v. Environmental Protection Agency*, No. 89-1511 (U.S. June 25, 1990) (1990 WL 73868) (*AISI*) (addressing post-closure permit/permit-by-rule issue).

16. 52 *Fed. Reg.* 45788 (Dec. 1, 1987).

17. *AISI*, 886 F.2d 390 (D.C. Cir. 1989), *cert. denied sub nom. American Mining Congress v. Environmental Protection Agency*, No. 89-1511 (U.S. June 25, 1990) (1990 WESTLAW 73868). *Accord Inland Steel Co. v. EPA*, 31 ERC 1527 (7th Cir. 1990) (exemption from RCRA definition of "solid waste" for point source discharges subject to permit requirement under Section 402 of the Clean Water Act does not exempt UIC wells from ambit of Section 3004(u)). The issue of EPA's authority to issue post-closure permits in the first place is currently being litigated in *In re Consolidated Land Disposal Regulations Litigation*, No. 82-2205 and consolidated cases (D.C. Cir. 1982).

18. 52 *Fed. Reg.* 23447 (June 22, 1987). The Proposed Rule would modify EPA's original financial assurance proposal somewhat with respect to the timing of financial assurance documentation, cost estimations, and allowable mechanisms.

19. 51 *Fed. Reg.* 37854 (Oct. 24, 1986). *See also* 52 *Fed. Reg.* 45791 (Dec. 1, 1987). Congress independently provided for, and EPA is establishing, corrective action programs at RCRA, Subtitle D (non-hazardous solid waste) facilities (*see* RCRA Section 4010(c), and 53 *Fed. Reg.* 33314 (Aug. 30, 1988)), and for underground storage tanks containing hazardous substances and petroleum products that are not wastes (*see* RCRA Section 9003(c) and 52 *Fed. Reg.* 12662 (April 17, 1987)). Those programs are discussed in part in Chapter VI, by M. L. Italiano et al.

20. Although EPA originally contemplated doing so, it has not established a date certain by which the property boundary of a facility is to be established for purposes of determining which SWMUs at that facility are subject to Section 3004(u). Arguably,

SWMUs located on property that is sold by a facility to a non-related entity prior to becoming subject to Section 3004(u) permit conditions or Section 3008(h) order conditions indicating otherwise are not within the purview of those authorities. EPA has addressed other transferred or contiguous property issues, *e.g.*, in lease and parent-subsidiary situations, in the Proposed Rule.

21. *See* EPA "Background Paper on Corrective Action" (Aug. 4, 1986); draft "National RCRA Corrective Action Strategy" (Oct. 14, 1986), pp. 3-4, 25 (hereinafter "Draft National Strategy").

22. EPA Memorandum, "Definition of Solid Waste Management Unit for the Purpose of Corrective Action Under Section 3004(u)" (July 24, 1987). The Proposed Rule provides examples of situations that EPA believes do or do not constitute "routine and systematic" releases. It is important to emphasize that EPA does not believe that its Section 3008(h) authority is confined to releases from SWMUs, but rather extends to releases of hazardous constituents anywhere within the property boundary of any facility that has ever operated under or been subject to RCRA interim status requirements. *See, e.g.*, Draft National Strategy, p. 5.

23. *See* Draft National Strategy, pp. 9-10.

24. "Region III Issues on Section 3004(u) Authority" (March 31, 1987), p. 2. Consistent with amendments to CERCLA in 1986 that extended the definition of "release" under that statute to include hazardous releases such as abandonment of closed receptacles containing hazardous substances (CERCLA, § 101(22)), EPA has stated, in the absence of a definition of "release" in RCRA, that it will interpret "release" for Section 3004(u) purposes to encompass also that situation (abandonment). Moreover, the Agency does not believe itself to be bound by any remaining limitations on the CERCLA definition. *See, e.g.*, 50 *Fed. Reg.* 28713 (July 15, 1985).

25. 55 *Fed. Reg.* 30798 (July 27, 1990). Because this publication went to press shortly after the Proposed Rule was published in the *Federal Register*, the preprint of the Proposed Rule was used by the author to prepare the discussion which follows; therefore, there are no further citations to the *Federal Register* for the Proposed Rule.

26. *See* note 7 *supra*.

27. For a general discussion of these principles and implementation recommendations, *see also* "RCRA Corrective Action Outyear Strategy," EPA, September 1989; RCRA Implementation Study, pp. 77-84.

28. *See* text at notes 13-14 *supra*.

29. *See, e.g.*, 40 C.F.R. § 262.34; 55 *Fed. Reg.* 22520, 22670 (June 1, 1990); 51 *Fed. Reg.* 10146, 10168 (Mar. 24, 1986); Memorandum from Marcia Williams, Director, EPA Office of Solid Waste, to Harry Seraydarian, Director, Toxic and Waste Management Division, EPA Region IX (June 17, 1986); and Memorandum from Marcia E. Williams, Director, EPA Office of Solid Waste, to Robert F. Greaves, Acting Chief, EPA Waste Management Branch (Dec. 15, 1987). Some states do not allow treatment in 90-day accumulation units.

30. *See* note 5 *supra*.

31. EPA's broad regulatory definition of *treatment*, together with the possibility of criminal enforcement action under Section 3008(d) of RCRA for knowing treatment of hazardous waste without a permit, is likely to further chill well-intended efforts at voluntary remediation. A crucial issue in many cases is likely to be whether the regulatory agency has sufficient evidence to demonstrate that the contaminated material being handled is a "hazardous waste" from a legal standpoint.

32. Unfortunately, 40 C.F.R. § 270.61 authorizes the issuance of such permits for 90 days only.

33. However, if the activity involved necessitates a permit modification or request for a temporary authorization, such an action would be required. *See, e.g.,* 40 C.F.R. §§ 270.41, 270.42, 270.72; 53 *Fed. Reg.* 37912 (Sept. 28, 1988).

34. Although the Agency appeared willing in earlier drafts of the Proposed Rule to grant conditional permitting exemptions for certain low-risk treatment activities in either of the two general scenarios described in the text, the Proposed Rule does not contain such an approach.

35. The preamble to the Proposed Rule states that EPA may also require an evaluation of whether a hazardous substance not listed in these two appendices has been released, based on the Agency's determination to use the statutory, rather than regulatory, definition of hazardous waste.

36. In order to counter criticism that EPA has employed inconsistent exposure and risk assessment assumptions at CERCLA sites nationwide, the Agency has drafted guidance intended to establish uniform procedures and standard criteria for assessing likely human exposure at such sites. *See* "Standard Exposure Assumptions", June 29, 1990 (draft). Given the considerable controversy that has arisen over the performance of risk assessments by potentially responsible parties at CERCLA sites, the level of Agency involvement in the RCRA risk assessment process is likely to be considerable.

37. *See, e.g., McLouth Steel Products Corp. v. Thomas,* 838 F.2d 1317 (D.C. Cir. 1988). (EPA groundwater model used in evaluating delisting petitions subject to attack in individual cases where EPA failed to provide notice and opportunity to comment upon it.)

38. It should be noted that EPA's "omnibus" regulatory authority in Section 3005(c) (3) of RCRA arguably provides the Agency with extraordinary authority to impose additional requirements beyond those stated in permit conditions, such that compliance with a permit no longer effectively acts as a shield against further regulatory encroachment. *See generally* 50 *Fed. Reg.* 28722 (July 15, 1985).

39. EPA apparently intends to use broad criteria relating to the multiplicity and complexity of sources, hazardous constituents, contaminated areas, release patterns, and remediation solutions to determine whether a streamlined or comprehensive alternative analysis is appropriate.

40. No action might be appropriate, for example, if hazardous constituents exceed action levels in a saline (*e.g.,* Class III) aquifer unfit for current or future human purposes, or the contamination involved originates from a source outside the facility. Because action levels are set at the more protective end of the acceptable cleanup risk range for carcinogens (*i.e.,* at the $1 \times 10^{-6}$ risk level), further actions may also be unnec-

essary if action levels have been exceeded but the constituent involved is present at a level within the acceptable cleanup range (*i.e.*, the $1 \times 10^{-4}$ to $1 \times 10^{-6}$ risk range). Conversely, the Agency intends to reserve authority to require a CMS in appropriate circumstances even where action levels have not been exceeded (*e.g.*, where multiple contaminants or sensitive environmental receptors exist).

41. Because no health-based or environmental-based levels are currently available to establish action levels for contaminated sediments in surface water, the Agency apparently intends to evaluate the need for a CMS to address such contamination on a case-by-case basis until such levels are established.

42. *See*, Vol. 55 30818 40 C.F.R. 264.521.

43. The latter approach would have made EPA more susceptible to "arbitrary and capricious" challenges to its decisionmaking, as EPA Regions set different risk levels at sites with similar characteristics without a rational basis for doing so.

44. 42 U.S.C. § 300f *et. seq.*

45. *See, e.g.*, 52 *Fed. Reg.* 3748 (Feb. 5, 1987) (proposed standards for regulating air emissions associated with equipment leaks and certain process vents at hazardous waste management units).

46. EPA has taken a similarly conservative approach for multiple contaminant sites in CERCLA cleanups. *See, e.g.*, "Interim Guidance on Compliance with Applicable or Relevant and Appropriate Requirements" (July 9, 1987), p. 9 (52 *Fed. Reg.* 32499 (Aug. 27, 1987)); Record of Decision for the Seymour, Indiana Superfund Site (September 25, 1987), pp. 28-36.

47. RCRA nowhere even discusses the location at which environmentally protective corrective action must be achieved. Section 121(d) of CERCLA arguably provides EPA discretion in at least some instances to define the point of exposure and, therefore, compliance, at the facility boundary or beyond. Moreover, neither statute specifies the length of time compliance with cleanup standards must be demonstrated. Although EPA has established a three-year period of compliance for groundwater corrective action for regulated units under 40 C.F.R. Part 264, Subpart F, the Agency at this point appears unlikely to set a specific time period in Subpart S in favor of a case-by-case approach employing designated decisional criteria.

48. *See* 47 *Fed. Reg.* 32299 (July 26, 1982).

49. The Proposed Rule would provide EPA Regions with the discretion to establish the groundwater point of compliance at the down-gradient boundary of the waste management unit when the waste is left in place (either in an individual unit or in several units in close proximity). On the other hand, EPA apparently recognizes that using the unit or facility property boundary as a compliance point would be unrealistic for air contamination because workers are protected by occupational safety standards and using the location of the most exposed individual, *i.e.*, the closest individual actually and most exposed on a long-term basis (typically beyond the facility boundary), is consistent with the actual risks posed by the facility. For surface water, the point of compliance would be set at the point the release enters the surface water. If a remedy for contaminated sediments is deemed necessary, EPA would specify on a case-by-case basis locations where compliance sampling would be performed.

50. These conditions are that: (1) cleanup standards are achieved for releases beyond the facility boundary as soon as practicable; (2) source or other controls effectively protecting against further significant environmental degradation are implemented as soon as practicable; (3) corrective action wastes are treated, stored, and disposed of in accordance with applicable management standards; (4) financial assurance is provided for the ultimate completion of cleanup; (5) adequate institutional controls (*i.e.*, engineered (*e.g.*, fences) or non-engineered (*e.g.*, prohibitions on groundwater use) controls) are implemented to prevent against exposure to remaining contamination within the facility boundary; (6) adequate monitoring is conducted to detect additional significant environmental degradation; and (7) all other measures necessary to protect human health and the environment are implemented. *See, e.g.,* 40 C.F.R. § 264.525 (d); 55 *Fed. Reg.* 30823 (July 27, 1990).

51. "Conditional" remedies are to be distinguished from two other corrective action concepts set forth in the Proposed Rule: (1) "phased" remedies, which are similar to CERCLA operable units in that they address only a portion of a contamination problem at a given point in time, and (2) "interim measures," akin to CERCLA removal actions, designed to deal with more immediate hazards in the short-term until a comprehensive remedy can be devised. *See, e.g.,* 40 C.F.R. § 264.525(f); 55 *Fed. Reg.* 30833 (July 27, 1990).

52. *See,* CERCLA, § 121(d)(4)(C); 40 C.F.R. § 264; 55 *Fed. Reg.*

53. Although RCRA does not include the statutory preference for "treatment" remedies found in Section 121(b) of CERCLA, the preamble to the Proposed Rule indicates that treatment of wastes will be strongly preferred to those remedies that offer more temporary, or less reliable, controls.

54. Earlier drafts of the Proposed Rule added a sixth factor — other relevant and appropriate federal requirements not explicitly provided for in RCRA — that was not included in the Proposed Rule.

55. *See* 55 *Fed. Reg.* 8666 (March 8, 1990); 40 CFR § 300.430(e),(f).

56. *See generally* RCRA Section 3006; 40 C.F.R. Part 271.

57. Significantly, EPA has stated that where groundwater cleanup standards can be achieved through natural attenuation within a reasonable time frame, a remedy schedule based on that process alone may be acceptable if the likelihood of exposure prior to attainment of those standards is low.

58. Another "timing" issue involves the length of time during which a facility must demonstrate compliance with cleanup standards. Rather than adopt the prescriptive approach EPA has employed for regulated RCRA units (*see* 40 C.F.R. § 264.96), the Proposed Rule opts for a more flexible approach, requiring the consideration of five specified factors on a case-by-case basis.

59. The issue of what constitutes a "hazardous waste" for regulatory purposes in the corrective action context is likely to be a very contentious one in at least some situations. *See generally* text at notes 13-14 and note 34 *supra*.

60. *See* RCRA Sections 3004(d)-(m) (LDRs); RCRA Section 3004(o) (MTRs).

61. Under the Proposed Rule, EPA Regions would not be authorized to modify performance standards, but only design and operating standards, and could not modify any statutory requirements (unless the statute so provides) or any requirements for incinerators or non-tank thermal treatment units. *See, e.g.,* 40 C.F.R. §§ 264.550, .551, .552; 55 *Fed. Reg.* 30840 (July 27, 1990).

62. *See, e.g.,* 54 *Fed. Reg.* 41566 (Oct. 10, 1989); 55 Fed. Reg. 8758-62 (March 8, 1990). Land disposal restrictions would apply when waste is removed from a CAMU or other unit for treatment or other purposes and the waste or treatment residuals are returned to the unit or to a different unit.

63. 55 *Fed. Reg.* 30846 (July 27, 1990).

64. Although a full discussion of public participation opportunities (which will likely extend to Section 3008(h) orders as well as to modifications of permits to include corrective action requirements) is beyond the scope of this article, suffice it to say that EPA is acutely sensitive to the public's interest in environmental contamination at RCRA facilities. *See, e.g.,* "Guidance on Public Involvement in the RCRA Permitting Program" (Jan. 1986); "Guidance for Public Involvement in RCRA § 3008(h) Actions" (May 5, 1987). In addition to the mailing list of interested parties for all Section 3004 (u) facilities, the information repository that EPA is contemplating for certain facilities subject to Section 3004(u) that are akin to CERCLA National Priorities List sites, and repeated opportunities for public comment, the Agency is apparently intending to require that permittees promptly notify in writing any person who owns or resides on land adjacent to a facility of the discovery of migration of hazardous constituents from a SWMU beyond the facility boundary in concentrations above action levels. Despite EPA's recognition that exceedances of action levels do not necessarily warrant corrective action or pose health threats, the ability of permittees to argue successfully for no action based on site-specific circumstances may be diminished substantially in light of public concern emanating from such disclosures.

65. *See* 53 *Fed. Reg.* 37912 (Sept. 28, 1988); 40 CFR § 270.41 (1990).

66. In order to obtain information necessary to assess the need for corrective action at interim status facilities, the Proposed Rule would require such facilities to include information about their SWMUs when they submit interim status closure plans for active hazardous waste management units.

67. *See also United States v. Indiana Woodtreating Corporation,* 686 F.Supp. 218 (S.D. Ind. 1988) (Section 3008(h) applies to facilities that treat, store, or dispose of hazardous waste after applicable date for interim status but fail to properly obtain interim status). The Agency has determined that protective filers, *i.e.,* those facilities that obtained interim status but never actually operated pursuant to it, are not subject to Section 3008(h). *See, e.g.,* 53 *Fed. Reg.* 23981 (June 24, 1988).

68. EPA's view has been upheld by at least one federal district court in *United States v. Clow Water Systems,* 701 F.Supp. 1345, 1356 (S.D. Ohio 1988).

69. These orders are typically akin to administrative orders issued under CERCLA and seek to impose similar burdens (*e.g.,* payment of stipulated penalties for failure to comply with schedules and inordinate limitations on review of EPA decisionmaking).

70. As of June, 1990, EPA had issued approximately 50 unilateral and over 100 consensual Section 3008(h) orders.

71. EPA has now promulgated final regulations establishing administrative hearing procedures for ISCAOs that have been upheld in court. 53 *Fed. Reg.* 12256 (April 13, 1988). *Chemical Waste Management, Inc., et al. v. U.S. Environmental Protection Agency,* 873 F.2d. 1477 (D.C. Cir. 1989). Although the type of hearing provided will vary depending upon the nature of the enforcement proceeding and order involved, facilities will not be afforded a full adjudicatory hearing (unless a Section 3008(a) action is involved), and may have a limited opportunity to supplement the administrative record upon which the Agency bases its decisions.

Environmental
Risk Management

# VI    Liability for Storage Tanks*

*Michael L. Italiano, Esq.*
*Gardner, Carton & Douglas*
*Washington, D.C.*
*Myron S. Rosenberg, P.E.*
*Camp Dresser & McKee*
*Cambridge, Massachusetts*
*and Peter W. Tunnicliffe, P.E.*
*Camp Dresser & McKee*
*Edison, New Jersey*

This chapter is intended to provide practical information and legal tools for responding to claims from leaking underground storage tanks, affectionately known as LUST. Cognizant in this era of new morality that "[h]ell has three gates, lust, anger, and greed,"[1] EPA changed its LUST program to UST. In order to bring some needed levity to a complex subject, this is one adverse precedent that will not be followed; in this chapter the authors continue to use the term LUST.

Given pending federal RCRA aboveground tank legislation and substantial litigation over releases from aboveground tanks, these case are covered as well. In fact, all of the material in this chapter is equally applicable to above and underground tanks.

Reported cases of LUST in the United States first appeared in the 1890s and concerned tanks at manufacturing facilities. With the on-set of the automobile and the need to store gasoline and other chemicals used in commerce, the number of tanks in use increased dramatically, see Figure 1 on the following page.

The incidence of leaks or releases increased along with the use of tanks, resulting in a substantial number of lawsuits to resolve liability or to enforce corrective action. Over 130 cases from 1890 to the

* This chapter is based on the book, Liability for Underground Storage Tanks, a Practicing Law Institute book (New York City:1987), and a new edition, Liability for Storage Tanks, scheduled for publication in 1991.

### Figure 1
### Underground Storage Tank Market End Users

Airports
Auto Dealers
Auto/Truck Rental
Auto Repair Shops
Banks
Carwashes
Cemetaries
Churches
Colleges
Commercial/Industrial Office
    Buildings
Construction Companies
County & Local Governments
   Fire Department
   Police Department
   Prisons
   Sanitation Department
   Public Bus System
   Water Treatment Plant
   Municipal Building
   Highway Department
Convenience Store
Delivery Services (UPS,
    Department Stores,
    Emery, etc.)
Distribution Companies
Elementary & High Schools
Farms
Federal Government
   Dams
   Federal Highway Department
   Military Bases
   Office Buildings
   Post Office Department
   Prisons

Home Owners
Hospitals
Hotels
Independently Owned Service
    Stations
Grocery Stores
Jobber Bulk Terminal
Major Oil Bulk Terminal
Major Oil Service Stations
Manufacturing Plants
Marinas
Mining Companies
Motels
Nursing Homes
Recreational Facilities
Residential Apartment Buildings
Restaurants
State Governments
   Prisons
   Highway Department
   State Office Buildings
School Bus Garages
Shopping Centers
Tire Stores
Transportation Services (Taxi,
    Limosine, Bus Lines)
Truck Stops
Trucking Firms
Utility Companies

*Source: Steel Tank Institute*

**Environmental**
**Risk Management**

present concerning leaking underground tanks are assessed in this text. These cases address liability in 11 main areas: negligence, contract, agency, strict liability, private nuisance, trespass to land, emotional distress, remedies, proof and causation of injury, defenses, and insurance. Figure 1 shows how tank use is pervasive in commerce by the substantial number of entities that are tank owners.

Government regulation of tanks is increasing concomitant with the number of known releases and the recognition that tanks will eventually leak if not replace before the design life of approximately 20 years, depending on soil and climatic conditions. Even with EPA and state regulatory programs in place there is a growing national awareness of ground water contamination induced by leaking underground storage tanks from reports in the news media, and from actions taken by state agencies, EPA and Congress. The Conference Report on the Hazardous and Solid Waste Amendments of 1984[2] projected that: (1)75,000 to 100,000 tanks that were leaking would expand to 350,000 by 1990, (2) substantial numbers of ground water contamination cases are attributed to LUST, and (3) LUST is a problem of national significance because one-half of the United States population depends upon ground water for drinking water. An EPA survey[3] reported 18-35 percent of approximately 1.6 million tanks are leaking; the Agency estimates that a leak of one gallon of gasoline can contaminate the water supply of a city of 50,000 people. State regulatory agencies reports of 12,444 leaks[4] show:

- 65 percent of the incidents were from retail gasoline stations;
- 95 percent involved operating as opposed to abandoned facilities;
- Mean age at the time of the leak was 17 years for tanks and 11 years for pipes;
- About one-half of the incidents were leaks from tanks and one-quarter from pipes; and
- 81 percent of the leaking tanks were steel and 19 percent were fiberglass.

Due to extensive EPA, state, and local requirements to address these problems, attorneys, engineers and managers must be able to decide what is the proper short- and long-term response to these rules. To assist in these efforts, legal precedents and technical considerations have been identified in the text. When there is litigation over alleged or actual releases from underground tanks, lawyers and managers will be faced with a combination of four factual settings with each requiring a different response: (1) one tank owner solely responsible for the alleged or actual release, (2) one tank owner with other known tank owners potentially responsible, (3) a single injured party, or (4) multiple injured parties. Strategies for addressing each and combinations thereof must be devised and each case will vary. This chapter is intended to provide some of the rudiments of how to respond.

When a tank owner's release has caused damage, the most effective response is to moot any claim by *in situ* or onsite remediation to the extent practicable. This can substantially reduce costs without sacrificing environmental protection because the scope and pace of work is not dictated by the government. Cleanup can therefore proceed more efficiently and expeditiously. Generally attempting to stonewall by filing briefs or other legal papers is more expensive to the client because the release may worsen and the opposing party or government agency involved will become antagonized and usually try to expand the scope of cleanup and damages. By analogy, experience with Superfund cleanups has shown that transaction costs can exceed cleanup costs when the primary focus is solely on litigation.[5]

The frequency of litigation will increase as more of the existing leaks are discovered as a result of increased tank testing and tank upgrades. Furthermore, there is the opportunity for success in litigation by an injured party to receive greater compensation since the tank owner's legal duty of care has been elevated by new comprehensive tank regulations. Litigation is not only occurring more frequently, but it is also becoming much more sophisticated even though the theories of liability are based on centuries old tort law. The sophistication in common law suits arise from the application of much more complex factual information. Such litigation is distinguished from EPA and state enforcement of tank rules that present not only factually but also legally complex issues.

Court and agency decisions on liability are more difficult today because concrete answers are rarely obtained from leak detection tests, groundwater monitoring, identification of product mobility, fate, effect and underground location, and prediction and assessment of health effects when there is exposure to chemicals. The real challenge in this area of practice is to know how to sufficiently obtain and discern material facts that can be convincingly applied to the law in the absence of true cause and extent of contamination, and effect on human health and environment.

When site investigation is required, the information at the end of this chapter is intended to guide strategies for assessing the onsite problem and extent of cleanup. When litigation is involved, the analysis of case law that follows is useful for identifying legal issues that concern the lawsuit. Only a brief introduction to federal and state statutes and regulations is provided because of the vast amount of rules being promulgated by EPA and the states and the many analyses thereof that have been conducted.[6]

## Federal Statutes

Approximately 2.5 million tanks are controlled by EPA's regulatory program.[7] EPA estimates that compliance and cleanup costs will average $4.84 billion per year.[8]

The Congressional intent in establishing an underground tank regulatory program (Figure 2) was to protect human health and envi-

---

**Figure 2**
**What the Law Requires**

- All Tanks
  - Release Detection
  - Recordkeeping
  - Reporting of Releases
  - Corrective Action
  - Reporting on Corrective Action Taken
  - Closure
  - Financial Responsibility

- New Tanks
  - Release Detection
  - Design and Construction
  - Installation
  - Compatability

- EPA must promulgate requirements "As May be Necessary to Protect Human Health and the Environment."

- EPA should consider impacts on small businesses taking into account current management practices.

ronment through "leak detection systems, inventory control systems (together with periodic tank testing) or comparable systems or methods of detecting releases."[9] However, "exclusive reliance on a dipstick method of inventory control (even with periodic tank testing) will not be sufficiently reliable to detect slow leaks."[10]

Section 9003 of the Subtitle I required standards for petroleum tanks, new non-petroleum chemical tanks, and existing non-petroleum chemical tanks. Rules for tanks include requirements for: (1) leak detection or inventory control and tank testing, (2) record-keeping and reporting, (3) corrective action, (4) closure and (5) financial responsibility for corrective action and third party liability. New tank performance standards include requirements for design, construction, installation, release detection, and compatibility.

Several state programs have been authorized under § 9004 since the state programs are "no less than the corresponding requirements promulgated by the Administrator pursuant to § 9003(a)."[11]

The federal and state petroleum and chemical UST programs are distinguished from EPA final rules for hazardous waste tanks promulgated in 1986. These regulations set standards for release detection, operation, corrective action, closure and post closure.[12] See a summary of requirements in Figures 3 through 9.

Federal regulation of aboveground tanks greater than 4200 gallons has been proposed in the RCRA reauthorization bill.[13] This program would be comparable to the RCRA Subtitle I requirements for underground tanks, and would be in addition to EPA's Clean Water Act rules for spill prevention control and countermeasures for aboveground tanks greater than 660 gallons and facilities with a total storage capacity of 1320 gallons or more.[14] The RCRA amendments would make tank owners strictly liable for corrective action taken by EPA to cleanup leaks,[15] and would allow EPA to prohibit the use of a facility after a release until adequate corrective action has been taken.[16]

The RCRA aboveground storage program would also authorize EPA to set aboveground tank standards for:
- Design, materials, fabrication;
- Installation, construction, siting;
- Placarding, maintenance, inspection;
- Release detection;
- Tank modification or repair; and
- Financial responsibility.

**Figure 3**
**Summary of Technical Standards — Petroleum Tanks**

• New Tanks
— Corrosion-protected single-wall systems
— Frequent to continuous monitoring
 (no less than monthly)

• Existing Tanks
— Upgrade/replace to new tank standards
 in 10 years
— periodic tank testing and inventory
 controls
— leak detection phase in 3 to 5 years

• Corrective Action
— Site-specific clean-up levels determined
 by field assessments

**Figure 4**

**Testing and Upgrading Existing Petroleum Tanks**

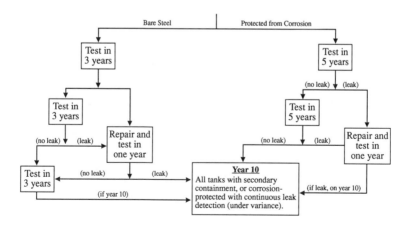

**Figure 5**
**Summary of Technical Standards**
**Chemical Tanks**

- New Tanks
  — Secondary containment and corrosion protection; or
  — Variance (based on detectability) allowing single-wall corrosion-protected systems and frequent to continuous monitoring

- Existing Tanks
  — Periodic tank testing and inventory controls until upgrading/replacement to new tank standards (mandatory at 10 years)
  — Leak detection phase-in 3 to 5 years
  — Upgrading/replacement to secondary containment if leak detection not available

- Corrective Action
  — Site-specific cleanup levels determined by field assessments

**Figure 6**

Testing and Upgrading Existing Chemical Tanks

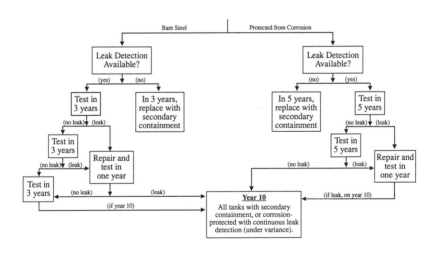

**Figure 7**

## SUMMARY OF FINANCIAL RESPONSIBILITY REQUIREMENTS

- Tanks Covered:

    - Petroleum USTs only
    - Rules for chemical USTs proposed. 53 Fed.Reg. 3818 (Feb. 9, 1988)
    - Legislation has been proposed for aboveground tanks

- Federal and State USTs are exempt

- $1 million coverage per occurrence for all types of USTs

- Aggregate coverage varies depending on number of USTs

- Owner or Operator, but not both, must demonstrate responsibility

- Numerous mechanisms are allowed: insurance, guarantee, indemnity contract, risk retention group, surety bond, letter of credit, State-required mechanism, or State fund

- Evidence and Certification of Compliance must be maintained for the operational life of a tank, and submitted with new tank notification, or within 30 days of release, or when coverage is terminated

## Figure 8

# <u>WHAT</u> DO YOU HAVE TO DO?  Minimum Requirements

You must have Leak Detection, Corrosion Protection, and Spill/Overfill Prevention.

### LEAK DETECTION

| | |
|---|---|
| **NEW TANKS**<br>*2 Choices* | • Monthly Monitoring*<br>• Monthly Inventory Control and Tank Tightness Testing Every 5 Years<br>(You can only use this choice for 10 years after installation.) |
| **EXISTING TANKS**<br>*3 Choices*<br>*The chart at the bottom of the next page displays these choices.* | • Monthly Monitoring*<br>• Monthly Inventory Control and Annual Tank Tightness Testing<br>(This choice can only be used until December 1998.)<br>• Monthly Inventory Control and Tank Tightness Testing Every 5 Years<br>(This choice can only be used for 10 years after adding corrosion protection and spill/overfill prevention or until December 1998, whichever date is later.) |
| **NEW & EXISTING PRESSURIZED PIPING**<br>*Choice of one from each set* | • Automatic Flow Restrictor  • Annual Line Testing<br>• Automatic Shutoff Device -and- • Monthly Monitoring*<br>• Continuous Alarm System  (except automatic tank gauging) |
| **NEW & EXISTING SUCTION PIPING**<br>*3 Choices* | • Monthly Monitoring*<br>(except automatic tank gauging)<br>• Line Testing Every 3 Years<br>• No Requirements<br>(if the system has the characteristics described on page 11) |

### CORROSION PROTECTION

| | |
|---|---|
| **NEW TANKS**<br>*3 Choices* | • Coated and Cathodically Protected Steel<br>• Fiberglass<br>• Steel Tank clad with Fiberglass |
| **EXISTING TANKS**<br>*4 Choices* | • Same Options as for New Tanks<br>• Add Cathodic Protection System<br>• Interior Lining<br>• Interior Lining and Cathodic Protection |
| **NEW PIPING**<br>*2 Choices* | • Coated and Cathodically Protected Steel<br>• Fiberglass |
| **EXISTING PIPING**<br>*2 Choices* | • Same Options as for New Piping<br>• Cathodically Protected Steel |

### SPILL / OVERFILL PREVENTION

| | |
|---|---|
| **ALL TANKS** | • Catchment Basins  -and- • Automatic Shutoff Devices -or-<br>• Overfill Alarms -or-<br>• Ball Float Valves |

| | | |
|---|---|---|
| * Monthly Monitoring includes: | Automatic Tank Gauging<br>Vapor Monitoring<br>Interstitial Monitoring | Ground-Water Monitoring<br>Other Approved Methods |

**Environmental**
**Risk Management**

Figure 9

# <u>WHEN</u> DO YOU HAVE TO ACT?   Important Deadlines

← ——————— For <u>WHAT</u> you have to do, see the chart on the left.

| TYPE OF TANK & PIPING | LEAK DETECTION | CORROSION PROTECTION | SPILL / OVERFILL PREVENTION |
|---|---|---|---|
| New Tanks and Piping* | At installation | At installation | At installation |
| **Existing Tanks**  |  |  |  |
| 25+ or unknown age | December 1989 |  |  |
| 20 - 24 years | December 1990 |  |  |
| 15 - 19 years | December 1991 | December 1998 | December 1998 |
| 10 - 14 years | December 1992 |  |  |
| Under 10 years | December 1993 |  |  |
| **Existing Piping** |  |  |  |
| Pressurized | December 1990 | December 1998 | Does not apply |
| Suction | Same as existing tanks | December 1998 | Does not apply |

\* New tanks and piping are those installed after December 1988
\*\* Existing tanks and piping are those installed before December 1988

## IF YOU CHOOSE TANK TIGHTNESS TESTING AT EXISTING USTs . . .

If you don't use monthly monitoring at existing USTs, you must use a combination of periodic tank tightness tests and monthly inventory control. This combined method can only be used for a few years, as the chart below displays.

Was the UST "upgraded", which means does it have corrosion protection and spill/overfill prevention devices?  →YES→  Was it "upgraded" <u>before</u> December 1988?  →YES→  Do monthly inventory control and a tank tightness test <u>every 5 years</u> until 1998; then do monthly monitoring.

↓NO     ↓NO

Do monthly inventory control and a tank tightness test <u>every year</u> until 1998; then "upgrade". For "upgraded" USTs, use the box on the right.    ← - -    Do monthly inventory control and a tank tightness test <u>every 5 years</u> for 10 years after "upgrading"; then do monthly monitoring.

**Liability for Storage Tanks**

EPA is required to provide more stringent rules for field-erected than shop-fabricated tanks. States may promulgate more stringent rules except for shop-fabricated tanks.[17]

Although not frequently used today, the 1899 Refuse Act can be enforced by the United States as a remedy for discharges from storage tanks to navigable waters.[18] Section 13 of the Statute makes it unlawful to deposit any refuse matter of any kind into navigable waters. The Statute provides for criminal liability without any need to establish intent or *mens rea*. In contrast, tank owners, operators, and suppliers have been found to be liable for civil, but not criminal, damages pursuant to § 311 of the Clean Water Act for discharges of hazardous substances into navigable waters.[19]

EPA has deferred regulation of product releases from underground tanks as hazardous wastes, and will regulate these releases under the corrective action provisions of the tank rules. The rules may apply, however, to releases from aboveground tanks depending on the hazardous substances released.[20]

## State Statutes

A survey of 22 states containing the greatest number of underground tanks shows that all have statutes which at a minimum provided for state response including penalties against a responsible party for unauthorized underground tank releases.[21] According to the American Petroleum Institute, about one-half of the states have tank permit or registration requirements and three-quarters have requirements for leak detection.[22]

## Common Law Liability Theories

Most LUST litigation is based on negligence, contract, nuisance, or trespass.

Negligence requires the defendant to compensate the injured party because of the defendant's carelessness or failure to do what a reasonable person would do under the circumstances. A successful negligence claim requires: (1) a duty to use reasonable care,[23] (2) a breach of duty,[24] (3) causation in fact and legal or proximate cause,[25] and (4) actual damages.[26]

Contract liability primarily arises through warranty, representation and indemnity (or hold harmless) provisions in leases between tank owners and operators. These agreements shield owners from liability from leaks when the owner has not committed a tort or wrong and the contract does not violate public policy.[27] Without these clauses, owners can be vicariously liable under agency theories. Indemnity and hold harmless agreements are invalid where void by statute[28] and where the owner commits a negligent act.[29]

Agency liability for underground tank releases extends to employers when the employee causes the release while acting within its scope of employment.[30] Employers using independent contractors are generally not liable,[31] unless they control the details of the contractor's work,[32] or assign an inherently dangerous activity,[33] or negligently hire. Notification of a release on behalf of a tank owner/operator may be made by its agent when the agent has actual or apparent authority to bind the owner.[34]

Strict liability holds tank owners and operators liable without proof of any negligence when the activity is inappropriate for the geographic locale[35] or an ultrahazardous activity.[36] It is the most indiscriminate liability theory for owners and operators.

Trespass is used when there is an intentional invasion interfering with possession of land. "Intentional" means knowledge to a substantial certainty that invasion will occur.[37] Trespass actions have been particularly successful when the release caused an explosion damaging plaintiff's property.[38] Nuisance liability requires the substantial, unreasonable interference with the use and enjoyment of land.[39] Unlike trespass, nuisance requires courts to balance the degree of harm with the importance of the activity to the regional economy, and if the harm outweighs the importance of the activity, liability can be found on non-negligent, unintentional conduct when there is ground water pollution.[40] Thus, when there is a nuisance, it is immaterial whether a tank owner or operator exercised reasonable care or foresight in the conduct of business, or whether it was non-negligent.[41] Well over 30 storage tank cases cover nuisance based on fire and explosion potential or actual damages. The decisive factor has generally been the proximity of the tanks to residential properties.[42]

## Common Law Remedies

The typical remedy for an underground tank release is money damages for ground water contamination, fires, or explosions. The burden of proving damages rests with the injured party,[43] and is usually based on the loss in property value,[44] which is classified as permanent damage for ground water because of the reduced rates of biological degradation, its slow movement and flushing times, and the adherence of petroleum to subsurface particles.[45]

Injured parties might mitigate damages by taking reasonable corrective action steps to reduce the harm such as cleaning up a release contaminating surface water.[46] However, there is generally no duty to mitigate damages to ground water by filtering or any other measures.[47] Pre-existing contamination of ground water is a factor to be determined by the trier of fact in setting the amount of damages. It does not include, however, contamination that is normally removed by water treatment.[48] Punitive damage awards to deter fraud or wanton conduct are not available for ordinary negligence,[49] but are awarded when there is a conscious indifference to consequences such as continuously exposing employees to gasoline vapors without any precautions.[50]

Medical monitoring costs may be considered as special damages that could potentially be awarded for chemical exposure from a LUST release when the weight of evidence from the exposure supports an increase in the risk of disease.[51]

## Proof and Causation of Injury

Direct cause and effect of underground tank releases contaminating ground water are the exception rather than the rule. Thus, injured parties must frequently use circumstantial evidence to meet their burden of proof.[52] A finding that the tank release was the cause of injury is a prerequisite to recovery of damages, and such a finding by circumstantial evidence will be based on facts from which deductions are drawn indirectly showing the facts to be proved, and excluding other reasonable hypotheses with a fair amount of certainty.[53] In the event scientific proof or expert opinion is used by either party, protection of work product from discovery is feasible under the attorney-client privilege and by protection of the documents prepared by or on behalf of the attorney in anticipation of litigation.[54]

## Defenses

The best defense likely to be favorably received by a court is for a tank owner to immediately rectify the release or mitigate any potential damages. Other defenses that can be used when applicable are limitation of actions including laches, assumption or risk, superseding cause, contributory negligence including unclean hands, and acts of God or third parties.

The statute of limitations can be a valid defense when the injured party fails to sue after the lapse of time prescribed by state statutes from the time the tort is complete.[55] When the injured party knowingly, willingly, and intentionally understands the nature, character and extent of the danger, the defendant can claim that the risk was assumed.[56] Assumption of risk as a valid defense for negligence, nuisance, and strict liability tort actions.

Superseding cause can be pleaded when a reasonably unforeseeable intervening act of a third party or other force causes the harm.[57]

Contributory negligence, as with assumption of risk, is an affirmative defense that must be pleaded and proved by the defendant to show that the injured party's negligence contributed to cause the harm.[58]

## Insurance — Duty to Defend and Judicial Determination of Coverage

Storage tank insurance case law almost exclusively has provided coverage for releases. The exception appears to be late notice of an accident by the insured to the insurer.[59] Another exception which has been decided for Superfund litigation is where the insured expected or intended the harm of the release.[60] (An extensive discussion of environmental insurance litigation can be found in Chapters XXVII by Russell and XXVIII by Heintz.)

An insurer's duty to defend a tank owner or operator is broader than the duty to indemnify for damages and includes defending any action that alleges facts within the terms of the policy,[61] and under recent law when a potential of insurer liability exists based on a reasonable investigation of the facts.[62] Courts have generally upheld coverage for insurers when an occurrence is defined in policies as:

> an accident, including injurious exposure to conditions, which results, during the policy period in bodily injury or property damage neither expected nor intended from the standpoint of the insured.[63]

Underground tank releases have been held to be covered by insurance policies when there was negligent installation and maintenance of tanks causing an accidental release,[64] when a release required the insured to excavate and dig trenches under court injunction,[65] when employee negligence resulted in loss of turpentine from damage to a valve appurtenant to a tank,[66] and when there is a release of hazardous substances resulting in CERCLA liability.[67] Critical to many of these areas is the court's interpretation of the "pollution exclusion clause," which existed in most policies from 1971-1986.

A personal property policy with an endorsement for oil in pipelines and a debris removal provision covered the cost of oil lost from a leaking tank as well as the cost of cleanup.[68]

Important issues related to insurance include bankruptcy, government disclosure requirements and risk assessment. The Supreme Court has determined that environmental cleanup costs take first priority in bankruptcy.[69] The Securities and Exchange Commission (SEC) requires companies registered to sell securities to disclose any demands, commitments, or uncertainty that affects the company's liquidity in any material way. The SEC has clarified that companies involved in Superfund sites cannot use uncertainty for failing to disclose and quantify the effect of potential cleanup.[70] Since many tank releases have been remediated under Superfund, the SEC disclosure requirement is likely to be applicable to cleanup of tank releases.

Risk assessment in the context of underground tanks arises in determining cleanup levels. It is frequently used in Superfund and tank corrective actions that are expensive or have a strong potential for human exposure to hazardous substances. Quantification of uncertainty in the risk assessment is being considered by EPA.[71] Since the degree of uncertainty in risk assessments is very high, the likelihood that risk assessments will be material factors in cleanup decisions will decrease to the extent uncertainty analysis is performed.

## Managing a Leaking Tank Case

Scientific evidence is essential in proving causation. It is obtained by applying monitoring techniques, leak detection methods, geologic and hydrologic assessment, well and surface water testing, and construction of borings and permanent wells.

Leak detection techniques were found by EPA to be less sensitive than previously reported by leak detection manufacturers. Manufacturers claimed to meet the National Fire Protection Association (NFPA) practice value of 0.05 gal./hr.; however, EPA determined that the best that could be performed at its Edison, N.J., test facility was 0.1 gal./hr.[72] This finding has increased research by manufacturers and resulted in voluntary standards to improve manufacturer disclosure of performance.[73]

The most expensive part of any case is corrective action or cleanup of releases that requires special care and attention to detail, technical and scientific assessment, and interface with regulatory agencies. Experts will be required to investigate contamination and any human exposure of hazardous substances.

EPA has assessed cleanup technologies addressing the most commonly encountered corrective action situations.[74] The American Petroleum Institute (API) has also provided a review of technology and characterization of petroleum products.[75] For recovery of free product from the water table, the most common methods are the trench method for water tables 15 feet or less from the surface and pumping wells for deeper releases.[76] Where it is useful to reverse ground water flow, e.g., to protect potable water supplies, the pumping well system can be used. Generally, free product recovery costs are affected more by the recovery method and equipment than the size of the release to ground water.

For removal of gasoline from unsaturated soils, the most widely used method is excavation and landfill disposal. In addition to the problems of increased landfilling costs, most soil contains hazardous substances which can subject the tank owner/operator to Superfund liability if problems develop at the landfill.[77] Consequently, excavation and disposal is most appropriate for small volumes. Enhanced volatilization, such as rototilling and aeration, can be very effective but explosion hazards can develop and emissions may need to be controlled. Incineration is used most effectively for smaller volumes due to costs. The combination of venting, such as vacuum extraction, and microbial degradation (bioremediation), can be the least costly and most effective technologies.[78] Figures 10 and 11 are worksheets that can be used to evaluate the feasibility of using these technologies in the unsaturated zone.[79] Figures 12 and 13 show the different phases of petroleum in the unsaturated zone that must be addressed and how to determine which phase exists.[80]

Hydrocarbons in ground water are typically removed by air stripping towers usually with granular activated carbon adsorption. Costs range between $350,000 to $500,000 per unit. Bioremediation is a much cheaper technology amenable to permeable substrata such as sandy formations.[81]

In order to maximize the effectiveness of cleanup/corrective action technology, basic data[82] should be obtained through a site assessment:

- What was released? Where and when?
- Where is most of the released product likely to be?
- How much product is likely to be present in different locations and phases?
- How mobile are the constituents of the contaminants and where are they likely to travel and at what rate?

Knowledge of subsurface transport of regulated substances can help answer these questions. The migration of these released substances depends on the quantity released, the physical properties of the leaked substance, and the structure of the subsurface.[83] Transport of liquids in the subsurface depends upon whether the liquids are in the saturated ground water zone, the capillary zone above, and the unsaturated (vadose) zone nearer the surface. In the saturated zone, contaminants travel in a dissolved and/or immiscible state. *Immiscible* means the fluids displace each other without mixing. In the capillary and unsaturated zones, substances are transported in solution in the water phase, as a constituent in an immiscible phase. However, flow in the capillary zone is primarily horizontal while in the unsaturated zone it is primarily vertical.

Figure 10

| WORSHEET FOR EVALUATING THE FEASIBILITY OF SOIL VENTING BEING EFFECTIVE AT YOUR SITE | | | | | |
|---|---|---|---|---|---|
| CRITICAL SUCCESS FACTOR | UNITS | SITE OF INTEREST ▼ | SUCCESS LESS LIKELY | SUCCESS SOMEWHAT LIKELY | SUCCESS MORE LIKELY |
| | | | | | Short |
| **SITE RELATED** | | | | | |
| • Dominant Contaminant Phase | Phase | | Sorbed to soil ○ | Liquid ○ | Vapor or Liquid ○ |
| • Soil Temperature | °C | | Low (< 10) ○ | Medium (10°- 20) ○ | High (> 20) ○ |
| • Soil Hydraulic Conductivity | cm/sec. | | Low (> $10^{-5}$) ○ | Medium ($10^{-5}$-$10^{-3}$) ○ | High (> $10^{-3}$) ○ |
| • Moisture Content | % | | Moist (> 0.3) ○ | Moderate (0.1 to 0.3) ○ | Dry (< 0.1) ○ |
| • Geological Conditions | — | | Heterogeneous ○ | — ○ | Homogeneous ○ |
| • Soil Sorption Capacity - Surface Area | $cm^2$/g | | High (> 50) ○ | — ○ | Low (< 5) ○ |
| • Depth to Ground water | m. | | Low (<3) ○ | Medium (3-15) ○ | High (>15) ○ |
| | | | | | |
| **CONTAMINANT- RELATED** | | | | | |
| • Vapor Pressure | mm Hg | | Low (< 10) ○ | Medium (10 to 100) ○ | High (> 100) ○ |
| • Solubility | mg/L | | High (> 1000) ○ | Medium (100 - 1000) ○ | Low (< 100) ○ |

**OTHER CONSIDERATIONS**

- Cost is from $15 to $60 per cubic yard.
- Effectiveness decreases after several months of treatment.
- Capable of removing thousands of gallons.
- Air emissions will likely need to be treated with GAC.
- Treatment can be done on-site
- Care must be taken to avoid explosions because vapors are concentrated
- Cleanup takes time so that this technology is not appropriate when emergency response is needed

Figure 11

## WORKSHEET FOR EVALUATING THE FEASIBILITY
## OF BIORESTORATION BEING EFFECTIVE AT YOUR SITE

| CRITICAL SUCCESS FACTOR | UNITS | SITE OF INTEREST ▼ | SUCCESS LESS LIKELY | SUCCESS SOMEWHAT LIKELY | SUCCESS MORE LIKELY |
|---|---|---|---|---|---|
| **RELEASE - RELATED** | | | | | |
| • Time Since Release | Months | | Short (< 1) ○ | Medium (1 - 12) ○ | Long (> 12) ○ |
| **SITE RELATED** | | | | | |
| • Dominant Contaminant Phase | Phase | | Liquid ○ | Vapor ○ | Dissolved ○ |
| • Soil Temperature | °C | | Low (< 10°C) ○ | Medium (10°- 20°C) ○ | High (> 20°C) ○ |
| • Soil Hydraulic Conductivity | cm/sec. | | Low (<10$^{-5}$) ○ | Medium (10$^{-5}$-10$^{-3}$) ○ | High (> 10$^{-3}$) ○ |
| • Soil pH | PH Units | | (< 6 or > 8) ○ | — ○ | (6 - 8) ○ |
| • Moisture Content | % | | Dry (<0.1) ○ | Moderate (0.1 to 0.3) ○ | Moist (>0.3) ○ |
| | | | | | |
| **CONTAMINANT- RELATED** | | | | | |
| • Solubility | mg/L | | Low (< 100) ○ | Medium (100 to 1000) ○ | High (> 1000) ○ |
| • Biodegradability - Refractory Index | Dimensionless | | Low (< 0.01) ○ | Medium (0.01 to 0.1) ○ | High (> 0.1) ○ |
| • Fuel Type | — | | No. 6 Fuel Oil (Heavy) ○ | No. 2 Fuel Oil (Medium) ○ | Gasoline (Light) ○ |

**OTHER CONSIDERATIONS**
• Cost is from $60 to $125 per cubic yard.
• Completely destroys contaminants under optimal conditions
• Effectiveness varies depending on subsurface conditions
• Biologic systems subject to upset
• Public opinion sometimes against putting more chemicals in ground
• Difficult to monitor effectiveness
• Minimizes health risk by keeping contaminants in ground and on site
• Takes long time to work—not for emergency response

Figure 12

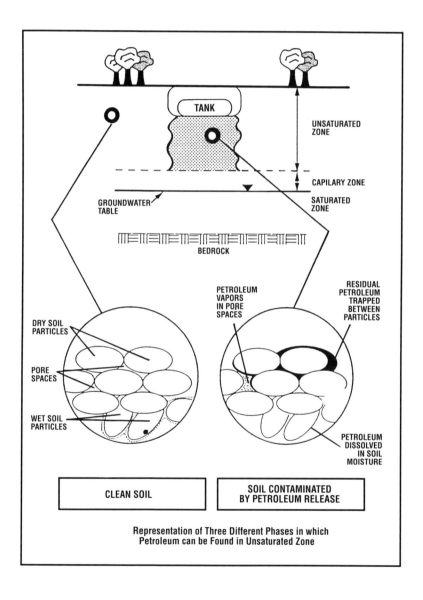

Representation of Three Different Phases in which
Petroleum can be Found in Unsaturated Zone

Figure 13

Rules-of-thumb* For Determining in Which Phase
Contamination Can Be Found


- Evidence of Residual Liquid Contamination:
    — High concentrations (>1% by weight) of contaminants in
      several soil analyses, i.e., petroleum makes up >1% of the
      weight of soil sample;
    — High concentrations (>10% by volume) of pure chemical
      vapor density in several soil gas analyses, i.e., contami-
      nant vapors are above 100,000 parts per million.

- Evidence of contaminant vapors:
    — Presence of residual liquid contaminants;
    — Significant concentrations in several soil gas analyses.

- Evidence of pore-water contamination:
    — Significant concentrations of contaminants in several anal-
      yses of pore water or ground water;
    — Presence of residual liquid contaminants **and** a significant
      soil moisture content.


*Sampling is required to apply these rules-of-thumb.*

---

Subsurface vapor transport requires dry soils and is governed by
vapor concentration and flux (vapor flow). The flux is away from areas of high concentration.[84]

# Future Trends and Emerging Issues

Liability for storage tanks is a rapidly evolving field of law, especially in areas of federal and state regulation, cleanup standards and
technology, medical monitoring, proof of causation, and insurance.
Perhaps even more dynamic is the underlying scientific understanding of the impacts of releases from tanks and the related analytical

methods used by the growing consulting and equipment manufacturing industries. Changes in science and technology are having the greatest effect in the areas of leak detection, site assessment of releases, cleanup methods, chronic health effects, and risk assessment.

The need for knowledge of the effects of releases is driven by the public's perceived risk of harm and the associated demand for regulation. Where corporate liability from ground water contamination or human exposure is concerned, the analogy holds true that "[a] small leak will sink a great ship."[85] Once there is a release to ground water, the problem is never easy to resolve. Acceptability of risks has been stated to be roughly proportional to the third power of the benefits of the activity involved. The exception is where the risk is voluntary, such as commercial aviation, skiing, or mountain climbing, and in these cases, the public will accept risks roughly 1000 times as great as involuntary hazards such as LUST releases, other pollution, or food additives.[86] In terms of overall perceived risks, LUST releases of hazardous substances rank high and can be equated to that of pesticides, which were ranked between four and nine out of 30 common activities or technologies (Figure 14 on the following page).

From the practitioner's perspective, the public and the courts will demand that responses to releases be given serious attention. Lawyers and managers working on LUST cases will be entering an arena frequently dominated by legal and scientific complexity and uncertainty, public controversy, and few demonstrated standards of performance. The parties that respond to the needs of this environment, especially with aggressive fact finding, will be able to control the outcome of a case because success in this evolving area of law, science, and technology is highly dependent on how much knowledge one wants to obtain through research and application. A tremendous amount of information is available from public sources outside of the normal discovery process, thus making cases not so much dependent on the fact known to both parties, but on the extent of facts brought to bear on the problem.

National regulation of tanks is a massive undertaking; it is the largest regulatory program at EPA. Some of the principles of common law and managing tank problems identified in this chapter may be used to provide not only guidelines for regulation , but also practical methods of resolving specific tank problems.

**Figure 14**

*Ordering of Perceived Risks of 30 Activities and Technologies*

| Activity or technology | League of Women Voters | College students | Experts |
|---|---|---|---|
| Nuclear power | 1 | 1 | 20 |
| Motor vehicles | 2 | 5 | 1 |
| Handguns | 3 | 2 | 4 |
| Smoking | 4 | 3 | 2 |
| Motorcycles | 5 | 6 | 6 |
| Alcoholic beverages | 6 | 7 | 3 |
| General (private) aviation | 7 | 15 | 12 |
| Police work | 8 | 8 | 17 |
| Pesticides | 9 | 4 | 8 |
| Surgery | 10 | 11 | 5 |
| Fire fighting | 11 | 10 | 18 |
| Large construction | 12 | 14 | 13 |
| Hunting | 13 | 18 | 23 |
| Spray cans | 14 | 13 | 26 |
| Mountain climbing | 15 | 22 | 29 |
| Bicycles | 16 | 24 | 15 |
| Commercial aviation | 17 | 16 | 16 |
| Electric power (non-nuclear) | 18 | 19 | 9 |
| Swimming | 19 | 30 | 10 |
| Contraceptives | 20 | 9 | 11 |
| Skiing | 21 | 25 | 30 |
| X-rays | 22 | 17 | 7 |
| High school and college football | 23 | 26 | 27 |
| Railroads | 24 | 23 | 19 |
| Food preservatives | 25 | 12 | 14 |
| Food coloring | 26 | 20 | 21 |
| Power mowers | 27 | 28 | 28 |
| Prescription antibiotics | 28 | 21 | 24 |
| Home appliances | 29 | 27 | 22 |
| Vaccinations | 30 | 29 | 25 |

Taken from Slovic, *Perception of Risk*, 236 SCIENCE 281 (1987).

**Environmental
Risk Management**

**Michael L. Italiano** has been responsible at over 100 waste sites for litigation, scientific and technical analysis, cleanup, and negotiation with federal and state agencies and industry. He has represented major national industry associations before Congress on environmental legislation. Mr. Italiano has over a decade of service with federal, state and local government and industry, has authored and served as editor of numerous environmental publications, and has written the book *Liability for Underground Storage Tanks*. His most recent public service was as Senior Analyst in the White House Science Office where he developed hazardous waste and environmental policy. He is Chairman of the Committee on Environmental Assessment which is developing consensus storage tank and environmental property transfer standards for the American Society for Testing and Materials, and is a member of the Environmental Liability Insurance Advisory Committee of the National Association of Insurance Commissioners. He is a member of the Bar in Pennsylvania and the District of Columbia.

**Dr. Myron S. Rosenberg, P.E.,** is a Vice President with Camp Dresser & McKee and since 1987, has served EPA's Office of Research and Development as Project Director for investigations concerning prevention, detection, and corrective action of hazardous materials released from Underground Storage Tanks (USTs). He has directed research ranging from evaluation of detection technologies to development of guidance for site evaluation and selection of soil remediation cleanup technologies. Dr. Rosenberg is serving as a member of the technical working groups of ASTM's Committee on Environmental Assessment developing storage tank and environmental property transfer guidance, practices, and standards. He has co-authored numerous articles on storage tanks. He is a Massachusetts registered Professional Engineer.

**Peter W. Tunnicliffe, P.E., J.D.** is a Senior Vice President with Camp Dress & McKee, a national and international environmental consulting firm. He directs environmental projects for numerous Fortune 500 companies. Mr. Tunnicliffe has been directly involved with major gasoline spill remediation projects on the East Coast, which included emergency remedial measures, product recovery, and long-term remedial measures. He has served as the senior officer for environmental audits, and assessments associated with compliance with the "due diligence" requirements for commercial property transfers. Mr. Tunnicliffe is a registered Professional Engineer in eight states and a member of the New York Bar.

## Endnotes

1. *Bhagavadgita* (Sanskrit), The Song of God 16, (P. Lal. trans.).

2. *H.R. Rep. No. 1133*, 98th Cong., 2d Sess. (1984).

3. EPA, Underground Motor Fuel Storage Tanks: A National Survey (1986).

4. EPA, State Incidence Report - Summary of State Reports on Releases from Underground Storage Tanks (1986).

5. Letter from J. Quarles and W. Gardner, Counsel for Mobay Chemical Corp., to U.S. Judge Scott O. Wright (Jan. 4, 1985), reprinted in 9 Chem. & Radiation Waste Litig. Rep. 436 (1985).

6. EPA, Summary of 1984 RCRA Underground Tank Requirements (Oct. 9, 1984 as corrected Feb. 1985); Lehman, Leaking Underground Storage Tanks; Leiter, Summary of Federal Underground Storage Tank Law, 135 Litigation and Administrative Practice Series, Amendments to the Resource Conservation and Recovery Act, 305 and 117 respectively (PLI 1985); R. Golemon, RCRA Provisions and EPA Proposed and Final Rules Regulating Underground Storage Tanks, Role of Local Governments in Pollution Control, Texas University Law School (Apr. 11, 1986).

7. *H.R. Rep. No. 1133*, 98th Cong., 2d Sess. (1984), 40 C.F.R. Part 280.

8. 52 *Fed. Reg.* 12765 (Apr. 17, 1987).

9. *Conf. Rep., H.R. Rep. No. 1133*, 98th Cong., 2d Sess. 128 (1984).

10. *Id.*, at 127.

11. 42 U.S.C. § 6991(c) (1984), and 52 *Fed. Reg.* 12853 (Apr. 17, 1987).

12. 51 *Fed. Reg.* 25470 (July 14, 1986), 53 *Fed. Reg.* 34086 (Sept. 2, 1988).

13. H.R. 3735, 101 Cong., 1st Sess. (Nov. 19, 1989).

14. 40 C.F.R. § 112.1 (1976).

15. H.R. 3735 § 9108.

16.  *Id.* § 9109.

17.  *Id.* § 9110.

18.  *U.S. v. Ballard Oil*, 195 F.2d 369 (2d Cir. 1952) (release of oil from a tank to the Connecticut River); *U.S. v. Standard Oil*, 384 U.S. 225 (1966) (discharge of jet fuel to the St. Johns River, Florida); *U.S. v. Esso Standard Oil*, 375 F.2d 621 (3d Cir. 1967) (release of petroleum to coastal waters of St. Croix); *U.S. v. Skil Corp.*, 351 F. Supp. 295 (N.D. Ill. 1972) (fuel oil discharge to the Chicago River); *U.S. v. General American Transportation*, 367 F. Supp. 1284 (D. N.J. 1973) (chemical and petroleum release from tank farm to the Arthur Kill).

19.  *U.S. v. General Motors*, 403 F. Supp. 1151 (D. Ct. 1975) (No. 6 fuel oil release from a tank to the Pequabuck River; nominal penalty award since defendant cleaned up the release); *U.S. v. Mackin Construction*, 388 F. Supp. 478 (D. Mass. 1975) (oil supplier breached duty of care resulting in release to the Mill River); *U.S. v. Mobil Oil*, 464 F.2d 1124 (5th Cir. 1972) (owner reporting release has statutory immunity from criminal violation of Clean Water Act); *U.S. v. Messer Oil Corp.*, 391 F. Supp. 557 (W.D. Pa. 1975) (owner not criminally liable for reporting release to Coast Guard).

20.  55 *Fed. Reg.* 11836 (Mar. 29, 1990).

21.  M. L. Italiano, Gardner, Carton & Douglas, *Legal Authority Governing Leaking Underground Storage Tanks*, Practicing Law Institute, N.Y., N.Y. (1984).

22.  American Petroleum Institute, Underground Petroleum Product Storage Tanks: State Requirements (1984). Under the federal program, all USTs were to have been registered by May, 1985.

23.  *Cooper v. Whiting Oil Co.*, 226 Va. 491, 311 S.E.2d 757 (1984).

24.  *Pryor v. Chambersburg Oil & Gas Co.*, 376 Pa. 521, 103 A.2d 425 (1954).

25.  *Bollinger v. Mungle*, 175 S.W.2d 912 (Mo. App. 1943).

26.  *Prosser & Keeton On Torts* at 165 (5th ed. 1984).

27.  *Phillipe v. Rhoads*, 233 Pa. Super. 503, 336 A.2d 374 (1975); *Govero v. Standard Oil Co.*, 192 F.2d 962 (8th Cir. 1951); *Darnell v. Taylor*, 236 So. 2d 57 (La. App. 1970).

28.  *Machen v. Gulf Oil Corp.*, 184 So. 2d 550 (La. App. 1965).

29.  *Town Pump, Inc. v. Diteman*, 622 P.2d 212 (Mont. 1981).

30.  *Pryor v. Chambersburg Oil & Gas Co.*, 376 Pa. 521, 103 A.2d 425 (1954) (explosion from a release).

31.  *Texaco v. Debusk*, 444 S.W.2d 261 (Ky. App. 1969).

32.  *Hennigan v. Atlantic Refining Co.*, 282 F. Supp. 667 (E.D. Pa. 1967) (leak and explosion beneath a refinery).

33.  *Bennett v. Imperial Oil Ltd.*, 28 D.L.R.2d 55 (Nfld. 1961) (gasoline contaminated well after faulty repairs).

34. *U.S. v. General American Transportation,* 367 F. Supp. 1284 (D. N.J. 1973).

35. *South Central Bell Telephone Co. v. Hartford Accident & Indemnity Co.,* 385 So. 2d 830 (La. App. 1980) (gasoline damaged phone cables); *Yommer v. McKenzie,* 255 Md. 220, 257 A.2d 138 (Md. 1969) (gasoline contaminated well); *McLaughlin v. Time Markets,* No. 336 (Con. Pleas Ct., Synder Co. Pa. May 8, 1987) (gasoline release to nearby municipal water supply).

36. *Moran v. Pittsburgh-Des Moines Steel,* 166 F.2d (ed Cir. 1948), *cert. denied,* 334 U.S. 846 (explosion of liquified natural gas tank results in strict liability as an ultrahazardous activity, citing § 520 of the Restatement of Torts).

37. RESTATEMENT (SECOND) TORTS §§ 268 comment i, 159(1)(1977).

38. *Pryor v. Chambersburg Oil & Gas Co.,* 376 Pa. 521, 103 A.2d 425 (1954); *Bonneau v. Ralph v. Martin Oil Co.,* 259 Pa. Super. 428, 393 A.2d 901 (1978).

39. RESTATEMENT (SECOND) TORTS §§ 821(d), (f), 822(a) & comment a.

40. *Wood v. Picillo,* 443 A.2d (R.I. 1982), *Cornell v. Exxon,* No. 59976 (N.Y. App. Div. June 28, 1990 on WESTLAW, New York database).

41. *Blais v. Callahan Oil Co.,* 18 Conn. Supp. 146 (Conn. C.P. 1952).

42. Annot., 50 A.L.R. 3d 209 (1989).

43. *Monroe "66" Oil Co. v. Hightower,* 180 So. 2d 8 (La. App. 1965).

44. *Continental Oil Co. v. Berry,* 52 S.W.2d 953 (Tex. Civ. App. 1932).

45. *Pan American Petroleum Co. v. Byars,* 228 Ala. 372, 153 So. 616 (1934).

46. *Bousquet v. Massachusetts,* 374 Mass. 824, 372 N.E.2d 257 (1978).

47. *Bean v. Sears Roebuck & Co.,* 194 Vt. 278, 276 A.2d 613 (1971).

48. *Cornell v. Exxon,* No. 59976 (N.Y. App. Div. June 28, 1990 on WESTLAW, New York database).

49. *Hudson v. Peavy Oil Co.,* 279 Or. 3, 566 P.2d 175 (1977).

50. *Hennigan v. Atlantic Refining Co.,* 282 F. Supp. 667 (E.D. Pa. 1967).

51. *City of Northglenn v. Chevron,* 5 Chem. & Radiation Waste Litig. Rep. (Computer Law Rep.) 639 (1983) (No.81-C-44 D. Colo. 1982) (release of gasoline to a residential sewer system). Accord, *Ayers v. Jackson Township,* 189 N.J. Super. 561, 461 A.2d (1983), *aff'd* in part *rev'd* in part 106 N.J. 557, 525 A.2d 287 (1987).

52. *Bennett v. Imperial Oil Co.,* 28 D.L.R.2d 55 (Nfld. 1961) (gasoline contaminated well), *Watson v. Great Lakes Pipeline Co.,* 182 N.W. 2d 314 (N.D. 1970) (gasoline from tank farm contaminated a well).

53. *Socony Mobil Oil Co. v. Southwestern Bell Telephone Co.,* 518 S.W.2d 257 (Tex. Civ. App. 1974) (release damaged underground cables).

54. CLEARY, MCCORMICK ON EVIDENCE § 96 (1972); *Dunning v. Shell Oil Co.*, 57 A.D.2d 16, 393 N.Y.S.2d (3d Dep't 1977).

55. *South Central Bell Telephone Co. v. Texaco, Inc.*, 418 So. 2d 531 (La. 1982); RESTATEMENT (SECOND) OF TORTS § 899 comment c (1977).

56. *Hennigan v. Atlantic Refining Co.*, 282 F. Supp. 667 (E.D. Pa. 1967); *South Central Bell Telephone v. Hartford Accident & Indemnity Co.*, 385 So. 2d 830 (La. App. 1980), *Cornell v. Exxon*, No. 59976 (N.Y. App. Div. June 28, 1990 on WESTLAW, New York database).

57. *Hennigan v. Atlantic Refining Co.*, 282 F. Supp. 667 (E.D. Pa. 1967); *United States v. White Fuel Co.*, 498 F.2d 619 (1st Cir. 1974).

58. *Texaco v. Debusk*, 444 S.W.2d 261 (Ky. App. 1969) (defense invalid by tank owner's conduct because the owner assured that there was no release but one subsequently occurred).

59. *Metal Bank v. INA*, Pa. Super 1987, Haz. Waste Lit. Rep. (Andrews) p. 10556 (Mar. 2, 1987).

60. *James Graham Brown v. St. Paul Fire & Marine Insurance*, No. 85-CI-06677 (Jefferson Cir. Ct. Ky. Feb. 17, 1988).

61. *United States Fidelity & Guaranty Co. v. Johnson Shoes*, 123 N.H. 148, 461 A.2d 85 (1983).

62. *C. D. Spangler Construction Co. v. Industrial Crankshaft*, No. 128PA88 (N.C. Feb. 7, 1990).

63. *American States Insurance Co. v. Maryland Casualty Co.*, 7 Chem. & Radiation Waste Litig. Rep. (Computer Law Rep.) 461, 463 (E.D. Mich. 1984).

64. *Allstate Insurance Co. v. Klock Oil Co.*, 73 A.D.2d 486, 426 N.Y.S.2d 603 (4th Dep't 1980).

65. *Taylor v. Imperial Casualty & Indemnity Co.*, 82 S.D. 298, 144 N.W.2d 856 (1966).

66. *W. J. Boyton & Son v. AETNA Insurance Co.*, 166 F. Supp. 199 (N.D. Fla. 1958).

67. *Intel Corp. v. Hartford Accident and Indemnity Co.*, Insurance Lit. Rep. H-6 (Mealey's 1988), *motion for reconsideration denied, Id.* at H-6.

68. *Lexington Insurance Co. v. Ryder System, Inc.*, 142 Ga. App. 36, 234 S.E.2d 839 (1977) (released oil was held to be within the plain meaning of debris, *i.e.*, waste material resulting from destruction of some article).

69. *Mid-Atlantic National Bank v. New Jersey DEP* [Quanta Resources], 475 U.S. 494 (1986), *citing Ohio v. Kovacs*, 465 U.S. 1078 (1985).

70. SEC release No. 6835, 54 Fed. Reg. 22427 (May 18, 1989).

71.  Resources for the Future, *Confronting Uncertainty In Risk Management* (1990).

72.  Memorandum from Jack Farlow, Chief, Technology Development Branch to Tom Young, Office of Underground Storage Tanks (1988).

73.  ASTM Standards on release detection for underground storage tanks (Phila. Pa., 1990).

74.  EPA, *Clean-up Of Releases From Petroleum USTs: Selected Technologies* (1988).

75.  American Petroleum Institute (API), *A Guide To The Assessment And Remediation Of Underground Petroleum Releases*, API Pub. 1628 (1989).

76.  EPA, *Clean-up Of Releases From Petroleum USTs: Selected Technologies* (1988).

77.  *Id.*

78.  *Id.*

79.  Camp Dresser & McKee and EPA, *The Role of Site Investigation in the Selection of Corrective Actions for Leaking Underground Storage Tanks* (1989).

80.  *Id.*

81.  EPA, *Clean-up Of Releases From Petroleum USTs: Selected Technologies* (1988).

82.  Camp Dresser & McKee and EPA, *The Role of Site Investigation in the Selection of Corrective Actions for Leaking Underground Storage Tanks* (1989).

83.  Rosenberg *et al.*, *An Overview of Transport of Contaminants from Leaking Underground Storage Tanks*, Proc., 2d Ann. Haz. Mat. Mgt. Conf. West (1986).

84.  *Id.*

85.  T. Fuller, M.D., Gnomologia 407 (1732).

86.  Slovic, Perception of Risk, 236 Science 280 (1987), citing Starr, 165 Science 1232 (1969).

# VII

# The Toxic Substances Control Act

## Alison A. Kerester, Esq.
## Beveridge & Diamond
## Washington, D.C.

Perhaps nowhere in the federal environmental statutory scheme is the concept of risk assessment and risk management more pervasive than in the Toxic Substances Control Act (TSCA). The goal of TSCA is the assessment and control of unreasonable risk of harm to human health and the environment from chemical substances and mixtures. In enacting TSCA to control these risks, Congress created a viable "cradle-to-grave" statutory scheme for controlling the risks from the manufacture, processing, distribution, use, and disposal of chemical substances. By seeking to regulate only those risks that are unreasonable, Congress implicitly recognized that society is not risk free. Moreover, by deliberately declining to define the concept of *unreasonable* risk, either in the statute or in the legislative history, Congress recognized that the concept of unreasonable risk is a dynamic one that reflects many factors and uncertainties, and ultimately requires a judgment call about the balance of risks and benefits.[1]

TSCA broadly defines the term *chemical substance* to include any organic or inorganic substance of a particular molecular identity, including those that evolve from a chemical reaction or occur in nature, and any element or uncombined radical.[2] The Environmental Protection Agency (EPA) has interpreted this broad definition to include certain micro-organisms and their DNA molecules. The definition, however, does not include those chemical substances, such as nuclear material, tobacco, pesticides, and drugs, which are regulated under other federal laws.[3]

The term *mixture* means any combination of two or more chemical substances if the combination does not occur in nature and is not, in whole or in part, the result of a chemical reaction. A mixture, however, does include a combination that is a result of a chemical reaction if none of the chemicals in the combination is a new chemical substance and if the combination could have been manufactured without a chemical reaction at the time the chemical substances were combined.[4]

TSCA provides EPA with a number of broad authorities to assess and regulate the unreasonable risks from chemical substances and mixtures. TSCA, however, is not a permitting or licensing statute like the Federal Insecticide, Fungicide, and Rodenticide Act (FIFRA) (See Chapter VIII by Heymann) or the Federal Food, Drug and Cosmetic Act or the Resource Conservation and Recovery Act (RCRA) (See Chapter V, Bourdeau). Thus, chemicals reviewed under TSCA are not deemed to be approved by EPA.

TSCA has been the sleeper environmental statute, little used as a regulatory tool by EPA in its efforts to control environmental harm. Recently, however, EPA has rediscovered TSCA's cradle-to-grave statutory scheme and implementing authorities and has begun using this statute to support not only the TSCA programs implemented by EPA's Office of Toxic Substances, but also to support the efforts of other Agency programs such as hazardous waste and clean air. The emergence of TSCA as a central linchpin in EPA's efforts to control environmental risks, coupled with EPA's extremely aggressive efforts to enforce this statute, are rendering TSCA a critical risk assessment and management tool for EPA.

## The TSCA Chemical Substances Inventory

TSCA essentially divides the universe of chemical substances into two components: new chemical substances and existing chemical substances. The nature of EPA's authority to regulate a chemical substance often hinges upon whether a chemical is a new or existing one. An existing chemical substance is a substance that is listed on the TSCA Inventory of Chemical Substances ("Inventory"). The Inventory, compiled and kept current pursuant to TSCA Section 8(b), is intended to be a master list of those chemical substances currently in U.S. commerce. Chemicals are added to the Inventory in two ways. First, the chemical may have been added at the time of the initial Inventory compilation. Manufacturers, importers, and processors were required, shortly after TSCA's enactment, to report to EPA on the chemicals that they were making and processing. Second, a chemical may be added after it has completed new chemical review under TSCA Section 5 (discussed below) and EPA is notified of its initial commercial manufacture or importation. Chemicals that are no longer in commercial production are routinely delisted from the Inventory after notice and comment.

In actuality there are two Inventories; the Public Inventory and the Confidential one. The Public Inventory, consisting of five volumes,[5] last published 1985 and most recently updated in 1990, contains the chemical identities of existing substances (either the specific identity or a more generic description in cases where the submitters sought to keep the exact chemical identity confidential). The Confidential Inventory (or Master Inventory) contains specific chemical identities that were declared confidential business information by submitters, and is not available to the public. A person who can demonstrate a *bona fide* intent to manufacture or import a chemical may request EPA to search the Confidential Inventory to determine whether the chemical is listed, obviating the need to submit a premanufacture notice.[6]

## TSCA Section 5: New Chemicals

TSCA Section 5 requires manufacturers (including, by definition, importers) of a new chemical substance to file a premanufacture notice (PMN) with EPA at least 90 days before the first commercial manufacture (or importation) of the chemical. The manufacturer must use the PMN form, which requires the submitter to provide information on the chemical's identity, intended production, potential worker and consumer exposure, and disposal methods. The submitter may claim any or all of the information in the PMN as confidential; if he does so however, he must also supply a sanitized version of the PMN, which will be available for public disclosure, in which all of the confidential business information has been deleted. Any test data in the submitter's possession or control also must be submitted along with the PMN. No new test data need be generated on the chemical.

There are a number of exclusions and exemptions from the process. By definition, chemical substances that do not meet the TSCA definition of chemical substance, such as those intended solely for use as a pesticide, food, drug, or cosmetic are exempt from the PMN requirements.[7] Chemicals used solely for research and development purposes, in quantities no greater than reasonably necessary, are exempt, provided that they are used under the supervision of a technically qualified individual, the potential risks are evaluated, and people potentially exposed to the chemical are notified of those risks.[8] No application for this exemption is necessary.

Test marketing activities are also exempt from the PMN requirements, provided that EPA grants a test marketing exemption (TME) application submitted by the manufacturer.[9] EPA will grant a TME if EPA is convinced the TME activity will not present an unreasonable risk of harm, and is for genuine test marketing purposes as opposed to an attempt to build up inventory prior to the PMN clearance. EPA generally grants a test marketing exemption for a period of one year.

EPA provides for a 21-day expedited PMN review period for low volume chemicals and certain polymers. The low volume exemption is available only to one manufacturer who will certify that he will manufacture the chemical in quantities no greater than 1,000 kilograms per year.[10] EPA must determine that the intended manufacture will not present an unreasonable risk before granting the low volume exemption. Because the low volume chemicals are not placed on the Inventory following commercial production, anyone who subsequently wants to manufacture the chemical must file a full PMN. The 21-day review period is also available for polymers meeting certain technical requirements.[11]

Certain types of new chemical substances are completely exempt from the PMN requirements. These include new chemicals used in or for instant film (the "Polaroid" exemption),[12] new chemicals imported as part of an article, impurities, byproducts, nonisolated intermediates, chemicals formed incidental to exposure to other chemicals, chemicals formed during the manufacture of an article,[13] and those formed incidental to the use of certain additives.[14]

No new chemical substance may be manufactured before the expiration of the minimum 90-day period. After expiration of this waiting time, or following approval from the USEPA, the manufacturer or importer must also file a formal notice of commencement of manufacture or import within 30 days after the first day of such manufacture or importation.[15] Failure to file a notice of commencement (NOC) has been a frequent basis of recent USEPA penalty assessments.

## Section 5(e): Regulation of New Chemicals

During the course of its new chemical review, if EPA determines that the new chemical: (1) may present an unreasonable risk to human health and the environment; or (2) will be produced in substantial quantities with resultant significant human exposure; and (3) EPA has insufficient information to conduct a reasoned evaluation of the substance, EPA may ban or otherwise limit the manufacture, distribution, processing, use, and disposal of the chemical under Section 5(e). EPA has developed quantitative risk triggers for determining whether a substance may present an unreasonable risk.

Pursuant to Section 5(e) EPA may issue a proposed administrative order banning or limiting the chemical pending the development of additional risk assessment information. The PMN submitter has the opportunity to file objections to the order. The filing of objections prevents the order from becoming effective. If after evaluating the objections, EPA still decides to ban or limit the chemical, it must seek a federal court injunction against manufacture before the lapse of the PMN review period.

EPA, however, typically negotiates a consent order regulating the chemical that may present a risk. Under such an order, the manufacturer and EPA agree to certain restrictions (such as the use of worker protective equipment) on the chemical and on the generation and submission of specified test data. Under this arrangement, the manufacturer can market the chemical while EPA is assured that the potential risk is reduced and that it will receive specified information necessary to continue EPA's evaluation of the chemical. On March 16, 1988 EPA proposed a model Section 5(e) consent order; it was later finalized.

## Section 5(f): Rules and Orders

When EPA finds that there is a reasonable basis to conclude that a chemical "presents or will present" an unreasonable risk to human health or the environment before it is able to promulgate a rule under Section 6, it shall take regulatory action to reduce that risk. EPA may issue an "immediately effective" proposed rule under Section 6 to limit (but not ban) the chemical. In effect, TSCA authorizes EPA to use the broad regulatory authorities of Section 6(a) to immediately regulate a new chemical substance that will present an unreasonable risk. Although technically a proposed Section 6 rule, Section 5(f) authorizes EPA to make that rule immediately effective upon publication in the *Federal Register*.

To date, EPA has proposed only three Section 5(f) rules banning the addition of four nitrosating agents to metalworking fluids.[16] Although these rules have never been made final, they were effective upon publication in the *Federal Register*.

If, however, EPA determines that the new chemical presents an unreasonable risk and that it is necessary to ban it from commercial manufacture, distribution, processing, use, and disposal, the Administrator may issue a proposed Section 5(f) order and apply for a federal court injunction. The proposed order takes effect upon the expiration of the premanufacture review period, unless the PMN submitter files objections. If the Administrator issues the proposed order, he must apply for an injunction in federal court before the lapse of the premanufacture review period, unless he determines on the basis of the objections filed by the submitter, that the chemical will not present an unreasonable risk.

### Section 5 (a): Significant New Uses

Section 5 also provides a mechanism that, in effect, converts an existing chemical into a new one, and subjects it to the equivalent of a PMN review.[17] This mechanism is called the "significant new use rule" or SNUR. Under the SNUR provisions, EPA may require manufacturers and processors of a chemical that will be used for a significant new use to file a notice with EPA (called a significant new use notice and functionally equivalent to a PMN) at least 90 days prior to beginning the manufacture or processing of the substance for that new use. This provision reflects congressional awareness that new uses of a chemical may produce potentially new risks that need to be evaluated by EPA.

TSCA does not define the term "significant new use" but requires EPA to consider "all relevant" factors, including: (1) the projected manufacturing and processing volume; (2) the extent to which the use changes the type of human or environmental exposure; (3) the extent to which the use increases the magnitude and duration of human or environmental exposure; and (4) the reasonably anticipated manner and methods of manufacturing, processing, distribution in commerce, and disposal.[18] "Significant new uses" may include increased production volumes, different manufacturing sites or disposal methods, or different types or increases in the extent of human or environmental exposure.

EPA established a list of activities that will constitute significant new uses, along with related recordkeeping requirements, with the promulgation of its "Generic SNUR" rule in 1989. When EPA designates an activity described by the standard list of activities as a significant new use for a chemical, it will list the substance and will reference which of the five following categories constitutes a new use. These standardized significant new uses include:

- Any method of manufacturing or processing associated with use of a chemical without establishing a program for protection in the workplace from dermal and respiratory exposure and demonstrating that chemical protective clothing is impervious;
- Any method of manufacturing or processing without establishing a hazard communication program, as described by EPA, to inform workers of potential risks from the chemical and the precautionary measures to be taken;
- Specified industrial, commercial, and consumer activities (such as manufacture, processing or use in a non-enclosed manner; use other than as a site-limited intermediate; commercial use);
- Disposal (designates specific ongoing allowable disposal methods with other methods deemed to be significant new uses); and
- Uses involving releases to water.[20]

EPA's Generic SNUR rule also established expedited procedures for issuing SNURs for chemicals subject to Section 5(e) consent orders.[21] In addition, EPA may use these expedited procedures for a chemical not subject to a final Section 5(e) order if EPA determines that activities other than those described in the PMN may result in significant changes in human exposure or environmental release levels, or is concerned about the substances' health or environmental effects. EPA has listed specific "concern" criteria in the rule, such as carcinogenic effects.[22]

## TSCA Section 6:  Existing Chemicals

Section 6 provides EPA with the authority to regulate risks imposed by chemicals already in commerce.  Under Section 6 EPA may ban or otherwise limit the manufacture, processing, distribution, use, and disposal of a chemical substance that "presents or will present" an unreasonable risk of harm.

Under Section 6(a), EPA has the following regulatory options for controlling unreasonable risk:

- Prohibit or limit the manufacture, processing, and distribution of a chemical;
- Prohibit or limit the manufacture, processing or distribution of a chemical for a particular  use or in specified concentrations;
- Require warnings and instructions with respect to the substance's use, distribution, or disposal;
- Require record keeping;
- Prohibit or limit disposal; and
- Require manufacturers to replace or repurchase a substance or to notify purchasers about the risks of the chemical.

In promulgating any regulation under Section 6(a), EPA must consider (and publish a statement on) the effects of the substance on human health and the magnitude of human exposure, the environmental effects and magnitude of environmental exposure, the benefits of the substance, the availability of substitutes, and the economic consequences of the rule.  EPA must also determine that the risks cannot be regulated more effectively under another environmental law.

Thus, EPA's regulatory hurdles for regulating unreasonable risks from existing chemicals are much greater than for new chemicals. EPA has interpreted the standard of "presents or will present" an unreasonable risk as requiring actual test data on the substance.  This standard has been extremely difficult to meet because little testing has been conducted on chemicals currently in commerce (a deficiency EPA is now trying to remedy  through issuance of increasing numbers of Section 4 test rules). This hurdle, coupled with the necessity of conducting a full benefit/cost analysis and determining that TSCA is the law best suited to regulate the risk, may explain EPA's failure to use its Section 6 authorities with any frequency.

Indeed, EPA has used the broad authorities of Section 6 only in a few instances — to regulate chlorofluorocarbons (CFCs), nitrosating agents in metalworking fluids, asbestos, hexavalent chromium chemicals in comfort cooling towers, and polychlorinated biphenyls (PCBs) . EPA, however, is now beginning a regulatory effort under Section 6 to control the risks from lead, and EPA has indicated that it will increase its use of its Section 6 authorities more aggressively in the future.

# TSCA Section 4:  Testing of Chemicals

TSCA Section 4 is designed to implement one of TSCA's major goals, that of requiring manufacturers, importers and processors to develop adequate data with respect to the human health and environmental effects of chemical substances and mixtures.[24] Pursuant to Section 4, EPA may require testing of substances and mixtures that may be hazardous to human health or the environment or that are produced in substantial quantities with resultant significant human or environmental exposure.

Section 4 also establishes an Interagency Testing Committee (ITC) to study and recommend those chemicals that should be priority candidates for testing.  The ITC reports its testing recommendations to EPA, designating various priorities for substances to be tested.[25] OTS has indicated that the 1990's will be the "decade of testing" of chemical substances and mixtures and that EPA will require testing to support Agency regulatory programs other than TSCA.

## Section 4 (a):  Grounds for Testing Requirement

There are two regulatory triggers for requiring testing under Section 4.  Section 4(a)(1)(A) is a risk-based testing trigger.  Under this risk trigger, EPA may require testing when it determines that:

- The chemical or mixture may present an unreasonable risk of injury to human health or the environment;
- Existing data on and experience with the chemical or mixture are insufficient to reasonably predict or determine the effects of the chemical substance; and
- Testing is necessary to obtain such data.[26]

In order to assess the risk associated with a substance, EPA considers such factors as case history data, the chemical's known physical and chemical properties, and data comparing the substance to other chemicals already demonstrated to adversely affect human health and the environment.[27] Under Section 4(a)(1)(A), EPA is required to base a finding of "unreasonable risk" on an "existing possibility of harm [that presents] reasonable and legitimate cause for concern."[28] However, while suspicion of possible exposure and toxicity must be more than theoretical, it is sufficient for EPA to base an "unreasonable risk" finding upon a suggestion of possible risk in existing scientific studies.[29]

EPA has not developed quantitative risk triggers for determining when a substance may present an unreasonable risk under Section 4 (a)(1)(A). Rather, EPA utilizes a qualitative approach to risk assessment. For example, EPA may determine that a substance may present an unreasonable risk based on structural analogy to another substance. Thus, if a structurally analogous substance presents a serious risk of harm to human health or the environment, EPA will likely require testing on the substance under review.

A second basis for requiring testing exists under TSCA Section 4 (a)(1)(B). Here, EPA may require testing if a substance or mixture is produced in substantial quantities and results in substantial environmental or human exposure and testing is necessary to determine the risks that may result from that exposure.[30] No express finding of risk is necessary under TSCA Section 4(a)(1)(B). Rather, the potential for risk is assumed to result from the substantial production and significant human and environmental exposure. The exposure levels required to meet the "substantial" standard have not been quantified by EPA. Instead, EPA has chosen to evaluate production and exposure on a chemical-specific basis.[31]

### Section 4: Test Rules

Once EPA determines that testing of a chemical substance should be required, EPA publishes a proposed test rule for public comment and a subsequent final test rule. The test rule sets forth the particular substance or mixture to be tested, the types of tests (and their protocols) required under the rule, and, if possible, the schedule for submission of data.

In addition, EPA has promulgated Good Laboratory Practice standards which specify in detail the minimum requirements that a laboratory and test sponsor must meet in order for a test to comply with a Section 4 test rule.[32]

Agency regulations require that any person subject to a test rule submit a letter of intent to comply with the test rule, or request an exemption from it, within 30 days of the effective date of the rule.[33] If another party has agreed to undertake the required testing, EPA typically grants the applied-for exemption.[34] However, if the planned testing upon which the exemption was contingent does not come to fruition, or if the testing is in some other way not completed satisfactorily, EPA may terminate an exemption.[35]

Parties who obtain an exemption from a testing requirement must reimburse those actually performing the required testing within the appropriate reimbursement period[36] for an amount agreed upon by the parties, or, failing such agreement, for an amount ordered by EPA pursuant to the reimbursement rule promulgated by EPA. [37] That rule requires that parties submit their dispute to an arbitrator, who will issue a proposed order, appealable to EPA, which applies a pre-established market share based formula.[38] A party may propose allocation factors other than market share if it can meet the burden of proving to EPA that a fair and equitable result will follow. If a test rule requires processors, as well as manufacturers and importers to conduct testing, the processors also will be required to reimburse those incurring testing costs.[39]

With increasing frequency, persons required by a Section 4 test rule to develop data regarding a chemical substance have agreed to undertake the testing as a joint venture, through which costs and testing responsibilities are shared pursuant to voluntary agreement. In such instances, potential conflicts that arise with respect to cost sharing and selection of test substance are addressed within the context of the participating or negotiating group.

### Consent Agreements for Testing

When EPA, the affected industrial participants, and interested parties participating in the negotiation process[40] agree on the necessary scope of testing to be required, enforceable consent agreements are sometimes executed in lieu of the promulgation of a test rule. Such consent agreements, when developed pursuant to EPA regulations,[41] are enforceable under TSCA Section 15(1) as orders issued under Section 4.[42]

### Post-Test Findings of Significant Risk

Upon receipt of test data generated pursuant to Section 4, EPA is required to evaluate the risk posed by the tested substance. If the data indicate a reasonable basis to conclude that a significant risk is posed by the chemical, EPA must either initiate regulatory action under TSCA Sections 5, 6, or 7 or publish its reasons for not taking such an action.[43]

# TSCA Section 8

In Section 8, Congress provided EPA with broad information gathering authorities regarding chemical substances and their possible effects. The powers granted to EPA's authorities under Section 8 are potentially far-reaching and have in fact become a useful tool for supporting regulatory activities of other federal programs with increasing frequency in recent years.

### Section 8(a): Activity Reports

Under Section 8(a), EPA has the authority to require current or prospective manufacturers and processors of chemical substances to maintain records and submit reports, as circumstances reasonably require. In cases where chemical substances are manufactured or processed only in small quantities for research and development, EPA's authority to impose reporting and recordkeeping requirements is more limited. EPA has used its Section 8(a) authority to impose record keeping and reporting requirements on specific chemicals, and has issued two sets of reporting rules applicable to multiple chemicals. EPA first issued the Preliminary Assessment Information Rule (PAIR), intended to gather preliminary exposure data from manufacturers and importers of listed substances.[44] Six years later, EPA issued the Comprehensive Assessment Information Rule (CAIR), which broadened the scope of reporting required to include processors and revised the format for reporting and the list of chemicals for which reporting was required.[45]

## Section 8(c): Records of Significant Adverse Reactions

Section 8(c) requires that a manufacturer, processor, or distributor of a chemical substance or mixture record any allegation that a significant adverse health or environment reactions has been caused by the chemical or mixture. Records of employee allegations must be kept on file for 30 years, while recorded allegations from any other sources must be kept for five years.[46] Types of adverse effects for which allegations must be recorded are listed by EPA in various regulations,[47] and certain alleged effects, such as human health effects already commonly recognized[48] or environmental reactions caused by a spill or discharge reported to the federal government pursuant to other applicable authority,[49] are exempted from the recording requirement. EPA has authority to require submission of the records maintained under Section 8(c).

## Section 8(d): Health and Safety Studies

Section 8(d) mandates the reporting to EPA of all unpublished health and safety studies on a chemical substance upon request by EPA. Persons who currently manufacture, import or process a chemical substance or mixture listed by EPA,[50] or who plan to do so, are subject to EPA's Model Reporting Rule.[51] That rule defines reportable studies to include monitoring reports that aggregate and analyze data, modeling studies that estimate actual or likely exposure based on best estimates of quantities and conditions, portions of company operations reports that discuss listed substances, clinical tests on employees that discuss implications beyond the individual employee, and studies of certain listed physical or chemical properties if they are intended to determine the environmental or biological fate of the Section 8(d) substance.[52]

Submission of studies not falling within the requirements set forth by EPA, or falling within one of several categories of exemptions,[53] is not required.

## Section 8(e): Substantial Risk Information

Section 8(e) imposes upon all manufacturers, processors and distributors of chemical substances or mixtures an affirmative obligation to report to EPA any information "which reasonably supports the conclusion that such substance or mixture presents a substantial risk of injury to health or the environment." Because private parties bear substantial reporting responsibility, and because EPA has undertaken more stringent and active enforcement of the provisions of Section 8(e) in recent months, the risk assessment issues raised in the context of Section 8(e) are critical ones.

Section 8(e) was enacted in reaction to a Congressional perception that some companies were withholding critical information on the potential health and environmental effects from workers, the public, and the government. Thus, under Section 8(e) Congress created a mechanism for the "immediate" reporting to EPA of risk information that rises to the level of "substantial." Neither the statute, nor the legislative history define precisely what constitutes a substantial risk. Although EPA has not issued regulations implementing Section 8(e), EPA issued a statement of Interpretation and Enforcement Policy in 1978 called "Section 8(e) guidance".[54]

According to EPA, a substantial risk is a risk of considerable concern because of the seriousness of the effect and the fact or probability of its occurrence. Economic or social benefits of the use, or the costs of restricting the use are not to be considered in determining whether information suggests a substantial risk under Section 8(e). Substantial risk information may arise from preliminary studies, from designed, controlled studies (e.g., *in vitro* experiments and tests), or from undesigned, controlled circumstances such as medical and health surveys. In its Section 8(e) guidance, EPA expressly emphasizes that "reasonable support" for a conclusion of substantial risk gives rise to reporting; a person does not need to have reached a definitive conclusion. Once that reasonable support is available, a Section 8(e) report must be filed, regardless of the study's conclusiveness.[55]

Although the statutory language of Section 8(e) suggests that companies must apply judgment as to what constitutes a substantial risk, EPA has expressly reserved judgement as to the significance of testing results to its own scientists.[56] EPA's reservation of risk determination along with informal indications of increasingly broad Agency determinations of what risks are substantial has resulted in some companies submitting virtually all data to EPA in order to avoid a potential enforcement risks. Under EPA's Section 8(e) guidance, risk information must be reported in writing to EPA Headquarters within 15 working days; emergency incidents of environmental contamination must be reported within 24 hours to the appropriate EPA Region. It is EPA's policy that officers and employees of a company who receive the type of information reportable under Section 8(e) and are capable of appreciating its significance are subject, as individuals, to the requirements of Section 8(e). However, companies that implement corporate Section 8(e) policies may relieve most individual officers and employees from Section 8(e) liability.

There are five exemptions from Section 8(e):

- Information that has been published by EPA in reports;
- Information that has been submitted to EPA pursuant to a mandatory reporting requirement of another law administered by EPA, such as RCRA;
- Information that has been published in the scientific literature and referenced in certain abstract services;
- Information that is corroborative of well established adverse effects; and
- Information that is contained in the spill notification provisions of Section 311(b) of the Federal Water Pollution Control Act.

## TSCA Section 11: Inspections and Subpoenas

Under TSCA Section 11(a), EPA is authorized to inspect any establishment, facility, or other premises in which chemical substances or mixtures are manufactured, processed, stored or held after their distribution in commerce.[58] In addition, EPA may inspect any conveyance used to transport chemicals. In conducting these inspections, EPA must present appropriate credentials and provide written notice of the inspection. The scope of EPA's inspection authority is very broad and extends to any records, files, papers, processes, controls, and facilities that bear on whether the requirements of TSCA have been complied with. An inspection also may extend to financial, sales, pricing, personnel or research data if described with reasonable specificity in the written notice.[59]

EPA may either conduct an inspection to determine compliance with a specific section of TSCA, such as the substantial risk reporting provision of TSCA Section 8(e), or to determine general TSCA compliance. EPA targets certain companies, such as those companies subject to TSCA Section 5(e) orders, for automatic TSCA inspection.

### Subpoenas

EPA is authorized to issue subpoenas as part of its TSCA enforcement efforts under TSCA Section 11(c). EPA may subpoena the attendance and testimony of witnesses as well as the production of reports, papers, documents, answers to questions and other information necessary to TSCA enforcement.[60] For example, EPA has issued subpoenas to corporations requiring production of their corporate Section 8(e) procedures and lists of subchronic and chronic tests conducted by or on behalf of the companies (as well as attendance and testimony of responsible corporate officials if necessary) as part of a large Section 8(e) enforcement effort.

EPA need not base its exercise of the subpoena power authorized in TSCA upon a discrete charge of a TSCA violation — it is sufficient that EPA wants assurance that the law is not being violated.[61] As a result, if EPA is in a position to argue that a subpoena is sought in pursuit of potential violations of TSCA, EPA may exercise its TSCA subpoena authority in a case although other environmental laws might be more appropriate to remedy the problem in the case. [62]

Congress did not limit the available enforcement and investigatory techniques granted to EPA to those explicitly listed in TSCA.[63] Consequently, courts have approved administrative searches by EPA after the *ex parte* granting of a warrant without hearing as reasonable and appropriate.[64]

## TSCA Section 16: Enforcement

Under the authority of TSCA Section 16(a), EPA can levy civil and criminal penalties for violations of the Act. EPA may assess civil penalties of up to $25,000 per day per violation of TSCA Section 15. TSCA Section 15 enumerates a list of violations of the Act, such as failure to maintain required records, or use of a chemical manufactured in violation of the Section 5 requirements. In determining civil penalties, EPA is to take into account the nature, circumstances, extent, and gravity of the violation, the violator's ability to pay, the effect on its ability to continue to do business,[65] history of previous violations, culpability and other factors "as justice may require."

EPA has developed an overall TSCA Civil Assessment Penalty Policy as well as separate civil assessment policies for Sections 4, 5, 8, 12 and 13 to guide EPA's imposition of penalties. Under these policies, EPA calculates a proposed TSCA penalty by first examining the nature, circumstances, and extent of the violation and calculates a "gravity based penalty."[66] EPA then adjusts the gravity base penalty upward if necessary to account for a company's history of previous violations. The penalty may be decreased to account for such factors as voluntary reporting of the violation, attitude, and steps that company has taken to insure that the violation will not reoccur.

The civil penalty provisions of TSCA have been pursued assiduously over the last three years with over 1,000 complaints being filed each year for principally three categories of violations:

- Premanufacture notification violations:
- Violations of PCB rules; and
- Failure to certify under § 13 respecting importation of chemical substances or give required export notification.

For example, during the first six months of 1986, 300 complaints were issued in the above referenced categories with proposed fines totalling $12 million.[67] It is likely that these will continue to be important enforcement target areas during the coming years.

**Premanufacture Notification Enforcement**

In 1989, UPACO Adhesives of Nashua, New Hampshire, paid $3.5 million for five PMN/NOC violations. P.D. George of St. Louis, Missouri, paid $1.9 million with respect to PMN violations involving three chemicals. U.S. Polymers, also of St. Louis, Missouri, paid $210,000 for PMN violations involving three chemicals.[68] Dow Chemical Company paid a $1 million penalty for failing to file a PMN on polycarbonate plastic in June of 1989.[69] The largest settlement in history continues to be that paid by BASF Corporation totalling $4.3 million for seven chemical infractions and three circumstances of new chemicals being processed into product.[70]

Recently, for example, McCloskey Corporation of Philadelphia was able to reduce a proposed penalty of $1.3 million to $615,000 for PMN infractions involving 26 chemicals by entering into a consent decree which provided, in part, for self-evaluation of other TSCA infractions. Cavedon Chemical of Woonsocket, Rhode Island, recently was assessed $85,000 of a $170,000 import certification violation based on immediate self-reporting.[71]

## PCB Enforcements

During the last year, the Public Service Commission of Colorado, Inc., paid $84,500 civil penalty for storage of improperly marked, leaking transformers.[72] During the same year C.R. Pacific Power Company paid a $23,000 penalty for failure to label and erect proper storage facilities for PCB transformers.[73] Boliden Metech, Inc., of Providence, Rhode Island, was fined $32,000 for improper disposal.[74] The largest PCB penalty collected thus far was from DeLonghi America, Inc., which imported radiators contaminated with PCB oils in contravention of the manufacture, distribution and use ban.[75] Recently five principals of Martha C. Rose Chemicals of Holden, Missouri, were indicted for illegal storage or disposal of 1.1 million pounds of capacitor cores.[76]

TSCA Section 16(b) also provides for the imposition of criminal penalties for those who "knowingly or willfully violate" any provision of Section 15, in the form of imprisonment for not more than one year, $25,000 per day of violation, or both.

## Export Notification

The EPA Office of Toxic Substances has also recently become active in enforcing 1983 regulations requiring written, seven day advance notification of intent to export certain designated chemical substances or mixtures outside the customs territory of the United States.[77] EPA is required to provide the foreign, importing country with information on the proposed shipment no later than five working days after receipt of export notification. Such notification is required for the following classes of chemical substances and mixtures:

- Chemicals or mixtures subject to TSCA Section 4 test rules;[78]
- Chemicals or mixtures which are the subject of TSCA Section 5 premanufacture notification consent orders or significant new use rules;[79]
- Chemicals or mixtures subject to TSCA Section 6 bans on distribution, sale or use of chemicals, such as asbestos or PCBs.[80]

The regulation specifically exempts "articles" except for articles containing PCBs.[81] The regulation also contains a limited exemption for

PCB or PCB articles which are exported only for the purpose of disposal.[82] Finally, on July 12, 1989, EPA proposed to amend the regulation so as to require notification only on the date of first export or on the first export in any calendar year.[83]

EPA has recently stepped up its enforcement efforts with respect to export notification in proportion to a dramatic increase in the number of such notifications over the last several years. Since 1984, there has been a nearly ten-fold increase in the number of export notices (524 notices in 1984 to an estimated 4,700 notices in 1989). EPA believes that in excess of 80 percent of such notices were triggered by TSCA Section 4 test rules.[84] During the same period EPA's Office of Compliance Monitoring has imposed significant penalties for failure to timely file export notification. The largest export notification fine to date was for $112,000 against 3-V Chemical Corporation of Charlotte, North Carolina.[85]

### Import Notification

In collaboration with the U.S. Customs Service, the EPA Office of Toxic Substances had been extremely active in the last several years in enforcing the "Customs Regulations Relating to Import of Chemicals under TSCA."[86] These regulations require the importer of a chemical substance imported in bulk or as part of a mixture to prepare and execute one of two different written certifications at the port of entry:

- For TSCA chemicals:
  I certify that all chemical substances in this shipment comply with all applicable rules or orders under TSCA and that I am not offering a chemical substance for entry in violation of TSCA or any applicable rule or order thereunder.

or

- For TSCA exempt chemicals:
  I certify that all chemicals in this shipment are not subject to TSCA.

Under the regulations, the primary basis for utilizing the second, or exempt status basis for import certification would be circumstances where all chemical substances are contained in "articles." The regulations do provide, however, that certification may nonetheless be required for chemical substances or mixtures as part of an article where specifically required by rule or order.[87]

Importers failing to comply with the certification requirements are subject to any and all civil penalties available under TSCA. In addition, the district director at the port of entry may detain chemical substances, mixtures or articles at the importer's risk and expense, among other circumstances, when the importer fails to certify compliance with TSCA or the district director otherwise has reasonable grounds to believe that the shipments not in compliance with TSCA. In July of 1989, for example, EPA's Office of Compliance Monitoring filed complaints seeking $112,000 and $10,000 respectively from 3-V Chemical Corp. of Charlotte, North Carolina, and Howard Hall International of Cos Cob, Connecticut in part, for failing to certify.[88]

## Future Trends and Emerging Issues

As the foregoing discussion illustrates, TSCA provides EPA with broad authorities to assess and regulate risks posed by chemical substances. Unlike some other environmental statutes, TSCA explicitly provides for a balancing of harm versus benefit in the determination of unreasonable risk and for consideration of economic costs in fashioning a solution to control those.

While EPA will continue its new chemical review program, it is likely that EPA will allocate increasing resources to assessing and regulating risks posed by chemicals currently in the marketplace. Such efforts, as for example EPA's current effort to regulate lead, will likely involve interaction among EPA, environmental groups, and the affected industry. EPA's choice of which existing chemicals to regulate may, as with lead, be driven by external forces, such as the environmental groups or Congressional pressure, rather than purely an Agency consensus.

To date, TSCA has not been widely used by EPA as a regulatory tool in controlling risks from chemicals. It now appears, however, that EPA, through its efforts at increasing TSCA enforcement, its focus on non-traditional chemical companies, such as electronics and aerospace firms, coupled with a pronouncement that the 1990's will be the decade of testing of chemicals, appears to signal a renewed effort at exercising its TSCA authorities.

## About the Author

Alison A. Kerester has eight years of experience in environmental matters at both the legal and policy levels. Using her J.D. from Cleveland State University and M.S. from the University of Michigan, she has done significant work on the Toxic Substances Control Act, pesticides, air toxics, risk assessments and dioxin areas. From 1987-1990 as a Senior Associate at Beveridge and Diamond, Washington, D.C., she worked on TSCA, FIFRA, Clean Air Act and published several articles on environmental issues. As Associate in the Environmental Law Department at McKenna, Connor & Cuneo from 1985-87, she was the principal author of "The TSCA Handbook." From 1982-85 she was a staff attorney at the U.S. EPA working on RCRA and TSCA. She is a member of the Ohio and Washington, D.C. bars.

## Endnotes

1.    "During the hearings, a number of witnesses recommended that the bill include a definition of unreasonable risk. Because the determination of unreasonable risk involves a consideration of probability, severity, and similar factors which cannot be defined in precise terms and is not a factual determination but rather requires the exercise of judgment on the part of the person making it, the Committee did not attempt a definition of such risk. In general, a determination that a risk associated with a chemical substance or mixture is unreasonable involves balancing the probability that harm will occur and the magnitude and severity of that harm against the effect of proposed regulatory action on the availability to society of the benefits of the substance or mixture, taking into account the availability of substitutes for the substance or mixture which do not require regulation, and other adverse effects which such proposed action may have on society."

Report by the Committee on Interstate and Foreign Commerce Together with Supplemental and Minority Views, 94th Cong. 2d Sess. H.R. Report No. 94-1341, pp. 13-14 (1976).

2.  TSCA Section 3(2)(A); 15 U.S.C. Section 2602(2)(A).

3.  TSCA Section 3(2)(B); 15 U.S.C. Section 2602(3)(2)(B).

4.  TSCA Section 3(8).

5.  **Volume I**: TSCA Inventory (Chemical Abstract Services Index, the CAS Index or Preferred names of substances).

Volumes II and III: Substance Name Index (alphabetical listing of all CAS index or preferred names, EPA submitter names and CAS synonyms);

Volume IV: Molecular Formula Index (lists all substances appearing in the Chemical Substances Identities section that have molecular formulas);

Volume V: UVCB Index, Section 4 Rule Index, Section 5(e) Order/Section 5(f)/ Section 6(a) Rule Index and Significant New Rules Index. (UVCB lists the CAS preferred names for all substances that lack a definite chemical structures or molecular formulas).

6. 40 C.F.R. Section 720.25.

7. In order to be excluded from the definition of chemical substance, the chemical must be intended for use solely as a pesticide, food, food additive, drug, cosmetic, or device. In those cases where the substance is manufactured for undifferentiated uses, EPA presumes that the substance is subject to TSCA. In addition, if the substance is generated for a dual purpose (*e.g.* fragrance for perfume and fragrance for a natural gas) the portion not intended for a non-exempt purpose (*e.g.* cosmetic purposes) is subject to TSCA.

8. TSCA Section 5(h)(3); 15 U.S.C. Section 2604(h)(3); and 40 C.F.R. Section 720.36.

9. TSCA Section 5(h)(1); 15 U.S.C. Section 2604(h)(1); and 40 C.F.R. Section 720.38.

10. 40 C.F.R. Section 723.50.

11. 40 C.F.R. Section 723.250. Polymers that have a number-average molecular weight greater than 1000 or are made from a specified list of reactants are eligible for this exemption. 40 C.F.R. Section 723.250(e).

12. 40 C.F.R. Section 723.175.

13. An article is a manufactured item which has been formed to a specific shape and whose end use is dependent upon that shape. Fluids intended to be removed from an article, like paint in a can, are not considered to be part of an article.

14. 40 C.F.R. Section 720.30.

15. *See* 40 C.F.R. § 720.102.

16. 40 C.F.R. Part 747.

17. TSCA Section 5(a)(1)(B); 15 U.S.C. Section 2604(a)(1)(B).

18. TSCA Section 5(a)(2); 15 U.S.C. Section 2604(a)(2).

19. 54 *Fed. Reg.* 31,298 (July 27, 1989).

20. *Id.* at 31,308 - 31,312; to be codified at 40 C.F.R. Section 721 Subpart B.

21. *Id.* at 31,314; to be codified at 40 C.F.R. Section 721 Subpart D.

22. *Id.* at 31,315; to be codified at 40 C.F.R. Section 721.170.

23. TSCA Section 2(b)(1); 15 U.S.C. Section 2601(b)(1).

24. TSCA Section 4(e); 15 U.S.C. Section 2603(e).

25. 50 *Fed. Reg.* 47,603, 47,604 (November 19, 1985). As of December 12, 1989, the ITC has issued twenty-five reports recommending a total of 90 chemicals and 20 groups of chemicals for testing.

26. TSCA Section 4(a)(1)(A);15 U.S.C. Section 2603(a)(1)(A).

27. 45 *Fed. Reg.* 48,524, 48,528 (July 18, 1980).

28. *Ausimont U.S.A. v. EPA*, 838 F.2d 93, 97 (3d Cir. 1988) Scientific curiosity was found inadequate grounds for requiring testing.

29. *Chemical Manufacturers Association v. EPA*, 859 F.2d 977, 988 (D.C. Cir. 1988) (substantial probability of existence of unreasonable risk of injury to health required to meet standard of TSCA Section 4(a)(1)(A)).

30. TSCA Section 4(a)(1)(B); 15 U.S.C. Section 2603(a)(1)(B).

31. 50 *Fed. Reg.* 20,652, 20,664 (May 17, 1985).

32. 40 C.F.R. Part 792.

33. 40 C.F.R. Section 790.80(a) and (b).

34. 40 C.F.R. Section 790.99.

35. 40 C.F.R. Section 790.93.

36. The reimbursement period starts "when the data from the last non-duplicative test to be completed under a test rule is submitted to EPA and ends after an amount of time equal to that which had been required to develop that data or after 5 years, whichever is later." 40 C.F.R. Section 791.3(h).

37. 40 C.F.R. Part 791.

38. 40 C.F.R. Section 791.40(b). That rule provides for proportional reimbursement based upon the exempted parties' shares of the total production volume of the test chemical.

39. In addition, a hearing officer may determine that equity requires that processors reimburse the testing parties. 40 C.F.R. Section 791.45(a).

40. EPA has promulgated regulations that allow members of the public to respond to EPA's publication of a *Federal Register* notice of the Agency's intent to negotiate a consent agreement. Such persons are then deemed "interested parties," and as such must consent to the agreement resulting from the negotiations before EPA will enter into it. 40 C.F.R. 790.22-790.24.

41. 40 C.F.R. Section 790.60(a).

42. However, such consent agreements are not enforceable as against non-signatories, and non-signatories are not subject to the reimbursement provisions of TSCA Section 4(c).

43. TSCA Section 4(f)(2).

44. 47 *Fed. Reg.* 26,992 (June 22, 1982) (codified at 40 C.F.R. Part 712, Subpart B).

45. 53 *Fed. Reg.* 51,698 (December 22, 1988) (to be codified at 40 C.F.R. Section 704.1-.225). Thereafter, on June 14, 1988 an additional 600 chemical substances trade names were added to the CAIR list, marginally applicable to substance purchases and processes, 54 *Fed. Reg.* 25,398.

46. 40 C.F.R. Section 717.15(d). If a firm ceases to do business and leaves no successor firm to maintain the Section 8(c) records, the firm must forward those records to EPA. 40 C.F.R. Section 717.15(e).

47. 40 C.F.R. 717.12.

48. 40 C.F.R. Section 717.3(c)(1).

49. 40 C.F.R. Section 717.12(d).

50. 40 C.F.R. Section 716.120.

51. 40 C.F.R. Part 716. Mandatory reporting of studies for 102 chemicals was required as of May 1, 1987; *see* 52 *Fed. Reg.* 16022.

52. 40 C.F.R. Section 716.50.

53. For example, studies of listed substances manufactured or processed only as impurities, studies analyzing data aggregated more than five years before the relevant substance was listed, and studies previously published in scientific literature, submitted by trade organizations or previously submitted to the Office of Toxic Substances are all exempt from the submission requirement. 40 C.F.R. Section 716.20.

54. 43 *Fed. Reg.* 11,110 (March 16, 1978).

55. *Id.* at 11,114.

56. Letter from Charles L. Elkins, EPA Office of Toxic Substances, A.E. Conroy, II, EPA Office of Compliance Monitoring, and Frederick F. Stiehl, Associate Enforcement Counsel for Pesticides and Toxic Substances, EPA to 700 companies. (Dec. 18, 1989) (clarification of EPA position regarding requirements of Section 8(e)).

57. Agricola, Biological Abstracts, Chemical Abstracts Dissertation Abstract, Index Medicux, National Technical Information Service.

58. TSCA Section 11; 15 U.S.C. Section 2610.

59. TSCA Section 11(b)(2); 15 U.S.C. Section 2610(b)(2).

60. TSCA Section 11(c); 15 U.S.C. Section 2610(c).

61. *EPA v. Alyeska Pipeline Serv. Co.*, 836 F.2d 443, 447 (9th Cir. 1988) (district court decision upholding EPA subpoena under TSCA based on arguable TSCA jurisdiction over site in addition to ongoing Clean Water Act permit investigation).

62. *Id.* at 448.

63. *Boliden Metech v. United States,* 695 F.Supp. 77, 81 (D.R.I. 1988) (an inspection warrant without a prior adversary hearing is sufficient protection of privacy rights and furthers the public interest in effective enforcement of environmental laws by EPA).

64. *Id.*

65. TSCA Section 16(a); 15 U.S.C. Section 2615(a).

66. Office of Toxic Substances Penalty Policy, 53 *Fed. Reg.* 312 U8 (August 17, 1988).

67. *See,* TSCA *Chemicals in Progress Bulletin,* "Bulletin," August 1986.

68. *See,* TSCA Bulletin (March, 1989).

69. *See,* TSCA Bulletin (September, 1989).

70. *See, TSCA Bulletin* (February 1989).

71. *See Pesticide News,* 17:38, p. 11 (July 26, 1989).

72. *See,* TSCA Bulletin (March 1988).

73. *Id.*

74. *See,* TSCA Bulletin (September 1989).

75. *See,* TSCA Bulletin (February 1987).

76. *See,* TSCA Bulletin (March 1989).

77. 40 C.F.R. § 707.60 *et seq.*

78. *See,* Section V-F *infra.*

79. *See,* Sections II-E and F *supra.*

80. *See,* Section V-A *infra.*

81. 40 C.F.R. 707.60(b).

82. § 707.60(c).

83. *See,* 54 *Fed. Reg.* 29524.

84. *See,* TSCA Bulletin (September 1989).

85. *Id.*

86. 19 C.F.R. § 12.118 *et seq.*

87. *See,* 19 C.F.R. § 12.121(b).

88. *See,* TSCA Bulletin (September 1989).

# VIII  The Federal Insecticide, Fungicide and Rodenticide Act

*S. Richard Heymann, Esq.*
*Foley & Lardner*
*Madison, Wisconsin*

The Federal Insecticide, Fungicide and Rodenticide Act, (FIFRA), 7 U.S.C. §§ 136 *et seq.*, is the primary source of regulatory authority over the numerous pesticides manufactured or used in the United States. Increased public concern with pesticide use, anxieties about increased presence of agricultural chemicals in the groundwater, fears of heightened cancer risk from pesticide residues in the nation's food supply, and apprehension concerning the consequences of introducing the products of biotechnology into the environment on a commercial scale, have focused renewed interest on this statute. It is the one with which the government has regulated pesticides in the United States since 1947, with major amendments in 1972 and additional, less substantial changes thereafter, most recently in 1988.

Generally speaking, FIFRA requires that all pesticides must be registered and calls upon the registrant to provide substantial data respecting the environmental and health risks that may be associated with the pesticide. FIFRA requires registration of facilities that manufacture, sell or distribute pesticides. EPA evaluates data submitted pursuant to the registration process to determine whether it is necessary to restrict or even prohibit use of a pesticide in order to protect human health or the environment. FIFRA also enables EPA to limit the risk a certain pesticide may pose by limiting its use to certified applicators only. FIFRA contemplates the need to re-evaluate the risks and benefits associated with individual pesticides and provides for periodic review of existing registrations and the data that supports them. It requires immediate notification of newly discovered evidence of new or increased dangers associated with a pesticide. FIFRA also contemplates the need to revoke registrations, or to impose greater restrictions in emergencies or similar circumstances where health and safety are endangered. FIFRA requires that detailed labels be affixed to pesticide products and regulates their content; any use of the pesticide inconsistent with those terms can result in severe penalties, thereby affording EPA both an enforcement tool and a point-of-purchase, point-of-use mechanism for emphasizing the limitations and restrictions. FIFRA also contains enforcement provisions and typical civil and criminal penalties.

## Registration

Section 3(a) provides that, with few exceptions,[1] "no person in any State may distribute or sell to any person any pesticide that is not registered under this Act." Section 2(u) of the Act defines a pesticide as:

> (1) any substance or mixture of substances intended for preventing, destroying, repelling, or mitigating any pest, and (2) any substance or mixture of substances intended for use as a plant regulator, defoliant, or dessicant [with certain exceptions].[2]

The focus of Section 2(u) is upon the intended use of a product, which the regulations define as follows:

> "A substance is considered to be intended for a pesticidal purpose, and thus to be a pesticide requiring registration if:
> > (a) The person who distributes or sells the substance claims, states, or implies (by labeling or otherwise);
> > > (1) That the substance (either by itself or in combination with any other substance) can or should be used as a pesticide; or
> > > (2) That the substance consists of or contains an active ingredient and that it can be used to manufacture a pesticide; or
> > (b) The substance consists of or contains one or more active ingredients and has no significant commercially valuable use as distributed or sold other than
> > > (1) use for pesticidal purposes (by itself or in combi-

nation with any other substance), (2) use for manufacture of a pesticide; or
  (c) The person who distributes or sells the substance has actual or constructive knowledge that the substance will be used, or is intended to be used, for a pesticidal purpose.[3]

*Pest* is defined (broadly) at Section 2(t) of the Act as:
  (1) any insect, rodent, nematode, fungus, weed, or (2) any other form of terrestrial or aquatic plant or animal life or virus, bacteria, or other micro-organisms  or other micro-organism (except viruses, bacteria, or other micro-organisms on or in living man or other living animals) which the Administrator declares [by regulation] to be a pest. . .

Exercising its regulatory authority, EPA has further defined the *pest* element of the Act's definition of *pesticide* as follows:
  An organism is declared to be a pest under circumstances that make it deleterious to man or the environment, if it is:
  (a) Any vertebrate animal other than man;
  (b) Any invertebrate animal. . .but excluding any internal parasite of living man or other living animals;
  (c) Any plant growing where not wanted. . . and any plant part such as a root; or
  (d) Any fungus, bacterium, virus, or other micro-organisms, except for those on or in living man or other living animals and those on or in processed food or processed animal feed, beverages, drugs (as defined in FFDCA § 201 (g)(1)) and cosmetics (as defined in FFDCA § 201(i)).[4]

All products which fit the definition of pesticide and do not fall into one of the exceptions set out in the regulations must be registered with the EPA before they can be manufactured or sold. The registration procedure is governed by Section 3(c) of the Act. Section 3(c)(5) sets forth the criteria determining whether EPA will register a pesticide. Specifically, Section 3(c)(5) **requires** EPA to register a pesticide if:
  (A) its composition is such as to warrant the proposed claims for it;
  (B) its labeling and other material required to be submitted comply with the requirements of this Act;

(C)  it will perform its intended function without unreasonable effects on the environment; and

(D)  when used with widespread and commonly recognized practice it will not generally cause unreasonable adverse effects on the environment.

Registration of any pesticide may be conditioned upon use restrictions, which are governed by Section 3(d)'s classification provisions and are discussed below. EPA may also issue "conditional" registrations under Section 3(c)(7) where:

(A)  "the pesticide and proposed use are identical or
substantially similar to any currently registered
pesticide and use" and no "unreasonable adverse
effect on the environment" would result, or

(B)  new uses are contemplated for a pesticide which is
already registered and no unreasonable adverse effects on the environment will result, or

(C)  there is a new active ingredient for which there
has been insufficient time to develop required data
(as for long-term toxicity studies) if the use of such
pesticide is in the public interest and no unreasonable adverse effect on the environment will result.
EPA has discretion to review all applications under either § 3(c)(5) or § 3(c)(7).

The principal advantage of the conditional registration process
is that it allows a registrant to avoid some of the data requirements under Sections 3(c)(1) and (2). The standards that determine whether EPA will review an application pursuant to the unconditional or conditional registration criteria are set forth at 40
C.F.R. § 152.111.  EPA publishes a priority list of chemicals for
which it will review data pursuant to the unconditional registration process.  Unless an applicant presents a new active ingredient
EPA generally does not deviate from its priority list and will accordingly review the application pursuant to the criteria for conditional registration set forth in sections 3(c)(7)(A) and (B) of the
Act.

Sections 3(c)(1) and (2) specify the information that an applicant
for registration must furnish to EPA in support of its application.

In particular, Section 3(c)(1) requires the applicant to submit six different types of information:
- the name and address of the registrant;
- the name of the pesticide for which registration is sought, including all trade names by which the pesticide is also known and the EPA registration number of the pesticide if one has been assigned (40 C.F.R. § 152.50(d));
- a complete copy of the pesticide's proposed label along with the statement of all claims to be made for the pesticide and directions for its use;
- the pesticide's complete formula;
- a request that the pesticide be classified for general or restricted use or both; and
- data which demonstrates that the pesticide conforms to the guidelines established by the EPA.

The data submitted by the registrant may stem from three different sources: it may be the result of tests run by the registrant for the express purpose of supporting its application; it may be a citation to data that appears in public literature; or it may be a reference to data previously submitted to EPA in conjunction with the application for a registered pesticide containing similar active ingredient(s).

The regulations provide two separate means by which a registrant may provide EPA with the required data. First, under the "cite-all method" the registrant receives a list of all data submitted by previous applicants with respect to the active ingredient(s) contained in the registrant's pesticide. The registrant must then contact the original applicant in order to receive authorization to use the data and make arrangements to compensate the previous applicant for its use. Under this method, the registrant must include in the application a general statement that he relied on all data specifically cited in the application and on any other data contained in the Agency's files that is related to the registrant's application. In addition, the registrant must include a general offer to pay for the use of such other data.[5]

A registrant's considerable investment in the generation of data is afforded a measure of protection by the provisions of Section 3(c)(1)(D), which limits the extent to which others may have access to or rely upon such data and which requires, under certain circumstances, applicants who rely upon previously submitted data to provide compensation to the original data submitter.

**The Federal Insecticide, Fungicide and Rodenticide Act**

For pesticides containing active ingredients first registered after September 30, 1978 registrants are entitled to the exclusive use of the data submitted in support of their registrations for a period of ten years. Section 3(c)(1)(D)(i). Otherwise, any data submitted after December 31, 1969 may be used by a subsequent applicant (i.e., a "me-too" applicant) to support its application for registration, however the original data submitter is entitled to compensation for such use of its data for a period of fifteen years after its submission. Section 3(c)(1)(D)(ii). That section also provides a binding arbitration procedure for determination of the amount of the compensation if the parties are unable to do so by agreement. FIFRA does not provide guidelines respecting calculation of appropriate compensation, leaving arbitrators with considerable discretion.[6]

The second data submission method is referred to as the "selective method." When using this method, the applicant must list all data requirements that would apply to the pesticide, its active ingredient(s) and use patterns, as if the pesticide were being proposed for registration for the first time. The registrant must demonstrate that it has satisfied each data requirement by one of the six following methods: documentation of a data waiver as governed by 40 C.F.R. § 152.91; submission of a new valid study; citation of a specific valid study previously submitted to the Agency;[7] citation to public literature or a government study; citation of all pertinent studies previously submitted to the Agency as specified in 40 C.F.R. § 152.95 (the "cite-all" method); or documentation of a data gap as defined in Section 152.96 of the regulations.[8]

The kinds of information and data required to support the registration of a pesticide are set forth at Part 158 of the regulations pursuant to Section 3(c)(2) of the Act. In order to make regulatory judgments about the risks and benefits of various kinds of pesticide products, EPA requires data respecting product chemistry, residue chemistry, environmental fate, toxicology, reentry protection, aerial drift evaluation, wildlife and aquatic organisms, plant protection, nontarget insects, product performance, and biochemical and microbial pesticides. Each kind of data is not required for each pesticide. Part 158 contains elaborate data requirement tables for various pesticide general use patterns. Separately, EPA publishes "Pesticide Assessment Guidelines" containing the standards for conducting acceptable tests, guidance on the evaluation and reporting of data, various definitions and timetables, and examples of acceptable protocols. As of July 1,

1989 EPA had issued twelve such documents, including "Product Chemistry", "Hazard Evaluation: Humans and Domestic Animals", "Environmental Fate", and "Residue Chemistry". The individual Pesticide Assessment Guidelines are listed at 40 C.F.R. § 158.108. In addition, EPA has promulgated regulations which dictate "Good Laboratory Practices" which must be followed in all testing intended to satisfy FIFRA data requirements.[9]

Because data generation and submission is expensive and ordinarily requires considerable time and effort, and because certain data requirements may not be applicable (or relevant) to some pesticide products, the regulations contain specific procedures for seeking waivers (§ 158.45) and implementing policies that permit less burdensome data submissions (§§ 158.35, 158.40, and 158.60). Since these policies do not appear in the regulations (and since in sufficiently unusual circumstances there will be no formal policy) applicants are urged by EPA to contact the Agency before embarking on a course of testing and data submission. Such ad hoc regulatory decision-making can be frustrating but it can also, as EPA asserts, be extremely helpful. At best it can save considerable time and money and even at worst it can avoid unpleasant surprises by discovering unanticipated Agency objections that would be all the more frustrating if discovered later in the registration process rather than sooner.

If the registrant is seeking to register a product that is composed exclusively from products which have been previou , ' registered with the EPA and which the applicant purchases from another producer, then the registrant is not required to submit data to the EPA. This exception is referred to as the "formulator's exemption."[10]

Applicants for registration are required to pay a registration fee,[11] as set out in 40 C.F.R. § 152.404 (July 1, 1989):

- new chemical                          $184,500
- new biochemical or microbial          $64,000
- new use pattern                       $33,800

- experimental use permit               $4,500
- old chemical                          $4,000
- amendment                             $700

The fee schedule is adjusted annually per § 152.410. Notice of application is published in the *Federal Register* and regulatory agencies, competitors, watchdog organizations, and others are given 30 days within which to comment.

EPA must notify an applicant within 45 days if the Agency determines that its application is incomplete and must grant or deny an application within 90 days. Section 3(c)(3)(B)(ii)(I) and (II). EPA has discretion to issue experimental use permits to allow use of an unregistered pesticide where EPA determines that such a permit is required to enable an applicant to accumulate information that is necessary for the registration of a pesticide pursuant to normal procedures.[12]

Section 6(a)(2) provides that "if at anytime after the registration of a pesticide the registrant has additional factual information regarding unreasonable adverse effects on the environment of the pesticide" the registrant must report such information to EPA within 15 working days.[13] "Unreasonable adverse effects on the environment" is defined by Section 2(bb) to mean "any unreasonable risk to man or the environment, taking into account the economic, social, and environmental costs and benefits of the use of any pesticide." Subpart D of Part 153 of the regulations provides more detailed reporting requirements, including section 153.66(a)(3)'s requirement that information be submitted which,

> if true, would be relevant, either by itself or in conjunction with other information, to an Agency decision regarding the risks and benefits of the pesticide, i.e. an Agency decision regarding the registerability of the pesticide or regarding the proper terms and conditions of the registration of the pesticide. . . .

There are exceptions for information previously submitted and for the opinions and conclusions of non-experts (narrowly defined).

## Classification of Pesticides

Section 3(d) requires EPA to classify pesticides as being for general use or restricted use, although by regulation EPA has acknowledged that most products will be classified as restricted use pesticides or will simply remain unclassified.[14] Section 3(d)(1)(C) requires EPA to classify a pesticide for restricted use if,

> when applied in accordance with its directions for use, warnings and cautions and for the uses for which it is reg-

istered. . . . or in accordance with a widespread and commonly recognized practice, [it] may generally cause, without additional regulatory restrictions, unreasonable adverse effects on the environment, including injury to the applicator. . . .

The technical criteria for making such determinations are set forth at 40 C.F.R. § 152.170. Pursuant to those criteria EPA has listed the uses of 44 specific, common active ingredients that are restricted to certified applicators or those under their direct supervision.[15]

A restricted use pesticide must be labelled in accordance with Section 156.10 of the regulations. Under Section 12(a)(1)(E) of the Act it is unlawful to sell or distribute a  misbranded[16] pesticide and under Section 12(a)(2)(G) it is unlawful to use any registered pesticide in a manner inconsistent with its labeling.  Section 156.10 requires that a label contain:

- the product name
- the name and address of the producer
- net weight or measure of contents
- product registration number
- producer's establishment number
- name and percentage (by weight) of active ingredients
- warning or precautionary statements (as required by § 156.10(h) of the regulations)
- directions for use (as governed by § 156.10(i))
- use classification.

If the EPA determines that a general classification should be changed to a restricted classification, it must provide a 45-day notice in the *Federal Register*.[17]  A registrant may also petition for a change from a restricted to general classification.[18]

## Re-Registration

Pursuant to the 1988 amendments to the Act, EPA has begun a re-registration process for each registered pesticide containing any active ingredient that was first registered prior to November 1, 1984. The re-registration process is carried out in five phases. In the first phase of the re-registration program, EPA must publish lists of all active ingredients registered before November 1, 1984 under a detailed time schedule. Priority is given to pesticides that are used in association with food, create residues in water or fish, or have a high likelihood of worker exposure. As the lists of active ingredients are published, the EPA is to give notice to each registrant whose pesticide contains one of the listed active ingredients.[19]

Phase two of the re-registration process requires the registrant to give notice whether it will seek re-registration. If the registrant decides to seek re-registration he must provide a list of all data required by current regulations for a pesticide's active ingredient(s), inform the Agency of any data not yet submitted with respect to the active ingredient, and commit to provide the missing data or offer to share the costs of anyone who has committed to develop such data. The registrant has three months to decide whether to seek re-registration.[20]

Phase three requires submission of various categories of information and data as necessary to satisfy the applicable data requirements in conformance with established guidelines, within express time limits.[21] Phase four requires EPA to review the information submitted by the registrant and determine whether the submissions are complete and adequate.[22] In phase five, the final phase of the program, EPA must determine whether to re-register a pesticide within one year from the time it receives all of the required data.[23]

## Reporting, Recordkeeping and Import Restrictions

Section 7 requires that each pesticide establishment be registered and that it submit an annual report revealing the amount of each pesticide produced and sold during the year. Section 8 requires producers to maintain records with respect to their operations and to produce these records for inspection. Section 9 authorizes EPA to inspect establishments in which pesticides are developed, packaged, labeled, and released for shipment.

Section 10 contains trade secret protection for certain information registrants are required to submit to EPA. The submitter bears the burden of designating material deemed to be confidential but the Agency makes an independent determination of confidentiality pursuant to 40 C.F.R. Part 2. EPA must provide 30 days notice if it intends to disclose information marked as confidential by the submitter, during which time a submitter must seek relief in federal court if it objects to the Agency's decision.[24] There are exceptions where public health considerations are at issue.

The Act does not apply to pesticides developed for export from the United States. This is proving to be a somewhat controversial issue and may be the subject of future amendments. It does apply, however, to imports and the Agency is notified by the Secretary of the Treasury when pesticides are to arrive in the United States. The Agency may then inspect the goods and may refuse admission of the pesticides into the United States.[25]

## Enforcement of the Act

Section 12 contains a list of unlawful acts, including the distribution or sale of an unregistered pesticide or a registered pesticide if its composition or the claims asserted in connection with its marketing differ from the representations which were made in connection with registration of the product. Section 12(a)(1)(E) also prohibits the distribution or sale of "misbranded" or "adulterated" pesticides. Section 156.10(a)(5) identifies labeling statements or representations that constitute "misbranding". They include false or misleading statements respecting the composition, effectiveness, or value of a pesticide, or any claim as to its safety (such as "safe", "non-poisonous", "non-injurious", "harmless", or "nontoxic to humans and pets") even if qualified by such language as "when used as directed." Section 12 (a)(2) also makes it unlawful for any person to fail or refuse to carry out or comply with the various labeling, reporting, record-keeping, and sale requirements and use restrictions contained in the Act, as well as to submit false data or registration information, or to use any registered pesticide in a manner inconsistent with its labeling. The latter prohibition, of course, makes careful draftsmanship of pesticide labels particularly important. EPA regulates label contents but does not approve label contents either explicitly or implicitly when it registers a pesticide.

Section 13(a) authorizes EPA to issue a "stop sale, use or removal" order to any person who owns, controls, or has custody of a pesticide which EPA has determined to be in violation of any provision of the Act, the registration of which has been suspended or cancelled, or even which is "intended" to be sold or distributed in violation of the Act. Section 13(b) authorizes seizure of a pesticide under such circumstances as when it is misbranded, unregistered, or "when used in accordance with the requirements imposed under this Act and as directed by the labeling, it nevertheless causes unreasonable adverse effects on the environment." A "stop sale, use or removal" order can be issued without prior notice or adjudication (and is therefore a favored enforcement tool). Seizures are accomplished by an action initiated by the Agency in federal district court.

Section 6(b) provides that a registration may be cancelled altogether,

> if it appears to [EPA] that a pesticide or its labeling or other material required to be submitted does not comply with the provisions of this Act or, when used in accordance with widespread and commonly recognized practice, generally causes unreasonable effects on the environment.

The 6(b) cancellation procedure is cumbersome, however, with formal notice requirements, consultation with the U.S. Department of Agriculture to assess the impact of cancellation upon food production and prices, and a hearing. The hearing may include referral to a Committee of the National Academy of Sciences for purposes of obtaining an independent scientific review. The decision is subject to review by the U.S. district court pursuant to Section 16 of the Act. Consequently it is used infrequently.

Streamlined procedures are provided to meet the "imminent hazard" requirement. It is enough if there is substantial likelihood that serious harm will be experienced during the year or two which would probably be required for the formal cancellation process to proceed.[26] Specifically, Section 6(c) allows EPA to issue an order suspending registration of a pesticide where "necessary to prevent an imminent hazard during the time required for cancellation . . ." The registrant is entitled to an expedited hearing of the imminent hazard issue. Emergency orders, immediately effective, are also available under Section 6(c)(3). Judicial review is provided solely to determine whether the order of suspension was arbitrary, capricious, or an abuse of discretion, or whether it was issued in accordance with applicable procedures.[27]

To further streamline the burdensome, highly adversarial process, the regulations provide still another procedure to address the issue of cancellation. Pursuant to 40 C.F.R. Part 154 EPA may conduct a "Special Review" to determine whether to initiate cancellation proceedings. The purpose of the review is to undertake a risk/benefit analysis following Agency determination that a pesticide, or certain of its uses, may pose significant risks. The substantive standards for initiating a Special Review, along with the review procedures, are set out in the regulations at 40 C.F.R. § 154.7 and §§ 154.21-35.

Predictably, the suspension or cancellation of a registration has tended to provoke litigation.[28] The effect of the 1988 amendments is apparent in the more recent case of *Ciba-Geigy Corp. v. EPA,*[29] which held that EPA may not cancel a registration without determining specific conditions under which a pesticide "generally" causes an unreasonable adverse effect on the environment. The court also emphasized, however, that EPA need only determine that a particular pesticide commonly causes unreasonable risks and creates significant probability that undesirable consequences may occur. At issue was EPA's attempt to ban the use of diazinon on golf courses and sod farms because of its risk to birds. Ciba-Geigy maintained that the "generally" adverse effects which justify cancellation under the Act require that EPA must find that birds are killed more often than not, or else cancellation would be improper. In an important clarification of the risk assessment which is required under FIFRA the court pointed out that a 30 percent risk of death, for example, may be a significant risk, even if actual bird kills are only infrequent.

The Act provides for both civil and criminal penalties for violations of its provisions. In general, any registrant, commercial applicator, wholesaler, dealer, retailer, or other distributor who violates any provisions of the Act may be assessed a civil penalty of up to $5,000 for each offense.[30] The penalty cannot be assessed unless the person charged has been given notice and an opportunity for a hearing. The amount of the penalty is determined by the EPA pursuant to written guidelines based on the impact upon the registrant's operation and the alleged severities of the violations. Criminal penalties include a fine of $50,000 and/or imprisonment of not more than one year for any registrant, applicant for registration or producer who knowingly violates any provision of the Act. All other persons violating provisions of the Act can be fined $25,000 and/or imprisoned for not more than a year or both.[31]

## Role of the States

Section 26(a) of the Act provides that the states shall have primary enforcement authority for pesticide use violations.[32] Otherwise EPA retains such authority, and retains authority as well to undertake enforcement action in instances of particularly serious violations or where state enforcement is inadequate, or in an emergency.[33]

Section 24(a) provides that:

A State may regulate the sale or use of any federally registered pesticide or device in the State, but only if and to the extent the regulation does not permit any sale or use prohibited by this Act.

Section 24(b) prohibits the states from imposing any labeling or packaging requirements in addition to or different from those contained in FIFRA. Within certain limits, Section 24(c) authorizes states to provide registration of a pesticide for uses in addition to those for which it is registered under Section 3 in accordance with local needs (provided EPA has not previously denied registration for such use or disapproved such use within 90 days after state approval).

States are left with authority to impose more stringent use restrictions upon pesticides than those which have been imposed by EPA, authority that several states have elected to exercise. The most dramatic example is the California initiative commonly referred to as "Big Green" which would, *inter alia*, phase out initially at least 19 pesticides. Part of the "Environmental Protection Act of 1990", scheduled to go on the November, 1990 ballot in California, the proposed pesticide section would phase out cancer-causing pesticides over five years and require the development of new standards for pesticide residues based solely upon human health risks without weighing any benefits achieved by a pesticide's use. California already maintains an extensive pesticide regulatory program.

## Future Trends

Many of the issues respecting pesticide use and regulation that seem likely to receive increased scrutiny during the 1990s are issues which involve traditional areas of state concern. Pesticide residues in groundwater, for example, and the disposal of pesticides are current topics of discussion between federal and state regulators. EPA appears likely to attempt to require states to promulgate groundwater management plans for each pesticide, without which sale of a pesticide would be prohibited in that state. Some states, such as Wisconsin, have already established strict groundwater laws. If the majority of states fail to do likewise it is possible that EPA may seek to amend FIFRA for the express purpose of addressing concerns over the widespread presence of pesticides in groundwater. Other such issues of state concern include the effects of pesticides on endangered species,[34] the establishment of standards for worker protection, and the regulation of "chemigation" (the passing of pesticides through an irrigation system, which raises practical considerations regarding the adequacy of labeling instructions).

Similarly, local communities are increasingly concerned about the pervasive use of pesticides, including spraying along roadways and utility easements. FIFRA allows **states** to regulate pesticide use but is silent as to local regulation. The cases have tended to deny local regulatory authority on grounds of federal pre-emption. In *Mortier v. Town of Casey*,[35] the Wisconsin Supreme Court held that local regulation of pesticide use was preempted by FIFRA. Certiorari was granted by the U.S. Supreme Court on January 14, 1991, *sub nom Wisconsin Public Intervenor v. Mortier*, (Case No.89-1905).

### About the Author

**Dick Heymann** is a partner with the 400-member law firm of Foley & Lardner. He graduated from the University of Wisconsin in 1966 and the University of Michigan Law School in 1969. He served as a law clerk for the Minnesota Supreme Court and, prior to practicing law, taught history and coached various sports at the Priory School in St. Louis. He is a senior member of Foley & Lardner's large environmental law practice group where he concentrates in general environmental counseling, particularly in connection with business and real estate transactions, and is also the firm's principal specialist in FIFRA matters. He has written and lectured extensively on environmental law topics and served on public and industry panels concerned with a variety of environmental regulatory problems. He lives and works in Madison, Wisconsin.

### The Federal Insecticide, Fungicide and Rodenticide Act

# Endnotes

1. The exceptions are set forth in the regulations at § 152.20 (pesticides regulated by other agencies, including certain human drugs regulated by the FDA), § 152.25 (certain pesticide-treated articles, such as treated wood, pheromones, vitamin hormones and other narrow specific exemptions), and § 152.30 (certain transfers of pesticides, experimental use permit pesticides under Section 5, pesticides sold or distributed under an emergency exemption, and existing stocks of formerly registered pesticides). 40 C.F.R. § 152.20-30.

2. The exceptions are: new animal drugs within the meaning of § 201(w) of the Federal Food, Drug, and Cosmetic Act, articles which Department of Health and Human Services regulations govern because they are determined not to be new animal drugs, and animal feed within the meaning of § 201(x) of the FFDCA.

3. 40 C.F.R. § 152.15.

4. 40 C.F.R. § 152.5.

5. 40 C.F.R. § 152.86.

6. *PPG Industries, Inc. v. Stauffer Chemical Co.*, 637 F. Supp. 85 (DC 1950).

7. For data supplied by a different registrant there may be an obligation to obtain written authorization and to offer to pay compensation. See Section 152.93 of the regulations and Section 3(c)(1)(D) of the Act. Both provisions are addressed below.

8. 40 C.F.R. § 152.90.

9. 40 C.F.R. Part 160.

10. Section 3(c)(2)(d) and 40 C.F.R. § 158.50.

11. Registrants are also required to pay an annual "maintenance fee" pursuant to Section 4(i)(5) of the Act in the amount of $425 per registration for the first 50 registrations held and $100 per registration for all additional registrations, subject to fee ceilings and to annual adjustment. Since the amount of the annual fee is designed, in the aggregate, to cover EPA's cost of the re-registration program, and since EPA has already cancelled approximately 20,000 registrations, it is likely the annual fees in future years will be increased and the fee ceilings for holders of large numbers of registrations increased as well.

12. FIFRA § 5.

13. 40 C.F.R. § 153.64(a).

14. 40 C.F.R. § 152.160.

15. 40 C.F.R. § 152.175. Section 11 of the Act provides for the training and certification of pesticide applicators. EPA has proposed (July, 1990) a new regulation to clarify what constitutes "direct supervision" by a certified applicator and to require that labels specify the level of supervision required. The proposed regulation will also upgrade applicator standards and streamline classification of applicators. Certification of pesticide applicators is covered by Part 171 of the regulations.

16. Section 2(g) of the Act contains a lengthy definition of "misbranded" which should be read in conjunction with Section 12(a)(1)(E) as the definition is, in reality, a blueprint for Agency enforcement of labeling violations.

17. Section 3(d)(2).

18. Section 3(d)(3).

19. FIFRA Section 4(c).

20. Section 4(d).

21. Section 4(e).

22. Section 4(f).

23. Section 4(g).

24. Sections 10(c) and (d)(3).

25. FIFRA § 17.

26. *Environmental Defense Fund, Inc. v. EPA*, 548 F.2d 998 (DC Cir. 1979), *cert. denied* 431 U.S. 925 (1979).

27. Section 6(c)(4).

28. *See,* for example, the early cases of *Environmental Defense Fund, Inc. v. EPA*, 465 F.2d 528 (DC Cir. 1972) (regarding efforts to obtain cancellation of the registrations of aldrin and dieldrin) and *Dow Chemical Co. v. Blum*, 469 F. Supp. 892 (CD Mich. 1979) (emergency suspensions of 2,4,5-T and Silvex based on a relatively meager record).

29. 874 F.2d 277 (5th Cir. 1989).

30. Section 14(a)(2).

31. Section 14(b).

32. To qualify for enforcement authority under Section 26, a state must have been determined by EPA to have adequate pesticide use laws or have entered into a cooperative agreement with EPA pursuant to Section 23. Most states have been approved for primary enforcement authority for use violations.

33. Section 27.

34. The Endangered Species Act requires EPA to protect endangered species from pesticides. The Agency may require states to develop individual management plans for endangered species much as they may be required to prepare groundwater management plans. Adoption of boilerplate regulations drafted by EPA is an alternative. Since species habitat, like groundwater geology, presents uniquely localized concerns, substantial state involvement in emerging regulation seems probable.

35. 452 N.W.2d 555 (Wis. 1990).

# IX
# Superfund Process and Progress — Superfund Liability Scheme

*Eric B. Rothenberg\**
*Partner*
*Morgan, Lewis & Bockius*
*New York, New York*

The Comprehensive Environmental Response, Compensation and Liability Act (CERCLA or Superfund), celebrated its tenth anniversary on December 11, 1990. The statute has been amended only once by the Superfund Amendments and Reauthorization Act (SARA), of October 17, 1986, which also increased the size of the Superfund from $1.6 billion to $8.5 billion. As a consequence of a last minute, October 28, 1990, House and Senate Budget Conference Committee compromise, the Superfund program was extended for an additional four years and the Superfund tax provisions for four years, entirely without substantive amendment.[1]

CERCLA establishes the Superfund, a fund of money that the government may use to finance cleanup activity at sites which have been the subject of formal investigation and assessment. The government may then sue to recover its costs. The government may also compel parties potentially responsible to clean up at their own expense. CERCLA also allows private parties to conduct cleanups and to sue other private parties for their cleanup costs, but not for personal injury or property damage. Potentially responsible parties are individually liable for the entire cleanup cost (joint and several liability) without regard to fault (strict liability). CERCLA is retroactive; it covers contamination events that may have occurred many years ago as long as there is a present effect of that past activity.

\*
*The author gratefully acknowledges the assistance of Kala Shah, who prepared the summary of state Superfund laws, and Michael W. Steinberg, a partner in the Washington, D.C. office of Morgan, Lewis & Bockius, who reviewed the text for substantive accuracy.*

Over the course of the last decade, a majority of the states have established their own Superfund programs to provide for cleanup at sites not remedied under the federal program. Not infrequently, these state programs establish a liability and enforcement scheme drawn directly from the Federal statute. In the aggregate, the state programs currently account for a majority of the ongoing cleanup efforts.

This chapter provides a summary of case law which has served to define the scope of liability under the Superfund statutes. The chapter next provides a current account of government enforcement and settlement efforts. The state Superfund programs are summarized in narrative form and also in a reference chart which is current as of September 1990. The chapter concludes with a brief commentary on Superfund trends under the Bush administration.

## Principles of CERCLA Liability

The original CERCLA did not provide expressly for joint and several liability or for contribution. However, courts interpreting CERCLA have held that, where site contamination cannot be apportioned among potentially responsible parties (PRPs) associated with site contamination, such PRPs are jointly and severally liable for cleanup or cost recovery.[2] Under such circumstances, PRPs who pay more than their fair share may have a right of contribution against others. CERCLA Section 113(f), added by the 1986 SARA amendments confirms existing case law by providing an express right of contribution.[3] Recent courts have suggested that they will divide liability given sufficient proof that the contamination can be apportioned.[4]

In *United States v. Cannons Engineering Corp. et al.*, the First Circuit reaffirmed that potentially responsible parties may be held strictly liable even in circumstances where to do so will result in disproportionate allocation of costs between potentially responsible parties as to degree of culpability.[5]

Following the SARA amendments, the government is required to demonstrate in its *prima facie* case: "A release or threatened release of a hazardous substance by a potentially responsible party (present or past site owner, substance generator or substance transporter) causing the government or a private party to incur response costs".[6]

The government need not show a nexus between a PRP's particular waste and the resulting harm, but only that PRP's waste was shipped to the site and that hazardous substances similar to that waste were at the site at the time of release.[7]

Only three defenses are expressly authorized by CERCLA.[8] These are: (1) Act of God; (2) Act of war; and (3) Demonstration that a release was caused **solely** by a third person with whom defendant had no contractual relationship **and** that defendant exercised due care with respect to the hazardous substances and took precautions against foreseeable acts or omissions of third parties (the third party defense). CERCLA Section 101(35), added by SARA in 1986, establishes conditions under which an innocent landowner — a landowner that acquired property without knowing or having reason to know of contamination on the property — may claim a **defense** to CERCLA liability. (This form of third party defense is treated at length in Chapter X by Heymann.)

## The Scope of Superfund Liability

The term *hazardous substance* incorporates by reference the definitions of toxics substances or hazardous wastes under the other major environmental statutes (Clean Water Act, Clean Air Act, RCRA and TSCA) and substances designated by EPA under CERCLA.[9] The government is authorized to undertake an emergency response under CERCLA § 104 with respect to imminent and substantial endangerment from a "pollutant or contaminant" — terms broadly defined to include any material which "may reasonably be anticipated to cause death or disease".[10]

Petroleum materials are not generally included under the CERCLA hazardous substances definition. EPA has indicated that used oil containing contaminants at concentrations above that normally found in refined oil does constitute a hazardous substance subject to CERCLA.[11] Conversely, normal constituents of gasoline do not render it hazardous.[12] The Oil Pollution Liability Act of 1990, a Superfund-like statute specifically directed towards releases of petroleum into "navigable waters" was passed by Congress on August 18, 1990.[13] Under the terms of that statute, the term *oil* is defined to include any petroleum material other than that which is regulated under CERCLA.[14]

A number of courts have recently considered whether asbestos is a hazardous substance. In circumstances where asbestos is released at a waste disposal site, courts have answered the question in the affirmative.[15] However, costs incurred in removing asbestos from buildings are not recoverable under CERCLA since asbestos installation does not constitute disposal.[16] Similarly, parties that remove asbestos containing materials may not maintain a CERCLA cause of action against asbestos manufacturers on the view that such manufacturers' initial sale of the products constituted waste generation.[17]

The term *release* includes virtually any means by which a hazardous substance might come in contact with the environment, including spilling, leaking, pouring, emitting, or discharging. CERCLA also covers threatened releases. Under SARA, the presence of hazardous substances at an abandoned facility constitutes a threat of a release.[18] Continued seepage from past spills of hazardous substances has been held to be a release.[19] Where a government response action is predicated on an actual release from a site, courts are divided on the issue of whether a the release must be in excess of some state or federal regulatory threshold.[20]

Incorporating by reference the definition at Section 1004(3) of RCRA, *disposal* constitutes any activity wherein hazardous or solid waste is emitted into the environment. The flow of hazardous substances into a river and leaching of hazardous substances through soil and into groundwater was found to be "disposal" in one recent case.[21]

Disposal need not be a one-time occurrence. Disposal may continue, for example, when hazardous wastes are moved, dispersed, or released during landfill excavations.[22]

CERCLA applies to **current owners** or **operators** of a contaminated site even if no hazardous substances were disposed of during their ownership.[23] However, when such past disposal activities do not result in actual or threatened releases following transfer of a contaminated site, courts have held that the subsequent passive owner is **not** a liable party.[24] Lessees will often be considered "operators" under the CERCLA definition.[25] Except where states or local governments acquired property involuntarily (through bankruptcy, foreclosure, tax delinquency, or abandonment), they may be liable under CERCLA as owners or operators to the same extent as other PRPs.[26]

More obviously, persons who owned or operated a site at the time when contamination occured (past owners) are liable.[27] Such an owner's liability is not extinguished by a subsequent transfer of property.[28] The class of potentially responsible prior operators includes other parties with authority over waste operations. One recent line of cases suggests, however, that environmental consultants and other independent contractors will not be considered operators, notwithstanding significant influence over the site.[29]

Remote generators (persons who by contract or otherwise arrange for disposal) and parties whose hazardous substances were shipped through multiple locations to the ultimate place of disposal through brokers or other intermediaries are liable for contamination of the disposal site. The generator need not have selected the disposal site in order to be held liable.[30]

A person who sells a hazardous substance may still be held liable under CERCLA, where the substance had no further use to the seller and was therefore a waste rendering the sale an "arrangement for disposal".[31] Sellers of new commercial products containing hazardous substances will not, conversely, be considered generators. In *Florida Power and Light Company v. Allis Chalmers*, for example, the Eleventh Circuit recently found that manufacturers of PCB equipment could not be held liable for cleanup costs when unforeseeable distant purchasers chose to dispose of the same.[32]

Brokers that make arrangements for disposal between a manufacturer and a disposal company may be liable even absent any role in the creation of the waste.[33]

Manufacturers that arrange with a formulator or reprocessor for tolled production of their chemicals are potentially responsible parties under CERCLA for cleanup of the derivative waste streams. Courts have found that chemical companies could be presumed to have expected that some chemicals would be discarded as waste in the production and reformulation process.[34]

A seemingly contrary viewpoint has been expressed by another court in the circumstances where more than one party may be involved in the generation and shipment of waste to a site which later became the subject of an enforcement action. In *Jersey City Development Authority V. PPG Industries*, the court held that liability would attach only to that company that makes the critical decision to ship such materials to the contaminated site.[35]

Pursuant to amendments added by SARA, federal, state and local governmental entities are fully liable as generators.[36] EPA has, however, recently issued a policy indicating that municipalities will not be held liable for generation of hazardous household solid waste absent site-specific evidence that such waste also contained hazardous substances of non-household (commercial, industrial or institutional) origin.[37]

Individual corporate officers and corporate employees, may be liable under CERCLA as operators if they personally participate in or make decisions about activities affecting hazardous waste disposal.[38] Some courts have recently held that liability will also attach to individuals with "ultimate authority to control" waste handling activities or the power to prevent a release, even in the absence of active management.[39]

A majority shareholder will accrue liability as an owner of a liable corporation, even absent actual management or control of operations. A minority shareholder may be liable as an operator if it controlled, managed, or supervised the company responsible for pollution.[40] Other courts have noted that shareholders in a closely held corporation may be liable depending upon the degree of control asserted including consideration of, among other things, participation in waste handling practices, whether the individual holds an officer, director or management position, and percentage of shares owned.[41]

Parent corporations that participate directly in day-to-day operations of their subsidiaries in a manner that affects hazardous waste disposal or that have the capacity to control such practices and do not prevent or abate contamination may be directly liable under Superfund as "operators".[42] As a separate basis of liability, parent corporations that significantly control or influence their subsidiaries or that use their subsidiaries in a manner contrary to the public interest may be liable for the activities of the subsidiary, as an "owner" based on "piercing the corporate veil."[43]

A corporation that acquires the stock of another corporation acquires the predecessor's CERCLA liability. Under recent cases, a corporation that acquires the **assets only** of another corporation may also acquire CERCLA liability pursuant to four exceptions to the rule of non-liability as set forth under state corporate law:

- The purchaser expressly or implicitly agrees to acquire the seller's liabilities;
- The transaction amounts to a consolidation or a merger of the two corporations;

- The purchaser is merely a continuation of the seller; or
- The transaction is fraudulent.

Courts have also applied a federal rule of decision (adopted a rule furthering the purpose of Superfund) thereby recognizing the four above mentioned exceptions to hold two successor corporations established through merger and consolidation liable under CERCLA for the debts of a predecessor that had caused contamination.[44] In several recent decisions, courts applied the "mere continuation" exception in extending liability to successors that served substantially the same customers, dealt in substantially the same products and maintained substantially the same facilities and staff as the predecessor corporation.[45]

Corporations no longer in existence may be held liable under CERCLA. In *United States v. Sharon Steel Corp.*,[46] the district court allowed a claim against a dissolved corporation owning property which it had contaminated with hazardous waste tailings from its operations. The court noted that while the company had been dissolved after it sold its assets, proceeds had not yet been distributed to shareholders. Subsequently, courts have dismissed claim against dissolved entities brought after reorganization was complete.[47]

Under a so-called lender's defense, the term *owner* does not include institutions which hold indicia of ownership (a security interest) without participating in management or operation of a contaminated site.[48] If they acquire contaminated property by foreclosure, lenders may be liable as owners.[49] Such lenders may, however, be eligible for settlement as *de minimis* parties under EPA's June 1989 *Guidance on Landowner Liability.*[50]

Potentially Responsible Parties have maintained CERCLA private actions against banks with loans to owners of contaminated parcels based on allegations that banks "assumed control of day to day waste management operations" such as by hiring environmental contractors or by assigning agents to evaluate or clean up the borrowers site, thereby destroying the lender's defense.[51] On the same theory, environmental enforcement agencies have directly sued lenders.[52]

On August 9, 1990, the 9th Circuit held in the case of *In re: Bergsoe Metal Corporation* that a CERCLA lenders defense will be breached only in circumstances where the holder of a security interest **actually** participates in the management of the contaminated collateral.[53] In

*Bergsoe*, The Port of St. Helens, Oregon, a municipality, through a sale lease back arrangement, held a mortgage on a piece of property including a lead recycling plant which subsequently became the subject of a EPA enforcement action. When Bergsoe Metal Corporation subsequently filed a Chapter 11 petition, its shareholders sued the Port alleging that certain rights contained in its mortgage and lease back documents manifested "management and control destroying the lender defense". The Bergsoe court rejected this argument, finding that no **actual** control or management had been asserted:

> What is critical is not what rights the Port had, but what it did. The CERCLA security interest exception uses the active "participating in management". Regardless of what rights the Port may have had, it can not have participated in management if it never exercised them.[54]

In an earlier case, *U.S. v. Fleet Factors*[55] the Eleventh Circuit took the contrary position in *dicta* that a non-foreclosing secured lender could be liable for cleanup of contaminated collateral even absent **actual control** if it had participated in the "financial management" of the facility to a degree sufficient to indicate the **capacity to control** waste operations (government action against factoring company whose equipment was located on contaminated property).

Concern over the widening scope of lender liability under Superfund, particularly potential liability of the Resolution Trust Corporation and Small Business Administration, resulted in the introduction of bills in both the U.S. Senate (S.2827, Jake Garn) and House of Representatives (H.R. 4494, John LaFalce). The Senate bill would have amended the Federal Deposit Insurance Act and the Federal Credit Union Act to protect deposit insurance funds and limit the liability of depository institutions, credit unions and other mortgage lenders acquiring real property through foreclosure or in a fiduciary capacity. The House bill would have provided a broad exemption for lenders who foreclose on contaminated property. Neither measure would have protected the non-foreclosing lender; though Federal Deposit Insurance Corp. Division of Liquidation director Steven Sellig sought amendments to S.2827 that would have provided such protection by allowing transfer of approximately 270 assets valued at $365 million, which are believed to be contaminated with hazardous waste, with full immunity for purchasers.[56] Such initiatives are likely to be reintroduced in the 102nd Congress. Meanwhile, a number of states are considering separate lender legislation. On April 5, 1990, for example, Colorado enacted lender liability legislation intended to protect those lenders who must foreclose on contaminated property. The legislation would exempt lenders from responsibility for remediation of contamination that occurred prior to foreclosure. Lenders would also be protected with respect to post-foreclosure contamination if lenders had conducted an environmental audit prior to foreclosure.

Assistant EPA Administrator James Strock announced before the Transportation and Hazardous Materials Subcommittee of the House Energy and Commerce Committee on August 2, 1990, that the EPA would draft a rule that would serve both to protect foreclosing lenders from Superfund liability and also define the nature of non-foreclosing conduct that would be deemed "participating in management" for Superfund purposes.[57] A non-public draft of a lender liability rule has been circulated within EPA since September 14, 1990. In its present form, the rule expressly rejects *Fleet Factors* and expressly recognizes a lender's right to engage in a broad range of non-management activities for the purpose of protecting its security interest, including:

- Performance of pre-loan environmental audits;
- Mandatory environmental remediation prior to or during the life of the loan;
- Periodic inspection of environmental conditions; and
- Imposition of environmental technology forcing requirements.

The policy also would allow a lender to engage in loan workout activities without compromising its defense and would regard foreclosure (and taking of title) as a non-ownership activity engaged in to protect a security interest **provided that** the lender has performed an audit in advance of foreclosure. Under the policy, CERCLA owner liability would not accrue even where a lender holds property after foreclosure for a period of time necessary to preserve the collateral's assets and wind up operations with the presumption that ownership in excess of six months would be outside the scope of the defense. Finally, the policy observes that federal governmental entities such as the Resolution Trust Corporation and the Federal Deposit Insurance Corporation would not need to perform pre-foreclosure audits in order to preserve their lender liability defense following foreclosure.

The automatic stay provisions of the Bankruptcy Code may be inapplicable to CERCLA enforcement proceedings,[58] including, in some circumstances, actions limited to the imposition of civil fines and penalties.[59] A trustee in bankruptcy may normally not abandon the contaminated property in contravention of state laws reasonably designed to protect health and the environment.[60]

Parties seeking contribution from debtors for cleanup costs may not enjoy the same rights as the government under the Bankruptcy Code. In one recent case, a party acquiring a debtor's property, which later became the subject of a Superfund action, was not be able to seek contribution because its claim was considered for contingent on future costs.[61] A bankruptcy trustee was recently held liable as an operator for "willful, intentional and/or negligent violations of laws governing the storage of hazardous wastes" in managing the bankrupt's estate.[62]

## Government Enforcement Authority

Superfund provides the Environmental Protection Agency with three mechanisms to effectuate site remediation. First, the EPA is authorized to act in response to the release or threatened release of hazardous substances into the environment.[63] EPA has broad discretion to determine when private parties may undertake the response action. Second, the Agency may order remedial or removal action in non-emergency circumstances.[64] Finally, the Agency may conduct cleanups and recover its costs from potentially responsible parties.[65] In all instances, the Agency is required to act in accordance with the National Contingency Plan and the regulations implementing CERCLA.

The National Contingency Plan (NCP) was issued by the EPA to establish guidelines for federal and state governments and private parties to conduct Superfund cleanups.[66] The NCP includes criteria for determining how much money will be spent on a site and methods for determining the appropriate extent of response actions. The first NCP that applied to CERCLA actions was issued in 1982.[67] EPA was required to issue the revised NCP in April, 1988, but the timetable slipped and it was recently issued on March 8, 1990.[68]

The NPL is EPA's list of priority sites requiring cleanup. It is a national list that EPA is required to update annually.[69] A site must be listed on the NPL if EPA intends to use Superfund money to finance a remedial action for the site.[70] EPA's decision to place a site on the NPL is extremely difficult to challenge.[71] A site is scored for the NPL using the Hazard Ranking System (HRS), a model that evaluates the relative potential of an uncontrolled site to harm human health or the environment. The HRS considers pathways of exposure in terms of numerical score, and those sites that score 28.50 or greater may be proposed for listing. SARA required EPA to revise the HRS so that "to the maximum extent feasible," it accurately assesses the relative risk to human health and the environment that the site poses.[72] EPA recently did so.[73] Although current NPL sites will not be re-scored, all new listings will be based on the revised HRS. The revised HRS is expected to increase the number of sites placed on the National Priorities List through greater emphasis on the risk of human contact with hazardous substances. According to one report, less than one quarter of sites presently on the NPL have been listed because of potential air and surface water pollution exposure hazards. Both types of exposure hazards and chronic exposures more generally, will receive increased consideration under the new HRS.[74]

The Preliminary Assessment (PA) determines whether a removal action is required, establishes priorities among sites for subsequent site inspections, compiles information necessary to develop preliminary and projected HRS scores, and eliminates sites from CERCLA remedial activity.[75] It is based primarily on analysis of readily available information about the site. The PA identifies the source, the nature of the release, and its magnitude and it may include review of data, such as site management practices, information from generators, aerial and site photographs, and interviews.

If warranted based on a PA review, a Site Inspection (SI) will next be conducted. A SI consists of a visual inspection of the site and collection of samples. The SI eliminates those releases that do not threaten public health or the environment; determines if nearby residents are threatened by a release; and collects data to determine whether a site should be included on the NPL.

Sites placed on the NPL following an SI, or which are the subject of a private party cleanup, are next subjected to a remedial investigation and feasibility study (RI/FS). The RI/FS defines the nature and extent of the release through sampling, monitoring, and exposure assessment and gathers sufficient information to determine the need for and the proposed extent of any remedy. The RI/FS establishes the approach to the remedial action, assesses the risk, and considers alternative approaches to remedying conditions at the site.[76]

Following the RI/FS, selection of remedy is based on comparison of alternatives under nine criteria grouped under three categories:[77]

**Threshold Criteria**
- Protection of human health and the environment;
- Compliance with Applicable or Relevant and Appropriate Cleanup Requirements (ARARs);

**Balancing Criteria**
- Long-term effectiveness and permanence;
- Reduction of toxicity, mobility of volume through treatment;
- Short-term effectiveness;
- Implementability;
- Cost;

**Modifying Criteria**
- State acceptance; and
- Community acceptance.

Of the balancing criteria, two criteria — (1) long-term effectiveness and permanence and (2) reduction of toxicity, mobility or volume through treatment — are to be given special emphasis. The alternative that meets the threshold criteria and affords the best combination of attributes of the balancing criteria is identified as the preferred alternative in the proposed plan. State and community acceptance are factored into a final balancing that determines the remedy and the extent of permanent solutions and treatment practicable for the site.

Under the threshold criteria, any remedy must assure adequate protection of human health and the environment and attainment of legally Applicable or Relevant and Appropriate Requirements (ARARs) for cleanup. CERCLA contemplates three types of ARARs:

- Ambient or chemical-specific concentration limits such as Maximum Contaminant Levels, National Ambient Air Quality Standards, Carcinogenic Potency Factors;[78]
- Performance, design, action-specific requirements such as RCRA regulations for closure of hazardous waste storage units; RCRA incineration standards; Clean Water Act pretreatment standards; and

- Locational requirements such as Federal and state siting laws for hazardous waste facilities; National Register of Historic Places.

In the remedial process, parties are first directed to determine chemical-specific, action-specific, and site-specific ARARs. If there are none, then pertinent health advisory levels (e.g., reference doses, carcinogenic potency factors) are identified. In this regard, the Agency for Toxic Substances and Disease Registry (ATSDR) is required by SARA to prepare profiles (including available toxicological information) on a minimum of 275 substances found at superfund sites. More than 100 such profiles have been issued to date.[79] State ARARs may next be considered, but are limited to those requirements that are promulgated, i.e., "laws imposed by state legislative bodies and regulations developed by state agencies that are of general applicability and are legally enforceable."[80] Requirements under other environmental laws may be either applicable or relevant and appropriate to a remedial action under CERCLA, but not both.[81]

The final NCP describes circumstances when water quality standards may be applied as ARARs: For Class III-type ground water that is not suitable for drinking, drinking water standards are neither applicable nor relevant and appropriate; For Class I-type and Class II-type ground water or surface water that is or may be used for drinking, the ARARs will be the maximum contaminant level goals (MCLGs), nine of which have been established under the Safe Drinking Water Act (SDWA),[82] (except where the MCLG is set at zero). In such circumstances, maximum contaminant levels (MCLs) set forth under the SDWA are the ARARs.[83] Federal Water Quality Criteria and RCRA Alternate Concentration Limits may be utilized provided that levels chosen do not exceed an acceptable risk range of 1/10000 ($10^{-4}$) to 1 in 10,000,000 ($10^{-6}$).[84] In June of 1990 a group of nine states filed petitions with the U.S. Court of Appeals for the District of Columbia challenging use of MCLs under the NCP in circumstances where the MCLG is set at zero.[85]

CERCLA Section 121(d)(4) provides that, under certain circumstances, an ARAR may be waived.[86] The above-referenced August 1988 Guidance sets forth specific examples when EPA will grant waivers. EPA may also select partial remedies or "operable units", which are consistent with but do not constitute a final remedy.[87]

In internal guidance circulated at EPA on June 29, 1990, the Agency has apparently proposed national standards for measuring likely human exposure to pollutants at Superfund sites. Such standards would largely supplant the ARARs and would need to be utilized at all Superfund sites unless local conditions warrant development of site-specific standards. The proposal was issued in response to criticism that inconsistent cleanup standards are used at otherwise comparable Superfund sites. The proposal also apparently includes maximum contaminant levels for soil.[88]  Also, on July 27, 1990 EPA proposed a regulation which would establish both RCRA corrective action trigger or action levels and cleanup levels for air, soil and water at contaminated sites.[89]

Section 300.400(e) of the NCP deals with regulatory permit requirements which could qualify as ARARs but would significantly impede cleanup progress. The NCP implements the SARA provisions in section 121(e), in this regard,  that no federal, state or local permits shall be required for removal or remedial action conducted entirely on site. In the NCP, EPA has defined *onsite* to mean the "areal extent of contamination and all suitable areas in very close proximity to the contamination necessary for the implementation of the response action." The term *areal* refers to both surface areas and the air above the site. EPA intends that the exemption applies to CERCLA activities, including investigations and CERCLA section 106 actions, conducted entirely onsite, before and after the remedy is selected, but not to "voluntary" private cleanups. This exemption extends to permits under RCRA. EPA will evaluate on a case-by-case basis whether to treat two non-contiguous facilities as one for purposes of the onsite permitting exemption. Wastes remaining onsite must comply with ARARs under federal law or state law, where more stringent. Onsite solutions must satisfy stringent water quality requirements established under the Safe Drinking Water Act and the Clean Water Act.

In the final NCP, EPA states its policy that an area of contamination consisting of continuous contamination of varying amounts and types at a Superfund site can be equated to a RCRA land disposal unit. EPA reaffirmed its interpretation that movement of wastes within such a unit will not, however, trigger the land disposal restrictions (LDRs). The LDRs are triggered only by **placement** of wastes into a unit.

EPA has been criticized for not compelling selection of permanent solutions by potentially responsible parties. The Office of Technology Assessment (OTA) has criticized EPA's remedy selection process as weighted toward considerations of cost and technical feasibility, resulting in the selection of land disposal and containment approaches in 42 percent of FY'87 remedies that EPA selected.[90] The OTA has gone as far as to suggest that potentially responsible parties should be barred from performing remedial investigation and feasibility studies, asserting that such parties have an inherent conflict of interest that would lead them to choose a low cost, non-permanent remedy.[91] The contrary view is expressed in a recent OSWER Report entitled "A Comparative Analysis of Remedies Selected in the Superfund Program During Fiscal Year 87 Through Fiscal Year 89",[92] indicating that treatment oriented remedies, rather than those relying on containment, have increased in number and now predominate. Treatment of highly toxic waste and utilization of innovative technologies are also reported to be common in the most recent remedial designs. Based on a paired analysis of EPA and PRP financed cleanups, the report concludes that remedies showed roughly the same percentage of treatment and containment remedies. The average cost of final source control remedies is reported to be $11.6 million.

## Government Settlements

EPA issues four types of notice letters that invite PRPs to settle:
- General notices;
- RI/FS special notices;
- RD/RA special notices; and
- Removal action notices.

All notices, with the exception of removal notices, are to be issued only to those parties for whom there exists sufficient evidence for EPA to make a preliminary determination of potential liability under CERCLA Section 107. The removal action notice is issued to all "readily identifiable PRPs" if the environmental threat is such that the removal action need not be initiated for at least six months.[93]

CERCLA Section 122(e) provides for a sixty day moratorium following receipt of a special notice, during which time, EPA may neither initiate response action nor file an enforcement action. If EPA receives a "good faith" proposal from the PRPs, it may continue the moratorium for 60 days in the case of a prospective remedial design/

remedial action (RD/RA) settlement or 30 days in the case of a prospective RI/FS settlement. When EPA considers a settlement "likely and imminent" it may grant a 30-day extension of the moratorium. Further extensions may be granted only by the OSWER Assistant Administrator.

The EPA Regions utilize notice letters in conjunction with a four-step settlement process. First, EPA regions are required to conduct PRP searches at the same time as the Site Investigation or NPL scoring.[94] The PRP search must be completed the year the site is proposed for the NPL. An administrative subpoena may be used to obtain necessary information or testimony.

General notice letters, which may include requests for information under Section 104(e), will then be sent to PRPs in advance of special notice letters allowing an "open negotiation period" free of moratorium complaints. EPA will conduct "informal" discussions or negotiations before issuing a special notice. EPA will prepare a negotiation strategy and draft a settlement document before issuing the special notice, and where appropriate, prepare an administrative order, RI/FS or draft consent decree.

A Nonbinding Preliminary Allocation of Responsibility (NBAR) is a preliminary allocation of responsibility among PRPs that EPA **may** prepare to facilitate settlement.[95] It is intended to allocate one hundred percent responsibility for site contamination, utilizing the following principles:
- Volume will be the primary basis of allocation, not toxicity;
- Percentage attributable to defunct or impecunious parties will be assigned to solvent parties;
- Responsibility will be allocated to financially viable owners and operators based on culpability; and
- Responsibility will be allocated to transporters based on volume, taking into account considerations such as packaging and placement of waste at a site (pass-through liability).[96]

EPA may prepare an NBAR if the following circumstances exist:
- A significant percentage of PRPs at the site request an NBAR;
- NBARs are required to ascertain a *pro rata* liability of federal, state, or municipal PRPs; and
- A large number of PRPs (including a sizable *de minimis* contingent) constitute a substantial portion of the site. NBARs may include *de minimis* and mixed-funding settlement approaches.

EPA has discretion to enter into settlements with *de minimis* PRPs that contribute hazardous substances in minimal amounts in comparison to the total amount of waste at site and where the waste is not significantly more toxic than other substances at the site. Also, *de minimis* claims can be resolved only where they involve a minor portion of total response costs.

EPA defines *de minimis* on a site-by-site basis.[97] Some EPA regions are using one to two percent volume as a starting point for negotiating *de minimis* settlements. EPA has also issued a *de minimis* settlement guidance for landowners who did not "conduct or permit the generation, transportation, treatment, or disposal of hazardous substances" at a site or otherwise "contribute to the release".[98] The guidance includes a model administrative order on consent and consent decree for *de minimis* landowner party settlement.[99]

*De minimis* settlements will be contained either in a judicial consent decree or administrative order on consent, contained a broad-form, covenant-not-to-sue and subjecting settling parties to enforcement in the event they fail to pay.[100] Approval of the United States Department of Justice is required if total site response costs will exceed $500,000. Numerous *de minimis* settlements have been reported since 1986.[101]

EPA may enter into a settlement in which total costs are paid in part by PRPs and in part by Superfund. In such cases, EPA is instructed to attempt to recoup the Superfund's share from the other PRPs. There are three types of mixed funding settlements that EPA recognizes:

- *Preauthorization* - in which the PRPs conduct the response action and the Agency agrees to allow a claim against the Fund for a portion of the response costs;
- *Cash-outs* - PRPs pay for a portion of the response costs up front, and the Agency conducts the response action; and
- *Mixed work* - PRPs and the Agency each agree to conduct discrete portions of the response activity.[102]

EPA's record on these funding settlements is mixed, at best. Virtually no cash-out settlements have been reported to date.[103]

In January of 1990, Bruce Diamond, Director of EPA Office of Waste Programs (OWPE), issued a directive requiring that Superfund settlements be embodied in two successive settlement documents: The Remedial Investigation/Feasibility Study (RI/FS) Administrative Order on Consent (AOC) and the Remedial Design/

Remedial Action Consent Decree.[104] A model RI/FS AOC contained in the directive has been criticized as extremely unfavorable to PRPs, *inter alia* because:

- The Agency retains virtual total control of the RI/FS content through the power to unilaterally revise interim drafts;
- Stipulated penalties accrue from the date of the submission of a deliverable which is later disapproved;
- Dispute resolution is only available as to the amount of stipulated penalties and as to whether a **force major** event has prevented performance by a PRP.[105]

Private non-settling parties have frequently challenged consent decrees. Courts have generally held that consent decrees will be approved and such challenges will be denied where they are "fair, adequate and reasonable and consistent with the public interest."[106] In those circumstances where courts have not approved Consent Decrees, the settlement was deemed "arbitrary and capricious" or was found to have departed from the requirements of the statute.[107]

EPA may recover costs "not inconsistent with the National Contingency Plan".[108] EPA's costs for removal and remedial actions are presumed reasonable and therefore recoverable unless a challenging party proves that costs are inconsistent.[109]

There has been substantial litigation over the types of costs which the Agency may recover. Courts have held that EPA may recover its **direct costs** of investigation, enforcement and cleanup, including attorneys' fees and litigation costs.[110] The Sixth Circuit has held that EPA may also recover **prejudgment interest**.[111] EPA may recover its **indirect** costs defined as "overhead" costs attributable to operation of Superfund program, including such items as salaries, rent, utilities and other administrative expenses.[112]

The government may also hold responsible parties liable for "damages for injury to, destruction of, or **loss of natural resources**".[113] Regulations providing standard procedures for natural resource damage assessments resulting from discharges into the coastal marine environments were promulgated on March 20, 1987.[114] These regulations were held invalid (at least in part) in the case of *State of Colorado v. Department of the Interior*.[115] where the court found that the regulations improperly restricted the damage estimate of loss to the economic value of the lost resources rather than the value of replacing or restoring the same.

An additional set of regulations applicable to all other types of natural resource damage were issued on August 1, 1986.[116] This second set of regulations were similarly held partially invalid as improperly limiting damages to the lesser of the cost of restoration or the economic value of the lost resource.[117] Revised regulations are due to be proposed before the end of 1990.

One court has recently held that a natural resource damage claim will not be available where such damage was previously identified and taken into consideration in an environmental impact statement submitted and approved pursuant to the National Environmental Policy Act or implementing regulations.[118] Natural resource damage claims are also not available with respect to damages occurring before CERCLA's enactment in 1980.[119] SARA also provided a three year statute of limitations for the filing of natural resource damage claims with respect to releases alleged to have occurred prior to the effective date of the amendments, are March 13, 1987. It is not clear whether judicial invalidation of the natural resource damages regulations will toll the statute of limitations in this regard.

CERCLA provides that the government is entitled to recover treble damages from a party who refuses to comply with an Administrative Order. One federal court has recently held, however, that the actual damage amount is to be calculated as the amount of actual damages multiplied by a factor of three, not by a factor of four as some parties had argued.[120]

The NCP provides that EPA must collect and maintain documentation to support all response actions, sufficient to provide accurate accounting of Federal costs incurred.[121] EPA's recovery of litigation costs may not be entitled to same deferential standard as cleanup costs.[122]

If a site poses an imminent and substantial endangerment to health or the environment, the government may compel PRPs to clean up through the issuance of an administrative order. Such actions may also be filed by state authorities seeking to compel performance of a specifically designated remedy.[123] Failure to comply with a cleanup order may result in treble damages and civil penalties up to $25,000 per day. EPA has sought such damages on 14 occasions thus far.[124] If a person complying with a cleanup order can establish it was not liable, it may recover its response costs.

CERCLA Section 107(a) allows private parties to recover from other PRPs the necessary costs of responding to a release of hazardous substances.[125] The elements of a private cost recovery action are the same as for a governmental cost recovery action except that a private party must prove that its response actions are **consistent** with the NCP.[126] In order to show consistency, plaintiff need not show that it complied with the precise criteria in the NCP but only that the response action, when evaluated as a whole, demonstrates substantial compliance with the NCP, is protective of human health, and meets the ARARS. The March 1990 NCP revisions supplant earlier cases, in this regard, which had required absolute consistency.[127]

A private party must have incurred **some** response costs in order to maintain an action.[128] Courts have stated that the only defenses available are those specifically set out in the statute.[129] Hence, contractual releases, representations, warranties and indemnities may not provide a defense to a CERCLA private contribution claim (though the same may be effective with respect to a state law claim).[130] *Caveat emptor* has been held not to be a defense to liability, but, rather among the equitable defenses that may affect the recoverability of damages.[131]

## State Superfund Law Summary

Thirty-seven states currently have some type of superfund law providing for a required 10 percent watch at federally funded CERCLA cleanups and ongoing remediation of hazardous substance contamination (sometimes limited to the cleanup of abandoned waste sites)[132] and/or immediate response to waste spills at non-federal sites). The survey as an appendix at page 247 provides a basic reference list of all state superfund program provisions that may affect business transactions. The survey is based on a review of actual state statutes in all fifty states, the District of Columbia and Puerto Rico. Information on state superfund lists (and the number of sites listed) is based in part on an EPA telephone survey conducted May to August 1989.[133] Citations are also given for states that have not yet promulgated lists but have the authority to do so.

A majority of states are patterned after the federal Superfund program and provide the strict, joint and several liability. Most also create funds through general revenue appropriations. Twenty-seven states maintain their own lists of hazardous waste or hazardous substance sites, while another nine, which have the authority to promulgate a separate state list, are in the process of developing them.

Certain trends are apparent in developing state superfund law. Given the cost and complexity of state enforcement proceedings, private superfund litigation appears to be increasingly encouraged by states. Only six states now have some limited governmental superlien provisions, while an increasing number, currently 23, permit private causes of action or actions for contribution among potentially responsible parties. Some of these private rights of action are limited to specific contamination events or types of waste released. In addition, the range of potentially responsible parties has been broadened considerably in many states.

The survey first identifies whether a state has a superfund law. In many cases, while a state does not have an exact counterpart to the federal superfund law, it will provide cleanup funds for ongoing remediation of abandoned sites or may fund the cleanup of unanticipated spills or releases which require immediate response. In the case of South Dakota, the superfund law appears to only authorize underground storage tank (UST) spill cleanup, but may be more broadly applied in actual enforcement.

The survey next identifies the potentially responsible parties (PRPs), the standard of liability, and defenses available, if any. The scope of responsible parties can include: owners, operators, generators, transporters, disposers, arrangers or contractors of disposal, storage or treatment of hazardous waste or substances, possessors, bailers, carriers, sellers, and in Washington state, persons responsible for writing waste handling usage instructions.

The liability standard, which is usually strict liability in almost all cases, is not, unlike the federal superfund law, always joint and several between responsible parties. In ten states liability is expressly not joint and several and in another seven states, liability can be apportioned among the parties if a responsible party can meet the burden of proof on its portion. A citation is provided for provisions establishing defenses for PRPs, if any, and/or recitation of types of parties excepted from the definition of PRPs. For many states, citations have been included at the end of the survey for state laws other than superfund laws which may impose additional liabilities on PRPs.

*Superliens* are liens placed on real (and sometimes personal) property of responsible parties who are found to be liable to the state for environmental cleanup recovery costs. Such liens have priority over even previously perfected security interests. A few states have recently removed the priority nature of these liens, reducing them to basic judgement liens. Some states have restrictions on the breadth of superliens, limiting attachment as a recovery remedy only for emergency response costs, or specifically excluding residential real estate, or municipal utility companies.

The definition of a *hazardous substance* under state superfund law varies according to the scope and intent of the law. Many states incorporate by reference, the definition of hazardous waste or hazardous substance as defined in federal statutes including the Comprehensive Environmental Response Cleanup Authority, the Resource Conservation Recovery Act, the Federal Water Pollution Control Act, the Clean Air Act, the Clean Water Act and the Toxic Substance Control Act. The inclusion of petroleum products in the definition is noted, since such materials are excluded from the federal Superfund statute. In addition certain types of substances or release events may be excluded from the scope of the state superfund authority through the definition of *hazardous substance* (citations are given in these instances).

Enforcement by the relevant state agency is not always authorized by the state superfund law. Most states include some type of cost recovery provision if the state has to clean up a hazardous release, but many states have a policy of requiring state environmental officials to first locate and order the responsible parties to cleanup and/or use federal CERCLA funds prior to using state funds for cleanup. The scope of such administrative orders and resultant enforcement varies much among states.

The existence of a private cause of action under the state superfund law may be limited to a right of contribution of a responsible party against another PRP or may generally allow a private citizen to initiate a suit under the law, which may also imply a right of contribution against a PRP; however, the authority for such causes of actions does not always exist in the same law and may be limited to specific acts or types of hazardous substance. Finally, the survey describes civil, criminal, and state punitive liabilities created under superfund and other state statutes (included in the Appendixes to each state following the survey).

# Future Trends and Emerging Issues Under Superfund

## CERCLA Under the Bush Administration

On June 14, 1989, EPA issued its 90-day management study of the Superfund Program, commissioned by William Reilly, EPA's Administrator, to respond to program criticism. Recommendations included strengthening Agency Superfund enforcement against private parties (particularly by issuing administrative orders); establishing priorities to deal with the most serious sites first; and phasing out contractors, instead of allocating $75 million to hire 500 new enforcement officers. In September, 1989, EPA announced its plans for implementing the study, setting 120 tasks to be accomplished by September 30, 1990.[134]

As of the close of 1990, OWPE Director Bruce Diamond has issued a new form Administrative Order on Consent which has been viewed by many industry representatives as severely curtailing PRP power over selection and implementation of site remedies.[135] In a related development, EPA Assistant Administrator Donald Clay announced on June 21, 1990, that EPA (rather than PRPs) would perform all future site risk assessments, even in circumstances where PRPs are performing lead cleanup activity under an approved RI/FS.[136] Finally, whereas in 1988 most site cleanups were performed pursuant to Consent Decrees, in 1989-1990 most were performed pursuant to unilateral administrative orders issued pursuant to Reilly's new Management Program. An informal report at the October 1990 Washington, D.C. meeting of the Information Network for Superfund settlements indicates that approximately 30 unilateral administrative orders have been issued thus far, almost exclusively for removal actions. Order recipients have noted that only a small number of potentially responsible parties have been sued, greatly complicating PRP organizational efforts. On the positive side, terms of the unilateral orders are more favorable than under the Agency's new model AOC, particularly to the extent that private parties retain more latitude in selection of remedy and negotiation on Agency cost recovery.

Potentially responsible parties will likely experience a dramatic increase in site remediation expense overt the course of the coming year as they are required to labor under the double impediments of Agency-controlled risk assessments and administrative orders on consent which virtually guaranty agency primacy over remedy selection. More flexible and cost-effective remedies will be available to such parties where cleanups are performed under state jurisdiction or are conducted pursuant to a federal unilateral administrative order.

The Agency appears to have instigated an increasingly large number of natural resource damage action claims in connection with Superfund cleanups. With revised natural resource damage regulations close at hand, it seems likely that many more of these actions will in fact be filed and prosecuted during the coming year.

Eleventh hour reauthorization of the Superfund Program in October of 1990 will put a significant damper on Superfund reform activities during the 102nd Congress. A number of groups have indicated that they will continue to pursue introduction of legislation which would result in amendment of the Superfund taxing authority. One such group is the American International Group (AIG), which has proposed a new tax in the from of a two percent surcharge on all commercial and industrial property and casualty insurance. AIG suggests such a tax would so dramatically increase the size of the Federal Fund, that the Agency would no longer need to pursue potentially responsible parties with respect to contamination which occurred before the enactment of Superfund in 1980.[137]

It seems likely that the U.S. EPA will issue its lender liability rule during 1991, providing, for the first time, norms of financial management which the lending community can follow with assurance that they will be exempt from Superfund liability. It is likely that issuance of a lender rule will catalyze the development and possible issuance of a similar rule for innocent land owners.

AK     The Oil and Hazardous Substance Release Response Fund was established within the state general fund by Alaska Stat. §§ 46.08.005 to 46.08.900 (1986). Other relevant implementation and enforcement provisions are Alaska Stat. §§ 46.03.758 to 46.03.900 (1989) and §§ 46.09.010 to 46.09.900 (1986).

AL     The Alabama Hazardous Substance Cleanup Fund is authorized and governed by Ala. Code §§ 22-30A-1 to 22-30A-11 (1990).

AR     Arkansas has two remedial funds. The Emergency Remedial Fund Act (ERFA) and the Remedial Action Trust Fund are authorized respectively by Ark. Stat. Ann. §§ 8-7-401 to 8-7-522 (1989) and §§ 82-4712 to 82-4724 (1987).

AZ     The Water Quality Assurance Revolving Fund is Arizona's only remedial fund and is authorized by Ariz. Rev. Stat. Ann. §§ 49-281 to 49-287 (1986).

CA     California has two remedial funds. Both the Hazardous Substance Account, established by Cal. Health & Safety Code § 25330 (1988) and the Hazardous Substance Cleanup Fund, created at § 25385.3 of the same code, are implemented by §§ 25350 through 25358 of the same code.

CO     The law which established Colorado's superfund, the hazardous substance response fund, has been repealed. It appeared at Colo. Rev. Stat. §§ 25-16-101 to 25-16-105 (1988) and incorporated CERCLA by reference. It may be reenacted or replaced by pending legislation. For cleanup authority over emergency spills, an Emergency Response Cash Fund was created under Colo. Rev. Stat. §§ 29-22-101 to 29-22-109 which includes cost recovery, civil and criminal penalty provisions. The UST Fund can be used to cleanup haz. substance leakage. Colo. Rev. Stat. § 25-18-109 (1989).

CT     The authorization for emergency spill response fund exists within the hazardous waste law at Conn. Gen. Stat. §§ 22a-114 to 22a-133g (1989) and 22a-451 and §§ 22a-450 to 22a-453 (1989).

DC     Although there is no superfund, the Hazardous Waste Management Act provides authority for some administrative orders and civil penalties for those who fail to take corrective action at D.C. Code Ann. §§ 6-701 to 6-712 (1984).

DE   Despite the lack of a superfund law, two separate acts authorize the Delaware Department of Natural Resources and Environmental Control to enforce waste spills and UST leakages. Del. Code §§ 7-6301 to 7-6318 (1989) and §§ 7-7401 *et. seq.* (1989).

FL   There are four funding sources for remedial action. The Pollution Recovery Fund is created by F.S. § 403.165 (1990) for restoration of "polluted areas" of Florida. The water Quality Assurance Trust Fund is created by F.S. § 376.307 (1990) for investigation and cleanup of inland sites contaminated with hazardous wastes that affect potable water resources. The Inland Protection Trust Fund is created by F.S. § 376.3071 (1990) for cleanup of contamination due to petroleum and other enumerated pollutants. The Florida Coastal Protection Fund, created by F.S. § 376.11 (1990), and the Port Trust Fund, created by F.S. § 376.22 (1990) are for prevention and abatement of pollutant discharges in coastal areas of Florida.

GA   Although no specific state superfund exists, both the Oil or Hazardous Material Spill or Release Act and the Hazardous Waste Trust Fund authorize the Director of the Environmental Division of Georgia's Department of Natural Resources to issue remediation orders and impose civil penalties. Ga. Code Ann. §§ 12-4-1 to 12-4-4 (1988) and §§ 12-8-60 to 12-8-83 (1979). The UST Trust Fund authorizes cleanup of releases of petroleum and other regulated substances from UST's and includes civil liability administrative order and cost recovery provisions. Ga. Code Ann. §§ 12-13-9 to 12-13-22 (1989). Finally, the Water Pollution Control Revolving Fund exists at Ga. Code Ann. § 12-5-38.1 (1986).

HI   The Environmental Emergency Response Revolving Fund is created and governed by the Hawaii Environmental Response Act at Haw. Rev. Stat. §§ 148-1 to 148-7 (1988).

IA   The Hazardous Waste Remedial Fund is created by Iowa Code § 455B.423 (1989). The Iowa Comprehensive Petroleum UST Fund is created under Iowa Code § 455G.3 (1989). Responsible Party Regulations were enacted under Iowa Admin. Code r. 10-133.3 through r. 10-133.5 (1989).

ID   No superfund exists. An emergency account allows for the neutralizing of hazardous waste under the state's Hazardous Waste Act at Idaho Code § 39-4417 (1988).

IL   The Hazardous Waste Fund and the Hazardous Waste Research Fund are governed by Ill. Ann. Stat. ch. 111 1/2, para. 1003.14 to para. 1043

(1989). Emergency response to hazardous substance releases are governed by Ill. Ann. Stat. § 750.301 to § 750.492. The UST Fund is established by Ill. Ann. Stat. ch 111 1/2 para. 1022.13 (1989).

IN     The Hazardous Substances Response Trust Fund is authorized by Ind. Code § 13-7-8.7 *et. seq.* (1990). The UST Trust Fund is established by Ind. Code § 13-7-20-30.

KS     The Kansas Superfund Law is located at Kan. Stat. Ann. §§ 65-3452 to 65-3470 (1989). A separate law governs leakage from UST tanks. *See* Kan. Admin Regs. §§ 28-44-1 *et. seq.* (1989).

KY     Although there is no state superfund, the Kentucky Environmental Protection Law provides for emergency cleanup of oil and hazardous substance discharges pursuant to FWPCA and includes cost recovery enforcement through the Hazardous Waste Management Fund. Ky. Rev. Stat. Ann. §§ 224.876 to 224.877 (Michie 1988).

LA     The Hazardous Waste Site Cleanup Fund has broader authority than its predecessor which addressed only abandoned hazardous waste sites. La. Rev. Stat. § 30:2205 (1987). Monies from the Site Cleanup Fund are allocated to the Environmental Emergency Response Fund which, along with the Hazardous Waste Protection Fund and the UST Trust Fund, provide authority for the remediation of emergency spills, releases or leakages. The authority for the latter three funds are, respectively, La. Rev. Stat. §§ 30:2034, 30:2198 and 1141:3.

MA     Both the Massachusetts Oil and Hazardous Material Release Prevention and Response Act and the regulations enacted pursuant to the act provide detailed cleanup enforcement provisions. The Act is located at Mass. Gen. L. ch 21E (1987) and the regulations can be found at Mass. Regs. Code tit. 310 §§ 40.001 to 40.620 (1989).

MD     The Hazardous Substance Control Fund was established by the Maryland Hazardous Substances Spill Response Law at Md. Health-Envtl. Code Ann. §§ 7-201 to 7-268 (1989).

ME     The Uncontrolled Sites Fund is a non-lapsing revolving fund established to oversee uncontrolled hazardous substance sites on a long-term basis by Maine Rev. Stat. Ann. tit. 38, §§ 1361 to 1371 (1989). A Ground water Oil Cleanup Fund was also established for remediation by Maine's Underground Storage Facilities Law at Maine Rev. Stat. Ann. tit. 38, §§ 561-570G (1989).

MI     The Environmental Response Fund is used to match federal CERCLA funds and to undertake response action at sites which are subjected to the risk assessment process. Mich. Comp. Laws Ann. §§ 299.601 *et. seq.* (1989). It has no directly-related enforcement provisions and is enforced by the Michigan Dept. of Natural Resources currently under the air, water and hazardous waste laws with whatever limited cost recovery, civil penalty and administrative order provisions exist within them.

MN     The Environmental Response, Compensation and Compliance Fund was established by the Minnesota Environmental Response and Liability Act at Minn. Stat Ann. §§ 115B.01 to 115B.37 (1988). Regulations governing the maintenance of a state list of sites according to the federal Hazard Ranking System are printed at Minn. R. 7044.0100 to R. 7044.1200 (1984).

MO     The Hazardous Waste Remedial Fund provides for Missouri's matching share of CERCLA funds for remediation of sites on federal list. Mo. Rev. Stat. § 260-480 (1990). It addresses primarily abandoned, uncontrolled sites and is enforced through the Hazardous Waste Act; the relevant provisions are Mo. Rev. Stat. §§ 260.350 to 260.480 and §§ 260.500 to 260.552 (1990).

MS     There is no specific superfund law. The general Pollution Emergency Fund contains monies that can be used for cleanup. Miss. Code Ann. § 49-17-68 (1989). Actual enforcement authority, however, exists within the Water and Air Pollution Laws and the Mississippi UST Act respectively at Miss. Code Ann. § 17-17-1 *et. seq.* (1988) and § 49-17-401 *et. seq.* (1988).

MT     The Environmental Quality Protection Fund was established by the Montana Hazardous Substance Remedial Action Law. Mont. Code Ann. §§ 75-10-701 to 75-10-715 (1987).

NC     The most sophisticated state fund is the Inactive Hazardous Substance Disposal Site Fund which is governed by N.C. Gen. Stat. § 130A-310 to § 130A.310.22 (1989). Two additional narrower remediation funds are the Emergency Response Fund created at N.C. Gen. Stat. § 130A-306 (1989), and the Oil or Hazardous Substance Pollution Protection Fund, created at N.C. Gen. Stat. § 143-215.87 (1989).

ND     Although there is no parallel state superfund, the Hazardous Waste Management Act and the N.D. Petroleum Release Compensation Act provide limited cleanup and enforcement authority for "imminent hazards" and are located, respectively at, N.D. Cent. Code §§ 23-20.3-01 to 23-20.3-10 and 1989 N.C. Sess. Laws H.B. 1297.

NE      There is no superfund in Nebraska. Very limited authority for cleanup and enforcement of ground water and some solid waste pollution exists within the Environmental Quality Act of Neb. Rev. Stat. §§ 81-1501 to 81-1533 (1989).

NH      The Hazardous Waste Cleanup Fund is as its title indicates limited in scope to redress hazardous waste pollution. N.H. Rev. Stat. Ann. §§ 145B:01-147B:11 (1989).

NJ      The N.J. Spill Compensation Fund is governed by the Spill Compensation and Control Act at N.J. Stat. Ann. §§ 58:10-23.1 to 58:10-23.10 (1989). Additional enforcement provisions are included in the N.J. Environmental Cleanup Responsibility Act at N.J. Stat. Ann. §§ 13:1K-6 to 13:1K-34 (1989). Rules enacted pursuant to the latter act are at N.J. Admin. Code §§ 7:26B-1.1 to 7:26B-11.1 (1989).

NM      Although there is no superfund, enforcement authority of cleanup of hazardous waste and UST releases exists under the New Mexico Hazardous Waste Act at N.M. Stat. An.. §§ 74-4-1 to 74-4D-8 (1987) and is implemented by the New Mexico Environmental Improvement Board, ch. 1, §§ 100 *et. seq.* (1989).

NV      Although there is no superfund, the hazardous waste management fund provides for cleanup monies and limited enforcement of hazardous waste pollution. Nev. Rev. Stat. §§ 459.400 to 459.600 (1987).

NY      New York has a limited superfund, created to cleanup inactive hazardous waste disposal sites which are placed on the state's separate list. N.Y. Envtl. Conserv. Law §§ 27-1301 to 27-1317 (McKinney 1989).

OH      The Hazardous Waste Cleanup Fund is a general purpose fund which supplies monies to enable enforcement of Ohio's Solid and Hazardous Waste and UST Laws. Ohio Rev. Code Ann. § 3734.28 (page 1989).

OK      The Controlled Industrial Waste Fund is not a superfund but rather authority for responding to "environmental emergencies and incidents." It exists at Section 1-2018 within Oklahoma's Controlled Industrial Waste Act and is more of a parallel to the federal RCRA statute. Okla. Stat. Ann. tit. 63, §§ 1-2001 to 1-2021 (1988). In addition, UST releases are regulated by the Okla. Corporation Commission Gen. R. & Regs. ch.1, Rs. 1 *et. seq.* (1990).

OR      The Hazardous Substance Remedial Action Fund is the ongoing remediation fund in Oregon. Or Rev. Stat. §§ 466.540 to 466.590 (1987). Additional emergency cleanup monies can be obtained under the Oil and Hazardous Material Emergency Response and Remedial Action Fund. Or. Rev. Stat. §§ 466.605 to 466.690 (1985).

PA    The Hazardous Sites Cleanup Fund was established under the Pennsylvania Hazardous Sites Cleanup Act. 35 Pa. Cons. Stat. §§ 101 to 1115 (1988).

PR    The Puerto Rico Superfund Law authorizes the Puerto Rico Environmental Emergencies fund which can be used to clean up "accidental or unauthorized intentional or attempted discharges." P.R. Laws Ann. Lit. 12, §§ 1271 to 1276 (1987).

RI    The Environmental Response Fund is limited to funding hazardous waste remediation and was created under the Hazardous Waste Management Act at R.I. Gen. Laws §§ 23-19.1-1 to 23-19.1-34 (1987).

SC    The Hazardous Waste Contingency Fund was created to redress the pollution of hazardous waste primarily at "uncontrolled waste sites." S.C. Code Ann. §§ 44-56-10 to 44-56-330 (1989).

SD    Although the Regulated Substance Response Fund was established as the South Dakota Superfund Law, it may be limited only to cleanup of storage tank releases. S.D. Codified Laws Ann. §§ 34A-12-1 to 34A-12-17 (1989). Some implementation regulations relating to petroleum cleanup (which is authorized by the state superfund) are printed under the South Dakota Petroleum Release Rules at S.D. Admin. R.74:32:01 *et. seq.* (1988).

TN    The Hazardous Waste Remedial Action Fund addresses more than hazardous waste cleanup. Tenn. Code Ann. §§ 68-46-201 to 68-46-221 (1985). Tennessee Superfund Regulations can be located at Tenn. Comp. R & Regs. ch. 1200-1-13 (1988).

TX    The Texas Spill Response Fund is governed by the Texas Hazardous Substances Spill Prevention and Control Act. Tex. Water Code Ann. §§ 26.261 to 26.356 (Vernon 1987). Additional enforcement authority exists under the Texas Solid Waste Disposal Act at Tex. Health & Safety Code Ann. §§ 4477-1-1 to 4477-1-13 91987).

UT    The Hazardous Substances Mitigation Fund was created under the Hazardous Substances Mitigation Act at Utah Code Ann. §§ 26-14d-101 to 26-14d-801 (1989).

VA   The Virginia Solid and Hazardous Waste Contingency Fund is author-
     ized by the Virginia Solid Waste Act and the Virginia Waste Manage-
     ment Act, located respectively at Va. Code Ann. §§ 10.1-1403 to 10.1-
     1457 (1988) and § 10-270 (1988). Emergency response actions can also be
     funded through the Virginia Disaster Response Fund and the Virginia
     Petroleum UST Fund authorized respectively at Va. Code Ann. § 44-
     146.37 (1989) and § 62.1-44.34:11 (1988).

VT   Although there is no ongoing cleanup fund, three funds can be used to
     cleanup spills or "unintentional" releases. The Solid Waste Contingency
     Fund establishes criminal and civil penalties for those parties who re-
     lease hazardous materials ( the definition of which includes petroleum
     and hazardous substance as defined by CERCLA) into the environment
     without notifying the Agency of Environmental Conservation. Vt. Stat.
     Ann. tit. 10, §§ 6601 to 6618 (1989). The cleanup of hazardous waste is
     also funded through this source. In addition, monies from the Petrole-
     um (UST) Fund and the environmental contingency fund can be uti-
     lized to respond to immediate threats to surface and groundwater, and
     are authorized respectively by Vt. Stat. Ann. tit. 10, §§ 1941 and 1283
     (1989).

WA   The Toxics Control Account is a fund created for ongoing remediation
     by the Washington Model Toxics Control Act. Wash. Rev. Code
     §§ 70.105D.010 to 70.105D.080 (1988). Washington Hazardous Waste
     Cleanup Regulations are located at Wash. Admin. Code §§ 173-336 to
     173-340 (1988).

WI   The Environmental Repair Fund provides for both immediate response
     to spills and solid waste facility post-closure remediation. Wisc. Stat.
     Ann. § 144.442 (1989). The Wisconsin Environmental Response Rules
     provide guidelines for implementing the fund. Wisc. Admin. Code
     §§ NR 550-01 to NR 550-50 (January 1987).

WV   The West Virginia Emergency Response Fund Act is a fund limited as
     its title suggests, to responding to hazardous waste emergencies. W.
     Va. Code §§ 20-5E-1 to 20-5E-24 (1990).

WY   Although there is no specific superfund, the Wyoming Environmental
     Quality Act contains enforcement mechanisms for the cleanup, cost re-
     covery and RP liability of polluted waters and polluting hazardous and
     solid wastes. Wyo. Stat. §§ 35-11-1 to 35-11-901 (1989).

| State | State Fund/Auth. for Fund [Cite] | PRPs/Liab. Std/Defenses | Super-Lien Prov. | "Haz. Subst." |
|-------|----------------------------------|--------------------------|-------------------|----------------|
| AK | Yes/AS 48.08.10 (1986) | Pers. "owning or having control over haz. subst." Ow/Op, D,T/S, J&S/ defenses: AS 46.03.822(b) | No; Reg. lien - AS 46.08.75 | inc. CERCLA and oil AS 46.03.826(5) |
| AL | Yes/AC 22-30A-3 (1990) | Ow/Op,G,T,D/ Proportional not J&S/S/I holder is not O, no 3rd P defense | No | inc. CERCLA-AC 22-30A-2 (6) |
| AR | Yes/RATFA:ASA 82-4715 (1987); ERFA: ASA 8-7-401 et seq (1986) | same as fed/proportional/S/I holder is not O: ASA 8-7-403(b)(2) | No-ASA 8-7-516(b); 8-7-417(b) (1989) | inc. CERCLA - ASA 82-4714 (h) |
| AZ | Yes/ARSA 49-282 (1986) "Water Quality Assurance Revolving Fund" | Same as fed./S, J+S unless RP meets b/p on its portion/ defenses and restrictions on RPs: ARSA 49-283 | No | Pollutant that may enter water exc. nuclear, workplace, engine emissions and fertilizer applic.; ARSA 49-281 |
| CA | Yes/CH&SC 25330 (1988) and CH&SC 25382 | Same as fed./S proportional acc to ct. and RP's meeting b/p | No | inc. CERCLA; CH&SC 25316 |

| Separate state List/No. of Sites | Implementing regs. | State Cost Recovery Prov/Adm. Order | PRP on Priv. Citizen c/a | Comments |
|---|---|---|---|---|
| Yes/1 | site specific consistent with NCP; AS 46.09.020 (1986) | Yes/Yes | Yes; A.S.46.03.822 | Civil and criminal penalties |
| No but auth. exists pursuant to AC 22-30A-5 | same as fed NCP guidelines | Yes/Yes 22-30A-5(1) | No | Notice and hearing reqd. before AO can be issued |
| Yes/5 | | Yes/Yes for info., site access and remediation | Yes; ASA 8-7-520 (1989) | treble damages; AO to anyone resp. for release or in control of site who has caused or contrib. to release or threatened release - ASA 8-7-409 (1989). |
| Yes/23 of which 5 are emerg. action sites | Fed. MCLs and Ariz. standards acc. to USEPA Survey | Yes/Yes-remediation, injunctive | Yes - ARSA 49-285.B | treble damages, civil penalty; surface and GW remediation only |
| Yes/328 on list with three tiers; also 1,000 unconfirmed sites on abandoned site program info. system (ASPIS) | State MCLs and Applied Action Levels (AALs) | Yes/Yes-info., site access and subpoena | Yes under Sep. Act: Proposition 65 | Civil and criminal penalties from hazardous waste management not specific superfund; treble damages |

| State | State Fund/Auth. for Fund [Cite] | PRPs/Liab. Std/Defenses | Super-Lien Prov. | "Haz. Subst." |
|-------|----------------------------------|-------------------------|------------------|---------------|
| CO | No Superfund-(repealed) | | No | |
| CT | Yes/CGS 22a-451(d) | "pers. or corp. which (in)directly causes pollution"/ S, J+S/CGS 22a-451 | Yes for emerg. cleanups- CGS 22a-452a | Haz. Waste, oil and gas; CGS 22a-452b |
| DC | No Superfund | | No | |
| DE | No Superfund | | No | |
| FL | Yes/FS: 403.165 (1990) | PRPs at least those in CERCLA, F.S. 403.727(4) (1990), but also broader, F.S. 403.727(1) (1990); Liability generally, 403.708 (1990), J/S liability, F.S. 403.141(2) (1990); Defenses, 403.727(5)-(8) (1990) | No | For cost recovery, follows CERCLA, F.S. 403.727(4) (1990), but statute defines much broader as anything hazardous to human health, F.S. 403.703(23) (1990) |

| Separate state List/No. of Sites | Implementing regs. | State Cost Recovery Prov/Adm. Order | PRP on Priv. Citizen c/a | Comments |
|---|---|---|---|---|
| None | | Yes/Yes - see comments | No | Enforcement authorization under Emerg. Resp. Fund |
| Yes/567 (inc. NPL) sites in inventory of hazardous waste disposal sites pursuant to CGS 22a-133c | | Yes/Yes | No | |
| None | | | No | Civil penalties and AO auth. for "imminent hazards" under haz. waste mgmt. law |
| Yes; 48 abandoned uncontrolled sites | | Yes/Yes (see comments) | No | Cost recovery and AO auth. for "imminent hazards" under resp. haz. waste mgmt. law and UST laws |
| Yes/over 500 - not scored | | Yes, F.S. 403.121(1) (1990)/Yes, F.S. 403.121(2) (1990); inspections and access authorized by F.S. 403.091 (1990). | No | Civil (F.S. 403.141(1) (1990)) and criminal (F.S. 403.161(3), (4) (1990) penalties. |

| State | State Fund/Auth. for Fund [Cite] | PRPs/Liab. Std/Defenses | Super-Lien Prov. | "Haz. Subst." |
|---|---|---|---|---|
| GA | No Superfund | | No | |
| HI | Yes/HRS 148.2 (1988) for Emerg. Resp. | Past and present Ow/Op, D,T/S, no J&S/defenses: HRS 143.6(4) | No | Not same as CERCLA; exc. engine, workplace and nuclear emissions; HRS 148.1 |
| IA | Yes/IC 455B.423 (1989) | T,"Pers. having control over haz. subst.,IC 455B.392/ltd. S, state arg. for J&S | No | Inc. RCRA and FWPCA-IC 455B. 381; exc. agricultural chems-IC 455B.419 |
| ID | No Superfund | | No | |
| IL | Yes/IAS ch. 111-1/2, para. 1022.2 | same as fed/state implied S, J+S/ IAS, ch.111-1/2, para. 1022.2(j) | Pending Legis. | Same as CERCLA; IAS ch. 111-1/2, para. 1003.14 |
| IN | Yes/IC 13-7-8.7-2 (1990) | same as fed/ S, J+S; also Guarantor if Ow,Op in bankruptcy | No | Same as CERCLA-IC 13.7.8.7-1. |

| Separate state List/No. of Sites | Implementing regs. | State Cost Recovery Prov/Adm. Order | PRP on Priv. Citizen c/a | Comments |
|---|---|---|---|---|
| Yes/753 | | | No | Double punitive damages, civil and criminal penalties under Waste Mgmt. Act. |
| Yes; not promulgatedas of 6/89 | Auth. pursuant to HRS 148.7 | Yes/Yes | Yes under HRS 342J-16, affected citizens have to intervene | Treble, punitive damages for failure of RP to remediate |
| Yes; 19 abandoned and uncontrolled sites (inc. NPL) | IA Adm. Code tit. 10, 133.1 et. seq. (1989) | Yes/Yes | Yes | No civil penalty, treble damages for RP's "willful failure" to clean up |
| None | | Yes/Yes; Only for emerg. conditions — see comments | Yes | Enforcement, cost recovery and priv. c/a provisions auth. by Haz. Waste Emerg. Resp. at IC 39-4413 to 39-4418 |
| Yes/29 | 35 IL Adm. Code 703.185 for GW Prot.; IAC 750.301 to 750.470 for Emerg. resp. | Yes/Yes | Maybe - refer to annot. to IAS ch.111-1/2, para. 1042 and 1022.2a(b) | Also RP Transfer Law |
| Yes; in development as of 5/89 | | Yes/Yes | Yes | Also RP Transfer Law and Hazardous Waste Disclosure IC-13-7-22.55 |

| State | State Fund/Auth. for Fund [Cite] | PRPs/Liab. Std/Defenses | Super-Lien Prov. | "Haz. Subst." |
|---|---|---|---|---|
| KS | Yes/KSA 65-3454a (1988) | "any pers. resp. for discharge"-KSA 65-3455/No J&S | No | Same as CERCLA-KSA 64-3452a |
| KY | No Superfund | | No | |
| LA | Yes/LRSA 30.2205 (1989) | OW + OP, G, T, D/S, not J+S, proportional if RP meets b/p-LRSA 30:2277 | No | Haz. Subst., no petroleum, LRSA 30:2272(4) |
| MA | Superfund enforc. but no specific fund: MGL ch. 21E | Ow/Op, T, Ker, "pers. who caused release"/S, J&S but proportional if RP meets b/p/MGL 21E-5(c) | Yes but some util. cos. are exc. MGL 21E-13 | inc. CERCLA and oil but not engine, nuclear or workplace releases, or fertilizer or pesticide applic. MGL 21E-2 |
| MD | Yes/MH-ECA 7-218 | Pres. non-govt OW/Op, past non-govt Op, G, "arrangers"/S, J+S but proportional if RP meets b/p/ MH-ECA 7-201(x)(2), 7-209 | No | "as defined by USEPA" MH-ECA 7-201(m) |
| ME | Yes/MRS tit. 38, 1364.6 (1987) | Past and pres. OW + OP, T/S, J+S/MRS tit. 38, 1367 | Yes but not over residential real estate - MRS tit. 38, 1371 | inc. CERCLA, waste oil, etc. - MRS tit. 38, 1362.1 |

| Separate state List/No. of Sites | Implementing regs. | State Cost Recovery Prov/Adm. Order | PRP on Priv. Citizen c/a | Comments |
|---|---|---|---|---|
| Yes/12 | | Yes/Yes | Yes-KSA 65-3450 est. rt. to intervene | Civil penalty, also UST regs. |
| None | | Yes/Yes - see comments | Yes - see comments | Enforcement under haz. waste mgmt. fund when emerg. arises |
| None as of 5/89 | | Yes/Yes for remediation | Yes - Ltd. to gen. cit. suits - LRSA 30:2226; PRP c/a 30:2076G | Treble damages and other liab. under other funds inc. UST Trust Fund |
| Yes/1,152 (inc. NPL) sites | Mass. Regs. Code tit. 310, 40.001 to 40.620 | Yes/Yes | Yes -MGL 21E-15 | Treble damages, civil and criminal penalties |
| None as of 5/89; Auth. exists:MH-ECA 7-223 | | Yes/Yes for entry and search not for info. or cleanup | No | Civil and criminal penalty provs. |
| Yes/317 (inc. NPL) sites of which 120 need no action, 6 have been cleaned up and 83 need cleanup | | Yes/Yes - also addit. emerg. powers under MRS tit. 38, 1368 | No | |

| State | State Fund/Auth. for Fund [Cite] | PRPs/Liab. Std/Defenses | Super-Lien Prov. | "Haz. Subst." |
|---|---|---|---|---|
| MI | Mich. Super-fund Law P.A. 307 § 12 (effective July 1, 1991). | Ow, Op, T, G/J&S but see "orphan share admin." & "alloc. process"/ defenses: P.A. 307 § 12A | No | Chem. or material injur. to h,s,w or envir., incl. CERCLA, Mich Haz. Waste Mgmt. Act, pertroleum as def. in Mich. Leaking UST Act |
| MN | Yes/MSA 115B.20 (1989) | Ow, Op,G,K'er,D, T or Possessor who knew or selected T or D/S, J&S but ct. can apportion/other parties: e.g. ER/ EE if neg.-MSA 115B.03, 115B.04(6)(7) | No-MSA (Vol. 8, Pub. Dom.) 514.671 | inc. haz. waste, FWPCA, CAA and RCRA, no gas or oil-MSA 115B.02(8)(9) but no "pollutants" or "contaminants"- MSA 115B.04(2) |
| MO | Yes/MRS 260.480 (1990) | "Pers. having control over a haz. subst." inc. bailee, carriers, etc. MRS 260.500(8)/S, no J&S/MRS 260.530.2 | No | inc. CERCLA and state haz. waste but not radioactive waste/MRS 260.500(5) |
| MS | No specific superfund Law | | No | |
| MT | Yes/MCA 75-10-704 | Ow,Op,G,T/ S,J&S unless RP meets b/p on its portion/75-10-715(5) | No | MCA 75-10-701(3) inc. CERCLA and petroleum products |

| Separate state List/No. of Sites | Implementing regs. | State Cost Recovery Prov/Adm. Order | PRP on Priv. Citizen c/a | Comments |
|---|---|---|---|---|
| Yes/2019 | | Yes, P.A. 307 § 12 | Yes, similar to CERCLA P.A. 307 § 15 | Amend. are effective July 1, 1991. |
| Yes/157 | inc. of fed. guidelines; MN R. 7044.0100 to R. 7044.1200 (1984) | Yes/Yes - info., access and injunctive | Yes - MSA 115B.08 | Civil penalty and witness and attorney's fees |
| Yes/54 abandoned, uncontrolled sites | Pending | Yes/Yes for site access and injunction | No | Criminal and civil penalties and treble punitive damages |
| None | | Yes/Yes - see comments | No | Criminal penalty and other enforcement provs. under water and air pollution and UST laws |
| Yes/149 | | Yes/Yes-info, site access, subpoena, injunctive | No | Civil penalty and punitive damages |

| State | State Fund/Auth. for Fund [Cite] | PRPs/Liab. Std/Defenses | Super-Lien Prov. | "Haz. Subst." |
|---|---|---|---|---|
| NC | Yes/NCGS 130A-310.11 (1989) | D, K'er, T, Arranger/S, no J&S/NCGS 130A-310.7(b) | No | Same as CERCLA/SARA-NCGS 130A-310 (2) but not pesticides under oil law |
| ND | No Specific fund | | No | |
| NE | No Fund | | No | |
| NH | Yes/NHRSA 147B:3 (1989) | same as fed/S/ NHRSA 147B:10-A | Yes; NHRSA 147B:10-b | Haz. Waste only; NHRSA 147B:2 VII |
| NJ | Yes/NJSA 58:10-23.11i (1988) | Discharger, any pers. in any way "resp." for dischg. of haz. subst./S, J&S | Yes/NJSA 58:10-23.11f(f) | Petroleum prods. and FWPCA; NJSA 58:10-23.11b(k) |
| NM | No general Su-perfund | | No | |
| NV | No specific Superfund | | No | |

| Separate state List/No. of Sites | Implementing regs. | State Cost Recovery Prov/Adm. Order | PRP on Priv. Citizen c/a | Comments |
|---|---|---|---|---|
| Yes/85 on State Priority List; 781 on inactive haz. waste innventory | | Yes/Yes | No but Yes under Oil and Hazardous Waste Pollution Law NCGS 143-215.89 | Civil and criminal penalties under Oil and Haz. Waste Pollution Law |
| None | | Yes/Yes - see comments | Yes under haz. waste law | No Superfund law; civil and criminal penalties and enforcement under haz. waste mgmt. act |
| No | | No/Yes for GW pollution - see comments | Only under solid waste disp. violations | No Superfund, NRS 81-1505 prohibits GW pollution and est. cleanup stds. |
| Yes/150-175 haz. waste sites | | Yes/Yes | No | |
| Yes/Auth. pursuant to NJSA 58:10-23.16 | NJ Admin. Code 7:26B-1.1 to 11.1; case by case | Yes/Yes | No | Treble damages |
| None | | Yes/Yes - see comments | No | civil, criminal penalties and enforcement through haz. waste act and UST releases |
| None | | Yes/Yes - see comments | No | Civil and criminal penalties under Haz. Waste Law enforcement |

**Superfund Process and Progress —
Superfund Liability Scheme**

| State | State Fund/Auth. for Fund [Cite] | PRPs/Liab. Std/Defenses | Super-Lien Prov. | "Haz. Subst." |
|---|---|---|---|---|
| NY | Yes but Ltd. to inactive haz. waste sites/ NYE-CL 27-1363 (1989) | same as fed/S, J+S | No | Haz. waste only - NYE-CL 27-1301:1 |
| OH | No Fund | | No | |
| OK | No Superfund | | No | |
| OR | Yes/ORS 465.380 (1989) | Ow,Op, "pers. who caused, contrib., or exacerbated release"-ORS 465.255/S, J&S un-der common law if harm indivisible | No | ORS 465.520(9) - inc. CERCLA and oil |
| PA | Yes/35 PCS 901 (1988) | Ltd. Ow,Op and others - 35 PCS 701/S, J&S/35 PCS 703, also excep-tions: 35 PCS 701(b) | No - ORS 465.335 | 35 PCS 103 - inc. CERCLA but exc. oil, workplace, nuclear and engine releases, fertilizer applic. |
| PR | Yes for emerg. resp. - PRLA 12-1271 (1987) | "any natural or juridicial pers. that exercises dominion...over haz. subst." - PRLA 12-1272(d) | No | "Any element, substance, compound or mixture that can cause harm to a liv-ing organism or to the environment" |

| Separate state List/No. of Sites | Implementing regs. | State Cost Recovery Prov/Adm. Order | PRP on Priv. Citizen c/a | Comments |
|---|---|---|---|---|
| Yes/1373 on inventory and registry of abandoned sites | | Yes/Yes | No | |
| Yes/430 (inc. NPL) sites on informal List | | Yes/Yes - see comments | Yes - see comments | Enforcement and strict liab. provisions exist in Ohio Haz. and Solid Waste Laws |
| Yes/11 | | No/Yes - see comments | No | Limited enforcement under Industrial Waste Act |
| Yes/under development as of 8/89 | OR Admin. R. 340-108-01 (1989) | Yes/Yes | Yes - PRP c/a for contrib. - ORS 465.255(5) | Punitive damages; civil penalty; notice of clean-up action reqd. 465.320 |
| None listed as of 8/89 | | Yes/Yes | Yes - 35 PCS 1115 | Treble damages |
| None | | Yes/Yes | Not in statute | |

| State | State Fund/Auth. for Fund [Cite] | PRPs/Liab. Std/Defenses | Super-Lien Prov. | "Haz. Subst." |
|---|---|---|---|---|
| RI | Yes but Ltd. to haz.,waste remediation/RIGL 23-19.1-23 | T, D, S/"absolute" as S, J+S | No | Haz. waste only - RIGL 23-19.1-4(4) |
| SC | Yes/Ltd. to remediation of hazardous waste | Ow,Op,G,T/not specified | No | Haz. waste only: SCCA 44-56-20(b) |
| SD | Yes but may be Ltd. only to UST releases/SDCL 34A-12-3 (1989) | Pres Op and Ow, Pers who "caused the discharge of a reg. substance"/S, no J+S | Lien over all except prev. perfected liens; SDCL 34A-12-13 (1989) | "Reg. subst." inc. CERCLA, CWA and petroleum - SDCL 34A-12-1(8) |
| TN | Yes/TCA 68-46-207(f) (1987) | Same as fed/S, no J+S, "equitably" proportional/TCA 68-46-207 | No - Lien ltd. to prospec- tive claims - TCA 68-46-208 | Same as CERCLA-TCA 68-46-202(3); but not applic. of pesticide - TCA 68-46-207(f) |
| TX | Yes/TWCA 26.265 (1985) | Past and Pres Ow, "any other pers. who causes, suf- fers, allows or per- mits a spill or dischg."/S, J&S but proportional if RP meets b/p on its portion | No - TH&SCA 4477-7-13(7) | as defined in CERCLA-TWCA 26.263(4) |

**Environmental
Risk Management**

| Separate state List/No. of Sites | Implementing regs. | State Cost Recovery Prov/Adm. Order | PRP on Priv. Citizen c/a | Comments |
|---|---|---|---|---|
| Yes/258 uncon-firmed abandoned/ uncontrolled sites | Pursuant to R.I.G.L. 23-19.1-24 | Yes/Yes - see comments | No | Punitive, treble damages, criminal penalty for violation of permit laws |
| Yes/42 | | Yes/Yes - site access, info. | No | Treble damages, civil and criminal penalties - disclosure requirements |
| No | USEPA stds. acc. to state auth.; also Petroleum Release Rules SD Adm. R. 74:32:01 - 74:32:05:13 | Yes/Yes - info., site access and injunctive | No | Civil and criminal penalties |
| Yes/281 of which 3 are in rule making stage, 800-900 suspected sites of which 688 have PA's done - list found at TCR&R 1200-1-13.03 | Tenn. Comp. R&Regs. ch. 1200-1-13 (1988) | Yes/Yes - info., access and re-medial response | No | Punitive damages of 150% of liab. amt. |
| Yes/28 | "Lowest cost alt. tech. feas."; state ARARs acc. to USEPA Survey | Yes/Yes injunctive | Yes/under solid waste act TH&SCA 4477-7-9 | double damages, civil and criminal penalties |

| State | State Fund/Auth. for Fund [Cite] | PRPs/Liab. Std/Defenses | Super-Lien Prov. | "Haz. Subst." |
|-------|----------------------------------|-------------------------|------------------|---------------|
| UT | Yes/UCA 26-14d-3 (1989) | Ow,Op,D,T except not common or K carrier/S, Proportional, express (not J+S)/UCA 26-14d-402 | No | Same as CERCLA - UCA 26-14d-102(9) |
| VA | Yes/VCA 10-270 (1988) | same as fed/not specified | No - VCA 10.1-1406.C | inc. CERCLA and petroleum products; VCA 10-105(c)(20) |
| VT | No Superfund | See comments | No | |
| WA | Yes/WRC 70.105D.070 (1989) | Ow/Op, Possessor, T,D,Seller, pers. responsible for written instructions for use/S, J&S/ WRC 70.105D.040 | No | inc. CERCLA and petroleum, etc. - WRC 70.105D.020(5) |
| WI | Yes but Ltd. to remediation of solid, haz. waste/ WSA 144.442 (1987) | Pres and Past OW and pers. whose actions caused or contributed to the conditions resulting in liab/ S, no express J+S- refer to common law | No | Haz. Waste only-WSA 144.43(2) |

| Separate state List/No. of Sites | Implementing regs. | State Cost Recovery Prov/Adm. Order | PRP on Priv. Citizen c/a | Comments |
|---|---|---|---|---|
| Yes reqd. by UCA 26-14d-501/but not promulgated as of 8/89 | Same as fed. guidelines - UCA 26-14d-601 | Yes/Yes | Yes/PRP c/a - UCA 26-14d-702(3) | civil penalty |
| No | | Yes/Yes | No | Civil and criminal penalty provisions under solid waste act |
| Yes/122 hazardous waste sites | | | No | VT. Solid Waste Mgmt. Law provides limited enforcement of hazardous waste cleanup |
| Yes/700 on state database inc. NPL, state and already cleaned up sites | Wash. Adm. Code 173-336 to 173-340 (1988) | Yes/Yes | Yes/priv. cit. c/a - WRC 70.105D.050 (5)(a) | Civil penalty and treble damages |
| Yes/60 | Wisc. Adm. Code NR 550.01 to NR 550.550 (Jan. 1987) | Yes/Yes | No | Civil and criminal penalties |

| State | State Fund/Auth. for Fund [Cite] | PRPs/Liab. Std/Defenses | Super-Lien Prov. | "Haz. Subst." |
|-------|----------------------------------|-------------------------|------------------|---------------|
| WV | Yes-Ltd. to haz. waste emerg. resp./WVC 20-5G-3 (1990) | G and others under haz. waste act/ not specified | No | Haz. waste only, WVC 2--5E-3(7) |
| WY | No Superfund | | No | |

| Separate state List/No. of Sites | Implementing regs. | State Cost Recovery Prov/Adm. Order | PRP on Priv. Citizen c/a | Comments |
|---|---|---|---|---|
| None | | Yes/Yes under Haz. Waste Act | Yes under Haz. Waste Act | Civil and criminal penalties |
| None | | Yes/Yes - see comments | No - only if c/a exists in fed. dist. ct. under Env. Qlty. Act | Enforcement and civil and criminal penalty provisions exist in the Wyo. Env. Qlty. Act as part of waste mgmt. law. |

## About the Author

Eric B. Rothenberg is a partner and New York Section Leader in the 80-lawyer Morgan, Lewis & Bockius Environmental Practice Group which has attorneys located in its New York, Washington, D.C., Philadelphia, Harrisburg, Miami and Los Angeles offices. He is a graduate of Harvard University (B.A.), the Harvard School of Public Health (M.P.H.) and Northeastern University Law School (J.D.). He was an environmental engineer and consultant for three years before practicing law. He is currently active in all areas of the firm's environmental practice including risk assessments in conjunction with lending, securities, financial and other business transactions, hazardous substance litigation and regulatory counseling.

## Endnotes

1. Inside EPA *Weekly Report*, Vol. 11, p. 1 (November 2, 1990). The additional year in the taxing provision comports with the rest of the budget deficit reduction package which terminates in 1995.

2. *See United States v. Chem-dyne, Inc.* 572 F. Supp. 802, 897 n.3 (S.D. Ohio 1983); *United ed States v. A & F Materials, Inc.*, 578 F. Supp. 1249, 1261 (S.D. Ill. 1984); and *Wehner v. Syntex Agribusiness, Inc.*, 616 F. Supp. 27, 30-31 (E.D. Mo. 1985).

3. *See U.S. v. Monsanto*, 858 F. 2d 160 (4th Cir. 1988) *cert. denied* 109 S. Ct. 3156 (1989).

4. *U.S. V. Northernaire Plating Co.*, No. G84-1113CA7 (W.D. Mich. 1989 (one third of cleanup cost allocated to owner of site while two-third allocated to electroplating facilities lessees and operators); *but see United States v. Monsanto Co.*, supra at 173 (defendant's volumetric evidence was insufficient to afford basis for dividing <u>harm</u> at the site); *U.S. v. Bliss*, No. 84-2086C-(i) (E.D. Mo. 1988); and *O'Neil v. Picillo*, 883 F.2d 176 (1st Cir. 1989), *cert. denied*, 110 S. Ct. 1115 (1990) (two non-settling defendants were held liable for all outstanding past & future costs, although each had sent minimal amounts of waste to site--they had not proved divisibility of harm.)

5. 899 F.2d 79 (1st Cir. 1990) (non-settlers asked by government to pay a premium were not allowed to challenge prior government settlements with *de minimis* parties on more favorable terms). *See, e.g. Levin Metals Corp. v. Parr-Richmond Terminal Co.*, 799 F.2d 1312, 1316 (9th Cir. 1986); *U.S. v. Northeastern Pharmaceutical and Chemical Co. (NEPACCO)*, 810 F.2d 726, 732, n.3 (8th Cir. 1986), *cert. denied*, 108 S. Ct. 146 (1987).

6. *See e.g. United States v. Bell Petroleum Services, Inc.*, 734 F. Supp. 771 (W.D. Tex. 1990). The italic terms are defined in Section III hereunder.

## Environmental
## Risk Management

7. *United States v. Monsanto Company*, 858 F.2d 160 (4th Cir. 1988) *cert. denied, supra.; Tanglewood East Homeowners v. Charles Thomas, Inc.*, 849 F.2d 1568 (5th Cir. 1988).

8. *See U.S. v. Stringfellow*, 661 F. Supp. 1053 (C.D. Cal. 1987), *United States v. Monsanto*, 858 F.2d 160 (4th Cir. 1988).

9. *See* CERCLA § 101(14).

10. *See* CERCLA § 101(33).

11. *See* Memorandum from F.S. Blake, EPA General Counsel to J.W. Porter, Assistant Administrator for The Office of Solid Waste and Emergency Response (OSWER) (July 31, 1987).

12. *See Wilshire Westwood Assoc. v. Arco*, 881 F.2d. 801 (9th Cir. 1989).

13. *See* P.L. 101-380, *Congressional Record* H6233 (August 1, 1990).

14. *See* Section 1001(23).

15. *See U.S. v. Nicolet, Inc.* (E.D. Pa.), Andrews, *Hazardous Waste Litigation Reporter* (*HWLR*), p. 17658 (August 7, 1989).

16. *3550 Stevens Creek Assoc. v. Barclays Bank of Ca.* No. CV87-20672-RPA, (9th Cir. October 3, 1990).

17. *See Dayton Independence School District v. U.S. Mineral Products Company* (5th Cir. 1990), 5 *Toxics Law Reporter (TXLR)* (BNA), page 345 (August 8, 1990).

18. *United States v. Northernaire Plating Co.*, 670 F. Supp. 742 (W.D. Mich. 1987). *See also Dedham Water Co. v. Cumberland Farms Dairy, Inc.*, 889 F.2d 1146 (1st Cir. 1989), (potential release of hazardous substances from deteriorating containers).

19. *United States v. Vertac Chemical Corp.*, 671 F. Supp. 595 (E.D. Ark. 1987), *Dedham Water Co. v. Cumberland Farms Dairy, Inc.*, Op. Cit. (continued leaching of hazardous substances from a pipeline).

20. *Amoco Oil Co. v. Borden, Inc.*, 889 F.2d 664 (5th Cir. 1989), (Some threshold must be exceeded).*But see City of New York V. Exxon Corp.*, No. 85 Civ. 1939(KC) (S.D.N.Y. Aug. 7, 1990). (A release in any amount or concentration is actionable.)

21. *Emhart Industries, Inc. v. Duracell International Inc.*, 665 F. Supp. 549 (M.D. Tenn. 1987).

22. *Tanglewood East Homeowners v. Charles-Thomas, Inc.*, 849 F.2d 1568 (5th Cir. 1988).

23. *Id., United States v. Stringfellow*, 661 F. Supp. 1053 (C.D. Cal. 1987).

24. *Kempf v. City of Lansing*, (W.D. Mich. 1990) 5 *TXLR* (BNA) 287 (August 1, 1990).

Similarly, in *Ecodyne Corp. v. Shah*, 718 F. Supp. 1454 (N.D. Cal. 1989) (a passive owner (Shah) who did not dispose of hazardous substances at a site was not responsible for subsequent release of such substances after conveyance of the property on the theory that Shah had never been an owner at the time of disposal).

25. *United States v. Monsanto*, 858 F.2d 160 (4th Cir. 1988); *United States v. Northernaire*, 670 F. Supp. 742, 748 (W.D. Mich. 1987) *aff'd sub nom. United States v. R.W. Meyer, Inc.*, 889 F.2d 1497 (6th Cir. 1990).

26. *United States v. Union Gas Co.*, 832 F.2d 1343 (3rd Cir. 1987), *aff'd*, U.S., 109 S. Ct. 2273 (1989).

27. *Sunnen Products Co. v. Chemtech Industries. Inc.*, 658 F. Supp. 276 (E.D. Mo. 1987).

28. *City of Philadelphia v. Stepan Chemical Co.*, 1987 Westlaw 16690 (September 3, 1987).

29. *Edward Hines Lumber Co. v. Vulcan Materials Co.*, 861 F.2d 155 (7th Cir. 1988). (Contractor that designed a facility, trained the facility's employees to operate the machinery therein, licensed the owner of the facility to use its trademark in connection with the facility's processes, and supplied the facility with raw materials, was held not to be an operator of the facility because the facility owner continued to exercise day-to-day control, hire employees, and make all production decisions.) In *Steppleworth v. Refuse Hideaway, Inc.*, (Wisc. Cir. Ct. 1990), an environmental consultant which disagreed and operated groundwater monitoring wells according to the State environmental agency's specifications was held not liable in a suit by adjoining landowners, *see* 5 *TXLR* (BNA) 816 (Nov. 28, 1990).

30. *United States v. Conservation Chemical Co.*, 619 F. Supp. 162 (W.D. Mo. 1985).

31. *United States v. A&F Materials, Inc.*, 582 F. Supp. 842 (S.D. Ill. 1984). (Liability for shipments of waste sodium hydroxide.)

32. *TXLR* (BNA) page 1156 (March 14, 1990). *See also United States v. Sharon Steel Corp.*, Civil No. 86-C-924J (D. Utah May 17, 1989), (seller of commercial unprocessed mining ores containing hazardous substances not liable for contamination resulting from purchasers use); *Amland Properties Corp. v. Aluminum Company of America*, 711 F. Supp. 784 (D.N.J. 1989), (sale of PCB transformers does not constitute generation of waste), and *Prudential Insurance Company v. U.S. Gypsum*, 711 F. Supp. 1244 (D.N.J. 1989), (sale of asbestos products did not constitute generation).

33. *United States v. Bliss*, 661 F. Supp. 1298 (E.D. Mo. 1987).

34. *United States v. Aceto*, 872 F.2d 1371 (8th Cir. 1989). (Company held liable for contamination caused by its pesticide formulator and refiner).

35. 655 F. Supp. 1257 (D.N.J. 1987) (company liable as generator for shipment of waste created by prior landowner), *aff'd*,___ F. 2d. (3d Cir. Dec. ___, 1988).

36. *United States v. Union Gas Co.*, 832 F.2d 1343 (3d Cir. 1987), *aff'd*, 109 S. Ct. 2273 (1989), (Corps of Engineers liable for contamination caused by damage to dike which also served as wall to waste containment cell.) *Dickerson Inc. v. U.S.* (11th Cir. 1989), 4 *TXLR* (BNA) 229 (August 2, 1989).

37. *Interim Municipal Settlement Policy*, 54 Fed. Reg. 51071 (December 12, 1989). The policy is intended to be consistent with a 1988 RCRA directive that household trash should not be considered a hazardous waste even if its contents would render it a "characteristic" material. The policy also observes that generators of sewage sludge and incinerator ash derived from household waste will be exempt from Superfund liability even though such waste streams may contain hazardous substances in sufficient concentrations to render them hazardous waste under RCRA criteria. The policy is intended to govern Federal enforcement only and specifically reserves to the courts a determination as to whether private parties may still maintain cost recovery actions or contribution claims against otherwise exempt municipal generators. The financial impact of the policy may be extremely significant in light of the fact that 25% of the sites on the National Priorities List contain waste from potentially exempt municipal generators. It is possible that at some sites which receive waste predominantly from exempt municipal generators, total volume of hazardous substances contributed by municipalities is actually greater than that contributed by industrial sources, even though such industrial contributions would have been in more concentrated form. For this and other reasons, the policy has been challenged by groups of industrial generators such as those associated with a Connecticut landfill in *B.F. Goodrich and Co. v. Murtha*, (D. Conn. 1989), *see* 5 *TXLR* (BNA), page 182 (July 11, 1990).

38. *United States v. NEPACCO Inc.*, 810 F.2d 726 (8th Cir. 1986), *cert. denied*, 108 S. Ct. 146 (1987); *U.S. v. Nicolet, Inc.*, 4 *TXLR* (BNA) 46 (E.D. Pa.); *United States v. Bliss,____ F. Supp.,___* 16 *Chemical Waste Litigation Reporter* (hereinafter *CWLR*) 1061 (E.D. Mo. September 27, 1988.)

39. *Michigan v. Arco Industries*, 723 F. Supp. 1214 (W.D. Mich. 1989). *But see Joslyn Mfg. v. T.L. James & Co.* 696 F. Supp. 722 (W.D. La. 1988), *aff'd* 893 F.2d 80 (5th Cir. 1990) (no officer liability absent actual personal participation), *United States v. Northernaire Plating Co.*, 670 F. Supp. 742 (W.D. Mich. 1987) *aff'd sub nom supra.*; *Vermont v. Staco*, 684 F.Supp. 822, 835 (D. Vt. 1988).

40. *U.S. v. McGraw Edison Co.*, (W.D.N.Y. 1989) 4 *TXLR* (BNA) 377 (49% owner liable).

41. *See Kelley v. Thomas Solvent Company*, 727 F. Supp. 1532, 1543-44 (W.D. Mich. 1989), *Quadion Corp. v. Mache et al.*, (N.D. Ill. 1990), Andrews, *HWLR* p. 19339 (July 2, 1990).

42. *U.S. v. Kayser-Roth Corp.* (1st Cir. 1990) 5 *TXLR* (BNA) 369 (August 15, 1990) (Parent held liable because it had the capacity to control subsidiary's waste disposal and other environmental matters including the release of hazardous wastes at the facility.) *State of Idaho v. Bunker Hill Co.*, 635 F. Supp. 665 (D. Idaho 1986), *see also, U.S. v. Nicolet Inc.*, (E.D. Pa. 1989), 4 *TXLR* (BNA) p. 46 (June 14, 1989). This "operator" theory of parent liability was recently recognized in *U.S. v. Allied Chemical Corp.* (N.D. Cal. 1990), 5 *TXLR* 286 (August 1, 1990) when the court denied motion for summary judgement by

parent. *Colorado v. Idarado Mining Co.*, 18 Env't. Rpt. Cas. (BNA) 20578 (D. Col. April 29, 1987).

43. Where a parent shared common officers and directors with its subsidiary and exerted "practical total influence" over finances and business activities, the parent was held liable as an "owner" for $850,000 in cost-reimbursement and future costs associated with the subsidiary's discharge and improper disposal of trichloroethylene. *United States v. Kayser-Roth Corp.* 724 F. Supp. 15 (D.R.I. 1989), 4 *TXLR* (BNA) 622 (October 25, 1989), *aff'd, see supra.* Another court applied a uniform federal rule of decision in refusing to pierce the corporate veil because the parent did not exercise the requisite degree of control over a subsidiary that it formed to purchase the assets of a company that caused PCB contamination. *In re Alleged PCB Pollution of Acushnet River*, 675 F. Supp. 22 (D. Mass. 1987). Most recently, the Fifth Circuit refused to pierce the corporate veil and hold the parent liable without a specific congressional directive or absent a showing that the subsidiary was established as part of a sham transaction (a directive which it did not find in CERCLA). *Joslyn Corp. v. James & Co. Inc.*, 893 F.2d 80 (5th Cir. 1990).

44. *Smith Land & Improvement Corp. v. The Celotex Corp.*, 851 F.2d 86 (3rd Cir. 1988), *cert. denied* 57 U.S.L.W. 3471 (Jan. 17, 1989), *In re Acushnet River and New Bedford Harbor*, 712 F. Supp. 1010 (D. Mass. 1989). A different result was reached, however, in *Anspec Co. v. Johnson Controls, Inc.*, 30 Env't Rep. Cas. (BNA) 1672 (E.D. Mich. 1989, appeal pending (6th Cir. 1990), where a court found that a merged company could not be held liable for the environmental contamination caused by one of its pre-merger component companies absent express statutory liability for "successor corporations".

45. *Kelle v. Thomas Solvent Company*, 727 F. Supp. 1532 (W.D. Mich. 1989), Andrews *HWLR* p. 13817 (January 2, 1989). *See also United States v. Vertac Chemical Corp.*, 671 F. Supp. 595 (E.D. Ark. 1987) (court applied "mere continuation" and "defacto merger" doctrines to hold successor corporation liable). In *Louisiana-Pacific Corporation v. Asarco*, however, the 9th Circuit dismissed an action against L-Bar Products, Inc., a company which acquired the assets of an Asarco predecessor which had marketed Asarco's slag waste (thereby resulting a Superfund liability) but where L-Bar did not continue the business of the predecessor which had resulted in the Superfund claim, *see* 909 F.2d 1260, 5 *TXLR* (BNA), page 251 (July 25, 1990). In *U.S. v. Western Processing* (W.D. Wash. 1990), the court denied a summary judgment motion by a successor to a dissolved waste disposal company alleged to be liable under a "federal common law mere continuation theory" 5 *TXLR* (BNA) 769 (Nov. 14, 1990).

46. 681 F. Supp. 1492 (D. Utah 1988). Sharon Steel has sought reconsideration of the court's denial of its motion to dismiss the government's Superfund claim, Andrews, *HWLR* 17660 (August 7, 1989).

47. *See Providence and Worcester Railroad Company v. The Penn Central Corporation*, 4 *TXLR* (BNA) 267 (D. Mass.) (August 9, 1989), *reh'g den.* 5 *TXLR* (BNA) 440 (August 29, 1990) where the Court dismissed an action against the post-reorganization successor to Penn Central Transportation Company. To the same effect, is a recent decision in *Kentucky v. Distler* (W.D. Ky.) dismissing a claim against a successor to a dissolved cor-

poration (all contamination had occurred prior to the time of dissolution), *see* Inside EPA's *Superfund Report*, p. 7 (March 28, 1990).

48. 42 U.S.C. § 9601(20)(A).

49. *United States v. Maryland Bank & Trust Co.*, 632 F. Supp. 573 (D. Md. 1986).

50. 54 *Fed. Reg.* 34235 (August 18, 1989).

51. *See Silresim Trust et al. v. State Street Bank & Trust et al.*, (D. Mass. 1989), Andrews, *HWLR*, p. 17170 (May 1, 1989), *Polger et al. v. Republic National Bank et al.* (D. Colo. 1989) Andrews, *HWLR*, 17169 (May 1, 1989); *Tanglewood East Homeowners v. Charles Thomas, Inc.*, 849 F.2d 1568 (5th Cir. 1988).

52. *Kelley, Attorney General State of Michigan v. Manufacturers National Bank of Detroit, et al.*, (W.D. Mich. 1990), Andrews, *Lender Liability Litigation Reporter* (LLLR) 3286 (August 14, 1990) (where the bank is alleged to have controlled waste management decisions as a member of the Borrowers Board of Directors); *see also United States v. Mirabile*, 15 Env't. Law Rep. 20994 (E.D. Pa. 1985).

53. 910 F.2d 668 (August 28, 1990).

54. *Id.* at 672.

55. 901 F.2d 1550 (11th Cir. 1990), *reh'g denied*, (July 17, 1990), Andrews, *LLLR* p. 19,196 (June 4, 1990).

56. *See* 5 *TXLR* (BNA) 324 (August 1, 1990).

57. Inside EPA *Superfund Report*, p. 1 (August 10, 1990).

58. *Ohio v. Kovacs*, 469 U.S. 274 (1985).

59. *See In re Commerce Oil Company*, 27 ERC 1801 (6th Cir. 1988), *but see In re: Chateaugay Corp. Reomar, Inc., The LVT Corp. et al.* 1990 U.S. Dist. LEXIS 2883 (S.D.N.Y. 1990) (costs related to a pre-petition release are dischargeable); *In re Wisconsin Barge Lines Inc.* (E.D. Mo. 1986) Andrews *HWLR* p. 13,514 (Nov. 7, 1988) (fine related to pre-petition conduct is dischargeable).

60. *Midlantic Bank v. New Jersey Department of Environmental Protection*, 474 U.S. 494 (1986), *but see In re Smith Douglas*, 75 B.R. 994 (E.D.N.C. 1987); *aff'd* 856 F.2d 102 (4th Cir. 1988) (abandonment allowed where debtor lacked unencumbered assets with which to finance cleanup and the government failed to show facility presented an imminent endangerment to health or the environment).

61. *See Juniper Development Group v. Kahn* (D.C.Mass. 1989), 4 *TXLR* (BNA) 655 (Nov. 1, 1989); *see also U.S. v. Fred Webb, Inc.* (D.C.N.C. 1989) 4 *TXLR* 652 (November 1, 1989) (Action against innocent purchaser of contaminated land acquired from bankruptcy estate.

62. *See Wisconsin v. Better Brite Plating, Inc.*, (Wisc. 1990), <u>appeal granted</u>, 5 *TXLR* (BNA), page 740 (November 7, 1990). On appeal, defendants have argued that no parties will be willing to serve as trustees if they may be charged with individual liability for hazardous substance contamination at the bankrupt's estate.

63. CERCLA Section 104.

64. CERCLA Section 106.

65. CERCLA Section 107.

66. 40 C.F.R. Part 300.

67. 47 *Fed. Reg.* 31180 (July 16, 1982).

68. 55 *Fed. Reg.* 8,666. Policy and guidance elucidating the NCP can be found in the final rule, the earlier proposed rule which appeared on December 21, 1988, 53 *Fed. Reg.* 51394, and in policy documents produced by the Office of Solid Waste and Emergency Response (OSWER) referred to from time to time in the text.

69. CERCLA Section 105(a)(8)(B).

70. *See* NCP, 40 C.F.R. § 300.425(a)(1). Any person may petition EPA to conduct a preliminary assessment of the site to determine its eligibility for the NPL. CERCLA Section 105(d). The state where the site is located must enter into an agreement with EPA to ensure its participation and financial commitment (50 percent for publicly owned or operated sites and 10 percent for all others).

71. *United States v. Eagle-Picher*, 759 F.2d 922 (D.C. Cir. 1985) (EPA's decision will be upheld unless arbitrary or capricious).

72. CERCLA Section 105(c).

73. Final revision signed on Nov. 11, 1990.

74. *See*, Inside EPA *Superfund Report*, p. 18 (July 4, 1990).

75. *See* EPA *Preliminary Assessment Guidance Fiscal Year 1988*, OSWER Directive 9345.0-01 (January, 1988).

76. *See* EPA *Guidance Conducting Remedial Investigations and Feasibility Studies Under CERCLA*, (Interim Final Draft) OSWER Directive No. 9355.3-01 (September, 1988).

77. 40 C.F.R. § 300.430(e)(9).

78. *See Superfund Public Health Evaluation Manual* (Dec., 1989).

79. *See* 4 *TXLR* (BNA) 663 (November 1, 1989).

80. 52 *Fed. Reg.* 32498 (August 27, 1987). The General Accounting Office has found that 26 states have promulgated numerical standards covering a total of 260 contaminants.

81. *See generally Interim Guidance on Compliance With Applicable or EPA Relevant and Appropriate Requirements* (ARARS), OSWER Directive 9234.0-05 (July 9, 1987), and *Draft Guidance on CERCLA Compliance With Other Laws*, OSWER Directive 9234.1-01 (August 8, 1988) (includes charts of potentially applicable ARARs).

82. *See* 40 C.F.R. § 141.50 through § 141.51 (40 new MCLGs proposed in 1987, 50 *Fed. Reg.* 46936).

83. Standards established for 30 new substances to date, 40 C.F.R. § 141.11 - § 141.16; 61 new MCLs were due by 1989 under the 1986 SDWA amendments.

84. *See* NCP 40 C.F.R. § 300.430(e)(2).

85. The states are New York, New Jersey, California, Kentucky, Ohio, New Mexico, Colorado, and Pennsylvania, *see Inside EPA*, page 4, (August 3, 1990).

86. *See* 40 C.F.R. § 300.430(f)(i)(ii)(c).

87. For groundwater operable units, *see* EPA *Draft Guidance on Remedial Actions do Contaminated Groundwater at Superfund Sites*, OSWER Directive No. 9283.1-2 (September 29, 1986).

88. *See* Inside EPA, *Superfund Report*, page 1, August 3, 1990.

89. 55 *Fed. Reg.* 30798.

90. U.S. Congress, Office of Technology Assessment, *Are We Cleaning Up?* OTA-ITE 362 (Washington, D.C.: U.S. Government Printing Office, June, 1988).

91. *See* U.S. Congress, Office of Technology Assessment *Coming Clean* (October 1989). *See also* Environmental Defense Fund, *Right Train, Wrong Track: Failed Leadership in the Superfund Clean-Up Program* (June 20, 1988).

92. OSWER directive 9835.13 (June 20, 1990).

93. *See* EPA *Interim Guidance on Notice Letters, Negotiations, and Information Exchange*, OSWER Directive No. 9834.10, 53 *Fed. Reg.* 5298 (February 23, 1988).

94. *See* EPA *PRP Search Manual*, OSWER Directive No. 9834.6 (August 27, 1987) for search specifications.

95. *See* CERCLA Section 122(e)(3).

96. *See* EPA *Interim Guidelines for Preparing Nonbinding Preliminary Allocations of Responsibility*, OSWER Directive No. 9839.1 (May 28, 1987).

97. *See* EPA *Interim Guidance on Settlement with De Minimis Waste Contributors under Section 122(g) of SARA*, OSWER Directive No. 9834.7, 52 *Fed. Reg.* 24333 (June 19, 1987).

98. CERCLA Section 122(g)(l)(B), *see*, *Guidance on Landowner Liability*, EPA (June 6, 1989).

99. *See* for example a recent settlement providing for a *de minimis* payment from current "innocent landowner" Kaiser Aluminum in *U.S. v. Deere and Co.* (DC N. Okl. 1989) 3 *TXLR* (BNA) 107 (June 28, 1989). A further guidance document "Methodologies for Implementation of CERCLA Section 122(g)(i)(A) *De Minimis* Waste Contributor Settlements" was issued on December 20, 1989, OSWER Directive No. 9834.7-1B to encourage the USEPA Regions to consider *de minimis* settlements.

100. *See* EPA "Model Settlement Document", 52 *Fed. Reg.* 43393 (November 12, 1987).

101. On August 21, 1987, EPA approved the first post-SARA *de minimis* settlement in *United States v. Ottati & Goss, et al.* (D.N.H. 1987). One *de minimis* PRP agreed to pay the federal government $270,000 and the State of New Hampshire $30,000, in exchange for which it obtained a complete release. *See* Andrews *HWLR*, p. 11,411 (September 7, 1987). EPA also approved a *de minimis* settlement for the Massachusetts and New Hampshire Cannon's Engineering Sites in which 313 parties will pay an estimated $14.6 million. *See* 53 *Fed. Reg.* 4070 (February 11, 1988), *TXLR* (BNA), page 338 (August 10, 1988). A settlement in connection with the McKin site in Gray, Maine, *See United States v. Dingwell* (D. Me. 1988), provides that 100 *de minimis* generators (responsible for less than 6,000 gallons) out of 320 PRPs will receive an expanded covenant in consideration for a 50% premium above their *pro rata* share. EPA approved a *de minimis* settlement in *United States v. Rohm & Haas Co., Inc.* (D.N.J. 1988) where 10 *de minimis* parties signed a partial consent decree providing $3.1 million for cleanup of a New Jersey landfill. *See* Andrews *HWLR* p. 13,095 (August 5, 1988). A consent decree filed in *U.S. v. Browning-Ferris Industries* (M.D. La. 1989), 4 *TXLR* (BNA) page 380 (Sept. 6, 1989) provides that BFI as a less than 1.6 percent volume low toxicity waste generator will receive a release from past and future USEPA cleanup claims in consideration for a $185,000 payment. Large quantity defendants remain liable for over $2.6 million in governmental costs incurred. A consent decree filed in *U.S. v. American Standard Co.* (W.D. Ark. 1989), provides for a broad, *de minimis* release of 6 defendants found to dispose of less than 12 thousand gallons of waste, Andrews *HWLR* 17,590 (July 17, 1989).

102. *See* EPA Guidelines for Mixed Funding Settlements under CERCLA, 53 *Fed. Reg.* 8279 (March 14, 1988).

103. Preauthorization settlements: (1) On August 24, 1987, EPA approved the first preauthorization mixed-funding settlement in *United States v. U.T. Alexander* (S.D. Tex. 1987) in which 22 of 24 companies agreed to perform a surface cleanup of the Motco site in Galveston, Texas at an estimated cost of $44.4 million. EPA has promised to reimburse PRP's 21% of the total cost. *See* Andrews *HWLR*, p. 11,413 (September 7, 1987); (2) On November 2, 1987, EPA approved a preauthorization mixed funding settlement in connection with the McAdoo, Pennsylvania Superfund site in which 64

companies agreed to be liable for 75% of an estimated $1.1-2.7 million dollar cleanup with an additional amount to be paid by Superfund. *See* Andrews *HWLR*, p. 11,903 (December 21, 1987); (3) In December, 1987, EPA preauthorized a claim against the Fund for 33% of an estimated $10 million cleanup in connection with the Harvey and Knotts Superfund site in Delaware, *United States v. General Motors Corp.* (D. Del. 1987). *See TXLR* (BNA) page 1343 (May 4, 1988). In June 1988, EPA filed suit seeking recovery of its past costs from non-signatory PRPs. *TXLR* (BNA), page 178 (July 6, 1988); (4) Under a Consent Decree filed December 21, 1988, eight PRP's agreed to fund 93% of an estimated $20 million cleanup, *U.S. v. New Castle County* (D. Del. No. 80-489), *TXLR* (BNA), page 1080 (Feb. 9, 1989); (5) Under a Consent Decree filed Feb. 9, 1989 in *U.S. v. Adac Corp.* (D. Mass. 1989), 223 companies agreeing to perform a $31 million cleanup were authorized to seek 31% of their costs from the Fund, an amount the Agency deemed proportionate to the share of 38 non-settling PRPs, 3 *TXLR* (BNA) 1166 (Feb. 22, 1989).

Mixed-Work Settlements: (1) Under a Consent Decree in *U.S. v. Stouffer Chemical Co.* (D. Mass. 1988), EPA agreed to use proceeds from the sale of property at the contaminated site to fund a portion of the remedy, 3 *TXLR* (BNA) 1119 (Feb. 15, 1989); (2) EPA has approved mixed-work mixed funding settlements in which it has agreed to bear the cost of the initial remedial investigation. *United States v. Air Products and Chemicals, Inc.* (D. Md.) and the Harold Dellett PCB Cleanup, Escondido, California. *See* 53 *Fed. Reg.* 9807 (March 25, 1988), Andrews *HWLR*, p. 12,336 (March 21, 1988); (3) In *United States v. Absolute Fire Protection Co.* (D.N.J. 1988), EPA's proposed consent decree provides that 226 companies will reimburse the United States for $5 million EPA incurred cleaning up the Kin-Buc landfill. The United States will pursue future costs from non-settlers; (4) A partial settlement in *United States v. Thomas Solvent Co. et al.* (W.D. Mich. 1986) provides for payment by defendant Grand Trunk Western Railroad of 75% of the government's response costs, with the remaining percentage and all future costs to be recovered from other defendants, *see* Andrews *HWLR*, p. 13,503 (Nov. 7, 1988); (5) A consent decree filed in *U.S. v. Ottati and Goss. Inc.* provides that the government will remain liable for groundwater remediation at a New Hampshire drum reconditioning site, *see* 4 *TXLR* (BNA) 241 (Aug. 2, 1989); (6) Under a consent decree approved in connection with PCB cleanup in *U.S. v. Pacific Hide & Depot, Inc.* (D. Idaho 1989), 4 TXLR 254 (Aug. 2, 1989), defendant Idaho Power Company will finance a site cleanup while non-settling defendants will remain liable for cost reimbursement, site maintenance and oversight.

104. *See* "Model Administrative Order on Consent for CERCLA Remedial Investigation/Feasibility Study" OSWER Directive No. 9835.3-1A (June 30, 1990).

105. *See* "A Critical Analysis of EPA's Model AOC for RI/FS Work," Information Network for Superfund Settlements (May 1990).

106. *United States V. Cannons Engineering Corp.,* 720 F. Supp. 1027 (D. Mass. 1989), *In Re Acushnet River & New Bedford Harbor,* 712 F. Supp. 1019 (D. Mass. 1989); *United States v. McGraw-Edison Co.,* 30 Env't Rep. Cas. (BNA) 1487 (W.D.N.Y. 1989); *United States v. Nicolet Inc.,* Civil Action No. 85-3060 (E.D. Pa., August 15, 1989); *Kelley v. Thomas Solvent,* Case No. 86-164 (W.D. Mich. June 5, 1989).

107. *In re Acushnet & New Bedford Harbor*, 712 F. Supp. 1019 (D. Mass. 1989), *United States v. Fairchild Industries*, Civil Action No. 88-2933 (D. Md. April 7, 1989) (Consent Decree did not provide for review of remedial decisions by EPA); *United States v. Rohm & Haas Co.*, 721 F. Supp. 666(D. N.J. 1989) (Arbitrary and capricious standard of review to be applied).

108. CERCLA Section 107(a)(4)(A).

109. *See* NEPACCO, 810 F.2d 726, 747 (8th Cir. 1986), *cert. denied*, 108 S. Ct. 146 (1987); *United States v. Northernaire Plating Co.*, 685 F. Supp. 1410 (W.D. Mich. 1988) *aff'd sub nom. United States v. R. W. Meyer, Inc.* (6th Cir. 1990). EPA *Superfund Cost Recovery Strategy*, OSWER Directive No. 9832.13 (July 29, 1988) (setting forth EPA's priorities and case selection guidelines for initiating cost recovery actions under CERCLA).

110. CERCLA Section 101(25); *Northernaire* at 1417.

111. CERCLA Section 107(a)(4) (interest accruing on all amounts recoverable under Section 107 from the later of the date of the written demand or the date of the expenditure). Northernaire at 1420.

112. In *United States v. R.W. Meyer, Inc.*, 889 F.2d 1497 (6th Cir. 1989), the court allowed recovery of overhead, administrative, costs, or those costs not directly attributable to specific sites. *See United States v. South Carolina Recycling & Disposal, Inc.*, 653 F. Supp. 984 (D.S.C.1984) (recovery allowed for administrative and legal expenses associated with cleanup and litigation); *NEPACCO* (costs recoverable include salaries and expenses); *Northernaire* at 1418-1420; *contra United States v. Ottati & Goss, Inc.*, No. C-80-225-L (D.N.H., slip. op. March 17, 1988) (Ottati & Goss) (indirect costs not directly attributable to site are not recoverable), *remanded* for clarification (1st Cir. April 1990).

113. CERCLA Section 107(a)(1-4)(c).

114. 52 *Fed. Reg.* 9042.

115. 880 F.2d 481 (D.C. Cir. 1989).

116. 51 *Fed. Reg.* 27674, 43 C.F.R. § 11.10 through 11.93.

117. *State of Ohio v. Department of the Interior*, 880 F.2d 432 (D.C. Cir. 1989).

118. *See Idaho v. Hanna Mining Company*, 882 F.2d 392 (9th Cir. 1989).

119. *In re Acushnet River v. New Bedford Harbor*, 716 F. Supp. 676 (D. Mass. 1989).

120. *See U.S. v. Parsons* (N.D. Ga.), 5 *TXLR* (BNA) p. 252 (July 25, 1990).

121. NCP, 40 C.F.R. § 300.160. *See also* EPA, *Cost Recovery Actions under CERCLA*, OSWER Directive No. 9831.1 (May 30, 1986) (comprehensive guidance to EPA regions regarding maintenance of a response action, including an exhaustive list of documentation EPA considers appropriate as proof that its actions followed NCP).

122. *Northernaire* at 1417; *Ottati & Goss*, slip opinion at 34, 38.

123. *See, Colorado v. Idarado Mining Co.* (D. Colo.) 3 *TXLR* (BNA) 1256 (March 8, 1989).

124. *See e.g., United States v. Fred Webb. Inc.* (C.N.C.) 4 *TXLR* (BNA) 652 (November 1, 1989) (Action for $325,000 and treble damages for failure to comply with § 106 Order).

125. *Cadillac Fairview, California v. Dow Chemical Co.*, 840 F.2d 691 (9th Cir. 1988).

126. *Artesian Water Co. v. New Castle County*, 659 F.Supp. 1269 (D. Del. 1987), *aff'd*, 851 F.2d 643 (3rd Cir. 1988).

127. *See eg., Cadillac Fairview*, 840 F.2d 691 (9th Cir. 1988).

128. *Brewer v. Ravan*, 680 F. Supp. 1176, 1179 (M.D. Tenn. 1988).

129. *Violet v. Picillo*, 648 F.Supp. 1283 (D. R.I. 1986).

130. *AM International Inc. v. International Forging*, 5 *TXLR* (BNA) 370 (August 15, 1990) (N.D. Ohio 1990).

131. *Smith Land & Improvement Corp. v. The Celotex Corp.*, 851 F.2d 86 (3rd Cir. 1988).

132. One recent account suggests that all states with the exception of Delaware and Nebraska, have an environmental fund of some sort if only limited to the purpose of providing the 10 percent federal match. *See* Anderson and McElrich, "The Environment and the Law," *Institutional Investor*, p. 7 (July 1990).

133. "An Analysis of State superfund Programs: 50 State Study", prepared by the Environmental Law Institute for the Hazardous Site Control Division in the Office of Emergency and Remedial Response of the EPA, EPA/540/8-89/011- Sept. 1989.

134. *See* Inside EPA's *Superfund Report*, Special Report (September 27, 1989).

135. *See* discussion *infra* at "Consent Decrees and Consent Orders."

136. *See* Inside EPA's *Superfund Report* Vol. IV, No. 14, p. 1 (July 4, 1990).

137. *See* Inside EPA's *Superfund Report* at page 17 (March 28, 1990).

Environmental
Risk Management

# X The Innocent Landowner Defense: One of the Few Ways a Company Can Manage Its Superfund Risk

*S. Richard Heymann, Esq.*
*Foley & Lardner*
*Madison, Wisconsin*

The so-called "innocent landowner defense" merits particular attention because it is the only defense under the Comprehensive Environmental Response, Compensation and Liability Act of 1980 (CERCLA or Superfund) that does not depend entirely upon circumstances beyond one's control. It affords the purchaser of real property an opportunity to assess the risk of potential CERCLA exposure prior to a transaction and to manage that risk by what has come to be known as "environmental due diligence." Qualifying for the innocent landowner defense is easier said than done. The defenses to CERCLA are severely limited: (1) an act of God; (2) an act of war; (3) an act or omission of a third party; and (4) any combination of the foregoing.[1]

The innocent landowner defense is found within a convoluted combination of definitions that comprise Section 107(b)(3)'s "third party defense." To establish that defense an owner or operator must prove "by a preponderance of the evidence" that:

> (1) the release or threat of release and. . . damages resulting therefrom were caused solely by. . .an act or omission of a third party other than an employee or agent of the defendant, or than one whose act or omission occurs in connection with a contractual relationship, existing directly or indirectly with the defendant . . .;

(2) he exercised due care with respect to the hazardous substance concerned, taking into consideration the characteristics of such hazardous substance, in light of all relevant facts and circumstances; and

(3) he took precautions against foreseeable acts or omissions of any such third party and the consequences that could foreseeably result from such acts or omissions.[2]

Section 101(35) specifically defines "contractual relationship" as used in subsection 107(b)(3) to include "land contracts, deeds or other instruments transferring title or possession" unless:

the real property on which the facility concerned is located was acquired by the defendant after the disposal or placement of the hazardous substance on, in, or at the facility, and. . .

(i) At the time the defendant acquired the facility the defendant did not know and had no reason to know that any hazardous substance which is the subject of the release or threatened release was disposed of on, in or at the facility.

The statute also explains that to establish that a defendant "had no reason to know" that a hazardous substance was disposed of at the property:

[T]he defendant must have undertaken, at the time of acquisition, all appropriate inquiry into the previous ownership and uses of the property consistent with good commercial or customary practice in an effort to minimize liability. . . .

[T]he court shall take into account. . .  commonly known or reasonably ascertainable  information about the property, the obviousness of the presence or likely presence of contamination at the property, and the ability to detect such contamination by appropriate inspection.

Nothing in this paragraph shall affect the liability under this Act of a defendant who, by any act or omission, caused or contributed to the release or threatened release of a hazardous substance.[3]

## Innocent Landowners Before SARA

Prior to the Superfund Amendments and Reauthorization Act of 1986 (SARA), EPA took the position that the existence of any contractual relationship between a current owner or operator and the party responsible for the release or threatened release (such as a contract for the purchase of real property or the deed itself) would eliminate the availability of the third party defense.[4] Arguably CERCLA liability was never intended to extend quite so far as EPA's interpretation would suggest. During the course of debate on the 1986 SARA amendments, for example, it was noted that innocent landowners "should not be held responsible. . .even under the current law."[5] One or two courts even appeared to fashion a *de facto* defense for innocent landowners. For example, *U.S. v. Mirabile* [6] implied that the third party defense was available to a defendant who unknowingly purchased land on which hazardous substances were placed, where the defendant did not add to the wastes and exercised "due care" with respect to the contaminants.[7] Most courts, however, agreed with EPA's position and, for all practical purposes, the third party defense to CERCLA liability was simply not available to current owners or operators of contaminated sites, even in cases where the property was contaminated by a prior owner or lessee.[8]

## Legislative History of the Innocent Landowner Defense

When Congress amended CERCLA in 1986 with SARA, it specifically addressed the predicament of the "innocent purchaser". According to the report of the Conference Committee, the "innocent landowner" defense was intended to "eliminate liability which might exist under §107 for landowners who acquired title to real property after hazardous substances, pollutants, or contaminants were deposited on the property and who, although they had exercised due care with respect to discovering such materials, were nonetheless ignorant of their presence."[9] As the courts begin to hear cases that address the uncertainties which the drafters left behind, the legislative history of the innocent landowner defense may prove helpful.

## The Innocent Landowner Defense: One of the Few Ways a Company Can Manage Its Superfund Risk

The objective of the innocent landowner defense was first articulated by Representative Barney Frank (D-Mass.) who proposed a separate innocent landowner amendment.

**Mr. Frank:** Part of having a tough and comprehensive program is having provisions that allow innocent individuals to be treated as innocent individuals. In other words, nothing can be more damaging to our efforts to have a program like this [Superfund] work, nothing is more damaging to a good regulatory scheme than having anything in it that could inadvertently sweep out within its coils innocent individuals. This amendment says that wholly innocent landowners will not be held liable. . . .

To get a release from liability under this section, a landowner must not have himself or herself allowed or permitted any storage, not have contributed to the release of any substance and, and this is very important, the landowner has the burden of proof to show that this landowner had neither actual nor constructive knowledge at the time of purchase that the property had been used for hazardous waste materials.

In other words, you can get a release under this only if you can show by the preponderance of the evidence that you not only did not contribute to it; you did not even know that when you bought it that it had this there.[10]

Following discussion of several specific cases in which innocent landowners had been held liable under CERCLA, Representative John Breaux (D-La.) concluded:

**Mr. Breaux:** It looks like we should try to craft some type of provision that really protects the innocent landowner who has not done anything to put the waste there, or who would have no way of knowing that the waste was there, and somehow wind up down the road years in advance that the property has toxic wastes on it. That person should not be held liable.[11]

The House agreed that a codified innocent landowner defense was necessary:

**Mr. Moakley:** . . . The Frank amendment establishes a fair policy toward dealing with the truly innocent landowner.

I believe that we all agree that those who are responsible for the illegal disposal of hazardous wastes should be held accountable. Unfortunately, under present law and EPA policy, we also hold an innocent landowner equally responsible. The Frank amendment will correct this injustice by establishing a fair policy for dealing with the truly innocent landowner. . . .[12]

The final version of the "innocent landowner" defense that emerged from Conference Committee, however, proved not to be an amendment to the liability provisions of Section 107 but a new definition of "contractual relationship."

This new definition of contractual relationship is intended to clarify and confirm that under limited circumstances landowners who acquire property without knowing of any contamination at the site and without reason to know of any contamination. . . may have a defense to liability under § 107 and therefore should not be held liable for cleaning up the site if such persons satisfy the remaining requirements of § 107(b)(3). A person who acquires property through a land contract or deed or other instrument transferring title and possession that meets the requirements of this definition may assert that an act or omission of a third party should not be considered to have occurred in connection with the contractual relationship as identified in § 107 (b) and therefore is not a bar to the defense.

In the limited circumstances identified in this definition, such landowners are entitled to the defense if they exercise the requisite due care upon learning of such release or threat of release. . . .

The conferees recognize that the due care requirement embodied in § 107(b)(3) only requires such person to exercise that degree of due care which is reasonable under the circumstances. The requirement would include those steps

**The Innocent Landowner Defense: One of the Few Ways a Company Can Manage Its Superfund Risk**

necessary to protect the public from a health or environmental threat. . . .

The duty to inquire under this provision shall be judged as of the time of acquisition. Defendants shall be held to a higher standard as public awareness of the hazards associated with the hazardous substance releases has grown, as reflected by this Act, the 1980 Act and other federal and state statutes. Moreover, good commercial or customary practice with respect to inquiry in an effort to minimize liability shall mean that a reasonable inquiry must have been made in all circumstances, in light of best business and land transfer principles.

Those engaged in commercial transactions should, however, be held to a higher standard than those who are engaged in private residential transactions. Similarly, those who acquire property through inheritance or bequest without actual knowledge may rely upon this defense if they engage in a reasonable inquiry, but they need not be held to the same standard as those who acquire property as part of a commercial or private transaction, and those who acquire property by inheritance without knowing of the inheritance shall not be liable. . . . [13]

It is clear from the legislative history that Congress believed certain purchasers of property ought not to be — and arguably were **never** intended to be — liable under CERCLA. Conceptually, Congress' concern is quite simple: it seems unfair to hold one responsible for cleaning up somebody else's mess if one did not know and could not reasonably have been expected to know that the mess even existed.

Unfortunately, the resultant language is not quite so simple. First, the landowner's **knowledge**, either constructive or actual, of the possible presence of hazardous substances on the property is scrutinized. He must prove that he undertook "all appropriate inquiry" regarding his property "consistent with good commercial or customary practice" and that, in spite of this inquiry, he did not know and had no reason to know of any hazardous substances on the property. Next, the landowner's **actions** are examined. He must prove that he did not conduct, permit, or contribute to the release or threatened release of hazardous substances, that he exercised "due care" with respect to those substances, and that he took reasonable precautions against a third party causing a release.

It is easy to be overly critical of the manner in which Congress ultimately structured the innocent landowner defense. Given Congress' desire to speed up the CERCLA cleanup process and to ensure that CERCLA remain an exceedingly "tough" statute it should come as no surprise that Congress turned a bit skittish when it came time to write into the statute a defense which, for the first time, might apply to more than a tiny handful of potentially responsible parties.

Congress' apprehensions, however, have resulted in sufficient ambiguity and uncertainty that its relatively straightforward desire to protect the innocent landowner from liability under CERCLA has emerged as a good idea which sounds better in theory than it has proved to be in practice. The only guidance provided by the statute is that courts, when determining whether a defendant has undertaken "all appropriate inquiry," must take into account: (1) specialized knowledge or experience of the defendant; (2) the relationship of the purchase price to the value of the property if uncontaminated; (3) commonly known or reasonably ascertainable information about the property; (4) the obviousness of the presence or likely presence of contamination at the property; and (5) the ability to detect such contamination by appropriate inspection.[14]

## Judicial Treatment of the Innocent Landowner Defense

Not surprisingly, the courts have found the statute's limited guidance respecting the requirements of an "appropriate inquiry" inadequate. The courts have generally taken cognizance of the five factors required by Section 101(35)(B), but they have tended to treat the entire issue more as a question of fact than a question of law, with the outcome turning on factual determinations made on a case-by-case basis.

One of the more striking examples is *BCW Associates Ltd. v. Occidental Chemical Corp.*[15] The plaintiffs in that case, BCW Associates and Knoll International Inc., were, respectively, the owner and lessor

## The Innocent Landowner Defense: One of the Few Ways a Company Can Manage Its Superfund Risk

of a warehouse previously used by Firestone Tire & Rubber Company to grind tires. The tire grinding operations released lead-contaminated dust into the air and coated the surfaces of the warehouse. Prior to acquiring the property, BCW Associates hired two separate engineering firms to perform environmental audits and Knoll independently hired a third engineering firm to conduct its own environmental assessment of the property. None of these inspections or audits discovered the contaminated dust in the warehouse.

The plaintiffs argued that they were "innocent landowners" within the meaning of CERCLA because their environmental site inspections of the warehouse constituted "appropriate inquiry" as required by Section 101(35)(B). The court devoted little attention to the operative provisions of the defense but did address those factors which CERCLA says a court must "take into account" in determining whether a purchasor has made "appropriate inquiry." Specifically, the court determined that Knoll's activities as the lessee contributed to the release of the lead-contaminated dust at the site and that BCW paid less for the property, which was purchased "as is", than it would have had to pay had the property been uncontaminated. (The court also noted that BCW received substantial collateral benefits from the cleanup and that its property, following cleanup, was worth more than it was when purchased.) Finally, and perhaps most importantly, the court noted that both BCW and Knoll were well aware of the excessive amounts of dust in the warehouse but that neither verified that the environmental assessment included an analysis of this dust. As a result, the court found that neither the owner nor the lessee were "innocent" and proceeded to apportion CERCLA liability evenly among the buyer, seller, and tenant.

BCW has not received favorable comment and its precedential value remains to be seen. It is nevertheless significant if for no other reason than because it indicates that mere performance of an environmental site assessment — by now a commonplace precaution in property transactions — is no guarantee of "innocence." The role of the environmental site assessment in qualifying for the innocent landowner defense is discussed further elsewhere in this chapter.

BCW is not the only case in which a reviewing court has proved unwilling to construe the innocent landowner defense broadly. In U.S. v. Hooker Chemicals and Plastics Corp.,[16] the innocent landowner defense was denied on grounds that those who are the "original disposers" of hazardous substances at a site cannot be innocent land-owners.[17]   In *Washington v. Time Oil Co.*,[18] the innocent landowner defense was denied because the landowner failed to exercise "due care" since it "had allowed" its tenant to run a sloppy operation that contributed to the release of hazardous substances at the site.[19]  In *Wickland Oil Terminals v. Asarco, Inc.*,[20] the innocent landowner defense was denied to a party claiming that it was unaware that the one million metric tons of metal slag on its property might be contaminated with lead and other heavy metals.

*Sterling Steel Treating, Inc.*[21] denied the defense on grounds that a purchaser's familiarity with the prior use of the property gave it reason to know of the contamination.  The court's only explanation, however, states that the purchaser was "aware of the industrial uses of the property." Although the decision does not purport to find as a matter of law that awareness of industrial usage alone demonstrates awareness of contamination, many lenders now require physical testing, whether or not there is evidence of contamination, whenever industrial property is to be acquired.  The defendant's actual knowledge of the operations conducted at a contaminated facility was also found to be determinative in *U.S. v. Monsanto Co.* [22]   In that case, Monsanto, the lessor, claimed that it was ignorant of the lessee's disposal practices and emphasized that it never inspected the lessee's facility.[23]   The court held, however, that since Monsanto knew that the lessee was engaged in the manufacture of chemicals it should have been aware that there might be problems at the site.  "The statute does not sanction such willful or negligent blindness on the part of absentee owners."[24]

Finally, *Kelly v. Thomas Solvents Co.*,[25] held that the innocent landowner defense was available only when the contamination at a facility was caused "solely" by the actions of the third party.  It was not enough to allege that the "bulk" of the contamination was caused by the third party.[26]

On the other hand, there are at least four reported cases which indicate that the adequacy of a landowner's efforts (if any) to ascertain contamination on property which he acquires are questions of fact and cannot be disposed of on motion for summary judgment. For example, in *U.S. v. Serafini*,[27] the court denied EPA's assertion that failure to conduct a site inspection could not, as a matter of law, constitute "due care" and "all appropriate inquiry."  EPA argued that a defendant who failed to conduct any site inspection at all could not assert the innocent landowner defense under any circumstances. The court pointed out, however, that the property had been purchased in 1969 and the issue, therefore, was whether **in 1969** failure to inspect the property constituted less than appropriate inquiry — a factual question. Undaunted, the EPA presented affidavits of experts claiming that the failure to inspect commercial property prior to purchase was not consistent with good commercial practice in 1969. Defendants countered with their own expert testimony that failure to inspect was standard practice in 1969 and the court emphasized, again, that the adequacy of a purchaser's efforts to detect environmental problems — including the lack of such effort — is a question of fact. Since there was a bona fide dispute respecting the factual issue of the adequacy of defendant's inquiry, the court refused to decide the availability of the defense on motion, setting it for trial.[28]

A similar case involved a landowner who had "reluctantly" permitted dumping to occur on his property.[29] As in the *Serafini* case, EPA requested partial summary judgment on liability claiming that the defendant's consent to dumping, as a matter of law, precluded the innocent landowner defense. The court disagreed with EPA and held that whether the defendant acted reasonably at the time that it permitted the dumping was a factual issue that should not be determined on summary judgment.[30]

*Westwood Pharmaceuticals, Inc. v. National Fuel Gas Distribution Corp.*[31] discusses the innocent landowner defense in some detail. In that case, the plaintiff claimed that the defendant could not assert the innocent landowner defense because the defendent sold the contaminated facility to the plaintiff, thereby establishing a "contractual relationship" within the meaning of Section 107(b)(3). That section, of course, permits the third party defense only when the contamination was caused solely by the act or omission of a third party other than "one whose act or omission occurs in connection with a contractual relationship, existing directly or indirectly, with the defendant. . . ."[32] The plaintiff argued that the defendant could not establish the defense because the sale of the property was a contractual relationship within the meaning of § 107(b)(3). The court disagreed:

> So construing the statute, however, would effectively render the "in connection with" language superfluous, and such construction should be avoided whenever possible. . .
> That a contractual relationship exists between the parties is

not disputed. . .however. . .not every contractual relationship precludes a former owner from invoking § 107(b)(3),
and [the former owner] is entitled, therefore, at least to
present proof that [the purchaser's] construction activities
at the site were not undertaken "in connection with" its
contractual relationship with [the defendant].[33]

The *Westwood* court recognizes, for the first time, that the "in connection with" language in the third party defense can be critical and im-
plies that a "contractual relationship" will only preclude the innocent
landowner defense if the contractual relationship was somehow connected to the activities that caused the release or threat of release. If
broadly applied, the reasoning of the *Westwood* court could provide
considerable comfort to sellers and purchasers of commercial property.

Finally, the only reported case in which the innocent landowner
defense has been granted on the merits is *U.S. v. Pacific Hide & Fur
Depo, Inc.*,[34] In that case, the defendants were family members who
had inherited ownership of a company that had caused contamination at a hazardous waste facility. Not surprisingly, the defendants
did not undertake an environmental audit of the company prior to
inheriting its stock. As in *Serafini*, EPA argued that, as a matter of
law, no inquiry at all could not satisfy the "all appropriate inquiry"
requirement of the innocent landowner defense. The court rejected
EPA's position and held that, particularly in cases of inheritance, "no
inquiry" may be sufficient.[35]

To summarize, the cases emphasize that the elements of the innocent landowner defense — whether the landowner has exercised
"due care", whether he made "appropriate inquiry" respecting the
condition of the property, whether his inquiry was "consistent with
good commercial practice", whether the purchase price was suspi-
ciously low, whether there existed "commonly known or reasonably
ascertainable information about the [condition of the] property", etc.
— are mostly factual issues, not legal ones. That in turn means that
the government (or a private plaintiff) which, but for the asserted innocent landowner defense, might otherwise have CERCLA liability
determined on motion for summary judgment will probably have to
forego the advantages of such a prompt procedure where a defendant believes it is entitled to the defense. On the other hand, the innocent landowner may not be able to prove his innocence without

first having to go through a trial on the merits which, presumably, would compel the landowner to incur the expense and burden of preparing for and enduring CERCLA litigation. The cost of avoiding CERCLA liability could, in the process, exceed the amount of the liability itself.

### EPA Guidance

In June of 1989 EPA issued a guidance document, providing additional insight into the Agency's interpretation of the innocent landowner defense.[36] The document focuses on the similarities between the criteria under section 122 governing entitlement to participate in *de minimis* settlements and the provisions establishing entitlement to the innocent landowner defense. EPA notes that demonstrating entitlement to the innocent landowner defense will generally require proof of much the same facts as establishing eligibility for *de minimis* settlement. EPA also points out that to establish the innocent landowner defense will generally require a trial on the merits, which can be a time consuming and expensive proposition. The *de minimis* settlement provisions of CERCLA, EPA reasons, are intended to enable a potentially responsible party, the quantity and toxicity of whose waste accounts for only a *de minimis* portion of the problem associated with a Superfund site, to avoid the burdens of litigation by entering into a settlement with the government at an early stage of the litigation.

Thus, since the *de minimis* settlement provision is intended to enable marginally culpable parties to avoid the exigencies of the CERCLA process, and since an allegedly innocent landowner may be no more culpable than a *de minimis* generator, EPA has determined to treat both categories of potentially responsible parties alike. The Guidance document instructs regional personnel to evaluate a landowner's probability of success in establishing entitlement to the defense at trial in assessing the appropriateness and terms of settlement under Section 122(g)(1)(B).

### Analysis of the Defense

It is difficult to take advantage of the innocent landowner defense both before it is too late to avoid CERCLA liability by becoming the owner of property which is not yet known to be contaminated and after contamination has been discovered and the property's owner has been identified as a potentially responsible party. An ounce of prevention being worth several pounds of cure in the context of CERCLA, it is far better to overcome the former obstacle than to have to overcome the latter.

CERCLA provides relatively little guidance respecting the extent of investigation (increasingly referred to as "environmental due diligence") necessary to satisfy the statute's "appropriate inquiry" requirement. Moreover, the appropriateness of inquiry only becomes relevant after the Superfund process is initiated by a release, or threatened release, of hazardous substances that were undetected by the buyer prior to purchase. At that time, with the clarity of hindsight, there likely will be considerable temptation to conclude that any inquiry which failed to detect such hazardous substances could not possibly have been "appropriate".

### Problems Encountered In Qualifying for the Defense

The initial decisions concerning the innocent landowner defense do not typically address the general concept of "appropriate" pre-purchase inquiry. The *BCW* case came close but it remains for the courts to roll up their sleeves and scrutinize the details of individual environmental site inspections that have become commonplace subsequent to 1986. Nor have the cases yet resolved the question of whether, prior to 1986, "good commercial or customary practice" required any environmental inquiry at all and, if so, of what sort. EPA officials, speaking off the record, have admitted that the Agency will be sorely tempted to attack the sufficiency of **any** environmental site assessment which fails to find contamination sufficiently serious to result in action under CERCLA but which is not discovered until a later date. Thus, it seems likely that, over time, more and more courts will have occasion to review the details and the appropriateness of environmental site inspections. In the process some of a buyer's more common concerns may be addressed, such as whether to undertake soil or groundwater sampling of any industrial property regardless of the absence of physical or documentary evidence of contamination, whether mere proximity to certain uses such as chemical manufacturing, landfills, etc. is alone sufficient to require greater scrutiny, and whether prior agricultural usage can be considered much as if the land had not been used at all.

Over time there may be enough litigation involving the innocent landowner defense to enable the courts to impart greater meaning to the notion of "appropriate inquiry." In the meantime, however, the statute provides inadequate guidance, the cases provide even less guidance, and the EPA Guidance provides less guidance still.

The opportunity to prove the adequacy of a landowner's site assessment may come at considerable cost — and risk. To the extent that there is any material factual dispute respecting the appropriateness of a landowner's pre-purchase inquiry, that issue will be decided only after a trial on the merits. Since Section 113(h) generally prohibits pre-enforcement judicial review, such a trial would likely occur only after response (and transaction) costs had been incurred. Thus a landowner wishing to assert his innocence must forego opportunities to settle with other PRPs, to settle with the government (possibly on a *de minimis* basis), and to reduce his exposure by participating in the CERCLA process. In *Reardon v. U.S.*,[37] for example, landowners sought to enjoin placement of a federal lien on their property pursuant to Section 107(l). They asserted (1) the innocent landowner defense, (2) that the lien was unconstitutional, and (3) that the lien was overbroad under Section 113(l). The court agreed to consider issue (2) but held that consideration of issues (1) (i.e., the innocent landowner defense) and (3) was precluded by Section 113.

If a landowner is unwilling to wait until trial to find out whether he qualifies for the defense, at present his options appear limited. One can always rely upon the kindness of others, i.e., seeking the acquiescence of EPA or other PRPs in an early determination of the applicability of the defense. Generally that will not be fruitful. Despite the reluctance of courts to consider the issue on motion for summary judgment, it nevertheless seems perfectly possible that the only question respecting an environmental site assessment might be its "adequacy," which is arguably a question of law, not fact, and therefore entitlement to the defense would be ripe for decision on motion for summary judgment. Thus, for example, if one could avoid such disputes as whether at a certain point in time it was customary to conduct any environmental site assessment at all, and if the parties could agree that the buyer hired a reputable firm which did no more and no less than what appears in its report, and that the only prepurchase evidence of contamination (i.e., the basis of the claim of inappropriateness) is as alleged, it seems possible that a court could conclude that there is no dispute as to material fact and it could proceed to determine whether the undisputed inquiry should have detected the undisputed prepurchase evidence (if any) of contamination.

If there is a dispute as to material fact, however (e.g., if the parties cannot agree respecting the evidence allegedly suggesting the presence of contamination which was available but overlooked at the time of the site assessment), then *de minimis* settlement under Section 122(g)(1)(B) as contemplated by the EPA Guidance document may be the most cost-effective, least risky solution, notwithstanding that *de minimis* setlements generally require payment of a premium and notwithstanding that under CERCLA an innocent landowner, unlike a *de minimis* generator, is not liable at all and therefore should not be obligated to make any payments, let alone to pay a premium.

## Future of the Defense

CERCLA reauthorization is scheduled to be considered by Congress in 1991. Amplification of the innocent landowner defense will presumably be on the agenda if Congress or EPA (administrative rule) hasn't by then already rectified the situation. The "Innocent Landowner Defense Amendment of 1989," H.R. 2787, was intended to clarify the innocent landowner defense. It provides that a "Phase I Environmental Audit", which includes a review of title documents, aerial photographs, and "reasonably obtainable" government records, a search for cleanup liens, and a "visual site inspection" would create a "rebuttable presumption" of appropriate inquiry. Other proposals to achieve a comparable result have been discussed as well, although prompt enactment seems unlikely since piecemeal amendment of CERCLA on the eve of reauthorization, potentially a time consuming and unpleasant exercise, will likely be unpopular with Congress. Nevertheless, initial efforts to amend CERCLA to limit the liability of lenders in the wake of the panel decision in *U.S. Fleet Factors*,[38] received considerable support in Congress and amendment of the innocent landowner defense might prove to be more practicable if undertaken in the context of clarifying the liability of lending institutions, which, Congress seems to feel, constitute a category of "innocent" bystanders much like the innocent landowners.

Most major environmental engineering firms have developed internal policies, complete with form documents, for undertaking environmental site assessments. Their focus tends to be objective and has resulted in a generally accepted practice of "Phase I, Phase II, and Phase III" audits. Phase I, depending upon the experience and ability of the firm, looks more or less like the "Phase I Environmental Audit" referenced in HR 2787. Phase II requires physical testing when the Phase I inquiry suggests possible problems. Phase III typically involves remediation of problems disclosed by the Phase II inquiry. In the absence of consistent Congressional or judicial interpretation their practices will presumably come to define the "good commercial or customary practice" standard of Section 101(35)(B).

Unfortunately the quality of performance varies substantially among consultants (due to their varying degrees of experience, the undersupply of seasoned personnel, deal-driven budget restrictions and similar factors), which deprives the marketplace of such commonality as would make it easier to predict what will be accepted as "customary."

Moreover, experienced environmental counsel have become increasingly uncomfortable with the "objective" approach of many consultants as it tends to result in overkill in the easy cases and ambiguous or inadequate site assessment reports in the hard ones. They tend to favor a more subjective approach that would base each investigation upon the focus of the statute (rather than an internal policy) and the peculiar facts of each individual case (rather than upon a form intended for use in all factual circumstances). Such an approach often tends to tailor the site assessment to the value of the transaction, which may decrease the cost of many investigations (though it does not sanction reduced effort where the likelihood of contamination is high, regardless of the value of the property) but may increase the risk of failure to qualify for the defense in others.

The American Society of Testing and Materials (ASTM) is in the process of developing a draft standard for performing environmental due diligence and anticipates a final draft in early 1991. (See Chapter XVII.) ASTM has the credibility to establish a standard that environmental professionals and the courts may accept.

Similar efforts have been undertaken by ASFE/The Association of Engineering Firms Practicing in the Geosciences, which published its own "recommended management procedures for consulting engineering firms" in a 1989 report entitled "Preacquisition Site Assessments". It recommends the checklist approach typically employed by environmental engineering firms and contains advice to engineering consultants intended to limit their own liability for failure to detect contamination. (Buyers, lenders, and others contracting for environmental site assessments should take care that their contracts require a site assessment which is "consistent with good commercial or customary practice", rather than specify any other, arguably less appropriate, inquiry such as might result from the multiple disclaimers which ASFE recommends).

In addition, the Federal Home Loan Bank System (FHLBS), regulating the savings and loan industry in 1989, now the Office of Thrift Supervision, and the Federal National Mortgage Association (Fannie Mae) and the Federal Regulatory Mortgage Corporation (Freddie Mac) have also issued guidance and checklists of their own, outlining environmental due diligence procedures that may influence future assessments of "good commercial or customary practice". Of their respective efforts, the "Thrift Bulletin 16" issued by the FHLBS Office of Regulatory Activities on February 6, 1989, entitled "Environmental Risk and Liability", is the more applicable to commercial transactions. It contains a "Description of Environmental Risk Reports" that is a useful general summary of customary environmental due diligence without many of the drawbacks associated with the all-purpose checklist.

EPA has said prospective purchasers aware of on-site contamination may be granted a covenant not to sue in return for a cleanup commitment or cash contribution under the contribution and apportionment provisions of CERCLA § 113(f)(1).[39] The first such "prospective purchaser" agreement was executed by USEPA Region X on August 9, 1989 in connection with the purchase by developer Von Roll Ltd. of a parcel owned by the City of Kellogg.[40] Similarly, in March of 1990, USEPA entered into an innocent landowner covenant not to sue with prospective purchaser Boliden Intertrade A.G. to allow reorganization. Boliden agreed to bear the cost of maintaining a wastewater treatment system during the six-month trial period.[41] In a similar proceeding, the State of New York granted a covenant not to sue to the purchaser of the Gladding Braided Products site in South Otselic, New York under a settlement that provided that a portion of the purchase price would be applied to the remediation of certain abandoned chemical wastes.[42] Such contribution-leveraged innocent landowner settlements may increase in number as prospective purchasers seek assurances that the defense will be viable after an acquisition.

**The Innocent Landowner Defense: One of the Few Ways a Company Can Manage Its Superfund Risk**

## About the Author

Dick Heymann is a partner with the 400-member law firm of Foley & Lardner. He graduated from the University of Wisconsin in 1966 and the University of Michigan Law School in 1969. He served as a law clerk for the Minnesota Supreme Court and, prior to practicing law, taught history and coached various sports at the Priory School in St. Louis. He is a senior member of Foley & Lardner's large environmental law practice group where he concentrates in general environmental counselling, particularly in connection with business and real estate transactions, and is also the firm's principal specialist in FIFRA matters. He has written and lectured extensively on environmental law topics and served on public and industry panels concerned with a variety of environmental regulatory problems. He lives and works in Madison, Wisconsin.

## Endnotes

1. 42 U.S.C. § 9607(b).

2. 42 U.S.C. § 107(b)(3)(a)-(c).

3. 42 U.S.C. § 9601(35)(b).

4. *See*, U.S. EPA "Guidance on Landowner Liability Under Section 107(a)(1) of CERCLA, *De Minimis* Settlements Under Section 122(g)(1)(b) of CERCLA, and Settlements with Prospective Purchasers of Contaminated Property," Memorandum from E.E. Reich, June 6, 1989 ("EPA Guidance Memo") at pp. 4-5.

5. 131 *Cong. Rec.* H1158 (Daily Ed. December 5, 1985).

6. *U.S. v. Mirabile* 15 ELR 20992 (E.D. Pa. Sept. 4, 1985).

7. *See also, U.S. v. Maryland Bank & Trust*, 632 F. Supp. 573, 581 (D. Md. 1986).

8. *See*, for example, *U.S. v. South Carolina Recycling & Disposal, Inc.*, 653 F. Supp. 984, 994 (D.S.C. 1986) (lessor liable for contamination caused by lessee); *U.S. v. Argent Corp.*, 21 ERC 1354, 21 ERC 1356; 14 ELR 20616 (D.N.M. May 4, 1984); *New York v. Shore Realty Corp.*, 759 F.2d 1032 (2d Cir. 1985) (current owner liable even if contamination caused by prior owner).

9. *See* Superfund Amendments and Reauthorization Act of 1986, Conference Report ("Conference Report") p. 186.

10. 131 *Cong. Rec.* H1158 (Daily Ed. December 5, 1985).

11. *Id.*

12. *Id.* at H1159.

13. Conference Report p. 187-188.

14. 42 U.S.C. § 9601(35)(B).

15. *BCW Associates Ltd. v. Occidental Chemical Corp.* (E.D. Pa. Sept. 29, 1988), 3 (BNA) *Toxics Law Reporter* 943 (Sept. 30, 1988).

16. *U.S. v. Hooker Chemicals and Plastics Corp.*, 680 F. Supp. 546 (W.D.N.Y. 1988).

17. *Id.* at 558.

18. *Washington v. Time Oil Co.*, 687 F. Supp. 529 (W.D. Wash. 1988).

19. *Id.* at 532.

20. *Wickland Oil Terminals v. Asarco, Inc.*, 19 ELR 20855 (N.D. Cal. Feb. 23, 1988).

21. *In re. Sterling Steel Treating, Inc.*, 94 Bankr. 924 (Banker E.D. Mich. 1989).

22. *U.S. v. Monsanto Co.*, 858 F.2d 160 (4th Cir. 1988).

23. *Id.* at 169.

24. *Id.*

25. *Kelly v. Thomas Solvents Co.*, 727 F. Supp. 1532 (W.D. Mich. 1989).

26. *Id.*

27. *U.S. v. Serafini*, 706 F. Supp. 346 (M.D. Pa. 1988).

28. *U.S. v. Serafini*, 711 F. Supp.197 (M.D. Pa. 1988).

29. *U.S. v. Moore*, 703 F. Supp. 460 (E.D. Va. 1988).

30. *See also, Jersey City Redevelopment Authority v. PPG Industries*, 655 F. Supp. 1257 (D. N.J. 1987) (triable issue as to what defendant knew and whether defendant's actions were reasonable).

31. *Westwood Pharmaceuticals, Inc. v. National Fuel Gas Distribution Corp.*, (W.D.N.Y. May 21, 1990), 5 (BNA) *Toxics Law Reporter* 221.

32. 42 U.S.C. § 9607(b)(3).

33. *Id.*

## The Innocent Landowner Defense: One of the Few Ways a Company Can Manage Its Superfund Risk

34. *U.S. v. Pacific Hide & Fur Depo, Inc.* 716 F. Supp. 1341 (D. Idaho 1989).

35. *Id.* at 1348-9.

36. "Guidance On Landowner Liability Under § 107(a)(1) of CERCLA, *De Minimis* Settlements under Section 122(g)(1)(B) of CERCLA, and Settlements with Prospective Purchasers of Contaminated Property."

37. *Reardon v. U.S.*, 731 F. Supp. 558 (D. Mass 1990).

38. *U.S. Fleet Factors* 901 F.2d 1550 (11th Cir. 1990).

39. *Guidance*, p. 26.

40. *Inside EPA Superfund Report*, Volume IV: 19, page 3 (September 13, 189).

41. *Inside EPA Superfund Report*, p. 3 (March 28, 1990).

42. *In re: Paris Industries Corporation* 106 Bankr. 339, (U.S. Bankr. Ct. Maine 1989), (BNA) *Toxic Law Reporter*, 548 (October 11, 1989).

# XI SARA Title III: The Emergency Planning and Community Right-To-Know Act Of 1986

*Richard A. Horder, Partner*
*and A. Jean Tolman, Senior Associate*
*Kilpatrick & Cody*
*Atlanta, Georgia*

President Ronald Reagan signed into law on October 17, 1986, the Superfund Amendments and Reauthorization Act (SARA). Included as Title III of that Act was the Emergency Planning and Community Right-to-Know Act of 1986 (EPCRA). While denominated an amendment to the Comprehensive Environmental Response, Compensation and Liability Act of 1980 (CERCLA), SARA Title III is, in reality, an entirely separate statute.

SARA Title III — herein referred to as EPCRA — was engendered in large part by the accidents at Union Carbide's Bhopal, India, chemical plant in December, 1984 and its Institute, West Virginia plant in August of 1985. The Bhopal incident, which resulted in death or injury to thousands of people, remains the chemical industry's worst disaster. The accident at the West Virginia plant, eight months later, brought the possibility of a similar tragedy occurring in the U.S. too close to home to be ignored by Congress and the public.

While the events in Bhopal and West Virginia served to spur the enactment of federal legislation in the area, environmental groups and many civic leaders had long held concerns about the presence of chemicals in communities and the lack of widespread information concerning the hazards they might pose. As a result, certain response programs already existed at various levels,[1] and many existing concepts were embodied in, and provided the framework for, the resulting statute.

The stated purpose of EPCRA is to promote emergency planning efforts at the state and local level and to inform residents and local governments of potential chemical hazards in their communities. In large part, EPCRA is an information transfer mechanism which requires that local officials be informed by business and industry of the "toxic" or "hazardous" chemicals present in the communities so that the responsible officials can be prepared to respond in the event releases of these chemicals take place. EPCRA is also designed to transfer information to the public sector, ultimately increasing the public's awareness of and access to information concerning chemicals in their localities. To accomplish this information transfer the Act imposes numerous reporting requirements on commercial and industrial facilities.

The promotion of local emergency planning and response is accomplished by Subchapter A (Sections 301 through 305) of EPCRA.[2] This portion of the statute requires that each state establish a state emergency response commission. The commission must in turn establish appropriate emergency planning districts and appoint local emergency planning committees. These local committees bear the responsibility of developing an emergency response plan for their particular localities.

To ensure that the committees have the information needed to develop and implement the emergency response plans, facilities are required to notify state and local officials of the presence of certain chemicals. In addition, immediate notification must take place if a release of a hazardous substance to the environment occurs. EPCRA also provides for training and educational programs for federal, State and local officials and provides for grants to state and municipal governments to improve emergency planning.

Subchapter B (Sections 311, 312, and 313) of EPCRA[3] addresses the information transfer and public awareness aspects of EPCRA. EPCRA requires that material safety data sheets (MSDSs) and emergency and hazardous chemical inventory forms be submitted by facilities to appropriate state and local officials so that they will be informed of the kinds, amounts and hazardous properties of chemicals present at the facilities. In addition, many facilities must submit annual reports estimating the amount of toxic chemicals they release each year into the environment.

The third and final subchapter of EPCRA (Sections 322 through 330)[4] contains a number of "general provisions," including penalties for violations of the Act, authorization for citizen suits to enforce EPCRA, trade secret provisions, and provisions for making information available to health professionals and to the public.

While this summary provides a brief overview of EPCRA's provisions, Title III is a complex piece of legislation and each section and its implementing regulations must be closely examined. The following provides a more detailed discussion of EPCRA's individual sections.

## Overview of Statutory Requirements

### Emergency Planning and Notification

Sections 301-305 of EPCRA are directed toward establishing emergency planning programs at the state and local levels, including the establishment of state emergency response commissions and local emergency planning committees.

*State Commissions, Planning Districts
and Local Planning Committees*

Section 301 of EPCRA evidences the statute's emphasis on local rather than national planning. It required that each state's governor appoint a state emergency response commission (SERC) by April 17, 1987.[5] Those serving on the SERC are to have expertise in emergency planning and response. By July 17, 1987, the commissions were to have designated emergency planning districts,[6] and local emergency planning committees (LEPCs) for each district were to be appointed by August 17, 1987.[7]

The local committees must include in their membership representation from each of the following groups: "elected State and local officials; law enforcement, civil defense, firefighting, first aid, health, local environmental, hospital, and transportation personnel; broadcast and print media; community groups; and owners and operators of facilities subject to the requirements of [EPCRA]."[8]

Each LEPC must establish its own rules and procedures, and such rules must include provisions for public notification of and participation in the LEPC's activities.[9] The LEPC must also establish procedures for providing information made available by EPCRA to the public.[10] The SERC is responsible for supervising and coordinating the LEPCs, along with providing procedures for receiving and processing requests from the public for information available from facilities under EPCRA.[11] Recognizing the need for a federal role in support of these local efforts, EPCRA establishes a means for providing training and education to emergency planning officials and authorizes the provision of grants to improve emergency planning by these entities.[12]

A primary responsibility of each LEPC was to prepare a "comprehensive emergency response plan" for its planning district by October 17, 1988; thereafter, the LEPC must review the plan at least annually and update it as required.[13] The plan must include, among other things: identification of facilities in the district subject to EPCRA and transportation routes likely to be used for extremely hazardous substances; procedures to be used by facilities and local emergency and medical organizations to respond to chemical releases; designation of facility and community emergency coordinators; and evacuation and training plans and notification procedures in the event of a chemical release.[14]

Guidance documents from EPA are available to assist local committees in preparing their emergency plans[15] and in carrying out their responsibilities under EPCRA.[16] In addition, in an effort to share information on successful practices with LEPCs, SERCs, and other EPCRA implementing agencies, EPA is publishing a series of bulletins offering examples of EPCRA implementation programs and strategies that are innovative or have proven to be effective.[17] A recent publication by the National Governors' Association describes how the states have implemented the requirements of EPCRA and documents the key problems and issues the states have addressed.[18]

While the state and local emergency planning programs described in the preceding paragraphs depend on the efforts of the SERCs and LEPCs in each state, they also depend on compliance by business and industry with certain emergency planning and notification requirements imposed on "covered facilities" by Sections 302, 303 and 304 of EPCRA.

*Emergency Planning and Notification Requirements*

Section 302(a) required EPA to publish a list of "extremely hazardous substances" (EHSs) and establish a "threshold planning quantity" (TPQ) for each listed substance.[19] The TPQ is the quantity of the chemical that will trigger EPCRA's emergency planning and notification requirements.[20] TPQs assigned by EPA range from one pound to 10,000 pounds.[21]

EPA is authorized to revise the EHS list and the TPQs, based on evidence as to a substance's hazardous properties and tendency to disperse in the environment.[22] Therefore, when determining whether a given chemical is an "extremely hazardous substance," care must be taken to consult the current EHS list.

Under Section 302(c) of EPCRA, a facility[23] subject to EPCRA's emergency planning notification requirement must have so notified the State Emergency Response Commission (SERC) by May 17, 1987, or within 60 days of becoming subject to the requirements.[24] A facility is subject to this requirement if a listed EHS is present in an amount equal to or exceeding its TPQ.[25]

To determine whether a facility has an amount of an EHS which meets or exceeds the TPQ set for that particular chemical, the facility owner or operator must calculate the total amount of the EHS present at the facility on May 17, 1987, or **at any time** after that date, "regardless of location, number of containers, or method of storage."[26] This calculation must also take into account the amount of the EHS present in mixtures or solutions. However, if an EHS is present in a mixture or solution at a level of one percent or less, the amount of EHS need not be counted in determining the total amount present at the facility.[27]

Section 303 of EPCRA requires that the facility designate a facility representative as the "facility emergency coordinator," who will participate in the local emergency planning process. This designation was due to the LEPC by September 17, 1987, or thirty days after establishment of the LEPC.[28] Any changes occurring at the facility that may be relevant to emergency planning must be reported to the LEPC, and the facility owner must provide information requested by the LEPC that is necessary for the local emergency plan.[29]

Under Section 304 of EPCRA,[30] facility owners or operators must "immediately" notify the LEPC's emergency coordinator and the SERC of a release[31] of a listed hazardous substance that exceeds the reportable quantity (RQ) for that substance.[32] In the case of a transportation release, or a release from storage which is incidental to transportation, notification to a 911 or similar emergency telephone number will suffice.[33]

The substances subject to Section 304 emergency release notification are those which are either subject to emergency notification under Section 103(a) of CERCLA, or on the list of EHSs.[34] The overlap of the two lists is confusing, and EPA is expected eventually to make the lists identical.

Facility owners and operators should be aware that many facilities not required to provide notice under Section 302 for emergency planning purposes will still be required to report releases under Section 304 if the RQ of the substance is exceeded. This is due to the fact that the threshold amounts for Section 302 reporting (the TPQs) are generally much larger than the RQs under Section 304.

Section 304 exempts from the release notification requirement releases which result in exposure only to persons solely within the facility boundaries.[35] It is important to recognize, however, that compliance with Section 304 does not obviate the need to report a release to the National Response Center under Section 103(a) of CERCLA.[36]

The emergency notification under Section 304 must: identify the substance released and whether it is on the EHS; give the time and duration of the release; estimate the quantity of hazardous substance released; indicate the media into which the release occurred; provide the name and telephone number of the person to contact for more information; and provide information on known or anticipated health risks, medical advice where appropriate, and precautionary measures to be taken.[37] All of this information must be provided immediately by telephone, and a written follow-up notice, containing updated information on response actions and health risk or medical information, is required as soon as practicable.[38]

Obviously, the detailed information required in the notification required under Section 304 is problematical. In an emergency situation, facility personnel are unlikely to have all of the information required, or be qualified to advise about health risks or to provide medical advice. Advanced planning by the facility is absolutely necessary in this area. The facility emergency coordinator should prepare emergency notifications for each substance present at the facility which facility personnel can then use in the case of a release.

For purposes of litigation defense, care should be taken in providing both the verbal and follow-up written notification, because each may contain damaging admissions that could be used in toxic tort suits arising from the release.

## Community Right-to-Know Reporting Requirements

The reporting requirements of Sections 311, 312 and 313 of EPCRA comprise the core of the "community right-to-know" component of EPCRA. It is helpful to consider the requirements of Sections 311 and 312 separately from those of 313, as the former two sections relate to hazardous chemicals present at the facility, while Section 313 concerns itself with the reporting of chemicals entering environmental media from the facility. Moreover, because the provisions are linked to different chemicals and thresholds, the facilities covered by Sections 311 and 312 may not be subject at all to Section 313.

### Hazardous Chemical Reporting, Sections 311 and 312

The reporting requirements imposed by Sections 311 and 312 of EPCRA[39] cover the largest number and types of facilities, because they potentially apply to nearly all employers. Sections 311 and 312 apply to facilities that must prepare or have available a material safety data sheet (MSDS) for a "hazardous chemical" under the Occupational Safety and Health Act (OSHA). OSHA broadly defines a hazardous chemical to mean "any chemical which is a physical hazard or a health hazard."[40] It has been estimated that as many as 50,000 chemicals are subject to Section 311 and 312 reporting because they meet the OSHA "hazardous chemical" definition.[41]

It is important to recognize, however, that certain hazardous substances are exempt from the OSHA Hazard Communication Standard (and, therefore, from both the MSDS and EPCRA Community Right-to-Know requirements). Eight specific exemptions are listed in the Hazard Communication Standard.[42] In addition, Section 311(e) lists several exclusions to the "hazardous chemical" designation which, if they apply, exempt the excluded substances from the reporting requirements of **both** Sections 311 and 312.[43]

If a business uses or stores hazardous substances at its facility that are **not** exempt, either under the OSHA Hazard Communication

Standard or Section 311(e) of EPCRA, such substances nevertheless may not be subject to reporting under Sections 311 and 312 because they do not meet the minimum reporting threshold amounts. EPA recently established the final thresholds for reporting under either Section 311 or 312 at 10,000 pounds of any non-EHS chemical, or the lesser of 500 pounds (or 55 gallons) or the TPQ of any EHS present at a facility.[44]

If a facility is subject to Section 311 reporting, on or before October 17, 1987, (or within three months after the facility first becomes subject to Section 311), the facility owner or operator was required to submit a copy of the MSDS for each such hazardous chemical present at the facility in amounts exceeding the minimum reporting threshold. The MSDS must be submitted to the SERC, the LEPC, and the local fire department.[45] An update must be submitted within three months anytime there is discovery of significant new information, or if an unreported hazardous chemical is present in a quantity exceeding the reporting threshold.[46]

Alternatively, the facility owner or operator may submit a list of chemicals for which an MSDS is required.[47] The list must include the chemical or common name of each substance as provided on the MSDS, and must identify the applicable hazard category [such as "immediate (acute) health hazard," or "highly toxic"], as defined in 40 C.F.R. § 370.2.[48] The facility owner or operator is under a continuing duty to update the MSDS information for which a list was submitted,[49] and to provide an individual MSDS if requested by the LEPC to do so.[50]

Section 312 of EPCRA, unlike Section 311, imposes an annual reporting requirement on facilities that are required to prepare or have available MSDSs for one or more hazardous chemicals.[51] Covered facilities are required to submit an inventory form on March 1 of each year if, at any time during the previous calendar year, the amount of the chemical present at the facility exceeded the minimum reporting threshold amount (which is the same as that established for Section 311 reporting.)[52] The inventory form must be submitted to the SERC, the LEPC, and the local fire department.[53]

The inventory form must contain an estimate of the maximum amount of each hazardous chemical present at the facility during the preceding year, an estimate of the average daily amount of hazardous chemical present, and the location of the chemicals at the facility.[54] Section 312 establishes two levels of detail for the required reporting. In "Tier I" reporting, information is provided in the aggregate, with general information on amounts and location of hazardous chemicals presented by categories of physical and health hazards established under OSHA regulations.[55] "Tier II" reporting is more detailed, with specific information provided on amounts, location and manner of storage of individual chemicals.[56] Under Section 312, Tier II information must be submitted only if requested by the SERC, the LEPC, or the local fire department.[57] It is available to the public by written request to the SERC or LEPC.[58]

Although the Tier II form is optional under federal law, EPA strongly recommends submission of the Tier II form. In addition, individual states may require the Tier II form be submitted instead of Tier I. For facilities using or storing non-exempt materials in excess of the reporting threshold, the due date for the Tier I (or Tier II) submission was March 1, 1990.

### Toxic Chemical Release Reporting, Section 313

The requirements of Section 313 apply only to those facilities in Standard Industrial Classification (SIC) Codes 20-39 (the manufacturing sector).[59] Covered facilities are those which, during the preceding calendar year, conducted manufacturing operations, had ten or more full time employees, and manufactured, imported, processed or otherwise used a listed toxic chemical in amounts greater than the applicable threshold quantity.[60]

The toxic chemicals subject to Section 313 reporting are listed in 40 C.F.R. § 372.65.[61] EPA may add or delete chemicals based on evidence as to their health effects, toxicity and persistence in the environment,[62] and the Agency has already used its discretionary authority several times to change the Section 313 list.[63]

In addition, any person may petition EPA to add a chemical to the list or delete a listed chemical,[64] to which EPA must respond within 180 days by either initiating a rulemaking procedure or denying the petition with a published explanation.[65] Section 313 also provides that when a state governor petitions to add a chemical, the chemical will automatically be added to the 313 list unless within 180 days from receipt of the petition EPA denies the petition or initiates rulemaking to add the chemical.[66]

The Section 313 requirements apply if a facility manufactures or processes more than 25,000 pounds of a listed toxic chemical during a calendar year.[67] If a facility "otherwise uses" a listed toxic chemical, without incorporating it into a product, the threshold quantity for triggering the section 313 reporting requirement is 10,000 pounds.[68]

Companies required to report under Section 313 must file a toxic chemical release form (Form R) for each reported chemical.[69] The Form Rs must be submitted to EPA, with a copy to the state, by July 1 of each year and report on toxic chemicals manufactured, processed or used at the facility in amounts exceeding the applicable threshold quantities during the previous calendar year.[70]

Form R is a complex and detailed document. It requires that the facility:

- establish the maximum quantity of the listed chemical present at the facility any time in the preceding year;
- estimate the amount released into the environment, including that from spills, by evaporation or from fugitive emissions;
- provide information about off-site disposal of waste and the quantity of each chemical present in such waste; and
- provide information regarding waste treatment and disposal methods.

Industry has found that it is no easy task to estimate the quantity of a chemical released to the environment from all sources at a facility. Section 313 requires that, in making its estimates, the facility use readily available monitoring data and other emissions measurements taken at the facility and other data the plant may have developed on its own. In the absence of such data, the facility may use other estimating techniques such as material balances, engineering estimates or published emissions factors.[71]

Effective January 1, 1989, a "supplier notification" requirement was imposed on any manufacturing facility (in SIC Codes 20-29) that manufactures, imports, or processes a Section 313 listed chemical and then sells or distributes a mixture or trade name product containing the chemical to a manufacturing firm or to a customer that sells it to a manufacturing firm.[72] A facility meeting these criteria is required to notify its customers in writing that the mixture or trade name product contains a toxic chemical(s) subject to Section 313 reporting.[73] This notification must be made regardless of whether the supplier triggers the Section 313 reporting requirement at its own facility.

There are several limited exemptions to the Section 313 reporting requirement:

- if the toxic chemical is present in a mixture at a *de minimis* concentration;[74]
- if it is present in an "article";[75]
- if it is used at the facility in certain described situations such as for janitorial or grounds maintenance;[76] and
- if it is manufactured, processed, or used in a laboratory at a covered facility;[77]

EPCRA requires that EPA use the data submitted under Section 313 to establish and maintain a "national toxic chemical inventory" in a computer data base.[78] Furthermore, these data must be made accessible to the public on a cost reimbursement basis.[79]

## Other General Provisions

### Pre-emption — EPCRA's Relationship to Other Laws (Section 321)

EPCRA does not preempt any state or local law, nor does it modify obligations or liabilities a person may have under any other federal law.[80] Section 321, however, requires that MSDSs required by any state or local law enacted after August 1, 1985 must be uniform in content and format with the MSDS required under Section 311. The state or locality may require supplemental information through additional sheets attached to the uniform data sheet.[81]

### Trade Secrets (Section 322)

An issue of importance to many companies and facilities is the effect that disclosure of confidential information required under EPCRA may have on the company's competitiveness in the market place. Section 322 addresses this concern by providing companies the right to make a claim of trade secrecy to withhold a specific chemical identity, except that no such claim can be made for emergency release information required under Section 304.[82] If a company's trade secrecy claim is found valid, the company need only provide the generic class or category of the chemical or substance in its required reporting. [83]

In order to make a claim of trade secrecy, a company must show that:

1) it has not disclosed the information to any person other than certain authorities or a person who is bound by a confidentiality agreement, and that the company has taken reasonable steps to protect the confidentiality of the information and intends to continue to take such measures;

2) the information is not required to be publicly disclosed or made available under any other federal or state law;

3) disclosure is likely to cause substantial harm to the company's competitive position; and

4) the chemical identity is not readily discoverable through reverse engineering.[84]

While the procedures for submittal of a claim for trade secrecy under Sections 303(d)(2) or (d)(3), 311, 312, or 313 vary slightly,[85] claims under all of these sections require the submittal of a completed standard substantiation form.[86]

Once a procedurally correct trade secrecy claim has been received by EPA, the alleged trade secret information is treated as confidential until EPA makes a contrary determination.[87] Upon petition for the release of the trade secret information by an outside party, EPA must immediately undertake a review to determine the validity of the trade secret claim.[88] EPA can also undertake such a review of a trade secret claim on its own initiative.[89]

Should EPA initially determine that the substantiation is insufficient, then the trade secret claimant may appeal the decision, or for good cause shown supplement the substantiation.[90] Because "good cause"[91] is not easily shown under this section, company's should take special care when initially completing the substantiation form.

### Disclosure to Health Professionals (Section 323)

Section 323 provides health professionals[92] the special right to obtain from the owner or operator of any facility any chemical identity, including trade secret information the facility has withheld from disclosure under Section 322, if this information is believed by the health professionals to be needed for diagnosis, treatment, or emergency medical care of an individual suspected to have been exposed to the chemical or substance.[93]  Also, a local government health professional can gain access to the information, including the trade secret information, for any of a number of medical treatment and preventive purposes.[94]

In all situations other than a medical emergency, the health professional must provide the company a written statement of need[95] and a written confidentiality agreement[96] stating that the information will not be used for any purpose other than the health needs set forth in the statement of need.[97]  After receiving a request, a company must promptly provide the requested information.[98]

In a medical emergency situation, no written request or written confidentiality agreement is necessary; however, only a treating physician or nurse can obtain this information.[99]

### Public Availability of EPCRA Information (Section 324)

Section 324 provides for public availability of all information submitted under the various provisions of EPCRA (other than trade secret information) during normal working hours at locations designated by EPA, the state governor or SERC, or the LEPC.[100]  The only exception is that the SERC or LEPC must withhold, upon the facility's request, the location of any specific hazardous chemical included by the facility in Tier II information required on the Section 312 chemical inventory form.[101]

Each LEPC must annually publish in local newspapers a notice stating that the information required under EPCRA has been submitted by facilities and is available to any member of the public for review at designated locations.[102]

### Citizen Suits (Section 326)

EPCRA provides for private citizen suits to be brought in the Federal District Court against a facility owner or operator for failure to 1) submit a follow-up emergency notice under Section 304, 2) submit an MSDS or list under Section 311, 3) complete and submit an inventory form under Section 312, or 4) submit a toxic chemical release form under Section 313.[103]  Before the action may commence, the plaintiff must give 60 days notice of the alleged violation to EPA, the state in which the alleged violation occurred, and the alleged violator.[104]  Also, no action may be commenced if EPA is diligently pursuing an enforcement action for the alleged violation.[105]

A citizen can bring a suit against EPA for failure to respond within 180 days to a petition to add or delete a Section 313 chemical, establish and maintain a computer data base as required by Section 313(j), or render a decision in response to a petition for trade secret disclosure within nine months after receipt.[106]   A citizen can also bring a suit against the EPA Administrator, a state governor or a SERC for failure to set up procedures and locations for public review of information,[107] and against the state governor or SERC for failure to respond within 120 days to a request for Tier II information.[108]

State and local governments are also given the right to commence civil actions against the owner or operator of a facility for noncompliance with several EPCRA provisions.[109]  Any SERC or LEPC may sue a facility owner or operator for failure to submit information under Section 303 or to submit Tier II information as required by Section 312.[110]  Also, any state may commence an action against the EPA for failure to provide information to the state regarding trade secrets as required under Section 322(g).[111]

### Transportation Exemption (Section 327)

Except for the requirements under Section 304 emergency release reporting, EPCRA does not apply to substances or chemicals in the course of transportation, including storage incident to transportation.[112]  The exemption includes the transportation and distribution of natural gas.[113]

# Enforcement Of EPCRA

### EPCRA Penalties (Section 325)

Section 325 of EPCRA[114] establishes civil, administrative and criminal penalties for noncompliance with the various requirements of EPCRA.  The consequences of noncompliance are severe, and to complicate matters, the applicable penalties vary with the section violated.

## Violation of Emergency Planning
### and Notification Requirements (Sections 302 and 303)

Section 325(a) provides that facilities covered by the emergency planning requirement of Section 302(c) and the information provision requirement of Section 303(d) may be ordered by EPA to comply with those requirements.[115] EPA's administrative order is enforceable by the appropriate U.S. District Court, and violation of such an order may subject the facility owner or operator to a civil penalty of up to $25,000.[116]

### Violation of Emergency Release Notification (Section 304)

Civil, administrative and criminal penalties are all available to address violations of the emergency notification requirements of Section 304.[117] EPA is authorized to assess a Class I administrative penalty of up to $25,000 for each violation of Section 304.[118] For each day the violation continues, EPA may assess a Class II administrative penalty of up to $25,000 per day.[119] In the case of a second or subsequent violation of Section 304, the administrative penalty may be increased to a maximum of $75,000 per violation for each day that the violation continues.[120] Adjudicatory hearings on the assessment of administrative penalties under Section 325 are governed by the Consolidated Rules of Practice published in the Code of Federal Regulations[121] including the Supplemental Rules of Practice for EPCRA penalty assessments.[122]

EPA may also bring an action in the appropriate U.S. District Court for judicial assessment of penalties of up to $25,000 per day for each violation of Section 304.[123] The penalty may be as high as $75,000 per day in the case of a second or subsequent violation of Section 304.[124]

Finally, if the violation of Section 304 was knowing and willful, the convicted facility owner or operator may be fined up to $25,000 per day and/or imprisoned for up to two years.[125] In the case of a second or subsequent conviction for violating Section 304, the criminal penalties may be increased to up to $50,000 per day and no more than five years imprisonment.[126]

*Violation of EPCRA Reporting Requirements*

EPCRA does not provide for criminal sanctions for violations of reporting requirements. Available civil penalties vary between the various provisions, and may be assessed by either administrative or judicial action.[127]

Sections 311, 323(b) and 322(a)(2) — Congress considered noncompliance with the requirements of Sections 311, 323(b) and 322(a)(2) to warrant less severe sanctions than the remaining sections. Violation of the reporting requirements of Sections 311 and 323(b) by any person other than a governmental entity, or violation of Section 322(a)(2) by any person, is punishable by assessment of a civil penalty of up to $10,000 per day.[128]

Sections 312 and 313 (Inventory & Toxic Release Reporting) — Noncompliance by any person other than a governmental entity with the reporting requirements of Sections 312 and 313 will subject that person to a civil penalty of up to $25,000 per day per violation.[129]

*Violation of Section 322 (Trade Secret Provisions)*

A trade secret claimant determined by EPA to have made a frivolous claim is liable for a judicial or administrative penalty assessment of $25,000 per claim.[130] More severe sanctions are available for those who knowingly and willfully reveal information protected under Section 322; they may be subject to criminal conviction and a fine of up to $20,000 and/or imprisonment for up to one year.[131]

*Special Enforcement Provisions for Section 323
(Information for Health Professionals)*

A health official who has not received requested information from a facility owner or operator may seek judicial enforcement of the information request in an appropriate U.S. District Court.[132]

**EPA Enforcement Response Policy For Section 313 of EPCRA**

In late 1988, EPA prepared a document for internal use entitled, "Enforcement Response Policy for Section 313 of the Emergency

Planning and Community Right-to-Know Act also known as Title III of the Superfund Amendments and Reauthorization Act (SARA)" (hereinafter the "Enforcement Response Policy").[133] The stated purpose of the Enforcement Response Policy was three-fold:

- to assure that Section 313 enforcement actions a,e fair, uniform and consistent;
- to see that the enforcement response is appropriate to the violation;[134]
- to deter persons from committing Section 313 violations.

The Policy describes four "level of action" enforcement alternatives and the circumstances under which they should apply:

- taking no action;
- issuing a Notice of Noncompliance (NON);
- seeking administrative or judicial civil penalties; and
- initiating criminal judicial action.[135]

According to the Enforcement Response Policy, "no action" is warranted under only very limited circumstances.[136] A Notice of Noncompliance (NON) is deemed an appropriate response to certain errors in Form Rs submitted on time to EPA and to late reports submitted 1 to 30 days after the due date of July 1, 1990.[137] To be considered a "late" report, however, the report must be submitted to EPA before any contact or inspection by EPA.[138] Additionally, an NON is inappropriate if the facility has received an NON for late reporting during any of the previous five reporting periods.[139]

An administrative civil penalty is deemed the appropriate response for non-reporting, incomplete reporting, failure to respond to or comply with an NON, repeated late reports, and repeat violations.[140] Although, as noted previously, EPCRA does not provide for criminal sanctions for violations of Section 313, 18 U.S.C. § 1001 makes it a criminal offense to falsify information submitted to the federal government. Additionally, the knowing failure to file a Section 313 report may be prosecuted as a concealment under 18 U.S.C. § 1001.[141]

EPA has constructed a matrix for determining the appropriate base penalty amount for any Section 313 violation. The total penalty is determined by calculating the penalty for each violation on a per chemical, per facility basis.[142] The matrix employs a "circumstance level" on one axis and a "penalty adjustment level" on the other. The circumstance level takes into account the seriousness of the violation with respect to the accuracy and availability of the information to

EPA, the states and the community.[143] The penalty adjustment level is based on the quantity of Section 313 chemical which is the subject of the violation and the size of the total corporate entity in violation.[144]

Once the gravity-based penalty is determined, upward or downward adjustments are made, considering the following factors:

- voluntary disclosure;
- culpability (including the violator's knowledge, control over the situation, and attitude);
- history of prior violations of EPCRA Section 313;
- ability to continue in business (ability to pay); and
- other factors as justice may require (such as environmentally beneficial expenditures in exchange for a penalty reduction).[145]

### EPA Interim Strategy for Enforcement of Title III and CERCLA Notification Requirements

On December 14, 1988, the EPA Office of Solid Waste and Emergency Response (OSWER) issued interim guidance concerning enforcement of Sections 302, 303, 304, 311, 312 and 322 of EPCRA and the Section 103 notification requirements of CERCLA.[146] The directive was prepared to provide the EPA regions an overall strategy for enforcing sections 302-312.[147]

*Section 304 Enforcement*

The strategy document suggests ways that the regional offices can identify potential violations of Section 304,[148] including the use of information requests and inspections authorized under Section 104(e) of CERCLA.[149] In discussing Section 304 enforcement priorities, the strategy document states that the regions should attempt to target a cross section of the regulated community, and should consider the following circumstances in assessing the priority of taking enforcement action against a particular violator:

- the volume and nature of substance released;
- the nature of environmental or health threats resulting from the release;
- the efforts made by the facility to comply with notification requirements;

- aggravating or mitigating circumstances, such as the facility's compliance with other EPCRA provisions;
- the significance of the violation to the SERC and LEPC; and
- the effect on the overall enforcement program.[150]

*Enforcement of Sections 302, 303, 311 and 312*

Although the strategy document emphasizes cases involving violations of Section 304, EPA regions are urged to coordinate with SERCs to identify potential violations of EPCRA Sections 302-303 and 311-312.[151] The strategy document describes sources of information to help identify facilities required to report under Section 302,[152] and notes that Section 302-303 and Section 311-312 violators may be identified by checking past accidental spill data in the Emergency Release Notification System.[153]

## EPA Administrative Enforcement Initiatives

EPA is taking seriously its job of enforcing EPCRA. On June 28, 1990, EPA announced that the number of EPCRA administrative complaints brought by the Agency totalled over 250, with proposed penalties of over $9 million.

EPA's first enforcement initiative was aimed at enforcing Section 313. In mid-February of 1990, EPA announced that during FY 1989, the first full year of enforcement of Section 313, the Agency issued 123 administrative complaints for failure to file annual toxic chemical release forms. An additional 44 complaints were issued in the first quarter of 1990. Over the same five-quarter period, more than $5 million in penalties were proposed. More recently, EPA announced that 80 civil administrative complaints had been issued during the first six months of 1990 for failure to meet Section 313 reporting requirements.

Although Section 313 initially received the greatest enforcement emphasis, enforcement of the other provisions of EPCRA has been far from ignored. On June 28, EPA filed multiple enforcement actions for violation of the emergency notification requirements of Section 304 of EPCRA and Section 103 of CERCLA.[154] (An action brought for Section 304 violations typically sets forth a violation of the corresponding emergency notification requirement of CERCLA section 103.)

In the June 28, 1990 enforcement initiative, twenty-three complaints seeking a total of $1,974,810 were filed simultaneously in all ten EPA Regional Offices.[155] In the majority of the cases, the complaints included counts for Section 311 and 312 violations as well (and one complaint was based solely on Section 311 and 312 violations).[156]

## EPCRA Cases

### Section 313

EPA Region VI obtained the first administrative determination of liability under EPCRA, and the first administrative decision awarding penalties under EPCRA in an Arkansas case involving failure to report under Section 313.[157]

Riverside Furniture Corporation (Riverside), an Arkansas furniture manufacturing facility, apparently was unaware that it was required to submit Form Rs by July 1, 1988, for Reporting Year 1987. On September 29, 1988, an EPA inspector discovered that Riverside had not filed Form Rs for any of six chemicals it had used during 1987 in amounts exceeding the applicable 10,000-pound threshold. Riverside immediately proceeded to file the forms, which were received by EPA on October 24, 1988.

On March 27, 1989, the federal administrative law judge (ALJ) granted EPA's motion for Partial Accelerated Decision, finding Riverside liable under EPCRA and holding that lack of knowledge is not a defense to liability for violating Section 313 of EPCRA. At the July 26, 1989 hearing on the assessment of civil penalties, Riverside protested EPA's proposed penalty of $126,000, contending that the amount should be $18,000 based on Riverside's lack of knowledge and prompt efforts to comply.[158] In ruling on the penalty assessment, the ALJ ordered Riverside to pay civil penalties amounting to $75,000. Although the ALJ found that the penalty was assessed in accordance with EPA's December 2, 1988 Section 313 Enforcement Policy, he disagreed with EPA's application of the policy's provision concerning "late report" versus "failure to report," with the latter having significantly higher penalties.

## Section 304

In the first EPCRA § 304 and CERCLA § 103 Class II administrative action for civil penalties brought by EPA, the federal ALJ granted EPA's motion for Partial Accelerated Decision, holding All Regions Chemical Labs., Inc. (All Regions) liable for violations of both statutory provisions.[160] In ruling on the penalty assessment proposed by EPA, the ALJ assessed an $89,840 penalty against All Regions for failing to notify EPA of two chemical incidents at its Springfield, Massachusetts, facility.[161] On June 17, 1988, All Regions had experienced two chemical releases involving a total of 180,000 pounds of chlorine gas, an EHS with an RQ of 100 pounds. All Regions did not notify the EPA National Response Center (NRC) immediately after the release as required under Section 103(a) of CERCLA. Further, All Regions did not provide written follow-up information required under Section 304 of EPCRA until 144 days after the releases.[162]

EPA proposed a total penalty of $122,000: $25,000 for the CERCLA violation and $97,000 for the EPCRA violation (which included daily penalties for each of the 144 days that All Regions had delayed giving notice). All Regions asserted that the EPA-proposed assessment was excessive and proposed a total penalty of no more than $6,000.[163] Noting that EPA has not as yet issued guidelines for assessing penalties for violations of CERCLA § 103 and EPCRA § 304, the ALJ relied upon the TSCA Penalty Guidelines[164] and EPA's General Enforcement Policy[165] for appropriate criteria. In imposing the $89,840 penalty, the ALJ took into account the company's cooperative attitude but emphasized the importance of the notification. The fact that the failure to notify had not compounded the damages and endangerment to public health and the environment had simply been "fortuitous" in this case.

## Sections 311 and 312

In December of 1988, EPA Region III brought the first enforcement action in the country under Sections 311 and 312 against Murry's Inc., located in Lebanon, Pennsylvania.[166] On July 12, 1988, Murry's failed to report a release of anhydrous ammonia as required by Section 102 of CERCLA and Section 304 of EPCRA.[167] EPA's subsequent investigation revealed that Murry's Inc. also failed to submit the required emergency planning documentation under Sections 311 and 312 of EPCRA.[168] EPA filed three administrative complaints against Murry's Inc., alleging various violations of CERCLA and EPCRA, including Sections 311 and 312. The total proposed penalty for all three complaints was $68,000. EPA and Murry's Inc. settled the cases for a total penalty payment of $51,250.

## Future Trends Under EPCRA

An unforseen but important issue that has arisen with respect to the formation of LEPCs is the legitimate concern of LEPC members, most of whom are volunteers, about protection from tort liability for their actions as members of the LEPC.[169] The question concerning many LEPC and SERC members is whether they will be protected under state statutes and case law from tort liability pursuant to an act or failure to act in the course of performing their duties.[170] The states, with the help of their attorneys general, are attempting to clarify and deal with this issue.[171]

The first three years of reporting under Section 313 have been learning experiences for affected facilities. According to EPA, the 1987 toxic release reporting data (submitted in July of 1988) contained a number of errors, resulting in inaccurate reporting of release estimates. The most common mistakes were the unnecessary reporting of neutralized acids and bases, the reporting of amounts of listed chemicals purchased rather than amounts released to the environment, and the reporting of chemical amounts generated prior to their being reduced by controls.

The accuracy of Form R submittal is expected to increase with time, especially as aids to Section 313 reporting develop. Several independent firms are marketing computer software products designed to help facilities meet their Section 313 reporting requirements, and many produce reports on magnetic media. EPA will accept Form R data on magnetic media provided they meet EPA's magnetic media format specifications.[172] Facilities may not use magnetic media, however, for submissions in which a chemical identity is claimed to be a trade secret, or for reporting of corrections to previously submitted Section 313 data.[173] States are not required to accept Form Rs submitted on magnetic media, so the possible use of mag-

netic media for state submittal must be discussed with and authorized by each state involved.

Industry has now had almost three years experience with EP-
CRA's implications. During the first two years, the main effort focused on complying with the numerous reporting requirements of
the law. This experience provides convincing evidence of both the
ambiguities inherent in EPCRA regarding what is to be reported and
how it is to be reported and the impact the reporting of releases has
on public awareness.

It seems evident from the discrepancies in the filed reports that
companies operating similar facilities may have differing interpretations of EPCRA's requirements, or at least have used differing assumptions in arriving at the calculations necessary to report the annual releases under Section 313.

In addition, EPA and the general public have expressed some surprise and dismay at the size of the emissions of toxic substances from
industrial facilities. This result was probably inherent in the evolution of EPCRA due to the raw nature of the information required to
be reported and the general lack of qualitative analysis required by
the Act. Industry did not help the situation because, in general, it declined to supplement the filed reports with explanatory information.

Raw information about pounds of chemicals emitted is, in reality,
of little use to either emergency planning committees or local citizens
evaluating the impact of such emissions on the community. It is likely that as SARA evolves, the law will require that more qualitative
information will be required to be furnished by industry about the
nature of its emissions.

Clearly, the environmental community and the general public now
have information provided to them by industry concerning the plant
down the street. This will continue to focus attention on industry in
general and can be expected to have an effect on the renewal of permits through the imposition of stricter emissions limits. Further, facilities that wish to avoid negative media attention and public scrutiny will be obliged to undertake voluntary efforts to reduce
emissions.

Siting and zoning issues for both new and existing facilities will
probably also be affected by the availability of EPCRA information.
Unfortunately, this will probably only exacerbate the "not in my back
yard" (NIMBY) syndrome. However, as the general public and local
communities become more adept at analyzing and understanding

the data reported, there may be some lessening of the usually adverse response to this information.

As Congress intended, the wealth of information generated under EPCRA since its inception in 1986 has already had a marked effect on public consciousness regarding hazardous chemicals and substances manufactured and used at local facilities. The flow of information to the public created by EPCRA has fueled toxic tort litigation and will continue to do so in the future. With industry itself providing information regarding its facilities' emissions, the ability of plaintiffs' attorneys to allege personal injury from exposure to these emissions will be enhanced.

Industry will likely continue to develop programs such as Community awareness and Emergency Response Program (CAER) developed in 1985 by the United State Chemical Manufacturers Association (CMA). (See Chapter XX by Mason.) CAER's primary goal is to promote the protection of public health and safety in the community by:

- developing community outreach programs that provide information on the chemicals used at local chemical manufacturing plants to the general public and
- assisting in local emergency response planning by coordinating the efforts of chemical plant emergency plans with the plans of other local entities.

International awareness of the need for community education and knowledge of potential dangers regarding hazardous substances manufactured and/or used at local facilities is also growing. In 1986, the United Nations Environmental Programme (UNEP) developed a handbook on Awareness and Preparedness for Emergencies at the Local Level (APELL), modelled after CMA's CAER program. (See Chapter XIII by Campbell.) APELL provides guidance to communities in all countries (particularly developing countries) to enhance community awareness and local emergency response to accidents resulting from the use of hazardous materials at local facilities.

‖

## About the Authors

‖

**Richard A. Horder**, a Partner in the Kilpatrick & Cody Law Firm, heads the environmental law practice group in the firm's Atlanta office. Prior to joining the firm, he was Associate General Counsel with Georgia-Pacific Corporation where he was responsible for toxic tort litigation and environmental compliance corporate-wide. Mr. Horder is a graduate of the University of Florida (BA 1968, JD 1971) the London School of Economics and Political Science (LLM 1974) and Georgia State University (MBA 1977).

**A. Jean Tolman**, a Senior Associate with Kilpatrick & Cody, is active in environmental litigation and compliance. She joined the firm after working as environmental scientist and program manager with the Florida Department of Environmental Regulation and the U.S. Environmental Protection Agency. Ms. Tolman is a graduate of Florida State University (MS 1974), and Georgia State University (JD 1987).

‖

## Endnotes

‖

1. An earlier response to public concern over the presence of chemicals in local communities was EPA's Chemical Emergency Preparedness Program (CEPP), which was developed in 1985 to increase state and local community awareness of the presence of chemicals in their communities and the possibility that accidental releases of extremely hazardous substances could occur. A second goal of CEPP was to contribute to the development of appropriate emergency response plans and capabilities at the state and local level for dealing with chemical releases.

2. 42 U.S.C. §§ 11001-11005.

3. 42 U.S.C. §§ 11021-11023.

4. 42 U.S.C. §§ 11041-11050.

5. 42 U.S.C. § 11001(a).

6. 42 U.S.C. § 11001(b).

7. 42 U.S.C. § 11001(c).

8. *Id.*

## SARA Title III: The Emergency Planning and Right-to-Know Act of 1986

9. EPA, in cooperation with the Federal Emergency Management Agency, has published a document aimed at educating local officials concerning how to respond to citizen questions about hazardous chemicals: *Risk Communication about Chemicals in Your Community, A Manual for Local Officials*, EPA 230/09-89-066, Sept. 1989.

10. 42 U.S.C. § 11001(c).

11. 42 U.S.C. § 11001(a).

12. 42 U.S.C. § 11005. In April of 1990, EPA announced the availability of $1.2 million in grant and cooperative agreement funds for state programs implementing EPCRA. EPA envisions awarding multiple grants of up to $150,000 each, to be used by the SERCs to help LEPCs enhance their effectiveness in a number of ways such as increasing LEPC public outreach programs and enforcement and compliance efforts. 55 Fed. Reg. 17924 (April 27, 1990).

13. 42 U.S.C. § 11003(a).

14. 42 U.S.C. § 11003(c).

15. *Hazardous Materials Emergency Planning Guide* (NRT-1), National Response Team, March 17, 1987; *Technical Guidance for Hazards Analysis*, U.S. EPA, FEMA, U.S. DOT, Dec. 1987.

16. *See also ,It's Not Over In October! A Guide for Local Emergency Planning Committees*, U.S. Government Printing Office, July 1988, 27 pp. Developed by 13 agencies and associations including the U.S. EPA, American Red Cross and U.S. Chamber of Commerce, this booklet offers suggestions to LEPCs for maintaining the momentum of their EPCRA efforts <u>after</u> the October, 1988 submittal of the comprehensive emergency plan.

17. *See e.g., Successful Practices in Title III Implementation.* CEPP Technical Assistance Bulletin, U.S. EPA, Office of Solid Waste and Emergency Response (OS-120), OSWER-89-006.2, Aug. 1989. *See also Why Accidents Occur: Insights From The Accidental Release Information Program*, U.S. EPA, Office of Solid Waste and Emergency Response (OS-120), OSWER-89-008.1, July 1989, 22 pp. This document was intended to help LEPCs establish a productive accident-prevention dialogue with local facilities. It uses information gathered from an EPA-established pilot program, the Accidental Release Information Program, to focus on the causes of chemical accidents, and passes information on to LEPCs on methods to prevent recurrences.

18. *Emergency Planning and Community Right-To-Know Act: A Status of State Actions-1989*, National Governors' Association, 120 pp. Included in the report is a detailed profile of each state, describing the state's SERC and LEPCs, including their membership, status of local plans, roles of agencies, enforcement, funding, liability and related laws.

19. 42 U.S.C. § 11002(a). The EHS list is published at 40 C.F.R. Part 355, Appendices A and B, with updates in the *Federal Register*.

20. 40 C.F.R. § 355.30.

21. *See supra* note 23.

22. 42 U.S.C. § 11002(a)(4). The most recent revision was published February 15 to be effective March 19, 1990. 55 Fed. Reg. 5544 (February 15, 1990).

23. A facility is broadly defined as: "all buildings, equipment, structures, and other stationary items which are located on a single site or on contiguous or adjacent sites and which are owned or operated by the same person (or by any person which controls, is controlled by, or under common control with, such person). For purposes of emergency release notification, the term includes motor vehicles, rolling stock, and aircraft." 40 C.F.R. § 355.20.

24. 42 U.S.C. § 11002(c) 40 C.F.R. § 355.30(b).

25. 42 U.S.C. § 11002(b).

26. 40 C.F.R. § 355.30.

27. 40 C.F.R. § 355.30(e)(1). *See also The Emergency Planning and Community Right-To-Know Act of 1986, Questions and Answers*, prepared by the EPA Emergency Planning and Community Right-To-Know Information Hotline, February 29, 1988, 52 pp., at 10-11. This informational document provides examples of threshold determinations and answers some commonly posed questions concerning the applicability of Section 302 notification requirements.

28. 42 U.S.C. § 11003(d) 40 C.F.R. § 355.30(c).

29. 42 U.S.C. § 11003(d) and 40 C.F.R. § 355.30(d).

30. 42 U.S.C. § 11004 and 40 C.F.R. § 355.40.

31. "Release means any spilling, leaking, pumping, pouring, emitting, emptying, discharging, injecting, escaping, leaching, dumping, or disposing into the environment . . . of any hazardous chemical, extremely hazardous substance, or CERCLA hazardous substance." 40 C.F.R. § 355.20.

32. 42 U.S.C. § 11004(a), (b).

33. 42 U.S.C. § 1104(b)(1). The "transportation exemption" provided in Section 347, discussed *infra*, is specifically not applicable to emergency notification under Section 304. 42 U.S.C. § 11004(d).

34. 42 U.S.C. § 11004(a).

35. 42 U.S.C. § 11004(a)(4).

36. 42 U.S.C. § 9603(a).

37. 42 U.S.C. § 11004(b)(2).

38. 42 U.S.C. § 11004(c).

39. 42 U.S.C. §§ 11021-11022.

40. Under the OSHA Hazard Communication Standard, a "physical hazard" includes chemicals that are combustible, reactive, corrosive, or otherwise dangerous because of their physical properties. A "health hazard" includes chemicals that are "carcinogens, toxic or highly toxic agents, reproductive toxins, irritants, corrosives or sensitizers," as well as chemicals that damage the nose, skin, eyes, or mucous membranes. 29 C.F.R. § 1900.1200(c).

41. *Title III List of Lists, Consolidated List of Chemicals Subject to Reporting Under Title III of the Superfund Amendments and Reauthorization Act (SARA) of 1986*, U.S. EPA, Office of Toxic Substances, Jan. 1989, 29 pp.

42. 29 C.F.R. § 1910.1200(b).

43. 42 U.S.C. § 11004(e). The five exemptions include: (1) any FDA-regulated food, food additive, color additive, drug, or cosmetic; (2) solid substances present in manufactured items such that exposure would not occur under normal usage; (3) substances used for personal, family, or household purposes, or present in the same form and concentration as products packaged for distribution and use by the general public; (4) substances used under technical supervision in a research laboratory or hospital or other medical facility; and (5) substances used routinely in agricultural operations or fertilizers for retail sale. *Id.*

44. For both Sections 311 and 312, the minimum reporting thresholds for the first two years of reporting were 10,000 pounds for any hazardous chemical, and the lesser of 500 pounds (or 55 gallons) or the TPQ of any extremely hazardous chemical (EHS), present at the facility. 53 *Fed. Reg.* 38344 (October 15, 1987), codified at 40 C.F.R. § 370.20(b). EPA established a zero threshold to become effective in the third year of reporting, intending that before then, it would conduct further studies and promulgate final reporting thresholds somewhere between zero and 10,000 pounds. *Id.* After conducting its study of alternative thresholds, EPA proposed final reporting thresholds in a "Notice of Proposed Rulemaking" in March of 1989. 54 *Fed. Reg.* 12992 (March 29, 1989). Failing, however, to meet the necessary time frame, EPA published an "Interim Final Rule," extending the previous thresholds for another year. 54 *Fed. Reg.* 41904 (October 12, 1989. Finally, in July of 1990, EPA published a final rule establishing final reporting thresholds for Sections 311 and 312. 55 *Fed. Reg.* 30632 (July 26, 1990).

45. 40 C.F.R. § 370.21(a).

46. *Id.*

47. 42 U.S.C. § 11021(a) and 40 C.F.R. § 370.21(b).

48. *Id.*

49. 42 U.S.C. § 11021(d) and 40 C.F.R. § 370.21(c).

50. 42 U.S.C. § 11021(c) and 40 C.F.R. § 370.21(d).

51. 42 U.S.C. § 11022(a) and 40 C.F.R. § 370.25.

52. 40 C.F.R. § 370.25(a).

53. *Id.*

54. 42 U.S.C. § 11022(d).

55. 42 U.S.C. § 11022(d)(1).

56. 42 U.S.C. § 11022(d)(2).

57. 42 U.S.C. § 11022(e) and 40 C.F.R. § 370.25(c).

58.   42 U.S.C. § 11022(e)(3) and 40 C.F.R. § 370.30(b).

59.   42 U.S.C. § 11023(b) and 40 C.F.R. § 372.22.

60.   *Id.*

61.   Some facilities have failed to recognize a chemical on the Section 313 list because they knew it under a different name. This problem can be avoided by consulting EPA's publication, *Common Synonyms for Chemicals Listed Under Section 313 of the Emergency Planning and Community Right to Know Act*, Office of Toxic Substances, U.S. EPA, January, 1988, 105 pp. Another "must have" publication is the *Title III List of Lists, supra* note 45. This document presents in tabular form the EPCRA Section 302 EHS chemicals, the CERCLA Section 103(a) chemicals, and the EPCRA Section 313 chemicals. All three lists are different, but many chemicals are found on more than one list. These overlaps become discernible in the consolidated list format. Not specified in the "List of Lists" are the more than 50,000 chemicals subject to Section 311 and 312 reporting requirements.

62.   42 U.S.C. § 11023(d).

63.   For example, effective February 14, 1990, EPA deleted non-fibrous forms of aluminum oxide, CAS No. 1344-28-1, from the list of toxic chemicals under Section 313 of EPCRA. Although fibrous forms of aluminum oxide will remain listed under section 313, facilities are relieved of their obligation to report releases of non-fibrous forms of aluminum oxide that occurred during the 1989 calendar year or after. 55 *Fed. Reg.* 5220 (February 14, 1990).

64.   42 U.S.C. § 11023(e).

65.   42 U.S.C. § 11023(e)(1).

66.   42 U.S.C. § 11023(e)(2). On January 9, 1990, the Natural Resources Defense Council and the Governors of New Jersey, New York and Vermont petitioned for the addition to the Section 313 list of 7 ozone-depleting chemicals based on carcinogenicity and other chronic health effects. 55 *Fed. Reg.* 10473 (March 21, 1990). In early 1990, EPA sought public comment on their addition. *Id.* Although 37 of the 39 comments EPA received were opposed to the addition of the seven chemicals, EPA decided not to deny the petition. The 7 chemicals were therefore automatically added to the Section 313 list on the July 8, 1990 statutory deadline, and the first Section 313 reports for these chemicals will be due on July 1, 1992 for the 1991 Reporting Year. 55 *Fed. Reg.* 31594 (August 3, 1990).

67.   42 U.S.C. § 11023(f) and 40 C.F.R. § 372.25. This is the threshold for Reporting Year 1989 and subsequent years. The threshold was 75,000 pounds for calendar year 1987, the first Section 313 Reporting Year, and 50,000 pounds for calendar year 1988.

68.   *Id.* The "otherwise used" threshold has remained unchanged at 10,000 pounds.

69.   42 U.S.C. § 11023(g) and 40 C.F.R. § 372.20. The Toxic Chemical Release Inventory Reporting Form (Form R) and instructions for its use are published at 40 C.F.R. § 372.85. Each year, however, EPA publishes much more detailed information and instructions, along with the Form R, in booklet form as the *Toxic Chemical Release Inventory Reporting Form R and Instructions*. The Revised 1989 Version (revised January 1990),

document No. EPA 560/4-90-007, known affectionately as "The Purple Book," contains 49 pages plus appendices. In addition, EPA yearly publishes a "Questions and Answers" document that supplements the Form R and instructions and provides additional explanation of the Section 313 reporting requirements: *Toxic Chemical Release Inventory Questions and Answers, Revised 1989 Version*, U.S. EPA Office of Toxic Substances, document No. EPA 560/4-90-003, Jan. 1990, 59 pp.

70.   40 C.F.R. § 372.30.

71.   "The Purple Book," *supra* note 73.

72.   40 C.F.R. § 372.45(a).

73.   40 C.F.R. § 372.45(b).

74.   40 C.F.R. § 372.38(a).

75.   40 C.F.R. § 372.38(b). "Article" is defined at 40 C.F.R. § 372.3.

76.   40 C.F.R. § 372.38(c).

77.   40 C.F.R. § 372.38(d).

78.   42 U.S.C. § 1132(j).

79.   *Id.* Section 313 data in the form of the Toxic Release Inventory (TRI) became available to the public on June 19, 1989 via the National Library of Medicine's Toxicology Data Network. In addition, the computerized TRI data base is available at 1,400 Federal Depository Libraries and 3,000 county libraries around the country. The 1988 TRI data are expected to be available on the data base by the Fall of 1990. EPA's Executive Summary of the 1987 Toxics Release Inventory was published in booklet form in June of 1989. *The Toxics-Release Inventory, Executive Summary*, document No. EPA 560/4-89-006., June, 1989, 25 pp.

80.   42 U.S.C. § 11041(a).

81.   42 U.S.C. § 11041(b).

82.   42 U.S.C. § 11042(a)(1)(A). A "trade secret" is defined as "any confidential formula, pattern, process, device, information or compilation of information that is used in a submitter's business, and that gives the submitter an opportunity to obtain an advantage over competitors who do not know or use it." 40 C.F.R. § 350.1.

83.   42 U.S.C. § 11042(a)(1)(B).

84.   42 U.S.C. § 11042(b)(1)-(4).

85.   Requirements for submitting trade secrecy claims under all EPCRA sections are found at 40 C.F.R. § 350.5.

86.   The "Substantiation to Accompany Claims of Trade Secrecy" form is found at 40 C.F.R. § 350.27. In completing the form, a trade secrecy claimant must answer all questions found at 40 C.F.R. § 350.7(a)(1)-(6). If a company finds it necessary to include information on the substantiation form which reveals the claimed secret chemical identity

or other confidential business information, the company must submit a "sanitized version" and an "unsanitized" version which includes all alleged sensitive information but clearly marks such information as either "confidential" or "trade secret." 40 C.F.R. § 350.7(d). Anything not marked will be disclosed without notice to the trade secret claimant.

87.   40 C.F.R. § 350.9(a).

88.   40 C.F.R. § 350.9(b). Procedures governing EPA review of a trade secrecy claim are found at 40 C.F.R. § 350.11.

89.   *Id.*

90.   40 C.F.R. § 350.11(a)(2).

91.   The provisions and criteria for a showing of good cause are found at 40 C.F.R. § 350.11(a)(2)(ii) and (iii).

92.   While the statute and applicable regulations do not define "health professionals," the term has been construed more broadly than doctors and nurses, and presumably includes other professionals such as x-ray technicians, physician assistants, and paramedics. *See* 53 *Fed. Reg.* 28771, 28797 (July 29, 1988).

93.   42 U.S.C. § 11043(a)(b).

94.   42 U.S.C. § 11043(c).

95.   The specifics regarding the written statement of need are found at 42 U.S.C. § 11043(c)(2) and 40 C.F.R. § 350.40.

96.   The specifics regarding the confidentiality agreement are found at 42 U.S.C. § 11043(d) and 40 C.F.R. § 350.40.

97.   42 U.S.C. § 11043(a), (c).

98.   42 U.S.C. § 11043(b).

99.   42 U.S.C. § 11043(b).

100.   42 U.S.C. § 11044(a).

101.   *Id.*

102.   42 U.S.C. § 11044(c).

103.   42 U.S.C. § 11046(a)(1)(A).

104.   42 U.S.C. § 11046(d)(2).

105.   *Id.*

106.   42 U.S.C. §11046(a)(1)(B).

107.   42 U.S.C. § 11046(a)(1)(C).

108. 42 U.S.C. § 11046(a)(1)(D).

109. *See* 42 U.S.C. § 11046(a)(2)(A).

110. 42 U.S.C. § 11046(a)(2)(B).

111. 42 U.S.C. § 11046(h)(1).

112. 42 U.S.C. § 11047. Storage in this context has been stated to mean "storage of materials which are still moving under active shipping papers and which have not reached the consignee." H. R. Conf. Rep. No. 96, 99th Cong., 2d Sess. (1986) 311.

113. 42 U.S.C. § 11047.

114. 42 U.S.C. § 11045.

115. 42 U.S.C. § 11045(a).

116. *Id.*

117. 42 U.S.C. § 11045(b).

118. 42 U.S.C. § 11045(b)(1).

119. 42 U.S.C. § 11045(b)(2).

120. *Id.*

121. 40 C.F.R. Part 22.

122. 40 C.F.R. § 22.40.

123. 42 U.S.C. § 11045(b)(3).

124. *Id.*

125. 42 U.S.C. § 11045(b)(4).

126. *Id.*

127. 42 U.S.C. § 11045(c)(4).

128. 42 U.S.C. § 11045(c)(2).

129. 42 U.S.C. § 11045(c)(1).

130. 42 U.S.C. § 11045(d)(1).

131. 42 U.S.C. § 11045(d)(2).

132. 42 U.S.C. § 11045(e).

133. EPA Memorandum, *Enforcement Response Policy for Section 313 of the Emergency Planning and Community Right to Know Act*, Office of Compliance Monitoring, December 2, 1988, 19 pp.

134. *Id.* at 1.

135. *Id.*

136. *Id.* at 2.

137. *Id.* The Agency allowed 90 days after the due date of July 1, 1988 and up to 60 days after the July 1, 1989 due date. *Id.*

138. *Id.*

139. *Id* at 3.

140. *Id.* at 5-6.

141. *Id.* at 6.

142. *Id.*

143. *Id.* at 7.

144. *Id.*

145. *Id.*

146. EPA Memorandum, *Interim Enforcement Strategy for Enforcement of Title III and CERCLA Section 103 Notification Requirements*, OSWER Directive #9841.0, December 14, 1988, 14 pp.

147. *Id.*

148. *Id.* at 7.

149. 42 U.S.C. § 9604(e).

150. *Id.* at 8.

151. *Id.* at 10.

152. One example given is *A Guide to Chemical Use in Industry: Extremely Hazardous Substance/Standard Industrial Classification (SIC) Code Crosswalks for the Emergency Planning and Community Right-to Know Act*, developed by the EPA Office of Waste Programs Enforcement (OWPE) based on information in the National Air Toxic Clearing House database Id. This document is now available from the OWPE. The document identifies chemicals used by various industries by their SIC codes. *Id.*

153. *Id.*

154. Environmental News Release, U.S. EPA Office of Public Affairs (A-107), R-109, June 28, 1990, 5 pp.

155. *Id.*

156. *Id.*

157. *In The Matter of Riverside Furniture Corporation*, EPA Docket No. EPCRA-88-H-VI-406S, September 28, 1989.

158. *Id.*

159. *Id.*

160. *In the Matter of All Regions Chemical Labs., Inc.*, Docket No. CERCLA-I-88-1089, December 1, 1989.

161. *Id.*

162. *Id.*

163. *Id.*

164. *See* 45 *Fed. Reg.* 59770 (September 10, 1980).

165. EPA Memorandum, General Enforcement Policy, #GM-22 (February 16, 1984).

166. *In Re Murry's, Inc.*, Docket No. EPCRA-III-001.

167. *Id.*

168. *Id.*

169. *See supra* note 21.

170. *Id.* at 13. The referenced report briefly describes the current status of state law and provides the results of a survey in which 35 state attorneys general responded with their interpretations of their respective state laws on this issue. *Id.* A more detailed discussion of the subject can be found in a recent EPA publication, *Tort Liability in Emergency Planning*, Technical Assistance Bulletin 7, Chemical Emergency Preparedness and Prevention, EPA Office of Solid Waste and Emergency Response (OS-120), Jan. 1989, 19 pp.

171. *Id.*

172. *See Toxic Chemical Release Inventory Magnetic Media Submission Instructions*, U.S. EPA, Office of Toxic Substances, document number EPA 560/4-90-008, Revised January 1990, 23 pp. As this booklet notes, facilities should be careful to select a software package that will produce a format meeting EPA specifications. Vendors can request EPA to validate their magnetic media formats, and EPA will, upon request, provide current information concerning software EPA recognizes as preparing valid magnetic media formats. *Id.*

173. *Id.*

# XII     OSHA Requirements for Safety and Health Risk Management Programs

## Mark N. Duvall, Esq.
## Union Carbide Chemicals and Plastics Co.
## Danbury, Connecticut

The Occupational Safety and Health Administration (OSHA), part of the U.S. Department of Labor, has embraced risk management programs as a crucial tool for protecting employee safety and health. OSHA has said that it:

> has concluded that effective management of worker safety and health protection is a decisive factor in reducing the extent and the severity of work-related injuries and illnesses. ... [S]ystematic management policies, procedures and practices are fundamental to the reduction of work-related injuries and illnesses and their attendant economic costs. . . .[1]

This approach has come about in part because of OSHA's recognition of the limits of its traditional strategy of effecting incremental changes in the workplace by adopting standards regulating specific hazards and then enforcing those standards. Each such standard has required enormous administrative resources and time, thus limiting OSHA's ability to adopt standards addressing more than a limited number of occupational safety and health hazards. It also means that the traditional strategy has overlooked the possibility of systemic changes, i.e., the creation of a network of protections in the workplace that anticipate hazards and prevent their appearance, and that do not wait for OSHA to mandate correction.[2]

In OSHA's view, a workplace safety and health risk management program should:

- Provide systematic policies, procedures, and practices that are adequate to recognize and protect employees from occupational safety and health hazards;

- Include provisions for the systematic identification, evaluation, and prevention or control of general workplace hazards, specific job hazards, and potential hazards which may arise from foreseeable conditions;
- Address compliance with applicable OSHA requirements;
- Address all hazards, even if compliance with law is not an issue;
- Be written to ensure clear communication of policies and priorities and consistent and fair application of rules, except possibly where the workplace is small and/or the hazards are not complex.[3]

The Occupational Safety and Health Act of 1970 (OSH Act) imposes two obligations on employers, both of which potentially require the use of safety and health risk management programs in some situations. Section 5(a)(1), 29 U.S.C. § 654(a)(1), known as the general duty clause, essentially requires employers to protect employees to the extent feasible from serious occupational hazards of which the employer is or should be aware. OSHA has taken the position that in some contexts this provision implicitly requires employers to implement safety and health risk management programs.

Section 5(a)(2), 29 U.S.C. § 654(a)(2), sometimes known as the specific duty clause, requires employers to comply with OSHA standards. In a number of standards OSHA has adopted explicit requirements for risk management programs. These include, among others:

- The hazard communication standard, 29 C.F.R. § 1910.1200;
- The hazardous waste operations and emergency response rule, 29 C.F.R. § 1910.120; and
- The proposed rule on process safety management of highly hazardous chemicals, proposed 29 C.F.R. § 1910.119.

OSHA's air contaminants standard table[4] is an example of a standard which does not have an explicit risk management requirement, although aspects of a risk management program exist (as under the substance-specific standards found at § 1910.1001 *et. seq.*) or are under consideration.

In addition to enforcing these mandatory duties, OSHA has encouraged employers to implement voluntarily safety and health risk management programs. OSHA has incentive programs for employers with superior safety and health risk management systems, known as the Voluntary Protection Programs.[5] It has published generic guidelines on development of safety and health program management.[6] And OSHA has encouraged employers in the petrochemical industry to implement process safety risk management programs.

### The General Duty Clause

Section 5(a)(1) of the OSH Act provides that each employer "shall furnish to each of his employees employment and a place of employment which are free from recognized hazards that are causing or are likely to cause death or serious physical harm to his employees". This general duty upon employers has some limitations:

- Only serious hazards are covered, those likely to cause death or serious physical harm;
- Only recognized hazards are covered (either constructive knowledge or actual knowledge will suffice).
- The requirement that employment and places of employment be "free" from recognized hazards is limited by the implicit requirement that abatement of the hazards be feasible.

The general duty clause imposes an obligation upon employers to become aware of serious workplace hazards recognized in their industry and to manage those hazards so as to protect their employees to the extent feasible. Any effective method of abatement is acceptable; thus, OSHA cannot explicitly require the use of risk management programs under the general duty clause if the employer effectively protects its employees from serious recognized hazards without the use of such programs. In practice, however, for complex hazards, employers may find it impossible to protect their employees as required by the general duty clause without the use of risk management programs. Referring to enforcement cases under OSHA standards and the general duty clause, OSHA has asserted that:

> The implication of these cases is that an employer has the duty to establish and maintain [safety and health risk] management practices, to the extent that they are necessary to ensure that safe and healthful working conditions are maintained and that safe and healthful work practices are followed.[7]

### OSHA Requirements for Safety and Health Risk Management Programs

The general duty clause has historically been considered to be preempted with respect to a particular hazard by an OSHA standard applicable to that hazard. Congress considered that specific standards would give employers superior notice of what their obligations are. This has sometimes created gaps in coverage, such as where an OSHA standard is unenforceable because it uses "should" instead of "shall."[8] But a relatively recent case has arguably expanded the scope of the general duty clause to cover situations where the employer knows that an OSHA standard applies but is inadequate to protect employees against the hazard. In *UAW v. General Dynamics Land Systems Div.*,[9] the D.C. Circuit held that the general duty clause cannot be preempted by a specific standard. Compliance with a specific standard may satisfy an employer's general duty obligation. But where the employer knows a specific standard to be inadequate to protect against the hazard, the general duty clause compels the employer to take additional steps to protect its employees from that hazard beyond those mandated by the standard.

The lesson of this case is that employers cannot rely upon compliance with standards as sufficient to execute their obligations under the OSH Act. If no standard applies, the general duty clause may apply. Even if a standard applies, the employer must remain alert to residual hazards not adequately addressed by the standard. This may require employers to develop risk management programs even where a specific standard applies and does not require one.

## The Hazard Communication Standard

The Hazard Communication Standard (HCS), 29 C.F.R. § 1910.1200, is a worker right-to-know (RTK) law.[10] OSHA adopted this standard partly in response to proliferating state RTK laws. Congress used it as a starting point for the federal community RTK law, the Emergency Planning and Community Right-To-Know Act of 1986 (EPCRA), also known as Title III of the Superfund Amendments and Reauthorization Act of 1986 (SARA).

The HCS is an early (1983) effort to require an occupational safety and health risk management program. It requires that the hazards of each chemical be identified by those in the best position to identify them, either the manufacturer of the importer of the chemical. It requires that the manufacturer or importer prepare a material safety data sheet (MSDS) for each chemical determined to be hazardous. Each MSDS must communicate the chemical's hazards and methods to protect against those hazards. The HCS also requires chemical manufacturers and importers to label containers of hazardous chemicals with an identity keyed to that on the MSDS, appropriate hazard warnings, and the name and address of a person to contact for more information.

MSDSs must be sent to customers with the first shipment of a hazardous chemical. Updated MSDSs must also be sent to customers. Distributors of chemicals are required to pass on to their customers the MSDSs they receive. If they repackage containers of hazardous chemicals, they must label the new containers with the necessary information. These requirements are intended to get hazard information into the hands of employers whose employees may be exposed to hazardous chemicals during use.

Employers whose employees are potentially exposed to hazardous chemicals must make hazard information available to employees by:
- Making MSDSs readily available to employees in their work areas during their work shift;
- Ensuring that the containers of hazardous chemicals are labeled with an identity keyed to that on the MSDS and appropriate hazard warnings, even if the chemicals are transferred from their original containers;
- Training employees in the recognition of hazards and how to protect themselves from those hazards.

Employers whose employees are potentially exposed to hazardous chemicals must also develop and implement a written hazard communication program which:
- Describes how the employer will meet the MSDS, labeling, and training requirements;
- Includes a list of all the hazardous chemicals known to be present in the workplace;
- Describes the methods the employer will use to inform employees of the hazards of non-routine tasks (e.g., cleaning reactor vessels) and of unlabeled pipes;
- Describes the methods used to communicate hazards to other employers present at the workplace (e.g., on-site contractors).

Significantly, the HCS does not require employers whose employees may potentially be exposed to hazardous chemicals to follow the manufacturer's recommendations on the MSDS or to take any steps other than communication of the hazard through training programs. But one purpose of the HCS is "to ensure that all employers receive the information they need. . . to design and implement employee protection programs."[11] Thus, OSHA expects that once employers receive information about safety and health hazards of chemicals, they will manage those hazards.

Under the general duty clause, employers are required, to the extent feasible, to provide employment and places of employment which are free from serious hazards which they recognize or should recognize. With the HCS, OSHA ensures that they do recognize chemical hazards, thus potentially triggering the obligations of the general duty clause. In addition, employers might face workers compensation liability, tort liability, and conceivably criminal liability for failure to use the hazard information to protect their workers.

When coupled with the general duty clause, the HCS is the single most important health standard issued by OSHA. It applies to all chemicals. It is evergreen, meaning that as new chemicals, new hazards and new methods to protect against hazards are identified, the HCS applies to them. It focuses on motivating employees to take responsibility for their own protection, while leaving legal responsibility for compliance on employers. It encourages employers to implement safety and health risk management programs by providing them with critical information to help them to do so.

## The HAZWOPER Rule

The Hazardous Waste Operations and Emergency Response (HAZWOPER) Rule, 29 C.F.R. § 1910.120, is an unusual OSHA standard in that Congress required its adoption and spelled out its major provisions in Section 126 of SARA.

Prior to 1986, Congress had enacted two statutes dealing directly with hazardous waste, the Resource Conservation and Recovery Act of 1976, as amended (RCRA), and the Comprehensive Environmental Response, Compensation, and Liability Act of 1980 (CERCLA). Both dealt with the safety and health of employees engaged in working with hazardous waste, but only tangentially. Under Section 7001 (f) of RCRA, 42 U.S.C. § 6971(f), EPA was directed to provide certain information concerning hazards faced by employees handling hazardous wastes to OSHA and the National Institute for Occupational Safety and Health (NIOSH), to assist them in carrying out their responsibilities under the OSH Act. Under Section 111(c)(6) of CERCLA, 42 U.S.C. § 9611(c)(6), Congress permitted funds to be used for a program to protect the safety and health of employees involved in responses to hazardous substance releases, the program to be developed jointly by EPA, OSHA, and NIOSH.

Those agencies plus the Coast Guard jointly developed a guidance manual, "Occupational Safety and Health Guidance Manual for Hazardous Waste Site Activities[12], OSHA also launched a special emphasis program for hazardous waste sites. OSHA Instruction CPL 2.70 (Jan. 29, 1986). Feeling that additional protections were necessary, in late 1986 Congress passed SARA, which contained detailed provisions on worker protection.

Section 126 required OSHA to adopt risk management standards for the safety and health protection of "employees engaged in hazardous waste operations." Congress also required that the standards include provisions for "a formal hazard analysis of the site and development of a site specific plan for worker protection"; training; medical surveillance; protective equipment; engineering controls; maximum exposure limits; informational programs; handling, transporting, labeling, and disposing of hazardous wastes; introduction of new technology for worker protection; decontamination procedures; and emergency response.

As required by Section 126, in 1986 OSHA adopted an interim final rule without conducting notice and comment rulemaking, then subsequently adopted a final rule after going through rulemaking. The final rule took effect on March 6, 1990.[13]

In drafting its rule, OSHA relied extensively on documents prepared by EPA and other agencies, as specifically directed by Section 126.[14]

In the rule OSHA interprets the term "hazardous waste operations" to include the following:
- Clean-up operations required by a governmental body involving hazardous substances that are conducted at uncontrolled hazardous waste sites (e.g., sites on the National Priorities List (NPL) or recommended for the NPL, state priority

sites, and sites being initially investigated before the presence or absence of hazardous substances has been ascertained);

- Corrective actions involving clean-up operations at sites covered by RCRA;
- Voluntary clean-up operations at sites recognized by governmental bodies as uncontrolled hazardous waste sites;
- Operations involving hazardous wastes that are conducted at treatment, storage, and disposal (TSD) facilities regulated under RCRA;
- Emergency response operations for releases of hazardous substances, or substantial threats of such releases, regardless of the location of the hazard, on the theory that once released a hazardous substance becomes a "hazardous waste".[15]

OSHA adopted separate requirements for operations at (1) uncontrolled hazardous waste sites and RCRA corrective actions, (2) operations at TSD facilities, and (3) emergency response operations. All three require the development and implementation of risk management programs.

At uncontrolled hazardous waste sites and RCRA corrective actions, employers must develop and implement a written safety and health program designed to identify, evaluate, and control safety and health hazards, and to provide for emergency response. Among other elements, the plan must include provisions for an organizational structures, a comprehensive work plan, a site-specific safety and health plan, a safety and health training program, a medical surveillance program, standard operating procedures for safety and health, and any necessary interface between general program and site-specific activities. Employers must meet other stringent requirements as well.

For hazardous waste operations at TSD facilities, the standard contains less-detailed requirements for development and implementation of a written safety and health program designed to identify, evaluate, and control safety and health hazards at TSD facilities, and to address site analysis, engineering controls, maximum exposure limits, hazardous waste handling procedures, and uses of new technologies, as appropriate. Employers must also develop and implement programs for hazard communication, medical surveillance, decontamination, new technology, material handling, training, and emergency response.

For emergency response operations, employers must develop and implement emergency response plans to handle anticipated emergencies prior to the commencement of emergency response operations. The plans must address pre-emergency planning and coordination with outside parties; personnel roles, lines of authority, training, and communication; emergency recognition and prevention; safe distances and places of refuge; site security and control; evacuation routes and procedures; decontamination; emergency medical treatment and first aid; emergency alerting and response procedures; critique of response and follow-up; and personal protective equipment and emergency equipment. The other requirements provide criteria for each of these items and cover related issues.

## Process Safety Management of Highly Hazardous Chemicals

OSHA has taken a series of steps to encourage employers with chemical-related operations that have catastrophic potential to develop sound risk management programs. The most recent of these is the publication of a proposed rule governing process safety management of highly hazardous chemicals.

Following the 1984 tragedy in Bhopal, India, and the incident at Institute, West Virginia, in 1985 and 1986 OSHA conducted a Special Emphasis Program for the Chemical Industry (ChemSEP).[16] OSHA conducted 40 in-depth inspections of chemical manufacturing facilities, focusing on safety and health management, including emergency preparedness. OSHA issued some citations for alleged violations of standards, but issued a comparatively large number of citations for alleged violations of the general duty clause and made many recommendations,reflecting its recognition that few OSHA standards address process safety.

The final report on ChemSEP recommended:

Performance-oriented standards for the industry should be considered to address the overall management of chemical production and handling systems. In essence, OSHA finds that safety is not only a matter of "having the right equipment," but that it is more nearly a function of the management activities which touch on use of the "right" equipment. Thus, standards for the chemical industry should. . .

## OSHA Requirements for Safety and Health Risk Management Programs

include [subjects such as] maintenance schedules for critical equipment, updating of operating procedures and process diagrams, emergency preparedness and response plans, and basic process safety considerations. Any such OSHA action would, of course, have to be closely coordinated with EPA guidelines and regulations on community awareness programs, chemical hazard information, and chemical releases.[17]

OSHA has made ChemSEP into a regular part of its inspection plan.[18] OSHA has issued a pamphlet informing employers of some of the lessons learned from ChemSEP.[19]

On October 23, 1989, a fire and explosion occurred at a Phillips polyethylene plant in Pasadena, Texas, which killed 23 employees, injured more than 130, and caused nearly $750 million in property damage. Secretary of Labor Dole promised a thorough investigation.

OSHA issued a final report on its investigation entitled "The Phillips 66 Company Houston Chemical Complex Explosion and Fire: A Report to the President" (Apr. 1990). It reviewed the history of ChemSEP and discussed the ongoing preparation of a standard. It also discussed the causes of emergencies at petrochemical plants generally. It found that "the primary causes of the accident were failures in the management of safety systems" at the Phillips plant. It encouraged companies in the petrochemical industry to institute chemical process safety management plans. It focused particularly on the heavy use of contractors in the petrochemical industry for maintenance work.

OSHA issued citations to Phillips and its contractor, which have been contested. Phillips received citations with a total of $5,666,200 in proposed fines, the second largest amount of penalties ever proposed against a company in a single inspection. The Phillips citations included 566 allegations of willful violations of the general duty clause, one for each of the employees potentially exposed, at a proposed penalty of $10,000 each, plus citations for alleged serious violations of OSHA standards. OSHA's general conclusion, according to the press release, was that "the plant's approach to safety and health has not been pursued with adequate management commitment to protect the lives and well-being of Phillips employees."

In both its 1987 ChemSEP final report and its 1990 Phillips investigation final report, OSHA found the need for a mandatory standard which would address process safety management of highly hazardous chemicals. OSHA recently proposed just such a standard.[20] The proposal is modeled after a 1988 document prepared by an industry consulting company, Organization Resources Counselors, Inc. (ORC), for use by OSHA entitled "Recommendations for Process Hazards Management of Substances with Catastrophic Potential".

The proposed rule would apply to the following:

- Processes which involve certain listed chemicals at or above the threshold quantities listed in an appendix (100 to 15,000 pounds);
- Processes which involve flammable liquids or gases onsite in one location in quantities of 10,000 pounds or more (with exceptions for fuel use and certain kinds of flammable liquids);
- The manufacture of explosives and pyrotechnics; and
- Processes which involve certain other highly hazardous chemicals.

The term *process* would include any manufacturing, storage, handling, use or movement. The proposed rule would include a list of highly hazardous chemicals and a method for identifying additional such chemicals in the future.

It would require the employer to develop and maintain a compilation of safety information to provide a foundation for identifying and understanding the hazards of processes involving highly hazardous chemicals. The information would cover the hazards of the chemicals handled, the technology of the process, and the equipment in the process.

The equipment for the process would have to comply with applicable consensus codes and standards, where they exist, or else recognized and generally accepted engineering practices. The employer would have to perform or update a formal hazard analysis every five years for identifying, evaluating, and controlling hazards involved in the process. Recommendations arising from that analysis would have to be implemented in a timely manner.

The employer would have to establish and implement procedures to manage changes to equipment design and operation technology prior to implementation of such changes, including the impact of the changes on safety and health.

The employer would have to develop and implement written operating procedures that address the steps for each operating phase, operating limits and safety and health.

The employer would have to train employees in an overview of the process and in the operating procedures. Retraining would be required annually.

Additional provisions would address relationships with contractors, pre-start-up safety reviews, mechanical integrity, hot work permits, incident investigations, emergency response, and compliance safety audits.

EPA has also been active in the issue of process safety. In Subtitle A of EPCRA (SARA Title III), Congress directed EPA to take a number of actions concerning emergency planning for a chemical release, and notification of certain kinds of releases. In particular, in Section 305(b) EPA was required to conduct a review of emergency systems for monitoring, detecting, and preventing releases of extremely hazardous substances. EPA's report to Congress under Section 305(b), dated June 1988, concluded that "[p]revention of accidental releases requires a holistic approach that integrates technologies, procedures, and management practices." This is very similar to OSHA's conclusion in the final ChemSEP report and in its Phillips report.

Around the time that SARA was enacted, EPA was developing a Chemical Accident Prevention Program, citing authority under CERCLA. Out of the Section 305(b) report and this program, EPA developed a Chemical Safety Audit Program to investigate the causes of releases at specific facilities, and the equipment, procedures, training, and management techniques utilized to prevent or mitigate those releases. The audits are also intended to enhance chemical safety practices at facilities by providing recommendations to management. EPA conducted its own chemical safety audit following the Phillips plant explosion, in addition to OSHA's extensive investigation.

In the future, OSHA and EPA are likely to be required to cooperate more closely in the area of process safety. OSHA has developed with EPA a memorandum of understanding for exchanging information between the two agencies and is developing joint enforcement inspections and strategies for chemical accidents. Moreover, legislation amending the Clean Air Act now before the President would require EPA to coordinate with OSHA in the promulgation of regulations governing risk management programs for facilities pro-

ducing, processing, handling, or storing extremely hazardous substances. EPA would be directed to promulgate rules mandating hazard assessments, and continuous monitoring as well as rules on the
prevention, detection, and response to chemical releases. In doing
so, EPA would be required to coordinate with OSHA in recognition
of OSHA's work on a process safety management rule.

## The Air Contaminants Standard

In contrast to the HCS, HAZWOPER, and process safety management rules, with their emphasis on written programs and comprehensive approaches to managing particular hazards, the air contaminants standard, 29 C.F.R. § 1910.1000, has no requirement for a risk
management program and it addresses only a few aspects of the hazard involved.

Typically, OSHA health standards address a variety of aspects on
controlling the hazards of a chemical. For example, the OSHA standard on formaldehyde, 29 C.F.R. § 1910.1048, has provisions governing permissible exposure limits (PELs), exposure monitoring, regulated areas, methods of compliance, respiratory protection, engineering controls, other protective equipment and clothing hygiene protection and housekeeping, emergency plans, medical surveillance,
and hazard communication. The result is a comprehensive risk management program for a single chemical. But OSHA has taken years
and required enormous resources to promulgate each of its approximately 25 substance-specific standards. At this pace, OSHA cannot
possibly establish control requirements for all health hazards.

The air contaminants standard focuses on only a few aspects of a
complete risk management program, but it covers 600 chemicals. It
establishes a PEL for each chemical and it prescribes a hierarchy of
controls to be used in achieving compliance with those PELs, with a
preference for engineering controls. Unlike EPA, OSHA does not
prescribe the technology to be used to achieve compliance, giving
employers flexibility to choose what works best for them.

Unions have sued OSHA to require it to adopt additional aspects
of a comprehensive risk management program requirement for each
of the 600 chemicals.[21] Even in the absence of a requirement to do so
however, many employers are likely to implement a risk manage-

ment program to facilitate compliance with the PELs. Generic OSHA standards that do prescribe aspects of a risk management program include the HCS, 29 C.F.R. § 1910.1200; respiratory protection, 29 C.F.R. § 1910.134; and employee emergency plans and fire emergency plans, 29 C.F.R. § 1910.38. OSHA has published voluntary guidelines outlining the elements of a recommended risk management program for several hundred of the covered chemicals.[22]

OSHA is considering adoption of generic standards addressing two aspects of a risk management program which would apply to some or all of the 600 chemicals covered by the air contaminants standard. The first concerns exposure monitoring, for which OSHA published an advance notice of proposed rulemaking (ANPR).[23] As a practical matter, employers often monitor to determine compliance, but currently for most chemicals there is no requirement to do so. OSHA published a list of analytical methods for most of the 600 chemicals to encourage monitoring.[24] The generic rule would impose monitoring requirements under certain conditions.

Similarly, OSHA has issued an ANPR on medical surveillance.[25] Most substance-specific standards have detailed requirements for medical surveillance on the theory that early detection of occupationally-related disease can lead to prevention, treatment or at least a limitation on further exposures. The generic rule would require medical surveillance under certain circumstances.

## Voluntary Guidelines Encouraging Employers to Adopt Safety and Health Risk Management Programs

In 1982 OSHA adopted Voluntary Protection Programs (VPP). There have been three purposes:
- Emphasizing the importance of employer-provided, site-specific occupational safety and health risk management programs;
- Encouraging the improvement of such programs; and
- Recognizing excellence in them.

VPP requirements have been amended over the years.[26] They provide recognition to qualified employers and remove them from lists

Environmental
Risk Management

of facilities to be inspected on a programmed basis. They still remain subject to inspections based upon incidents and employee complaints.

The principal program, STAR, requires excellence in injury incidence rates and the following components of a risk management program: management commitment and planning; assessment of hazards; correction and control of hazards; safety and health training; employee participation; and evaluation of safety and health programs. The other program, Merit (formerly "Try"), has similar requirements which are less rigorous.

In 1983 OSHA announced a comprehensive workplace health programs policy intended in part to stimulate establishment of comprehensive systems of protection against workplace health hazards.[27] It set forth briefly 13 elements of workplace health protection systems. The main incentive provided in the program was cutting back on programmed inspections where the employer could demonstrate that it had implemented such a workplace health risk management program. This Reagan Administration proposal led to Congressional criticism and eventual abandonment of the incentive, but the idea of encouraging comprehensive workplace health risk management programs continued.

In 1989, OSHA issued voluntary occupational safety and health management guidelines.[28] They are applicable to general industry, shipyards, marine terminals, and longshoring. They supplement earlier guidelines on safety and health program management in the construction industry, OSHA Instruction STD 3-1.1 (June 22, 1987). Major elements include:

- Management commitment and employee involvement;
- Work site analysis of existing hazards, and conditions and operations in which changes might create hazards;
- Hazard prevention (by effective design of the job site or the job), where feasible, and elsewhere hazard control;
- Safety and health training.

## Future Trends and Emerging Issues

In summary, for several years OSHA has sought to promote occupational safety and health hazard management programs through the general duty clause, standards, and voluntary programs. These efforts are likely to continue, especially in light of the rulemaking proposals OSHA currently has out for comment, and OSHA's recent use of general duty clauses in the Phillips case.

## About the Author

Mark N. Duvall graduated *magna cum laude* from Amherst College in 1974, where he was elected to *Phi Beta Kappa*. He received his law degree from the University of Virginia School of Law, where he was elected to the Order of the Coif. Currently he is Health and Safety Counsel in the Law Department of Union Carbide Chemicals and Plastics Company Inc., responsible for federal, state and foreign laws pertaining to health and safety. He is a member of the District of Columbia and Connecticut Bars and the American Bar Association.

## Endnotes

1. 54 *Fed. Reg.* 3904, 3908-09 (Jan. 26, 1989).

2. *See, e.g.,* 48 *Fed. Reg.* 54546, 54547 (Dec. 5, 1983).

3. *See* 54 *Fed. Reg.* at 3909.

4. 29 C.F.R. § 1910.1000.

5. *See* 53 *Fed. Reg.* 26339 (July 12, 1988).

6. 54 *Fed. Reg.* 3904 (Jan. 26, 1989).

7. 54 *Fed. Reg.* 3904, 3910 (Jan. 26, 1989).

8. *See, e.g., A. Prokosch & Sons Sheet Metal, Inc.,* 8 O.S.H. Cas. (BNA) 2077 (OSHRC 1980).

9. 815 F.2d 1570 (D.C. Cir.), *cert. denied,* 484 U.S. 976 (1987).

10. Identical standards also appear at 29 C.F.R. § 1915.99, 1917.28. 1918.90, and 1926.59.

11. 48 *Fed. Reg.* 53280, 53281 (Nov. 25, 1983).

12. DHHS (NIOSH) Publication No. 85-115 (Oct. 1985).

13. *See* 54 *Fed. Reg.* 9294 (Mar. 6, 1989), **corrected**, 55 *Fed. Reg.* 14072 (Apr. 13, 1990). *See also* 54 *Fed. Reg.* 26654 (June 23, 1989) (application to state and local employees of states without state plans); 55 *Fed. Reg.* 2776 (Jan. 26, 1990) (proposed rule on accreditation of training programs for hazardous waste operations).

14. *See* 51 *Fed. Reg* 4565 (Dec. 19, 1986); 52 *Fed. Reg.* 29620, 29621 (Aug. 10, 1987).

15. *See* 54 *Fed. Reg.* 9294, 9297 (Mar. 6, 1989).

16. *See* OSHA Notice CPL 2 (Mar. 17, 1986).

17. OSHA, "Chemical Special Emphasis Program Final Report" (1987) at 24.

18. *See* OSHA Instruction CPL 2-2.45 (Sept. 6, 1988).

19. OSHA 3091, "Safety & Health Guide for the Chemical Industry" (1986). *See also* OSHA 3088, "Emergency Response in the Workplace" (1984).

20. Proposed 29 C.F.R. § 1910.119, 55 *Fed. Reg.* 29150 (July 17, 1990).

21. *AFL-CIO v. OSHA*, No. 89-7185 at al. (11th Cir.)

22. "Occupational Safety and Health Guidelines for Chemical Hazards," DHHS, (NIOSH) Publication No. 81-123 (Jan. 1981), as supplemented by DHHS (NIOSH) Publication No. 88-118 and No. 89-104 (1988).

23. 53 *Fed. Reg.* 37591 (Sept. 27, 1988).

24. 54 *Fed. Reg.* 2332, 2960 (Jan. 19, 1989).

25. 53 *Fed. Reg.* 37595 (Sept. 27, 1988).

26. *See* 53 *Fed. Reg.* 26339 (June 12, 1988) (Current version).

27. 48 *Fed. Reg.* 54546 (Dec. 5, 1983).

28. 54 *Fed. Reg.* 3904 (Jan. 26, 1989).

# XIII International Environmental Risk Management

## Laura B. Campbell, Esq.*
## Morgan, Lewis & Bockius
## New York, New York

In 1970, Earth Day was an American event expressing the American public's concern over the environment. Earth Day 1990 was a global phenomenon in which people from countries around the world participated. Activities focused on both domestic and international environmental problems recognizing that air and water pollution do not respect national boundaries. Multilateral treaties, foreign domestic legislation, and recent U.S. judicial decisions reflect the growing perception that environmental issues are global problems requiring international solutions.[1] Increasing international concern about the environment presents a unique challenge to U.S. companies operating abroad.

Today, an interdependent global economy requires industry to be international in order to be competitive. In an era of increasing environmental concern, however, overseas operations pose difficult questions about the applicability of environmental standards and effective risk management. As discussed below, a recent international treaty on waste export favors imposing the prevailing standards of industrialized countries on disposal activities in developing countries. Personal injury suits arising out of activities conducted in foreign countries are being brought in U.S. courts where damage awards are higher and proof of causation is easier than in the host country. Even cases tried in foreign courts, such as those brought against Union Carbide by the Bhopal plaintiffs, can have severe financial and public relations consequences.

* The author wishes to acknowledge Tamara Crickett for her valuable assistance in researching this article.

Effective management of environmental risk by a multinational corporation, therefore, requires assessment of the risks posed by both foreign and U.S. operations and implementation of a program designed to minimize these risks. Designing a program to minimize environmental risks of offshore operations requires consideration of international treaties and codes of conduct, judicial decisions concerning U.S. activities abroad, and foreign environmental legislation.

This chapter discusses current developments in international environmental law, a recent case brought in an American court based upon the activities of U.S. companies operating abroad, and environmental legislation in the European Community and Japan. Finally, the chapter presents a basic outline for designing an effective international environmental risk management program.

# Recent Developments
# In International Environmental Law

## Protection Of The Ozone Layer —
## The Vienna Convention and Montreal Protocol

In March 1985, a framework for control of chemicals which damage the ozone layer of the earth's atmosphere was established with the adoption of the Vienna Convention for the Protection of the Ozone Layer. With the subsequent passage of the Montreal Protocol on Substances that Deplete the Ozone Layer in 1987, countries from every region of the world agreed to take significant steps towards reducing emissions of ozone-depleting chemicals. The Montreal Protocol limits the production and consumption of specific chlorofluorocarbons (CFCs) and halons that contribute to the depletion of ozone in the stratosphere. Ozone depletion would lead to increased human exposure to harmful ultraviolet radiation which is associated with higher rates of skin cancer and cataracts and possible suppression of the immune system. Additionally, CFCs have been linked with an increase in global warming. CFCs are used in a variety of products, including aerosols, refrigerants, foaming agents and solvents.

The Montreal Protocol calls for a freeze on the production and use of certain CFCs at 1986 levels with additional reductions of 20 percent and 50 percent in the early 1990s. The production and use of halons covered by the Montreal Protocol are frozen at the 1986 levels. The amended Protocol, as of June 29, 1990, calls for a 50 percent cut in CFCs by 1995, an 85 percent cut by 1997, and a total phase-out by the year 2000. Developing countries were granted a ten-year grace period. The participants also agreed to a 50 percent reduction in the use of halons by 1995, with a total phase-out by the year 2000.

The United States ratified the Montreal Protocol by promulgating regulations under the authority of Section 157 of the Clean Air Act. The United States also amended the Internal Revenue Code in 1989 to impose an excise tax on the sale or use of certain ozone-depleting chemicals by producers, manufacturers or importers. The tax, which was effective January 1, 1990, is imposed not only on pure chemicals, but on mixtures and products containing designated CFCs and halons.

In 1989, the European Community agreed in principle to eliminate the production and use of CFCs by the year 2000, sooner than required by the Montreal Protocol. The European Community also agreed to cut CFC production by 85 percent as soon as possible, moving beyond the 50 percent reduction set forth in the Montreal Protocol.

The Montreal Protocol is an example of the length to which countries became willing to go in the 1980s in order to prevent environmental problems which had not yet fully manifested themselves. At the same time, the division of opinion between industrialized and developing nations expressed during the negotiation of the Montreal Protocol may be indicative of similar differences of opinion which will arise during development of future international environmental agreements. Large developing nations, such as India, China, Mexico and Brazil expressed reluctance to take measures which might impede their economic development in order to mitigate environmental problems which they view as having been caused by industrialized countries. Developing countries also want access to the technology to manufacture alternatives to CFCs as a condition of signing the Montreal Protocol. In this respect, the amended Protocol established a $160 million fund to assist developing countries in switching to substitutes. Moreover, an additional $80 million was earmarked for assistance to new signatories that are developing countries: an obvious incentive for India and China to now ratify the amended Protocol.

Companies in industrialized countries want assurances that they will be able to profit from developing alternatives to CFCs, a costly and difficult process. Mechanisms for protecting the interests of companies which create alternatives to CFCs as well as schemes and funding for making CFC substitutes available to developing countries in order to elicit their support for the Montreal Protocol raise complex and difficult issues concerning intellectual property rights and market access. One thing is clear, however, in order to make any international environmental treaty work, both industrialized and developing countries must support such an agreement.

### Export of Hazardous Waste — The Basel Convention

Partially as a result of increasingly stringent domestic regulation of hazardous waste disposal in industrialized countries, hazardous waste export to developing countries has increased. Developing countries eager to obtain foreign currency have accepted industrialized countries' hazardous waste for disposal. Widely publicized incidents involving transport of chemical waste from France to several African nations were particularly influential in highlighting the increasing problem of hazardous waste export. While waste export can be both financially and environmentally beneficial when waste is imported by a country with more efficient disposal technology than the exporting country, problems arise when the country of import lacks the technology and expertise to safely dispose of the waste.

In response to increasing concern over the international transport of hazardous waste, the United Nations Environmental Program (UNEP) held an *ad hoc* work group meeting in 1984 to develop guidelines concerning international management of hazardous waste. The so-called "Cairo Guidelines" were adopted by UNEP on June 17, 1987. Among other things, the Cairo Guidelines directed UNEP to draft an international treaty on the transboundary movement of hazardous waste to be adopted by early 1989. Accordingly, UNEP drafted a convention on the transboundary movement of hazardous (and some non-hazardous) waste and on March 22, 1989, participants from 116 countries assembled in Basel, Switzerland, to adopt the convention.

The Basel Convention on the Transboundary Movement of Hazardous Wastes and Their Disposal regulates international waste export by holding exporting countries accountable for the management of their waste in importing countries. The Basel Convention also gives those countries through which waste is transported the authority to restrict such transit, encourages waste minimization, and promotes the sharing of information and technology for safe waste disposal practices.

The Basel Convention requires that exporting nations provide notice of waste shipments to importing countries and receive consent to the import before the waste leaves the country of origin. More importantly, however, the Basel Convention seeks to impose the environmental standards of the nation exporting the waste in the country of ultimate disposal. While such a policy would be difficult to enforce, it is worth noting that many countries have agreed to the concept of applying the prevailing standard in an industrialized country to activities which take place in a developing country.

### Global Warming

For the past several years, increasing concern over the so-called "greenhouse effect," the effect of certain gases to trap heat in the earth's atmosphere, has been growing. Some of the gases which appear to contribute to global warming are carbon dioxide, CFCs, ozone in the lower atmosphere, nitrous oxide and methane. One possible result of an increase in global temperature is a significant rise in sea level which would cause flooding of low-lying coastal areas that are heavily populated. While the scientific certainty about the extent and danger of global warming continues to be debated, particularly within the Bush Administration, there is strong international pressure to adopt a convention on global warming similar to the one dealing with ozone depletion.

European countries, Australia, and New Zealand feel more strongly than the current U.S. Administration about the likelihood of global warming and the damage it would cause. At the meeting of the G-7 nations during the week of July 10, 1990, in Houston, Texas, the United States was alone among western nations in opposing curbs on carbon dioxide emissions. One possible reason for American reluctance to reduce carbon dioxide emissions is its heavy reliance on fossil fuels for power generation, a major source of carbon dioxide. Deforestation, particularly of tropical rain forests, is also a potential factor in global warming. Living plants absorb carbon dioxide, while decaying vegetable matter is a net emitter of the gas.

While the science remains uncertain, UNEP, in cooperation with another United Nations organization, the World Meteorological Association, has begun to prepare for negotiations on a global convention on climate change. At this time, it appears likely that a convention will be adopted at the United Nations Conference on the Human Environment which is to be held in Brazil in June of 1992.

As with the Montreal Protocol, developing countries resist reducing the use of fossil fuels or taking other actions which would interfere with the industrialization process in order to protect the global environment. Without the support of developing countries such as China, the largest user of coal in the world, a global warming treating will be ineffective. In negotiating for their support of a treaty, developing countries are pushing for financial aid and technology transfer to enable them to comply with the terms of the agreement.

## Judicial Developments

On March 28, 1990, the Texas Supreme Court ruled in *Dow Chemical Company v. Alfaro*, (Texas Supreme Court No. C-7743) that Costa Rican farm workers, who alleged they suffered personal injuries from exposure in Costa Rica to a pesticide manufactured in the United States, may sue the manufacturers in Texas. The plaintiffs in the case alleged that exposure to dibromochloropropane or DBCP, a pesticide manufactured by Dow Chemical and Shell Chemical, resulted in irreversible sterility. Because the maximum recovery permitted under Costa Rican law is less than $1,500 per person, the plaintiffs filed suit in Texas where Dow operates the country's largest chemical manufacturing plant and Shell has its world headquarters. DBCP was banned for most uses in the United States in 1977 based on scientific data submitted to the U.S. Environmental Protection Agency.

The Texas Court's split decision was based on the statutory abolishment of the doctrine of *forum non-conveniens* under a Texas statute.[2] Section 71.031 of the Texas Civil Practice and Remedies Code provides:

> an action for damages for the death or personal injury of a citizen of this state, of the United States, or of a foreign country may be enforced in the courts of this state, al-

though the wrongful act, neglect, or default causing the death or injury takes place in a foreign state or country if... in the case of a citizen of a foreign country, the country has equal treaty rights with the United States on behalf of its citizens.

The United States and Costa Rica agreed to reciprocity and open access to the courts of each others' countries in the Treaty of Friendship, Commerce and Navigation of July 10, 1981.

The five-four decision of the Texas court was accompanied by a strongly worded dissent, stating that the decision would make Texas "an irresistible forum for all mass disaster law suits." The dissent also stated "Bhopal-type litigation with little or no connection to Texas will add to our already crowded dockets, forcing our residents to wait in the corridors of our courthouses, while foreign causes of action are tried."

The state statute that abolished the doctrine of *forum non-conveniens* for suits brought by citizens of a country which has entered into a treaty with the United States was passed in 1913 and since that date has not resulted in a significant number of lawsuits in Texas by foreign plaintiffs. Therefore, it is not certain, as asserted in the dissenting opinion, that the decision in the *Alfaro* case will greatly increase the number of suits based on activities of U.S. corporations in foreign countries to be brought in Texas courts.

The *Alfaro* case is significant, however, because trial of the case in a U.S. court opens corporate defendants to huge personal injury judgments and application of U.S. standards for proving causation. American plaintiffs in personal injury and other product liability claims have increasingly relied on scientific and medical data developed for regulatory agencies to prove causation. The increasing willingness on the part of U.S. courts to use epidemiological data to prove individual causation has made it easier for plaintiffs alleging injury due to exposure to toxic substances to prevail in personal injury and product liability claims. If suits against U.S. companies based on foreign activities are entertained by American courts, scientific and medical data generated for regulatory purposes may be used to show negligence or strict liability under U.S. law. Being subject to such suits would be tantamount to requiring U.S. companies to meet American environmental standards while operating abroad. The decision in *Alfaro*, therefore, provides strong impetus for U.S. multinationals to consider U.S. law in planning environmental risk management programs for overseas operations.

# Foreign Environmental Legislation

### The European Community

The European Community was founded in 1957 by a group of countries known as the European Economic Community (EEC). The EEC was created by the Treaty of Rome and included the following six countries: Belgium, France, the Federal Republic of Germany, Italy, Luxembourg, and the Netherlands. The EEC, the European Atomic Energy Community, which was also created by the Treaty of Rome, and the European Coal and Steel Community, created by the Treaty of Paris in 1951, have now effectively combined into what is known as the European Community (EC). The EC currently consists of twelve countries (Member States) including the original six members of the EEC, Denmark, Ireland, and the United Kingdom, who acceded to the EC in 1973, Greece, who acceded in 1981, and Portugal and Spain, who acceded in 1986.

The goal of the Treaty of Rome is to create a European common market without trade or tariff barriers between Member States. The Single European Act, enacted January 7, 1987, amended the Treaty of Rome to create a unified "internal market" providing for the free movement of goods, people, services, and capital throughout the EC by December 31, 1992. This 1992 deadline is commonly referred to as the "1992 integration" of the EC. To achieve this 1992 goal, the Single European Act provides for the creation of vigorous mechanisms to remove trade barriers that currently interfere with the creation of this internal market.

The EC is a regional organization which confers some powers on a coordinated, centralized EC government while allowing other powers to remain with the individual Member States. The EC bureaucracy, responsible for administering the Treaty of Rome, has four governmental bodies: the Council of Ministers (Council), the Commission of the European Community (Commission), the European Parliament (Parliament), and the European Court of Justice (ECJ or Court).

The Council is a ministerial-level organization composed of representatives from each Member State. Although the Treaty of Rome established only one Council, in practice there are several Councils which may operate simultaneously. These numerous Councils exist because various EC responsibilities are delegated to separate groups of ministers. For example, the Member States' environmental ministers combine to comprise the Environmental Council, the Member States' transportation ministers combine to comprise the Transport Council, and the Member States' agricultural ministers combine to comprise the Agriculture Council.

The Council, as established by the Single European Act, consists of the heads of state of each Member State. The Council meets biannually to adopt or reject legislation proposed by the Commission. The members of the Council represent their Member States' interests rather than the combined interests of the EC. The Council presidency rotates among the Member States in six month intervals with changes on January 1 and July 1 of each year.

The Commission, consisting of seventeen individuals, is the executive branch of the EC. The Commissioners represent the entire EC and are under oath to act independently and not to follow instructions from their own countries. The Commission develops and proposes legislation to the Council and is responsible for overseeing and enforcing EC laws. The seventeen Commissioners are appointed by the Member States: the five largest members assign two Commissioners each and the seven smaller members assign one Commissioner each. The Commission is supported by a staff that functions in a manner similar to United States' regulatory agencies. Each Commissioner is responsible for one or two of the 24 administrative groups, which are known as directorates-general (DGs). Environmental matters, along with consumer protection, are delegated to DG XI.

The members of Parliament, each elected to a five-year term, represent neither the EC nor their respective countries but, rather, the individual citizens who elected them to office. In this way, the Parliament resembles the United States House of Representatives in that its 518 members are elected by voters from the Member States. The Parliament, which sits in Strassbourg, France, is divided into political parties rather than by national groupings. For example, some members of Parliament refer to themselves as members of the Green Party rather than representatives of a specific country. This structure provides a forum and allows the political parties, who are highly fragmented at the national level, to speak with a much louder voice in the European Parliament.

The Parliament's powers are restricted because it has only an advisory role to the Council and Commission. The Parliament must be consulted before laws and policies are approved and has the right to propose amendments or, in some circumstances, compel the adoption of amendments to proposed EC legislation. The Parliament's most common tactic is to delay resolution of measures of which it disapproves. For example, the Parliament successfully delayed creation of the European Environment Agency (EEA) because it preferred conferring both enforcement and advisory powers on the Agency rather than just an advisory capacity as advocated by the Commission and Council.

The European Court of Justice (Court or ECJ) is comprised of thirteen judges, each appointed for a six-year term by agreement among the Member States. The ECJ has no authority to impose penalties for noncompliance with EC environmental laws and policies. ECJ decisions have been persuasive, however, when the Commission has brought cases before the Court contending that Member States have failed to implement Directives on environmental matters. Complaints are often brought before the ECJ to compel Member States' to pass implementing legislation and to enforce EC environmental directives.

The EC utilizes several types of legislation to address environmental issues at the Community level. These tools include Regulations, Directives, Decisions, and Recommendations. EC legislation is enacted by following either a "consultation procedure" or a "cooperation procedure". The consultation procedure begins with a proposal for legislation being initiated by the Commission. While at this level, the EC bureaucracy and outside interests are allowed considerable input in the formation of the proposal. If the Commission decides to go forward with the proposed legislation after completion of the consultation process, the proposal is forwarded to the Council for its consideration. If adopted by the Council, the proposed legislation becomes EC law. The cooperation procedure, created by the Single European Act, requires that proposed legislation from the Commission be reviewed by both the Council and Parliament. Adoption of EC legislation under the cooperation procedure requires close coordination and compromise throughout the EC bureaucracy.

A regulation enacted by the Council has immediate impact on Member States and does not require any additional action (implementing legislation) by the Member States. To date, few significant environmental measures have been enacted in the form of a regulation. Growing concerns over the diverse Member States' environmental policies and laws, however, are leading the EC to consider environmental regulations as tools for future environmental legislation. If this occurs, the Member States will be given less flexibility in how they implement and enforce EC-mandated environmental policies and laws.

Directives are adopted by the EC and addressed to the Member States who are responsible for enacting national legislation to achieve the goals established by the directives. Member States, which are given considerable flexibility in deciding how to achieve these goals, often miss or ignore deadlines stipulated in the directives. Further complications arise when a Member State enacts national legislation to implement a directive but interprets the directive in a manner which diverges from the original intent of the Commission's drafters. For these reasons, the EC is considering moving away from utilizing directives as the major tool for EC environmental legislation. There are currently, however, over 250 EC directives which deal with the environment.

Decisions are binding communications from the EC to individual parties in regard to specific cases. The parties to a decision can be Member States or individuals.

Recommendations are not binding on the Member States and do not give rise to legal obligations. The purpose of recommendations, which are usually initiated by the EC institution issuing them, is primarily to encourage Member States' adoption of EC policy initiatives.

The European Investment Bank (EIB) was established by the Treaty of Rome and delegated the responsibility for distributing financial resources to encourage development of the EC. The EIB is located in Luxembourg and is operated by the Board of Governors which is comprised of the Ministers of Finance of each Member State.

The EIB operates on a nonprofit basis and makes loans to EC Member States for three types of projects: (1) those promoting the less developed regions of the EC; (2) those fostering the integration of the EC; and (3) those of common interest to the Member States. Environmental protection is often included in one of the three types of projects funded by the EIB and has, therefore, evolved into a significant component of EIB lending activities. For example, the EIB recently funded environmental clean-up and restoration projects in

Portugal and Spain, allocated funds for clean-up of the Mediterranean Sea, and is currently financing the construction of infrastructure projects which take the environment into consideration.

Environmental issues are high on the political agenda of almost every country in Europe. Politicians in the United Kingdom, Germany, Belgium, the Netherlands and France, for example, have been persuaded by intense and sustained pressure from their constituents to take up the mantle of environmental protection. Some Member States subject to demands created by rising environmental activism among their constituencies nevertheless have a poor record of enforcing EC environmental legislation. As a result, there is increasing support for granting the EC stronger enforcement powers for ensuring compliance with EC environmental laws. This view is widely held by members of Parliament who support a more centralized environmental program for the EC. As a result, stricter environmental controls are being proposed at both the national and EC levels.

The future course of environmental controls to be instituted by individual European countries is difficult to predict because of rapid changes in environmental laws currently being proposed at both the EC and Member State levels. One complication involves the responsibility given to Member States to implement EC environmental directives: Member States interpret the goals of EC environmental directives and then enact national legislation in accordance with achieving their perceived goals. This procedure leads to fundamentally different, and often conflicting, environmental programs within the twelve Member States.

For these reasons, it is important for U.S. corporations doing business in Europe to understand environmental laws in both the EC and its individual Member States. The EC's role in environmental affairs is in the process of change and Member States themselves are initiating vigorous national environmental programs. In addition, environmental issues are increasingly viewed by Member States as international problems requiring international solutions.

The EC's authority for environmental protection is based on two rationale contained in the Treaty of Rome: (1) the need to preserve free trade by removing market barriers among Member States; and (2) the need to protect the environment, human health and natural resources. The legal basis on which an environmental regulation is based determines the role various EC institutions play in its development as well as the Member States' authority to enact stricter requirements. Therefore, the legal basis for a particular piece of environmental legislation is often as controversial as the content of the law itself.

From 1957 until 1987, Article 100a of the Treaty of Rome was the sole basis for EC environmental controls. Article 100a gives the EC authority to enact legislation to preserve and remove barriers to the EC internal market. For example, if cars manufactured in Italy cannot be sold in the Netherlands because they do not meet the Dutch emission standards, environmental regulation has created an impediment to trade.

Articles 130r-t of the Single European Act establish the framework for EC regulation based on environmental concerns. Article 130r established protection of the environment and human health as an independent basis for EC regulation. Article 130s gives the EC powers to adopt and implement environmental policies for the EC. Article 130t allows Member States to adopt environmental laws more stringent than the EC. As a result, countries with strong environmental laws such as Denmark or West Germany favor EC environmental legislation based on Article 130 because they are allowed to implement national standards which are stricter than those of the EC. Article 130 has enabled the EC to pursue a more coordinated environmental policy and encouraged debate over the type and extent of environmental programs the EC should institute.

On May 7, 1990, a regulation establishing a European Environment Agency was adopted by the Council. EC officials indicate that the new Agency is not intended to be an enforcement agency with responsibilities similar to those of the U.S. Environmental Protection Agency. Rather, it is planned as an information gathering and scientific and technical body with the role of advising the Commission and Council regarding environmental matters.

Some countries within the EC, such as the United Kingdom, question the Commission's motives in establishing the Environment Agency. They believe that the creation of an advisory agency is merely the first step toward establishing a centralized EC environmental organization with enforcement capabilities. The Parliament has strongly supported efforts to establish such a centralized environmental agency with authority for enforcement. This conflict over the role and powers of the new Agency delayed its creation. Under the terms of an agreement reached in March 1990, the Council deferred further discussion of the enforcement issue for at least two years, at which time the EC Commission must provide a report on the Agency's progress and suggest changes in its structure.

Presently, establishment of the Agency is being delayed until the Member States can agree on where it should be located. Eleven of the twelve Member States have offered to host the Agency in their country. The most likely current contenders for hosting the Agency are Berlin, Copenhagen or Brussels.

The air pollution control program established by the EC is similar to, but less extensive than, that of the United States. The EC has promulgated air pollution directives for establishing air quality standards and emission standards for vehicles, fuels, and facilities. The EC air quality standards regulate levels of sulfur dioxide, particulate matter, nitrogen oxide, and lead. The vehicle emission standards regulate carbon monoxide, nitrogen oxide, and hydrocarbon releases from motor vehicles. Fuel standards include allowable amounts of lead in petroleum products and sulfur content of gas and oil.

The 1984 Directive on Air Pollution from Industrial Plants establishes an overall framework to guide Member States in regulating emissions from industrial plants. The Directive requires developing and executing a program to prevent and reduce air pollution from specified industries. The Directive identifies sulfur dioxide, nitrogen oxides, carbon monoxide, organic compounds, heavy metals, dust, asbestos, glass and mineral fibers, chlorine compounds, and fluorine compounds as specific pollutants targeted for regulation. Member States are free to restrict additional pollutants if they so choose. The Directive also requires any regulated industrial plant to receive authorization from the applicable Member State before undertaking any substantial alteration of the plant. Standards for the reduction of emissions from new and existing facilities are controlled by the 1988 Directive on the Limitation of Emissions of Certain Pollutants into the Air from Large Combustion Plants (31 O.J. Eur. Comm. (No. L 336) 1 (Dec. 7, 1988)).

Since the early 1970s, the EC has recognized the need for uniform controls on emissions of carbon monoxide, hydrocarbons, and nitrogen oxides to prevent barriers to free trade in vehicles. The early controls were dominated by the interests of Italy, France, and the United Kingdom in having the least stringent standards possible. The lobbying efforts of these countries effectively barred adoption of more stringent controls for several years.

In the late 1980s, however, countries such as Denmark succeeded in their efforts to impose more stringent standards on emissions from vehicles. Council Directives 88/76 and 88/77 established standards for emissions from automobiles and heavy vehicles. The EC establishes the framework of standards that Member States may impose on vehicle emissions so as to limit creation of trade barriers within the EC. The EC has also addressed amounts of lead allowed in gasoline (Council Directive 85/210 of 20 March 1985, 28 O.J. Eur. Comm. (No. L 96) 25 (Apr. 3, 1985)) and has even allowed Member States to restrict the sale of leaded gasoline (Council Directive 87/416 amending Directive 85/210, 30 O.J. Eur. Comm. (No. L 225) 33 (Aug. 14, 1987)). The EC is slowly moving toward establishing stricter standards on emissions from motor vehicles as evidenced by the Proposed Amendment to Directive on Motor Vehicle Emissions 89/662 (Jan. 5, 1990) which reflects the evolution of stricter controls for vehicle emission standards in the EC.

In an effort to address problems associated with acid rain, Council Regulation 528/86 of 17 November 1986 (29 O.J. Eur. Comm. (No. L 336) 1 (Dec. 7, 1988)) permits the collection of data and monitoring of acid levels in water bodies throughout the Community. Since 1984, the EC has adopted more stringent measures dealing with air pollution from new and existing municipal waste incinerators. A June 1988 Directive will restrict emissions of sulfur dioxide and nitrogen dioxides from large combustion units over the next fifteen years. For new plants, this Directive requires compliance with emission levels as a prerequisite to obtaining a license. Unlike other Directives, this one specifies specific emission limitations for certain industries, rather than leaving it up to Member States to determine the appropriate limitations.

The EC's water pollution program is similar to that of the United States' Clean Water Act in that various EC Directives designate water pollution goals to be achieved and delegate authority for achieving these goals to the Member States. This authority allows Member States to designate segments of waterways for particular uses and to establish and apply criteria to achieve these classifications. The EC water quality standards include standards for surface water, drinking water, bathing water, and water used for the cultivation of freshwater fish and shellfish. Member States' compliance with EC water quality standards is less than optimal; a majority of the Member States routinely violate several of the water quality Directives.

Council Directive 76/464 (19 O.J. Eur. Comm. (No. L 129) 23 (May 18, 1976)) is the EC's framework law for dealing with pollution discharges into waterways. This Directive establishes a "Black List" of toxic pollutants to be eliminated from effluent discharges and a "Gray List" of substances to be severely curtailed. The success of this Directive has not been uniform throughout the EC and eleven of the twelve Member States have been cited for noncompliance with it. In addition to the Member States' infractions, the EC has frustrated full implementation of the Directive by not adopting specific discharge requirements for many pollutants. Although the "Black List" includes 129 dangerous substances to be eliminated from effluent discharge, the Commission established, as of 1989, specific requirements for only 12 of these substances.

The European Community has issued a number of directives dealing with various aspects of waste transportation, treatment, storage, and disposal. Rules for the disposal of waste within the borders of a Member State are generally left to control by the respective Member State. The EC takes a more active role, however, in regulating the shipment, handling, and disposal of waste which involves two or more Member States. Likewise, the EC is more likely to regulate hazardous or toxic waste at the Community level and allow solid waste problems to be administered at the Member State and local levels.

Similar to the air and water pollution directives, the waste management directives rely on Member States to implement and enforce the EC waste management goals. As a result, local authorities are designated responsibility for directing the disposal of household wastes. Council Directive 75/442 of 15 July 1975 (18 O.J. Eur. Comm. (No. L 194) 39 (July 25, 1975)) guides Member States in regulating waste disposal within their own borders. The Member States are given considerable flexibility in controlling the disposal of waste inside their national borders. A 1988 proposal to amend the aforementioned directive would provide stricter EC controls on waste disposal and management activities of the Member States.

The EC has adopted detailed directives for the disposal of toxic and hazardous waste. As compared to the solid waste directives, the directives dealing with toxic and hazardous waste grant less authority to the Member States.

A Council directive dated June 16, 1975 relates to the disposal of waste oil. The purpose of this Directive is to create an efficient and uniform EC system for managing waste oil by regulating the treatment, discharge, deposit and collection of oil by requiring the harmonization of Member States' laws relating to waste oil disposal.

An April 6, 1976 Council directive regulates the disposal of poly-chlorinated biphenyls and polychlorinated terphenyls. This directive provides for disposal of PCBs and PCTs at facilities authorized by the competent authorities of Member States.

Council directives enacted in 1978 and 1984 deal with the EC supervision, control, and disposal of transfrontier shipments of hazardous waste within the EC. A 1988 Council resolution addresses the transfrontier movement of hazardous waste to third countries and advises EC Member States on how to deal with such shipments of waste. These directives provide a framework for regulating transportation and disposal of waste within the EC and have the goal of ensuring that national regulations are not used as barriers to trade and EC economic integration.

The 1978 Council Directive regulates disposal and handling of toxic and dangerous waste by requiring Member States to prohibit un-permitted and uncontrolled discharges of toxic and dangerous waste. The Directive is the fist step toward a coordinated EC permit system governing the transportation and disposal of toxic and dangerous waste. Amendments calling for a more harmonized approach to disposal and handling of EC waste are expected to be enacted in the near future.

A directive governing waste transport within the EC requires compulsory notification and use of a manifest for all transfrontier shipments of hazardous waste between EC countries. This directive was inspired by an uncontrolled and unauthorized transfrontier shipment of hazardous waste from an industrial accident in Seveso, Italy in 1976. Forty-one barrels of waste collected from a Seveso chemical plant explosion were found illegally discarded on a French farm after several nations refused to take the waste. Public outrage over the illegal disposal prompted EC investigation into problems associated with transfrontier shipment of wastes throughout the EC.

A 1988 EC resolution concerning transfrontier shipment of hazardous waste to third countries stresses the importance of creating an international agreement which would ensure effective management of transfrontier shipments of hazardous waste and their ultimate disposal. This resolution was passed by the Commission after a great deal of adverse publicity over Member States' export of hazardous waste to African countries. Although this resolution has no binding effect, it does set forth certain steps which the Commission intends to pursue to avoid the continued export of hazardous waste to countries which do not have the technology for safe disposal.

The Seveso industrial accident which spurred EC adoption of the transfrontier waste directive also provided impetus for passing an EC directive on the classification, packaging, and labeling of dangerous substances. A defective safety valve burst as pressure built up in a reactor at the Hoffman Larouche subsidiary plant in Seveso, Italy, resulting in a cloud of trichlorophenol which spread four and one-half miles, carrying 4.5 pounds of TCDD dioxin. The plant manager of the facility failed to inform local authorities until 27 hours after the release, apparently hoping that rain would wash it away. The presence of dioxin was not disclosed for another seven days. The entire area was eventually evacuated and the company paid $80 million for cleanup costs and personal injury and property damages.

Following the Seveso incident, increased concern over control of chemicals led to the passage of an amendment to the chemical directive. This directive restricts the marketing and use of dangerous chemicals and substances. It requires that manufacturers and importers notify the affected Member State(s) prior to marketing a new chemical or chemical substance. This notification must be given 45 days prior to marketing of a new chemical or chemical substance and must include: first, the technical data necessary to evaluate risks associated with the chemical or substance; second, a declaration of any known adverse health effects; third, a proposed classification label (i.e., whether the chemical will be classified as an explosive, corrosive, or toxic) for the chemical; and fourth, any recommended safety precautions. The Member State who receives the notification is responsible for notifying other Member States of the new chemical and/or substance.

Prior to notification and marketing, the chemicals or substances must be tested according to uniform procedures which are intended to avoid imposition of differing laws throughout the Member States. The testing requirements mandated by the Directive are proportional to the volume of product marketed. For example, when marketing exceeds 1,000 tons per year, long-term carcinogenicity studies, biodegradation, and exotoxicity studies are required. In addition, each Member State may impose additional restrictions on marketing and use of chemicals or chemical substances.

The Directive defines a new chemical or chemical substance as one which was not sold in the EC prior to September 18, 1981. An inventory of pre-1981 chemicals are listed in the European Inventory of Existing Commercial Chemical Substances (EINECS). Although pre-

1981 chemicals must be classified and labeled according to the Directive, they are not subject to the testing requirements.

An amendment to the chemical Directive was proposed in January 1990. The proposal focuses on chemical hazards to the general environment, imposes new testing requirements for chemicals, and requires the assembly and distribution of safety information for 1,300 listed dangerous chemicals. The proposal would require the use of an ecological hazard label inscribed with the warning "dangerous to the environment" as illustrated by a leafless tree and a dead fish.

Adopted in June 1990, the Directive on Freedom of Access to Environmental Information is similar to the U.S. Freedom of Information Act in that it allows any individual to obtain, upon request to a public authority, information regarding the environmental impact of proposed public and private sector projects. Under the Directive, any Member State that collects or assimilates environmental data would be required, upon written request, to provide that information to the public. One result is that information generated by private companies and then reported to Member State or EC authorities, either voluntarily or pursuant to mandated reporting requirements, will become subject to public record and release. The Directive provides an exception for confidential information and specifies the type of information classified as confidential.

The June 1985 Directive on environmental impact assessment requires evaluation of potential environmental impacts of proposed projects. The Directive stresses that a solid environmental policy depends on preventing environmental pollution and nuisances and insists that assessment of projects' environmental impacts will help further integration of pro-environmental measures into the planning and decision-making processes at an early stage. The Directive requires environmental assessment of the environmental effects of significant public and private projects and takes into consideration the nature, size, and location of the proposed project.

The Directive is similar to the U.S. National Environmental Policy Act but its implementation relies heavily on Member States' local planning and zoning procedures. The implementation, oversight, and enforcement of the Directive is delegated to the individual Member States who are given considerable flexibility in providing exemptions to complete the environmental impact assessments. The Directive specifically requires that the assessments include the following elements:

    (1) a description of the project;

    (2) an outline of alternatives to mitigate environmental impact;

    (3) a description of the types and extent of environmental contamination caused by the existence of the project;

    (4) a nontechnical summary of the above information; and

    (5) an explanation of any difficulties encountered by the developer in compiling the aforementioned information.

The proposed Directive on Civil Liability is controversial because it establishes a framework for expensive controls and costly litigation similar to what has developed in the U.S. under the Superfund laws. The proposed Directive would apply the "polluter pays principle" to ensure that victims of damage from waste are fairly compensated and that polluting industries are forced to include the cost of environmental contamination in the price of their products. The Directive would further impose liability on producers and importers of waste or on the entity in "actual control" of the waste, thereby potentially applying to those responsible for the production and temporary storage of waste products, including manufacturers, importers, and transporters of waste products. If several waste producers and/or importers are involved, they will be held jointly and severally liable for any damage caused by the chemical. If adopted, parties subject to the Directive would be liable for personal injury, property damage, and environmental contamination caused by release of their wastes. The proposed Directive allows any injured person to pursue compensation from the responsible party. Although there is an exemption provision for oil and nuclear wastes, there is no such exemption from liability for solid or hazardous wastes.

The major difference between liability imposed under the EC directive and U.S. Superfund is that EC generator liability ends when the waste reaches an approved disposal site.

The Commission plans to propose in early 1991 a directive requiring private corporations to complete audits of their operation's environmental impacts on air, land, water, and the local community. The full extent of the proposed Directive is currently not known but implementation of it, like other EC environmental laws, will probably be carried out by the Member States.

## Eastern Europe

The opening of Eastern Europe has exposed serious and pervasive environmental problems adversely affecting human health and polluting the region's air, water, and land.  As a result, governments and businesses in both Western and Eastern Europe are allocating substantial resources to address these environmental problems.

Serious threats to human health and severe degradation of natural resources and environmental quality have created international concern over Eastern Europe's environmental problems.  The need for stricter environmental regulation will undoubtedly affect the path of Eastern Europe's ongoing social, economic, and political changes.  Private sector activities such as the establishment of international joint ventures in Eastern Europe will be affected by the development of East European environmental regulatory schemes. Therefore, companies planning business ventures in Eastern Europe should consider environmental controls during the project development stage.

## Environmental Protection and Western Financial Assistance

The success of Eastern European development is heavily dependent upon financial assistance from the West.  The United States, Japan, and several Western European countries are contributing significant resources toward the creation of Eastern European democracies and market economies.  Much of this Western assistance takes Eastern European countries' environmental problems into account through direct funding of environmental projects or by imposing environmental requirements on other economic development activities.

For example, the United States has undertaken the retrofitting a coal-burning power plant in Poland to reduce air emissions; Sweden has funded capital improvements of state-owned power plants in an effort to decrease transfrontier air pollution; and the Federal Republic of Germany is undertaking significant revitalization of the formerly East German waterways.  Similar initiatives have been funded by the United Kingdom, France, Finland, Japan, Australia, and Canada.

Each country's rationale for funding environmental restoration and clean-up project varies. The countries of Western Europe are adversely affected by transfrontier pollution originating in Eastern Europe. Many Western European nations can achieve a cleaner environment, at a lower cost, by investing in pollution reduction in

Eastern Europe rather than their own countries. In addition, Eastern Europe has been used as a waste disposal site for Western Europe for decades. Thousands of shipments of Western waste have crossed the borders into Eastern Europe where they have been subjected to few, if any, environmental controls.

In addition to the aforementioned bilateral assistance, multilateral aid to Eastern Europe is being provided by the World Bank and the newly created Bank for European Reconstruction and Development.

The World Bank's environmental program began in the 1970s with creation of an Environmental Advisor and the Office of Environmental and Health Affairs. The Bank signed the Declaration of Environmental Policies and Procedures Relating to Economic Development in 1980. By 1985, however, the Bank had only one environmental professional on its staff and had done little to integrate environmental concerns into its lending policies. With the selection of Barber Conable as president of the World Bank in 1986, the Bank entered a new stage of environmental activity. Recent efforts have resulted in the creation of an Environment Department responsible for coordinating the Bank's environmental policy and research efforts, a detailed environmental agenda for the Bank, and creation of a Global Environment Facility targeted at financing environmental projects.

The World Bank will likely be an active player in providing financial assistance for Eastern European development. It is uncertain, however, what kind of environmental controls Eastern European nations will be required to meet as conditions of obtaining loans from the World Bank.

The Bank for European Reconstruction and Development (BERD) was created specifically to address the economic, political, and social development of Eastern European nations. BERD, created in May 1990, by 44 charter members, is headquartered in London. BERD anticipates extending its first loan in March 1991. Forty percent of the Bank's loans are to go to public sector redevelopment projects and the remaining sixty percent are dedicated to private sector initiatives.

Environmental protection was specifically addressed in the Bank's enabling statute. This makes BERD the first multilateral development bank to identify support of environmental protection as one of its primary responsibilities. The full extent of BERD's environmental program is still not known. However, it is anticipated that environmental protection requirements, guidelines and procedures for environmental impact assessments and the organization of an environmental affairs office will be published in late 1991.

In the "Support for East European Democracy Act of 1989" (SEED Act) the U.S. EPA and the U.S. Department of Energy are given responsibility for overseeing development of environmental protection programs in Poland and Hungary. Specifically, Congress assigned the U.S. EPA the authority to work with Hungarian officials in establishing a regional center in Budapest, Hungary with responsibilities "for facilitating cooperative environmental activities between governmental experts and public and private organizations from the U.S. and Eastern and Western Europe."

The appropriation of resources and expertise to deal with Eastern Europe's environmental problems is a source of business opportunity. Hundreds of Eastern European power plants and industrial facilities will be retrofitted or reconstructed in the next decade in order to meet new environmental goals. Czechoslovakia, for example, plans to spend $800 million on cleaning-up its power plants by 1995. Additionally, revitalization and decontamination of natural resources will receive significant attention in the next few years. Construction of infrastructure projects such as sewage works and water treatment facilities will involve significant reliance on Western technology and expertise.

### Japan

Japan's scheme of environmental regulation reflects a history of serious incidents of human exposure to air pollution and toxic chemicals during the 1950s and 1960s. Perhaps the most famous of these incidents is that involving mercury poisoning resulting from a chemical company's discharge of organic mercury into Minamata Bay, located on the southern island of Kyushu in a small fishing village. Local residents of Minamata who ingested shellfish containing mercury, suffered severe neurological effects and a number of victims died. Another similar incident of mercury poisoning in a northern area of Japan called Niigata also contributed to an overwhelming public fear of exposure to mercury and other toxic chemicals which ultimately led a group of affected victims to bring a large-scale suit against a Japanese polluter in 1967.

Also during the 1950s and 1960s, a chemical company's industrial effluent containing cadmium and other toxic chemicals bioaccumulated in fish and soil, resulting in extensive human ingestion of this substance. The result of such exposures to the "itai-itai" disease or "it hurts, it hurts" disease added to the Japanese concern over the effects of Japan's postwar industrialization. Other major incidents involving human health damage from pollution include: wide-spread respiratory disease caused by extremely heavy air pollution in the Tokyo-Osaka corridor where the majority of Japan's industry is concentrated and the contamination of rice oil with polychlorinated biphenyls (PCBs) from a leaking heating pipe in a rice oil production vessel.

In addition to the aforementioned cases, other serious incidents of human exposure to chromium and arsenic set the stage for the courts to develop legal doctrines which arose from victims' suits against the polluting industries. The basis for the development of environmental policy in Japan was the need to prevent human exposure to heavy metals, toxic chemicals, and conventional air-pollutants. These early cases resulted in the establishment of strict pollution control laws and the basic legal principles of joint and several liability governing claims for compensation of health injuries from air and water pollution. Thus, the occurrence of these environmental catastrophes caused Japanese environmental law to focus heavily on regulating the pollutants which have historically caused the greatest problems in Japan.

In 1967, the Japanese Diet passed the "Basic Law for Environmental Pollution Control," which established the foundation for environmental policy in Japan. This Basic Law provided the legal basis for establishing standards for regulating air, noise, soil, water and other forms of environmental pollution. In 1970, the Japanese Diet enacted or substantially amended fourteen additional environmental laws. These new laws, which included the Water Pollution Control Law and the Air Pollution Control Law, provided a comprehensive framework for Japanese environmental protection. After 1970, Japan entered a new era of environmental pollution control which paralleled that of many other industrialized countries.

The Environment Agency, created in 1970, is the primary organization responsible for setting environmental standards and policies in Japan. The Environment Agency is a cabinet-level agency established as a special department of the Prime Minister's Office rather than as an independent ministry. The primary functions of the Agency are to control environmental pollution and to promote administrative measures for nature conservation.

The Environment Agency maintains jurisdiction over the planning, drafting, and promotion of environmental policies, the coordination of various branches of government ministries responsible for the environment, the coordination of budgetary policies for pollution-related expenditures, and centralized management of appropriations for environmental research and development. The Agency is headed by a Director-General. Within the Agency there are four bureaus: (1) the Planning and Coordination Bureau, responsible for planning, implementation, and coordination of environmental policies and measures and environmental impact assessments; (2) the Nature Conservation Bureau, responsible for all policies relating to conservation; (3) the Air Quality Bureau, responsible for setting air quality standards and enforcing air pollution control laws; and (4) the Water Quality Bureau, responsible for setting water quality standards and enforcing water pollution control laws. Enforcement of environmental laws and regulations takes place at the prefectural or municipal level with funds supplied by the central government.

Two additional departments under the direction of the Agency are the Environmental Health Department and the National Institute for Environmental Studies. The Environmental Health Department is largely responsible for enforcing the Pollution-Related Health Damage Compensation Law and for coordinating efforts to promote scientific study of health damage induced by pollution. The National Institute for Environmental Studies is designed to carry out interdisciplinary research on matters relating to the environment.

Other ministries also play a very important role in the development and enforcement of Japanese environmental law. In fact, it is sometimes argued that these ministries exert a more powerful influence over Japanese environmental policy than the Environment Agency and thus should not be overlooked. They include:

(1) the Ministry of Health and Welfare, which has authority for solid and hazardous waste management policy;

(2) the Ministry of Construction, which has authority over disposal of wastes used for land reclamation;

(3) the Ministry of Agriculture, Fisheries and Forestries, which regulates pesticides; and

(4) the well-known Ministry of International Trade and Industry, which has general authority over all industrial plants in Japan.

The major laws governing air pollution in Japan are the Basic Law for Environmental Pollution Control and the Air Pollution Control

Law. The Basic Law sets ambient air quality standards based on the protection of human health and conservation of the environment. Prior to the enactment of the Basic Law in 1967, air pollution control consisted of emission controls on individual sources of pollution. Regulating only individual emissions was largely ineffective in Japan because of the heavy concentration of factories in urban areas. Since the promulgation of the Basic Law, Japan has set air quality standards for sulfur dioxide, carbon monoxide, suspended particulate matter, nitrogen dioxide and photochemical oxidants.

The Air Pollution Control Act, enacted in 1968 and subsequently amended in 1970 and 1974, provides a broad basis for controlling emissions of pollutants into the air. Under the provisions of this law, restrictions are imposed on facilities emitting sulfur oxides, nitrogen oxides, dust particulates and certain toxic substances from stationary sources. Emission limitations can be imposed by the central government on stationary sources on an individual basis. Prefectural governments are allowed, however, to impose more stringent standards when necessary to protect human health and the environment. The toxic air pollutants which are regulated under the Air Pollution Control Act are cadmium and its compounds, chlorine and hydrogen chloride, fluoride and hydrogen-fluoride, silicon-fluoride and lead and its compounds. Standards for emissions of toxic air pollutants apply to only a limited number of industrial facilities.

Sulfur dioxide is one example of Japan's success in substantially reducing pollution from stationery sources since the early 1970s. From a peak concentration of 0.059 parts per million (ppm) in 1967 (average values recorded at 15 monitoring stations in Japan), sulfur dioxide concentration had been reduced to 0.012 ppm by 1984. Nitrogen dioxide, while greatly reduced since 1967, remains a concern because of the large  percentage of such emissions which come from mobile sources.

The major laws governing waste management in Japan are the Waste Disposal and Public Cleansing Law and the Law on the Prevention of Marine Pollution and Maritime Disaster. The Waste Disposal Law, enacted in 1971, deals with domestic and industrial waste separately. Standards for the collection, transportation, treatment and disposal of domestic waste are set by municipalities. The prefectures set standards for storage collection, transportation, treatment and disposal of industrial wastes and technical standards for the construction and operation of disposal facilities. Under these technical standards, three types of industrial waste landfills are provided for: 1) isolated type landfill for the most dangerous waste, 2) leachate controlled landfills, and 3) the leachate un-controlled landfills.

Japan's waste management scheme relies heavily on incineration and resource recovery. For example, as early as 1983, about 70 percent of Japan's domestic waste was being incinerated. The Law on the Prevention of Marine Pollution and Maritime Disaster was enacted in 1970. The purpose of this law is to regulate ocean dumping of waste. Subsequently, the law has been amended to comply with international treaties in 1983 and 1986.

The three major laws which regulate water quality in Japan are the Basic Law for Environmental Pollution Control, the Water Pollution Control Act and the Waterworks Act. The Basic Law establishes water quality standards for the protection of human health and for the conservation of the living environment. The water quality standards enacted to protect human health are those governing cadmium, cyanide, organic phosphorus, lead, chromium, arsenic, mercury, and PCBs. The Waterworks Act sets drinking water standards with regard to these substances. The water quality standards issued to protect the living environment are established for a number categories depending upon the use of an individual body of water.

The Water Pollution Control Act establishes effluent limitations for specific pollutants. Effluent limitations for individual sources are based on the national standards as well as the total pollution load of a specific body of water. An industrial source may be required to reduce its effluent if the stream to which it discharges has exceeded its pollution load for a specific substance. In addition, prefectures are allowed to impose more stringent requirements than the national government under the Water Pollution Control Act.

Generally, Japan has been quite successful in reducing discharges of heavy metals and certain toxic substances into its waters. Major areas of contamination from past disposal practices, particularly in coastal areas, continue to be a problem. These areas of contamination result primarily from two activities: 1) discharge of industrial effluent which preceded the enactment of current water pollution control laws, such as the mercury discharges into Minamata Bay, and 2) reclamation of land along the coastal areas with contaminated sludge from sewer treatment plants.

Serious water quality problems in Japan result from a lack of sewage treatment plants. In 1986, estimates showed that only 36 percent of the Japanese population was served by sewage treatment plants. As a consequence, many large inland bodies of water are seriously polluted by organic waste.

Prior to the enactment of many of Japan's environmental laws in 1970, victims of severe exposure to pollution won several major court battles over compensation for pollution-related health damage. As a result of this successful litigation and the recognition by Japanese policymakers that compensation for persons whose health had been damaged by pollution was a necessary element of Japan's environmental legislation, the 1973 Law for the Compensation of Pollution-Related Health Damage was enacted. This law:

(1) established mechanisms for financing compensation;
(2) designated polluted regions;
(3) designated pollution-related diseases;
(4) developed medical criteria for determining whether individuals injuries were pollution-related; and
(5) provided for grievance procedures for persons who wish to appeal a compensation award or denial of a claim.

The law was substantially amended in 1987 to eliminate compensation for respiratory injuries for which claims were made after 1987.

Funding for compensation under the law is provided for in two ways: 1) by a tax on sulfur dioxide emissions in the case of areas designated for heavy air pollution, and 2) by the industry which discharged the substance causing the damage in the areas designated for toxic substance pollution.

The Compensation Law has always been a source of controversy in Japan. Many industry groups believe that it has accomplished its purpose and should be repealed. As noted above, substantial restrictions on new compensation in air pollution areas have already been enacted.

Environmental Impact Assessments in Japan have been required by means of administrative guidance only on a case by case basis. Historically, the environmental impact assessment process has not been widely adopted in Japan.

In 1975, the "Report on an Environmental Impact Assessment System" was issued by the Central Council on Environmental Pollution Control, an advisory body to the Environment Agency. Subsequently, the Environment Agency drafted a bill based on the report. Due to internal political strife, the bill was never enacted into law. Thereafter, many local authorities passed ordinances on environmental impact assessment resulting in disparate treatment for different projects. Therefore, in 1984, the Japanese government adopted a formal decision on the "Implementation of Environmental Impact Assessment," which covers the following public projects:  road construction, new dam construction and river conservation works, railway and airport construction, land reclamation and drainage, land rezoning, and new housing and industrial zone development. In 1985, in response to the 1984 government decision, all competent ministries and agencies issued Directives establishing guidelines for projects subject to environmental impact assessment process.

## Future Trends and Emerging Issues

The most important purposes of an international environmental risk program are:
- To limit potential liability for environmental or health related damages caused by foreign operations;
- To avoid increased regulation; and
- To enhance the public opinion concerning overseas operations.

U.S. industries operating abroad have recognized these issues and responded by creating and participating in several organizations aimed at including business concerns in the development and implementation of international codes of conduct and environmental treaties. Some recent developments in this area are discussed briefly below.

In the wake of the Exxon *Valdez* disaster, U.S environmental groups joined with institutional investors controlling approximately $150 billion of assets to develop the Valdez Principles of Good Environmental Practice. Under the Valdez Principles, companies agreed to reduce waste generation, market safe products, assume responsibility for harm caused by their activities include environmentalists on their corporate boards and make the results of annual environmental audits available to the public.

The Global Environmental Management Institute (GEMI) was recently created as a response to the challenge which environmental groups presented to industry to meet its commitment protecting the environment. Nineteen major U.S. corporations are currently members of GEMI, whose stated purpose is to participate in the development of the "Charter for Sustainable Development" being created by the International Chamber of Commerce and to represent emerging ideas and knowledge concerning environmental management practices.

The major goal of GEMI is to encourage the development of quality environmental management practices from within its corporate membership and thereby avoid the imposition of additional regulatory controls or the occurrence of environmental accidents.

GEMI is administered by an organization affiliated with the U.S. National Committee of the International Chamber of Commerce. GEMI also facilitates coordination among other world business organizations such as the International Chamber of Commerce's International Environmental Bureau.

The International Environmental Bureau (IEB) was established by the International Chamber of Commerce for purposes similar to those of GEMI. The IEB's membership, however, is broader than that of GEMI.

Development of an effective international environmental risk management program requires consideration of international codes of conduct, foreign environmental legislation, international environmental treaties and U.S. environmental regulation. As discussed in earlier sections, a growing trend to impose standards applicable in the country in which corporate parent is cited is reflected in recent judicial decisions such as *Dow v. Alfaro* and the structure of new international treaties such as the Basil Convention. Complying with local environmental regulation, in the country of operation may no longer be sufficient to minimize potential environmental liability for foreign operations. Development of a global environmental risk management scheme and periodic environmental audits of overseas operations can serve to minimize liability under international, foreign and U.S. environmental laws.

# Appendix A

## Major Environmental Legislation of the European Community

*Air Pollution*

1. *Council Directive 70/220 of 20 March 1970 on the Approximation of the Laws of the Member States Relating to Measures to Be Taken Against Air Pollution by Gases from Positive Ignition Engines of Motor Vehicles,* **O.J. Eur. Comm.** (No. L 076) 1 (1970), amended by **O.J. Eur. Comm.** (No. L 159) 61 (1974); (No. L 223) 48 (1978); (No. L 197) 1 (1983); (No.036) 1 (1988); (No. L 214) 1 (1988); (No. L 226) 1 (1989).

This Directive relates to measures to be taken against air pollution by gases from engines of motor vehicles. This Directive sets forth emission control standards for motor vehicles with positive ignition engines.

2. *Council Directive 72/306 of 2 August 1972 on the Approximation of the Laws of the Member States Relating to the Measures to Be Taken Against the Emission of Pollutants from Diesel Engines for Use in Vehicles,* **O.J. Eur. Comm.** (No. L 190) 1 (1972).

This Directive Sets forth emission control limits for motor vehicles with diesel engines.

3. *Council Directive 75/716 of 24 November 1975 on the Approximation of the Laws of the Member States Relating to the Sulphur Content of Certain Liquid Fuels,* **O.J. Eur. Comm.** (No. L 307) 22 (1975), amended by **O.J. Eur. Comm.** (No. L 091) 19 (1987).

This Directive requires member states to take certain actions to require the use of low-sulphur gasoline.

4. *Council Directive 80/779 of 15 July 1980 on Air Quality, Limit Values and Guide Values for Sulphur Dioxide and Suspended Particulates,* **O.J. Eur. Comm.** (No. L 229) 30 (1980), amended by (No. L 319) 18 (1981).

This Directive sets forth ambient air quality standards for sulphur dioxide and suspended particulates.

5. *Council Directive 85/210 of 20 March 1985 on the Lead Content of Petro*, **O.J. Eur. Comm.** (No. L 096) 25 (1985), amended by (No. L 372) 37 (1985); and (No. L 225) 33 (1987).

This Directive sets forth maximum permissible lead content in gasoline.

6. *Council Directive 75/324 of 20 May 1975 on the Approximation of the Laws of the Member States Relating to Aerosol Dispenses*, **O.J. Eur. Comm.** (No. L 147) 22 (1975).

This Directive sets forth labelling and marketing requirements for aerosol containers.

7. *Council Decision 80/372 of 26 March 1980 Concerning Chlorofluorocarbons in the Environment*, **O.J. Eur. Comm.** (No. L 090) 45 (1980).

This Decision requires member states to ensure that certain CFC production capacity is not increased and that not later than December 1981, industry within member states achieve a 30 percent reduction compared with 1976 levels in the use of CFCs in the filling of aerosol cans.

8. *Council Decision 82/795 of 15 November 1982 on the Consolidation of Precautionary Measures Concerning Chlorofluorocarbons in the Environment*, **O.J. Eur. Comm.** 29 (No. L 329) (1982).

This Decision requires member states to cooperate with the EEC in conducting research on CFCs.

9. *Council Regulation 3322/88 of 14 October 1988 on Certain Chlorofluorocarbons and Halons Which Deplete the Ozone Layer*, **O.J. Eur. Comm.** (No. L 297) 1 (1988).

*Council Resolution of 14 October 1988 for the Limitation of Use of Chlorofluorocarbons and Halons*, **O.J. Eur. Comm.** (No. C 285) 1 (1988).

*Commission Recommendation 89/349 of 13 April 1989 on the Reduction of Chlorofluorocarbons by the Aerosol Industry*, **O.J. Eur. Comm.** (No. L 144) 56 (1989).

These regulations pose mandatory requirements on all member states concerning the production and use of CFCs and halons.

10. *Council Directive 85/210 of 7 March 1985 on Air Quality Standards for Nitrogen Dioxide,* **O.J. Eur. Comm.** (No. L 087) 1 (1985), amended by **O.J. Eur. Comm.** (No. L 372) 36 (1985).

This Directive sets forth ambient air quality standards for Nitrogen Dioxide.

11. *Council Directive 82/884 of 3 December 1982 on a Limit Value for Lead in the Air,* **O.J. Eur. Comm.** (no. L 378) 15 (1982).

This directive sets an ambient air quality limit for lead in the air based on the need to protect human health.

12. *Council Directive 88/609 of 24 November 1988 on the Limitation of Emissions of Certain Pollutants into the Air from Large Combustion Plants,* **O.J. Eur. Comm.** (No. L 336) 1 (1988).

This Directive sets forth emission limits for nitrogen oxides and sulphur dioxide from combustion plants with thermal import equal or greater to 50MW regardless of the type of fuel utilized by the plant.

13. *Council Directive 89/369 of 8 June 1989 on New Municipal Waste Plants,* **O.J. Eur. Comm.** (No. L 163) 18 (1989).

This Directive sets out emission limitations and pollution prevention requirements for new municipal waste incineration plants.

*Water*

1. *Council Directive 73/404 of 22 November 1973 on the Approximation of the Laws of the Member States Relating to Detergents,* **O.J. Eur. Comm.** (No. L 347) 16 (1973), amended by **O.J. Eur. Comm.** (No. L 109) 40 (1982).

*Water Pollution*

1. *Council of European Community's Directive on Detergents, November 22, 1973*

This Directive requires member states to ban the use and marketing of detergents in which the surfactants are less than 90 percent biodegradable.

2. *Council Directive 74/440 of 16 June 1975 Concerning the Quality Required of Surface Water Intended for the Abstraction of Drinking Water in the Member States,* **O.J. Eur. Comm.** (No. L 194) 26 (1975), amended by **O.J. Eur. Comm.** (No. L 271) 44 (1979).

*Council Directive 80/778 of 15 July 1980 Relating to the Quality of Water Intended for Human Consumption*, **O.J. Eur. Comm.** (No. L 229) 11 (1980), amended by **O.J. Eur. Comm.** (No. L 319) 19 (1981).

These three Directives set forth drinking water quality requirements.

3.  *Council Directive 82/176 of 22 March 1982 on Limit Values and Quality Objectives for Mercury Discharges by the Chlor-Alkali Electrolysis Industry*, **O.J. Eur. Comm.** (No. L 081) 29 (1982).

This Directive establishes effluent limitation and water quality objectives for water affected by mercury and its compounds.

4.  *Council Directive 84/156 of 8 March 1984 on Limit Values and Quality Objectives for Mercury Discharges by Sectors Other than the Chlor-Alkali Electrolysis Industry*, **O.J. Eur. Comm.** (No. L 074) 49 (1984).

This Directive sets forth initial limitation and water quality values for mercury discharges for industries other than the chlor-alkali electrolysis industry.

5.  *Council Directive 83/513 of 26 September on Limit Values and Quality Objectives for Cadmium Discharges*, **O.J. Eur. Comm.** (No. L 291) 1 (1983).

*Council Resolution of 25 January 1988 on Community Action Programme to Combat Environmental Pollution by Cadmium*, **O.J. Eur. Comm.** (No. C 030) 1 (1988).

These Directives elicits emission limitations for cadmium for industrial plants and establish a Community program to combat environmental pollution caused by cadmium.

6.  *Council Directive 84/491 of 9 October 1984 on Limit Values and Quality Objectives for Discharges of Hexachlorocyclohexane*, **O.J. Eur. Comm.** (No. L 274) 11 (1984).

This Directive lays down emission limitation values and water quality objectives for HCH in the aquatic environment.

7.  *Council Directive 80/68 of 17 December 1979 on the Protection of Groundwater Against Pollution Caused by Certain Dangerous Substances*, **O.J. Eur. Comm.** (No. L 020) 42 (1980).

This Directive lists dangerous substances whose discharge to groundwater must be controlled and licensed by individual member states.

*General*

1. *Council Directive 85/337 of 27 June 1985 on the Assessment of the Effects of Certain Public and Private Projects on the Environment,* **O.J. Eur. Comm.** (No. L 175) 44 (1985).

This Directive requires assessment of the environmental effects of both public and private projects.

# Appendix B

## Japanese Environmental Laws

### Air Pollution

*Air Pollution Control Law;* Law No. 97 of 1968, as amended by Laws No. 18, 108 and 134 of 1970, No. 88 of 1971, No. 84 of 1972, No. 65 of 1974 and No. 33 of 1989.

*Noise Regulation Law;* Law No. 98 of 1968, as amended by LawsNo. 18, 108 and 135 of 1970 and No. 88 of 1971.

*Vibration Regulation Law;* Law No. 64 of 1976.

*Offensive Odor Control Law;* Law No. 91 of 1971.

### Water Pollution

*Water Pollution Control Law;* Law No. 138 of 1970, as amended by Laws No. 88 of 1971, 84 of 1972, No. 47 of 1976, No. 68 of 1978, No. 41 of 1980, No. 58 of 1983, No. 61 of 1984, No. 90 of 1985 and No. 34 of 1989.

*Law Concerning Special Measures for Conservation of the Seto Inland Sea;* Law No. 110 of 1973, as amended by Laws No. 35 and 47 of 1976, No. 68 of 1978 and No. 34 of 1989.

*Law on the Prevention of Marine Pollution and Maritime Disaster;* Law No. 136 of 1970, as amended by Laws No. 137 of 1970, No. 54 and 84 of 1973, No. 95 of 1975, No. 47 and 68 of 1976, No. 87 of 1978, No. 41 of 1980, No. 85 of 1980, No. 58 of 1983, No. 25 of 1984, No. 102 of 1985 AND No. 40 OF 1987.

*Industrial Water Law*; Law No. 146 of 1956, as amended by Laws No. 99 and 161 of 1962, No. 168 of 1964, No. 98 of 1966, No. 88 of 1971 and No. 88 of 1972.

*Law Concerning Special Measures for the Water Quality of Lakes Law*; Law No. 61 of 1984, as amended by Laws No. 69 of 1986 and No. 34 of 1989.

*Water works Law*; Law No. 177 of 1957;

*Sewerage Law*; Law No. 79 of 1958, as amended by Law No. 97 of 1987.

### Pesticides

Agricultural Chemicals Regulation Law; Law No. 82 of 1948, as amended by Laws No. 155 of 1949, No. 113 of 1950, No. 151 of 1951, No. 161 of 1962, No. 87 of 1963, No. 1 and 88 of 1971, No. 27 and 87 of 1978, No. 45 of 1981, No. 57, 78, 83 of 1983 and No. 23 of 1984.

### Waste Management

*Waste Disposal and Public Cleansing Law*; Law No. 137 of 1970, as amended by Laws No. 71 of 1974, Nos. 47 and 68 of 1976 No. 43 of 1983 and No. 87 of 1987.

*Agricultural Land Soil Pollution Prevention Law*; Law No. 139 of 1970, as amended by Laws No. 88 of 1971 and No. 87 of 1978.

### Chemicals

*Law Concerning the Examination and Regulation of manufacture, etc. of Chemical Substances*; Law No. 117 of 1973 as amended by Laws No. 68 of 1975, No. 57 of 1978, and No. 44 of 1986.

### Miscellaneous

*Basic Law for Environmental Pollution Control*; Law No. 132 of 1967, as amended by Laws No. 132 of 1970, No. 88 of 1971, No. 111 of 1973, No. 84 of 1974 and No. 78 of 1983.

*Law Concerning the Compensation of Pollution-Related Health Damage*; Law No. 111 of 1973, as amended by Laws No. 85 of 1974, No. 8 of 1976, No. 10 of 1978, No. 16 of 1980, No. 16 of 1983, No. 78 of 1983, No. 15 of 1985, No. 43 of 1987, No. 97 of 1987 and No. 7 of 1988.

*Nature Conservation Law*; Law No. 85 of 1972, as amended by Laws No. 73 of 1973, No. 87 of 1978 and No. 58 of 1987.

*Natural Parks Law*; Law No. 161 of 1967, as amended by Laws No. 140 and 161 of 1962, No. 13, 61 and 140 of 1970, No. 88 of 1971, No. 52 and 85 of 1972, No. 73 of 1973 and No. 87 of 1978.

*Law for the Punishment of Crimes Relating to Environmental Pollution Which Adversely Affects the Health of Persons*; Law No. 142 of 1970.

*Pollution Control Works Cost Allocation Law*; Law No. 133 of 1970, as amended by Law No. 43 of 1988.

## Appendix C — Bibliography

1. Vienna Convention for the Protection of the Ozone Layer, Final Act; United Nations Environment Program; Mar. 22, 1985.

2. Montreal Protocol on Substances that Deplete the Ozone Layer; 52 Fed. Reg. 47,515-47,523; December 14, 1987.

3. Protection of the Stratospheric Ozone, 40 C.F.R. Part 82.

4. "IRS Issues Guidance Implementing Excise Tax on Ozone-Depleting Chemicals;" p. 1510; Environment Reporter, Bureau of National Affairs; January 5, 1990.

5. "Environment Council, Ozone Layer: EC Negotiating Position in Favor of Strengthening of Montreal Protocol Provisions--the Timetable and the Financial Provisions"; *Europe*; June 9, 1990.

6. Proposal for a Council Regulation (EEC) on substances that deplete the ozone layer; Official Journal of the European Communities; April 4, 1990; No. C 86/4.

7. Thomas David, "Cost Put at up to Rs20bn for India to phase out use of CFCs"; *Financial Times*, page 4; May 4, 1990.

8. Hunt, John; "India set to sign protocol on CFCs"; *Financial Times*, page 22; June 30/July 1, 1990.

9. Cairo Guidelines and Principles for the Environmentally Sound Management of Hazardous Wastes; U.N. Doc. UNEP/GC. 14/17.

10. *Stockholm Declaration on the Human Environment,* reprinted in *Reporter of the United Nations Conference on the Human Environment,* U.N. Doc. A/CONF.48/14 and Corr. 1 (1972), U.N. Sales No. E. 73 II.A.14 and corr., reprinted in 11 **I.L.M.** 1416 (1972), and in **United Nations Environment Programme, Stockholm Declaration, Environmental Law Guidelines and Principles No. 1** (1972); *United Nations Conference on the Human Environment,* G.A. Res. 2994, 27 U.N. GAOR Supp. (No. 30) at 42, U.N. Doc. A/8730 (1972).

11. Convention on the Control of Transboundary Movement of Hazardous Wastes and Their Disposal, U.N. Doc. UNEP/1G.80/3; March 22, 1989.

12. Treaty of Rome, Article 100A; March 25, 1957.

13. Single European Act, Articles 130R-T; June 29, 1987.

14. World Commission on Environment and Development, *Our Common Future* (1987).

## About the Author

Laura B. Campbell is an Associate with Morgan, Lewis & Bockius, specializing in assessing and allocating the environmental risks associated with project financings, mergers, acquisitions, joint ventures, and other banking and corporate transactions. She also counsels multinational companies on foreign and international law affecting the acquisition and operation of businesses abroad. Since 1987, she has taught International Environmental Law at the National Law Center, George Washington University. Ms. Campbell received a B.S. from the University of Notre Dame and a J.D. from George Washington University. She is admitted to the New York and District of Columbia Bars.

## Endnotes

1. The term International Law as used in this paper refers to law governing relations among different countries. International law can be bilateral, between two nations, or multilateral, among three or more nations. Domestic Law refers to the internal law of a country and the term Foreign Domestic Law refers to the internal law of a foreign country.

2. The doctrine of forum non-conveniens states that a case may be dismissed even when the court has jurisdiction if the form is not convenient for the parties to the dispute.

# XIV Implementing an Environmental, Health and Safety Audit Program for Loss Exposure Reduction

*J. David Sullivan*
*Manager, Browning-Ferris Industries*
*Houston, Texas*
*Director, Environmental Affairs*
*BFI Pharmacetical Services*
*Houston, Texas*

An audit is a thorough, systematic, mostly objective, documented, periodic review by an entity of operations and practices related to meeting various requirements, goals, regulations, policies and standards imposed from within or without the organization for self-evaluative purposes.[1]

*Audit* is a word that has a somewhat negative connotation. As an auditor, I stand accused of criticism, deserved or not; nitpicking; bean counting; and job justification. I subscribe to the above definition of an audit, adapted from EPA's policy statement on environmental auditing[2] and ADL.[3] Audits are conducted by qualified, proficient personnel from within the organization or hired for this specific task from outside sources. Audits follow well defined protocols and procedures worked out in advance of execution using agreed standards and criteria sometimes referred to as the rules of engagement. Audits require from auditors independence of thought, action and reporting while exercising due professional care. Audits require gathering, testing, documenting and verifying data and evidence which must be thoroughly evaluated, then formally and clearly reported. Timely and appropriate follow-up to initiate and complete corrective action for all audit deficiencies and exceptions is essential.[4] Audits should be used to identify and correct problems and to constantly review and improve the quality of performance, systems and resource allocations to assure not only compliance with the law but also limitation or elimination of potential or real adverse effects of business decisions.

There are several types of Environmental Health and Safety (EH&S) audits which may be further categorized as follows:

- Compliance audits;
- Risk assessment surveys, including vendor audits;
- Due diligence or acquisition audits;
- Management systems audits;
- Property transfer or divestiture audits;
- Opportunity assessments, such as waste minimization audits;
- Environmental impact assessments; and
- Other special purpose audits (SEC audits).

These categories are neither mutually exclusive nor exhaustive or even generally accepted terminology.

The profession of auditing in this context has not yet matured to the point where even the terminology is standardized, although attempts are being made from several quarters to move the process of definition and standardization along at a more rapid pace.[5] An interesting and fairly exhaustive discussion of the history of environmental auditing pegs the genesis of environmental auditing as a 1979 report to EPA known as the ACUREX report, Assessment of Innovative Enforcement Procedures,[6] although ACUREX was preceded by several SEC investigations between 1977 and 1980. The 1984 ADL report to EPA, titled "Current Practices in Environmental Auditing,"[7] identifies 1976 as the earliest known corporate program. With such disagreement about historic facts from well recognized practitioners, it is easy to see why no generally accepted standards have emerged.

The touted benefits of auditing are also diverse, much discussed and with little general consensus; however, there is strong agreement that auditing is worthwhile.[8] The inventory of such benefits includes:

- Regular documentation of compliance status for possible defensive use;
- Identification and correction of noncompliance prior to initiation of regulatory enforcement;
- Increasing awareness and expertise of line managers and staff in the audited areas;
- Risk identification and management;
- Improvement of operations and maintenance practices;
- Increasing managers' attention and commitments to proper management;

- Cross-training and sharing of techniques that yield good results; and
- Cost savings from sharing cost-effective opportunities between audited units.

However, one may find that the true benefit of audits is peace of mind for the managers and executives in the environmental, health and safety departments.

Even the federal government is now initiating and staffing audit programs for its own facilities. The Department of Energy has an aggressive program to evaluate their facilities' compliance status and offsite impacts, consisting of "tiger teams" dispatched to the audited facility by national management.[9] The Nuclear Regulatory Commission and the Tennessee Valley Authority have practiced self-evaluative audits for a number of years.[10] The Department of Defense has also begun to encourage its facilities management units to conduct audits.

Compliance audits usually focus on areas of involvement where there are explicit regulatory, statutory or permit requirements placed on facility operations. Usually, these are accomplished utilizing the regulations as a guide and the regulatory compliance monitoring methods as references. Depending entirely on the scope and complexity of regulatory requirements applicable to a specific operation, this type of audit can require from two to three workdays up to two workmonths of effort.

The auditors selected for these activities usually include personnel who have both training and experience in the technical areas to be evaluated, as well as some legal background or access to an attorney. The technical areas to be evaluated may include air pollution control, water pollution control, waste management, hydrogeological evaluation, safety and health practices for both physical and chemical hazards, transportation control, financial assurance and many others. If the objective is an exhaustive evaluation, as many as nine to ten different auditors may be needed for varying lengths of time.

Risk assessment surveys are usually quick, low-cost surveys of a particular facility or operation with the objective of identifying and documenting the incidence of specified risks or named perils. Pollution liability insurance risk assessment surveys used by insurance underwriters and vendor due diligence audits fall into this category. Although fairly structured in scope, those audits may actually be quite flexible in execution if well qualified and experienced auditors conduct them. That is, experienced auditors will usually be able to form supportable, first-sight opinions on relative risk by quick recognition of both potential hazards and management systems flaws with minimal need for verification of details. These audits can be accomplished with two to five workdays of effort on average.

Due diligence or acquisition audits can be the most demanding type of audit, again depending on the scope and complexity of both the facilities and the environmental, health and safety standards involved. Most practitioners are now using a phased technique to evaluate acquisition risks.[11] Phase I consists of records reviews, regulatory contacts, evaluation of previous site usage and monitoring data and brief onsite inspections. Phase I should be thorough enough to characterize both general compliance status and management systems adequacy, as well as estimate risks of environmental contamination, indoor air pollution, toxic tort claims and other major needs for monitoring or corrective actions. Phase I due diligence audits may expend anywhere from five to ten workdays to two to three workmonths of effort.

Phase II or site characterization, sampling and analysis is designed to define the severity and extent of any contamination or thoroughly assess the risk of future claims. Phase II costs and resource demands can only be estimated after preparation of a sampling and analysis work plan with well-defined data acquisition objectives.[12]

Phase III audits are actually initial remedial activities dictated by either the laws affecting property transfer or by the risk management or cleanup options negotiated between the buyer and seller of a property. These activities, while possibly costly, can only be accurately estimated at the close of Phase II. Again, depending on applicable laws, costs of Phase III may be assumed by either the buyer or the seller but are usually jointly funded and supervised.[13]

Management systems audits are targeted to verify and document the status of the subject company's EH&S management organization, structure, personnel, communication, policies, procedures, budgets, delegations, etc. These audits may be initiated at the impetus of either regulators or by internal quality improvement efforts. While somewhat subjective and lacking generally accepted standards of practice, these audits can be quite useful in targeting both improvements and budget adjustments.[14] Cost of these audits is variable, but usually comparable to that of a compliance audit of the same unit.

Property transfer assessments (PTAs) or divestiture audits are similar in design to due diligence acquisition audits, but are initiated and programmed by the seller rather than the buyer. The purpose of these audits is to make an independent, verified record of the property condition prior to transfer in order to assure compliance with applicable property transfer laws and to verify any claims, representations and warranties made by seller to buyer before closing. If agreeable, the buyer and seller may jointly contract with a disinterested, qualified third party to conduct a PTA in order to reduce the cost of duplicative efforts, as well as to avoid situations where opposing experts may disagree. Costs are usually similar to acquisition audit costs. In some instances, initiation of Phase II and Phase III PTAs may be necessary.

Opportunity assessments previously have involved waste minimization, cost avoidance or pollution prevention evaluations for the most part. However, opportunity assessments may be tailored to evaluate any subdivision of management for unrecognized opportunities or quality improvements. Costs are dependent on the extent of the evaluation effort, but may be held to levels comparable to a compliance audit with acceptable results.[15]

Environmental impact assessments are evaluations usually required by state or federal law when siting or permitting a new facility or when modifying some land use limitation or permit for an existing facility. The process required for federal projects under the National Environmental Policy Act (NEPA) or the Tanner Process in California are examples of this type of audit. This audit has been practiced for a number of years in response to demand first generated in 1970 by the passage of NEPA and is quite well defined in most jurisdictions. Therefore, the costs and time frames are determined from previous experience. For average business projects, as little as two workweeks or as much as three to six workmonths may be required depending on the type of project and the sensitivity of the surrounding environment. Environmental assessments are intended to analyze, predict, minimize, eliminate or mitigate potential impacts of proposed actions. Recently, this concept has been extended to existing facilities with the intent of minimizing or eliminating the offsite impacts of continued operation of the existing unit. This can be a very effective risk management tool.

## The Audit Team

The audit team should be selected from well trained, well qualified individuals who are both independent in mind set and sensitive to the interpersonal relationships and the valid concerns of the parties being audited.[16] Auditors should have not only educational background in a field of study related to the technical area being audited but also should have enough experience and direct operational involvement to establish their credibility. Auditors should be trained in the practices, techniques, standards and procedures for auditing. While a thorough, in-depth understanding of the laws, regulations and concepts affecting a facility is necessary in some disputed cases, a general and broad working knowledge with some applications experience will usually suffice for staff auditors. The audit team leader not only must possess exemplary training, experience and qualification in the audit target areas but also must have a good understanding of management principles and practices, as well as good interpersonal and motivational skills. The team leader must clearly establish reliability and credibility for the team. A personal rapport with the facility personnel should be cultivated in order for the audit team to be assured quick access to complete, detailed information.

Use of both internal and external auditors are acceptable practices for most of the types of audits discussed. There are pros and cons attendant to each approach. There are many consulting services organizations that offer audit services using well-qualified, experienced personnel; however, with some exceptions, use of external consultants usually costs 20 to 50 percent more than using internal staff. If qualified, proficient internal staff is not available, then training costs may offset the price differential. If audit demand is short-term or of indefinite frequency or staff budgets are limited, use of external consultants may become attractive.

Although auditor registration and certification programs are becoming available, there are no generally accepted standards to be applied for qualification and testing of auditors. While these registration and certification programs are steps in the right direction, until a consensus is achieved and a unifying national organization is chartered to maintain these standards, the benefits of registration and certification will remain somewhat debatable. California has the first program authorized by law but, so far, no legal requirements mandate use of registered and certified individuals.[17] Other relevant programs for certification are offered by the National Association of Environmental Professionals, the Institute of Hazardous Materials Management, the Institute for Environmental Career Advancement and the National Environmental Training Association. The Institute for Environmental Auditing, the Environmental Auditing Roundtable and the Environmental Auditing Forum recently proposed to merge. This action may promise to be the first potentially successful movement toward a national unifying organization.[18] Both the Water Pollution Control Federation (WPCF)[19] and the American Society for Testing and Materials (ASTM)[20] have been active in proposing and publishing guidance related to environmental auditing. (See Chapter XVII, Italiano.) WPCF published a manual of practice for auditing last year, and ASTM is actively encouraging formation of a subcommittee to propose and adopt standards for property transfer audits.

We are therefore left with only some old but sage advice when selecting consultants for environmental audits; *caveat emptor*. The buyer of these services should be as careful in this selection as in selecting an attorney or accountant. The need for well informed opinions, professional work ethics and discretion are quite similar among these three professions.

## Audit Procedures

Audit procedures involve several stages of activity that may be useful to discuss. These procedures may be implemented from either generic or customized protocols. In this context, I use the term "protocol" to define an activity plan and guide, and the term "procedure" to define either a written standard applicable to one specific set of requirements or a checklist.

The protocol should include consideration of audit purposes and goals, audit planning and logistics, priorities and resource needs in the first stage. Audit planning may include one or two onsite visits to assure that standards are agreeable, logistics are covered and resources will be adequate. These pre-audit visits are also recommended to allow the audit leader to begin establishing rapport and credibility with the facility staff. Short of actual visits to the site, several telephone calls will be necessary to discuss details. Onsite audit activities should first include a general orientation and health and safety briefing for the auditors by the facility staff. Close physical inspection, sampling, monitoring and measurement activities may be necessary to fully accomplish all audit goals. A general site walkover will help the auditors visualize

physical facilities and unit operations. All onsite audits involve common elements of:
- Reviewing organization and systems;
- Gathering physical, documentary, testimonial and observational evidence;
- Systematically evaluating evidence against standards and practices;
- Reviewing adequacy of evidence;
- Drawing conclusions; and
- Communicating conclusions to the appropriate facility personnel.

The last item is essential to successful completion of an audit. Should specific deficiencies be documented, early notification to the responsible manager can result in immediate corrections. Failure to fully discuss audit findings upon completion of site activities can result in miscommunication, erroneous conclusions and loss of rapport with the facility personnel.

After the visit, the final stage is audit report preparation and follow-up of corrective actions. A draft report should be prepared by the auditors within seven to 30 days from the conclusion of site activities. The draft is provided to the audited facility to allow rebuttal of misinterpretation on facts or erroneous conclusions and provision of further relevant information that was either unavailable or overlooked during the audit. When comments on the draft are received, the auditors should proceed expeditiously to a final report correcting all known errors and implementing all credible suggestions from the audited facility.

All successful audit programs include major emphasis on follow-up and correction of deficiencies, also known as audit response. Audit exceptions left uncorrected represent potential liabilities. Quick and appropriate corrective actions are imperative. Doing no audit may be better than doing one and forgetting or neglecting the audit response. In evaluating an audit or audit program, end results are what count. Successful loss limitation hinges on successful audit responses.[21]

Other key elements of successful programs include:
- Timely and complete reporting;
- Full, voluntary disclosure to the auditors by the facility personnel;
- Multimedia, cross-media and offsite evaluations, not strictly compliance;

- Open minds on both sides of the audit;
- Clear channels of communication;
- Well-defined methods of dispute evaluation and resolution;
- Well-understood and widely disseminated goals and objectives which are promoted by upper management; and
- Well-defined rules of engagement for the audit.

When the audit procedures are defined in the contract rules of engagement, then there is consistent agreement by all parties on protocol, standards and requirements. Audit procedures and checklists may be developed for specific units, the operating division or the company as a whole. While certain requirements are ambiguous or in a state of flux, strict procedures and checklists are of marginal value. When requirements and standards are fairly fixed, those tools can allow broad, thorough coverage of audited requirements by personnel who may be less than experts in a given area. Standard Operating Procedures (SOPs) and checklists also serve as a memory jog, a training aid and a standardization tool. Development of such aids can result in significant savings of time and costs, as well as promoting quality improvement.

## Audit Confidentiality, Disclosure Requirements and Information Management

Confidentiality of audit work product presents somewhat of a moral dilemma. Certainly some protection of information relevant to a business' competitive position, marketing strategies and proprietary methods, techniques and equipment is prudent, as is protection of information gathered for the purpose of preparing legal defense against civil or criminal actions before the courts or expected to be placed before the courts; however, overly zealous protective measures run the risk of encouraging a perception with the public, regulators, legislative bodies and public prosecutors of an intent to hide or cover up damaging information. Informed opinion on this issue is currently mixed. Some express the opinion that such protective measures are futile, counterproductive and a waste of effort and money.[22] Others maintain that taking full advantage of all protections offered by law is merely prudent business practice. Close attention to the evolution of law and practice by professionals is warranted over the next few years. Meanwhile, here are several considerations to be made when setting policy or procedure on this issue:

- There is no legal means to assure that audit reports will remain confidential;
- There is yet no statutory or common law directly on point;
- Ordinarily, otherwise available privileges afforded to documents and communications in certain relationships do not apply to information used in furtherance of criminal or fraudulent activities;
- There are many legal duties to disclose certain information to various governmental agencies, the omission of which can result in civil or criminal charges;
- Indemnification and hold harmless agreements are important contract provisions relative to errors and omissions for violation of confidentiality;
- Under current rules of procedure and concepts of case law, facts themselves are not protected by **any** privilege; only opinion, advice, strategy or self-incriminating statements;
- Once recorded, any information in any file may be discoverable under the rules of civil procedure and may be impounded if so authorized by a criminal search warrant.[23]

Activities are under way to further define the extent of protections that may be exerted in defense of confidentiality of audits. The state of Colorado was reportedly considering the adoption of a bill expressly recognizing self-evaluative privilege in specific circumstances, within certain time limits; however, the bill was vetoed by the governor. EPA's audit policy statement expresses the intent that self-evaluative documents not be used in enforcement proceedings unless they are the direct result of audits required by enforcement case settlement agreements and a reasonable grace period for corrective action has expired.

Meanwhile, certain precautions continue to be prudent and make sense:[24]

- Limit the number of copies of audit working papers and reports to the absolute minimum;
- Limit accessibility and distribution of such documents to only those parties with a true need to know;
- Route correspondence through legal counsel with a request for review and advice prior to distribution;
- Have all audits initiated at the express request of counsel;

- Maintain a log of all copies, establish a records retention and destruction policy and retrieve and shred all copies when no longer needed or at the dates specified in the retention policy;
- Divide reports into sections discussing facts, those discussing analyses and those discussing plans for corrective action;
- Limit availability of the facts section to counsel only;
- Clearly establish that the auditors are either an investigative arm of counsel's office or acting as agents of counsel in these matters;
- Train all individuals made privy to these documents in the requirements necessary to avoid unintentional waiver of privilege;

Some possibly useful case law relevant to these issues are listed in Table 1:

---

### Table 1

**Attorney-Client Privilege**
  *Upjohn Co. v. United States*, 449 U.S. 383,394 (1981) .
  *Admiral Insurance Co. v. United States District Court for the District of Arizona*, 881 F.2d 1486,1492 (9th Cir. 1989) .
  *W.R. Grace & Co. v. Pullman, Inc.*, 446 F. Supp. 771,776 (W.D. Okla. 1976).

**Attorney Work Product**
  *In re International Systems and Controls Corp. Securities Litigation*, 91 F.R.D. 552,556 (S.D. Tex. 1981).
  *In re Grand Jury Proceedings*, 601 F.2d 162,171 (5th Cir. 1979).
  *Hickman v. Taylor*, 329 U.S. 495 (1947); *Fed. Reg. Civ. P.* 26 (b) (3).

**Self-Evaluative Privilege**
  *Bredice v. Doctors Hospital, Inc.*, 50 F.R.D. 249 (D.D.C. 1970).
  *Webb v. Westinghouse Electric Corp.*, 81 F.R.D. 431 (E.D. Pa. 1978).
  *Lloyd v. Cessna Aircraft Co.*, 74 F.R.D. 518 (E.D. Tenn. 1977).
  *New York Stock Exchange, Inc. v. Sloan*, 22 Fed. Reg. Serv.2d 500 (S.D.N.Y. 1976).

**Ministerial Agents**
  *TRW, Inc.*, 479 F. Supp. 160 (D.D.C. 1979), aff'd, 628 F.2d 207 (D.C. Cir. 1980); c.f., *United States v. IBM Corp.*, 66 F.R.D. 154 (S.D.N.Y. 1964).

**Investigative Agents**
  *United States v. Arthur Young & Co.*, 677 F.2d 711 (2d Cir. 1981).

## Implementing an Environmental, Health and Safety Audit Program for Loss Exposure Reduction

Cases are frequently cited in discussions of the privileges associated with attorney-client communication, attorney work product doctrine and self-evaluation. Counsel should be consulted to assist in setting policy on these issues prior to any attempts to assert privilege.

As discussed above, there are specific legal duties to disclose information to the government and public under certain federal and state laws.[25] These exist in addition to any common law requirements to mitigate hazards or to fully disclose liabilities during certain transactions. Information and facts gathered during an audit may in some circumstances activate a self-reporting obligation. Lead auditors and legal counsel should be aware of these obligations and review each audit report against these requirements. Standardized tools such as report review checklists can be used to facilitate a thorough detailed review against requirements.

Confidentiality concerns may be exacerbated by the use of automated data mangement systems, FAX machines, computer modems and the like.[26] Any data management or records imaging system stores a retrievable, readable copy of the documents input to it either in standard code or graphic form. Therefore, confidentiality concerns may dictate full control of all forms of storage media, as well as physical copies of the sensitive documents. Such media include floppy disks, hard disks, mass storage media on mainframes such as tape and large capacity hard disks, as well as compact laser disks — read only memory. Not only must appropriate measures be taken to assure security and access control for those media but when no longer useful, data destruction measures must be taken such as magnetic wipes, sector overwrites or actual physical destruction of the media. However Draconian this may seem, these measures are necessary to assure protection of privilege. Anything less leaves a large chink in that armor which is already known to some regulatory agencies.

Information management systems are invaluable and readily adaptable to use in audit program management. Proper design and application of such systems can result in significant savings for operating an audit program, as well as assurance that audit exceptions and corrective action schedules are implemented and followed up to appropriate closure with little risk of neglect or memory lapse. Currently automated systems lend themselves to report preparation, summaries, systematic time management and response schedule management.

Many efforts have begun to systematically reduce some audit data acquisition and review procedures to expert or knowledge-based logical programs.[27] These will facilitate audit reviews being accomplished by moderately experienced auditors, with the same results and quality as if an expert had done the work. A few expert systems are already available on the open market. Commercial personal computer software has also been used with some success to custom program some elements of expert or schedule tracking systems. However, the complex, multilevel logic involved in expert systems may be too demanding for current PC-based data processors to run quickly with few errors.

This topic is so timely that the Center for Energy and Environmental Management developed a seminar on the topic and has presented it in multiple locations over the last few years.[28] There has been an environmental software directory[29] published and even a journal of environmental software.[30] Several technical publications and journals have also begun to publish annual review or monthly columns on the subject.[31] Managers implementing an audit program should seriously consider the usefulness and cost recovery of such programs.

## The Need for Auditing

Numerous authors have presented multitudinous answers to the question "Why audit?" in many forums ranging from mass media, scholarly journals, and continuing education symposia to the halls of Congress and the annals of the United States Executive Branch — the *Federal Register.* However, all this rhetoric reduces to the one word answer: "self-preservation." Businesses and even government agencies, by their audits or lack thereof, are sorting themselves into two categories: the Quick or the Dead.

The degree of responsibility, accountability and liability now being imposed on American corporations and their employees by the public and all levels of government for proper management of their environmental, health and safety affairs can be likened to those expected of fiduciary managers for public trust funds. In many cases, the penalties for failure and the attendant public opprobrium are closer to those heaped on a person convicted of a heinous crime. While there are supporters on both sides of this proposition, the realities are that the expectations of the governments involved, of the public and of corporate shareholders are very high and climbing.

In the past, corporations were accused of practicing social Darwinism, survival of the fittest, where their decisions affected their employees or the public. Now, this concept is being applied to corporations by the public. Many shareholders seem to be voting with their feet more and more on these issues. The "Green Movement," radical and activist environmental groups, grass-roots and *ad hoc* organizations and special interest groups abound. Concepts like "environmental terrorism" and "not in my backyard" (NIMBY) have entered the forum of public debate. As a 15-year environmental professional, this glare of public attention leaves me with mixed feelings, as I'm sure it does board members of some corporations which have experienced major environmental or safety incidents over the last several years. Remembering the adage of *carpe diem*, however, I hope we can avail ourselves of the opportunities being given us.

To answer the question, "Why audit?" in a more pragmatic vein, several reasons for environmental, health and safety audits come to the forefront:

- Risk, liability and loss reduction;
- Self-evaluation and quality improvement;
- Control of EH&S costs;
- Improved customer service and customer relations (I include regulators and the public, as well as purchasers of goods and services, in the category of customers;)
- Education, training and networking within the organization; and
- Performance standardization in the organization.

Perhaps the seminal documents for current discussions of environmental auditing were conceived in 1980, little more than two years after the inception of that endeavor, by Arthur D. Little's (ADL) Center for Environmental Assurance. Although several firms were already auditing in 1980, as documented by the "Survey,"[32] these concepts had not entered the general stream of corporate or government environmental management thinking. ADL's efforts to communicate with EPA's Office of Regulatory Reform and Office of Enforcement and Compliance Monitoring led to EPA's adoption of its "Policy on Inclusion of Environmental Auditing Provisions in Enforcement Settlements" on November 14, 1986,[33] which reiterated most, if not all, of the concepts in an interim policy statement previously issued on November 8, 1985.[34] This final policy remains in effect today and is being considered for inclusion in all settlements of EPA enforcement actions.

From these documents and many settlement decrees and orders entered since 1985, it is clear that EPA firmly believes in the concept of self-evaluative EH&S audits. If accurately performed and well supported by corporate culture, these activities can significantly reduce EH&S risks, liabilities and loss exposures for most businesses.

## Corporate Policy and Commitment to Environmental, Health and Safety Procedures

Paradigms are a popular topic of discussion today. (*Paradigms* are not to be confused with *paragons*. *Webster's* says that *paradigms* are "typical examples or archetypes," while *paragons* are "models of excellence or perfection." When discussing business, I much prefer paradigm to paragon, since the only paragon of business I can recall is the biblical Good Steward of his master's ten talents of silver.) In this context, *paradigm* is a particularly appropriate word for what is implied, as well as what is expressed. Arthur D. Little presents three paradigms, although unattributed, for environmental management philosophies:
- "Problem Solving" or Reactive Management;
- "Managing for Compliance" or Compliance Assurance Management;
- "Managing for Environmental Assurance" or Proactive Management.[35]

EH&S audit programs are usually part of compliance assurance management organizations, seldom part of reactive management organizations, and almost always part of proactive management organizations.

Others have characterized these paradigms as follows. The reactive style ". . . deal(s) with trouble as it comes. They lurch from problem to problem and wonder why they waste money, burn out good people and anger board members. They agonize over poor media coverage. The neighbors mobilize."[36] The compliance assurance style "try(ies) to meet the minimum requirements. They find out what the

## Implementing an Environmental, Health and Safety Audit Program for Loss Exposure Reduction

law requires and do some careful engineering to stay on the right side of it. If they are accused of pollution, they have the comfort of being able to say they tried. "Unfortunately, the law keeps changing and they are unable to anticipate the changes. Consequently they buy land or buildings (or other companies), hire engineers and architects, spend large amounts of money designing projects and. . .processes, and then have to redesign and duplicate costs because they have no overall approach to environmental protection."[37]

The proactive style "manage(s) for environmental protection. They strive to bring environmental impacts to a minimum level or eliminate them. They make pollution abatement and resource conservation a primary goal of project concept and design, and they reward environmentally sensitive approaches. They do 'preventative' lawyering to determine with certainty from whom they must obtain permits to do what. They do more than is required by laws and regulations. This way they stay abreast of new government requirements, away from lawyers and lawsuits, and ahead of the competition. By adopting good ideas before the law requires them, and designing them into projects, they force the competition to catch up."[38]

When reduced to a word, the difference between these management styles is *ethics*. Ethics is not a popular topic among most businessmen. You more often hear terms like return on investment, P to E, bottom line, market share and stockholders' equity and return. They find discussions of these topics enjoyable because it means profits, without which no one gets paid. What these businessmen need to learn is that without good, sound environmental ethics behind the financials, no profits will be made. Some recommend a "holistic" cost accounting method; an assessment of "environmental management and environmental accounting systems and methods. The purpose of these assessments is to reduce production costs, decrease pollution control and disposal fees, minimize liability and enhance environmentally sound business practices."[39] This should include "(1) Management Assessment, (2) Compliance Review, and (3) Opportunity Identification" stages.

Ethics need not be cost-ineffective. Indeed, avoided and ignored costs often mean the difference between success or failure in today's market. And that means risks and consequences must be considered: an unethically "avoided cost" is an environmental risk with potentially serious consequences. In a roundtable discussion published last summer in *Chief Executive* magazine,[40] Peter Huber of

Manhattan Institute of Policy Research and Jonathan Cannon, formerly of EPA, made it clear that knowledge of and compliance with the law is no defense from tort claims, but noncompliance and ignorance are almost insurmountable barriers to a successful defense. Those who go beyond the law have a much better defense. George Pilko of Pilko and Associates, an environmental consulting firm, offered poignant advice. Establish a policy actively supported by the chief executive. Clearly and frequently communicate it to all staff. Conduct audits and risk assessments. Fix the identified problems quickly and with appropriate priority. To do otherwise risks catastrophe. In the same discussion, John Hall estimated Ashland Oil's losses from the Pittsburgh diesel fuel spill on January 2, 1988, to be about $21 million with a class action suit still pending.

CERES, the Coalition for Environmentally Responslble Economies, published last year the Valdez principles named for the Exxon *Valdez* incident.[41] CERES is an organization of over 350 socially conscious investors (both individual and institutional) controlling more than $150 billion of investments. Such money talks to businessmen. CERES proposes to review and rate the environmental conduct of publicly held corporations using the ten Valdez principles, which include annual publication of a self-evaluative progress report and annual environmental audits made publicly available. These annual ratings would be published by CERES presumably as guides to "green investments." Although still in draft, the guidelines stipulate that an annual fee of up to $15,000 be paid to CERES by each rated company. Nonparticipating or low-rated corporations would be placed at disadvantage in today's "green" marketplace. While these guidelines are still in draft form, this should be sounding alarm bells in the board room as it represents a new "high" in coercive tactics used by otherwise arm's-length, common stockholders concerned about management practices.

In the same vein, EPA issues annual enforcement accomplishment reports.[42] These reports reflect that between mid-1988 and the end of 1989, over $35 million in civil penalties were imposed by EPA cooperating with the Department of Justice (DOJ), with over $110 million since 1984. EPA penalties can range from $200 to $50,000 per day of violation, up to $1,000,000 per violation. EPA's civil penalty policy allows upward adjustment of penalty amounts for bad faith, consistent noncompliance or severe impacts of the violation. It also allows downward adjustments in converse circumstances.

**Implementing an Environmental, Health and Safety Audit Program for Loss Exposure Reduction**

The real kicker is the mandate to recover the economic benefit of noncompliance. This means "avoided costs" plus interest will be EPA's initial, minimum offer in penalty negotiations.

Ethical questions can become toxic tort risks in today's litigious society. Asbestos from Manville Corporation, Agent Orange and superabsorbent tampons top the list of products, the distribution of which led to bankruptcy, reorganization or hostile asset plundering.[43] Cause-in-fact is not always the standard of proof used for these claims; instead, speculation and poorly supported opinions from unqualified experts have won the day in recent times.[44] Community and employee right-to-know statutes and toxic release reporting requirements, as well as citizen civil suit enforcement authorizations, make these risks even larger.

Vicarious liability for offsite consequences of business decisions has become tighter. Recent decisions, such as *Waste Conversion Inc. v. Pennsylvania,*[45] allow pass-through of liability from independent offsite contractors back to the original shipper, generator or owner of hazardous materials involved in spills or releases.

The joint and several liability imposed by Superfund is being actively enforced by EPA and DOJ. Thirty-nine of the 50 states now have their own state-authorized, abandoned waste site cleanup programs similar to Superfund, which independently impose similar duties and liabilities to the federal Superfund. Five states now have Superlien laws affecting the transfer of real property and seventeen states bave nonpriority environmental liens.[46] These laws impose strict, no-fault liability on current property owners for complete and thorough cleanups prior to closing any property transfer. New Jersey's Environmental Cleanup Responsibility Act (ECRA) represents the most mature program in this area, as well as one of the toughest. In the six years since enactment, ECRA cleanups have cost business over $207 million.[47]

Innocent landowner liability for cleanup costs can be substantial. However, the 1986 Superfund Amendment and Reauthorization Act (SARA) offered some defense from these actions to landowners who can prove they "did not know and had no reason to know that any hazardous substance which is the subject of the release or threatened release was disposed of on, in or at the facility."[48] Also, innocent landowners must establish that they have not caused or contributed to the contamination and have met acceptable standards of due diligence in their transactions.[49] Trustees, executors, successors and oth-

er parties legally empowered to exert control over facility operations have also been held liable.[50] This latter category has been interpreted to include governmental agencies controlling release response actions, both state and federal.[51] The combination of these liability concepts is making the Federal Deposit Insurance Corporation, the Resolution Trust Corperation and most public and private
lenders very uneasy.[52] Department of Energy facility cleanup plans
are rapidly progressing. A proposed consent decree for the DOE's
Fernald, Ohio, installation was announced last year, which is projected to cost over $1 billion.[53] The total DOE cleanup costs may run
as high as $1 trillion over the next 50 years.

Laws and regulations requiring disclosure of environmental liabilities generally evolve from two regulatory arenas, the public
health and environmental control agencies and the agencies responsible for control of publicly held companies and their statements of
financial condition; e.g., the Securities and Exchange Commission.
In the first instance, the law imposes specific responsibilities and liabilities on the owner and operator of a facility subject to regulation
to monitor, record and report data pertinent to its own compliance
with those regulations; e.g., air emissions, water discharge monitoring or waste generation reports. Failure to make accurate, complete
reports results in both civil liability and, in cases of willfulness or
neglect, criminal liability.[54]

In the second instance, the law requires full disclosure of any
business situation which may affect "materially" the financial statements of net worth or profit and loss by any publicly held corporation.[55] While current SEC interpretations of "materially" include
only liabilities already "recognized" under the dictum of Generally
Accepted Accounting Principles (GAAP), efforts are starting among
consumer groups and business watchdog organizations to lobby for
a requirement to include contingent liabilities on the balance sheet.
Such contingent liabilities include 100 percent funding of cleanups
at each state or federal Superfund site where the company may be
involved above the *de minimis* level, estimated number of toxic tort
liabilities for releases reported to the government under SARA-Title
III, estimated product liability claims for new products amortized
over each product's viable lifetime, estimated costs of construction
and operation of new pollution control devices required by authorized control programs being implemented in phases at net current
worth, and the like. These disclosures may be real eye openers for
some stockholders.

**Implementing an Environmental, Health and
Safety Audit Program for Loss Exposure Reduction**

While risk management techniques exist that allow companies to transfer or share certain risks by insurance, risk retention pools or self-insurance, the hard market for pollution liability insurance and surety bonds has resulted in 80 percent to 90 percent of companies that handle, manage or clean up pollution to retain their loss exposures. Those companies that are successful in obtaining third-party coverage often find that the rates are somewhat prohibitive and that the insurers often impose intrusive risk management requirements as conditions of coverage. (See Chapter XXIII, Telego.) Market forces will continue to move toward the proactive style of environmental risk management.[56]

Employee and community right-to-know programs such as SARA-Title III and OSHA's Employee Right-to-Know will not only require regulatory reports of potentially damaging information but will also sometimes require that specific, written notice be given to employees, customers and the public.[57] These notices may increase the risk of initiating toxic tort claims. In today's litigious social and judicial framework, such claims are often successful with diminishing burdens of proof on plaintiffs.[58] State programs such as California's Proposition 65 are increasing the burden and consequences of trade in hazardous materials.[59]

The parameters which define the form of successful attempts to penetrate the corporate veil, to attach personal liability to corporate officers for business activities controlled by those officers, have been interpreted recently to the main advantage of those attempting such penetration.[60] Although most articles of incorporation and other chartering agreements usually afford indemnification from such claims to corporate officers, this indemnification is likely to be preconditioned on successful defense of these claims.

Finally, and perhaps the most significant area of liability for individuals in this business, successful investigation and prosecution of alleged criminal violations of environmental, health and safety law has rapidly expanded since 1983, from negligible to very significant. As governmental resources devoted to pursuing such actions have increased, so have the penalties to convicted violators. (See Chapter XII, Duvall.)

From 1983 to mid-1989, EPA's Office of Criminal Investigations and DOJ's Environmental Crimes Section have pursued 540 indictments, winning 412 pleas or convictions with fines totaling over $23 million and with sentences imposed totaling over 250 years, of which actual time served was over 88 years.[61] With more than 65 Special Agents, about 20 attorneys and some 50 technical specialists on call, the EPA Office of Criminal Investigations is becoming a major actor not only in enforcement after-the-fact but also in promoting voluntary compliance.[62] The DOJ staff in Environmental Crimes, taken with EPA's resources and the joint training and investigation initiatives with the FBI and state and local law enforcement agencies, places an intimidating array of people, equipment and techniques in the effort to pursue and prosecute environmental violators.

The most frequent prosecution targets for these agencies were the actual decision makers in illegal activities. The targets included 12 percent managers, 5 percent officers, 20 percent vice presidents and 33 percent presidents of the companies involved. This totals 70 percent; i.e., 70 percent of the targets of these investigations were not the blue-collar workers actually conducting illegal acts, but were the managers and executives ultimately responsible.[63]

While the incidence and success rate of criminal prosecutions have increased, so also have the penalties. The maximum penalties available to the prosecutors and the courts now include on first offense up to $1,000,000 and fifteen years for felony violations of the Resource Conservation and Recovery Act and up to $50,000 and three years for felony violations of Superfund, the Clean Air Act and the Clean Water Act.[64]

Broad constructions of proof of criminal intent or neglect have been successfully argued in many cases of late.[65] An evil heart and mind are no longer essential elements of proof for negligent violations. The courts may assume that, since a defendant is doing business in such a highly regulated area of endeavor, this mere fact predisposes that thorough knowlege of the law and regulations is readily available to him.[66]

Some regulators and prosecutors now view criminal charges as the first avenue of choice when evaluating prosecutable merit of enforcement cases.[67] Other enforcement officers show little sympathy for negligent violators, much less intentional violators, saying that criminal penalties are now just another of the many costs of doing business in America.[68] While there continues to be disagreement and controversy over the severity of penalties and fines, recent severe sentences (for which all avenues of appeals have yet to be exhausted) imposed by courts for offenses subject to the Uniform Sentencing Guidelines make it clear that judicial centrists and reformers are using the guidelines as written.[69] Some cases before sitting judicial activists may cast doubt on some aspects of the guidelines' intent and language, but government appeals of anomalous sentences can result in uniform implementation. The guidelines, albeit possibly revised, are here to stay.[70]

In one recent case, a first offense of unpermitted filling activity in a regulated wetland area on private property resulted in a sentence for the property owner and developer which was more severe than some sentences allowed under the same guidelines for a bank robber.[71] Mr. Pozsgai was sentenced to 36 months in prison and a fine of $202,000 for cutting timber, bulldozing and filling a forested wetland area on his own property, after repeated warnings and notifications of the possible illegality of such actions. The area involved was less than 14 acres. Even given the recalcitrant nature of this defendant, the sentence seems somewhat harsh and at disparity with the true social and environmental consequences of the illegal act.[72] However, on consideration of the cumulative worldwide impacts and the consequence of such small incursions into natural systems, such activities need to be curbed. The fact that sentencing in such cases will remain controversial is the only conclusion which may be drawn.

Overall, as stated at a recent conference on RCRA Reauthorization, it seems that executives in charge of environmental compliance may now be alternatively titled "vice presidents in charge of taking the rap and cooling your heels in the slammer."[73] Personal liabilities, including monetary fines and jail time, are "working their way up the corporate ladder" according to a staff attorney for the DOJ Environmental Crimes section.[74] (See Chapter XXX, Reich.)

EPA is not the only actor in expanding personal liability for corporate executives. State and local prosecutors have been meeting mixed success in prosecution of executives for knowing violation of state worker health and safety statutes.[75] Although appeals are not complete, the president, plant manager and foreman of Film Recovery Systems, Inc. in Cook County, Illinois, were convicted of murder in the job-related death of a worker at the company's plant which recovered silver salts from waste photographic and x-ray film by using cyanide baths.[76] Similar cases have been spawned from this trial in a number of states. *New York v. William Pymm*,[77] and the State of New Jersey's actions against Cylinder Recon Co., Special Hazards Management Co. and Carmelo Vasi.[78] In October of 1989, the explosion and fire at Phillips Petroleum Co.'s plant in Pasadena, Texas, killed

23 people and resulted in $750 million in estimated property damage. In April of 1990, the Federal Occupational Safety and Health Administration proposed $5.7 million in penalties against Phillips and $724,000 in penalties against Fish Engineering and Construction, Inc., the primary maintenance contractor for Phillips. So, without knowing the full extent of the toxic tort claims (including natural resource damage) or wrongful death claims nor that of lost revenues or equipment replacement cost overruns, the projected damages subtotal has been estimated at about $760 million and rising.[79]

Given the current risks, liabilities and exposures accounted above, consistent loss control and risk management (not to mention avoidance of jail time) cannot be successfully practiced by corporations, their officers, executives and managers, without a strong and constantly reinforced environmental, health and safety ethic. This ethic must be inculcated into the roots of corporate culture so that no manager or line employee needs to ask when faced with otherwise "gray-area" decision making. If it doesn't feel "right," don't do it. The risks are too high. This view is gaining much support among business professionals, as well as professional environmental, health and safety managers and scientists.[80] To do otherwise can put companies out of business and individuals in jail and in bankruptcy.

## Corporate Management Systems for Environmental, Health and Safety Affairs

Which systems are necessary for appropriate management of EH&S affairs today? This question must be answered by any business executive considering, initiating or maintaining an EH&S program. There are several fairly definitive texts available that specifically discuss the various views on answering this question.[81] They present a consensus on the necessary elements for successful programs.

First and indispensable, there must be strong commitments and policies supporting proactive management of these areas from the chief executive officer and the board of directors, communicated well and frequently through upper and middle management to the line managers and line employees.

Business plans must include goals, policies, procedures and budgets for adequate resources. Upper management must give clear di-

## Implementing an Environmental, Health and Safety Audit Program for Loss Exposure Reduction

rection and middle management must develop, implement and over-view the goals, procedures and accomplishments in these areas. Adaptable, adequate budgets must be made and tracked to assure that both operating and capital expenditures are planned and made in a timely manner to address all priority needs. Delayed and avoided costs in these areas will not only result in higher eventual costs, but may also result in perceptions by the public and regulators that the company does not seriously pursue compliance. That's an image easy to acquire, but hard to live down.

Organizational structure and personnel staffing the positions must be appropriate to meet both line and mid-level needs for enough, well-qualified staff who understand their roles and responsibilities. Guidance and direction must be thorough, concise, understandable and available. Flexibility and adaptability are critical in the face of constant changes. Methods for coordination, prioritization, delegation, motivation and standardization must be well planned, readily available and routinely used. Resources for methods and availability of communication opportunities must be adequate and frequently used and reviewed up, down and laterally within tbe organization. The same applies to communication with parties outside the organization. The regulatory community, Congress, state governments, the public, the press, customers and special interest groups must all be kept informed.

Quality of effort must be constantly measured and reviewed. Performance evaluation, problem identification, corrective action programming, rewards and sanctions must be systematically addressed.[82] Business systems, policies, procedures and guidance must be defined in all of these areas. There are many methods and organizational structures that can accomplish these tasks, both centralized and decentralized. In large and diverse organizations, decentralized matrix management structures often work well.

Organizations and systems can be structured at any level to serve the critical needs. Several critical elements are easily thought of in archetypical terms. Terms that describe some of these elements are Compliance Management and Technical Assistance; Engineering and Special Services; Training, Recruiting and Employee Development; Communication, Internal and External; Management Data and Information Systems; Legal Services; Risk/Loss Control; and Auditing. Breakdowns or deficiencies in any of these elements can cause effects throughout the system and can result in negative feedback loop effects amplifying the consequences across the whole business. The goal of wise business managers today should be to assure in-time delivery of all of these services to their decision-makers and line managers in a cost-effective manner.

## Risk Management Reviews — Future Needs

EH&S audits, opportunity assessments and other special purpose audits are becoming a standard part of most proactive risk management programs. The government's perspective was presented at a joint meeting of three audit professional organizations in December, 1989.[83] The government view seems to be that as a part of EPA's effort to foster cooperative environmental management, to depart from the command and control style of regulation and to encourage proactive management of these issues by nongovernmental means (deregulation or regulatory reform), the agency considers compliance audits, management systems reviews and opportunity assessments as indispensable tools to prudent professional environmental risk managers.[84]

Suggestions have been made that these requirements are so substantial and important that "a third-tier" of professional, independent "regulatory specialists, attorneys and environmental 'accountants' who would audit, measure and certify compliance to the federal and state government" would be beneficial to all involved.[85] Indeed, standardization, registration and certification of professional auditors and managers of environmental, health and safety systems is not only recognized as a need, attempts are being made to initiate the process.[86] The registration and certification of environmental engineers, safety professionals, industrial hygienists and hazardous materials managers are already available and widely accepted. However, we run the risk of having too many voluntary certification organizations using different standards, causing conflict and uncertainty in the establishment of the worth and reliability of such certifications. An overall unifying body and principles or standards are needed that generally sanction or accredit such voluntary programs. Development of specially targeted protocols and procedures for opportunity assessments is another area where needs will escalate. Waste minimization auditing techniques are fairly well documented

## Implementing an Environmental, Health and Safety Audit Program for Loss Exposure Reduction

at present. More definition of overall pollution prevention systems criteria, management systems review methods and specific risk limitation and avoidance measures is needed.

EH&S risk quantitative methods need research and development funding and encouragement. Further analysis and development of systems failures, risks, consequences and cost models is necessary. Such models are required to allow proper prioritization, budgeting and scheduling for incident prevention in as many different sectors as there are clearly distinguishable categories of risk and liability. There are many such subdivisions. Attempts are being made further to mount this effort.[87]

Finally, there is sorely needed an open, well-publicized and continuing dialogue on ethical conduct in an accessible forum. Such dialogue cannot be influenced by coercive tactics, threats of legal actions or self-interested publicity. Such a forum should have as its charter the definition, nurture and dissemination of ethical standards of conduct for professionals in technical fields, planners, managers and evaluators of environmental, health and safety management systems in both business and government. The heretofore adversarial relationship of business and government and special interest institutions should be put aside as a precondition of admission to any discussions in this forum. Recognition of an egalitarian right to expression without fear of repression, as well as of the basic commonality of goals and objectives, must be a prerequisite for membership. For the good of the public and of the professions, partisan positions must be subordinated to the will of the body after appropriate open debate.

The current systems of elective body legislation, executive body direction and enforcement and judicial review (all subject to the winds of public opinion, the lures and lumps of special interest, political action groups and the pressures from sometimes reactionary, uninformed or venial antagonists) have resulted in systems that are sometimes misdirected, ill conceived, very costly, uncoordinated and often at cross-purposes. In this time of increasing demands and shrinking resources, we cannot afford such inefficiencies, but must recognize the rights of the public and of individuals to influence the outcome.

A utopian viewpoint such as the public interest in natural resource allocation, conservation and preservation has not been well served by the present systems and laws. The need to ensure a livable world for our progeny dictates that we act now to begin correcting not only past excesses but also current inefficiencies.

**J. David Sullivan** is an environmental scientist and manager who has been involved in the science, government and business of environmental protection since 1976. For six of eleven years with the U.S. Environmental Protection Agency, Region VI, he served in the Region's Environmental Services Division as a multi-media environmental compliance inspector. He was included in a team of investigators and attorneys awarded the EPA's Bronze Medal for Commendable Service for outstanding contribution to the Agency's Criminal Enforcement Program in 1989. Most recently employed as Manager, Facility Environmental Audits with CECOS, the hazardous waste disposal affiliate of Browning Ferris Industries, Inc., and as the Manager of Environmental Affairs for CECOS, he is now Director of Environmental Affairs for BFI Pharmaceutical Services.

## Endnotes

1. Principles for Conducting Environmental, Health and Safety Audits (Discussion Draft), Arthur D. Little — Center for Environmental Assurance, Cambridge, Mass. (1988).

2. "Environmental Auditing Policy Statement," 50 *Fed. Reg.* 46,504 (Nov. 8, 1985).

3. *Environmental Auditing Fundamentals and Techniques*, Greeno, Hedstrom, and Diberto, Arthur D. Little — Center for Environmental Assurance, Cambridge, Mass. (2d ed. 1985).

4. Principles for Conducting Environmental, Health and Safety Audits (Discussion Draft) , Arthur D. Little — Center for Environmental Assurance, Cambridge, Mass. (1988).

5. "Defining Our Vocabulary," J.K. Deuel and J. D'Aloia, Jr., *Environmental Auditor*, New York, N.Y., Vol. 1, No. 1 (1989), pp. 33-38.

6. "Environmental Auditing: Past, Present and Future," John Palmisano, *Environmental Auditor*, New York, N.Y., Vol. 1, No. 1 (1989), pp. 7-20.

7. "Current Practices in Environmental Auditing," a report to U.S. EPA, Arthur D. Little — Center for Environmental Assurance, Cambridge, Mass. (1984).

8. "Benefits of Environmental Auditing," a report to U.S. EPA, Arthur D. Little — Center for Environmental Assurance, Cambridge, Mass. (Dec. 1984).

9. Tiger Team Assessment of the Mound Plant, Miamisburg, Ohio, Department of Energy, Washington, D.C. (Dec. 1989), NTIS Order Code, DE-90005756/WEP.

## Implementing an Environmental, Health and Safety Audit Program for Loss Exposure Reduction

10. "Framework for a Corporate Environmental Auditing Program: The TVA Experience," John R. Thurman, *Environmental Auditor*, New York, N.Y., Vol. 1, No. 1 (1989), pp. 55-58.

11. "Environmental Site Assessments for Commercial Real Estate Transactions," Douglas G. Schubring, Environmental Auditor, New York, N.Y., Vol. 1, No. 1 (1989), pp. 59-68.

12. "Industry Drafts Phased Pollution Assessment Rules to Limit Cleanup Liability," *Inside EPA*, Washington, D.C., Vol. 11, No. 31 (Aug. 3, 1990), p. 10.

13. *Ibid.*

14. Greeno, Hedstrom, and Diberto, *op. cit.*, p. 3.

15. "Waste Minimization: Incentives and Disincentives for Meeting a New Environmental Goal," Robert L. Kerr, *Environmental Auditor*, New York, N.Y., Vol. 1, No. 1 (1989), pp. 25-31.

16. Principles for Conducting Environmental, Health and Safety Audits (Discussion Draft), Arthur D. Little — Center for Environmental Assurance, Cambridge, Mass. (1988).

17. "Registering Environmental Assessors in California, USA," Kirk C. Oliver, *Environmental Auditor*, New York, N.Y., Vol. 1, No. 1 (1989), pp. 21-24.

18. "Environmental Managers Launch First Group to Set Environmental Professional Standards," *Inside EPA*, Washington, D.C., Vol. 11, No. 32 (Aug. 10, 1990), p. 2.

19. Environmental Audits — Internal Due Diligence, MOP FD-18, William J. Librizzi and Catherine N. Lowery, Co-Chairmen, Water Pollution Control Federation, Alexandria, Va. (1989).

20. "Industry Drafts Phased Pollution Assessment Rules to Limit Cleanup Liability," Inside EPA, Washington, D.C., Vol. 11, No. 31 (Aug. 3, 1990), p. 10.

21. "Environmental Liability: From Pinstripes to 'Pen' Stripes," James V. Faulkner, Jr., *The Generator Journal*, Houston, Tex. (Summer 1989), p. 14.

22. *Environmental Audits*, Lawrence B. Cahill, Ed., Government Institutes, Inc., Rockville, Md. (5th ed. 1987), p. 28.

23. "Confidentiality and the Environmental Audit," remarks by David B. Weinberg, Wald, Harkrader & Ross, at the Environmental Auditing Conference, sponsored by The Energy Bureau, Inc., Washington, D.C. (Oct. 20, 1982).

24. *Ibid.*

25. "Sizing Up Your Audit Program," Arthur D. Little — Center for Environmental Assurance, Cambridge, Mass. (1983), pp. 14-15 and "Environmental Liability: From Pinstripes to 'Pen' Stripes," James V. Faulkner, Jr., *The Generator Journal*, Houston, Tex. (Summer 1989), p. 14.

26. "Computers in the Decision Process: Legal Implications of Electronic Data Transfer and Data Management Systems," Jeffrey C. Worthington, Tech Law, Inc., Lakewood, Colo. (1989).

27. "Regulations and Compliance Expertise (RACE) Knowledge-Base System: Description and Users Guide," D.K. Mann, G.R. Franczak, L. Pritchard, and D.H. Wiggins, Construction Engineering Research Lab. (Army), Champaign, Ill. (Dec. 1989) , NTIS Order Code, AD-A218091/7/WEP.

28. "How to Automate Environmental Information Management," a seminar sponsored by the Center for Energy and Environmental Management, Fairfax Station, Va. (March/April 1990).

29. *Environmental Software Directory*, Elizabeth Donley and Alice Cobey, Ed., Donley Technology, Garrisonville, Va. (1989).

30. *Environmental Software*, a journal sponsored by The Computational Mechanics Institute, Billerica, Mass., USA.

31. "Microcomputer Software Reviews," in the Journal of the Air & Waste Management Association, published monthly by Air & Waste Management Assoc., Pittsburgh, Pa.

32. "A Survey of Environmental Auditing," Arthur D. Little — Center for Environmental Assurance, Cambridge, Mass. (1980).

33. "Final EPA Policy on Inclusion of Environmental Auditing Provisions in Enforcement Settlements," Memoranda, From: Thomas L. Adams, Jr., To: EPA Enforcement Officials, Washington, D.C., Dated: November 14, 1986.

34. "Environmental Auditing Policy Statement," 50 *Fed. Reg.* 46,504 (Nov. 8, 1985).

35. Greeno, Hedstrom, and Diberto, *op. cit.*

36. "Managing for Environmental Protection," Gregor I. McGregor, *Waste Tech News*, Denver, Col., Vol. 1, No. 8 (Jan. 16, 1989), pp. 10 - 12.

37. *Ibid.*

38. *Ibid.*

39. Assessments That Address The Economics of Environmental Management," Gaston & Snow *Environmental Advisor*, Boston, Mass., Vol. II, No. 36 (May 1990), pp. 1-3.

40. "CE Roundtable — The $150 Billion Question," *Chief Executive*, No. 52 (July/August 1989).

41. "Can the Valdez Principles Green Corporate America," *The Environmental Forum*, Vol. 6, No. 2 (March/April 1990).

42. "Overview of EPA Penalty Practices," an EPA Report, Compliance Policy and Planning Branch, Office of Enforcement and Compliance Monitoring, Washington, D.C. (March 1988).

## Implementing an Environmental, Health and Safety Audit Program for Loss Exposure Reduction

43. "Remarks of Edmund B. Frost before the Energy Bureau Conference on Environmental Auditing," Edmund B. Frost, Kirkland & Ellis, at the Environmental Auditing Conference, sponsored by The Energy Bureau, Inc., Washington, D.C. (Oct. 20, 1982).

44. *Christophersen v. Allied Signal Corp.*, CA-5, No. 89-1995-CV.

45. *Waste Conversion Inc. v. Pennsylvania, Pa.*, Commw. Ct., No. 647 C.D. 1989 (Jan. 8, 1990).

46. "Is the Great Superlien Scare Finally Over?" William J. Hamel, an analysis and perspective article in *Environmental Reporter*, Washington, D.C., Vol. 21, No. 18 (Aug. 31, 1990), pp. 853-855.

47. "New Jersey's ECRA: Problems, Policies, and Future Trends," I. Leo Motiuk and Daniel J. Sheridan, an analysis and perspective article in *Environmental Reporter*, Washington, D.C., Vol. 21, No. 11 (July 27, 1990), pp. 549-556.

48. Comprehensive Environmental Response, Compensation and Liability Act of 1980, as amended, Title I, Section 101(35) (A) (i), 42 U.S.C.A. Section 9601(35) (A) (i).

49. "Innocent Landowner Liability," Gaston & Snow *Environmental Advisor*, Boston, Mass., Vol. I, No. 25 (Dec. 1989), p. 2.

50. "Trustee Executor Liability under Superfund," Steven L. Leifer and Nancy E. Allin, an analysis and perspective article in *Environmental Reporter*, Washington, D.C., Vol. 20, No. 42 (Feb. 16, 1990) , pp. 1786-1789 and "Successor and Parent Corporations: Liability for CERCLA Response Costs," David E. Dering, an analysis and perspective article in *Environmental Reporter*, Washington, D.C., Vol. 20, No. 41 (Feb. 9, 1990).

51. "State of California Liable in Stringfellow Superfund Case," *The Hazardous Waste Consultant*, Lakewood, Col., Vol. 8, No. 3 (May/June 1990), pp. 3-5.

52. Testimony of Steven A. Seelig, director FDIC division of liquidation before the Senate Banking Committee, July 19, 1990. *See* "FDIC, Resolution Trust Corp. Seek Protection in Senate Bill Limiting Exposure under CERCLA," *Environmental Reporter*, Current Developments, Washington, D.C., Vol. 21, No. 13 (July 27, 1990), pp. 533-534.

53. "$1 Billion Consent Decree Proposed for DOE Facility in Ohio," *Pesticide and Toxic Chemical News*, Washington, D.C., Vol. 18, No. 23 (Apr. 11, 1990), pp. 19-20.

54. "Disclosure of Environmental Liabilities to Governmental Agencies and Third Parties," James R. Arnold, Pettit & Martin, from "The Impact of Environmental Law on Real Estate and Other Commercial Transactions," a course of study of the American Bar Institute, Washington, D.C. (Sept. 23-24, 1988) .

55. *Ibid.*

56. "Corporate Environmental Risk Management Strategies, the EIL Risk Assessment Process and Risk Financing Alternatives," D. Jeffery Telego, from the Conference on Environmental Risk Management Strategies, sponsored by *Inside Superfund*, Washington, D.C. (Oct. 1988).

57. *Ibid.*

58. *Christophersen v. Allied Signal Corp.*, CA-5, No. 89-1995-CV.

59. Telego, *op. cit.*

60. "Drawing the Liability Line," Barry S. Shanoff, *World Wastes*, Atlanta, Ga., Vol. 33, No. 7 (July 1990), pp. 137-138.

61. "Getting Tough on Environmental Crime," Laurie A. Rich, *Resources*, a publication of the Environmental Resources Management Group, Exton, Pa., Vol. 11, No. 5 (Oct. 1989), pp. 9-11.

62. "Enforcement Targets Corporate Executives," Gaston & Snow *Environmental Advisor*, Boston, Mass., Vol. I, No. 16 (July 1989), pp. 1-3.

63. *Ibid.*.

64. *Ibid.*

65. "Criminal Enforcement of Environmental Laws," Kevin L. Call, Deckerd, Price & Rhodes, Environmental Law Update, (Nov. 1989), pp. 3-4.

66. *United States v. Hayes International Corp.*, 786 F.2d 1499 (11th Cir. 1986).

67. "Only Criminal Sanctions Can Insure Public Safety," E. Dennis Muchniki, *The Environmental Forum*, Vol. 6, No. 3 (May/June 1990), pp. 31-32.

68. "A New Cost of Business for Environmental Violators," Paul Thomson, *The Environmental Forum*, Vol. 6, No. 3 (May/June 1990), pp. 32-33.

69. "A System Spinning out of Control," Kevin A. Gaynor, *The Environmental Forum*, Vol. 6, No. 3 (May/June 1990), pp. 28-29.

70. "Environmental Protection or Enforcement Overkill," Paul D. Kamenar, *The Environmental Forum*, Vol. 6, No. 3 (May/June 1990), pp. 29-30.

71. *Ibid.*

72. "Pozsgai's Swamp, A Tale without Heros," John G. Mitchell, *Audubon*, New York, N.Y., Vol. 92, No. 4 (July 1990), pp. 112-124.

73. "How to Avoid Criminal & Civil Liability under RCRA," Christopher Harris in conference remarks at "RCRA Reauthorization and Implementation — Preparing for the 1990 Debate," sponsored by *Inside EPA* and Risk Management Technologies, Inc., Washington, D.C. (April 3-4, 1990).

74. "Getting Tough on Environmental Crime," Laurie A. Rich, *Resources*, a publication of the Environmental Resources Management Group, Exton, Pa., Vol. 11, No. 5 (Oct. 1989), pp. 9-11.

75. "The Corporate Safety, Health and Environmental Professional: Responsibilities, Liabilities, and Conflicts," Jerry M. Keys, *SemiConductor Safety Association Journal*, (Sept. 1989), pp. 40-45.

## Implementing an Environmental, Health and Safety Audit Program for Loss Exposure Reduction

76. *State of Illinois v. O'Neill*, 83 C-11091 (Cir. Cook County 1985).

77. *People of the State of New York v. William Pymm*, N.Y. Sup. Ct. App. Div., Indictment No. 930186.

78. "Company, Former President Charged in Worker's Death," *Occupational Health & Safety News*, Waco, Tex., Vol. 5, No. 22 (Jan. 8, 1990), pp. 1-2.

79. "OSHA Probe Leads to Recommendations for Safety Program for PetroChemical Industry," *Chemical Regulation Reporter*, Washington, D.C., Vol. 14, No. 5 (May 4, 1990), pp. 150-151.

80. "Business Ethics: Action Needed," Jay A. Sigler and Joseph E. Murphy, *The National Law Journal*, Vol. 11, No. 12, (Nov. 28, 1988), p. 13.

81. "Environmental Auditing and Environmental Management," Frank B. Friedman, *Practical Guide to Environmental Management*, Environmental Law Institute, Washington, D.C. (1990), pp. 63-90.

82. Principles for Conducting Environmental, Health and Safety Audits (Discussion Draft), Arthur D. Little — Center for Environmental Assurance, Cambridge, Mass. (1988).

83. "Environmental Auditing in the 1990s: A Government Perspective," Tapio Kuusinen, Working Papers, Newsletter of the Institute of Environmental Auditing, Washington, D.C., Vol. 3, No. 3 (Winter 1989), pp. 1-4.

84. *Ibid.*

85. Environmental Compliance, Is the System Working?" Gaston & Snow, *Environmental Advisor*, Boston, Mass., Vol. I, No. 15 (July 1989), p. 4, quoting Bill Drayton, President of ASHOKA.

86. "Environmental Managers Launch First Group to Set Professional Standards," *Inside EPA*, Washington, D.C., Vol. 11, No. 32 (Aug. 10, 1990), p. 2.

87. "Quantitative Surveillance Model for System Risk Class Assessment," Richard B. Jones and Robert L. DeMichell, *Environmental Auditor*, New York, N.Y., Vol. 1, No. 1 (1989), pp. 39-48 and "Evaluating Health, Safety and Environmental Auditing Requirements using a Simple Risk Model," William A. Yodis, *Environmental Auditor*, New York, N.Y., Vol. 1, No. 1 (1989), pp. 49-54 and "A Risk Assessment Method for Waste Generator Due Diligence Evaluations of Hazardous Waste Facilities," Kevin D. Grant, *Environmental Auditor*, New York, N.Y., Vol. 1, No. 3 (1989), pp. 153-166.

# XV

# Waste Reduction Audits

*Robert B. Pojasek, Ph.D.*
*Vice President*
*Geraghty & Miller, Inc.*
*Andover, Massachusetts*

Consultants and industry have long been familiar with environmental compliance and loss control auditing practices and procedures. It was quite natural to seek to describe waste reduction audits in a manner similar to those practices and procedures.

Another traditional influence is also present in most waste reduction audits — the environmental engineer's focus on the end-of-the-pipe. The focus is on identifying all wastes and tracking them back to their source instead of focusing on the process to determine what wastes may be created. This latter approach is the preferred method of the process engineer. By understanding the process, it is possible to learn how waste generation may change with production volume or by process upset.

Many states have passed toxics use reduction legislation. The focus of this answer to the public's fear of chemicals (i.e., chemophobia) is controlling the use of toxic chemicals in the workplace. A heavy emphasis will be placed on the examination of process flow and materials balance; however, these are also good tools to utilize in waste reduction programs. The better understanding of the process that results from following this approach will lead to the discovery of numerous opportunities to reduce wastes (or prevent losses). An excellent reference describing the use of the process flow diagram and materials balance has been published by the Ontario Waste Management Corporation.[1]

The term *waste* in this chapter will include process "losses" to all media. *Waste reduction* for the purposes of this chapter refers to in-plant practices that reduce, avoid, or eliminate the generation of waste at the source.  Each of these practices is derived from an understanding of the process, including the following:

- Good operating practices — which include management initiatives, improved operations and maintenance (including preventive maintenance) of existing facilities, waste stream segregation, scheduling and materials handling improvements and spill and leak prevention;
- Input substitution or input materials modification — which involves replacing a toxic substance used in a process with a nontoxic or less toxic substance or using a purified or modified material;
- Technology modification — which refers to improved controls, energy and water conservation, process redesign, process modification, and equipment changes;
- Closed-loop recycling — which includes instances when waste is directly and immediately reused, and never leaves the process for storage or purification; and
- Product substitution — which refers to a change in the final product that allows less waste to be generated.

The conduct of a waste reduction audit must rely on a schematic drawing of the manner in which the process operates — the process flow diagram or a table such as Table 1.  A companion item is the materials balance which is one of the most basic and widely used principles of process engineering.  It accounts for all the inputs into a process and balances them with what comes out both as product and losses.  Using these items, the process engineer can conduct a waste reduction audit by observing, measuring and recording process-related data, collecting and analyzing samples, and asking questions of those who operate and manage the process.

To be effective, this program must be conducted methodically and thoroughly under the direction of an experienced process engineer.  Some people have relied on detailed questionnaires as a substitute for this experience; however, it should be clear that there are numerous drawbacks to this approach.

This chapter will address the derivation of a process flow diagram and a materials balance.  The use of a tracking system to collect and maintain the data is highlighted.  Using this information as the starting point, a verification inspection can be conducted.  This is at the heart of a waste reduction audit.  Finally this material can be subjected to an independent audit very much like the way the financial information of the firm is reviewed.

**Table 1**
**Typical Format for an**
**Environmental Compliance Audit**

Before Site Visit
- Organize Audit Team
- Prepare and Submit
  Pre-visit Questionnaire
- Review Relevant Regulations
- Define Audit Scope
- Develop Detailed Site
  Visit Agenda
- Review Audit Protocols

Conduct Site Visit
- Initial Briefing
- Review Records/Documentation
- Interview Staff
- Physically Inspect Facilities
- Closing Briefing

After Site Visit
- Develop the Audit Report
- Develop/Assess Action Plan
- Close Out Audit

## Constructing the Process Flow Diagram

Within every industrial facility there are a number of distinct operations, which, when combined in the proper sequence, lead to the production of a product. The process engineer refers to these as unit processes. To properly begin a waste reduction audit, it is necessary to list all the unit processes and assemble as much information on them as possible. This information should include the following:

| | |
|---|---|
| Facility | Name of unit operation |
| Department | Operation type |
| Product line | Located on-site (Y/N) |

## Waste Reduction Audits

Information on the operation type includes the following categories:

| | |
|---|---|
| Material storage | Waste storage |
| Manufacturing process | Waste blending |
| Waste air emissions | Recycling |
| Wastewater emissions | Waste treatment or disposal |
| Other releases | |

Other information that should be collected on the process can be found in Table 2. Care must be taken to include all intermittent processes, such as cleaning, make-up, blow-down, and tank dumping in the inventory process.

---

**Table 2**
**Process Information**

- Process description
- Equipment lists and specifications
- Operating manuals
- Piping and instrumentation diagrams
- Facility layout and elevation plans
- As-built drawings
- Equipment operating conditions (temp., pressure, etc.)
- Physical locations where materials are added to the operation
- Physical locations where emissions result
- Types of measurements made and recorded
- Analyses and assays performed
- Utilities affecting the process
  (steam, vacuum, coolant, nitrogen, wastes, etc.)
- All process reactions (stoichiometric description)
- Material/Energy balance (design and operating)
- Cleaning steps and operations
- Frequency of operation

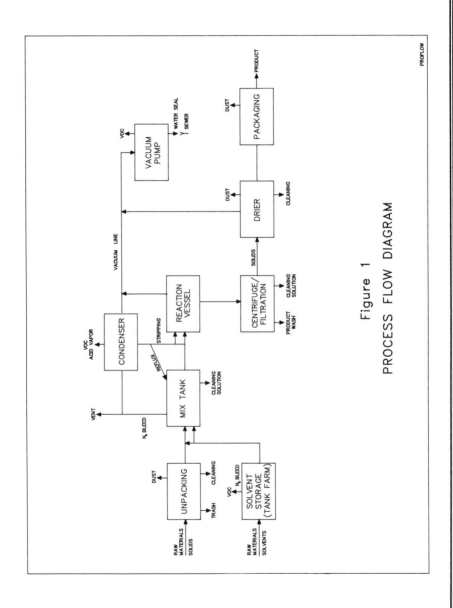

Figure 1

PROCESS FLOW DIAGRAM

While it may be obvious that a reactor or plating bath is a unit process, it is quite important to include all ancillary features such as the following:

| | |
|---|---|
| Storage areas | Powerhouses and boilers |
| Laboratories | Cooling towers |
| Pumping stations | Warehouses |
| Maintenance shops | Pollution control devices |
| Garages | |

Discretion is required when considering the level of detail to include in this information; however, before a decision is reached to narrow the focus, the process engineer must ensure that this is done from a basis of sound understanding of the process involved. It must also be kept in mind that waste can occur before or after the actual unit process itself.

Once all the unit operations are listed, a process flow diagram can be prepared to describe the interconnections between the individual process components. Intermittent processes such as cleaning must be indicated by proper labelling. Figure 1 on the previous page shows an example of a simplified process flow diagram.

If the facility already has a process flow diagram, the audit process will proceed with the refining and verification of this document. This chapter assumes that an adequate process flow diagram must be constructed essentially from scratch.

## Establish a Materials Tracking System

Once the process flow diagram is in place, a procedure to account for material flows to and from each unit process must be put into place. One of the most fundamental principles of process engineering is that of a material balance. The material balance is defined in the *Superfund Amendments and Reauthorization Act [(Section 313 (l) (4)]* as follows:

> For the purposes of this subsection, the term 'mass balance' means an accumulation of the annual quantities of chemicals transported to a facility, produced at a facility, consumed at a facility, used at a facility, accumulated at a facility, released from a facility, and

transported from a facility as a waste or as a commercial product or by-product or component of a commercial product or by-product.

It is useful to have a system that facilitates the tracking of all material usage, losses and production to specific unit operations. The following information should be included in the materials tracking system:
- Material purchases and usage by unit operation;
- Material movement between unit operations;
- Generation of losses (wastes) from each unit operation;
- Classification of the losses with respect to regulations;
- Production outputs.

Special accounting allowances must be made for certain complex situations. For example, there is the possibility of double counting for certain losses when wastes are processed through treatment, storage and disposal operations or multiple waste streams are blended together. A detailed knowledge of process flow is required to allocate waste management costs to the proper department. Throughout this process, it is important to have knowledge of how specific products relate to material usage and process losses.

Information which should be collected on the process inputs is summarized in Table 3. Information needed on the products may be found in Table 4 and the information on losses may be found in Table 5. Data sheets for use in gathering and recording this information have been published by the U.S. Environmental Protection Agency[2]. 

Once the information is collected, it is possible to complete a preliminary materials balance. The data can be tabulated as in Figure 2 on the following page. The individual and sum totals making up the material balance must be reviewed to determine information gaps or inaccuracies. Significant imbalances point out the need for further investigation. Measurement and estimating errors can contribute significantly to an imbalance. In addition, various inputs and losses (e.g. evaporation) may have been understated or missed altogether. The compilation of accurate, comprehensive data is essential to a successful waste reduction audit.

**Table 3**
**Input Materials Information**

- Name of material
- Source/supplier
- Component/attribute of regulatory concern
- Annual consumption rate
  — the process unit
  — overall
  — component(s) of concern
  — purchase price, $ per unit
  — overall annual cost
- Delivery mode
- Shipping container size & type
- Storage mode
- Transfer mode
- Empty container disposal/management
- Shelf life
- Supplier would:
  — accept expired material (Y/N)
  — accept shipping containers (Y/N)
  — revise expiration date (Y/N)
- Acceptable substitute(s), if any
- Alternate supplier(s)

Attention must be paid to accounting control in a material balance program. Documentation must reflect each of the following points:

- Completeness — all inputs, outputs and losses are recorded
- Validity — all recorded items adequately represent what actually takes place in the process
- Accuracy — each material is in the correct amount and is recorded on a timely basis
- Maintenance — records are properly controlled after entries are made
- Physical Security — access to the records is restricted to authorized people

This documentation can be independently audited later if these points are considered.

### Table 4
### Products Information

- Name/identification of product or by-product
- Component/attribute of regulatory concern
- Annual production rate
  — overall
  — component(s) of concern
- Annual revenues
- Shipping mode
- Shipping container size & type
- On-site storage mode
- Containers returnable (Y/N)
- Shelf life
- Rework possible (Y/N)
- Customer would:
  — relax specification (Y/N)
  — accept larger containers (Y/N)

---

### Table 5
### Losses Information

- Last Name/identification
- Process Unit Source
- Loss Leaves Process as
  — Air emission
  — Wastewater
  — Solid Waste
  — Hazardous Waste
  — Release
  — Other
- Waste Characteristics
- Component attribute of regulatory concern
- Occurrence
  — continuous or discrete
  — periodic, sporadic, non-recurring
- Generation Rate
  — Annual
  — Maximum
  — Average
  — Frequency
- Management Methods
- Cost of Management

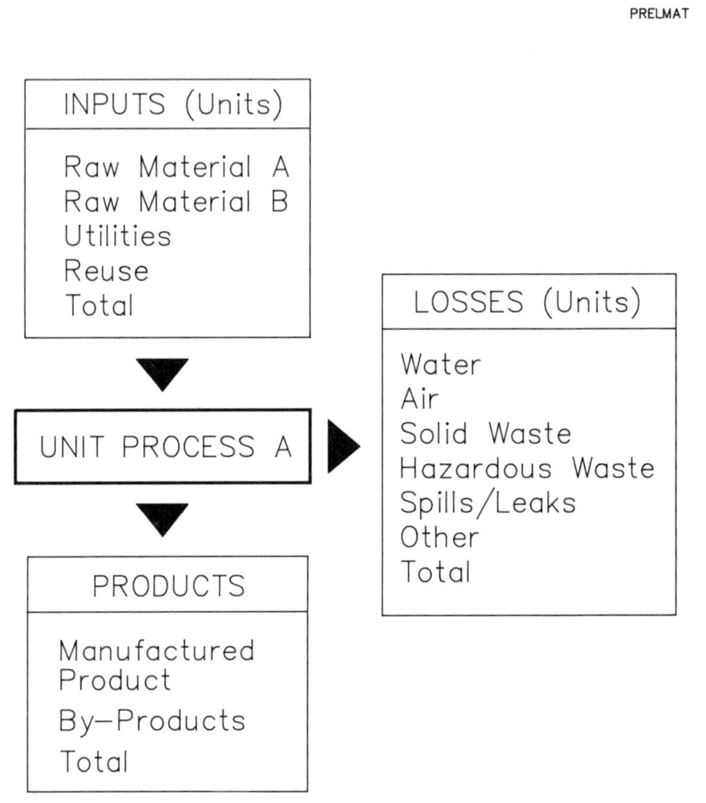

PRELMAT

INPUTS (Units)

Raw Material A
Raw Material B
Utilities
Reuse
Total

UNIT PROCESS A

LOSSES (Units)

Water
Air
Solid Waste
Hazardous Waste
Spills/Leaks
Other
Total

PRODUCTS

Manufactured
Product
By—Products
Total

Figure 2

PRELIMINARY MATERIALS BALANCE
FOR UNIT PROCESSES

Much of the data gathering done to this point in the waste reduction audit could be accomplished without actually visiting the facility. However under ideal circumstances, the process flow diagram and materials balance were constructed by someone who is familiar with the facility's operations. Now it is time for the process engineer to verify the information. This is at the heart of the waste reduction audit because it is often in this step that the opportunities for waste reduction as described in the definition (found above in the introduction) are identified for further action.

First the inspector will verify that the process flow diagram correctly depicts the actual process in the facility. Careful documentation and photographs should be used to show any corrections that may be required. Each unit process must be carefully observed by the inspector while it is in operation.

The design and operating characteristics of a unit process will determine to a great extent its potential for the loss of hazardous constituents. During the facility investigation, the actual potential for releases must be determined. The investigator should determine whether the unit has engineered features that are designed to prevent losses from the unit. If such features are in place, an evaluation as to whether they are adequate (in terms of capacity, engineering, etc.) to prevent losses must be prepared.

During the verification inspection, the process engineer should examine the unit's operating history to obtain information that indicates what losses typically take place. There are several operational factors that influence the likelihood of losses:

- Operating life of the unit. Units that have been operating for long periods of time are generally more likely to have losses than newer units (i.e., low waste and nonwaste technology);
- Operating status of the unit. In some cases, the operating status of a unit (e.g., continuous flow, batch, intermittent use, etc.) may have an effect on the relative likelihood of losses; and
- Operating procedures. Maintenance and inspection records should indicate whether a unit is likely to have losses. Units which production personnel inspect regularly and properly maintain are less likely to have releases than units that have been poorly maintained.

Now the attention should shift to verification of the materials balance. Each of the items covered in Table 6 are important to the opera-

**Table 6**
**Verification of the Materials Balance**

- Process entity — materials utilized, produced or lost are separate and distict from other operations.
- Verifiable sampling and analysis — all samples were taken and analyzed in accordance with a written sampling plan utilizing designated standard methods.
- Units of measure — consistent with the item being examined and normalized correctly to production.
- Objectivity — evidence must support the recording of all data.
- Materiality — relative comparisons are made to determine the significance of each item to the materials balance.
- Conservatism — all estimates are conservatively prepared
- Going concern — facility is expected to keep the process.
- Periodicity — definition of the operating cycle and the impact on the materials balance.
- Consistency — materials balance is prepared on a basis which is consistent with preceding years.

tion.  Careful notes must be taken on items which deviate substantially from the rigor demanded in this process.  A summary report will later recommend changes which will improve the materials balance information to the extent that it might create more waste reduction opportunities.

In the conduct of the verification inspection, the process engineer should record all opportunities for waste reduction.  Standardized forms could be developed so that this information could be utilized by the engineer conducting the waste reduction feasibility study.

# Independent Audit
# of Waste Reduction Program

It is often useful for facility's to have someone with a more detached outlook to monitor their waste reduction programs and look for problem areas and pressure points.  In a manner similar to an independent financial audit, a waste reduction professional can pro-

# Environmental
# Risk Management

vide a detailed report on the firm's waste reduction systems and meet with the people involved to suggest improvements.

A process flow diagram and materials balance is like a financial accounting system. The independent audit can verify that the diagrams represent what is actually occurring at the facility. This audit should be able to check on where the materials balance numbers came from and test the validity of the measurements and assumptions utilized to derive the data.

One approach to such an audit includes an ongoing study of the facility's waste reduction information system. In this manner, there is prompt recognition of when a system is too overloaded and outdated for the facility's present phase of growth. If growth is not very rapid, an independent review of the process flow diagrams and materials balance could be performed on a two-year rotational basis.

Good process auditors should be highly involved in a successful waste reduction program. They get to know the facility's business, people and waste reduction program thoroughly. They are trained to balance production objectives and issues against considerations of efficiency and practicality. Besides providing sensible, responsive audit services, they should act as a sounding board for the facility's management group. A thorough system review should lead to improvements in the waste reduction program and actually generate new opportunities to reduce losses in the process.

Some day there may be a Waste Reduction Accounting Standards Board similar to the Financial Accounting Standards Board which issues FASB guidance. However until that time, a facility will have to rely on the experience and integrity of the individuals retained to do this work.

The process flow diagram and materials balance should be the basis for a waste reduction audit. A prepared questionnaire such as that used in a regulatory compliance audit not only has no logical place in a waste reduction audit but it also does not help an inspector (experienced or otherwise) to locate all the waste reduction opportunities. There are instances where a checklist can be useful to be certain that all information sources were covered before leaving a facility.

By verifying the process flow diagram and the materials balance under the direction of a process engineer, information on waste reductions opportunities will be documented in a form useful to those involved in the feasibility study. It will also save time in that the people conducting the feasibility study will not have to conduct another preliminary site investigation before proceeding in their search for options to reduce the wastes.

If adequate documentation is prepared during the waste reduction audit process, it can be independently audited on a periodic basis in a manner similar to a financial audit. Given the proliferation of toxics use and waste reduction legislation as well as other demands placed on industry by the public and the shareholders, this independent auditing may be a good idea whose time has come. Some companies (e.g. Boeing, 3M and Polaroid) release an Annual Report on Waste Reduction. Such a report is far more creditable with the statement of an independent auditor.

## About the Author

**Robert B. Pojasek, Ph.D.** is a Vice President at Geraghty & Miller, Inc. From his office in Andover, Bob directs the pollution prevention engineering efforts in the company's 42 regional offices. He is a member of the American Institute for Pollution Prevention and is a nationally recognized expert in the field. His office is located at One Corporate Drive, Andover, Massachusetts (508) 794-9470.

## Endnotes

1. Ontario Waste Management Corporation. *Industrial Waste Audit and Reduction Manual*, Toronto, Ontario, September, 1987.

2. U.S. Environmental Protection Agency. *Waste Opportunities Assessment Manual*, Publication No. 625/7-88/003, Cincinnati, Ohio, July, 1988.

# XVI Risk Assessment Process

*Curtis Haymore, President*
*Environomics, Inc.*
*Vienna, Virginia*

This chapter describes the approaches many analysts use to assess risks in health and environmental studies. The chapter identifies the essential steps to perform risk analyses and provides a few sample calculations. The methods and procedures shown here reflect current standard practices, rather than controversial approaches or complex analyses. The chapter covers two general approaches to developing risk assessment estimates: deterministic, point estimate models and probabilistic models. This chapter is a primer of risk assessment methods and is meant for a new practioner or reviewer of a risk assessment. The chapter concludes by speculating on developments that may change practices.

The chapter focuses on risks to human health and how analysts estimate risks from both carcinogenic and noncarcinogenic toxic chemicals.[1] The chapter discusses only briefly how risks to the environment are assessed, mainly to highlight the differences between health and environmental assessments and alert the reader to the need for better methods for assessing environmental effects.[2] This chapter does not discuss how to assess risks related to industrial safety or to technologies (such as nuclear power).

This chapter discusses the mechanics of simple, quantitative approaches to risk assessment. There is a continuing need for analysts to identify possible weaknesses, underlying assumptions, and risks that are not yet susceptible to quantitative analysis. A single chapter, however, cannot include all the caveats that are needed. Please be warned that though these qualifications are excluded, they are important in any risk assessment upon which decisionmakers might base their judgments. Similarly, this chapter excludes a discussion of how qualitative assessments are integrated and balanced with quantitative analyses.

## Identifying Hazards, Estimating Exposures, and Characterizing Risks

There are three steps in environmental and health risk assessment.[3] The analyst must first identify the hazards of concern, and if present, must use some measure of their danger. Second, the analyst must estimate the exposure to these chemicals. Finally, the analyst must characterize the risk that results from the exposure.

### Hazard Identification

The risk assessment analyst must determine which chemicals pose a possible risk and determine what is known about their toxicities. Identifying the chemcials that may pose a risk in a given situation can be simple (for example, if the analyst is examining the effects of only a single chemical) or difficult (for example, if the analyst is examining many compounds and needs to apply rigorous screening criteria). The analyst generally can include only those chemicals for which there are both toxicity and exposure data.[4]

Final risk estimates are usually expressed and incremented in order of magnitude (ten-fold) steps, and thus even high-toxicity chemicals in low concentrations or high concentrations of low-toxicity chemicals may not affect the result. For example, in estimating the risks of toxic chemicals in indoor air, researchers have identified hundreds of chemicals. Even so, there are many fewer chemicals that researchers know to be toxic, which have reported toxicities accepted by federal agencies, and which are commonly found in significant concentrations, and which have high enough concentrations and toxicities to affect risk assessment calculations. The important questions to keep in mind are the following:

- What chemicals are present?
- Are there data on their toxicity?
- Is information available on exposure levels or can reasonable assumptions be made?
- Does the combination of toxicity and exposure levels warrant inclusion?

There are many ways for analysts to characterize the toxicity of chemicals, although they most commonly use only a few. Quantitative risk assessments rely on available published data and most usually rely only on potency data approved by a governmental agency such as the U.S. Environmental Protection Agency (EPA). The list of available toxicity data is, therefore, finite. For example, there are about 45 chemical and physical agents for which there is accepted evidence of carcinogenicity to man. There are many more noncarcinogenic compounds that researchers know or believe to be toxic to man in varying degrees, but the volume is a very small fraction of the chemicals present in the environment and in industrial production. There is a growing consistency in the potency values researchers ascribe to carcinogens and noncarcinogens and most risk assessments use these values. Analysts who use values other than those in common sources usually defend their judgments with extensive toxicological rationales.

Analysts express risks from cancer and those from other toxic, but noncancer-causing agents using different measures. Analysts commonly use "unit risk factors" (standardized measures of potency) for human carcinogens. For other toxic chemicals, a common measure is the "reference dose," a daily dose level that EPA generally uses as acceptable. Most risk assessments use values for toxicity that are point estimates, though the range of possible values is widely accepted to be large. Analysts also sometimes use point estimates to indentify bounds or ranges to better capture the variability implicit in the estimates.

## Exposure Assessment

Analysts must estimate what amount (dose) actually results from exposure to toxic chemicals. In most risk assessments, it is in the assessing of exposure that the analyst introduces more variables, calculations, and judgments (Figure 1 on page 450). The more direct the measurement of exposure, the less error is likely to be introduced in the calculations. The best case is when the dose and background levels can be directly measured. It is more usual, however, to only have monitoring data available on the ambient concentration levels in air, water, or soil, requiring analysts to estimate the dose and background levels. When estimating situations that do not yet exist (evaluating potential changes in regulations or the introduction of new chemcials in a production process, for example), analysts usually estimate many more steps, perhaps starting as far back in the chain as the amount of chemicals released or the amount generated. The less direct the derivation of dose estimates, the more assumptions are necessary to derive an estimate, increasing the potential for error.

### Risk Characterization

The final step in a risk assessment is to put the pieces together and characterize the risks posed. This step involves multiplying the toxicity values times the derived dose values, and making appropriate conversions to put the result in the appropriate measure of risk.

# Point Estimates Versus Probability Distributions

Analysts commonly use point estimates in assessing health and environmental hazards and in estimating exposures. For example, toxicity data are most often available and used as point estimates. Point estimates also are easy to use in calculations and to explain to readers. Sometimes analysts use point estimates to represent the typical case — a mean or median of the possible values, for example. Sometimes they use them to represent a "conservative" number that is unlikely to be exceeded. Sometimes they use point estimates in pairs to bound a range of possible or likely values.

Almost every variable really is **variable**. Analysts use point estimates to represent the range of values (or the end points of a range) that a variable can take. This approach unfortunately loses much important data. Unless the variable is an exact quantity (for example, a conversion factor), these variables are better represented by a description of the variable's probability distribution. Any phenomenon that is measured or estimated has a probability of being several other, perhaps extremely close, values. Estimates of releases of chemicals, their fate and transport through the environment, and their uptake into biological systems are not fixed or precisely known.

Risk assessments require the multiplication of hazard estimates and exposure estimates. In almost all cases, probability distributions and their summary measures (such as means and percentiles) cannot be multiplied as are point estimates. The most common technique for performing these calculations is Monte Carlo simulation. Monte Carlo simulation selects a value from each variable's distribution according to the probability of that value, multiplies (as appropriate) the values selected for each variable, and reports a single, point estimate result. The process is then repeated (usually a minimum of 100 times to as high as a few thousand times). The result of these numerous calculations is that the analyst generates a new probability distribution. Summary statistics are computed from the generated data rather than derived mathematically from the original distributions.

Another complicating factor is that many environmental processes are nonlinear, dynamic, chaotic. Researchers have traditionally thought that most distributions of variables are small perturbations about a single "true" or real value. Researchers believed that the variation they witness in actual measurements is the result of independent, random influences that eventually cancel each other out or become dissipated as the variable settles down to its "true" value. In such a world, the use of a single point estimate for a mean, for example, makes sense in that it probably represents the "true" underlying value.

A new science of chaos shows that the linear systems upon which most scientists have built their theories and that model builders have used as a basis in their deterministic models are probably the exception in the natural world. In looking at weather, biological populations, dispersion through turbulence, and numerous other examples, it is now apparent that many systems react severely to small changes, leading to wildly different results over a short time and that many natural systems do not oscillate around an underlying single value, but perhaps two, three, or hundreds of values. The result is that information about the distribution of variables is absolutely critical in making projections about many environmental phenomena.

The advantages of using probabilities rather than point estimates are the following:

- This approach estimates distribution and summary statistics correctly;
- Provides a distribution of the possible values and the probability of each value gives policymakers more information; and
- Allows for the visual display of distribution data in an uncomplicated and intuitive way to present information about the uncertainty of the results.

## Health Risk Assessment

Human health risk assessments usually follow the pattern in Figure 1 on the following page. The following sections discuss each step and show examples of how calculations are performed in a hypothetical situation.

## STEPS IN THE RISK ASSESSMENT PROCESS

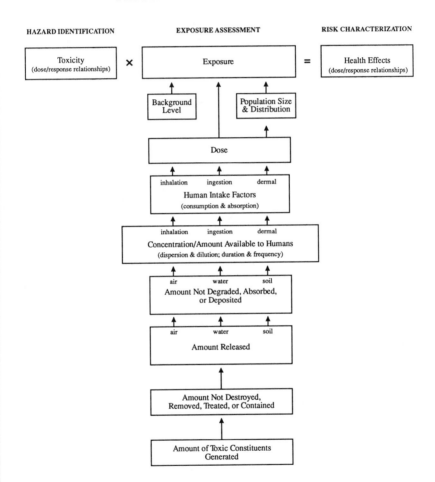

## Hazard Identification

For simplicity, this example assumes we know the toxic constituents of concern, one hypothetical compound that causes cancer and another that has toxic effects (perhaps liver malfunction) but is not a carcinogen. For each compound, there is a single route of exposure, inhalation.

### Types of Risk

Carcinogens are confounding substances. Their effects, though real, occur in such small percentages in human populations that establishing tight estimates of the response to different doses is impossible. Researchers presume most carcinogens to be human carcinogens because they produce tumors in studies on animals. Risk assessments generally assume that administering high doses to animals and translating the results to low doses in humans is appropriate. The data, however, fit equally well any of several mathematical models that extrapolate from the actual high doses administered to the low doses usually found in the environment. The scientific community commonly uses models that generate essentially linear responses to dose at low doses. This linearity conveniently allows scaling to human weights and extension of risk estimates to larger populations.

Noncarcinogenic toxic substances produce effects that differ in the organs that are affected, the type of effect produced (such as dysfunction or changes in weight), when the effects occur (acute or chronic), and the dose at which these effects occur. Several carcinogens also produce other toxic effects, requiring their effects to be considered separately.

### Risk Measures

There are many possible measures of the risks of a carcinogen (Figure 2). Figure 2 on the following page shows two alternative situations that could result from hypothetical regulatory alternatives. To display both situations, the risk for each person exposed to risk was calculated and the risk level each faced was put in rank order, left to right, in the graphs. Risk is the vertical axis (presented here as an ab-

## Figure 2
### Situation A

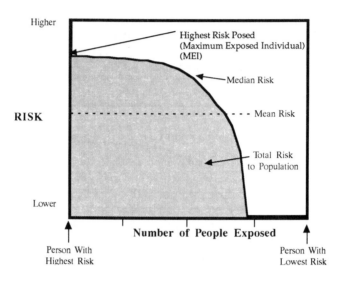

### Situation B

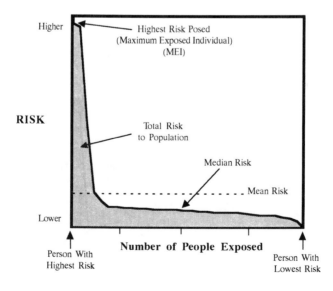

solute scale for visual reasons). The lifetime risk for each individual is the height of the curve above the horizontal axis.

One common measure is that of the risk to the most exposed individual (MEI).[5] Figure 2 shows this as the intercept with the risk axis. Another possible measure is the number of people exposed to any risk. Figure 2 shows this as the intercept with the bottom axis. On either of these two bases, Situation A is the preferable alternative (a lower MEI and fewer people exposed).

Another possible measure is the risk to the whole population, usually expressed as the expected number of cancer cases for carcinogens. Figure 2 displays this as the area under the curves (because cancer risk is assumed linear at these levels). Another common measure is a characterization of the "average" risk posed. Figure 2 shows two ways of measuring averages: the median risk (half above and half below) and the mean risk posed. Using either a concept of average risk or of total risk posed, situation B is preferable to situation A.

The choice of the risk measure, obviously, can greatly influence the outcome. Because of this, many risk assessments routinely report more than one measure, such as the MEI and the population risk.

All noncarcinogens are assumed to have some dose, the threshold level, below which there is no adverse effect.[6] Although these toxic chemicals have dose-response functions above this level, most risk assessments for easy comparability of chemicals use this threshold level, adjusted by safety levels, as the value for comparing with exposure levels. The "reference dose," a measure established by EPA, is a usual measure of the acceptable daily dose for individuals. Projected exposure levels are divided by the reference dose and the ratio is the "hazard index." Any quotients over one are generally considered to pose undue risk. The smaller the ratio under one, the larger the margin of safety is over any possible effects.

## Exposure Assessment

In most risk assessments, the exposure assessment is the bulk of the analysis. Even when good monitoring data are available, many assumptions have to be made and calculations performed to derive exposure estimates for typical cases or scenarios. If data on ambient concentrations are available, it may be important to subtract out background levels to examine the impact of particular actions. Modeling is the only approach for estimating risks in advance of particular actions. The analyst must estimate the release of hazardous chemicals and project the fate and transport of the chemicals. Many ground-water, surface-water, and air models exist that estimate the dispersion and degradation of chemicals in the environment. Analysts must estimate each medium separately (for example, air, surface water, and ground water). Some complex risk assessments require the combination of several models to track fully the dispersion of a chemical through the environment.

Analysts often must construct several scenarios of exposure. For example, one scenario might aim to represent the exposures that affect observers and bystanders, another might represent the danger from ingesting downstream surface water or contaminated fish or shellfish, others might represent consuming food from contaminated gardens or contaminated venison, and yet others may represent drinking from potentially contaminated water wells. Scenarios also may reflect expected routine exposures, extreme cases of high exposures,[7] and large-scale, accidental releases. Fault trees are sometimes constructed that attempt to identify the possible sequences of actions and the collective probability of each course through the tree. The risk assessment should cover the chemicals, sequence of possible release and fate and transport of the chemicals, and routes of exposure for each scenario.

Risk assessments of carcinogens have a computational advantage over noncarcinogens. The number of expected cases of cancer from carcinogens is presumed to be linear with dose. The same amount, whether administered in large doses to a few or distributed among many people in small doses, results in the same number of projected cancer cases. The values are scalable. For risk assessment of noncarcinogens, by contrast, the analysis often must address more precisely who gets what dose. The need to specify when threshold levels are exceeded, by how much, and by how many is crucial to whether there is great risk or no risk.

A final caution about building models and estimating parameters. The increasing knowledge base on dynamic systems provides additional theoretical reasons why simple deterministic models are inelegant tools, but it also provides evidence that deterministic models lead to misunderstandings of natural systems and incorrect results.

It requires us to examine carefully all the variables in risk assessments and ask what is really known about the underlying probability distributions. Variables that have multiple likely values or that have seemingly unpredictable wide variations must be properly interpreted for a risk assessment to be meaningful and not misleading.

## Risk Characterization

### Carcinogens

The analyst must combine the hazard identification data and the exposure assessment data to characterize the risks posed. Figure 3 shows the calculations for a very simple risk assessment for a hypothetical carcinogen. This example assumes an inhalation route of exposure, and for simplicity, assumes that all the carcinogen a person breathes results in a dose. Examples for the dermal and ingestion routes of exposure would be similar in approach.

The first calculation in Figure 3 is the general formula for computing lifetime individual risk. It shows that the hazard identification step uses a single factor, the cancer potency (expressed as the inverse of milligrams of chemical per kilogram of body weight per day). The Exposure Assessment in this example has three components: ambient concentration of the chemical in air (expressed here in milligrams of chemical per cubic meter of air); the rate people inhale air (expressed in cubic meters per day); and the weight of a person (expressed as kilograms and needed to scale the cancer potency factor to human proportions). The result is a dimensionless factor of the additional risk to an individual of being exposed to that concentration for a lifetime. A result of $1 \times 10^{-6}$ would mean that a person would have a one-in-a-million additional risk of contracting cancer because of the exposure.[8]

The next calculation is an example using a point estimate approach. For each variable, a single number is used in the calculation. In this example, these variables represent the mean values of their respective distributions. The result of these values is a point estimate of $1 \times 10^{-3}$, or a one in a thousand additional risk of contracting cancer from this exposure.

The next calculation shows how using probability distributions would work through to an estimate of individual lifetime risk.[9] In this approach, each variable has a distribution shown as a probability

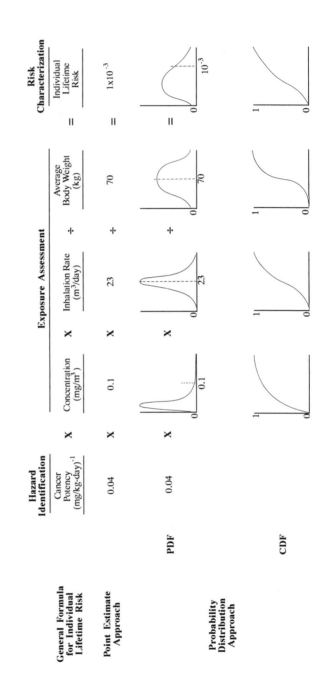

Figure 3

Sample Calculation of Individual Lifetime Risk
From Inhalation of a Hypothetical Carcinogen

density function or PDF. The analyst applies a Monte Carlo technique that allows repetitive calculations using different values from each distribution according to its probability. The repetitive calculations generate a new probability distribution from which summary statistics can be calculated. Accompanying each PDF is the cumulative density function (CDF). The CDF is helpful to identify quickly important measures (not shown here) such as the median risk (50th percentile) and other percentile risk levels (such as the 95th percentile). The amount of information available using the probability distribution approach is vastly more than that available using point estimates and gives a risk manager the ability to assess directly the uncertainties.

Other routes of exposure use different exposure assumptions. For ingestion of water and food, the analyst must assume the typical amount of water or food consumed per day. For dermal exposures, penetration rates are available for some chemicals.

A risk assessment estimates risks to the population for carcinogens by building upon the estimate of lifetime individual risk. Figure 4 shows the general formula for annual population risk. The lifetime individual risk is multiplied by the population exposed and divided by an average life expectancy to obtain the annual number of cancer cases expected. The point estimate approach generates a single value (in this example, 50 excess cases per year). The probability distribution approach, however, can show much more information. It can show, for example, the range within which the annual number of cases has a 90 percent chance of being, the most likely number of cases, and the median. This variation derives from the variation in a just few exposure parameters.

### Noncarcinogens

The analysis of noncarcinogens is similar to that of carcinogens. Figure 5 shows the general formula for calculating the risk from a noncarcinogen. The inverse of the reference dose is multiplied by the concentration and the inhalation rate and divided by the average body weight to arrive at a Hazard Index. If the Hazard Index exceeds one, there are assumed to be cases of people affected by the exposure. Results below one indicate the relative acceptability of the exposure. In our point estimate example, the Hazard Index is computed to be 0.5, or below the trigger value of one. The Probability

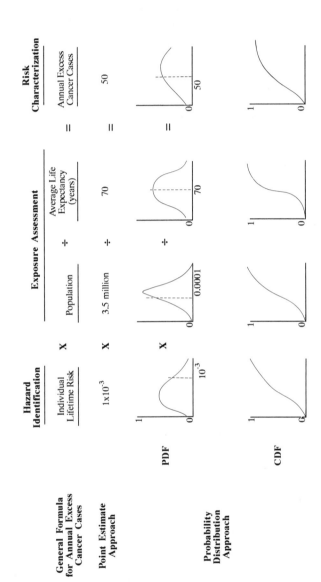

**Figure 4**

**Sample Calculation of Annual Excess Cancer Cases
From Inhalation of a Hypothetical Carcinogen**

**Figure 5**

**Sample Calculation of a Hazard Index
From Inhalation of a Hypothetical Noncarcinogen**

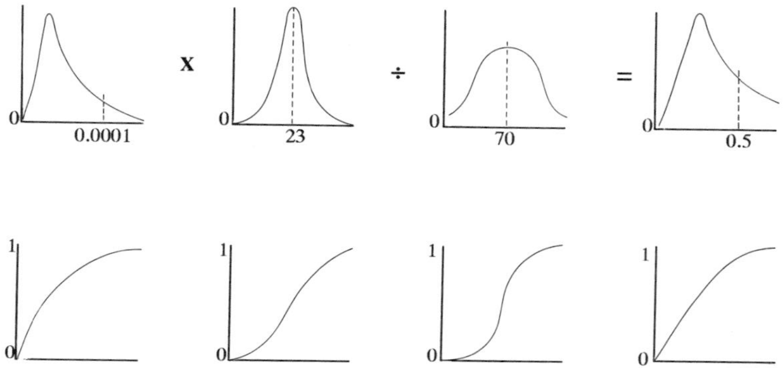

Distribution Approach, however, shows that there is a significant chance of the value being over one. Following the thread into the estimate for population risks, the point estimate approach projects that no people would be affected. The Probability Distribution Approach, however, suggests that some of the population may be affected by this exposure.

## Severity Indices

In some risk assessments, important distinctions lie in the differences between the effects of the different chemicals. In such cases the use of a measure to standardize or weigh the importance of the effects is necessary. These "severity indices" are difficult for analysts to defend because they involve pure value judgments. When these are used, analysts often use several versions of the weights so that readers have more of an opportunity to find a weighting approach that closely matches their own. The results can range, by necessity, between the lowest risk posed by a chemical to the highest risk posed by a chemical.

## Top-Down Checking

Once your preliminary assessment is completed, it is good to compare the results with other findings for reasonableness. One example is to compare the estimate of annual cases of a particular cancer against the actual number of cases reported (when you are attempting to measure the effects of real world exposures). If the projected value greatly exceeds actual cases, or accounts for a seemingly disproportionate amount of the cancers, a reexamination of the assumptions and calculation would be prudent. Whether cross-checking the reasonableness of carcinogens or noncarcinogens, analysts prefer to compare computed results to real world data.

Another use of a top-down approach is for analysts to compare results against other estimates. This use of top-down approach has severe limitations. Comparisons to other estimates are usually meaningless. One way to avoid mistaken judgments is to ask, in advance, what differences between the existing values and new values would lead you to do. For example, if the results of this risk assessment are significantly under other estimates or projections, are you led to believe that the new estimates are low or that the existing estimates are high? If your risk assessment generates results above current pro-jections, do you assume your estimates are faulty, or that the situation is more dangerous than you thought? If the only estimates that will be accepted are those that are near other existing projections, no new risk assessment is needed: defer instead to the existing data.

Repeated refinement of assumptions to "calibrate" models to more closely match other assessments brings into question why a new assessment is needed.

## Environmental Risk Assessment

This discussion of environmental risk will be even more general than that for human health risk. The approaches are, however, similar. In the Hazard Identification, there are several new ways of looking at risks. First, representative species are used for most calculations. Although there are many studies of toxicity to animals, it is unusual to find good studies that have been performed on the important species in a given study area. For example, birds are often used as surrogates for amphibians and reptiles. Also, generally only a few species are used to represent the vast number of plants and animals present in most areas. Very little quantitative data exists on effects on plant life, resulting in most of these presentations being narrative. There is some standardization in identifying threatened and endangered species, although the presence of adverse effects usually precludes the alternatives being considered, and precise quantification is usually unnecessary.

Work on other types of risk is accelerating. Unfortunately, little scientific work on the environment can now be used for risk assessment. Well-tested, easily administered, and commonly accepted measures of ecological damage do not exist. There is great attention now being given to acid rain and climate change, but there is little of practical use for those who wish to identify cumulative and potentially global problems in advance.

## Future Trends

Where is risk assessment policy headed? There are now many commonly used assumptions about how to use data in risk assessments. This is in spite of the great scientific debates being waged on almost every assumption or significant study conclusion. Researchers are slowly settling these differences. Below are my predictions for the near-term future of risk assessment.

- The process of performing risk assessments will grow more complicated. Many advances will require specialized treatment to handle different situations. For example, as alternative biological mechanisms are accepted for some carcinogens, researchers probably will revise the no threshold assumption. Another example is that chemicals that are found to be synergistic will require special treatment in analyses.
- Many changes will lower the estimates of risks that are estimated. Many of the assumptions commonly used were selected because they are prudent and protective in the face of great uncertainty. As better data are available, some of these assumptions will be relaxed.
- Researchers will place even greater reliance on published guidelines to establish acceptable procedures.
- Fate and transport modeling will become more complicated by the better understanding of dynamic, chaotic systems. The increase in uncertainty these changes produce may lead to more simplified forms of risk assessments that need less precision and rely more heavily on personal values.

## About The Author

**Curtis Haymore** has analyzed environmental and human health risks, economic impacts and policy issue for 16 years. He worked on hazardous waste regulations at the U.S. EPA, and has consulted with EPA, Department of Energy, and several other general agencies before forming Environomics, Inc. Mr. Haymore also teaches graduate courses in environmental policy and environmental impact assessment at the University of Virginia. He holds degrees in Economics from the University of California and in Environmental Planning from the University of Virginia. He serves as the 1991 President of the National Capital Area Chapter of the Society for Risk Analysis.

## Endnotes

1. This chapter uses the term *chemicals* very generally to refer to all toxic chemicals, compounds, and wastes.

2. In this chapter, I use the term *environmental risks* to mean those risks that are not direct risks to human health, for example, risks to wildlife and the ecology.

3. The sequence, number, and names of the steps in risk assessment often differ, but most follow the steps presented here. In any event, the concepts and labels are easily translated into this construct.

4. If other chemicals, for which no toxicity or exposure data are available, are of special concern, a narrative discussion is possible. Such a discussion can only be speculative, however, and cannot be the basis for a risk calculation.

5. Many argue for the exclusive use of the MEI as a risk measure. Several laws incorporate the concern expressed by many rural lawmakers and environmental groups that the use of any other measure tends to devalue people in less densely populated areas. However, decisions to lessen risk by avoiding highly populated areas are routinely made, for example in routing hazardous materials and low-level military training flights.

6. There are many methods used to establish this level, but most conceptually simple and the basis for the rest of the discussion is the "no observed effects level" or NOEL. This is the highest dose at which no effects have been documented.

7. "Worst case scenarios" developed a bad reputation as being wildly unrealistic and usually impossible because of compounding very unlikely events. The National Environmental Policy Act regulations, for example, specifically do not require worst case analysis. It is common, and in some cases required, that risk assessments do examine unlikely, but realistic possible events.

8. For some carcinogens (for example, components of tobacco smoke), the risk is often expressed as cancer deaths, not just cases. Analysts usually do not take into account improved survival rates for some cancers.

9. An excellent discussion of using probability density functions and cumulative density functions to present more information in risk assessments is in Adam M. Finkel's *Confronting Uncertainty in Risk Management: A Guide for Decision-Makers*, a report for the Center for Risk Management, Resources for the Future, January 1990, Washington, D.C.

# XVII Environmental Due Diligence Process in Business and Real Estate Transactions

*Michael L. Italiano, Esq.*
*Gardner, Carton & Douglas*
*Washington, D.C.*
*and Richard D. Jones*
*Pepe & Hazard*
*Hartford, Connecticut*
*and William P. Gulledge*
*Front Royal Group*
*McLean, Virginia*

This chapter provides an overview of good commercial practices for environmental assessment of commercial real estate transactions and of national activities in this regard for development of corporate due diligence standards. These standards have been developed to avoid Superfund liability and improve the quality of environmental assessments.

In order to develop good commercial practices pursuant to the Superfund Innocent Landowner Defense,[1] the American Society for Testing and Materials (ASTM) Subcommittee on Environmental Assessments in Commercial Real Estate Transactions was established. Standard commercial practices are needed because of the confusion created in the commercial real estate industry, as well as in the consulting community, by vague statutory requirements for the Defense and the lack of guidance from court decisions regarding liability of financial institutions for Superfund cleanup costs.

As EPA continues to step up its enforcement of Superfund cleanup actions, the confusion will increase if there is no consensus on environmental due diligence standards. EPA has developed a draft interpretative rule for secured creditors and parties seeking the Innocent Landowner Defense that will require lenders and financial institutions to exercise environmental due care when involved in acquisition, loan origination, workout, and foreclosure situations where real estate is involved. The level of such due care is expected to be defined by the ASTM Standards. ASTM has been setting standards for business and government since the turn of the century for such diverse subjects as steel, cement, robotics, security systems, textiles, resource recovery, hazardous waste treatment, sports equipment, and medical devices.

The views in this chapter about the ultimate nature of the ASTM standard, which has yet to be finalized by the subcommittee, reflect the views of the authors and not necessarily the conclusions of the subcommittee. As an overview of environmental due diligence in commercial business transactions, the rest of this chapter covers the following:

- Background on due diligence;
- Superfund liability;
- ASTM Standard Development;
- Scope and Principles of Good Commercial Practices;
- Fundamental Level of Environmental Assessment;
- Phase I Trigger;
- Phase I Assessment;
- Phase II Trigger;
- Phase II Sampling and Analysis;
- Phase III Trigger, Cleanup and Corrective Action; and
- EPA Interpretative Rule for Secured Creditors and Innocent Landowners.

## Background on Due Diligence

As environmental law and regulation at the national, state and local level have mushroomed, the frontier of environmental liability has expanded, creating a compelling need for business to develop effective risk management strategies for commercial real estate transactions.

Perhaps the greatest impetus to the development of industry based practices and procedures to manage environmental risk has been the need to avoid Superfund liability. But Superfund liability is not by any means the only reason why all prudently conducted commercial transactions should include comprehensive environmental due diligence. Whether a party to a commercial transaction is exposed to personal liability or not, if property in which it has an investment is environmentally contaminated, market value will be impaired if not destroyed. This is true for lenders, developers, tenants and owner-occupiers alike. Nonetheless, it is Superfund liability and the attendant Innocent Landowner Defense which is galvanizing the industry to develop an environmental due diligence standard.

In light of the government's abandonment of any effort to define good commercial practices under Superfund, one must almost conclude that the government has invited industry to fill this definitional vacuum by itself articulating what are "good commercial or customary practices in the industry." Industry has finally responded to this implied invitation with the organization of The American Society for Testing and Materials (ASTM) Subcommittee on Environmental Assessments in Commercial Real Estate Transactions. Since the inception of the subcommittee on March 20, 1990, it has met numerous times and has benefitted by the contribution of over 400 individuals and institutions from the real estate and environmental consulting community, devoting thousands of hours to the effort to develop a standard for environmental due diligence. While the driving force behind the organization of this subcommittee was without doubt the compelling need for certainty in the Innocent Landowner Defense, the Subcommittee has a broader charge:

*To ensure informed and prudent decisionmaking in environmental risk management by developing a due diligence tool designed to identify, quantify and address environmental contamination.*

The ASTM Subcommittee is developing a standard that will recognize that environmental due diligence is a continuum stretching from a very low level of due diligence to a very high level of inquiry. Along the continuum, increasing effort should result in additional information. This process is also governed by the law of diminishing returns; the standard recognizes that at some point the additional expenditure of effort to obtain additional information is not worth the resulting incremental increase in knowledge. The standard also recognizes that there is no such thing as perfect due diligence and that no practical or reasonable protocol can or should be expected to discover all potential contamination. There is always uncertainty in environmental assessment. The objective of the Subcommittee and the objective of the resulting standard is to reduce uncertainty. The Subcommittee has never been and cannot be focused on the elimination of uncertainty.

The standard will be developed using a decision tree model. This means that as the user moves up the due diligence continuum through Phases I, II, and III, from limited to more extensive inquiry, the standard will, at each interstice, indicate that (1) no further inquiry is necessary and hence the underlying real estate transaction can be completed or (2) that prudence requires further inquiry. This approach recognizes that due diligence is a combined technical, legal, and business decision, the extent of each being dependent upon the nature of the property and transaction.

What makes the process of developing a workable standard difficult is the legal context of environmental due diligence. CERCLA's Innocent Landowner Defense is predicated upon the conduct of a certain level of inquiry. Other legally significant due diligence standards exist under state law.[2]

The standard contains an important feature stipulating that compliance by a user with the standard will constitute "best industry practices" and consequently, establish the Innocent Landowner Defense under CERCLA. In other words, if a user appropriately employs the standard and pursues additional inquiry until such time as its qualified consultant concludes that no further inquiry is needed, the user will have met the burden of the Innocent Landowner Defense.

# Superfund Liability

Under Superfund, liability of land owners is strict, joint and several, retroactive, perpetual and, for practical purposes, unlimited.[3] This requires some definition. *Strict liability* is essentially liability without fault or the need to prove negligence. *Joint and several* means a landowner could own, for example, one-fiftieth of a Superfund site or have contributed one drum to the site, but would still be liable for cleanup of the entire site unless its liability can be apportioned, which is difficult to do. In other words, any party is liable for the entire cleanup cost. *Retroactive liability* means the owner could have had hazardous substances deposited on the property with full government sanction before the enactment of Superfund, but still be liable. Two of the few exceptions to this liability are the secured creditor exemption, and SARA's Innocent Landowner Defense that requires "all appropriate inquiry into the previous ownership and uses of the property consistent with good commercial or customary practice."[4] That definition left *appropriate* and *good commercial practice* to be defined by the courts.

The secured creditor exemption provides a defense to liability where the party, without participating in the management of a facility, holds indicia of ownership primarily to protect its security interest in the facility.[5] While lenders have a certain level of insulation under the secured creditor exemption,[6] the defense is of limited utility because in order to realize its collateral the secured lender must be able to foreclose and dispose of real property security. To the extent a lender's collateral is burdened by environmental risk from contamination, it will be unable to convey such collateral to third parties who cannot succeed to the protection of the secured creditor exemption. In this sense, its secured creditor rights are illusory; see the discussion of the initial draft of the EPA Interpretive Rule below and in Chapter IX by Rothenberg.

## ASTM Standard Development

The lack of a definition of good commercial practice serves to underline the need for a standard. The standards under development are intended to apply to all nonresidential property and exclude the rental or purchase of a single-family home, apartment, condominium or cooperative.

A draft standard has been prepared by the ASTM subcommittee setting forth procedures for environmental assessment of commercial transactions. The standard recognizes that assessments can reveal some hazardous substances, but they can be at levels or remediated to levels that do not appear to present potential harm to public health and environment. The fact that contamination was not discovered does not demonstrate that the inquiry was not appropriate. As we have said before, there is always uncertainty in environmental assessments; the objective is to reduce uncertainty as much as possible.

The standard will not radically change the substance or nature of the inquiry customarily know as a Phase I, Phase II or Phase III assessment. There are, in large measure, established catechisms for these levels of environmental inquiry and the job of the Sub-committee is not to radically reform or reinvent the nature of due diligence but to categorize and rationalize "best existing commercial practice." Hence, much of the substance of or the body of the standard will be familiar to most sophisticated real estate participants.[7]

The fundamental level of due diligence is the pre-Phase I or screening minimum environmental assessment. It can be relied on without requiring a Phase I, only if it results in a conclusion that there is a low probability of contamination, e.g., a lack of prior or existing industrial or manufacturing activities.

Most transactions will continue to need a Phase I environmental assessment. The purpose of a Phase I is to identify existing information about the subject site and adjoining property through a records search, site inspection, and report. The goal in Phase I is to identify the likely presence of those substances which are or may be hazardous substances.

The Phase I due diligence environmental assessment can also encompass elements of an environmental audit. A Phase I environmental due diligence audit focuses on the environmental management practices employed at the site, including a visual inspection of the facility, a review of the plant's environmental management, an historical records search and regulatory documentation (permit and compliance data, general and multimedia inspection reports, etc.) and an evaluation of the process unit operations and waste management practices. A partial list of specific data that is evaluated includes raw materials and hazardous substances, constituents/waste handling and characterization, environmental setting (site characterization), potential receptor populations, and environmental policies and guidelines.

The Phase II assessment determines the presence and concentration of hazardous substances based principally on sampling and analysis. The purpose of a Phase II assessment is to develop quantitative information about the site which was not readily available in Phase I. Phase II determines if there is the presence of hazardous substances and hazardous materials at levels not protecting public health and environment.

Phase III is the cleanup/corrective action phase necessitated when Phase I and/or Phase II identify the presence of hazardous substances that must be remediated in order to protect public health and environment. The purpose of a Phase III assessment is to identify, plan and implement the means of correcting or remediating identified hazards. When a property is subject to a Phase III, defenses to Superfund liability are preserved if the hazard is removed or remediated before or during acquisition.

## Scope and Principles of Good Commercial Practices

The ASTM standard applies to commercial real estate transactions. It defines practices necessary to qualify for the Innocent Landowner Defense to federal Superfund liability, i.e., what constitutes all appropriate inquiry into the previous ownership and uses of the property consistent with good commercial or customary care. The standard also outlines business practices for the environmental assessment of properties that are the subject of commercial real estate transactions.

The objectives guiding the development of these standards are:
- To ensure the efficiency and integrity of commercial real estate transactions;
- To facilitate compliance with applicable governmental requirements or environmental protection;
- To improve the quality of environmental assessments;
- To clarify the legal responsibilities associated with commercial real estate transactions, and
- To ensure that the standard of inquiry is practical and reasonable.

At any level of due diligence, eventually a choice must be made among:
- Closing the transaction if the property is reasonably clean;
- Conducting further assessment to clarify decisions to be made;
- Remediating contamination before completing the transaction; and
- Declining to go forward with the transaction.

## Environmental Due Diligence Process in Business and Real Estate Transactions

An environmental assessment is a means by which the parties to a commercial real estate transaction attempt to identify releases or threats of releases of hazardous substances and to assess the risks associated with identified hazardous substances. The assessment of properties that are the subject of commercial real estate transactions are broader than the practices necessary to qualify for the Innocent Landowner Defense to federal Superfund liability because the parties to a transaction may well want to be aware of environmental risks that would not necessarily subject them to Superfund liability. Such risks include hazards not or not uniformly subject to Superfund regulation:

- Radon;
- Asbestos in buildings;
- Wetlands;
- Certain Department of Transportation (DOT) designated hazardous materials;
- Earthquakes;
- Lead paint; and
- Lead in drinking water.

Whether the ASTM standard will address some or all of these non-CERCLA issues is as yet not resolved.

Appropriate inquiry can be accomplished within a reasonable time and at reasonable cost consistent with the goals of Superfund, the goal of establishing the appropriate scope of environmental assessments, and the goal of preserving the innocent landowner and secured creditor defenses to Superfund liability. Not every property will warrant the same level of assessment. The appropriate level of environmental assessment will be guided by issues such as the type of property, whether there are any facts actually known or discovered in previous steps that indicate potential threats to human health and the environment, and the location of the property.

## Fundamental Level of Environmental Assessment

For purposes of discussion, this level is referred to as a Pre-Phase I or transaction screening assessment. It applies when the party seeking the assessment has no knowledge of matters that would make a reasonable person believe that there are hazardous substances on the property at levels which would not protect public health or the environment or which require further investigation to determine whether the conditions would threaten public health or the environment. Knowledge of such conditions or "triggers" requires a Phase I assessment.

Present or previous use of the subject property or any adjoining property that involves the generation of hazardous substances, which includes almost all commercial and industrial land uses, would also indicate to the buyer and other interested parties that a pre-Phase I is not likely to be sufficient "appropriate inquiry." A Phase I is also required when there are any pending judicial proceedings or final administrative or judicial decisions citing violations of federal, state or local laws regarding hazardous substances on the subject property, unless there is administrative or judicial determination that violations regarding hazardous substances have been remedied.

Furthermore, a Phase I assessment is required where present or previous use of the subject property or adjoining properties required a permit which indicates the presence of hazardous substances. Such a permit might be issued under the Resource Conservation and Recovery Act, Clean Water Act, Clean Air Act or other federal, state or local law requiring a permit or other entitlement for use from a public agency regarding use, handling, treatment, storage, disposal, recycling/reuse, discharge, manufacture, processing or distribution of hazardous substances on the subject property. A Phase I may not be required, absent other triggers, if investigation shows that no activities on the property presently require such permits and that the permitting agency has not provided written notice of or found violations of permits presently required.

A Phase I is required where the property or any adjoining properties are listed on the National Priorities List, the CERCLIS list, the RCRA Notifiers list or the list of contaminated sites identified pursuant to the state superfund laws. Communications or notices from the owner or any tenant or other user of the property or adjoining property regarding any hazardous substances on the property would be an indication that the assessment is likely to go beyond pre-Phase I into at least Phase I.

The discussion above indicates the importance of determining past as well as present uses of the property and adjoining properties during the fundamental assessment. One especially good source is Sanborn maps, which show the subject property in historical perspective and should be obtained for as far back as they are available. Where Sanborn maps are not available, zoning maps and/or land use maps and aerial photographs should be obtained for as far back as they are available. Geographical Information Systems (GIS) can also be used to aggregate and evaluate site data geographically through computerized overlays.

Another requirement of the screening assessment is the site reconnaissance. This is an important feature of the screening process and one which clearly distinguishes it from a Phase I. The purpose of the walk-through is fundamentally the same as in a Phase I: to note any conditions which would cause a reasonable person (a non-professional in environmental matters) to believe that hazardous substances are or are likely to be present on the property that would threaten public health or the environment. If any of these conditions is observed, a Phase I assessment should be performed using a qualified professional environmental consultant.

## Phase I Trigger

Examples of conditions which would require a Phase I assessment are existing or potential levels of hazardous substances in locations which may not be protective of public health and environment. These would include:

- Historical information about prior use suggesting contamination;
- Vegetation or wildlife that is visibly distressed;
- Pits, ponds or lagoons;
- Metallic or plastic 55-gallon drums;
- Storage tanks;
- Tranformers or capacitors with possible PCB's;
- Asbestos in friable or potentially friable condition;
- Landfills;
- Evidence of waste disposal or listed waste sites;
- Characteristics suggesting lead based paint or lead in drinking water; and
- Communications, postings, or notices regarding hazardous substances on the property.

Components of the Phase I assessment include the following:
- Site classification based on use;
- Multi-family use determination;
- Records search;
- Site reconnaissance; and
- Report preparation.

Site classification consists of categorizing the assessed property as vacant or unimproved land, improved land with or without hazardous substances, or as a special case. This classification is based on the Pre-Phase I walkthrough.

Next a record search should look at historical land use records and then at environmental agency documents and records at the federal, state and local levels. Standardized pre-visit questionnaires can be developed to assist in identifying these records.

Based on physical and historical observations, the purpose of site reconnaissance or a site visit is to render an opinion on the possible presence of hazardous substances generally without any sampling or testing. All observations and findings should be documented.

The assessor should review the site within the determined boundaries and indicate any visual signs of potential releases of hazardous substances, indicating the methods used and limitations thereof. The general site environmental setting should identify:
- Descriptions of abutters and operations of concern;
- Nearby potable water supplies within half a mile and other sensitive receptors;
- Potential sources of contamination within a quarter-mile for urban areas and a half-mile for non-urban areas unless circumstances dictate otherwise;
- Geologic, hydrogeologic, hydrologic, meteorologic, and topographic setting;
- Site utilities and power lines; and
- Surface water drainage patterns.

If structures are present, the assessor should make interior and exterior observations concerning the use/reuse, generation, storage, or disposal of hazardous substances.

Interior observation should identify the following:
- Processes carried on at facility;
- Operations which use hazardous substances;
- Product, byproduct and waste storage areas and handling and disposal procedures;
- Approximate quantities of hazardous substances used and waste generated;
- Floor drains and other potential discharge points;
- Storage tanks;
- Source of heat and water supply; and
- Transformers.

Exterior observations should identify the following:
- Product and waste storage areas;
- Evidence of underground or aboveground storage tanks (fills, vents, patches in pavement);
- Dry wells, catch basins, retention ponds, etc.;
- Onsite surface water (creeks/rivers);
- Areas of surface staining, leachate breakouts, or distressed vegetation;
- Septic and sewer systems;
- Transformers;
- Utility trenches;
- Evidence of previous buildings;
- Extensive filling or grading (including fill from offsite);
- Evidence of stacks and sources of air emissions; and
- General waste management practices.

Based on the information obtained and the onsite observations, the assessor shall make inquiries/interviews of site personnel. The assessor should interview long-time, knowledgeable personnel, top management, the plant manager, maintenance and environmental personnel, purchasing agents, owner/operator, and possibly community representatives, concerning past and present activity that would generate hazardous substances. The assessor should also review the following:
- Both physical and historical evidence that would suggest a potential release of hazardous substances by various routes to the environment;

- The property owner/operator records for the property and structures, including building plans and construction details; and
- Records and permits that relate to the hazardous substances used, generated, stored, or disposed of that could present a potential release to the environment.

The Phase I Environmental Site Assessment Report should include an introduction consisting of the purpose of the document and the scope of services; it should provide conclusions and recommendations that relate to the extent of the perceived environmental hazards associated with the subject property.

Special considerations apply to the use of multifamily properties which must be considered as an integral part of the environmental assessment. Hazards associated with multi-family properties are different than those pertaining to industrial properties and therefore, a different scope of inquiry in a Phase I environmental assessment may be warranted in most cases. Circumstances associated with the use of multifamily property which may warrant heightened focus in a Phase I environmental assessment include the following features:

- Some populations spend considerable time in multi-family properties, i.e., they eat, sleep and live there;
- These are sensitive populations, such as children, senior citizens, the disabled, the infirm and pregnant women;
- Special conditions and or materials may present particular hazards on multifamily properties such as lead paint, lead in drinking water, radon, PCBs, ureaformaldehyde, asbestos and maintenance chemicals.

## Phase II Trigger

A Phase II assessment is required where the Phase I assessment shows the presence or potential presence of hazardous substances above background levels and at locations not protective of public health and environment. The Subcommittee intends to complete work on the assessment process through the Phase II triggers before beginning work on the contents of a Phase II type assessment.

## Environmental Due Diligence Process in Business and Real Estate Transactions

The purpose of Phase II is to quantify the location and concentrations of hazardous substances by using proven sampling and analysis methods with specified measures for quality control and quality assurance. Since parts per billion levels of some substances can present potential environmental problems, very small technical errors can cause substantive and costly problems. For this reason, existing consensus or government standards that have been peer reviewed should be used in all sampling and analysis.

## Phase II Sampling and Analysis

A number of existing standards for Phase II activities have been developed by ASTM, various associations and committees. ASTM Committee D-18 has soil and groundwater sampling and analysis standards including 35 under development with EPA support. EPA's RCRA Technical Enforcement Guidelines contain several methods of performing Phase II sampling and analysis. As another example, EPA has also issued test methods for evaluating solid waste.

ASTM standards used in soil and groundwater sampling and analysis include the following:

C 150       Specification for Portland Cement;

D 421       Practice for Dry Preparation of Soil Samples for Particle-Size Analysis and Determination of Soil Constants;

D 653       Terms and Symbols Relating to Soils and Rock;

D 1452       Practice for Soil Investigation and Sampling by Auger Borings;

D 1586       Method for Penetration Test and Split-Barrel Sampling of Soils;

D 1587       Method for Thin-Walled Tube Sampling of Soils;

D 1785       Specification of Poly (Vinyl Chloride) (PVC) Plastic Pipe, Schedules 40, 80, and 120;

| | |
|---|---|
| D 2113 | Method for Diamond Core Drilling for Site Investigation; |
| D 2434 | Test Method for Permeability of Granular Soils (Constant Head); |
| D 2488 | Practice for Description and Identification of Soils (Visual-Manual Procedure); |
| D 4220 | Practice for Preserving and Transporting Soil Samples; |
| D 4448 | Guide for Sampling Groundwater Monitoring Wells; |
| D 4750 | Test Method for Determining Subsurface Liquid Levels in a Borehole or Monitoring Well (Observation Well); and |
| F 480 | Specification for Thermoplastic Water Well Casing Pipe and Couplings Made in Standard Dimension Ratio (SDR). |

Conducting a Phase II assessment does not necessarily mean that the transaction is denied the benefit of the Innocent Landowner Defense: it will be common for the assessment to identify some hazardous substances which are at levels or remediated to levels not presenting a threat to public health and environment before the transaction is completed, thus preserving the Defense.

## Phase III Trigger, Cleanup and Corrective Action

A Phase III assessment or cleanup is required where Phase II data indicate the presence of hazardous substances constituting a threat or potential threat to public health and environment. The purpose of a Phase III assessment is to identify and plan the means of remediating identified hazards constituting a threat to public health and environment, and effecting such remedial or corrective action.

When a property is subject to Phase III, defenses to Superfund liability can be preserved if the hazard is removed or remediated before or during the acquisition, consistent with the National Contingency

Plan's (NCP's) goal of protecting public health and the environment. Such a defense is contemplated by EPA's guidance on landowner liability due to potential environmental benefits where "the prospective purchaser participated in a cleanup" with "appropriate environmental safeguards."[8]

Hazardous substance cleanup also falls within the realm of exercising due care required in CERCLA § 107(b)(3), the third party defense. As noted in the Superfund legislative history:

> The Conferees recognize that the due care requirement embodied in Section 107(b)(3) only requires such person to exercise that degree of due care which is reasonable under the circumstances. The requirement would include those steps necessary to protect the public from a health or environmental threat.[9]

Due care is clearly exhibited by remedial action protective of public health and the environment. This is consistent with the stated purpose of Superfund "to ensure cleanup of abandoned chemicals and protect human health and the environment."[10] By definition, the statute and NCP remove liability after completion of appropriate cleanup protective of public health and environment. The CERCLA liability provisions encourage private parties to conduct cleanup because "the resources of the Fund alone are simply insufficient to provide an adequate remedy to the national problem of hazardous waste disposal."[11]

The statute removes liability for parties specified in CERCLA §107 if releases have been cleaned up or remediated consistent with the standards of CERCLA §121 so there is no "imminent and substantial endangerment to the public health or welfare or environment" pursuant to CERCLA §106 abatement actions, or no "imminent and substantial danger to the public health or welfare" pursuant to CERCLA §104 response authorities.

This defense to liability for cleanup protective of public health and environment is consistent with the other defenses available to the parties potentially liable as identified above in § 107(a). Its importance is underscored by the large number of parties that are and have been conducting cleanup attendant to commercial transactions. Many transactions in urbanized areas are contingent on such cleanup activities. This is a practice that good public policy should encourage. In fact, CERCLA, EPA and the courts recite the importance and need for private cleanup. Consequently, a clear defense to liability is a necessary result of these cleanup activities taken by parties to commercial transactions in order to reduce uncertainty regarding potential liability. The process of conducting cleanup protective of public health and environment is usually determined by the following:

- Assessing location, extent and type of hazardous substances present and their inherent hazard, fate and effect;
- Assessing potential pathways and human or environmental receptors and their proximity;
- Identifying the risk to public health and environment presented by the substances at their present location;
- Evaluating remedial alternatives; and
- Conducting remedial or removal action.[12]

The standard developed by ASTM should provide a solid working base-line not only for assessing properties in general but also for assessing those properties that will require a certain level of remediation. It is the certainty provided by an industry-wide, agreed upon standard which will allow remediation activities to go forward with the certainty that when completed the property will meet the industry standards for due diligence in general and the Innocent Landowner Defense in particular.

The Subcommittee intends to develop the standard as to the screening assessment and Phase I assessment up to the Phase II triggers completely before turning to the work of defining Phase II and Phase III procedures and protocols. However, the structure of these portions of the standard should follow logically from the work currently being undertaken on the screening and Phase I issues and should build rationally upon that base.

## Future Trends and Emerging Issues

In August of 1990, the EPA announced that it intended to resolve some of the uncertainty caused by the *Fleet Factors* case by providing guidance as to what a secured lender can and cannot do in connection with the lending relationship while remaining within the protective safe harbor of the secured creditors exception to liability under CERCLA. Ever since the inception of CERCLA, the boundaries of the secured lenders exception to liability have been at best unclear and the recent case law has suggested, not only to all sensible commentators but to Congress and the EPA as well, that some additional guidance was necessary. An interpretive rule was transmitted by EPA to the Office of Management and Budget for review in September of 1990 and as of the date these materials were written, has not yet been released by OMB for publication in the *Federal Register*. Nevertheless, copies of the text of the proposed Interpretive Rule have been in circulation since September and have been widely discussed.

This Interpretive Rule imposes an affirmative duty on secured creditors to conduct due diligence during loan origination, and/or before acquisition of realty by purchase (before workout), and in foreclosure where the lender will be acting to protect its security interest.[13] Mitigative or preventative measures that are environmentally responsible are protected by the rule.[14] This new due diligence standard set up as the price of admission to the proposed anti-*Fleet* safe harbor is promulgated with even less guidance as to what level of due diligence is contemplated than that which exists in CERCLA itself. Is it more extensive in the due diligence required to meet the requirements of the innocent landowner's defense; is it the same; or is it less? While it appears there is little or no statutory support for many of the provisions of this new interpretive rule, the real estate finance industry must be prepared to deal with it. The significance of the rule is now greater in that Superfund has been recently reauthorized without the LaFalce and Garn amendments which would have expanded and clarified the lender liability provisions of the statute.

There is little analytical support for a new, separate and distinct standard of environmental due diligence for this Interpretive Rule and for this reason it would seem that the due diligence necessary for the Innocent Landowner Defense and that needed under this new secured lender safe harbor should be the same. In this event, the ASTM standard can serve as protection both for the general user and for the secured lender.

Superfund liability and the inconsistent quality and application of many environmental assessments have driven the real estate industry and the real estate finance industry to develop standardized practices for environmental assessments of commercial transactions. The standard will codify the best current commercial practices. As such, it should be ultimately accepted by the government as the touchstone for the Innocent Landowner Defense. To the extent the new secured lender safe harbor rules gain currency, it should similarly provide some certainty in accessing the defense. The ASTM process was born from a driving need to obtain certainty, not just as to Superfund liability but also with respect to environmental risk more generally. The industry will now develop a standard. It will be workable and efficient and affordable. While it will always be impossible to eliminate all environmental risk, the development and broad use of the ASTM standard will enormously reduce the uncertainty of environmental risk management today and thereby assist in the efficient operation of real estate markets everywhere.

## About the Authors

**Michael L. Italiano** has been responsible for litigation, scientific and technical analysis, cleanup and negotiation for over 100 waste sites with federal and state agencies and industry. He has represented major national industry associations before Congress on environmental legislation. Mr. Italiano has over a decade of government and industry service, and has written the book *Liability for Underground Storage Tanks*. His most recent public service was as Senior Analyst in the White House where he developed hazardous waste and environmental policy. He is Chairman of the Committee on Environmental Assessment, which is developing consensus storage tank and environmental property transfer standards for the American Society for Testing and Materials, and is a member of the Environmental Liability Insurance Advisory Committee of the National Association of Insurance Commissioners. He is a member of the Bar in Pennsylvania and the District of Columbia.

**Richard D. Jones** is chairman of Pepe & Hazard's real estate and commercial finance group. He is a well-published author whose practice includes structuring, documenting and closing commercial real property transactions for lenders and borrowers, and structuring and documenting joint venture and partnership arrangements. He has lectured nationwide on real estate, environmental and construc-

## Environmental Due Diligence Process in Business and Real Estate Transactions

tion lending. He is a graduate of Washington and Lee University, B.A. in Economics, and received his J.D. from University of Virginia and an L.L.M. in Taxation from Boston University. He is a member of the Mortgage Bankers Association of America and currently serves as their Vice Chairman of the Income Property Committee's Environmental Issues subcommittee. He is Vice Chairman of the ASTM Committee on Environmental Assessment.

**William P. Gulledge** is Vice President, Front Royal Group, Inc., Environmental Insurance Management, Inc. in McLean, Virginia. He has 15 years of experience in environmental management projects, has worked as a senior environmental engineer and program manager for energy development and hazardous waste disposal projects. He currently provides technical direction, new product development, risk management guidance, and underwriting and claims support to Front Royal Insurance Company. He has over 30 management and technical papers to his credit and is Chairman of the ASTM Technical Section, Environmental Assessment of Commercial Property Transactions. He has an M.S. in Environmental Sciences and Engineering and a B.A. in Political Science from The American University in Washington, D.C.

# Endnotes

1. CERCLA § 101(35). CERCLA is the Comprehensive Environmental Response, Compensation and Liability Act, or Superfund, 42 U.S.C. § 9801 *et seq.* as amended by the Superfund Amendments and Reauthorization Act (SARA) Pub. L. No. 99-499, 100 stat. 1613 (1986).

2. For example, Connecticut and New Jersey have property transfer acts and more recently, EPA has proposed yet another legally significant due diligence standard as the "price of admission to its new Anti-*Fleet* Material Participation Safe Harbor Rule."

3. CERCLA § 107(a) and case law interpreting this liability provision, *see* Chapter IX, *supra* at p. 223.

4. *Id.*, as amended by SARA.

5. CERCLA § 101(20)(A), *see* Chapter IX, *supra* at p. 223.

6. *See U.S. v. Mirabile*, 23 Env't. Rep. Cas. (BNA) 1511 (E. D. Pa. 1985); *Guidice v. BFG Electroplating and Manufacturing Co.*, 30 Env't. Rep. Cas. (BNA) 1665 (W.D. Pa. Sept. 1,

1989); *U.S. v. Nicolet, Inc.,* 29 Env't. Rep. Cas. (BNA) 1851 (E.D. Pa. 1989); *U.S. v. Fleet Factors Corporation,* 901 F. 2d 1550 (11th Cir. 1990). *In re: Bergsoe Metal Corporation,* 910 F.2d 668 (9th Cir. 1990).

7.  American Society of Testing and Materials Subcommittee E50.2 on Environmental Assessments in Commercial Real Estate Transaction, draft document, Appendix A, "Legal Background to Federal Law and the E50.2 Standard On Environmental Assessments in Commercial Real Estate Transactions," defines terms as follows:

Due Diligence: That level of inquiry about a property that goes beyond Superfund's "appropriate inquiry" and which may be prudent to undertake by a party to certain commercial real estate transactions before closing or as a condition to the transaction. Different levels of due diligence apply to different properties.

Environmental Site Assessment: The process by which certain levels of appropriate inquiry or due diligence are conducted for a parcel of property. An environmental site assessment may include more inquiry than that required to meet "appropriate inquiry" for certain properties.

Environmental Audit: The investigative process to determine if an existing facility is in compliance with applicable environmental laws and regulations. The term audit should not be used to describe the ASTM E50.2 standards(s), although audits may in particular circumstances include or be part of an assessment.

8.  54 *Fed. Reg.* 34241 (Aug. 18, 1989).

9.  H.R. Rep. No 99-253 (1) 99th Cong., 2d Sess. 4, reprinted in 1986 U.S. Code Cong. & Admin. News 2835,2836.

10.  *Id. at 2836.*

11.  *Dedham Water Co. v. Cumberland Farms Dairy, Inc.* 805 F. 2d 1074, 11082 (1st. Cir. 1986).

12.  *See EPA Guidance on Preparing Superfund Decision Documents, 1989.*

13.  EPA Draft Interpretive Rule for Secured Creditors and Innocent Landowners. 40 C.F.R. Part [], p. 13.

14.  *Id.,* p. 15.

**Environmental Due Diligence Process in Business and Real Estate Transactions**

# XVIII

## Investigation Techniques for Allocation of Superfund Liability

*Bart M. Schwartz*
*Senior Managing Director and Counsel*
*Kroll Associates*
*New York, New York*
*and Scott G. Vincent, Esq.*
*Cleveland, Barrios, Kingsdorf & Casteix*
*New Orleans, Louisiana*

The Comprehensive Environmental Response, Compensation, and Liability Act (CERCLA or Superfund) was enacted by Congress in 1980 as a means to redress the environmental and health dangers presented by the existence of thousands of hazardous waste sites throughout the country. The legislative intent behind the act was to hold responsible for the cost of cleanup those persons who were involved in creating hazardous wastes and those who profited from its disposal. Under CERCLA, as amended in 1986 by the Superfund Amendments and Reauthorization Act of 1986 (SARA), the Environmental Protection Agency (EPA) may require "responsible parties" to cleanup locations where contamination has been determined to be of concern or potential threat to human health and the environment, or it may undertake the remedial operations itself, where the responsible parties do not respond to the contamination. In the latter instance, the remedial operations are funded by the Superfund, and the federal government may seek reimbursement of its expenditures from the responsible parties.

Although CERCLA does not expressly delineate the standard of liability thereunder, the act defines the term *liable* or *liability* as "the standard of liability which obtains under section 1321 of Title 33

[Clean Water Act], which does impose strict liability. The courts have consistently imposed strict liability in CERCLA cases.[1]

One of the more alarming aspects of CERCLA is that it imposes liability retroactively to activities and operations occurring long before its enactment that were legal and generally acceptable at the time of their occurrence.[2] Thus, liability is also absolute; a party may be responsible for the remediation of a contaminated site even though the party was acting in accordance with then-accepted waste handling and disposal procedures.

CERCLA imposes liability for the cleanup of a site on four categories of "potentially responsible parties" (PRPs):
- Current owners or operators of the site;
- Former owners or operators of the site;
- Generators of hazardous substances sent to the site for treatment or disposal;
- Transporters of hazardous substances sent to the site for treatment or disposal.[3]

Liability under CERCLA has been broadly and liberally construed to impose liability against:
- A landowner for contamination caused by a previous owner;[4]
- Previous owner for contamination occurring during its ownership;[5]
- A lessor for the operations of its lessee;[6] a foreclosing lender;[7]
- A developer and lender who financed the development of a subdivision located on contaminated property;[8]
- A successor company for contamination caused by the company with which it merged;[9]
- Directors, officers, and stockholders;[10] and
- A parent company for the activities of its subsidiary.[11]

The strict liability imposed on a PRP is virtually unavoidable, unless the party can establish that the release of hazardous waste and resulting damage were caused by an act of God, an act of war, or an act or omission of a third party.[12] Although Congress deleted the specific terms *joint and several* liability contained in preliminary House and Senate versions of the legislation from the final version of the act, CERCLA has been interpreted to impose joint and several liability upon a responsible party unless the party can prove that the environmental injury is divisible and that there is a reasonable basis for apportioning the harm.[13] Thus, a party responsible for only a small fraction of the hazardous waste at a particular site may be responsible for the cleanup cost of the entire site. This makes it attractive for the EPA to focus its enforcement efforts on large, national "deep pocket" companies responsible for only a portion of the contamination and which end up paying for the share of cleanup costs that should have been borne by others who are unable to pay or who cannot be located.

The harshness of this rule is somewhat alleviated by the right of a party to seek contribution from other responsible parties.[14] The act contains no guidelines for the allocation of response cost among liable parties but rather, leaves this matter to the courts.[15] The factors which the courts have taken into account in allocating liability among responsible parties include:

- The ability of the parties to demonstrate that their contribution to a discharge, release or disposal of a hazardous substance can be distinguished;
- The amount of hazardous substance involved;
- The degree of toxicity and mobility of the hazardous substance involved;
- The degree of involvement by the parties in the generation, transportation, treatment, storage, or disposal of the hazardous substance;
- The degree of care exercised by the parties with respect to the hazardous substance concerned, taking into account the characteristics of the hazardous substance; and
- The degree of cooperation by the parties with federal, state or local officials to prevent harm to the public health or the environment.[16]

In light of liability that can be both strict and joint and several, a PRP should undertake to develop a factual basis for one of the limited defenses to liability under CERCLA and to establish a reasonable basis for dividing the harm and shifting, to the extent possible, the liability therefore to other responsible parties. It is for this purpose that the environmental investigation becomes necessary.

## Selecting the Appropriate Environmental Investigation Agency/Firm

In choosing an investigative agency to gather the necessary background information on a site in order to locate and identify additional responsible parties, a number of factors should be considered. The first is the size of the investigating firm. Environmental investigation firms range in sizes from one-person operations to national and international firms. Although a one-person firm may be suitable for a very limited PRP Search, it is extremely important that there be enough experienced environmental investigators to handle the tasks that arise during the course of the investigation. A firm that routinely handles other types of investigations may have many investigators on staff, but few, if any, with environmental experience.

The most important quality to look for in an investigation firm is experience with the type of project involved. The more experienced the investigation firm, the more it will be able to understand and anticipate the needs of the client. The members of the firm must have a basic understanding of the rudimentary provisions of the environmental law, such as the allocation of liability under CERCLA, that are implicated by the project so that they may better accomplish the purpose of the project, i.e., to identify and locate other responsible parties for the allocation of liability. An investigation firm that lacks environmental law familiarity is simply unacceptable.

An investigation firm bidding on the project should be able to provide a list of similar projects completed by the firm. A party searching for an environmental investigation firm should ask each prospective firm for the names of the project managers who will be involved in the investigation, their experience, and a brief description of how the investigation will be conducted.

Unlike most other types of investigation, the complexities and sheer volume of facts that must be gathered and substantiated in an environmental investigation is mind-boggling. With hundreds and even thousands of interviews to conduct and leads to follow, it is easy to become inundated and miss important information that may be critical to the case. To efficiently and effectively handle the tremendous volume of facts, figures and data, an electronic filing capability is a valuable asset for an environmental investigation firm.

Computers utilized during the investigation should be capable of recording and relaying information as well as providing cross-referencing on a real time basis so that the client can be up to date on the project as constant evaluation and direction by the client may be required.

It is also important to select a company with a knowledge of waste practices and waste streams. The company must be familiar with waste characteristics and understand to some degree which processes create what kind of waste product.

This is particularly true in cases of abandoned waste sites where there may be little available information. More traditional investigative capabilities are required, such as being able to identify and locate witnesses and to conduct interviews of witnesses in order to obtain pertinent information.

Managing a PRP investigation requires constant supervision. It is important that the investigative agency be capable of managing a large investigation and that the agency maintain a constant line of communication with its field investigators. The investigative agency should be able to generate periodic reports involved in the investigation. The end result of the investigation performed by the chosen agency should be a final report that provides factual support for the identification of other responsible parties and for the allocation of liability among the responsible parties.

## Investigation Techniques for the Allocation of Superfund Liability

Oftentimes a party who is only minimally at fault for the condition of a site, such as a party responsible for the placement of a small portion of the hazardous waste on the site, or technically at fault, such as a current landowner failing to satisfy the innocent landowner defense for hazardous substance placed or released on his property prior to its acquisition, is called upon by the EPA to remedy a site or pay the expenses for the remediation of the site. The innocent landowner could then possibly seek contributions from other responsible parties.

Upon being named a responsible party by the EPA, a party should not be dismayed by the initial absence of available records and should not start out the investigative process with the pre-conceived notion that there are no records and information anywhere and if there are such records, they are not locateable or are sketchy at best. Experience shows that, more often than not, there are records which, if the appropriate course of investigation is followed, will be located. One of the first steps of a site investigation should be the accumulation of background information about the history of the site as well as an on-site inspection. An understanding of the past uses of the site is essential to estimate the potential environmental exposure associated with the facility and is a helpful tool in initially formulating the breadth and depth of the environmental investigation.

A review of in-house records maintained on behalf of the facility may uncover changes of ownership of the facility, usages of the property, past operations, environmental violations, and other pertinent information. Of typically lesser benefit, but necessary, is a title search of the property which will reveal the chain of ownership of the property, although such a search rarely uncovers the actual usages of the property.

Other sources of background information are newspaper and journal accounts pertaining to the site. Aerial photographs of the site, if available, depict the development and uses of a facility over the years. On a large site with heavy disposal activity, aerial photographs can reveal the commercial concerns operating on the site and their location on and use of the site, as well as transporters of waste to the site. These photographs are also useful in interviewing witnesses. For example, if a witness gives a description of the property or an account of a disposal that is inconsistent with or affirmatively disproved by the photographs, that individual's statement should be given little, if any, credence. The photographs might also refresh a witness's recollection of facts concerning the site and corroborate his statement.

A review of the files maintained by the applicable federal, state, and local environmental agencies can disclose a wealth of information concerning present and past waste disposals on the site. On the federal level, the EPA is the primary source of file information. On the state level, the primary source of file information is the state counterpart to the EPA. The records of such state environmental agencies should contain copies of manifests, i.e., notices required under the laws of most states that must be filed by a generator, transporter, and receiving agency of disposable, hazardous or "special" waste, indicating essentially the type and volume of waste being disposed on the site.

The manifests, if accurately completed and filed, indicate each instance of waste disposal, the type and volume of the substances involved, the generator of the waste, the transporter, and the recipient of the waste, and are therefore, one of the best documents to be used in the process of identifying other responsible parties and of allocating responsibility for the cleanup of the site.

Unfortunately, the filing of a manifest in connection with waste disposal and the creation of a centralized state department or agency such as a Department of Environmental Quality did not come into play in most states until the late 1970s or early 1980s. For records of contamination prior to then, there may be no central state office to contact for a file search, and the records may be disbursed throughout other state agencies, such as the Department of Water Quality Control, the Department of Natural Resources, Department of Air Quality Control, and the State Health Department. In dealing with the various state agencies, it should be kept in mind the provincial tendency associated with some departments of not sharing records and files with another. An elevator ride in a state office building from one agency to another may prove to be very rewarding. On the local level, the police department, sheriff's department, and fire department are other sources of information.

An excellent source of information often overlooked is the records of other responsible parties who have been designated by the EPA to clean up a site. A cooperating PRP may be able to provide much of the background information mentioned above.

After the site history has been compiled, the investigative field work comes next. This phase of the project should include three steps, developing a list of potentially informative persons (PIPs), locating PIPs, and conducting interviews.

The investigator must first formulate a list of PIPs, that is, those individuals who are likely to have information concerning the facility. Eyewitness accounts are the most convincing and vivid sources of information and provide pertinent details not found in reports. Eyewitness accounts may be the only source of information concerning a disposal or other contaminating occurrence, especially one occurring 40 or 50 years ago. Typical categories of PIPs include former site owners, past and present owners of neighboring property, former site employees, former truck drivers and radio dispatchers of transporters, present and former employees of PRPs, present and former neighbors and area residents, present and former inspectors, various personnel of government agencies, and fire and police personnel who worked in the site area. Other categories of PIP also include past and present insurance brokers and/or agents and insurance carriers. Normally, the most informative of these categories are previous owners, operators, site employees and drivers for the haulers who delivered to the site.

After PIPs have been identified, they must be located. Since many of these potential witnesses will have moved since their association with the site, some persons several times, especially prospective witnesses to disposals occurring 40 to 50 years ago, it is necessary to track down and locate a current address for each of these witnesses. This facet of the investigation can often be the most costly and time consuming and should, to the extent possible, be assisted by computerized information processing.

After PIPs have been located, they must be interviewed. Interviews should be conducted by an experienced investigative team with a thorough understanding of waste streams and waste-handling practices. For most projects, the optimal team consists of individuals with environmental investigative background experience and, at certain times during the investigation, a member with technical expertise. The investigator provides the capability of locating witnesses and records and of conducting the interviews. The member of the team possessing a technical background can assist in evaluating the information collected and by providing questions and follow-up questions of a technical nature to ask during an interview. This inter-disciplinary approach minimizes the risk that a crucial discovery inquiry will be omitted during the interviewing process.

Interviews should be structured to determine the type of waste and the amount of waste deposited at the site. Careful attention to detail is necessary regarding the pick up and disposition of waste. The interviewer should employ site maps and aerial photographs when questioning witnesses and should elicit as much pertinent detail as possible. A decision should be made in the planning stages as to whether statements given by witnesses should be taped (with permission) or written. In any event, interview summaries should be made by the investigation team and forwarded to the manager of the investigative agency responsible for the project for review and consultation with the client.

Once the investigation phase is completed, the information gathered should be analyzed and processed, preferably with the assistance of a computer, and the appropriate reports should be generated. The final report to be submitted to the client should include a detailed site history and a summary of the facts developed by the investigation, presented in such a way as to be easily verified. The report should be prepared so that the client does not have any additional investigation to perform should the report's contents be challenged by the new PRPs found. It should also disclose the quantity and type of all waste known to have been deposited at the site by each generator. Equipped with this information, the client can approximate the portion of the waste it is responsible for, and more importantly, the portion for which other parties are responsible and take the appropriate action to shift the cleanup costs to other parties.

## Recurring Concerns in Verifying Sources of Data

A recurring problem encountered in the course of the investigation process is forged, incomplete, or inaccurate documents. These document problems, if left undetected, can lead to inadequate and inaccurate conclusions in the investigation report. Manifests are sometimes forged or completed with misleading information. For example, a transporter who has been paid by a generator to transport and dispose of waste at an approved facility could dispose of the waste in a ditch or creek and forge the signature of the intended disposal facility, thereby pocketing the funds intended for the disposal costs. As a result of this scheme, the manifest would inaccurately reflect that the waste had been disposed of at the intended site. Another example of fraudulently executed manifests would be where a generator lists another chemical company as the generator in an attempt to avoid being tracked down, through the paper trail, as being a PRP. A third example, which takes place with some frequency, occurs when a generator records a substance with a lower toxicity level than that actually transported or writes down a lesser quantity in the manifest report.

The problem of fraudulent documents can be alleviated by verifying and substantiating the information contained in the document. Just because a manifest states that X quantity of Y substance was transported from a particular generator to a particular facility does not necessarily mean that the information is true. The truck drivers working for the transporting company and the employees at the receiving site at the time of the disposal reflected in the manifest should be contacted and interviewed to verify the information contained in the record. It is a good practice, where possible, to get multiple confirmation from various witnesses on the same incident.

A second area of concern involves the verification of information submitted by other PRPs. In a large, heavily contaminated site, it is not unusual for two hundred to three hundred companies to be named PRPs by the Federal EPA or state Superfund agency. More often than not, a committee is formed by the PRPs and the members submit their records and files to the PRP committee, i.e., allocation subcommittee, which in turn, makes a determination as to the allocation of liability. There is a natural tendency for the individual PRPs to minimize their past involvement. Therefore, although the proper PRPs may be named by the EPA, the documentation furnished by some of the PRPs may not reflect the accurate frequency at which the PRP disposed of waste on the site or the proper quantity of waste disposed on a particular occasion or the proper substance disposed on a particular occasion. The best way to remedy this problem is to spot-check the documentation submitted to the PRP committee. Dispatchers and drivers for the hauling companies and supervisors and employees of the disposal facility should be interviewed to get a general idea as to what companies disposed what substance on the site and how frequently and to see if this information matches the information furnished by the individual PRPs.

A third recurring problem, briefly touched upon in the third section of this chapter, involves the relatively new existence of centralized state environmental agencies, such as the Department of Environmental Quality or the Department of Environmental Protection, and of the requirement of filing disposal notices or manifests with these centralized agencies. Manifests, if completed accurately and truthfully and in all instances of waste disposal, would chronicle all of the disposals occurring at a particular site. For information about possible disposals prior to the late 1970's it is necessary to search the files of predecessor agencies, such as the Department of Natural Resources, the Department of Water Quality Control, the Department of Air Quality Control, and the State Health Department, and the files of various local agencies, such as the police department, fire department, and sheriff's department, and to interview potentially informative persons.

A witness's changing his version of the facts subsequent to the taking of his statement is another problem encountered in environmental proceedings. The best way to protect against this is to pin the witness down as much as possible by obligating him to give fact-specific, detailed information and to confirm his statement through interviewing other witnesses. When interviewing a truck driver, for example, the interviewer should ask the witness to describe the trucks driven, the route taken, his driving schedule for the time period involved, the storage facility on the generator's site from which the waste was taken, and the precise location on the receiving site where the waste was disposed. The truck driver should be asked to draw a sketch of the generator's facilities as well as of the recipient's facilities. This information should be confirmed by asking other drivers working for the same hauling company the same questions.

A fifth area of concern, albeit one that does not deal with the verification of sources of data, is the protection of the confidential information gathered as a result of the investigation. It is essential that an attorney direct the work of the investigation team in order to cloak the information under the attorney-client privilege and/or work product privilege.[17] (See Chapter XIV, Sullivan.) Greater protection has been afforded to information discovered through the use of independent, outside counsel than information discovered through the use of in-house, corporate counsel.[18] For this reason, the contract engaging the environmental investigation agency should be with the attorney, not the client.

## Future Trends and Potential Impact on Superfund PRP Cost Allocations

When CERCLA was passed in 1980, the Superfund had $1.6 billion to be spent over a five-year period.[19] When CERCLA was reauthorized in 1986 by SARA, the amount authorized for the Superfund over the next five years was increased to $8.5 billion.[20] This seemingly large amount of money has proven hopelessly inadequate.

The EPA has identified over 27,000 sites as candidates for cleanup under the Superfund program, while the General Accounting Office employed by Congress believes that up to 425,000 sites should be added to this list. [21] The average cost of investigating and cleaning of a site placed on the EPA's national priorities list has been estimated to be $15-$20 million per site.[22] A congressional report has estimated the cost at between $21 million and $30 million per site.[23]   The total national cleanup bill was projected in late 1989 to be roughly $500 billion.[24] Many of these estimates are now thought to be very conservative.

With a present funding gap of approximately $491.5 billion, the EPA has increased its enforcement efforts to identify and locate PRPs and recoup remedial expenditures from them.

As the liability of a PRP is retroactive, strict and joint and several, there is little, if any, incentive on the part of the EPA to undertake a full and complete investigation to determine all of the responsible parties.  Rather than go through this extremely costly process, the EPA typically conducts a precursory investigation, consisting principally of a review of the manifests pertaining to the site and of a limited field investigation, leaving it to the named PRPs to conduct a more definitive investigation in order to locate additional PRPs and to assess liability amongst themselves.

Faced with potential remedial costs ranging in the tens of millions of dollars per site and the distinct probability of the existence of additional, unnamed PRPs, there has been a growing trend on the part of named PRPs to combine their resources and form a PRP committee.  The purpose of the committee is to locate other responsible parties and to allocate responsibility for cleanup costs amongst the responsible parties.  To accomplish the end, the committee retains the services of an environmental investigation agency to undertake a complete environmental investigation of the site.  As the cost of investigating and cleaning up of a site has grown astronomically over the years, PRPs have found it necessary to increase their reliance on investigations in order to protect their interests.  There is every reason to believe that this cost-effective trend will continue.

## About The Authors

**Bart M. Schwartz** served as Chief of the Criminal Division for the U.S. Attorney's Office, Southern District of New York, under Rudolph Giuliani from 1983 to 1985. Mr. Schwartz was previously a partner in a law firm specializing in federal litigation. He has also served as Assistant U.S. Attorney in the Southern District of New York. He has extensive experience in the planning and conducting of investigations of all kinds, including civil and criminal environmental inquiries. Mr. Schwartz received a B.S. from the University of Pittsburgh in 1968 and a J.D. from New York University in 1971.

**Scott G. Vincent** is a member of the law firm of Cleveland, Barrios, Kingsdorf & Casteix in New Orleans, Louisiana, where he heads the firm's environmental law section. He graduated *cum laude* from Louisiana State University. He was selected as an honors graduate for and received a Master of Laws degree (LL.M.) at Tulane University. He served as law clerk to the Honorable Edwin F. Hunter, Jr., of the United States District Court for the Western District of Louisiana.

## Endnotes

1. *United States v. Marisol, Inc.,* 725 F.Supp. 833 (M.D.Pa. 1989); *United States v. Aceto Agr. Chemicals Corp.,* 872 F.2d 1373 (8th Cir. 1989); *United States v. Monsanto Co.,* 858 F.2d 160 (4th Cir. 1988); *Tanglewood East Homeowners v. Charles - Thomas, Inc.,* 849 F.2d 1568 (5th Cir. 1988); *New York v. Shore Realty Corp.,* 759 F.2d 1032 (2nd Cir. 1985).

2. *O'Neil v. Picillo,* 833 F.2d 176 (1st Cir. 1989); *United States v. Northeastern Pharmaceutical & Chem. Co.,* 579 F.Supp. 823 (W.D.Mo. 1984), *aff'd in part, rev'd in part,* 810 F.2d 726 (8th Cir. 1986); *United States v. Hooker Chemicals & Plastics Corp.,* 680 F.Supp. 546 (W.D.N.Y. 1988); *Mayor and Board of Aldermen of Boonton v. Drew Chem. Corp.,* 621 F.Supp. 663 (D.C.N.J. 1985); *United States v. Shell Oil Co.,* 605 F.Supp. 1064 (D.Col. 1985). But see *Idaho v. Bunker Hill Co.,* 635 F.Supp. 665 (D.Idaho 1986); *Brown v. Georgeoff,* 562 F.Supp. 1300 (N.D. Ohio 1983).

3. 42 U.S.C. § 9607(a). Prior owners are liable only if they owned or operated the facility at the time of disposal of hazardous substance. *BCW Associates, Ltd. v. Occidental Chemical Corp.,* 1988 Westlaw 102641 (E.D.Pa. September 29, 1988).

4. *Smith Land & Improvement Corp. v. Celotex Corp.*, 851 F.2d 86 (3rd Cir. 1988); *New York v. Shore Realty Corp.*, 759 F.2d 1032 (2nd Cir. 1985); *United States v. Stringfellow*, 661 F.Supp. 1053 (C.D. Cal. 1987).

5. *United States v. Monsanto Co.*, 858 F.2d 160 (4th Cir. 1988).

6. *United States v. Monsanto Co.*, 858 F.2d 160 (4th Cir. 1988); *United States v. Northernaire Plating Co.*, 670 F.Supp. 742 (W.D.Mich. 1987), *aff'd*, 889 F.2d 1497 (6th Cir. 1989); *International Clinical Laboratories v. Stevens*, 710 F.Supp. 466 (E.D.N.Y. 1989).

7. *New York v. Shore Realty Corp.*, 759 F.2d 1032 (2nd Cir. 1985); *United States v. Maryland Bank & Trust Co.*, 632 F.Supp. 573 (D. Md. 1988); see also *Guidice v. BFG Electroplating and Manufacturing Co., Inc.*, 732 F.Supp. 556 (W.D.Pa. 1989). See also *United States v. Fleet Factors Corp.*, 901 F.2d 1550 (11th Cir. 1990).

8. *Tanglewood East Homeowners v. Charles - Thomas, Inc.*, 849 F.2d 1568 (5th Cir. 1988).

9. *Smith Land & Improvement Corp. v. Celotex Corp.*, 851 F.2d 86 (3rd Cir. 1988).

10. *United States v. Multi-Chem, Inc.*, No. 84-0159-BG(CS), Chem. Waste Lit. Rptr. (Computer L. Rptr.) 1185 (August 1, 1989); *Michigan v. ARCO Industries Corp.*, 721 F.Supp. 873, 723 F.Supp. 1214 (W.D.Mich. 1989); *Kelley v. Thomas Solvent Co.*, 727 F.Supp. 1532 (W.D.Mich. 1989); *United States v. Conservation Chemical*, 628 F.Supp. 391 (W.D.Mo. 1985); *United States v. Northeastern Pharmaceutical & Chem. Co.*, 579 F.Supp. 823 (W.D.Mo. 1984), *aff'd in part, rev'd in part*, 810 F.2d 726 (8th Cir. 1986); *United States v. Ward*, 618 F.Supp. 884 (E.D.N.C. 1985); *United States v. Carolawn Co.*, 14 Envtl. L. Rep. 20699 (D.S.C. 1984); *Idaho v. Bunker Hill Co.*, 635 F.Supp. 665 (D.Id. 1986); *United States v. Bliss*, 667 F.Supp. 1298 (E.D.Mo. 1987).

11. *United States v. Kayser-Roth Corp.*, 724 F.Supp. 15 (D.R.I. 1989); *Idaho v. Bunker Hill Co.*, 635 F.Supp. 665 (D.Id. 1986); *United States v. Nicolet*, 712 F.Supp. 1193 (E.D.Pa. 1989). But see, *Joslyn Corp. v. T. L. James & Co., Inc.*, 696 F.Supp. 222 (W.D.La. 1988), *aff'd*, 893 F.2d 80 (5th Cir. 1990); *F. M. C. Corp. v. Northern Pump*, 668 F.Supp. 1285 (D.Minn. 1987).

12. 42 U.S.C. § 9607(b)(1-3). The SARA Amendments of 1986 added the "innocent landowner" defense as a part of the "third party" defense. *See* 42 U.S.C. § 9601(35). These defenses are more fully discussed in Chapter X.

13. *United States v. Western Processing Co., Inc.*, 734 F.Supp. 930 (W.D. Wash. 1990); *O'Neil v. Picillo*, 883 F.2d 176 (1st Cir. 1989); *In re Acushnet River & New Bedford Harbor*, 722 F.Supp. 893 (D.Mass. 1989); *United States v. Marisol, Inc.*, 725 F.Supp. 833 (M.D.Pa. 1989); *United States v. Rohm & Haas Co.*, 721 F.Supp. 666 (D.N.J. 1989); *United States v. Monsanto Co.*, 858 F.2d 160 (4th Cir. 1988); *United States v. Northeastern Pharmaceutical & Chem. Co.*, 579 F.Supp. 823 (W.D.Mo. 1984) *aff'd in part, rev'd in part*, 810 F.2d 726 (8th Cir. 1986); *United States v. Conservation Chemical Co.*, 589 F.Supp. 59 (W.D.Mo. 1984); *Idaho v. Bunker Hill Co.*, 635 F.Supp. 665 (D.Id. 1986); *United States v. Bliss*, 667 F.Supp. 1298 (E.D.Mo. 1987); *United States v. Miami Drum Services, Inc.*, 25 Env't. Rep. Cas. (BNA) 1469 (D.Fla.).

14. 42 U.S.C. § 9613 (f)(1).

15. "In resolving contribution claims, the court may allocate response costs among liable parties using such equitable factors as the court determines are appropriate." 42 U.S.C. § 9613 (f)(1).

16. *United States v. A & F Materials Co.*, 578 F.Supp. 1249 (S.D.Ill. 1984); *United States v. Monsanto Co.*, 858 F.2d 160 (4th Cir. 1988).

These factors are sometimes referred to as the "Gore factors" since they are derived from an unsuccessful amendment to CERCLA offered by then Representative, now Senator Albert Gore of Tennessee in 1980.

17. *Cf. Gold Metal Process Co. v. Aluminum Co. of America*, 7 F.R.D. 684 (D.Mass. 1947); *Conforti & Eisele, Inc. v. Div. of Bldg. and Const.*, 170 N.J.Super. 64, 405 A.2d 487 (1979).

18. *Upjohn Co. v. United States*, 101 S.Ct. 677 (1981); *United States v. Charles George Trucking Co.*, 642 F.Supp. 329 (D.Mass. 1986); *In re Grand Jury Subpoena*, 599 F.2d 504 (2nd Cir. 1979); *United States v. Reserve Mining*, 412 F.Supp. 705 (D.Minn. 1976).

19. 42 U.S.C. § 9631.

20. 42 U.S.C. § 9611(a).

21. *Hazardous Waste Report 3*, Vol. 9, No. 11 (February 8, 1988); Ortiz, *The Hazardous Waste Services Industry - A Market of Opportunity*, 2 Envtl. Waste Mgmt. World 3 (March 1988).

22. *9 Hazardous Waste Report 3* (April 18, 1988).

23. *9 Hazardous Waste Report 3* (April 18, 1988); Chem. Waste Lit. Rptr. 1073 n.5 (1988).

24. Congress of the United States, Office of Technology Assessment, *Coming Clean: Superfund Problems Can Be Solved* 27 (1989).

502

# XIX Pollution Prevention Progression

*Robert B. Pojasek, Ph.D.*
*Vice President*
*Geraghty & Miller, Inc.*
*Andover, Massachusetts*

It is easy to get the impression that there is a distinct battle[1] going on between those who use the terms *waste minimization*[2] and *waste reduction*.[3] This notion, however, would preclude the concept that there may be an evolutionary transition taking place that would bring industry from one level to the next. In the related fields of environmental management[4] and quality control,[5] arguments have been made for similar transitions.

*Waste minimization* as it has been put in practice is often one-dimensional. The primary focus is on regulated hazardous wastes. It is the environmental engineer who is trying to stem the quantity of those wastes and the resultant costs and liabilities associated with them. Because hazardous wastes often pose the greatest costs of all environmental emissions for a given facility, it is obvious why the early focus is on waste minimization.

*Waste reduction*, on the other hand, involves a much more direct means to prevent waste discharges to any media (i.e., air, water, solid waste, hazardous waste, and other releases) at the source. It takes additional skills to bring waste reduction beyond the use of good operating practices. The environmental engineer must seek assistance to examine a variety of in-plant practices that can reduce the generation of those wastes.

These practices include the following: input substitution or input materials modification, technology modification, closed-loop recycling and product substitution.

A new regulatory term has been brought forth in a number of states (e.g., Oregon, Massachusetts and Maine). It's called Toxics Use

Reduction. Whether this falls under the heading of waste reduction or not may be open to debate; however, it is clear that both of these terms are driving industry to the full use of pollution prevention in every aspect of its business.

This chapter will explore how a facility program can evolve from a waste minimization focus to emphasis on waste reduction and pollution prevention. A historical perspective on the use of each of these terms is presented.

The pollution prevention progression is presented along with the 15 milestones that a firm will take to move along this progression.

Finally, the concept of a waste reduction audit will be examined from the perspective of the pollution prevention progression. The details of an advanced audit format are presented in Chapter XV.

## Historical Perspective

National environmental statutes and regulatory programs implemented by the U.S. Environmental Protection Agency (EPA) constitute a waste management by media approach to environmental protection. Hazardous constituents are lost to the air, water and land as a result of production process operation in industry.

The strategy employed to protect the environment has invariably been to try to affect the loss by controlling those hazardous constituents individually by media after they have been produced and have the potential to move among the media.

This has fostered the growth of a pollution control culture. A generation of environmental engineers have been trained in this culture.

It is interesting to note that the Federal Water Pollution Control Act and the Clean Air Act, both passed by Congress in the early 1970's, had explicit provisions for waste reduction.

Waste reduction aspects of individual environmental statutes are analyzed in detail in the Office of Technology Assessment report [6] on waste reduction.

Despite the apparent flexibility of those provisions, waste reduction gave way to pollution control because it did not involve penetrating into the confidentiality of or disrupting the operation of industrial processes. Furthermore, it did not pose a direct threat to product quality.

The concept of waste minimization was formally introduced in a regulatory fashion with the passage of the Hazardous and Solid Waste Amendments of 1984 (PL 98-616; November 8, 1984). Within Section 1003 the concept is clearly stated as follows:

> The Congress hereby declares it to be the national policy of the United States that, wherever feasible, the generation of hazardous waste is to be reduced or eliminated as expeditiously as possible. Waste that is nevertheless generated should be treated, stored, or disposed of so as to minimize the present and future threat to human health and the environment. . . minimizing the generation of hazardous waste and the land disposal of hazardous waste by encouraging process substitution, materials recovery, properly conducted recycling and reuse, and treatment . . .

This statute did not explicitly define waste minimization and EPA did not define it in the regulations. As a result, not only the choice of actions but also the determination of what actions constitute waste minimization has been left up to industry.

Effective September 1, 1985, hazardous waste generators were required[7] to confirm that they had a program:

> . . . Unless I am a small quantity generator who has been exempted by statute or regulation from the duty to make a waste minimization certification under Section 3002(b) of RCRA, I also certify that I have a program in place to reduce the volume and toxicity of waste generated to the degree I have determined to be economically practicable and I have selected the method of treatment, storage, or disposal currently available to me which minimizes the present and future threat to human health and the environment.

There was confusion within the regulated community on what constituted a waste minimization program. On June 12, 1989, the EPA issued draft guidance[8] to hazardous waste generators on the elements of such a program. The key elements in this guidance are listed in Table 1.

Table 1
Key Elements of Waste Minimization Plan

1. Obtain Top Management Support
2. Install a Waste Accounting System
3. Conduct Periodic Waste Minimization Assessments
4. Develop a Cost Allocation System
5. Encourage Technology Transfer
6. Provide for Program Evaluation

The EPA began the transition of its move to waste reduction with its release of a proposed policy statement[9] on January 26, 1989. It states:

EPA's proposed policy encourages organizations, facilities, and individuals to fully utilize source reduction techniques in order to reduce risk to public health, safety, welfare and the environment. . .

If such a transition was possible within the EPA, perhaps such a transition could take place in industry. In this manner, an evolutionary switch would be made from waste minimization to source reduction and pollution prevention.

## Pollution Prevention Progression

There have been documented transitions which have occurred in the related fields of environmental management and quality management. Table 2, on the next page, shows how the stages in those areas may compare with the stages a company experiences in its progress towards pollution prevention.

Table 2
Comparisons of Previously Studied Evolutionary Programs to
the Pollution Prevention Progression

| Stages | Quality Management Maturity | Environmental Management Development | Pollution Prevention Progression |
|--------|------------------------------|--------------------------------------|----------------------------------|
| One | Uncertainly | Beginner | Damage Control |
| Two | Awakening | Fire Fighter | Pollution Control |
| Three | Enlightenment | Concerned | Waste Minimization |
| Four | Wisdom | Pragmatist | Source Reduction |
| Five | Certainty | Proactivist | Pollution Prevention |

In the Damage Control Stage a facility responds to a complex and piecemeal body of environmental regulations with a "hit-or-miss" approach to compliance. Typical characteristics in this stage involve the following:
- Applying temporary fixes to systemic problems
- Meeting compliance deadlines at the last minute
- Shifting pollutants from one media to another
- No recognition of prevention at the management level

The pollution prevention function, if it exists at all, is found deep in the recesses of the "overhead function" with a person who performs environmental compliance activities on a part-time basis.

This limitation creates a self-fulfilling prophecy that pollution prevention will never be part of a company which remains in this stage.

The Pollution Control Stage is more progressive, but no less frustrating when it comes to pollution prevention. Here management realizes that government enforcement efforts and environmental accidents jeopardize facility operations.

Pollution prevention could help the organization, but management is unwilling to devote the time and money necessary to make it happen. Emphasis is placed on end-of-the-pipe solutions.

Waste Minimization usually appears with the decision to follow the U.S. EPA guidance[10] associated with the signatory on the hazardous waste manifest form.

This focus on hazardous wastes is logical because it is this waste which often poses the greatest financial liability to the company. There is also a good potential to save the company money because of the escalating costs of hazardous waste management and the ever-broadening umbrella of what is covered under these regulations.

The company may or may not have a formal policy at this point; however, someone is designated to lead the waste minimization crusade and resources are allocated to this task.

At some point the group starts involving other departments to help track the wastes back to their sources where the potential for waste minimization is greater.

Other wastes, such as air emissions and water discharges, also may receive some consideration in an advanced Waste Minimization Stage. Emphasis is placed on good operating practices.

Source Reduction represents another matter altogether. People are deeply involved in a multi-disciplinary, multi-media program and take the time to learn more about the subtleties of the philosophy of pollution prevention. The company can begin working on the 15 milestones to move to pollution prevention.

Source reduction projects may need some incentive to compete for capital spending requests; however, those projects which are funded will bring back healthy financial returns.

In the final stage, pollution prevention becomes an absolutely vital part of the company management. Pollution prevention becomes a company policy, well known to everyone in the organization.

It is each person's responsibility to identify opportunities to prevent pollution. The drive for pollution prevention is reinforced every day in meetings and other company functions.

In this stage, the company is revisiting the 15 milestones which it went through to get here.

## Fifteen Milestones to Pollution Prevention

In order to reach pollution prevention on the pollution prevention progression, a number of milestones must be attained; fifteen sample milestones are presented in Table 3. The exact number of milestones and the order in which they are achieved may vary from facility to facility. This transition should have a lot of built-in flexibility; however, in the author's experience, each of the milestones presented must be addressed in some manner in order to achieve pollution prevention status.

### Table 3
### Fifteen Milestones to Pollution Prevention

1. Promulgation of Management Initiatives
2. Assembling the Pollution Prevention Implementation Teams
3. Select the Pollution Prevention Program Elements
4. Determine How Pollution Prevention Will Be Measured
5. Establish a Solid Economic Base
6. Prepare Process Flow Diagrams and Materials Balances
7. Establish a Materials Tracking System
8. Provide for Technology Transfer
9. Set Specific Pollution Prevention Goals
10. Verify the Process Flow Diagrams and Materials Balances
11. Establish Pollution Prevention Teams at the Worker Level
12. Provide Engineering and R&D support
13. Implement Pollution Prevention Options
14. Give Recognition to Those Involved
15. Do It Over Again

## Promulgation of Management Initiatives

The company should prepare a pollution prevention policy which articulates management's commitment to implementing the planned activities and achieving established goals. This policy statement should be signed by the highest-ranking operational manager at each facility. By having facility management which is personally committed to participating in the program, the level of visibility and the assurance of everyone's cooperation are essentially guaranteed. In the end, the acid test of strong management support for pollution prevention must be reflected by timely integration of the policy and program considerations into the facility's decision-making process. Unfortunately, reluctance among facility managers to change past practices is often the first barrier to overcome. Often, documenting and quantifying potential environmental vulnerabilities and their related costs (as well as what environmental releases have cost similar companies or what other companies have profited by pollution prevention) have helped to make top management more receptive. Clear articulation of the benefits of pollution prevention must be the subject of effective communication with the management. This support is very important in determining where a facility will fit into the pollution prevention progression. Having minimal support from upper management, the program is limited to waste minimization and the use of good operating practices.

### Assembling the Pollution Prevention Implementation Team

Just as it takes a variety of professional skills to manage and operate a facility effectively, the same principle holds true in running a pollution prevention program. Department managers have the ultimate responsibility for performance in each of these skill areas (e.g., accounting, purchasing, scheduling, production, maintenance, legal, etc.). To the extent possible, the early participation of these people is very important. Members of the team must have the ability, commitment, authority and resources to get the program going. They must also possess or have ready access to the wide variety of experience required. At the proper management levels they can develop formal pollution prevention reporting relationships within the department and across the departmental lines. It is they and the people who work for them that make the program work. This team should select a leader to act as its spokesperson. To enhance the effectiveness of a high-level team, an outside person knowledgeable about pollution prevention may be brought in to facilitate the meetings. The facilitator role should incorporate the following characteristics:
- Is a neutral servant of the group
- Does not evaluate ideas
- Focuses energy of group on a common task
- Suggests alternative methods and ideas procedures
- Protects individuals and their ideas from attack
- Encourages everyone to participate
- Helps the group find win/win solutions
- Coordinates pre- and post-meeting logistics

Using an experienced facilitator can help accelerate progress in the pollution prevention progression.

### Select the Pollution Prevention Program Elements

These milestones represent the logical program elements in a pollution prevention effort; however, at this early stage it is important to determine the ordering of elements and the extent to which each one will be addressed at a given location. Each milestone represents a series of activities from barely responsive to exhaustive. At this time, the implementation team can determine where to start in each case. Special attention must be given to the following items: prioritizing target processes or wastes; framework for prioritizing waste reduction opportunities; structure of the feasibility study phase; implementation schedules and targets; monitoring, evaluation and documentation of the program; and the means for ensuring ongoing management and worker support. One technique that works quite well is to have a "menu" of program elements prepared by someone knowledgeable about pollution prevention which describes each element, the range of activities possible, the point at which an effort should be started, and the benefits provided by the element. From this menu, the team can structure a customized program for the facility or the company as a whole.

### Determine How Pollution Prevention Will Be Measured

There is an old saying, "If you don't want to win, why keep score?" Because "winning" is what pollution prevention is all about, there are innumerable ways to measure progress. Included are the following measurement categories: absolute, production normalized, throughput normalized, and economic. The selection of the measurement tool depends primarily on the manner in which the program results are to be aggregated at the corporate level. Formalizing the company's measurement system strengthens the verification and auditing functions and assures proper management. This also sets up the paper trail. By placing the results of measurements in highly visible charts, a company or facility firmly establishes the foundation of its entire pollution prevention program. Progress, when it occurs, can now be clearly shown to all who may be concerned; however, it is very important to have a well-documented base year to which progress will be compared.

### Establish a Solid Economic Base

In the past, environmental management has been treated simply as a "cost of doing business." These costs were often incorporated into the fundamental economic strategy of the firm. More competitive firms are now using pollution prevention to lower those costs without jeopardizing their compliance status. They are charging departments fully-loaded waste management costs, factoring in liability, compliance and oversight costs. There is even a cost associated with putting a pollution prevention program into place. A simple financial plan sets out the amount of money that is to be spent on the program during a fiscal year. A more comprehensive financial plan would detail the yearly funding requirements, the projected sources and uses of funding, and the expected savings from pollution prevention efforts. It would provide computational guidelines for the financial evaluation of pollution prevention projects and detail financial control mechanisms such as spending authorizations and limits. There are a variety of computerized financial models available which are specific to pollution prevention programs. Active participation of the comptroller in using this information is strongly advised.

### Prepare Process Flow Diagrams and Materials Balances

The best way to understand all processes which utilize chemicals is to prepare flow diagrams and materials balances. The procedure for accomplishing this milestone is described in Chapter XV. Information will have to be gathered from many places in the firm to complete this task; however, this is a good means to ensure that all the necessary data is located without using a "previsit" questionnaire which asks for everything. This procedure examines all the inputs and outputs to each process unit. Emissions and wastes are treated as losses. Utilizing the discipline of this approach, company personnel will better understand the workings of all of their processes.

### Establish a Materials Tracking System

Tracking systems for hazardous materials management can vary widely in scope. As a minimum, the system may track only hazardous wastes using a paper manifest system. Comprehensive systems track raw material usage, production, and wastes (i.e., losses) to all media. These systems can be computerized and integrated with the facility's accounting and inventory control systems. Comprehensive systems allow for backcharging of the costs of pollution control and waste treatment/disposal directly to the production units that produced the losses. Various system modules may be implemented in phases as the facility's program and data needs grow.

**Provide for Technology Transfer**

It is important that everyone involved in the pollution prevention effort be on constant watch for useful information. State and federal agencies are publishing a great deal of information on this topic. So, too, are the trade organizations. The literature is gaining in this developing, topical area. There are even computerized databases specializing in pollution prevention. Rarely will these information sources provide magic answers; however, opportunities for pollution prevention and some of the various options available to realize these opportunities will help the team move forward in the milestones below. Companies with multiple facilities may consider establishing an electronic mail network to share information internally and to enhance communication between the facilities regarding pollution prevention.

**Set Specific Pollution Prevention Goals**

These goals set forth the facility's expectations for the amount of waste reduction that is expected to be achieved. They should also specify a timetable for the achievement of these goals. Typically, a facility looks to accomplish goals on a two-year (short-term) and a five-year (long-term) basis. It is important that the goals be specific and capable of being achieved. Having the goals broken down into a quarterly reporting format enables management to review the accomplishments and disappointments of the waste reduction effort on a regular basis. During this review, the program leader can state the objectives for the next 90 days and how the implementation group intends to achieve them. This process also ensures frequent involvement from top management who participate in these reviews.

**Verification of Process Flow Diagrams
and Materials Balance**

With the process flow diagrams and materials balance, tracking system and goals in place, it is now time to actually visit the unit processes to verify the information and observe the process in operation and interview the operators. With a complete understanding of the unit from the visit, opportunities for pollution prevention can be clearly identified. This procedure is discussed in more detail in Chapter XV.

### Establish Pollution Prevention Teams at the Worker Level

Active employee involvement greatly increases the program's chances for success. Pollution prevention can be implemented within a "Quality Circle" activity. This passes ownership of the effort from the plant management to the employees. Working in this manner it is easier to take pollution prevention opportunities and test their ability to be implemented. The workers can "fine tune" many of the options to make them more successful yet. Some level of training will be required to implement this program. The tracking system, which should be in place by now, will help monitor the progress.

### Provide Engineering and R&D Support

Once an opportunity has been identified to substitute or eliminate a chemical or to change the production process, it is necessary that a proper feasibility study and pilot testing be conducted to make sure that this change is warranted in the pollution prevention program. Everyone wants to make certain that the reliability of the process or the quality of the product will not be changed. In smaller operations, outside assistance will be required. R&D can be utilized to develop new technologies and products that help solve the pollutant loss problems (e.g. cryogenic cooling coils around the top of a solvent dip tank to keep vapors contained). A pollution prevention design review should be built into all new process lines. A company should opt for manufacturing processes that have the least possible impact on the environment consistent with the pollution prevention program. R&D can assist in the selection of environmentally compatible and recyclable material in connection with the development and manufacture of the firm's products. Active involvement in the pollution prevention program will help this to happen.

### Implement Pollution Prevention Options

Many great ideas make it through the feasibility study and pilot tests only to fall flat during implementation. Milestones numbers 11 and 12 help better prepare the option for implementation; however, a proper implementation program must address each of the following items:
- Prequalification process for chemical and equipment suppliers;
- Preparation of detailed plans and specifications;

- Conducting a sound bidding process;
- Contracting;
- Construction management and shake-down oversight;
- Operation and maintenance training; and
- A program to document the results.

A strong engineering approach as embodied in these items will help ensure proper implementation. Outside process engineering support may be required if company personnel do not have the time available to dedicate to this very important task.

### Give Recognition to Those Involved

Award programs should be established to recognize those who meet the goals set by the facility or production unit, or individuals who perform outstanding acts. The prizes or awards need not be financial. Recognition is what is important. Designation as "employee of the month", a photograph in the annual report or company newsletter, a certificate with a letter to the personnel file--all these items provide genuine recognition of performance which will be appreciated by all those involved. Workers will continue to support the program whether or not they as individuals, participate in the awards. Recognition cannot be absent from a successful pollution prevention program.

### Do It Over Again

Pollution prevention takes time. It is a good idea to re-evaluate the program on an annual basis. In order to make pollution prevention a lasting part of the corporate culture, the management based team should prepare an annual report for upper management and revisit each of the milestones which need strengthening in the year to come. At all levels, improved performance must be encouraged. It is wise to have a comprehensive, consistent, and fair pollution prevention auditing program in place. Management can audit the program. Those involved in the program can undertake self audits; however, a third party audit by a qualified, outside pollution prevention professional should be sought. These auditing activities will provide objective performance data and generate meaningful information to allow those involved to foresee, identify, and resolve significant production issues and problems in a timely manner. Repetition of the 15 milestones makes the pollution prevention program perpetual. If pollution prevention isn't ingrained in the organization, it will never reap the benefits the program envisioned.

## Conducting the Assessment

An assessment is the process of evaluating the prospects for pollution prevention at the facility. In the early phases of the pollution prevention progression, a facility assessment is conducted like an environmental compliance audit. Because the focus is on minimizing the waste streams, a detailed understanding of the process is not likely. Waste reduction options are suggested based on the experience of the people involved in the assessment program and from what they are able to locate in the literature. If this experience involves the design of waste treatment devices, there is a natural tendency to utilize minimization simply to scale down the size of the pollution control or waste treatment option which may ultimately be recommended. One of the greatest risks faced by an environmental engineer involved in this assessment is that a means may be found to eliminate a waste stream for which a pollution control device has been recently designed. Also, in this early phase, many of the options selected involve drying, concentrating, or separation without in-process reuse.

Toxics use reduction legislation at the state level is an attempt to move the assessment away from a focus on the wastes. Instead, the focus is shifted to the toxic materials utilized by the facility with specific attention paid to the process utilizing these regulated materials. A toxics use reduction program would not be much better than a waste minimization program if it were limited to minimizing process inputs without an eye towards how the process operates. In this manner, it is possible to consider substitutes for various inputs or to eliminate certain hazardous materials (e.g. cleaners) altogether.

It is important to move past the concept of tracking wastes and emissions or using environmental compliance audit questionnaires when implementing a pollution prevention program. Begin to think of the process flow diagrams and materials balances as an accounting system upon which the production operations are based. Using these systems provides a logical means for conducting an assessment without the often superficial means described above. Think of this practice as being subject to independent audit. More details of this concept may be found in Chapter XV.

## Conclusion and Future Trends

Any industrial facility is a complex entity requiring a number of individual skills to ensure proper operations (i.e. management, financial, marketing, purchasing, scheduling, labor, etc.). Implementing pollution prevention practices is every bit as complex. It takes the same sense of teamwork to make it happen.

An outside consultant can "facilitate" the process; however, there must be a strong effort from within the firm. Pollution prevention ethic must be incorporated into every activity conducted at the facility. Each activity must be scrutinized as follows:

- How does it contribute to the process flow and materials balance?
- How can it be modified to improve the process flow and materials balance?
- How can new information be found to further improve the process flow and materials balance?

Working on these issues with an internal and integrated team takes advantage of the synergies and individual skills that the team brings to the effort. It is teamwork which is essential to the success of the pollution prevention program.

It is necessary to get the facility management, and therefore mid- and lower management, to consider pollution prevention as a leading part of the operation. Then, they must explain what pollution prevention is all about so that anyone can understand it and enthusiastically support it. After all, why should the facility sacrifice resources to remove pollutants from process emissions when it may be possible to prevent these pollutants from being emitted in the first place?

Unfortunately shareholders are often more interested in short-term profitability than in long-term sustainability. Also, sporadic government enforcement efforts and the highly unpredictable nature of environmental accidents do not compel management to focus available resources on a program perceived to be intangible and not immediately pressing.

Pollution prevention is not hard to do — it is just hard to sell to management. It asks them to commit money this year to prevent future pollution. A training program that costs money now may produce benefits in the future.

Fortunately, many managers now have had the experience of seeing that their investment was a wise one and are spreading the word.

A facility can expect many specific benefits from a well-planned and executed pollution prevention effort, especially when coupled with other plant programs. These benefits may include:

- Reduced costs — pollution control facilities that did not have to be built;
- Reduced operating costs — existing pollution control facilities;
- Reduced manufacturing costs — improving product yields and process efficiencies;
- Retained sales of products that might otherwise have been taken off the market because of environmental problems;
- Income or savings derived through the sale or reuse of wastes;
- Reducing or eliminating inventories and spills;
- Reduced exposure to future liability costs;
- Increased environmental awareness by plant personnel and management;
- Reduced environmental compliance costs; and
- Enhanced corporate image and enhanced competitiveness.

These benefits should appear attractive to any firm. By following the guidelines presented in this chapter all these benefits should be realized.

## About the Author

**Robert B. Pojasek, Ph.D.**, is a Vice President at Geraghty & Miller, Inc. From his office in Andover, Mr. Pojasek directs the pollution prevention engineering efforts in the company's 42 regional offices. He is a member of the American Institute for Pollution Prevention and is a nationally recognized expert in the field. His office is located at One Corporate Drive, Andover, Massachusetts, (508) 794-9470.

## Endnotes

1.  U.S. Congress, Office of Technology Assessment. *From Pollution to Prevention,* OTA-ITE-347, U.S. Government Printing Office, Washington, D.C., June, 1987.

2.  U.S. Environmental Protection Agency. *Report to Congress: Minimization of Hazardous Waste,* EPA 530-SW-033, Office of Solid Waste and Emergency Response, Washington, D.C., October, 1986.

3.  U.S. Congress, Office of Technology Assessment. *Serious Reduction of Hazardous Waste,* OTA-ITE-317, U.S. Government Printing Office, Washington, D.C., September, 1986.

4.  Hunt, Christopher B. and Ellen R. Auster. "Proactive Environmental Management," *Sloan Management Review,* 31(2), Article No. 7, Winter, 1990.

5.  Crosby, Philip B. *Quality is Free,* Mentor Books, New York, NY, 1979.

6.  *Id., supra* at 3.

7.  U.S. Environmental Protection Agency in 50 *Fed. Reg.,* 28729 (July 15, 1985).

8.  U.S. Environmental Protection Agency in 54 *Fed. Reg.,* 25056 (June 12, 1989).

9.  U.S. Environmental Protection Agency in 54 *Fed. Reg.,* 3845 (January 26, 1989).

10.  *Id., supra* at 8.

# XX Improving Performance — The Chemical Industry's Approach to Pollution Prevention

*Ann M. Mason, Associate Director*
*Waste and Release Reduction*
*Chemical Manufacturers Association*
*Washington, D.C.*

This chapter describes the quiet revolution that the chemical industry is conducting within its own operations to improve its performance. First, it will describe the Responsible Care® Initiative* and the six Key Elements. Second, it will present a summary of the implementing activities approved as of July 1990. Third, it will detail efforts intended to reduce the impact of industry's operations on employees and the public — the pollution prevention and environmental areas.

Other industries may choose to examine the Responsible Care® Initiative and its implementing programs for use as a framework for improving the performance of their industry or facility operations. CMA welcomes discussions with improvement-oriented companies and industries and extends an invitation to join CMA as Responsible Care® Partners.

## Responsible Care® — A Framework for Improved Performance

Since the chemical release in Bhopal, India, in 1985, the chemical industry has reexamined its operations and intensified its efforts to improve its overall performance. Between 1986 and 1989, many voluntary programs were developed by the Chemical Manufacturers Association (CMA) using CMA's consensus-building process.

---

* In 1988, the chemical industry launched an innovative new program to respond to public concerns. The program is called Responsible Care®.

In 1988, the U.S. chemical industry adopted many of the principles from a similar program the chemical industry launched in Canada in 1984. Within CMA the Responsible Care® program is an obligation of membership.

Under CMA's bold Responsible Care® Initiative, the chemical industry commits to improve performance in health, safety, and environmental protection and to support that promise with tangible actions. To fulfill this commitment, the chief executives of CMA's member companies designed a program with six Key Elements. Each of these elements addresses critical aspects of the Initiative to assure the success of Responsible Care®. The six elements are:

- Guiding Principles
- Obligation of Membership
- Codes of Management Practices
- Public Advisory Panel
- Self-Evaluation
- Executive Leadership Groups.

### Guiding Principles — Obligation of Membership

To ensure a sound cornerstone for Responsible Care®, CMA's chief executives developed and signed ten guiding principles that provide the framework for improving industry performance (Table 1). The executives affirmed the importance of operating in conformance with these Guiding Principles by amending the CMA By-laws to require companies to adhere to these principles **as an obligation of membership** in CMA. This condition makes the Responsible Care® Initiative unique. In a sense, these ten guiding principles establish a contract between the public and CMA member companies as the basic framework for operating in the U.S. Companies who fail to operate in accordance with this commitment will be expelled from CMA by their industry peers.

### Codes of Management Practices

Codes of Management Practices are the framework for industry to implement the Guiding Principles. They delineate proper and acceptable practices in specific areas of industry operation that are intended to improve performance in health, safety, and the environment.

Guiding Principles for

# RESPONSIBLE CARE

## A Public Commitment

As a member of the Chemical Manufacturers
Association, this company is committed to
support a continuing effort to improve the
industry's responsible management of
chemicals. We pledge to manage our
business according to these principles:

■ **To recognize and respond to community concerns about chemicals and our operations.**

■ **To develop and produce chemicals that can be manufactured, transported, used and disposed of safely.**

■ **To make health, safety and environmental considerations a priority in our planning for all existing and new products and processes.**

■ **To report promptly to officials, employees, customers and the public, information on chemical-related health or environmental hazards and to recommend protective measures.**

■ **To counsel customers on the safe use, transportation and disposal of chemical products.**

■ **To operate our plants and facilities in a manner that protects the environment and the health and safety of our employees and the public.**

■ **To extend knowledge by conducting or supporting research on the health, safety and environmental effects of our products, processes and waste materials.**

■ **To work with others to resolve problems created by past handling and disposal of hazardous substances.**

■ **To participate with government and others in creating responsible laws, regulations and standards to safeguard the community, workplace and environment.**

■ **To promote the principles and practices of Responsible Care by sharing experiences and offering assistance to others who produce, handle, use, transport or dispose of chemicals.**

CHEMICAL
MANUFACTURERS
ASSOCIATION

Currently, CMA's Responsible Care® Initiative includes plans for five Codes of Management Practices that implement the Guiding Principles. Each code covers a specific aspect of industry's operations and provides specific implementing guidance. As of July 31, 1990, the CMA Board of Directors approved two Codes. Industry groups are developing the remaining codes.

*Status of the Codes of Management Practices*

Community Awareness and Emergency Response (CAER) — approved January, 1990.

Waste Reduction and Management:
1. Waste and Release Reduction — approved April 1990.
2. Waste Management — under development.

Safe Plant Operations:
1. Process Safety — approval third quarter 1990.
2. Worker Health and Safety — under development.

Distribution — approval third quarter 1990.

Product Stewardship — under development.

**Public Advisory Panel**

In CMA's Responsible Care® program, the public defines the term *responsible*. CMA asked a third party to assemble an independent, diverse group of public opinion leaders to share the public viewpoint with CMA. The identity of the Panel members is anonymous, although individual panel members may choose to reveal his/her involvement in shaping the Responsible Care® Initiative. The panel consists of independent thought leaders from across the United States and includes a doctor, a farmer, an ethicist, a futurist, an environmental leader, and a League of Women Voters leader.

Through the Public Advisory Panel, the public is directly involved in developing practice codes. The Panel provides a key role in reviewing, commenting, and shaping all of the implementing programs outlined in the Codes of Management Practices. The Public Advisory Panel reviews the concepts in each Code during the drafting phase and provides guidance about whether the Code adequately addresses public concerns.

## Member Self-Evaluation

Inherent in any program is the need to measure and track implementation progress. Responsible Care® requires that each company submit an annual progress report for each Code through the Code's Self-Evaluation Form.

Currently, the Code Self-Evaluation Form has six implementation stages:

| | |
|---|---|
| Stage I | No Action |
| Stage II | Evaluating company practices against Code practice. |
| Stage III | Developing action plan to implement Code practice. |
| Stage IV | Implementing action plan. |
| Stage V | Code management practice in place. |
| Stage VI | Implementation reviewed and reaffirmed this year. |

CMA members designed the Self-Evaluation Form as an internal management tool to track progress, both within each company and as an industry. As companies implement the Codes of Management Practices, the CMA steering committee for Responsible Care® will evaluate the effectiveness of this reporting mechanism and modify it as needed. The ultimate measure will be improvement in industry performance in both real and perceptive terms.

## Executive Leadership Groups

Member company chief executives recognized that they must provide top level commitment to ensure the success of CMA's Responsible Care® Initiative. They developed ten regional Executive Leadership Groups to provide a mechanism for mutual assistance between companies, problem identification and solution, and code review. The Chairperson of each Executive Leadership Group is a present or past member of the CMA Board of Directors.

Using regional meetings, top company executives meet with their peers to discuss corporate-wide Responsible Care® implementation activities.    Through the Executive Leadership Groups, the CMA Board of Directors has a mechanism to monitor continued company commitment to the Responsible Care® Initiative and to review industry's progress toward improved performance.

# The Codes Of Management Practices —
# Steps To Improve Industry Operations

To date, CMA members have approved two Codes of Management Practices:   Community Awareness and Emergency Response (CAER) and Waste and Release Reduction.

### Community Awareness and Emergency Response — Planning, Preventing, Communicating and Responding.

The CAER Code provides the framework for the outreach and communication activities for all of the other Codes.   The key concepts in the CAER Code, communicating, planning, preventing, and responding, were established as a voluntary CAER Program activity in 1985.   Building on existing company programs, the voluntary CAER program provided an industry-wide mechanism to incorporate facility emergency response plans with those of the community and to improve industry responses to emergencies when they occur.

Under the Responsible Care® Initiative, the CAER Code embodies two sets of Management Practices.   One set relates to companies initiating and maintaining a community outreach program.   The goals of community outreach include establishing open communications with the community and responding to public concerns.

The second set of Management Practices in the CAER Code requires companies to establish an emergency response program and to respond rapidly and effectively to emergencies.

To date, over 1,400 facilities have been actively involved in implementing the CAER program.   Many companies have incorporated CAER activities into their world-wide operations.   Under the Responsible Care® Initiative, more companies and facilities will join the ranks of those already participating in the CAER network.

Because listening to and talking with the public are key features of the Responsible Care® Initiative, the CAER outreach efforts are critical to its success. Company CAER Coordinators face added challenges and new opportunities for communication as they open dialogues with the public relating to the other Codes under Responsible Care®.

## Waste and Release Reduction — Building on Ongoing Efforts.

The Waste and Release Reduction Code builds on, expands, and consolidates four existing CMA programs: Waste Minimization, Air Quality, SARA Title III Reporting, and Chemical and Release Reduction.

**Waste Minimization.** CMA's Waste Minimization Program, established in 1986, had four program elements: industry support (workshops, resource manuals); communications; measurement and tracking; and advocacy and outreach.

**Air Quality.** CMA's Air Quality Control Policy of 1986, covered both process emissions and accidental releases. For process emissions, the policy encouraged companies to implement four steps:
1. Develop an inventory of existing emissions of toxic air pollutants;
2. Assess the impact of these emissions on employees and the surrounding community and determine the adequacy of the current control technology;
3. Reduce these emissions as needed to safeguard employees, public health, and the environment;
4. Communicate the results of these actions to appropriate community representatives and governmental agencies.

**SARA Title III Activities.** CMA's Title III program is designed to help assure industry-wide compliance, strengthen outreach activities with the communities, and make Title III work at the local level. CMA instituted a massive education and awareness campaign through newsletters, meetings, seminars, booklets, and video-taped materials.

**Chemical Release Reduction Policy.** Designed for local implementation, CMA established the Chemical Release Reduction Policy in 1989. The goal of the policy included extending reduction efforts to all environmental media and striving for long term continuous improvement in making reductions. Four broad elements included:

1. Inventory releases to all environmental media starting with the pollutants listed in SARA Title III, Section 313. Members were encouraged to include other chemicals in their inventories, as appropriate.
2. Establish reduction priorities for the inventoried releases based upon factors such as their potential health and environmental impact and the level of community concern.
3. Develop a release reduction plan based on the reduction priorities developed in the previous step. While reductions may be achieved by many methods, preference is given to making the reductions using the following order: source reduction, recycle/reuse, and treatment.
4. Communicate release reduction progress and future plans to employees and the public.

### Waste and Release Reduction — Charting New Directions under Responsible Care®

The Waste and Release Reduction Code forms one part of a two-part Code designed to improve industry efforts for environmental protection. This code combines and expands upon the four previously described programs. One important expansion is that implementation of the Code is an obligation of CMA membership.

This first part, the Waste and Release Reduction Code, moves beyond existing industry programs by setting two far-reaching goals:

1. Ongoing, long-term reductions in the amount of all contaminants and pollutants released to the air, water, and land.
2. Ongoing reductions in the amount of wastes generated at facilities.

An important aspect of this Code is the definition of the term *waste*. Based upon input from the Public Advisory Panel, CMA adopted a broad definition for waste.

*Waste — Any gas, liquid, or solid residual material at a facility, whether hazardous or non hazardous, that is not used further in the production of a commercial product or provision of a service and which itself is not a commercial product.*

The second part of the Code is under development and will address management of the remaining materials left after implementation of the Waste and Release Reduction Code, company wastes handled by contractors, and remediation of sites.

CMA member companies recognize that achieving ongoing, long-term reductions requires the commitment and expenditure of substantial human and financial resources. By adopting the Waste and Release Reduction Code, companies are charting a new course toward source reduction.

**Waste and Release Reduction —
Providing a Framework for Progress.**

The Waste and Release Reduction Code contains ten management practices that provide a framework for reducing waste generation and releases.

Practice 1 — Commit the Organization.
*A clear commitment by senior management through policy, communications, and resources, to ongoing reductions at each of the company's facilities, in releases to the air, water, and land and in the generation of wastes.*

Management commitment forms the foundation for the entire Responsible Care® Initiative and its reduction program. Company implementation will range from an informal verbal company policy to well established written policy. Each company and/or facility must determine the best way to achieve the fundamental change in corporate culture and attitude required by the Responsible Care® Initiative and its related Codes.

Practice 2 — Inventory Wastes and Releases.
*A quantitative inventory at each facility of wastes generated and releases to the air, water, and land, measured or estimated at the point of generation or release.*

Establishing an inventory is essential to identifying and understanding what reduction opportunities exist. Many companies in CMA are covered by the release reporting requirements of the Emergency Planning and Community Right-to-Know Act of 1986, also called SARA Title III. Most of these companies will use these inventories as the foundation for the inventory required by the Code. The Code encourages facilities to evaluate their inventories and expand them to cover all substances and wastes.

CMA, EPA, and others offer resource materials to estimate or measure releases and wastes. Two areas in which CMA expended considerable effort include measuring equipment leaks (fugitive emissions) and estimating releases from ponds and spill areas (secondary emissions). Guidance documents are available for each of these release types. In addition, CMA experts developed a software package to capture the fugitive data (POSSE) and developed a series of models for estimating secondary emissions (PAVE).

Practice 3 — Evaluate Potential Impacts.
*Evaluation, sufficient to assist in establishing reduction priorities, of the potential impact of releases on the environment and the health and safety of employees and the public.*

Under this practice, facilities must evaluate the potential impact of the wastes generated and releases on employees and the public. Many facilities may expand to the public the occupational health evaluations conducted for employee protection. Some facilities may choose to conduct testing in communities using either a short-term survey or long-term monitoring. Some facilities may choose to use modelling to estimate the impact of the facility on employees and the public. Ultimately, the concerns of employees and public will determine the type of evaluation.

Practice 4 — Educate and Listen to Employees and the Public.
*Education of, and dialogue with, employees and members of the Public about the inventory, impact evaluation, and risks to the community.*

Using the outreach mechanism established in the Community Awareness part of the CAER Code, companies must seek the input of employees and the public. Listening to concerns is the key concept in this practice. Gaining input from employees and the public is the goal. Inherent in this practice is an educational process so that employees and the public can understand the technical terms and concepts used to describe plant operations, the inventory, the impact evaluation, and the risks.

Companies that have established an outreach mechanism under the CAER Code and companies that have engaged the public in conversations about the SARA Title III releases know that establishing these public contacts are important. Sometimes both facilities and the public find establishing open communication mechanisms a daunting and challenging opportunity.

There is no best way to establish an outreach mechanism. CMA offers many written resources and a support network for facilities.

Practice 5 — Establish a Reduction Plan, Goal, and Priorities.
*Establishment of priorities, goals and plans for waste and release reduction, taking into account both community concerns and the potential health, safety, and environmental impacts as determined under Practices 3 and 4.*

Only after developing the inventory, performing the evaluation, and listening to the employees and public should a facility develop a reduction plan. When the company executives included this practice in the Code, they recognized the importance of incorporating the results of practices 2, 3, and 4 into developing the facility reduction plan.

Each company and facility is beginning the implementation of the Waste and Release Reduction Code at a different point because many companies and facilities have implemented reduction projects for a long time. In fact, some companies instituted a formal corporate or facility reduction program over ten years ago. Therefore, each company and/or facility must identify its own reduction opportunities, identify the concerns of its own public, determine the reduction priorities and goals, and develop and implement its own reduction plan.

Practice 6 — Implement the Reduction Plan.
*Ongoing reduction of wastes and releases, giving preference first to source reduction, second to recycle/reuse, and third to treatment. These techniques may be used separately or in combination with one another.*

The U.S. Environmental Protection Agency has endorsed the hierarchy: source reduction, recycle/reuse, and treatment.

Under the Waste and Release Reduction Code, each waste and release source must be evaluated for its reduction potential. This evaluation will reveal the priorities for reduction. Once identified, the

**Improving Performance — The Chemical Industry's Approach to Pollution Prevention**

hierarchy requires that facilities preferentially try to implement reduction projects for source reduction before recycle/reuse or treatment.

Each company must identify its own reduction priorities and implement a reduction plan to meet company/facility-set goals. Technical infeasibility is only one of several facility and/or waste specific criteria that can lead to selection of a reduction project involving recycle/reuse or treatment. When developing their reduction priorities, companies/facilities may choose to consider other criteria including: risk/benefit mechanisms; public concern; size of the facility; economics; and other factors such as conservation of resources.

Practice 7 — Measure Progress.
*Measurement of progress at each facility in reducing the generation of wastes and in reducing releases to the air, water, and land, by updating the quantitative inventory at least annually.*

Tracking and measuring progress are important features of the Waste and Release Reduction Code. Facilities must have some mechanism to measure progress against the facility's reduction plan and its goal. Inherent in the Waste and Release Reduction Code is the understanding that facilities will discuss general reduction techniques and assumptions as part of the public education and dialogue process.

Practice 8 — Communicate Progress.
*Ongoing dialogue with employees and members of the public regarding waste and release information, progress in achieving reductions, and future plans. This dialogue should be at a personal, face-to-face level, where possible, and should emphasize listening to others and discussing their concerns and ideas.*

Practice 8 provides the feedback loop to employees and the public. Using the outreach mechanism established in the Community Awareness part of the CAER Code, facilities communicate actions and progress toward resolving concerns that were identified in Practice 4. CMA emphasizes listening to employees and the public.

Practice 9 — Integrate Reduction Concepts in Planning.
*Inclusion of waste and release prevention objectives in research and in design of new or modified facilities, processes, and products.*

Incorporating reduction concepts into the business planning process will aid progress toward source reduction. Business units considering new products, expansions, major modifications, or process retrofit are good candidates for source reduction. Hence, it is essential that those concerned with planning these activities know about the corporate reduction objectives.

Practice 10 — Outreach.
*An ongoing program for promotion and support of waste and release reduction by others.*

Under this practice, companies have some flexibility in the types of activities they choose to conduct. Some examples of activities that represent industry outreach include:

a. Sharing of technical information and experience with customers and suppliers;

b. Supporting efforts to develop improved waste and release reduction techniques;

c. Assisting in establishment of regional air monitoring networks;

d. Participating in efforts to develop consensus approaches to the evaluation of environmental, health, and safety impacts of releases;

e. Providing educational workshops and training materials;

f. Assisting local governments and others in establishment of waste reduction programs benefitting the general public.

## Measuring Industry-Wide Progress

As part of the Waste and Release Reduction Code, companies are required to send three reports to CMA or its designated agent:

1. Self-Evaluation Form.

   Each year companies must send a report that identifies the number of facilities in each of the six implementation stages. CMA will compile these data to determine industry-wide progress.

## Improving Performance — The Chemical Industry's Approach to Pollution Prevention

2. Release Trend Data.

   Each year companies must send CMA release data based upon the Toxic Release Inventory that most members submit to the Environmental Protection Agency under the SARA Title III requirements.

3. Waste Data.

   Each year since 1981, CMA has collected data on waste generation from members on a voluntary basis. Beginning with the 1990 reporting year, members are required to complete the waste survey.

# Implementing Opportunities For Waste and Release Reduction

Many challenges face the chemical industry as it travels down the implementation pathway. Some, quite frankly, arise from within the industry; many arise from outside the industry. This section presents a few of the challenges we expect.

### Changing the Corporate Culture

Responsible Care® represents a major shift in the way the chemical industry historically approached its business. Now, manufacturing a product and making profits, while still important, must be incorporated with being a good neighbor. For some companies this represents a change in corporate perspective. For other companies this represents only a minor adjustment of existing corporate policies.

The top executives are committed to this change. They are willing to face their employees, the public, and the stockholders in defense of improved industry performance.

### Challenging Industry Employees to Own the Program

Success of the Waste and Release Reduction Code relies upon all employees of the chemical industry — manufacturers, researchers, planners, and association staff — to adopt a waste and release reduction attitude as we work. Most reduction projects spring from simple, every day actions, for example, turning off the continuous flow of water, recycling paper and plastics, running the production process at more optimal conditions, and performing preventative maintenance. While it is true that some projects will cost millions of dollars, employees can make important contributions to the reduction effort.

Education, clear goals, and motivation are all concepts that are easier to discuss than to achieve. The Environmental Protection Agency has a slogan, "Think Globally, Act Locally." For success in the Waste and Release Reduction Code, all employees must adopt the basic reduction concepts.

### Challenging Regulators to Allow Source Reduction

In today's regulatory climate, the technology, command and control approach exists. Permit writers generally find that it is easier to use a technology based approach than the alternative — a performance based approach. Reviewing a permit application, already a cumbersome and time-consuming task for all concerned, is easier when the prescribed control technology is used on the end of the pipe. Applicants who propose source reduction strategies report that the entire permit process either stops or slows to a snail's pace.

Failure to obtain a permit(s) in a timely manner causes serious problems including the possibility of stopping production in one or more sections of a facility. If a facility needs a permit to operate and a permit is impossible to obtain when a source reduction project is proposed, facilities are less willing to propose source reduction projects. Such permit impediments hinder source reduction projects. Regulators interested in promoting source reduction projects can help motivate industry by closely examining the entire permitting process and removing unnecessary barriers where they exist.

### Everyone Benefits from Early Reductions

The chemical industry firmly believes that early reductions benefit society, respond to public concerns, and reduce the opportunity for exposure to pollutants.

Figure 1 shows the cumulative benefits of early reductions for a source that releases 50 tons of pollutants per year. This means that over eight years this source will release the cumulative total of 400 tons. In this example, the 50 ton facility voluntarily implemented some waste and release reduction projects that reduced their releases by 80 percent (40 tons). This reduction means that, after the implementation of the reduction projects, the facility will release 10 tons to the environment. Over the same 8 year period, the facility will release the cumulative total of 80 tons (instead of 400 tons). The net result is that through early implementation of reduction projects the facility did not release 320 tons of pollutants. The environment and the public benefits.

Now suppose that at year 8, the facility is required to comply with a regulation that requires a 90 percent reduction on top of its existing release levels. (90 percent of 50 tons allows the facility to release five tons.) If the facility waited until year 8 to implement reduction projects, the opportunity to eliminate 320 tons would have been missed. But this is exactly what would have resulted if the regulators had required a technology-based approach rather than grant a permit based on performance based standards and source reduction.

### Creating Expansion Opportunities
### In a Reduction-Oriented Climate

Generally, as facilities reduce, their permits are rewritten to reflect the reductions — tighter permit limits.

To illustrate the significance of the tighter permit, consider two identical facilities, A and B, releasing 100 tons per year (Figure 2). These facilities are competitors. Facility A reduces releases 80 percent and is given a new permit (of 20 tons) that reflects the early reductions. Facility B reduces nothing and continues to release 100 tons per year. Production levels at the two facilities remain the same. Now, to compete in the world market, both facilities A and B want to increase production. Both facilities propose to use the same process modification and achieve the same production level. Facility A applies for a process modification asking for a slight increase in the level of permitted releases (assume an increase of 5 percent or 1 ton per year) to accommodate the expansion. Facility B applies for a process modification declaring a net reduction in emissions of 75 percent (25 tons). Who gets the permit?

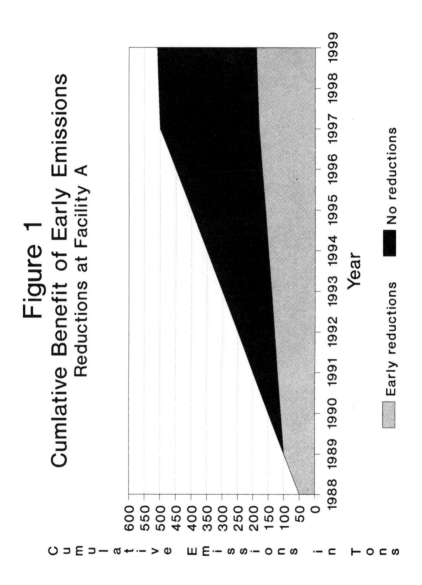

Figure 1
Cumlative Benefit of Early Emissions
Reductions at Facility A

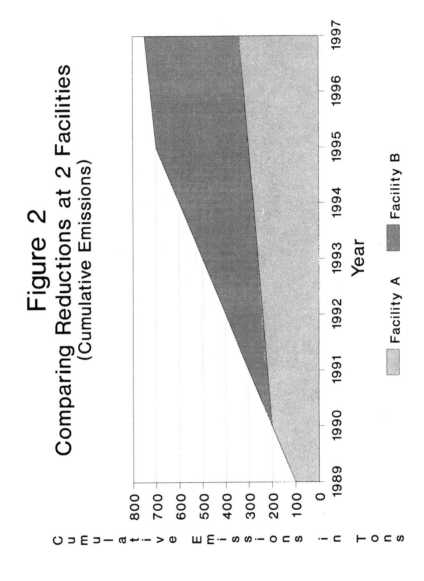

Figure 2
Comparing Reductions at 2 Facilities
(Cumulative Emissions)

If regulators and society in general reward the do-nothing facility and penalize the reduction-oriented facility, they are sending industry and society the WRONG message — It is OK to pollute. When companies that aggressively search for ways to reduce releases are thwarted from competing in the world market because they cannot expand production due to a tightened permit, the permit becomes a disincentive for voluntary reductions.

Regulators who are trying to create incentives for facilities to use source reductions or to go beyond the required control technologies must recognize that the existing system creates some disincentives.

## Future Trends

In this chapter, we provided an overview of the Responsible Care® Initiative and described the Waste and Release Reduction Code of Management Practices. We also previewed some of the implementation challenges that industry, regulators, and the public must address.

Under Responsible Care® the chemical industry embraces the goal of long-term reductions in the amounts of wastes generated and compounds released to the environment. Alone, industry can not achieve this goal. We must have assistance. Regulators must address some of the disincentives for early, voluntary reductions. In fact, industry, already committed to reductions, will respond eagerly to regulatory and legislative incentives. Similarly, a critical part of the program is listening to our employees and to the public. The public is invited to share their concerns with us.

Under Responsible Care® the chemical industry commits to an entire cultural change and a realignment of priorities. In implementing the initiative, we don't claim to be responsible; rather we expect to be held responsible for our performance. It will take a lot of time, money, and hard work. As we move down this road, we invite others to pick up the challenge and join us.

## About the Author

**Ann M. Mason,** Associate Director, Chemical Manufacturers Association, manages CMA's Waste and Release Reduction and Management Program — an industry effort to encourage companies to implement waste and release reduction programs. Over the last 18 years, Ms. Mason has acquired wide experience in environmental management in air, water, groundwater, wastewater treatment, spill response and cleanup, contract management, and consensus building.

#  XXI    Risk Communications Issues

*Robert E. O'Connor, Ph.D.*
*University of Pennsylvania*
*University Park, Pennsylvania*

Risk communication is an interactive process of exchanging information and opinion about the nature of risk, about risk messages, or about the arrangements for risk management.[1] Effective risk communication is a key component of any risk management program. Poor risk communication contributes to unwarranted tension between communities and industry.[2] The consequences include greater difficulty in licensing, permitting and siting, and more lawsuits.

Other chapters of this desk reference detail industry efforts to demonstrate its commitment to good risk management practices (e.g., the CMA's Responsible Care® Program) and to thorough preparations for potential, if highly unlikely, environmental emergencies. These risk communication efforts are in part responses to the difficult social and political situation for environmental risk management.

This chapter provides:
- An overview of risk communication in today's difficult regulatory climate;
- An examination of the qualitative factors that affect community sentiment;
- Guidelines for developing and implementing an effective risk communication program; and
- A look at emerging trends in environmental risk communication.

## Overview: Risk Communication in a Hostile World

The 1990s are a difficult environment for risk communicators due to heightened concern with health and safety risks from technology, and to lack of trust in institutional managers. Despite real advances in health and safety, the American people are more concerned than ever before about their health.[3] As millions of Americans have attained economic security, they have become more concerned with technological threats to the environment and to their personal security.[4] As people worry less about feeding their families, they worry more about risks from the local chemical company. The fact that the chemical company is operating more safely than ever before does not change their heightened concern about health and safety risks.

A generation ago "chemicals" symbolized progress and a better quality of life for all. Now many people overestimate risks from chemicals and prefer to live away from industries.[5] A similar, but even greater, over estimation of risk exists when nuclear facilities are involved.[6] Quality of life for many means bucolic images, not proximity to facilities that use or manufacture hazardous materials. In the 1990s, nuclear power plants are not perceived as the safe, clean, non-polluting energy source that their proponents envision, but as a threat to the quality of life of everyone in their vicinity.

If the heightened concern with health were accompanied by great trust in institutions that manage technologies perceived as risky, the climate for risk communication still could be friendly. If people worry about their health and view chemicals as extremely hazardous, they may still have little problem with living near a large facility if they trust management to do its job well.

Unfortunately for risk managers, since the mid-1960s trust in every major American institution, including the chemical industry, has fallen.[7] For example, in 1966, 55 percent of adults had a great deal of confidence in business leaders; by 1986, only 16 percent rated business leaders highly.[8]

The government fared no better. By 1986 the "great deal of confidence" figure for the executive branch of the federal government was 18 percent; for Congress, 21 percent; for the leaders of state government, 19 percent; and for local government leaders, 21 percent. Large majorities have only some confidence or hardly any confidence at all in the leadership of American institutions. These figures suggest that Americans are skeptical both toward the claims of businesses that they will handle their complex and dangerous technologies responsibly and toward the statements of government bureaucrats that they can be trusted to protect the interests of the public. With such widespread distrust, it is not surprising that many citizens say they do not want industries that utilize technologies perceived as risky coming into their communities.

Governments responded to popular concerns by requiring industry to operate in a more open fashion and by mandating public involvement in the following:
- EPCRA emergency planning requirements;
- EPCRA right-to-know requirements;
- RCRA and CERCLA public participation requirements; and
- State and local right-to-know laws.

The Emergency Planning and Community Right-to-Know Act (EPCRA) passed in 1986 as part of the Superfund Amendments and Reauthorization Act (SARA). EPCRA requires chemical manufacturers to develop emergency plans with nearby communities and to inform workers and the public about chemical risks at the facility. Many state and local laws have imposed more extensive reporting requirements. Regarding hazardous waste, federal laws (Resource Conservation and Recovery Act, or RCRA, and the Comprehensive Environmental Response, Compensation and Liability Act, or CERCLA, better known as Superfund) and their amendments, require public hearings before new permitted hazardous waste (i.e., treatment) facilities can be sited and before cleanup plans can be implemented. Again, state laws have often expanded the rights of citizens to participate in what used to be private decisions by chemical companies.

Concerns about accidents have generated two other responses:
- APELL, a United Nations Handbook for developing a process for responding to technological accidents, and
- CAER, the Chemical Manufacturers Association's (CMA) initiative to improve community/industry emergency response efforts.

Awareness and Preparedness of Emergencies at Local Level (APELL) is a 1988 document from the United Nations Environment Programme (*sic*). The intention is to encourage a partnership among national authorities, industry, local authorities, and other leaders of the community to identify potential accidents and plan responses. Community Awareness and Emergency Response (CAER) began in 1985 as a voluntary program to encourage its members to develop emergency response plans with community leaders. In 1989 the CMA formally adopted the CAER code, obligating its members to work with communities to plan for emergencies. CAER commits the industry to a risk communications program, but cannot ensure that the effort will be successful.

The 1990s provide a difficult climate for risk communication activities. The emergency preparedness programs and laws mandating public involvement in formerly private decisions reflect public concerns. The public views many technologies as dangerous and has great trust in neither the industry nor government regulators. The "Not In My Back Yard" (NIMBY) response is rife. Nevertheless, not every risk communication situation involves community outrage, and there have been many successful risk communication programs.[9]

## Explaining Community Outrage

Some risk communication situations are more difficult than others, usually for reasons having little to do with the actual degree of risk at a site. Outrage factors also often are substantially beyond the control of risk communicators. When several of these factors are present, environmental risk managers face a great challenge.[10] Recognizing the factors that explain community outrage is necessary to design and implement an effective risk communication program.

The level of community concern and even outrage is by no means directly related to the actual risk associated with a facility. Although this fact may be frustrating to environmental risk managers, ignoring the factors that do influence public risk perceptions will not lead to effective risk communication. Refusing to recognize and respond to popular perceptions engenders hostility and makes successful risk communication unlikely.

*Involuntary* risks engender outrage while voluntary risks are more acceptable. Individuals who smoke may protest the opening of a nuclear power plant. Some of the smokers will dispute claims that smoking is an unhealthy habit. Others will agree that the risk to their health from smoking is greater than from living near the plant, but will argue that the comparison is irrelevant because they choose to smoke, but had no role in approving the licensing of the plant. Similarly, a community that is coerced into accepting a facility is likely both to become angry and to inflate their risk assessments. Anger and overestimation of risk increase as communities feel powerless in the face of big business and big government.

*Uncontrollable* risks are less acceptable than risks under a person's or community's control. Most people feel safer driving than riding as a passenger. People are more comfortable dealing with environmental risks if they have some personal way of observing or monitoring the risk than if they are totally dependent on government regulators.

Risks of *catastrophic potential* are less acceptable than those with deaths and injuries spread over time and space. The image of a facility exploding and killing thousands in a release of lethal gases is much more frightening than the image of a facility that creates a hazardous product that kills more people over a number of years. Environmental risk managers can demonstrate statistically that the second facility is much more dangerous than the first, but their arguments are unlikely to be convincing.

*Unfair* risks are less acceptable than fair ones. It is a question of equity, with justice defined as benefits commensurate with risks. An unfair risk involves perceptions that the benefits from the facility are going elsewhere — to out-of-town owners, stockholders, and users of the manufactured products — while the risks associated with the facility are borne locally.

*Dreaded* risks are less acceptable than others. A facility whose products are associated with cancer will be less acceptable than one with a worse record of potential fatalities from emphysema. Cancer is a dreaded disease; emphysema is not.

*Exotic* risks are less acceptable than familiar ones. People are less concerned with risks from their household cleansers than with minute releases of the same chemicals from a new, modern chemical research facility.

*People-created* risks are less acceptable than natural risks. Communities may become enraged at discovering high radon levels caused by mill tailings used in the construction of their homes; they are much less likely to demonstrate alarm when the high levels come from natural sources. At a public meeting, one risk communicator told people that they should not be upset at their industrially caused high radon levels because other people, with much higher naturally caused radon levels in their homes, were not worried. The audience became enraged.

Risks associated with *untrustworthy institutions* are less acceptable than are risks involving institutions with better reputations. Some companies and agencies are trusted more than others. Risks associated with institutions with poor reputations are less likely to win community support.

*Undetectable* risks are scarier than detectable ones. When the effects are long-term or the culprit invisible (e.g., radioactivity, odorless and colorless gases), the community is more likely to oppose a facility than when the risks are immediate and detectable.

Finally, risks viewed as *ethically objectionable* are less acceptable than those seen as emanating from constructive activities. To many people, chemical weapons are morally wrong. A community is likely to be more accepting of risks associated with a pharmaceutical company than with a chemical weapons facility.

The more of these outrage factors present in an environmental risk management situation, the greater the potential for strong public concern about the risk. This is not to say that communities ignore all scientific information, but that outrage factors combine with an understanding of scientific information to produce public opinion. Environmental risk managers too often focus so heavily on risk assessment data that they ignore outrage factors. Nevertheless, a review of risk communication experiences demonstrates successes as well as errors called horror stories. Several guidelines for developing effective risk communication programs can be drawn from the experiences of successful programs.

## Guidelines For An Effective Risk Communication Program

Effective risk communication depends upon adherence to six guidelines:

1) Identify goals, plan, and commit resources;
2) Recognize that communication is a two-way process;
3) Know your audience;
4) Be open, honest, frank, and compassionate;
5) Involve other credible sources; and
6) Work with the media to present your story.

These guidelines may seem to be both obvious and common sense, yet they are frequently violated in practice with unfortunate results. Adherence to the guidelines does not guarantee full community acceptance of industry positions. Adherence to these guidelines will increase the likelihood that the public will be informed, reasonable, collaborative, and oriented toward solutions.[11]

1. **Guideline: Identify Goals, Plan, Commit Resources**
   - **What do you want to achieve?**
   - **What can be accomplished by what date?**
   - **Who is the spokesperson?**
   - **Are the staff trained?**
   - **How is outstanding work rewarded?**
   - **Is the program working? Did you succeed?**

An effective risk communication program requires organizational commitment to that achievement. Every organization involved in technologies perceived as risky is engaged in a risk communication process, even if the company pays little attention to risk communications. For example, the failure to respond to a local official's request for information communicates a message to that official regardless of company intentions. The message is that the company either does not care about local opinion or is so incompetently organized that citizen inquiries are lost. Firms with a "let-sleeping-dogs-lie" attitude toward risk communications may save some overhead expenses immediately, but are likely to engender community outrage that could be avoided.[12]

Goals may be long-term or immediate. They may involve compliance with legal requirements (e.g., provide EPCRA-required information), the achievement of a desired result (e.g., gain formal community support for licenses required for plant expansion), or successful conflict resolution (e.g., reaching an agreement with a concerned community group regarding air quality monitoring). Without clarity on goals, planning is impossible.

Once goals are set, management must identify (or hire) spokespersons with good interpersonal and presentation skills, train staff in communications skills, and reward outstanding work. Brilliant scientists are not necessarily good risk communicators. It is often easier for a good communicator who lacks a technical background to learn the necessary information than for a poor communicator with a technical background to develop good communication skills.

Regardless of who is doing the communicating, a key to success is clarity that management views the work as important, that outstanding work will be rewarded. Too often technical experts, asked to do risk communications, consider the assignment an unfortunate diversion from their "real" work for the company.

The final point under the general guideline of organizational commitment is that the company needs periodic evaluations of its risk communication program. A program that does not directly generate a cash flow may be more difficult to audit than an income-generating department; nevertheless, the effort and expense to perform a thorough communications audit is worthwhile. The absence of a complete evaluation communicates a message that the firm is not fully committed to effective environmental risk management.

Realization of objectives such as rewarding outstanding work also requires evaluation. Other benefits include both identifying areas where stronger efforts are needed and noting where savings are possible. Good intentions in the absence of hard-nosed analysis is unlikely to result in an effective risk communication program.

**2. Guideline: Recognize That Communication Is A Two-way Process**
- **Share information and views;**
- **Recognize that citizens have a right to participate;**
- **Involve the community early;**
- **Grant community concerns legitimacy; and**
- **Identify interests, not positions.**

The conventional, traditional meaning of risk communication has been the transmission of technical or scientific information from elites to the general public.[13] The new definition, that risk communication is a two-way process, is accepted by organizations as diverse as the Army Corps of Engineers[14] and the National Research Council (1989). Risk communication includes elites explaining their views of the risks associated with a project, but also involves citizens explaining their feelings and values about a proposal. Risk communication has expanded beyond technical information to include other information and opinion deemed relevant by potentially affected parties. People are concerned not just with the nature and degree of risk, but with questions of who has what right to decide how risks should be shared.

This broader approach to risk communication came about in response to citizen demands for a role in decisions affecting their communities. If citizens interpret a company or agency's risk communication program as merely an effort to teach them about risks so they share the organization's views of what constitutes acceptable risks at the facility, they most likely will become angry and will harden their views into an us-against-them mentality. Instead, effective risk communications involves listening as well as making presentations. The company or agency learns the community's concerns and desires. The public learns what the organization is considering and why the company has reached the conclusion that the tentative plans pose no unreasonable costs to anyone, but should be beneficial.

A two-way model of risk communication entails communicating intentions early. This signals the firm's respect for citizen involvement and its sincerity in seeking public input. If at an initial meeting, citizens see a finished plan or a license application that is about to be submitted, they will view the company's message as a statement of its intentions with no opportunity for public input. They will understand that they can "comment" all they want, but, because the plans are finished, nothing will be changed. Instead, by requesting comments before final plans are drawn up, the organization demonstrates a receptive attitude toward the community's concerns.

Too often, spokespersons for an organization have been unwilling to recognize the legitimacy of community concerns that are either technically naive or entirely nontechnical. A community group may be quite concerned that releases of small quantities of a toxic chemical into the air will, over time, bring significant health problems. An unfortunate response would be to lecture to the citizens that their fears are technically foolish and that there is nothing more to be said. A better response to strong concerns of this nature is first, of course, to explain why even small releases are extremely unlikely. Then, a dialogue on ways to respond to continuing fears might include a discussion of devising a monitoring procedure that would permit the citizens' group itself periodically to check instruments that would record even small releases. Citizen monitoring programs have built community support in a number of cases.[15]

Non-technical community concerns are legitimate. A typical example of an unfortunate risk communication situation involves extremely emotional testimony at a public meeting about personal fears for the family and children if a proposed facility is built. The poorly-trained spokesperson for the organization that wants to build the facility is uneasy during this testimony. He is a scientist trained to focus on data, not on feelings or values. At the conclusion of the testimony, the spokesperson asks if anyone now has any factual questions or comments. By this response, the spokesperson has rejected the testimony as irrelevant and also demonstrated how he or she views the communication process. A better response is to acknowledge the person's feelings by simple statement such as, "I can see that you're angry about this new proposed facility because. . . What do you think might be done to. . ." By demonstrating a willingness to discuss concerns beyond those based on risk estimates, the spokesperson both respects the legitimacy of the community's concerns and demonstrates an acceptance of two-way communication.

In the risk communication process, the search for solutions to risk management problems is facilitated when the focus is on interests rather than positions.[16] For example, the position of a community group is that the facility not be built in the community and the position of the company is to build it on a particular plot of land. By focusing on the stated positions of the two parties, progress is difficult. By focusing on the interests of the two, however, the risk communication process might bring out that the community's interest is that the stream running by the proposed site for the facility not become polluted, and the company's interest is to build the facility close to railroad tracks. A solution might be for the community to trade public land near the railroad, but away from the stream, to the company in exchange for its riverside property. If the risk communication process had focused on positions rather than interests, this solution would not have been reached.

The guideline of recognition that an effective risk communication program is a two-way process does not entail acquiescence to citizen demands. Learning citizen values, feelings, and concerns does not mean agreement with their positions, but acknowledges that they have a right to participate in decisions that affect their community. After listening to the community's concerns, industry representatives sometimes find that citizens are more willing to give the company's technical information more credence. Also, many times firms identify minor modifications that can be made to meet community concerns. In these situations firms have reached successful outcomes to siting and other controversial disputes through their willingness to make minor changes.

3. Guideline: Know Your Audience
   • Identify all community groups with an interest;
   • Learn their concerns and values; and
   • Determine which issues are important and how best to present your message.

Companies frequently assume they know what the community knows and wants based upon the experiences of other firms with similar situations and from the statements of elected official and self-defined neighborhood spokespersons. The tendency is for companies to overestimate the degree of agreement among citizens and to view these united citizens as unambiguously either supportive or in opposition. The actual situation is invariably much more complex. Public opinion is divided: there are strong supporters, strong opponents, people permissive toward the agency's proposal, "show me" people with qualms about change, and many people who have no opinion at all. This "silent majority" is neither necessarily supportive nor in opposition, but generally open to persuasion.

Learning as much as possible about community concerns begins with looking at newspaper clippings and informally talking to people. When major controversies are possible, more systematic techniques of information gathering such as focus groups and surveys are worthwhile.

In a focus group, a trained moderator meets for two to three hours with eight to twelve people for an in-depth discussion of their views. The participants for each focus group are selected on the basis on a shared characteristic (e.g., farmers, hunters) of relevance to a potential dispute. Focus groups provide information into the reasons for actual and potential support and opposition.

The limitation of focus groups is that they provide depth at the cost of breadth. They cannot measure how typical and widespread in the community are the views expressed by the focus group participants. Focus groups are useful, however, in the preparation of questions for use in phone or door-to-door surveys. For this reason, focus groups and surveys are complementary methods of ascertaining public opinion.

Surveys are helpful in mapping community opinion both as it exists and in testing "what if" communication options.[17] Surveys can be designed to provide valid inferences to whatever population parameters are important (e.g., residents of particular neighborhoods, community leaders), as well as to the community as a whole.

Focus groups and surveys are easy to do poorly. Although the methodology of survey research may seem to be simple, there are so many potential problems in measurement and sampling that it is almost impossible for amateurs to design and conduct a quality survey. Poorly designed and implemented focus groups and surveys provide information that is unreliable and often misleading, and may engender community opposition. If appropriately trained public opinion specialists are not available in house, one of the many firms experienced in environmental risk management surveys should be hired.

The attempt to identify all groups "with an interest" includes both meanings of *interest*: having a stake in the particular risk in question and expressing concern about the risk. There is a large number of histories of risk communication efforts when an agency prepared extensively to respond to the concerns of existing community organizations, only to be surprised by the appearance of *ad hoc* groups.[18] Typically in a controversy involving environmental risks, a new group will form composed of people from a neighborhood potentially threatened. By asking who is likely to believe that they have a significant stake in the risk decision, an agency or company may anticipate their concerns.

Knowing the audience enables risk communicators to become aware of political and economic issues that may overlay health and safety concerns. By being able to put health and safety concerns into a broader context, risk communicators are likely to recognize hidden agendas and avoid unnecessarily antagonizing citizens. The National Research Council concluded, "Solving the problems of risk communication is as much about improving procedures as improving content."[19] Knowing the audience is a key component of understanding how to improve both procedures and content. By understanding each audience, risk communicators can design both procedures and messages that will address the most salient citizen concerns in the manner most likely to bring about a constructive dialogue.

4. Guideline: Be Open, Honest, Frank, And Compassionate
   - Admit when you don't know the answer, commit to finding out;
   - Tell what is underway, what is possible, what cannot be done;
   - Only promise what you can do, and do what you promise;
   - Avoid abstract, cold language about risks and death; and
   - Recognize feelings and values.

At their worst, risk communicators adopt the role of "expert" and attempt to limit discussion to the "data" showing a project or facility is reasonably safe. As noted above, people who ask technically naive questions are sometimes disparaged and emotional statements are viewed as irrelevant. Instead, by recognizing the legitimacy of public concerns and discussing options for addressing those concerns, progress toward mutual respect and an informed public is possible. By respecting values and feelings, risk communicators have found that community members become more receptive to technical information.

If the risk communication involves potential risks associated with a planned action (e.g., cleanup of a hazardous waste site or building a new facility), releasing information while the risk management options are tentative sends the message to the community that their input is important. At the same time, the risk communicator should clarify that citizen participation does not mean community control, but the right of citizens to participate in decisions that affect them. The message is that the chemical company has the right to make chemicals, and intends to do so in a manner that poses no unreasonable risks to the lives, property, and other values of residents. The participation of the community to ensure that these objectives are met is welcome.

The guideline for honest and open communication calls for the release of preliminary studies and bad news as well as supportive information. This recommendation flows not just from moral or ethical considerations, but from practical experience.[20]

In controversies, the existence of preliminary studies almost invariably becomes known to the public. If the spokesperson refuses to release results, the popular assumption is that there is something to hide and that the organization does not trust the community to react responsibly. If the eventually released results are somewhat negative, these suspicions are confirmed. A wiser choice is to release preliminary results with honest *caveats* that the results are indeed preliminary. If additional studies are likely to show the preliminary results to be misleading, the spokesperson should explain the basis for this expectation.

Data should be withheld only when the results are part of a series of tests, and cannot be interpreted until further results are available. When releasing information in a piecemeal fashion makes no sense, the rule is to explain this and to give a date when the results can be released.

Nobody likes to release bad news. Nevertheless, it is far preferable that the organization provide the information than attempt to suppress it. The practical reason is that, in environmental risk management controversies, efforts to suppress information rarely succeed.[21] As some negative information leaks out to concerned citizens, the media is likely to conjure possibilities much worse than the actual results. If the press does not get information from the organization, reporters will find other sources who are likely to be neither accurate nor supportive. When citizens learn that the organization has not been forthcoming with information, the credibility of the organization and its representatives will be damaged. In some cases, the withholding of information may also violate right-to-know laws.

When the risk information relates to an accident at a facility, the emergency response procedures set through the CAER or APELL process should be expeditiously followed. Failure to follow those procedures sends a message to the community that the CAER process was more an attempt to mollify local critics than to involve the community in emergency preparedness.

5. **Guideline: Involve Other Credible Sources**
   - **Identify other sources; and**
   - **Involve them in the process.**

Regardless of how honest and fair a spokesperson is in communicating risks, community people are not likely to view the information as "objective." They understand that chemical companies are not disinterested in the outcome of the risk communication process. They assume that even the most honest representatives of outstanding corporations still have an unavoidable tendency to slant information in directions favorable to the company's wishes. One way to enhance the credibility of both the information and the process is to involve respected outsiders such as physicians, university scientists, civic leaders, and professional meeting facilitators.

In environmental risk management disputes, two types of people are frequently asked to participate. One type is brought in to improve communications between the organization and concerned citizens and to apply conflict resolution techniques.[22] The work includes moderating public meetings and working with the different interests to develop paths toward agreement. The history of the controversy and other case-specific information determines the advisability of involving different individuals. Some people asked to participate may live outside the community and are selected because of their training and experience in helping resolve similar conflicts. Others may be respected local officials asked to moderate meetings. Besides reducing the adversarial nature of environmental risk management conflicts, involving local officials has often also had the benefit of increasing their understanding of, and support for resolving, disputes. Before involving others, however, care should be taken to ensure that they actually are viewed as credible by significant community groups. Frequently local officials lack credibility in environmental risk management disputes because they are assumed to favor the interests of developers over those of potentially affected homeowners.[23]

The other use of credible sources has been to provide an independent technical review of company or agency reports. Many environmental risk management disputes have been settled as a result of the review of technical reports by scientists who do not work for the company. Independent reviewers function to explain the report to concerned citizens, answer their questions, focus attention on real uncertainties rather than on less serious problems, and help the company understand the nature of the citizens' concerns. With citizens unlikely to trust chemical companies to provide accurate risk assessments, only an independent review can raise the credibility of those assessments. Congress has recognized the utility of independent technical reviews in improving the risk communication process. The Superfund Amendments and Reauthorization Act of 1986 (SARA) provides authorization to fund citizen groups to hire their own technical advisers to review documents.

6. **Guideline: Work With The Media To Present Your Story**
   - **Be accessible to reporters;**
   - **Help reporters do their jobs;**
     - **help define the story;**
     - **provide information; and**
   - **Praise reporters for good stories.**

More risk communications takes place through the media than public hearings, direct mail, and all other forms of contact. Therefore, what the media report is critical to successful risk communication. Although an effective program of risk communication cannot control what the media present, understanding the structural biases of the media provide an opportunity to help the company's positions get a fair hearing.[24]

The media cover **news stories** so your task is to define the news before others define it. Reporters, who generally have weak technical backgrounds, will appreciate your help in generating a story that will get them column inches or airtime.

A news story is more than just information. A television news producer and a newspaper editor must decide what will be reported from among many happenings that could be covered. The media try to be interesting because consumers have alternatives for their entertainment attention and advertisers can spend their money elsewhere too.

Stories are interesting to the extent they involve danger (e.g., a threat to the community), suspense (i.e., we know a lot, but there is missing information or future adventures), human emotion (e.g., a mother wants to protect her child's health), anger, conflict, and a villain (e.g., the big company or agency that may be threatening the community). Any story that can provide these elements is likely to reach the news. For television, good visuals (e.g., angry citizens confronting company representatives, rusting barrels of hazardous waste) also increase the likelihood of coverage. Important matters such as the federal deficit or the savings and loan scandal receive less coverage than less significant stories because the former do not easily lend themselves to interesting melodrama.

Conflicts in environmental risk management situations lend themselves to extensive media coverage because all the elements of a good story are present. The problem for environmental risk managers is that the obvious villain is the company or the agency. Unless environmental risk managers plan ahead to attempt to engender a different story, the likely story will portray corporate officers/bureaucrats insensitive to risks threatening the community.

Dealing with the media involves helping reporters do their jobs by providing them with stories such as the company's struggle to bring jobs to the area, the advances in safety procedures that demonstrate the organization's priorities, and the company's request for citizen input before plans for expansion are finalized. Developing good relations with reporters and good communication to the community through the media cannot wait until there is a conflict. If you wait, others who have good relations will define the story to reporters before the company has presented its views. Then the structure of the media will make it unlikely that the organization can avoid assuming the role of the villain.

Maintaining good relations with the media requires contact on an ongoing basis. After a story appears, environmental risk managers should contact the reporter with appropriate praise and criticism of inaccuracies. Building long-term relationships of trust with editors and reporters is worth the effort.

Adherence to these six guidelines requires patience and commitment. Chemical companies are most comfortable making chemicals, not dealing with community health and safety concerns that experts typically view as exaggerated or ridiculous. Agencies are most comfortable implementing laws, not answering questions at public meetings. Nevertheless, the benefits of effective risk communication are so substantial — and the costs of failure so great — that effective risk communications must become an integral part of any environmental risk management program.

## Trends in Environmental Risk Communication

Three trends of recent years seem likely to continue:
- More state mandates for public information programs and for public involvement in licensing and siting decisions;
- Strong enforcement of right-to-know and reporting requirements; and
- Increased use of conflict resolution techniques that depend on the risk communication process.

Many local governments have discouraged the siting of facilities that deal with hazardous materials. Particularly difficult is the siting of treatment, storage, or disposal facilities for hazardous or radioactive wastes. In response to the intransigence of local governments and the inability to site needed hazardous waste facilities anywhere, many state governments have enacted siting procedures that override local zoning ordinances. These siting procedures have requirements for extensive risk communication and public involvement. Typically siting commissions are required to hold public hearings at different stages of the process. The state governments have decided that it will be possible to site unwanted facilities, but that the process will involve ongoing risk communication.

A second trend that also means extensive risk communication is the rigorous enforcement of the new right-to-know and reporting requirements.[25] For example, an administrative law judge for the U.S. Environmental Protection Agency fined a furniture manufacturer $75,000 for failure to file forms reporting releases of six chemicals.[26] The judge agreed that the company was unaware of the requirement and filed promptly upon learning of the obligation. Nevertheless, in setting the fine the judge ruled that the company had the responsibility to keep abreast of EPCRA and its regulations.

The third trend is for the government to encourage more extensive use of conflict resolution techniques such as facilitated meetings, mediation, and negotiated rulemaking. These techniques depend on environmental risk communication to define issues in ways that facilitate reaching agreements through finding common ground. In the 1980s the Conservation Foundation was a leading advocate for expanded use of these methods of reaching agreement. Its head during this period, William K. Reilly, became Administrator of the U.S. Environmental Protection Agency in 1989.

The bottom line is that effective risk communication has become part of the definition of effective environmental risk management.

## About the Author

Dr. Robert E. O'Connor specializes in environmental risk communications. While a senior associate at ICF Incorporated, O'Connor managed support services for Superfund community relations policy development at U.S. EPA headquarters. His other clients included the U.S. DOE Office of Civilian Radioactive Waste Management, several state agencies, and numerous private firms. His current work incudes communicating climate change (for the U.S. EPA) and assessing the impacts of citizen environmental risk perceptions on land-use options (for the New Jersey Department of Environmental Protection). O'Connor has published widely in journals as diverse as the *Policy Studies Journal, Administration and Society, Food Technology,* and the *American Political Science Review.* A member of the political science department at the Pennsylvania State University, he also is affiliated with the Environmental Resources Research Institute at Penn State and Environomics, Inc., of Vienna, Virginia.

## Endnotes

1. National Research Council, 1989. *Improving Risk Communication.* Washington, D.C.: National Academy Press.

2. Hance, B. J., C. Chess, and P. M. Sandman, *Improving Dialogue with Communities: A Risk Communication Manual for Government.* Trenton: Division of Science and Research Risk Communication Unit, New Jersey Department of Environmental Protection, 1988.

3. Dunlap, R. E., "Public opinion and environmental policy," *In Environmental Politics and Policy: Theories and Evidence,* J. P. Lester, ed. Durham: Duke University Press, 1989.

4. Inglehart, R. "Values, Objective Needs, and Subjective Satisfaction Among Western Publics," *Comparative Political Studies,* 4:428-458, 1977.

5. Mazmanian, D., and D. Morell, "The 'NIMBY' Syndrome: Facility Siting and the Failure of Democratic Discourse," In *Environmental Policy in the 1990s,* N. J. Vig and M. E. Kraft, eds. Washington, DC: CQ Press, 1990.

6. Slovic, P., Fischhoff, B., and S. Lichtenstein, "Perception and Acceptability of Risk From Energy Systems," in Public Reactions to Nuclear Power: Are There Critical Masses?, W. R. Freudenburg and E. A. Rosa, eds., Boulder: Westview, 1984.

7. Lipset, S. M., and W. Schneider, The Confidence Gap: Business, Labor, and Government in the Public Mind. New York: The Free Press, 1983 and "The Confidence Gap During the Reagan Years, 1981 - 1987," *Political Science Quarterly,* 1-23, 1987.

8. L. Harris, Inside America. New York: Vintage Books, 1987.

9. Covello, V. T., P. Slovic, and D. von Winterfeldt, *Risk Communication: A review of the Literature.* Washington, DC: National Science Foundation, 1987.

10. Hance et al., *supra,* note 4; also, *see also,* Covello, V. T., P. M. Sandman, and P. Slovic, *Risk Communication, Risk Statistics, and Risk Comparisons: A Manual for Plant Managers.* Washington, DC: Chemical Manufacturers Association, 1986.

11. Covello *et al., supra,* note 9.

12. Hance *et al., supra,* note 4.

13. Krimsky, S., and A. Plough, *Environmental Hazards: Communicating Risks as a Social Process.* Dover, MA: Auburn House. 1988.

14.  Mazmanian, D., and J. Nienaber, *Can Organizations Change?: Environmental Protection, Citizen Participation, and the Corps of Engineers.* Washington, DC: Brookings, 1979.

15.  Bord, R. J., "The low-level radioactive waste crisis: Is more citizen participation the answer?" In *Low-Level Radioactive Waste Regulation: Science, Politics, and Fear,* M. E. Burns, ed., Chelsea, MI: Lewis, 1988.

16.  Fisher, R. and W. Ury, *Getting to YES: Negotiating Agreement Without Giving In.* Boston: Houghton, Mifflin, 1981.

17.  Covello *et al., supra,* note 9.

18.  Hance *et al., supra,* note 4.

19.  National Research Council, p. 147.

20.  *Id.*

21.  Hance *et al., supra,* note 4.

22.  Bingham, G., *Resolving Environmental Disputes: A Decade of Experience.* Washington, DC: Conservation Foundation, 1986.

23.  Bord, R. J., D. J. Epp, and R. E., O'Conner, *Achieving Greater Consistency Between Subjective and Objective Risks.* Washington, DC: U.S. Environmental Protection Agency, 1989.

24.  Graber, D. A., *Mass Media and American Politics.* 3rd ed. Washington, DC: CQ Press, 1989.

25.  Conn, W. D., W. L. Owens, and R. C. Rich, *Communicating with the Public About Hazardous Materials: An Examination of Local Practice.* Washington, DC: U.S. Environmental Protection Agency, 1990.

26.  *In the Matter of Riverside Furniture Corporation,* U.S. EPA Region VI, Docket Number: EPCRA-88-H-VI,406S, 1989.

# XXII Crisis Management, The Frequently Missing Risk Management Program Segment

*Richard H. Soper\**
*Soper & Associates*
*Palos Verdes Peninsula, California*

All too frequently, creative risk and insurance management programs lack the vital, but elusive, Crisis Management Plan segment. It is inconceivable that many organizations currently devote from one to six percent of their gross revenue to insurance purchasing, risk funding and loss control as well as internal and external risk management administrative activities yet do not have an effective Crisis Management Plan in place. However, this is the existing situation in many organizations in both the public and private sectors.

Even when logical, proven risk and insurance management techniques and effective loss control activities are utilized, disasters must still be anticipated. The results of a loss can definitely be minimized through the adoption of a Crisis Management Plan which encompasses formulation, implementation and operation of appropriate management techniques.

The crucial question must be asked, "How can an executive responsible for risk funding and loss control activities focused on operational continuity and financial survival justify not having a Crisis Management Plan for the funded anticipated perils and fortuitous events, the inevitable crisis?"

## Defining Crisis Management

In the true concept of contingency planning, crisis management should not be construed as the traditional "Band-Aid" approach to an insured (or uninsured or uninsurable) event involving only a simple emergency plan. Effective crisis management should be conceived of as a broad approach to major catastrophe exposure containment interfacing with operational continuity as well as business and financial survival. In summary, the definition of crisis management must remain broad in nature and not become inhibited by the traditionally narrow considerations of only those perils addressed by standard commercial insurance policies.

### Crisis Management Plan Definition

As a segment of an operating Risk Management Program, *Crisis Management Plan* may be defined as a strategic technique to reduce the adverse effects of a loss incident (emergency and/or catastrophic) through risk identification, measurement, loss mitigation and management accountability as well as possessing emergency response capability with a primary focus on pre-loss planning and post-loss recovery.

### Crisis Management Strategy Defined

*Strategy*, in the systems context of crisis management plans (involving disaster avoidance, loss mitigation and maximizing recovery), is a structured methodology designed to meet immediate objectives as well as long-term goals. Crisis management strategy[1] entails two equally important and interrelated tasks: (1) strategy formulation and (2) strategy implementation.

## Crisis Management Awareness

"Recent surveys show that fewer than half the Fortune 1,000 companies have either crisis management staff or even a plan in place"[2] thus emphasizing the serious magnitude of this risk management program void. This critical situation concerning the missing Crisis Management Program segment must be rectified.

## Environmental
## Risk Management

Dr. Frank Press, President of the National Academy of Sciences, has remarked on numerous occasions about the necessity of mitigating the consequences of natural hazards such as earthquakes, hurricanes and floods. The importance of crisis management is further emphasized by the fact that he has called for the establishment of an international "Decade of Natural Hazards" in order to focus attention on the interdependency of so many industrial activities. No longer can events be considered isolated in nature: all of us have a stake in the total crisis management process.

### News Media Focus

The news media continue to focus on the broad area of major crisis exposures, including actual crisis situations, which continue to generate public awareness for such significant events as:
- Earthquakes (e.g., Philippine Islands, San Francisco area, Mexico City, U.S.S.R., Japan, Peoples' Republic of China);
- High rise building fires (e.g., several recent major office buildings and hotels);
- Severe weather (e.g., hurricane, tornado, snow and/or ice storms);
- Product contamination (e.g., cyanide laced medication capsules);
- Pollution (e.g., toxic gases in Bhopal, India and the tanker oil spill in Prince William Sound, Alaska);
- Nuclear reactor accidents (e.g., Chernobyl and Three Mile Island);
- Adverse political activity (e.g., South Africa, Iran, Peoples' Republic of China, Nicaragua); and
- Hostile takeover (e.g., Kuwait, Cuba).

### Lack of Industry Awareness

Even with the increased awareness caused by the high efficiency of the news media reporting, there is only a limited commitment being exercised by business executives and the risk management and insurance community to prepare for the inevitable crises. Following are typical risk and insurance management industry stakeholders who, all too often, do not include the illusive Crisis Management Program segment as an integral part of their risk management plan:

- **Risk Managers and Chief Financial Officers** frequently do not have a formulated emergency plan involving a pre-rehearsed, detailed response action plan.
- **Insurance Brokerage Firms** clients' comprehensive risk and insurance management programs are typically devoid of emergency non-business hour contacts and recommended pre-crises and post-loss procedures including suggested contingency plans.
- **Insurance Underwriters** regularly issuing policy contracts with virtually no instructions regarding an action plan to be implemented in the event the loss, which is insured, should occur.
- **Risk Management Consultants** performing audits of existing risk and insurance management programs and, subsequently, developing findings and recommendations, all too often, fail to suggest structuring a Crisis Management Program.
- **Accounting Firms** routinely complete major corporation annual audits and issue reports with statements concerning the adequacy of insurance, but often neglect to address the lack of a Crisis Management Program.

## Crisis Management Plan Objectives

Crisis Management Plan objectives should interface with the identified needs of the operating entity and involve a broad focus encompassing life safety, pre-loss planning, post-loss recovery, asset conservation, revenue production maintenance, with the ultimate goal of financial survival.

The thrust of the Crisis Management Plan pre-loss planning and post-loss recovery task objectives should be broad in scope and identify with:

**Pre-Loss Task Objectives:**
- Life Safety
- Crisis and Loss Exposure Identification, Assessment and Control
- Maintenance of Existing Services, Operations and Revenue Producing Activities
- Protection of an Uninterrupted Earnings Flow
- Conservation of Assets

**Environmental
Risk Management**

- Retention of Market Position
- Preservation of Established Image
- Pollution Exposure Management and Loss Abatement

**Post-Loss Recovery Task Objectives:**
- Re-establishment Capability of Services, Operations and Revenue Production
- Pollution Containment and Cleanup
- Containment of Loss Expenses
- Minimize Lost Operating Time
- Maximize Financial Recoveries
- Maintain an Effective Defense Posture
- Capitalize on Post Crisis Image Enhancement Opportunities

## Crisis Management Plan Strategy

The ultimate goal of the Crisis Management Plan is to provide the corporation with maximum life safety for both employees and visitors, operational continuity and financial survival. The assumption must be made that key management responsibility is the same during a crisis situation. It must be an accepted fact that the normal management "job description" is applicable for conditions which are better or worse.

The Crisis Management Plan is recommended to be operated and governed via the structured management committee approach. The Crisis Management Committee has the responsibility of formulating, implementing and operating the Crisis Management Plan.

The primary purpose of a Crisis Management Committee system is to provide a technique by which to attack and resolve specific task problems associated with the operation of a Crisis Management Plan. The committee approach involves a high level of efficiency, provides for back-up committee membership and cross training.

### Committee Approach

The committee approach allows for a concentrated time commitment by concerned management to function efficiently in operating the Crisis Management Plan. Furthermore, the committee approach involving several different operational management levels may concisely interface with normal existing management policies and procedures.

Major segments of the Crisis Management Plan may be divided and organized in specific, identified crisis management committees, subcommittees, task activity groups and emergency response teams. Within the identified Crisis Management Committee area should be specific pre-assigned responsibilities. The Emergency Response Team should be responsible for immediate management of any developing crisis situation.

The committee concept for the Crisis Management Plan is somewhat similar to the Loss Control Committee approach; however, the following significant differences must be noted:

- Operational goal is to focus on life safety, business continuity and financial survival rather than workers compensation claim frequency and severity;
- A significantly higher level of management is represented on the committee, thus allowing for effective decision-making while responding to the established line of authority.

### Predetermination of Priorities

Predetermination of sequential task actions, establishment of appropriate priorities and delegation of management authority are essential ingredients in the formulation and implementation of an effective Crisis Management Plan strategy. Emergency action in an organization with formulated Crisis Management Plan policies and procedures simply becomes a case of immediately implementing the previously established action plans. This involves a logical sequence of activities with predetermined priorities.

## Crisis Management Plan Responsibilities

The Crisis Management Plan should be considered an integral component of existing management responsibilities and interface with business and operating objectives, policies and procedures as well as long-term revenue goals. Operational authority should be provided through the utilization of a Crisis Management Committee composed of senior staff members. Each committee member should be backed up by an actively involved alternate committee member.

### Crisis Management Committee

The Executive Crisis Management Committee must have authority and responsibility for formulating, implementing and operating the Crisis Management Program. The committee should be composed of senior staff managers who function with authority and have a performance record of project completion. Furthermore, the committee system approach should operate within the existing line of authority, immediate objective and long-term goals. This committee systems approach has been extremely successful and allows for a minimal time commitment by concerned management to function efficiently in operating the Crisis Management Program.

Crisis Management Subcommittees should be established for handling specific task assignments. Task assignments may include, but should not be limited to, administration, communications, news media coordination, executive succession planning, alternate headquarters site selection, alternate headquarters operating strategy, offsite computer center operations, offsite valuable record storage including retrieval capabilities as well as developing alternate operational resources. Other crisis management subcommittees will be accountable to a specific cost center, geographic location or operational function (e.g., production or transportation) or will be responsible for special activities (e.g., management information systems, vital record duplication, unique raw material sourcing).

### Emergency Response Team

The primary objective of the Emergency Response Team is to provide an immediate, qualified group to perform emergency operations before outside help arrives. Continued assistance at the scene is also expected of the team. The Emergency Response Team should operate in the interim, prior to the arrival of outside assistance (police, fire, paramedic, utility company, etc.) and, in the event outside help is not readily available due to a major area catastrophe (e.g., earthquake, power failure, flood, hurricane, etc.) should have the additional responsibility and training to provide required interim emergency services. Responsibilities range from management of a full employee evacuation to suppression of a minor fire as well as provision for cardio-pulmonary resuscitation. The Emergency Response Team should answer directly to the Crisis Management Committee.

In selecting team members, age and physical condition is of great importance. Prior emergency experience, military training and/or knowledge of first aid are desirable prerequisites.

## Crisis Management Plan Organization

A Crisis Management Plan Organization Chart has been developed, illustrating an overview of operational authority, chain of command as well as committee operations, task assignments and responsibilities. The chart delineates the Crisis Management Committee reliance upon the operational manual and policy statement as well as identifying the various responsibilities and task assignments. There are four recommended Crisis Management Plan task responsibility categories:

- Emergency Response Team;
- Operations during a crisis impairment;
- Crisis plan task assignments; and
- Recovery plan assignments.

These task responsibilities should generally function independently of each other prior, during and following a crisis.

The Crisis Management Plan (Figure 1) concerning strategy applicable to formulation and implementation of an operating organizational chart is on the facing page.

## Crisis Management Plan Components

Crisis Management Plans, appropriate for most major organizations, should include the following key strategic components.

### Executive Policy Statement
Crisis Management Policy Statement that interfaces with the identified crisis needs, responds to the organizational goals and has the endorsement of executive management.

**Environmental
Risk Management**

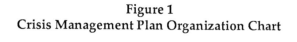

Figure 1
Crisis Management Plan Organization Chart

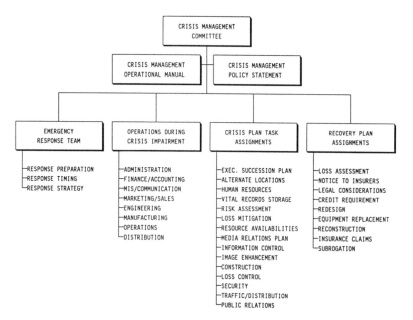

## Crisis Management Committee

Crisis Management Committee composed of key management personnel who have the authority and responsibility for the program. The primary purpose of the committee is to provide a technique to manage and resolve task problems associated with the crisis management program. The Crisis Management Committee is to operate with an effective, strategic plan providing policies, standards and procedures consistent with operational, service, marketing and profit goals.

Crisis Management Subcommittees should be organized by and report to the Crisis Management Committee and operate with the responsibility of such vital task assignments as contingency relocation planning, alternate site administration capability, computer systems backup, communication systems alternatives (internal and external), vital records backup including offsite storage retrieval capability, production contingency planning, alternative inventory sources, transportation and distribution, as well as sales and marketing plan modification.

### Emergency Response Team

Emergency Response Team shall provide for immediate emergency response capabilities at the time of crises. The team is to operate on its own in the interim before outside assistance such as fire department, paramedics, utility services and police arrive and to continue to assist until relieved.

The Emergency Response Team has the additional responsibility of providing support emergency services required at such times as public assistance is unavailable or will be delayed (e.g., earthquake, civil commotion, power failure, flooding and severe weather). There should be an Emergency Response Team organized for each definite physical (geographic) area of responsibility.

### Operational Crisis Management Manual

Develop and maintain a Crisis Management Manual intended for the key Crisis Management Committee and Emergency Response Team participants. Contents should include, but not be limited to policy, procedures, pre-loss contingency planning, emergency response strategy, resource directory and recovery plans.

A key feature of the manual is the emergency response strategy action guides identifying specific task responsibilities to be performed prior, during and following a crisis (e.g., bomb evacuation, fire, earthquake, flood, utility failure, explosion, product contamination, etc.). Another key component of the Crisis Management Manual is the development of a crisis management directory organized to contain vital information essential for effective operation of the Crisis Management Program during non-business periods as well as normal business hours. The directory should include emergency services, medical services, utility services, support services, insurance services, brokerage services and key executives. Other sections of the directory should include, but not be limited to, Crisis Management Committee membership, Crisis Management Subcommittee membership, Emergency Response Team as well as appropriate contractors, sub-contractors and support services (of a pre-arranged and pre-selected nature).

The main intent is for the Crisis Management Manual to be used as a procedural guide during a major crisis or catastrophe situation. In addition, the manual should be used as a guide associated with crisis preparation, assessment and containment. The manual is also intended as a training guide for newer participants in the Crisis Management Plan.

### Vulnerability Assessment and Continuous Crisis Assessment

Vulnerability reduction programs (loss control, fire protection, safety engineering, etc.) should be established and maintained in order to mitigate or eliminate the identified crisis and loss exposures. The Executive Crisis Management Committee shall develop analytical capabilities and resources for the purpose of identification, measurement, potential magnitude assessment and forecasting anticipated crises.

### Recovery Plan

A Recovery Plan should be organized to facilitate a post-loss assessment analysis and prompt, effective recovery. The plan should be composed of the required task modules allowing for the re-establishment capabilities regarding services, operations and revenue producing activities. In addition, the recovery plan should focus on expense containment, minimizing lost operating time, maximizing recoveries and pursuing warranted subrogation opportunities.

In summary, a continuing crisis management education program maintained with dual emphasis on specific response capabilities and general emergency preparedness is a key ingredient to the success of the Crisis Management Plan. The actual training program should
be organized on a regular meeting basis with a long-range plan encompassing appropriate training topics.

An effective evaluation system is the utilization of a Crisis Management Audit Committee operating continuously in order to assure attainment of objectives and identification of program areas requiring improvement, modification or enhancement.

## Crisis Management Plan Timing

Crisis Management Plan Timing should be formulated to focus on four defined time periods: (1) prior to crisis, (2) during crisis, (3) immediately following crisis and (4) post-crisis recovery.

The major attribute of success under the Crisis Management Plan will be a focus of pre-loss planning which would be "prior to crisis." The primary area of responsibility for the Emergency Response Team action is "during crisis" and "immediately following crisis." The greatest opportunity for expense and time loss containment associated with re-establishing operations is the "post-crisis recovery." Also included in "post-crisis recovery" is full reconstruction, filing of appropriate claims and warranted subrogation activities.

The following Figure 2, "Sequential Plan Timing," identifies the four distinct time periods.

Figure 2
Sequential Plan Timing

## Emergency Response Team Responsibilities

The Emergency Response Team shall have the ability to respond immediately to any developing emergency at the time of crisis. The team is to operate on its own in the interim prior to arrival of outside assistance. During a major crisis such as a widespread natural disaster, the Emergency Response Team may be the only organized, qualified group available to provide emergency assistance. Consequently, they, together with the Crisis Management Committee, will be responsible for handling major emergencies without the assistance of the local fire department, paramedics and police department.

The following Figure 3, "Emergency Response Team Responsibilities" illustrates an overview of the responsibilities, operating strategy and reporting relationship.

**Figure 3**
**Emergency Response Team Responsibilities**

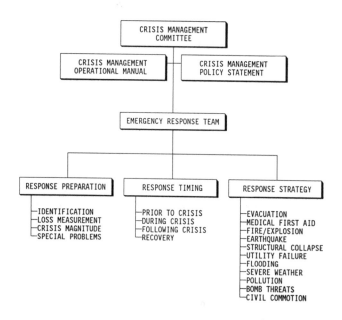

The Emergency Response Team should answer directly to the Crisis Management Committee. The Emergency Response Team is the "line" operating group responsible for physically carrying out the plan at the direction of the Crisis Management Committee. The Emergency Response Team should have the capability of initiating emergency procedures appropriate for virtually any crisis situation including, but not limited to evacuation, first aid, fire, explosion, earthquake, bomb threats and/or utility failure.

## Emergency Response Action Guide

A major responsibility of the Crisis Management Committee and Emergency Response Team is to formulate and implement a chronological emergency plan guide listing specific actions to be taken in the event of a crisis. The guide should be used in the regular training efforts of the Crisis Management Committee and the Emergency Response Team.

### Response Task Modules Development

The Emergency Response Action Guide should be structured to include the following vital information as warranted:
- General assessment of loss exposure;
- Technical information concerning each significant identified loss exposure;
- Loss exposure identification and measurement;
- Crisis magnitude potential forecasting; and
- Managing special loss exposure problems.

The Emergency Response Action Guide should be formulated to include specific time periods including action prior to, during and immediately following the crisis. The format should be structured so that during an emergency there is a pre-established priority combined with a chronological listing of responsibilities. The developed emergency response strategy must fit the existing situation, such as a twenty-four-hour petrochemical processing facility as opposed to a limited use distribution center complex. Time and effort should not be spent on developing emergency response strategies for situations unlikely to happen, such as structural problems related to snow loading in Southern California.

**Environmental
Risk Management**

**Emergency Response Task Modules**

The following is a directory of the chronological action guides being used by a client for its autonomous manufacturing facilities in the Northeast United States. This directory would be considered appropriate for most organizations:
- Evacuation, including alarm procedures;
- First aid medical emergencies;
- Fire, smoke detection and/or explosion;
- Electrical power failure emergencies;
- Boiler and machinery emergencies;
- Flooding emergencies;
- Structural collapse and/or earthquake;
- Severe windstorm emergencies; and
- Bomb threats.

# Crisis Management Manual Overview

An operational Crisis Management Manual is critical to an effectively implemented Crisis Management Plan.

**Contents Overview**

Primary sections of the Crisis Management Manual should include, but not be limited to:
- **Manual Administration**
  Issuing identification and serial number, provision for revision record, explanation of format and statement concerning "in-house" proprietary usage.
- **Policy Statement**
  Policy statement concerning crisis management, risk management and overall objectives.
- **Program Overview**
  A summary overview of the intended formulation and implementation method, role of the Crisis Management Committee and Emergency Response Team.
- **Operational Crisis Management Plan**
  Responsibilities of committees, emergency response plan, operations during a crisis impairment, crisis plan task assignments.

- **Emergency Response Action Guide**
  A strategic plan for each identified primary peril involving action prior to crisis, action during crisis and action immediately following crisis (i.e., evacuation, medical first aid, fire, earthquake, bomb threats, etc.).
- **Directory**
  Identified major internal/external resources, committee members, Emergency Response Team members and pertinent insurance program information data.
- **Recovery Plan**
  Procedures concerning loss assessment, legal considerations, reconstruction, subrogation and recovery.

### Manual Format

It is suggested that the manual be distinctly colored and in a loose leaf fashion readily adaptable to refinement, revisions and updates. The key sections of the contents should be separated and identified by colored "thumb tabs" index sheets. Key members of the committee and response team should have two manuals thus allowing for offsite storage as crises do not always occur during normal business hours.

## Managing a Comprehensive Crisis Management Plan

The managing of the Crisis Management Program in a large, multi-location organization is dependent upon provision of adequate procedures and ability to adapt to unique local problems.

The Crisis Management Committee with the sole responsibility of the operation becomes the Executive Crisis Management Committee. Each physical location has a Crisis Management Committee to address local management responsibilities and special situations. The Emergency Response Team is composed of local staff and should be prepared for anticipated problems associated with the operation. If the operation, such as a petrochemical facility, runs twenty-four hours a day, then there should be a fully competent Emergency Response Team organized on each work shift.

An organization chart has been developed in order to identify the operational authority, chain of command, general responsibilities and specific task assignments. The chart delineates the Crisis Management Plan reliance upon the Crisis Management Procedure Manual as well as corporate and crisis management policy statements. The organizational chart ultimately identifies the executive authority as derived from the Board of Directors, Executive Committee. Please refer to Figure 4, "Crisis Management Geographic Plan Organization" on the following page.

## Managing Highly Sensitive Crisis Exposures

Highly sensitive crisis exposures including, but not limited to kidnap, product extortion associated with toxic contamination and product recall, should be handled as confidential exposures. These sensitive exposures should be confronted and associated crisis management contingency plans developed. Because of the highly confidential nature of the sensitive crisis exposures, the plans and procedures should not be circulated as part of an operational manual or distributed indiscriminately throughout the organization. The nature of the highly sensitive exposures is such that only a few individuals, in conjunction with the Board of Directors Executive Committee, should be involved in the project.

Figure 5 has been developed to provide an overview of a feasible solution for handling highly sensitive crisis exposures and indicates the warranted task responsibilities, strategic plan with regard to scope and chronological order.

In order to develop and refine their management ability associated with highly sensitive crisis exposures, many organizations utilize one of several specialized consulting organizations. Preventive contingency planning is recognized by many organizations as a means of minimizing risk and safeguarding assets.

The various highly specialized consulting firms are normally qualified to prepare detailed contingency plans designed for specific needs, provide staff briefings and take into account the laws and practices of the countries involved. An important facet of the specialized consulting activity is establishing a liaison between appropriate authorities so that if and when a crisis does occur, it can be resolved effectively with minimal commercial damage and loss of good will as well as providing for a post-crisis image enhancement opportunity.

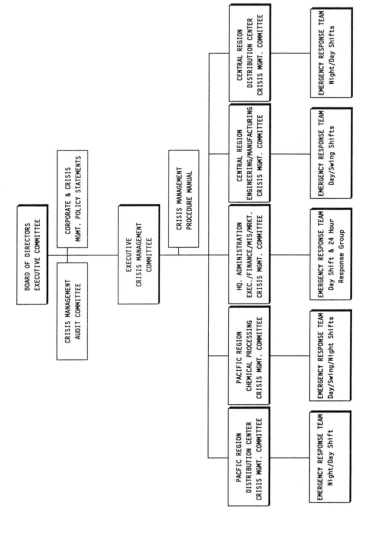

Figure 4
Crisis Management Geographic Plan Organization

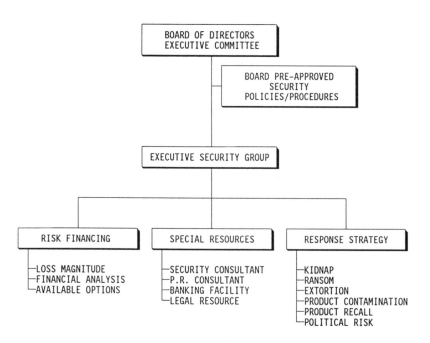

Figure 5
Highly Sensitive Crisis Exposures Strategy

In many cases, when insurance coverage, such as kidnap and ransom, is in place, the policies may be structured to provide a credit toward specialized consulting activities. Normally, this credit is a fixed percentage of the total annual premium amount.

## Creating an Environmental Crisis Management Plan

The proposed Crisis Management Plan methodology, as outlined, is readily adaptable for any range of identified crises as well as for the narrowly focused situation involving environmental impairment. An effective Environmental Crisis Management Plan segment should involve certain key success task activities which would include, but not be limited to, anticipated exposures, action tasks, qualified and trained response team, identified resources and news media management plan.

## Crisis Management, The Frequently Missing Risk Management Program Segment

## Environmental Crisis Management Strategy

In expanding upon environmental crisis management planning considerations, the emphasis must be placed on pre-event planning and comprehensive analysis of the anticipated exposures. Anticipated exposures should identify the breadth of problems that may occur, the economic loss exposure, the effect on the exposed population, environmental impact damage, recovery duration and post-crisis image problems as well as image enhancement opportunities.

The news media management plan is a crucial factor relating to public acceptance of an environmental problem, an improved legal defense posture and post-crisis image enhancement. At the time of an environmental crisis, there should be a general, conceptual press release, developed before the anticipated occurrence, indicating management concern, an aggressive recovery plan and management compassion associated with the environmental impact. The news media action plan should be developed prior to any environmental crisis and portray a responsible position assumed by Executive Management. There is an opportunity for post-crisis image enhancement through the effective implementation of an aggressive environmental crisis management program. Key factors in the media program should be that press releases and interviews are only to be provided by designated members of the Executive Crisis Management Committee.

The pre-occurrence selection of a litigation and claims management organization to handle claims as well as selection of a major law firm with a proven track record in the environmental field is critical. The organization of a litigations control plan should be formalized to interface with the existing environmental loss exposures.

The Environmental Crisis Management Plan should be a component of the overall organizational crisis management program. The Environmental Crisis Management Plan objective should interface with the identified needs of the organization and encompass life safety, environmental protection, pre-loss planning, post-loss recovery, asset conservation, effective recovery and post-situation enhancement.

**Environmental Crisis Management Plan Key Components**

An environmental crisis management plan appropriate for most exposure situations should include the following key strategic components:

- **Executive Environmental Policy Statement**
Environmental crisis management policy that interfaces with the identified loss exposures, responds to the organizational goals, has the endorsement of Executive Management and provides for post-crisis image enhancement.
- **Crisis Management Environmental Committee**
The Environmental Crisis Management Committee should report directly to the Executive Crisis Management Committee of the overall program. The environmental crisis management committee is to develop the strategic pre-and post-loss plans as well as to provide appropriate policies, standards and procedures consistent with organizational objectives.
- **Environmental Response Team**
Provide for an Emergency Response Team which is adequately and properly trained for the identified environmental crises.
- **Continuous Environmental Loss Assessment**
The Crisis Management Environmental Committee should possess analytical capabilities and resources for the purposes of identification, measurement, magnitude assessment and forecasting as associated with intervention in the anticipated environmental crises. Continuous assessment of environmental crises should include, but not be limited to life safety, health considerations, botanical and zoological concerns, duration of incident and recovery time.
- **Vulnerability Reduction**
The Environmental damage vulnerability reduction program should be established in order to mitigate or eliminate the identified environmental crises and loss exposures.
- **Crisis Management Directory**
The environmental crisis management directory should be a subpart of the overall organizational crisis manage-

**Crisis Management, The Frequently Missing
Risk Management Program Segment**

ment directory. The intent of the directory is to provide vital information essential for effective environmental crisis management during non-business periods as well as normal operating hours. The directory should be the major source of identified and developed resources in order to cope with a major environmental crisis.

- **Environmental Action Plan**
  A chronological action plan identifying specific task responsibilities to be performed during and following a contamination event would include prompt action and major reliance on developed resources. Key to the action response is the prompt implementation of an effective recovery plan. Essential in the response and training aspects of the plan is an appropriately focused and detailed Crisis Management Program Procedure Manual.
- **Continuing Environmental Exposure Education**
  Environmental education crisis program should be maintained with dual assessment of loss exposures, response capabilities and recovery.
- **Environmental Crisis Management Plan Audit**
  The Environmental Crisis Plan should be subject to periodic audit reviews in order to assure objective obtainment and identification of program areas that require improvement, modification or enhancement.

The preceding are considered the minimum key considerations for Environmental Crisis Management Plan criteria as components of a major organizational Crisis Management Program. The topical outline of key components as delineated must not be considered as the panacea for all environmental emergency situations, but merely a discussion guide.

## Loss Exposure Assessment

Frequently, the risk management planning formulation process is myopic in defining the magnitude of probable maximum loss exposures. A significant task in the Crisis Management Plan strategy formulation should be to broadly identify and measure the various potential crises and loss exposures. To accomplish this task, the extent of a specific loss must be determined through a review of probable loss frequency and severity. Severity can be categorized in one of three levels of loss magnitude which range from an accidental event that is effectively funded under the risk management program to a major unfunded or underfunded catastrophe that could threaten the ultimate financial survival of the organization.

Significant perils to be considered include fire, flood, earthquake, severe windstorm, building collapse, contamination, embezzlement, theft, disability, death and torts. Less traditional, but potentially severe exposures, include kidnap, appropriation of assets (foreign or domestic), product extortion or product recall. Some organizations have not survived the adverse publicity following a serious product liability loss and/or recall situation.

### Evaluating Crises Exposures

In the process of evaluating crises exposures, a determination concerning probability of loss should be developed concerning the following factors:

- **Frequency**
  Simply a measurement of how often a particular type of loss may occur.
- **Severity**
  Relates to magnitude of loss, including life, assets or ability to maintain operations.
- **Variation**
  Identification of various "trending" factors which are applicable in determining total crises loss considerations and include such factors as inflation, changes in laws, increased seasonal or business cyclical activity, technological advances, market fluctuations and socio-economic considerations.
- **Impact**
  Identifies the risk bearing capability of a particular entity; loss magnitude may be determined by (1) whether or not a loss is easily handled within the insurance program, (2) whether or not there is a serious financial inadequacy in the overall insurance funding arrangement and/or (3) whether or not the loss actually threatens financial survival of the entity. A key impact consideration is proper

loss vulnerability identification of unusual exposures such as unique resource material, limited supply of custom built parts, extended duration of supply time, single distribution center susceptibility to loss situations and/or political risk problems.

### Insurance Adequacy

A continuous review of the risk and insurance management funding program should be maintained. Key items such as breadth of insurance coverage, significant exclusions, deductible exposures, self-insured retentions, limits of coverage including total available annual aggregate considerations should be continuously assessed. Other factors include the financial integrity of the insurance market utilized as well as the competency of the responsible insurance brokerage firm and assigned account executive team.

The process of establishing adequate insurance limits should involve planning and analyzing for the maximum foreseeable crises. Consideration must be given to the accumulation of deductibles, self-insurance financial loss exposure and ultimate modification of experience-rated insurance policies.

An effective vehicle for determining adequate limits of coverage and realistic recovery time is the utilization of a "Think Tank" analysis session that involves concerned senior management. For example, in determining the limits for a manufacturing facility, including recovery time and possible contingent business interruption exposures, the formal meeting would involve the Chief Financial Officer, Director of Manufacturing, Director of Taxation and other concerned executives. The mission would be to pursue a hypothetical worst case loss scenario and to actually develop vital information such as replacement cost values, alternate temporary manufacturing capabilities, extra expense exposure, business interruption time period as well as any problems associated with contingent business interruption or inability to meet contractual obligations.

### Comprehensive Analysis

In projecting for the probable maximum foreseeable event, it is important always to combine several exposures in order to achieve a realistic hypothetical impact on the corporate operating and financial abilities.

A hypothetical situation in a manufacturing facility could involve a boiler explosion with an ensuing fire, injury to both employees and third parties with pollution and fire damage occurring in the immediate exterior perimeter. It is important to consider such event refinements as structural collapse affecting a number of self-insured fleet vehicles. In analyzing a major crisis situation, it is important when reviewing natural hazards to extend the impact on the corporation finances to the effects of major losses against either the self-insured or experience-rated group benefit plans.

Consideration should be given to other specific adverse exposures such as hostile takeover, product extortion, product contamination, product recall, pollution, limited resource interdependency, government regulatory problems, destructive union and strike activities as well as hostile media situations. In addition, the crisis and loss exposure assessment must remain broad in nature and not become inhibited by the traditionally narrow considerations of only those perils addressed by standard commercial insurance policies.

### Unique Loss Vulnerability Identification

Even more important than the mere potential of crises is the unique exposure vulnerability which adversely impacts and influences loss magnitude.

A flow analysis is frequently the quickest and simplest way to identify a critical vulnerability exposure. When analyzed in a flow analysis, a simple manufacturing distribution operation with retail outlets could identify a critical distribution link. An example would be 12 manufacturing facilities supplying 85 retail outlets. The vulnerability point would be that all completed manufactured items are accumulated, stored and shipped from a single distribution center. The ultimate consequences of a distribution center loss impact manufacturing, since completed product cannot be shipped, and impact retail sales, since there is no longer is an inventory supply.

Typical identified vulnerability problems include unique resources used in processing or manufacturing, limited quantity of custom-built parts utilized in product assembly, extended duration of raw material supply time, labor strike exposures concerning manufacturing and shipping, political risk problems affecting foreign source materials, one-of-a-kind single manufacturing machines, annual seasonal operations developing cyclical business peaks and valleys, hostile competition via patent infringement, and loss of communications capability over an extended period of time.

## Loss Magnitude Categories

An ongoing responsibility of the Crisis Management Committee is to identify and measure potential loss situations on a continuing basis in order to categorize them as to the degree of seriousness. Loss magnitude categories can be established by defining probable maximum loss exposure with respect to market position, financial impact (cash flow and earnings), disruption of operations and/or duration of business interruption as a result of the event.

Levels of loss which face the organization may be defined as follows:

- **Magnitude I**

    The first category is one in which the actual survival of the organization is at stake. For example, major earthquake or catastrophic accident affecting the facilities, operation or staff. Such disasters could result in casualties, destruction of property as well as the loss of computer and communications facilities and critically important records. Magnitude I losses would be beyond the point of recovery for the typical organization. Fortunately, the chances of a Magnitude I loss occurring are remote.

- **Magnitude II**

    A Magnitude II loss can be defined as one with a **significant** impact on life safety, revenue and existing assets, but without the major threat to the financial stability of the organization. For example, a major fire results in significant damage to the contents and structure of a manufacturing facility. A Magnitude II loss would affect no more than 50 percent of the revenues. Such a loss could cause a partial relocation or a significant change in manufacturing operations and would certainly be identified in the annual report to stockholders. It would affect annual forecast results and profit, but would not pose an ongoing financial burden.

- **Magnitude III**

  A Magnitude III loss is one that is easily manageable within the risk-bearing capacity of the organization. For example, a flood or fire at a retail or production location does not result in significant asset loss or business interruption. Other examples include an accident involving a company vehicle resulting in injuries and establishment of medical or disability reserves or an adverse legal judgement in a product liability case which results in significant, but not substantial, product recall.

## Crisis Management Recovery Plan

In the prior loss planning mode, there should be the development of a strategic recovery plan. Primary task assignment should be Crisis Management Committee assumption of responsibility.

Important considerations include, but are not limited to, notice to insurers, legal considerations, credit requirements, redesign, equipment replacement, reconstruction and image protection. Final recovery task items should be the presentation of insurance claim documents, termination of alternate temporary location facilities as permitted, restoration of all operations and focusing on any post-crisis image enhancement opportunities.

### Immediate Post-Loss Assessment

After a crisis has occurred and prior to beginning a strategic recovery program, it is essential to complete a loss assessment analysis. Factors to consider in the Crisis Management Recovery Plan and preliminary assessment of loss should include, but not be limited to, the items identified in Table 1 on the following page.

## Table 1
### Recovery Plan Assessment Considerations

**Impact on staff**
    Injury severity and frequency
    Fatalities
    Status of dependents
    Access to facility
    Other mitigating concerns

**Operating status**
    Destroyed area
    Heavily damaged area
    Limited damage area
    Unaffected area
    Operating capability
    Service capability
    Communications capability
    MIS capability
    Contractual obligations
    Credit and cash availability

**Third party loss exposures**
    Life safety
    Pollution incident
    Breach of contracts
    Inability to comply with contractual obligation
    Service interruption
    Exterior property damage
    Care, custody and control situations

**Claim Value Considerations**
    Building values
    Lost operating time
    Lost earnings
    Extra expense items
    Payroll attributed to cleanup
    Normal operating payroll
    Overtime payroll
    Stock, contents, inventory and equipment expense
    Rental expense, including emergency equipment
    Differential contract product manufacturing expenses
    Alternate facility rental expense
    Lease of service equipment
    Purchase of service equipment
    Other unclassified expenses

**Recovery Considerations**
    Applicable insurance
    Funded self-insurance
    Self-insured retention exposure
    Subrogation opportunities

The loss assessment analysis should be supplemented with a narrative report concerning the crisis and its effect on employees, facility, production, inventory, transportation, merchandising, market plan and administration. In addition, extensive photograph records are invaluable in a loss assessment situation and most beneficial in settlement negotiations and frequently assist in maintenance of an adequate defense posture and subrogation activities. The crisis assessment analysis will enable management to establish actual recovery goals.

**Loss Recovery Management**

The second phase of the strategic recovery plan is the formulation, implementation and assignment of action plans. The process is a management tool which will provide for written accountability, status and identification of problem areas associated with recovery tasks. Two prevalent management-oriented scheduling techniques used in the application of recovery plans are PERT (Program Evaluation Review Technique) and CPM (Critical Path Method).

Crisis Management Committee task assignments regarding loss recovery management should include, but not necessarily be limited to the following:

- Notice to insurers;
- Legal considerations;
- Credit and cash requirements;
- Redesign;
- Equipment replacement;
- Reconstruction;
- Insurance claims recovery; and
- Subrogation activity.

Following the recovery, the Crisis Management Committee should evaluate the entire crisis project from pre-crisis planning through completion of recoveries and enhance ongoing crisis management as warranted.

## Maintaining An Effective Crisis Management Plan

Maintenance of an effective Crisis Management Plan requires committees with an effective membership, continuous identification and measurement of loss exposures; and an aggressive training program. These elements ensure that the Crisis Management Plan is effective, responsive to emergencies and capable of reaching the agreed-upon objectives as well as ultimate goal attainment.

### Crisis Management Audit Committee

A vital ingredient of ensuring program effectiveness is the utilization of an audit program using a Crisis Management Audit Committee. It is essential that the chairperson of the Crisis Management Audit Committee report to someone other than the chairperson of the Crisis Management Committee, who is the director of the plan. In order to eliminate bias and to provide for total objectivity, the Audit Committee Chairperson should report to the Executive Committee of the Board of Directors.

### Crisis Management Education Topics

A typical continuing education plan for the Crisis Management Committee and Emergency Response Team should encompass the following training topics:
- Evacuation procedures;
- Medical emergencies;
- Search and rescue;
- Fire suppression methods;
- Automatic sprinkler emergency operations;
- Earthquake preparation and/or simulated emergencies;
- Structural collapse and/or earthquake;
- Hazardous materials management;
- Communications systems and alternatives;
- Crisis management policy and authority;
- Primary and secondary command posts;
- Operation of emergency equipment;
- Computer center failure and/or damage emergencies;
- Salvage operations — prevention and recovery;
- Protection of vital records;
- Electrical power failure emergencies;
- Boiler and machinery emergencies;
- Flooding emergencies;
- Severe weather; and
- Bomb threats or explosions.

### Crisis Management Education Methods

The most effective, proven method of Crisis Management Plan training involves an appropriate case study with presentation of a catastrophe scenario, a crisis management solution and a critique on the effectiveness of the solution. The following education methods are also appropriate techniques for utilization in Crisis Management Plan training activities:
- Disaster simulation models;
- Delphi techniques;
- Game simulations; and
- Actual field exercises.

In selecting training topics and educational methods to be used, emphasis must be placed on appropriateness for the staff involved and the identified needs of the organization. Training in areas where there is little or no likelihood of occurrence should be minimal.

## Crisis Management Plan Advantages and Opportunities

The advantages and opportunities associated with an effective implemented Crisis Management Plan are numerous and include, but are not limited to the following:
- Increased focus on life safety considerations;
- Improved legal defense posture;
- Negligence litigation exposure control;
- Insurance expenses reduction;
- Continuous crisis assessment;
- Loss vulnerability reduction;
- Retention of market position;
- Asset conservation;
- Earnings flow protection;
- Loss expenses containment;
- Maximizing financial recovery;
- Minimizing lost operating time;
- Pollution loss reduction;
- Post-crisis image enhancement for stakeholders; and
- Protect Directors and Officers from negligence litigation.

## Crisis Management, The Frequently Missing Risk Management Program Segment

An effectively implemented Crisis Management Plan presents an outstanding advantage for the risk manager when he deals with the insurance brokerage firm's marketing and renewal efforts.

## Crisis Management Consulting

Crisis Management Program consulting frequently involves a systems approach producing a strategic action plan that should be formulated and implemented prior to the occurrence of crises. The Crisis Management Program consulting strategy is developed in a logical sequence of task activities thus interfacing with the identified crisis exposures.

A successful consulting project scope frequently encompasses a five-phase modular system utilizing the following approach:

- **Feasibility Study, Phase I**
  Project definition including determination of scope, warranted program magnitude and strategic plan requirements;
- **Assessment, Phase II**
  Project scope including identification, measurement, assessment and definition of crisis management requirements, including the evaluation of the existing risk management program and insurance coverages (an audit of existing funding arrangements in force);
- **Formulation, Phase III**
  Project formulation including decision analysis, program formulation (including creation of a specific Crisis Management Program Operational Manual) and development of appropriate strategies;
- **Implementation, Phase IV**
  Project implementation including executive and management briefings as well as implementation seminars for involved staff; and
- **Management, Phase V**
  Project maintenance including Crisis Management Program operation, monitoring and assessment of management and staff participation and preparedness.

Environmental
Risk Management

It is significant to note that consulting expenses associated with the formulation and implementation of a Crisis Management Program are frequently offset by generated premium savings as a result of underwriting credits. The most significant credits are generally associated with business interruption, extra expense, contingent business interruption and excess umbrella liability coverages.

## Crisis Management Program
## Advantages and Opportunities

The Crisis Management Program results in a net savings, even without the occurrence of a catastrophe. The Crisis Management Program may be compared to an automatic sprinkler system that provides ongoing premium credits and which will respond automatically to any fire situation. The results of a catastrophic loss can definitely be minimized through the utilization of an effective Crisis Management Program. Furthermore, the probability of Directors and Officer negligent litigation exposure should be substantially reduced.

The advantages and opportunities associated with an effectively implemented Crisis Management Program are numerous and include, but are not limited to the following:

- Increased focus on life safety considerations;
- Improved legal defense posture;
- Negligence litigation exposure control;
- Insurance expenses reduction;
- Continuous crisis assessment;
- Loss vulnerability reduction;
- Retention of market position;
- Asset conservation;
- Environmental emergency management ;
- Earnings flow protection;
- Loss expenses containment;
- Maximizing financial recovery;
- Minimizing lost operating time;
- Post-crisis image enhancement for public and customers; and
- Protect Directors and Officers from negligence litigation.

# The Future of Crisis Management

A Crisis Management Plan should be considered as an absolute essential in organizations that involve complex manufacturing processes, limited resources of critical items, service activities involving life safety considerations, distribution activities with reliance on centers involving accumulation of stock (unique inventory, single source items, critical resources, etc.), operations subject to adverse publicity, seasonal fluctuation, cyclical economic impacts or multi-national organizational activities.

A non-structured crisis management approach attacking catastrophic situations as they occur is neither prudent nor acceptable in our current socio-economic climate. Executive management must accept the responsibility on behalf of employees and investors to identify and manage the inevitable crises.

Predetermination of sequential task actions, establishment of appropriate priorities and delegation of management authority are essential ingredients in the formulation and implementation of an effective Crisis Management Program strategy. Emergency action in an organization with formulated Crisis Management Program policies and procedures simply becomes a case of immediately implementing the previously established action plans. This involves a logical sequence of activities with pre-determined priorities.

From a personal standpoint, the executive, chief financial officer, risk manager, insurance broker, and underwriter should view an effective Crisis Management Plan as a vital career safeguard, thus providing for professional growth in their area of responsibilities that are associated with life safety, asset conservation, revenue protection and ultimate financial survival.

Crisis management, as an evolving discipline, must come of age and become a required segment of creative and responsible risk management programs which, in turn, must focus on the operational continuity and financial survival of the organization.

## About the Author

Richard H. Soper is a Principal of Soper & Associates, Palos Verdes Peninsula, California. Mr. Soper's Risk and Insurance Management Society (RIMS) activities have included Chairman and Vice Chairman of the National Education Committee; President, San Francisco Chapter; Director, Los Angeles Chapter; and National Director. Mr. Soper has previously served with several major corporations in a risk management capacity. He has held risk and insurance management teaching appointments at the University of California Berkeley Extension, University of California Los Angeles Extension, and at Golden Gate University.

## Endnotes

1. Richard G. Hamermesh, Editor, *Harvard Business Review; Strategic Management*, Harvard Business Review Executive Book Series, (John Wiley & Sons, Inc., New York: 1983) p. 2.

2. Ian I. Mitroff, Ph.D., School of Business Administration at the University of Southern California.

## Crisis Management, The Frequently Missing Risk Management Program Segment

# XXIII

# Risk Financing: Insuring Potential Pollution Exposures

## *Dean Jeffery Telego*
### *President*
### *Risk Management Technologies, Inc.*
### *Washington, D.C.*

Risk management involves the business of managing the future. The role and responsibilities of the corporate risk manager are dynamic, multi-disciplinary and constantly evolving. The cornerstones of risk management are protection and preservation of corporate assets, net income and public image from potential loss exposures and liabilities. In many corporate organizations and industrial establishments, the risk managers are becoming responsible for the environmental, health and safety issues as well as for managing the property and casualty insurance and company benefits program. This chapter identifies the process and protocol for integrating these multiple responsibilities: identification of environmental risk and the handling of that risk through transfer (i.e., insurance) and retention mechanisms.

Environmental Stewardship, Total Quality Management, Pollution Prevention Pays, Responsible Care Program and the Valdez Principles represent some of business management's concepts, codes and principles currently being implemented as proactive environmental risk management by corporations, associations and institutional investors in support of pollution prevention and control.

The modern risk manager's decision-making process has expanded beyond a linear risk management process. Management of environmental and personal injury loss exposures and liabilities requires contemporaneous safeguarding of officers and directors from allegations of civil or criminal actions or other third party tort claims. The process is used often; with every environmental crisis comes new corporate awareness and new demands from institutional investors, shareholders and the general public.

Companies that generate, transport, treat, store, dispose, reclaim, or recycle/reuse hazardous materials, wastes, constituents, contaminants or substances face regulatory compliance hurdles and potential legal obstacles. These challenges demand innovative and integrative management practices as well as workable standards and achievable pollution prevention or control technologies that both demonstrate savings and reduce risks.

There are three overwhelming environmental forces affecting the way companies do business today. First, multinational and national companies are witnessing major government and industry directives requiring pollution prevention, waste reduction, and recycling. Simultaneously, more stringent government environmental and occupational laws and regulations are being promulgated with stiffer civil and criminal sanctions against companies. Second, American citizens have more direct access to environmental data than ever before under environmental laws such as the Clean Water Act (i.e., discharge monitoring reports), Superfund (i.e., remedy selection and citizen suits) and SARA Title III, OSHA, RCRA (i.e., Right-to-Know, siting and permitting) and, new Clean Air Act Amendments of 1990 (i.e., compliance monitoring reports). Companies that are able to reach or plan to attain "zero discharge" goals will reduce the costs of risk management and potential liability resulting from such citizen disclosures.

Market force number three is economics. Industry's bottom line is profit and cost control. According to a recent government report, between $90-$100 billion was spent last year for pollution control of toxic substances and hazardous wastes compared to $27 billion in 1972.[1] As risk managers become more responsible for their companies' pollution exposures, they will be in the ideal position to determine which risks need to be transferred and those that can safely and cost-effectively be retained and managed.

## The Corporate Risk Management Program

A company's commitment to proactive environmental risk management becomes the basis for a successfully executed risk financing program. The environmental risk management structure should ideally be based upon an understanding of the potential pollution exposures (perceived and real), followed by installation of corrective measures or remedial actions where they are needed.

Company financial officers and/or risk managers in the regulated community who are concerned about the potential of Superfund or toxic tort liability should look to creative risk financing alternatives. The risk financing alternatives described in this Chapter employ pollution insurance mechanisms. As the property and casualty market continues to expand during 1991, insurance facilities are emerging that underwrite and provide coverages for both first party and third party pollution legal liability on a monoline policy[2] basis and with niche product lines from specialty insurance markets.

Seventy to eighty percent of companies that generate or handle hazardous substances and wastes will continue to retain their potential pollution loss exposures as a result of the conditions taking place in the business community and pollution liability insurance marketplace. The potential adverse effects of statutory and common law actions are driving companies to minimize their potential pollution loss exposures through pollution prevention techniques as part of their basic loss prevention or risk control. No matter whether a company decides on a self funded program or to transfer the potential pollution risks, careful risk management and risk assessment will be the key to dealing with potential and actual loss exposures. Central to systematic management of pollution exposures is undertaking steps to identify, evaluate, control, prevent and ultimately to eliminate the risk. Industry and government initiatives toward pollution prevention (i.e., source reduction) and waste minimization (i.e., recycling) will make for insurable risks with less restrictive terms and conditions.

Companies generating and/or handling hazardous materials and/ or wastes may still face reduced insurance capacity and restrictive pollution policy language until the insurance underwriters can determine the predictability and extent of the risk. The pollution liability insurance market will provide more capacity if private industry can demonstrate solid environmental risk management programs that reduce the possibility of future Superfund or toxic tort activities. Those pollution liability insurers who have realized impressive profits from the pollution insurance marketplace have done so through the use of careful underwriting procedures. Accordingly, at this time, commercial liability insurance or liability risk retention groups will be available only to those companies that can demonstrate solid corporate and environmental waste management practices and can afford to pay the premiums above unusually high deductibles and/or meet capitalization requirements.

This chapter will first explore the legal framework that defines the environmental roles and responsibilities of the risk manager in evolving a corporate environmental risk management program that can result in the successful identification, control and transfer of potential pollution loss exposures. This chapter will next focus on the important role qualitative risk assessment plays in the transfer and retention of risk followed by a detailed analysis of those key insurance markets presently providing domestic and foreign pollution insurance. The risk financing alternatives and financial responsibility requirements for owners and operators of treatment, storage, disposal and reclamation/recycling (TSDR) facilities and underground storage tanks, will also be evaluated in this chapter. The final segment of this chapter offers an analysis of future environmental trends and emerging pollution insurance issues facing the corporate risk manager.

## Air Pollution Control Overview

Thirty-two billion dollars per year is spent for implementing the existing Clean Air Act regulations.[3] Thirty to fifty billion dollars is projected to be spent each year by industry to implement the new Clean Air Act Amendments passed by Congress and signed by President Bush on November 15, 1990.[4] There are approximately 800 pages and 11 titles to the new Clean Air Act. The eight most important titles include auto standards, clean fuels, nonattainment, air toxics, acid rain, chlorofluorocarbons, permit requirements and enforcement. The regulatory requirements will be phased in over a ten to forty-year period. The statute will strengthen the authority and increase the resources of air quality control agencies at both the federal and state levels. The amendments will create a new universe of regulations requiring installation of more advanced and expensive pollution control equipment and other key changes in industrial operations and regional transportation systems. The central goal of the Clean Air Act still remains the attainment of the National Ambient Air Quality Standards.[5]

The Superfund program is complex and expensive. It affects all segments of our society. The Comprehensive Environmental Response, Compensation and Liability Act of 1980 (CERCLA) and its amendments of 1986, Superfund Amendments and Reauthorization Act, known as SARA, are collectively called Superfund. This body of law provides for the removal and cleanup of abandoned and inactive contaminated sites and the containment and cleanup of actual or threatened releases of hazardous substances. Superfund has been reauthorized for a four-year extension as part of the Omnibus Budget Reconciliation Act. The taxing provisions extend for four years and the program authorization for three years with no relief from the liability scheme and harsher enforcement to be seen under Section 106 with increased number of unilateral administrative orders (UAOs). (See Chapter IX on Superfund Process and Progress — Superfund Liability Scheme, by Rothenberg.)

The goal of the Superfund program is to protect human health and the environment from exposure and harm caused by potential or actual pollution from hazardous waste sites. Critics of Superfund believe that in the weaving of the Superfund web, too many transactional and cleanup costs have been incurred while too few sites have been settled or permanently cleaned up. A Superfund study conducted by the Centers for Disease Control issued to Congress indicated only 11 percent of 951 Superfund sites studied posed any real risk to human health.[6] The Superfund program has a voracious appetite for potentially responsible parties (PRPs) who are destined to pay for the cleanup of waste sites. The legal framework is based on absolute/perpetual, strict, joint and several, and retroactive liability. The Superfund program has expanded its list of new types and forms of PRPs beyond past and present owners and operators, generators and transporters to now include lenders, real estate developers, bankrupt parties, and governmental entities. For those corporations cited as PRPs, we now have case law that holds dissolved corporations, parent companies, company directors and officers, shareholders, successor companies and absentee owners liable for Superfund cleanup costs. Add to this group parties never sued in the governmental actions who are nonetheless sued in private party cost recovery actions by named recalcitrant PRPs.[7]

Superfund also entangles the primary, excess and reinsurance property and casualty carriers when they are sued by the PRP insureds. These carriers are in turn suing each other as well as the PRPs as a way to reserve rights, transfer risks and allocate their share of the liability.

PRPs at hazardous waste sites are also subject to (Section 310) citizen suits against PRPs alleging cleanups inconsistent with National Contingency Plan (NCP) and third party toxic tort actions for alleged bodily injury and property damages or from the "sleeping giant," trustee claims for natural resource damages.

EPA has extensive enforcement and settlement tools in its war chest to compel PRP initiated cleanups. These tools include Section 106 actions to enforce an order to collect a penalty or compel a cleanup. EPA can also use the Superfund trust fund and perform the cleanup and seek (under Section 107) cost recovery actions for contribution or punitive damages.

The risk manager should be mindful of ten major areas of concern that affect Superfund settlements and the cleanup process that need immediate attention and resolution by policymakers, regulators and private parties. These include:

- The EPA model consent decree for conducting Remedial Investigations/Feasibility Studies and Remedial Design/ Remedial Action may lead to fewer settlements and more 106 Unilateral Administrative Orders (UAOs).
- EPA's inconsistent cleanup methods and standards appear to be confounding the remedy selection process; cost appears not to be considered uniformly in remedy selection.[8]
- The revised hazard ranking system expands the environmental harm considerations by adding new exposure pathways or threats that assess direct contact of humans with contaminated soils and contaminated human food chain. This will expand the number of NPL sites.[9]
- EPA regions will have complete control of the risk assessments and therefore control "how clean, clean should be." With this move, the cost of cleanups may go up and the process may slow down with the overprediction of risk.
- The shortfall in new or innovative technologies appears to have led to an overuse of containment rather than treatment as the preferred alternative.
- The settlement process appears in considerable disarray with an inordinate amount of time required to resolve negotiated

consent decrees, covenants not to sue, mixed funding or *de minimis* buy out options. This may worsen with the increased use of EPA model documents.

- EPA will increasingly coordinate actions against PRPs with other federal agencies such as natural resource damage claims, (NOAA) on securities filings (SEC) and on Title III reporting.
- Response action contractor (RAC) liability and indemnification still has not been resolved. The RACs effectiveness is threatened due to uncertainty in cleanup standards, indefinite performance standards, and the perceived or real shortfall in adequate risk financing alternatives.
- At this time, it appears that the availability of affordable and less restrictive pollution insurance may be determined primarily by the courts in continued litigation between policyholders and their primary and excess carriers. Unless there is a legislative resolution to this litigation, the reinsurers who are the backbone of such a market (and now also becoming litigants and participants in Superfund arbitration cases) will continue to stay away from reinsuring potential pollution risks.
- Lastly, the Superfund oversight hearings will need to address finding solutions to problems with the EPA remedy selection process, discretionary apportionment of liability by the courts, lender liability, protection for fiduciaries in asset management and the avoidance of benefits to recalcitrant PRPs.

One of the hottest issues on Capitol Hill and within EPA and the board rooms of many commercial banks and S&Ls is the lender liability issue. This issue involves the "secured creditor" exemption in the statute and defines what constitutes protection of a lender's security interest in its collateral. Also at issue is the definition of innocent landowners and the defensible standards of due diligence needed to demonstrate appropriate inquiry. Key segments of the financial services industry are affected, such as the commercial and institutional lenders, real estate developers and quasi-government agencies like the Small Business Administration, Federal Deposit Insurance Corporation, and Resolution Trust Corporation. These entities are awaiting EPA and OMB action on the interpretive administrative rule affecting the "secured creditor" exemption. All organizations will be required to perform due diligence as a defense against future liability at the pre-loan during and prior to foreclosure.

## The Management of Solid and Hazardous Wastes

One of the most complex bodies of government regulations involved with the management of solid and hazardous wastes is embodied in the Resource Conservation and Recovery Act (RCRA) and its 1984 Hazardous and Solid Waste Amendments (HSWA). These laws created over 72 rules and regulatory deadlines with many soft and hard hammers that have been the driving force behind the management of solid and hazardous wastes.

Over 500,000 companies and individuals in the U.S. that generate over 200 million metric tons of hazardous waste each year must comply with the RCRA regulatory program at a cost to industry of about $11-$15 billion per year. RCRA is a regulatory statute designed to provide "cradle-to-grave" control of hazardous waste by imposing management requirements on generators, transporters and owners and operators of treatment, storage, disposal and recovery/recycling facilities.

The most significant subtitles of RCRA are Subtitle C for hazardous waste, Subtitle D for nonhazardous wastes, and Subtitle I for underground storage tanks.[10] Tank management will also be paramount with the implementation of technical and financial responsibility requirements. Government financial responsibility requirements for owners and operators of treatment, storage, disposal and recycling/reuse (TSDR) facilities and underground storage tanks (USTs) have forced corporate risk managers to deal head on with assessing numerous government financial assurance instruments and options in order to meet facility corrective action, closure and post closure, as well as liability requirements.

## Risk Financing Requirements and Alternatives

### Statutory Financial Responsibility Requirements

Under RCRA § 3004(a)(6) of Subtitle C, owners and operators (O/O) of treatment, storage, disposal and reuse/recycling facilities are required to demonstrate financial responsibility against potential third party claims resulting from bodily injury or property damages.[11] These regulations call for owners and operators to demonstrate financial assurance during the operating life of the facility. The shortfall in pollution legal liability insurance was most forcefully witnessed in late 1984 for both sudden and gradual loss incidents and exposures. Key market forces lead to the perceived and real lack of insurance capacity of both general liability and environmental impairment liability (EIL) coverage.

Adverse judicial interpretations of comprehensive general liability (CGL)[12] policies, the withdrawal of the excess and reinsurance carriers and their capacity, coupled with cash flow underwriting by insurers and the cyclic nature of the insurance and economic marketplace led the EPA to promulgate additional financial responsibility mechanisms in September of 1988.[13] Companies can now meet their RCRA financial assurance requirements by employing financial instruments that include liability insurance, surety bonds, a financial test, a corporate guarantee from a parent corporation, cross stream and multi-tier corporate guarantees, letters of credit and combinations of these mechanisms. Limits for owners/operators of treatment and storage facilities are required to demonstrate $1 million per incident and $2 million in the aggregate. Owners/operators of land disposal facilities, including surface impoundments, waste piles, underground injection wells and land disposal facilities are required to demonstrate $3 million per occurrence and $6 million in the aggregate for nonsudden and gradual incidents in addition to the sudden and accidental coverages, exclusive of legal defense costs, with first dollar coverage provided by the insurer. Certain states like Louisiana and Massachusetts have set more stringent financial responsibility requirements for limits of liability insurance.

The financial instruments used most often to meet the financial assurance requirements for third party liability are insurance or insurance in combination with a financial test or a corporate guarantee and insurance. TSDR facilities are also required to demonstrate financial assurance for closure and post closure activities. Many facilities employ irrevocable letters of credit, trust funds or bonds as financial instruments in order to meet their requirements for facility closure and post closure.[14]

Owners/operators of petroleum-filled USTs also are required to demonstrate financial assurance under Section 205 of SARA, amending Subtitle I of RCRA for USTs. These owners/operators need to demonstrate financial responsibility for both third party claims as well as onsite cleanup or corrective action against onsite leaks or releases. Those owners/operators of 100 petroleum tanks or fewer need to maintain $1 million per occurrence and $1 million in the aggregate while those owners/operators of over 100 tanks need a $1 million per occurrence and $2 million in the aggregate. Nine financial assurance instruments are available to them. In addition, the rules require owners of USTs with monthly throughputs of under 10,000 gallons per year to secure $500,000 per occurrence or claim and $1 million in the aggregate. EPA has extended the financial assurance compliance deadline for UST owners/operators of between 13 and 99 tanks at multiple sites to April 26, 1991. Owners/operators of tanks have until October 26, 1991, if they have fewer than 13 tanks at multiple sites or fewer than 100 tanks at one site.[15]

The demand on owners/operators to meet regulatory requirements has been weak due to both the lack of government enforcement for noncompliance and the perceived shortfall in traditional insurance markets. The availability of alternative risk financing mechanisms like state assurance trust funds has proved to be a viable short-term risk financing alternative to commercial insurance. In some states, insurers have established wrap around programs with the approved state trust funds aimed at providing the required administrative skill or capacity.

## Risk Financing Alternatives

A corporate environmental risk management program and strategy should require the risk manager to identify and evaluate toxic and hazardous pollutant exposures, design loss control and prevention programs in order to reduce or eliminate such exposures and/or transfer the potential for future environmental loss exposures through a pollution insurance risk financing alternative.

Companies that generate or handle hazardous constituents need to employ risk assessment as part of their risk control and finance program in order to facilitate commercial pollution insurance (i.e., Environmental Impairment Liability or EIL) or a self-funded insurance program that considers group or association insurance (i.e., captives or risk retention groups).

## Risk Assessment Survey and Insurance Application Process

For those insurers providing coverage for pollution risks, the risk assessment is the critical tool for underwriting and rating pollution exposures. The combination of negative market and pollution insurance conditions; stringent legislative, regulatory and common law actions; and the uncertain court actions against general liability and EIL insurers has led to a limited growth both in primary, reinsurance and excess insurance capacity from the traditional and specialty markets. The risk assessment survey therefore becomes the company's essential technique for both identifying and correcting pollution exposures and making insurance available.

Risk assessment surveys are usually required in order to bind pollution liability insurance from both the commercial specialty and non-traditional pollution insurance carriers. All phases of the survey depend heavily on the cooperation of the proposed policyholders, the broker/agent, primary insurer (in some cases the reinsurer or excess carrier), and the expertise and technical judgment of the consulting risk assessment firm. Key phases of the survey include:

- Raw material, hazardous substance, constituent or waste inventory and characterization;
- Previous claims history, records search, compliance and permits review;
- Corporate interview and site survey of the environmental setting, facility description of conditions and receptor population(s) exposures, corporate and facility environmental management policies and practices.

Where required by the insurer in policy conditions, follow-up surveys are also conducted to ensure observations or recommendations for corrective measures have been implemented.

The risk assessment also provides the potential policyholder with a qualitative judgement/assessment of the potential loss exposures and liabilities associated with past and present activities. The assessment is based in part upon the inherent risks of the hazardous materials or substances handled or produced onsite, and their potential for causing harm to receptor populations. The assessment also evaluates the efficacy of the current environmental risk management program; the degree of control, prevention and minimization exercised in materials/wastes processing, handling and storage, current practices for waste treatment; and the adequacy of corrective measures or remedial action for past loss exposures.

Some key benefits and advantages of having a risk assessment include:

- Independent verification of corporation compliance with statutory and regulatory requirements and how the corporations are perceived by company management and employees, as well as by the government and third parties;
- Determination of the extent to which community or worker health and safety may be impaired from hazardous material or wastes, irrespective of the status of compliance with applicable standards;
- Determination of the extent to which employees are adhering to corporate and plant management policies and guidelines regarding environmental protection and worker health and safety;
- The protection of assets and net income through a proactive environmental risk management plan.

The risk assessment process as discussed hereunder is consistent with the protocol used by EIL carriers in the United States, Canada and selected European countries. Single and multiple site surveys are generally initiated by contacting a licensed broker or agent about pollution insurance. Some insurers are direct writers (i.e., First Environmental Review Insurance Co.) and do not use brokers or agents to market or facilitate the underwriting of the risk. When a broker/agent is used, the broker/agent advises his or her client about those specialty markets (traditional and non-traditional), and the insurance options available to the client. The client must complete a standard pollution insurance application. If a broker/agent is used, the carrier will provide the broker/agent a copy of the policy application and a list of acceptable risk assessment consulting firms.

Insurance coverage is site specific. The nature of the company's operation and the number of sites to be insured will determine the assessment schedule. In some cases not all sites are surveyed; some are "paper audited" the first year and site visited in the following year based on risk factors identified through company documentation, telephone interviews and regulatory contacts. A recently performed risk assessment may be acceptable for underwriting purposes depending on when it was done and by whom.

The next step involves either the broker/agent or the potential policyholder securing bids for performance of the required risk assessments and/or paper audits. The potential policyholder then evaluates a risk assessment firm based on its level of experience and expertise in performing risk assessment surveys. The evaluation process includes the examination of the individual risk assessor(s) that will be performing the assessments. Key questions that should be asked: "Are we getting a risk assessor who understands our operation?" and "Are we getting a senior level person whose experience will be respected by facility management?"

The range of prices for a risk assessment vary according to the location of the sites, the nature and complexity of the operations, number of sites to be assessed, and the time schedule for completing the project. The cost of the risk assessment is usually borne by the potential policyholder. Risk assessment findings usually need to be determined prior to or as a condition of binding coverage. The turnaround time for completion of a risk assessment is between three and five weeks, again dependent on the complexity and availability of data about the facility. Some carriers are now using their inhouse risk assessors and passing the costs of the survey on to the insured in the price of the premium.

For potential policyholders with multiple sites using an outside risk assessment firm, the firm or the client's broker will coordinate all site visits. Pre-site questionnaires are sent out to request inventory lists of raw materials, products, byproducts and hazardous wastes, compliance records and process and permit information, a copy of the policy application, site plots, 10(K) and annual reports, and notices of any violations.

There may be an interview with the company's top management in order to evaluate corporate procedures and policies related to their environmental risk management program and their overall commitment to risk control, and prevention of pollution by toxic and hazardous materials and substances. Final selection of sites to be surveyed is negotiated between the insured and the insurer. The number of sites visited and depth of information sought may be influenced by preexisting treaty agreements between the primary carrier and their reinsurers.

All scheduled site visits involve a thorough interview with plant management and a site walk-through of the plant facility and its grounds. The risk assessors use generic and tailored checklists. Normally the site visit involves one or two days onsite with one or two senior level risk assessors and the plant and/or environmental managers. A representative from corporate or the insured's brokerage firm may also attend.

The risk assessment survey should fulfill several specific objectives:

- To accurately document and inventory actual onsite conditions, operations and named perils. This includes identifying and evaluating potential for nonsudden and/or sudden hazardous substances releases;
- To compare site conditions via an independent verification of compliance to established statutory, regulatory, loss control, and operational requirements;
- To identify and evaluate the toxic or hazardous substances that have potential for release, the subsequent pathways for exposure, and the inherent hazard(s) associated with the material(s) and constituents located onsite;
- To determine accuracy in reporting and recordkeeping programs;
- To address the effectiveness of management control systems (e.g., risk control program information management systems, pollution prevention or waste minimization programs);
- To informally debrief management on cost-effective source reduction or process engineering alternatives or waste handling/waste minimization options and areas of concern needing possible corrective or remedial actions;
- To qualitatively assess potential lossexposures and areas of liability associated with past and current site activities.

After the site visit is conducted, the assessor(s) will compile all site data, perform background technical/engineering data analysis, and make regulatory agency contacts. A draft report is developed by the risk assessor(s) for the client's evaluation and comments. Client technical comments are reviewed by the risk assessor(s) and, where appropriate, incorporated or appended to the final report. Depending on the report findings and confidentiality considerations, the report may go to corporate or outside counsel or to the proposed insured who in turn directs it to their broker/agent or directly to the insurance carrier for consideration.

The risk assessment may call for the entire site to be underwritten or specify unit operations to be covered. Conditions or contingencies may be identified and placed on potential loss exposures that may result in endorsements to exclude or add an operation based upon remedial measures being undertaken. If pollution insurance is denied, the risk assessment report can serve as a loss control tool and in some cases as an environmental audit for future environmental risk management planning.

Companies subject to the risk assessment process often wish to prevent disclosure of confidential business and environmental information to regulators or the general public. The proposed insured may wish to seek all legal control possible for the confidentiality of all written, verbal or oral communications. The potential policyholder may also seek to maintain control of how the risk assessment survey is staffed, the scheduling of site visits and cost. Finally, the potential policyholder should evaluate the report for accuracy (i.e., process waste stream information). The report and its findings and observations are based on established standards and requirements and expert professional judgement. The risk assessment firm, if challenged by insurance underwriters, regulatory agencies or in a court of law should be prepared to justify its review of available data. Sampling and analysis is beyond the normal scope of a typical risk assessment survey. However, if sampling and analysis is requested, the data should be reproducible and therefore defensible.

The following qualitative risk assessment data should be gathered and assessed as part of the survey:

- Examine management plans and policies, housekeeping, recordkeeping, permitting and contingency planning and documentation;
- Examine overall facility description and environmental setting;
- Conduct an inventory of potentially hazardous constituents, characteristics of the raw materials, products, by-products, and wastes and then quantitatively characterize the hazardous materials, or constituents or wastes for their potential chemical, physical and toxicological properties, fate and effects (referring to Title III form R filings);
- Determine the flow of chemicals that the facility uses and characterize the various unit process operations, storage practices, and waste disposal operations and areas;

- Assess the site characteristics (i.e., topography, geological formations, onsite land use activities and offsite land uses;
- Inspection for signs of pollution, such as stained soil, distressed vegetation, noxious odors, fill or vent pipe indicators of abandoned underground storage tanks;
- Review ancillary operations (non-process management control);
- Assess point and non-point sources of storm/waste water discharges, stationary point source and fugitive air emissions, surface water discharges and solid non-hazardous and hazardous waste generation, groundwater conditions and groundwater monitoring data;
- Review the current practices in engineering design, facility operations, management, employee training, maintenance of pollution controls for hazardous waste treatment, storage, and disposal operations and areas;
- Evaluate any hazardous waste minimization/recycling plans and audits and note future pollution prevention plans;
- Enumerate and identify population distribution centers along potential pathways of exposure, including high risk groups;
- Address non-human populations and the potential for natural resource(s) damages;
- Make note of occupational health and safety considerations and conditions from material safety data sheets on the nature of chemical toxicity and hazards and OSHA 200 forms that reflect the potential for worker exposure as well as how conditions may lead to worker error and result in a sudden and accidental pollution release as well as business interruption;
- Assess facility sensitivity to crisis management, risk communications and overall community political risk by examining the company program to address SARA Title III requirements, (i.e., community right-to-know laws, emergency and contingency planning) the Hazard Communication program, and process safety management of highly hazardous chemicals;
- Certain insurers require that regulatory agencies be contacted to verify compliance and permit conditions (i.e., notices of violation and other environmental data);

- Finally, all risk assessment data and related information should be summarized by risk categories from the survey findings and observations to determine the potential for non-sudden and sudden environmental impairment and named perils.

The rating matrix used by various insurers may emphasize or prioritize exposure units differently; however, there is overall uniformity in addressing categories of risk. The effect on the overall rating of favorable and negative factors is assessed by the underwriter in order to determine the potential for sudden or non-sudden releases of hazardous or toxic substances, environmental impairment and named perils related to the facility site. Observations or recommendations are developed for risk control, pollution prevention and waste reduction/minimization purposes as well as for corrective measures or remedial action of particular exposure units being assessed for first party and/or third party insurance coverage. Potential policyholders with a cited or questionable loss exposure will negotiate specific terms and conditions (e.g., contingencies, exclusions and endorsements) of coverage. The pollution concerns must be addressed or rectified either prior to or as a condition of pollution insurance coverage.

## Top Management Commitment

An extremely important factor in the qualitative risk assessment process includes assessment of overall corporate philosophy, policies, procedures, and/or guidelines related to the proactive management of toxic and hazardous wastes. Such an evaluation both addresses top management's commitment and support of pollution prevention and control and also identifies key personnel in the organization responsible for the environmental risk management activities.

Top management's philosophy and concern about a facility's operation is reflected in the plant's overall concern and participation in quality control and quality assurance. Top management's commitment to a proactive environmental risk management program is witnessed by effective lines of communication from the President/CEO down and reflected by line management's awareness, action and accountability. Incentives need to be offered to all employees to participate in the pollution prevention activities and waste minimization programs within the plant and in the community.

Companies that have a centralized organizational structure allow their top management to have greater influence over environmental pollution issues. Decentralized organizational structures (companies with division, group or unit operations presidents) need even greater integration of communication and commitment to environmental compliance. Senior management responsible for these efforts must develop policies, commit resources, delegate responsibilities and enforce or hold senior line managers accountable for results (i.e., management by results). Production and risk management personnel should be provided with incentives and rewarded by top management based on their implementation of environmental safeguards, pollution prevention (source reduction, material substitution, process refitting), and waste minimization techniques (recycling/reuse) that ultimately provide cost savings while protecting assets from claims or suits. It is essential that production line management be rewarded for environmental cost savings just as they are for meeting production quotas.

Top management's responsiveness to the needs of and candid communications with individual plant personnel reflect the overall attitude of the organization toward potential pollution exposures and liabilities. With increased civil and criminal sanctions reflected in most environmental and occupational requirements and increased public access to information, the impact of laws under SARA's Title III and OSHA's Hazard Communications Standard (Worker Right-to-Know) laws, top management needs to be even more sensitive to potential personal and corporate liability resulting from disgruntled employees, government inspectors or citizen actions for perceived and actual mismanagement of toxic or hazardous substances. A company's effective communication skills will be one of the determining factors in preventing loss exposures from becoming liabilities.

The risk assessment process should be part of a company's overall environmental risk management program for purposes of loss control as much as for risk transfer. The environmental risk management challenges of tomorrow will call for company officers and their risk managers to be more accountable, not only to their shareholders but also to their public (i.e., Valdez Principles). This will demand more effective risk communication regarding potential and actual pollution exposures.

Because the pollution insurance market is slow to expand, a company generating and/or handling hazardous materials and/or wastes will in the short term need to retain much of its potential pollution liability. Risk transfer options involving commercial liability insurers or alternative mechanisms like liability risk retention groups or purchasing groups will be available only to those companies that can demonstrate solid corporate and environmental waste management practices and can afford to pay the premiums and/or meet the capitalization requirements.

Corporate management will continually be faced with establishing a balance between production quotas and environmental protection. An environmental risk management program prudently developed can turn risk control and loss prevention costs into production savings. Implementing pollution prevention and waste minimization programs, risk assessment and environmental auditing, information management systems and preemptive strategies to anticipate regulatory or legal/judicial actions will go a long way toward protecting corporate assets, reducing loss exposures and liabilities and insuring against pollution incidents.

## Pollution Insurance Marketplace

The demand and availability of pollution insurance took a dive in the mid-1980s as a result of increased losses, inconsistent risk assessment standards, cash flow underwriting, and judicial interpretations making **comprehensive** general liability (CGL) insurance policies adverse to insurers. The demand for pollution coverage is based on the need for liability protection, financial responsibility requirements, indemnification for onsite cleanup costs (first party), and as an alternative to the absolute pollution exclusion on the **commercial** general liability (CGL) form.

### Past and Present Developments

The property and casualty market is cyclic by nature. Commentators have observed that the demand by companies for EIL insurance has been limited by restrictiveness of the policy coverages, by weak government enforcement of financial responsibility regulations (especially for the underground storage tanks), by high premium prices, by a perception that the product was unavailable at affordable prices, and by the desire of many companies to employ either self-insurance or an alternative risk financing program.

At one time in late 1984 there were as many as 16 viable markets underwriting EIL coverage on a monoline basis with a combined pollution insurance (EIL) capacity that exceeded $165 million. Among them were included Evanston Insurance Company through Shand Morahan; Hartford Steam Boiler Insurance Company; Great American Surplus Lines Co. through Stewart Smith; St. Paul Surplus Lines; American International Group Companies, i.e., National Union and American Home Assurance; The Home Group and the 49 member companies of the Pollution Liability Insurance Association (PLIA). With the withdrawal from the U.S. market of key reinsurers like SCOR, Swiss Re, Zurich Insurance and other European insurance companies, the reduction in capacity, market demand and increase in claims and IBNRs (incurred but not reported) liability exposures, the market shrank to two major players. In late 1987, Reliance National Risk Specialists, a Reliance Holding Group Company, came onto the EIL scene with Environmental Compliance Services, Inc., (ECS) as their managing general agency. In 1991, U.S. capacity is restricted to about $30 million in true EIL insurance with additional capacity for limited named perils coverage coming from one domestic excess insurance association and several offshore excess captive insurance carriers. With the passage of the Liability Risk Retention Act of 1986, two EIL markets, the Environmental Protection Insurance Company (EPIC) and Petromark, Inc., emerged to provide some coverage for owners and operators of TSDFs and USTs. However, lack of demand and inadequate capitalization resulted in their demise and runoff in early 1990.

Today we have principally two key EIL markets: AIG underwriting through one of its companies, Commerce & Industry, Inc., (formerly American Home/National Union) and Reliance National (formerly Reliance National Risk Specialists). Other companies like St. Paul and the Chubb Group have reentered the pollution insurance market, but only to fill a niche, custom tailored market product line needs and on an accommodation basis (adding a line of coverage to a pre-existing, multiple line of coverage) offering limited capacity to their insureds. Other insurers like Lloyds and the ILU Companies offer substantial limits, up to $50 million, but the coverage is restrictive and appears to include only named perils for sudden and accidental pollution liability coverage. Highlighted in this chapter are the other niche markets like United Coastal, United Capital, St. Paul Fire & Marine Insurance Co., Front Royal Insurance Company, First Environmental Review Insurance Co., and London (NAS Services) KILN syndicate who target key accounts and fill market niche demand.

The EIL carriers for pollution insurance are currently targeting niche or custom tailored markets such as response action contractors, environmental engineering and consultants, tank removers, lenders, environmental laboratories, property developers, low risk association business and hospitals, etc. Generators representing heavy industry and manufacturing seeking EIL coverage have found many of the coverage provisions to be too restrictive and expensive. The EIL carriers, too, are restricting their offerings, due to the litigious market conditions affecting the pre-1986 comprehensive general liability and EIL carriers.

### ISO Pollution Exclusion and Endorsement

Adverse judicial decisions based on interpretations of CGL insurance policies issued prior to 1986 lead the Insurance Services Office (ISO) and other insurance organizations to modify the CGL policy to exclude pollution coverage from CGL policy forms on an absolute basis. (See Chapters XXVII, Russell and Chapter XXVIII, Heintz). Effective in 1986, the ISO came out with the "new" pollution exclusion for the CGL form which excludes all pollution no matter whether it is gradual/nonsudden or sudden and accidental.[16] The CGL policy categorically excludes coverage for pollution, except for products completed operations and certain other offsite exposures. The exclusion is incorporated in both the "occurrence" and "claims-made" versions of the policy. It makes no distinction between sudden and gradual emission of pollutants. It excludes coverage for:

"Bodily injury" or "property damage" arising out of the actual, alleged or threatened discharge, dispersal, seepage, migration, release or escape of pollutants:

    (a) At or from any premises, site or location which is or was at any time owned or occupied by, or rented or loaned to, any insured;

(b) At or from any premises, site or location which is or was at any time used by or for any insured or others for the handling, storage, disposal, processing or treatment of waste;

(c) Which are at any time transported, handled, stored, treated, disposed of, or processed as waste by or for you or any person or organization for whom you may be legally responsible; or

(d) At or from any premises, site or location on which any insured or any contractors or subcontractors working directly or indirectly on any insured's behalf are performing operations:

    (i) if the pollutants are brought on or to the premises, site or location in connection with such operations by such insured, contractor or subcontractor; or

    (ii) if the operations are to test for, monitor, clean up, remove, contain, treat, detoxify or neutralize, or in any way respond to, or assess the effects of pollutants.[17]

Coverage for emissions from the insured's premises, whether gradual or sudden, will be provided under the CGL policy by use of special forms and endorsements.

The ISO filed in 1989 CGL modifications or buy-back options to the pollution exclusion that allows on a limited basis endorsements or coverage. Insurers at their discretion on an individual account basis can provide these buy-back options. The three options include:

- Pollution liability coverage extension endorsement CG0422, that deletes the pollution exclusion for bodily injury and property damage and can be attached to either an "occurrence" or a "claims-made" policy, and continues to exclude cleanup costs;
- Pollution liability coverage form (designated sites) CB0039, providing coverage on a "claims-made" basis only, with its own limits; and
- Pollution liability limited coverage form (designated sites) CG0040, limits coverage to damages because of bodily injury or property damage only and excludes coverage for cleanup and related costs.

These policy revisions essentially recognize a separate pollution policy for the exposures described.

The ISO and organizations like the Risk and Insurance Management Society and other insurance and bar associations are presently working to amend the wording. Pertinent coverage can be expected to be modified periodically with additional endorsement wording.

### Liability Risk Retention Act of 1986

To fill the shortfall in available pollution liability insurance, Congress passed in 1986 the Liability Risk Retention Act (LRRA). LRRA allows risk retention and purchasing groups to be developed and licensed "onshore", contingent upon compliance with the technical and financial requirements of any one state, therefore potentially preempting the admission requirements of other states. With the enactment of the LRRA, and the 1986 Tax Reform Act and subsequent amendments, the momentum has been shifting away from offshore captives and toward the formation of domestic risk retention and purchasing groups. The LRRA does not allow, in all cases, the preemption of the RCRA financial responsibility requirements for those states where permit provisions require that insurance be provided by licensed carriers in that state. As a result of the LRRA, several pollution risk retention groups (RRG) were capitalized and made operational in 1988. As noted above, two of the most notable facilities shut down operations due to under-capitalization of reserves to pay losses (Petromark) and lack of demand for the product (Environmental Protection Insurance Company). Petromark, an RRG operated by the Planning Corporation, underwrote owners and operators of petroleum underground storage tanks and the Environmental Protection Insurance Company (EPIC), an RRG for USTs and a broader range of pollution risks, officially closed their doors in early 1990. Petromark's book of business was assumed by various Lloyds syndicates, while EPIC dissolved operations due to the lack of profitability.[18]

There are risk retention groups presently underwriting pollution type risks (i.e., USTs), but on a limited basis. Terra Insurance Corporation Limited is one risk retention group based in Vermont that provides professional liability insurance for response action contractors on a limited basis. Terra Insurance and its subsidiary Demeter Ltd. were founded to provide limits of E&O and EIL coverage for professional engineering firms. Demeter, Ltd. is a Bermuda-based stock insurance company offering $1 million in limits of EIL insurance. The initial success of these non-traditional markets (risk retention groups) has not been promising for the pollution type risk. To date, there has been little demand due to capitalization requirements and cited restrictiveness of policy language.

## Insurance Alternatives

The need for alternatives to commercial pollution liability insurance for small as well as large businesses can in part be met through the development of non-traditional insurance programs that include both mutual and stock captive insurance companies, risk retention and purchasing groups, pools, and reciprocal insurance exchanges that offer primary and excess general liability and pollution liability insurance coverage. To date there is a handful of profitable captive insurance companies underwriting excess liability coverage that includes sudden and accidental pollution coverage with limits up to $300 million for key industry risks.

### *Captives*

One successful risk financing mechanism created for catastrophic loss has been the excess captive. A captive insurance company is a company formed to insure the risks of its shareholders. The captive can take the form of a pure captive (sole owner), association captive (more non-insurance entities) or a rent-a-captive (fronting type program). To date the two most successful applications of an association captive facility have been Marsh & McLennan and Morgan Guaranty's American Casualty Excess Insurance (ACE) facility and its younger brother, X.L. Insurance Company, Ltd. Both excess casualty facilities have matured in the marketplace with a strong billion (s) dollar equity base while providing underwriting stability in price and policy forms for the potential excess and catastrophic risk.

Captives need to be licensed in every state in which they wish to write insurance. This is dependent on the type of captive insurer and the state insurance requirements. The LRRA may, on the other hand, allow a trust-funded offshore captive to serve as a non-admitted insurer of a purchasing group if it is done through a licensed broker acting according to the surplus lines laws of that state where the purchasing group is located.

*Key Markets*

There are dedicated markets for pollution legal liability insurance. They are AIG (Commerce & Industry, Inc., formerly National Union/American Home Insurance Companies) and Reliance National (Environmental Compliance Service, Managing General Agency). Both provide sudden/gradual, third party personal/bodily injury and property damage (PI or BI/PD), claims-made coverage on a primary and excess basis. AIG's liability limits are $20 million per incident and $20 million in the aggregate, while Reliance National's limits are $5 million/$10 million. They both will consider underwriting a broad range of risks that include hospitals, utilities, light and heavy manufacturers, electroplaters, TSDFs, recyclers, mining, oil and gas, etc. Both offer pollution legal liability, two forms of contractor pollution liability (CPL) coverage, transporters pollution liability, Response Action Contractors (RACs) errors and omissions (E&O) coverage, TSD pollution liability, an environmental consultants E&O coverage, and soon a lender liability product.

Reliance National offers those products discussed above plus hospital pollution liability, professional liability for environmental laboratories, and a first party pollution cleanup program geared to the property purchaser or borrower and its lender.

A new entry into the pollution insurance marketplace is First Environmental Review Insurance Company, a First City Financial Corporation subsidiary that offers a claims-made $2 million aggregate policy for first party coverage designed to provide environmental remediation insurance for environmental risks associated with developed and undeveloped property.

Lloyds and the ILU Companies currently offer $50 million in limits of sudden/accidental pollution liability through Leslie & Godwin on a monoline claims-made basis. This facility will cover risks on a named perils basis as in transportation risks, collision, and overturn of road and railroad vehicles.

*Specialty Markets*

Specialty insurance carriers offer pollution coverage products for niche markets. These insurers include United Capitol and United Coastal. They offer limits ranging from $1 million per occurrence and $1 million in the aggregate to $5 million per occurrence and $5 million in the aggregate for professional E&O for environmental engineers and consultants. United Capitol is alleged to be one of the largest underwriters for owners and operators of sanitary landfills.

Other liability markets include St. Paul Fire & Marine Insurance Company who underwrites aboveground pollution liability, 72-hour trigger on a sudden and accidental basis. Front Royal Insurance Company, a Virginia domiciled carrier, underwrites petroleum, offsite non-petroleum and Directors and Officers (D&O) pollution coverages. Front Royal currently underwrites low risk association business. Front Royal is in the process of developing a lender liability product.

Finally, there are other specialty carriers like the Chubb Group and London (NAS Services) KILN syndicate that offer niche products to insureds. Chubb Energy Resources Group currently underwrites oil and gas pollution liability for sudden and accidental incidents on a claims-made form for limits of $1 million in the aggregate. The coverage is only for property damage. The KILN syndicate, through NAS Services, provides a bankers environmental legal exposure reimbursement coverage tailored for banks, S&Ls, and other financial institutions. It covers legal expenses in defending insureds against allegations of damage by pollution or contamination originating from property acquired through foreclosure of loans made by the institution or which the institution holds in trust. Law suits and Superfund administrative procedures are covered. Limits of coverage are $1 million per claim and $1 million in the aggregate. There are many carriers that provide limited pollution insurance on an accommodation basis, such as The Travelers and The Home Group.

### UST Markets

There are presently 18 markets for UST risks. All carriers except AIG and Travelers appear to meet EPA's financial responsibility requirements by offering limits of $1 million per occurrence and $2 million in the aggregate and providing for onsite corrective action. Of those 18 markets, 14 represent the more traditional carriers, while four are represented by non-traditional carriers such as a purchasing group or risk retention group.

The Great American, Agricultural Excess Surplus Insurance Company (AESIC) program appears to offer more complete coverage or capacity on a per location basis. The carriers like Oilmen's, General Star (General Re) or the new Lloyds facility (formerly Petromark, the risk retention group) will underwrite the UST coverage. Carriers like AIG and Tank Owners Insurance Company perform wrap-around programs with the state insurance trust funds.

Thirty-seven states have passed legislation for establishing trust funds that are competing head-on with the traditional insurance carriers. Fourteen states have EPA-approved facilities. States like Iowa offer three types of programs: a guarantee program: insurance and onsite cleanup.[19]

*Foreign Markets*

Foreign insurers in Europe generally do not exclude sudden/accidental or nonsudden/gradual coverage from the CGL policies, except for Italy.[20] Presently there are half a dozen European carriers underwriting pollution risks for industry association business. Also, countries like France, Italy and The Netherlands maintain active insurance pools underwriting pollution insurance for certain industrial risks.[21] New pollution liability insurance products are emerging in the European marketplace from carriers such as AIU and Zurich Insurance Company. AIU is coming out with a new pollution insurance policy for industrial risks with limits of coverage targeted at $10 million per policyholder.[22] Also Swiss Re will continue to be an active participant in providing EIL coverage as they have over the last 15 years. Currently Swiss Re offers $9.4 million in aggregate EIL insurance for British chemical companies through its Palatine Insurance Co. Ltd. subsidiary. Risk assessments will be performed by the insured prior to binding coverage.

The Zurich Insurance Company will introduce the new "Europolicy" to provide corporations up to $91 million in property damage and $36.3 million in liability coverage. At this writing, it is uncertain how much pollution liability coverage will be offered through the Zurich facility. Historically, Zurich has provided to its insureds on an accommodation basis, sudden and accidental coverage for named perils. Zurich Insurance has been a key reinsurer of American carriers who provide environmental impairment liability insurance. Their presence in both the American and European markets has been that of a conservative underwriter of potential pollution risks. Zurich Insurance employs rigorous underwriting criteria based on a systematic risk engineering program. An acceptable risk must reasonably and adequately cover critical steps undertaken in the Zurich

Hazard Analysis Methodology.[23] The general liability coverage underwritten by Zurich Insurance typically covers the potential pollution exposures for only sudden and accidental incidents arising from specific named perils such as fire, explosion, implosion, tanks, and associated piping and transportation incidents. Zurich provides this type of coverage for their multinational clientele who have operations (risks) in both Europe and the United States.

At this time, European industrial establishments demonstrate limited demand for pollution coverage underwritten on a monoline basis. As the liability standard changes from a fault-based standard to strict liability, the demand may go up voluntarily or be mandated for high hazard industrial establishments.[24]

Companies seeking pollution liability coverage on a worldwide basis can secure limits up to $300 million (time tested sudden/accidental coverage). For U.S. operations, on a claims-made basis, $30 million in coverage is available from the specialty markets providing EIL, notably AIG (Commerce & Industry, formerly underwritten by National Union and American Home Assurance Company), and Reliance National through Planet Insurance Co. via their managing general agency, Environmental Compliance Services, Inc. (ECS). Structuring a program in excess of $30 million would call for securing time-tested sudden and accidental named perils coverage from either American Excess Insurance Association, better known as the AEIA (American Slip), or from non-traditional offshore captive excess casualty insurers such as X.L., Ltd., and ACE. X.L., Ltd., will attach limits as low as $15 million up to $100 million, while ACE will provide up to $200 million in limits in excess of a $100 million underlying limit.

European companies, with operations in both Europe and the U.S., will find pollution liability coverage generally available, on occurrence-made forms, under their general liability policies except for in Italy, where pollution coverage is excluded in the general liability policy. The layering of coverages would come from both traditional carriers or from offshore markets.[25]

These coverage contracts will be contingent upon the business relationship, industry segment, loss/claims history, accommodated lines of coverage, liability standard in the respective country, other underwriting criteria, and industry segment.

Many European carriers are beginning to limit pollution coverage to claims-made, sudden and accidental incidents on a named peril basis, in light of the changing standard of liability in Europe for pollution risks.

## Analysis of Key Markets

*American International Group*

American International Group, Inc., (AIG) has shifted its pollution insurance book of business from National Union Fire Insurance Co., of Pittsburgh, Pennsylvania, over to Commerce & Industry, Inc., a division of AIG. The pollution legal liability is broad pollution third party liability insurance offered as a monoline coverage on both a primary and excess basis. AIG writes on a claims-made policy with limits of $20 million per claim or incident and $20 million in the aggregate covering both sudden and accidental incidents as well as gradual pollution. Gradual pollution coverage can be written separately. Coverage is site-specific, named locations. Third party bodily injury and property damages are covered with a one-year extended reporting period and no retroactive date. Exclusions on the third party policy include no coverage for sold, closed or onsite cleanup; non-owned disposal sites; known prior acts; sites owned, but not operated, by the insured; pollution occurring during waste transportation; pollution stemming from defective products; and punitive damages. Underground storage tanks may be endorsed onto the third party policy if the tanks are part of the operation.

The AIG program for TSDRFs complies with EPA federal and state financial responsibility requirements with defense costs outside the underlying limits capped at 25 percent of the aggregate limit. Defense costs can be covered within policy limits at the policyholder's discretion. The minimum premium is $17,500 for $1 million of coverage with a $25,000 self-insured retention. This AIG coverage is written for the potential catastrophic risk. AIG/C & I will perform location as well as account underwriting. Account underwriting considers type of business, total locations, exposure locations, types of facilities, sales volumes, experience and environmental staffing. Location underwriting involves surrounding environment, site features, waste streams, raw materials, finished products, site history, management and regulatory compliance. A risk assessment survey is required prior to binding coverage or as a condition of coverage. AIG uses an exposure rated model and 25 factors in determining premium calculations. Company financials are instrumental in establishing premium price.

AIG will consider a broad range of risks to underwrite. They include hospitals, utilities, mining, oil and gas operations, paper and pulp, recyclers, electroplaters, light and heavy manufacturing, owners and operators of treatment, storage and disposal facilities. AIG has also developed coverages for response action contractors on a blanket basis and project basis. The blanket Contractors Pollution Liability (CPL) policy is offered for two years completed operations. Subcontractors and generals are excluded. There is a minimum premium of $25,000 and minimum retention of $50,000. This blanket coverage is for remediation work offered on a claims-made basis for sudden and gradual incidents. This onsite and offsite third party coverage has defense costs inside the limit.

This policy can also provide coverage for tank installers and removal liability. Limits for the blanket coverage are set at $5 million per incident and $5 million in the aggregate. CPL coverage is also offered on a project basis with similar terms and conditions as the blanket policy except for the following features: coverage limits are $10 million per claim and $10 million in the aggregate. This policy is geared for the EPA Superfund contracts where EPA can indemnify the RAC above the $10 million aggregate or self-insured retention (SIR). Defense costs are covered either within or outside policy limits at the policyholder's discretion. Defense costs covered outside policy limits are capped at 25 percent of the aggregate limit similar to the third party coverage. AIG will provide transporters pollution liability insurance for auto liability on a claims-made basis for sudden and accident incidents. Defense coverage is provided as supplemental with no retroactive date. This coverage is tailored for those haulers on an ISO form. The pollution exclusion is removed for those transporting hazardous materials/wastes over the road. Limits are set at $1 million per claim and $1 million in the aggregate. They will write excess of $4 million above a $1 million self-insured retention or in excess of preexisting limits.

AIG also underwrites response action contractors' E&O coverage for Superfund project work only. (See Chapter XXIV, Dybdahl.) This professional liability coverage sets a minimum premium at

$100,000 for $1 million in coverage. Aggregate limits that are offered are set at $5 million. AIG's newest pollution insurance product is an environmental consultants' E&O coverage. It is offered on a claims-made basis with limits of $2 million per incident and $2 million in the aggregate. These limits are expected to be $5 million per occurrence and $5 million in the aggregate. Minimum deductible and premium is $100,000 unless the insured has other coverage with AIG, then these prices are one-half the set minimum.

AIG currently underwrites and administers three types of EIL programs for owners and operators of underground storage tanks (USTs). The first program is a third party bodily injury/property damage (BI/PD) coverage developed for insureds that have greater than 25 USTs. No first party cleanup coverage is provided for corrective action. Defense costs are outside the limits. Program limits are $5 million per incident and $5 million in the aggregate. Minimum premium is $10,000 with a $10,000 deductible. This is site specific coverage. This is offered in all states; however, in its present form, it does not meet EPA's UST financial responsibility requirements.

AIG also underwrites through Sedgwick James of Pennsylvania a UST program called Enviroguard aimed at owners/operators with 25 or fewer USTs. The same policy features apply as the other UST program; however, limits for this program are set at $1 million per incident and $2 million in the aggregate. Minimum premium and deductible is $1,000. AIG also provides wraparound programs for states that have established a residual market for USTs. Currently AIG is providing program administration for the Florida UST insurance facility.

AIG risk management may still offer through subsidiary companies, American Home and National Union Insurance, pollution risk management and sudden and accidental coverage programs for both gradual and nonsudden as well as sudden and accidental exposures together with voluntary first party pollution cleanup. The policy is on an "indemnity" basis as opposed to "pay on behalf of" with normal policy limits to be negotiated. This coverage is subject to a completed financial review and satisfies action of certain collateral requirements under a budget stabilization program or promissory note program. The program provides for the development of an off-balance-sheet reserve or fund through reinsurance. This fronting program can be employed for insureds on an accommodation basis using the standard commercial general liability policy without the absolute pollution exclusion.

**Risk Financing: Insuring Potential Pollution Exposures**

AIG through Commerce & Industry is coming out with two new insurance products, one to be environmental remediation insurance for real estate transactions and the other program is to be underwritten as portfolio coverage for lenders and financial institutions.

*Reliance National*

Reliance National is the second largest underwriter of pollution insurance in the United States. Reliance National provides first party and third party liability insurance through Environmental Compliance Services, Inc. (ECS). ECS is a managing general agency, performing the underwriting, pricing, binding and servicing of accounts for Reliance National, part of the Reliance Insurance Group. All coverages are provided on a claims-made policy written on Planet Insurance Company paper. Reliance National/ECS pollution liability limits are $5 million per incident and $10 million in the aggregate. All covered locations must be scheduled onto the policy. ECS will perform monoline and account underwriting on a claims-made basis for both sudden and gradual pollution incidents. Defense costs are usually covered within policy limits, except where prohibited by the applicable state law.

ECS is responsible for underwriting and administering a program of insurance for companies on environmental exposure. Insurance coverages arranged under the program include: general liability, automobile liability and physical damage, contractors environmental liability, consultants environmental liability, pollution legal liability, property pollution cleanup, professional liability and excess liability coverage. ECS has also added programs in hospital pollution liability and professional liability for environmental laboratories.

Hazardous waste/hazardous materials transporters whose business operations consist of a minimum of 25 percent of gross receipts involved in the transportation of hazardous materials and waste, including asbestos, are considered for the ECS "Auto Pollution Liability" program. The policy covers sudden and accidental incidents on a claims-made form, no retroactive date. Limits of coverage are $1 million per occurrence and $5 million excess. The coverage is first dollar (no deductible) and does not seek reimbursement from the insured on cleanup. The policy form is an ISO business auto form with a pollution exclusion, which is also required by the government for liability coverage.

The generators and owners and operators involved in the treatment, storage, disposal and reclamation/recycling (TSDR) of hazardous wastes as defined under federal or state environmental laws are covered under the ECS third party pollution legal liability form. Limits of coverage are $5 million per incident and $10 million in the aggregate. No retroactive date is specified, and defense is provided as a supplemental limit when required by statute. The minimum premium is $20,000 and minimum retention is $25,000. Both sudden and gradual coverage is provided on a claims-made basis.

Hazardous waste contractors involved in the cleanup, removal or treatment of hazardous wastes at sites that encompass response (remedial) action contractors, emergency response/spill cleanup and mobile treatment or disposal units are covered under two contractor pollution liability (CPL) programs. One CPL program is tailored to provide blanket coverage for sudden/gradual releases with defense costs within the limits. Subcontractors and the insured's clients can be covered as additional insureds. There is a retroactive date provision. Both first party and third party liability is covered under $5 million limits per claim/incident and $5 million in the aggregate. There is a completed operations coverage of two to five years with the same retroactive date and a one-year extended reporting period for claims. Minimum premium is $20,000, while the minimum retention is $25,000. Other types of contractors are considered such as construction, electrical and tank removal contractors. ECS also offers this product on a project basis with the same policy provisions as the blanket coverage, except the aggregate limits can be raised to $10 million in order to meet certain government Superfund contract requirements. Both CPL programs are written on a claims-made policy.

ECS also offers special niche coverage for hospital pollution liability, sanitary landfills, metal/solvent recyclers and specialty companies. In addition, ECS has launched a consultants' environmental liability (CEL) claims-made policy with coverage that includes first party and pollution cleanup with defense costs within policy limits. Coverage is provided for pollution and professional liability for both "paper" and "hands on" consultants on a blanket or project basis. Limits of coverage vary depending on whether it is provided on a blanket or project basis. If blanket coverage is desired, the limits are $5 million per incident and $5 million per aggregate, and on a project basis, limits to up to $10 million on an aggregate basis. Minimum retention is $25,000 and minimum premium is $25,000 for a $1 million coverage. A one-year extended reporting period is offered. ECS also offers an environmental consultants' professional liability coverage for "paper" consultants. This policy offers the same coverage provisions with a minimum premium of $20,000 based on a $1 million limit.

One of the more recent ECS products is their first party pollution cleanup policy written on a claims-made basis for onsite sudden/ gradual releases. The coverage indemnifies the insured for cleanup costs incurred by an insured at an owned and scheduled location in response only to a legal obligation imposed through a government action. The coverage is targeted for the operator, purchaser, borrower and the financial institution, who would be an additional insured. Coverage is only available on a site specific basis, no blanket policies are offered, and a risk assessment by an ECS-approved firm will be necessary as a condition to binding coverage.

ECS/Reliance National now offers environmental laboratories liability insurance if 50 percent of their business is comprised of environmental analyses. The coverage is claims-made. E&O insurance is also provided with a one-year extended reporting period option. The limits of coverage are $500,000 per claim with a $500,000 aggregate or a $1 million per claim and $1 million aggregate. Defense costs are within policy limits. For the $500,000 limit policy, anticipate the minimum premium to be $15,000.

Finally, ECS also offers general liability coverage on the ISO claims-made form, automatic five-year discovery period, unlimited supplemental defense costs and includes an absolute pollution exclusion. Liability limits above $5 million can be arranged.

### Niche Markets

There are numerous niche markets evolving in the pollution insurance field to fill the demand for specialized primary and excess coverages. Discussed below in more detail are some of those markets.

*First Environmental Review Insurance Company*

First Environmental Review Insurance Company (First Environmental) is a California licensed insurer that provides coverage for specific environmental risks discovered in soil, ground water and surface water at developed and undeveloped real property. First Environmental offers first party coverage designed to provide environmental remediation insurance for sellers, purchasers, and their lenders for environmental risks associated with developed and undeveloped real property transfer. The product covers parties in a real property transaction against the costs associated with the investigation and remediation of hazardous substances not previously discovered on the subject property. The policy is claims-made with aggregate limits of $2 million for two years of coverage from the date of the site inspection.

The coverage will be provided on properties from vacant land to large industrial complexes. Their target market is commercial and retail establishments, office and light industrial facilities, and new residential developments. Coverage is contingent on a Phase I and/or Phase II environmental assessment to be performed prior to binding coverage. Deductibles range from $10,000 to $25,000, depending on policy limit, and premiums range from $5,000 to $25,000, depending on the potential risk to be covered. The policy form does contain a 24-hour notice requirement from the time that the pollution discovery becomes known to any person in control of the insured's property. The trigger of coverage for a claim also becomes actionable based on this named or additional named insured reporting the incident or having it reported as a result of government action.

First Environmental is a direct writer; therefore, at this time does not use brokers or agents to market/sell its product. This program became effective for underwriting potential pollution risks in October of 1990. Reinsurance is provided by Lloyds of London and associated company markets and United Reinsurance Company.

*United Capitol Insurance Company*

United Capitol Insurance Company is an Atlanta, Georgia, domiciled liability carrier that provides general liability coverage for contractors that install, repair or remove chemical and petroleum tanks. United Capitol historically has aligned itself with Commercial Casualty in order to underwrite EIL risks, asbestos abatement contractors and UST installers and owners/operators of USTs. According to market indicators, they are one of the largest providers of coverage for owners/operators of sanitary landfills. Their policy is claims-made coverage for contractors pollution liability. Onsite cleanup is covered and defense costs are within policy limits. Policy limits are $1 million/$1 million with a minimum premium of $100,000 and $10,000 deductible. United Capitol also offers professional liability E&O coverage on a claims-made basis for environmental consultants, asbestos consultants and engineers. Limits are $1 million per incident and $1 million in the aggregate; defense costs are within policy limits; a minimum deductible of $25,000 and minimum premium of $40,000 is provided.

### United Coastal

Based in New Britain, Connecticut, United Coastal offers contractors pollution liability for sudden and accidental pollution with defense costs within policy limits. The minimum deductible is $5,000; the minimum premium is $60,000. They also offer professional liability E&O coverage on a claims-made basis for environmental consultants and engineers. Both pollution liability and E&O coverage can be combined. Limits are set at $5 million per occurrence and $5 million in the aggregate with defense costs within policy limits. The minimum deductible is $5,000 and minimum premium is $40,000. United Coastal is a surplus lines carrier licensed in Arizona in 1985.

### St. Paul Fire & Marine Insurance Company

St. Paul Fire & Marine Insurance Company currently offers on a claims-made policy aboveground pollution liability coverage with limits of $1 million per occurrence, $1 million aggregate. The minimum premium is $25,000 up to $50,000 and the minimum is negotiable. A risk assessment is required prior to binding coverage. It features only sudden and accidental coverage that includes bodily injury and property damage caused by the omission, discharge, release or escape of pollutants from the insured's premises or work site. Such a pollution incident must occur above ground, result from an accident, begin and end within a 72-hour period after the retroactive date, and result in environmental damages. The coverage can be purchased on a stand alone basis or as part of the general liability policy. When purchased with the general liability policy, separate aggregate limits would apply. St. Paul can be most competitive when pricing this coverage as part of the general liability.

*Chubb Group*

The Chubb Group also offers an oil and gas pollution liability policy through Chubb Energy Resources Group. The coverage is for sudden and accidental incidents offered on a claims-made basis with limits of $1 million aggregate. This policy covers only property damage with minimum premium of $2,500 and minimum deductible set at $10,000.

## Insurance Markets For Underground Storage Tanks

The discussion of UST markets below is not intended to be an exhaustive analysis, but is aimed at providing the reader with a snapshot of who is out in the market underwriting tanks. Even though the commercial market is expanding, the demand for the product is limited due to weak government enforcement of the financial responsibility requirements and competition for premium dollars from the residual markets (state trust funds). The policies are claims-made and most of the markets perform rigorous underwriting and tank testing and tank assessments.

*Agricultural Excess and Surplus Insurance Company (AESIC)*
*Through Great American Insurance Company*

AESIC is a surplus/excess lines carrier that appears to comply with all EPA-UST financial assurance requirements. The facility offers per site limits of $1 million/$1 million or $1 million/$2 million per location. If 14 locations had tanks, then the limits go to $14 million aggregate coverage with $1 million per site. Their minimum deductible is $5,000 and minimum premium is $3,500 and their target audience is the major petroleum companies (CONACO, Exxon). They will write UST owner/operator risks on private and government entities (petroleum marketers, non-marketers, e.g., municipalities). Potential policyholders must meet technical requirements specified in EPA regulations for retrofitting an UST and tank management program. The policy offers a 12-month extended reporting period at no extra cost. Defense costs are outside policy limits. AESIC writes in all states except Delaware and New Hampshire.

*Front Royal Insurance Company*

Front Royal Insurance Company (Front Royal Group) is a surplus/excess lines carrier, licensed in Virginia and eligible to transact business in 23 states. Its limits are $1 million/$2 million annual aggregate per policy for petroleum marketers. Limits of $500 thousand/$1 million per pollution incident are offered for non-marketers. Front Royal writes stand-alone coverage, claims-made, with defense costs outside policy limits. Front Royal meets EPA compliance for limits of liability, onsite, offsite/third party coverage. There is a 12-month extended reporting period option. They employ a computer inventory analysis and site assessments are required. The minimum premium is $2,500 per site, and for limits of $1 million/$2 million there is a $25,000 deductible. Their target audience is petroleum marketers and non-retail manufacturers, as well as association business.

*General Star Indemnity Company, Subsidiary of Gen Re*

General Star Indemnity Company offers an EIL policy available nationwide by appointed wholesalers. They have limits of $1 million/$2 million. They appear to comply with EPA standards. General Star covers onsite and offsite cleanups as well as third party bodily injury/property damage (BI/PD) with an extended reporting period of 12 months. A tank tightness test is required to qualify for coverage. Their deductibles range from $10,000 to $50,000 with minimum premium of $3,500. General Star will cover up to $250,000 in defense costs above policy limits.

*Shand, Morahan & Company, Inc.*

Shand, Morahan & Company, Inc., is a surplus lines wholesaler and underwriting manager for the petroleum storage tank cleanup and liability insurance program insured though the Evanston Insurance Company. The Shand UST program is being written on a claims-made basis with coverage that includes both cleanup (onsite and offsite) and liability for BI/PD caused by an UST release on the scheduled premises. Liability coverage is $500,000 per claim and $1 million in the aggregate, and limits include defense costs capped at $100,000 per claim and $200,000 in the aggregate. A minimum premium for $500,000 of coverage is $5,000 and $13,000 for $100,000 in coverage. They require the tanks to be tested using Shand-approved methods. The policy is designed for municipalities, school districts and public agencies.

### Oilmen's

Oilmen's insurance plan is a Bermuda captive that reinsures pollution policies written by Fireman's Fund Insurance Company. Oilmen's provides property and casualty (P & C) insurance for petroleum marketers, petroleum wholesalers and retail distributors only. Their current policy limits are $1 million per occurrence and $2 million per aggregate using a claims-made form. There is a separate $500,000 cap on defense limits outside policy limits and a $25,000 minimum deductible. Tank statistical/reconciliation testing is required prior to binding coverage. The program will work around state funds. Oilmen's works with an exclusive distribution system of agents/brokers in certain states. The Oilmen's program appears to meet EPA's financial responsibility requirements.

### Universal Underwriters

Universal Underwriters is a Zurich Insurance Company-owned carrier domiciled in Kansas City, Missouri, that currently provides pollution insurance for owners and operators of aboveground storage tanks and soon for USTs, with limits set at $1 million per incident and $1 million in the aggregate. Their target market is auto dealerships. Zurich Insurance Company's program is provided on an accommodation basis with very stringent underwriting conditions.

### Federated Mutual Insurance Company

Federated uses the ISO broad pollution form for covering USTs and aboveground storage tanks containing petroleum and hazardous (regulated) substances. They provide coverage to groups that include petroleum marketing firms, auto dealers, farm and industrial equipment dealers, contract and sheet metal operators. The minimum premium for petroleum marketers is $5,000 and for non-marketers it is $1,000. Their policy standards comply with EPA's on-site cleanup as well as third party BI/PD. Site assessments are required for tanks, soil and tank tests. Federated has been offering limits of $1 million per incident and $2 million in the aggregate, exclusive of defense costs. They write coverage in 38 states on an accommodation basis only and offer a six-month renewable policy. They have been one of the largest insurers for USTs, providing coverage for over 80,000 tanks at 25,000 locations. This has been reduced; state insurance funds are competing for their business and placing restrictions on their program. They will not write coverage in certain states.

### American International Group

As discussed earlier in the chapter, AIG offers three UST insurance products, none of which comply with EPA UST requirements. These include Enviroguard, operated by Sedgwick James of Pennsylvania, for buyers with 25 tanks or fewer, where first party coverage is restricted. AIG also provides $5 million per occurrence and $5 million in the aggregate for third party coverage only for owners of 25 tanks or more. Defense costs are outside the limit and minimum premium is $25,000. Finally, AIG does offer state wraparound programs for their UST state trust funds, such as their present wraparound program for Florida.

### Other Markets

Lloyds of London (20 syndicates) presently underwrites USTs through the Planning Corporation. This program was formerly operated through the now failed Petromark risk retention group. Policy limits of $1 million per claim and $2 million in the aggregate can be written on a primary or excess basis attaching excess of $1 million per claim and $2 million in the aggregate. Defense costs are outside policy limits. The minimum premium is $2,500 and deductible at $25,000.

Other UST markets that offer coverage and appear to meet EPA tank minimum requirements include Illinois Union, a CIGNA company, through Associated Excess/Surplus Underwriters; Northern Commercial Insurance Company through Cowan Surplus Lines; Environmental Impairment Purchasing Group through Presidential Fire & Casualty; the Chubb Corporation for clients on accommodation; American Environmental Purchasing Group through Belaire Group Casualty Association; and the Homestead Insurance Company, a purchasing group.

There are a few facilities that provide state wraparound programs such as the Tank Owners Insurance Company (risk retention group) and London Sphere-Drake/CE Heath. The London Sphere program insures deductibles on state trust fund tank programs and will issue separate policies for each state to dovetail with their state regulations.

Finally, Travelers offers an UST program targeting bulk oil distributors and petroleum marketers with pollution coverage written in conjunction with other property and casualty coverages. The limit of coverage is $1 million; the coverage is third party only.

The state financial assurance funds are providing stiff competition to the commercial insurers. Three types of programs are offered by the states in the forms of guarantees, insurance (like the private market) and onsite cleanup (state fund). To date 37 states have passed UST legislation. Fourteen state programs have been approved by EPA, but may not completely meet all financial responsibility requirements.[26] States like Iowa have model programs with a fund to pay for old tank cleanups, an insurance program and a loan program for small business. The major problem with the state programs is inadequate funding and administration.

### Excess Markets for Pollution Coverage

*American Excess Insurance Association*

American Excess Insurance Association (AEIA), better known as American Slip, is an excess lines insurer that requires no capital contribution and uses a stand alone form. The policy excludes pollution, although there is a limited buy-back granted for some pollution coverage for unintended fire, explosion, lightning, collision, overturned automobile or railroad vehicle. Such pollution must be a single or intermittent discharge, dispersal, release or escape which ceases within seven days of its first commencement. Limits of coverage are up to $75 million excess of a $25 million attachment point (umbrella coverage effective when the first $25 million is paid). Member companies include Travelers, Crum and Forster Co., Aetna Casualty and Surety Co., CIGNA, Chubb Group, Zurich Insurance Group, NAC Re Corporation, General Accident Insurance Company, the Home Insurance Group and AIG.

*North American Casualty Excess Insurance Company*

North American Casualty Excess Insurance Company (ACE) is an excess captive insurance company created by Marsh & McLennan (M&M) and Morgan Guaranty Trust to stabilize insureds' costs and to handle the catastrophic loss, like its traditional insurance cousin, American Slip. ACE is domiciled in the Cayman Islands and managed from Bermuda. ACE will offer limits up to $200 million aggregate excess of $100 million in increments of $10 million. Attachment can go as high as $1 billion. ACE writes on a claims-made form. ACE has over 375 policyholders with annual premiums of $230 million and policyholder surplus over $1 billion. ACE has a quota-share reinsurance in place stating that reinsurers will share from the first dollar any losses had by ACE. ACE also writes a stand alone form that offers limited pollution coverage for sudden and accidental releases. Discovery period must be within seven days of the first known release of pollutants. The insured must notify ACE in writing within 20 days of first release. Claims are arbitrated in London. ACE has a diverse membership: industrial manufacturing (50 percent); utilities, transportation and construction (20 percent); financial services (12 percent); and waste management services and others (18 percent).

*Exel, Ltd.*

Exel Ltd. (X.L. Insurance Company, Ltd.) is an excess captive insurance company also created by M&M and Morgan Guaranty, domiciled and managed in Bermuda. X.L. provides $75 million excess over $25 million for liability or a lesser amount, such as $15 million, depending on the risk. X.L. has purchased a $150 million excess over $50 million to protect itself against situations in which two or more of its insureds are involved in a single incident. At this time there are over 100 shareholders and over 55 policies in force with $757.4 million in capital and total assets of over $1.4 billion. X.L. uses an occurrence reported form that can be converted to a full occurrence form by annually purchasing an unlimited discovery endorsement. Pollution is sudden and accidental, similar to ACE. As with ACE, X.L. uses a financial model for their rating schedule based on seven hazard groups. Policyholders include chemical, pharmaceutical, industrial, manufacturing, utilities, hotels and auto manufacturers.

### Tortuga - Reiss Organization

Tortuga is an excess liability insurance company designed to take advantage of unused capacity in the participant's own captive insurance company. Tortuga's limits are $50 million excess of $25 million on a claims-made policy. Tortuga is domiciled in the Cayman Islands and managed in Bermuda. Sudden and accidental pollution coverage is offered as part of this line of coverage.

### Associated Electric and Gas Insurance Services, Ltd.

Associated Electric and Gas Insurance Services, Ltd., (AEGIS) is a non-accessible captive mutual insurance company owned by its policyholders. Established in 1975, AEGIS operates as a surplus lines insurer in the U.S. for the public utility industry. AEGIS writes excess general liability and auto liability on a claims-made basis. Policy limits have been $25 million with a $200,000 deductible. Pollution coverage is available on a sudden/accidental and gradual release (or time test) basis. AEGIS restricts coverage for pollution from hazardous waste disposal sites. AEGIS will endorse certain UST risks.

### Energy Insurance Mutual (EIM)

Energy Insurance Mutual (EIM) is a utility risk retention group developed to underwrite excess liability insurance coverage of $25 million excess over $25 million underlying for multiple lines of coverage. EIM was formed in Barbados in 1986 and is now domiciled in Tampa, Florida, as a licensed insurance company. Coverage is provided on a claims-made basis with a five-year additional claims period. Pollution coverage is limited for PCBs to sudden and accidental incidents.

## Alternative Risk Financing Programs For Pollution Risks

### Commonwealth Risk Services

Commonwealth Risk Services (Mutual Indemnity) is a risk management company developed to provide risk financing for companies and/or their captives and rent-a-captives using their funding application through their Insurance Profit Center. The Insurance Profit Center (IPC) program (rent-a-captive) places business through numerous

**Risk Financing: Insuring
Potential Pollution Exposures**

insurers including Mutual Indemnity, Ltd., of Bermuda or through IPC's subsidiary, Mutual Risk, and uses fully funded fronting programs/insurers such as United National or Agricultural Excess & Surplus Insurance Company. Commonwealth can do high risk product liability, casualty, pollution liability, and architects and engineers. Commonwealth uses an EIL, claims-made policy offered through Mutual Indemnity. After claims, if any, are paid, the insured would receive underwriting profit plus investment income. Commonwealth will also issue manuscript forms. Limits of $1 million per incident and $1 million per aggregate for pollution risks are offered. Mutual Indemnity, Ltd., has capital funds in excess of $20 million and assets in excess of $161 million.

### Foreign Commercial Markets

The general demand for EIL coverages is low in industrialized countries of North America and Europe. The demand for EIL may be on the upswing as a result of pollution insurance coverage vanishing from the general liability policies in several European countries and markets.[27] This is the result of the slow but pressing change from a fault based negligence standard to require strict liability in the event of environmental damage. The "polluter pays principle" is the basis of control and this development is most effectively being realized in Germany (formerly West Germany) and the United Kingdom.[28]

### United Kingdom

Pollution liability insurance in the United Kingdom (UK) is generally available on claims-made policies for sudden and accidental incidents. Most insurers in the UK exclude only gradual and nonsudden pollution claims and are silent on pollution relative to sudden and accidental incidents. Under the influence of U.S. environmental statutory and common law standards of liability, many UK carriers are introducing restrictive language and/or exclusions regarding unintended or unexpected sudden and accidental claims. Much of this pressure to exclude/restrict coverage is due to pressure from reinsurers and restrictions stated in the insurance treaties. Over the next five years it can be expected that the UK insurers will employ more stringent underwriting criteria for potential sudden and accidental pollution liability risks. Currently, major insurers that write all lines of public liability policies have no exclusion for pollution risks. Each risk tends to be underwritten on a case-by-case basis with major risks primarily restricted to only sudden and accidental coverage. Gradual pollution coverage appears to be disappearing except where risks are not perceived to have pollution exposures.[29]

The UK demand also apparently is low for EIL (sudden and gradual) insurance except from high industrial risks such as chemical companies. The British Chemical Industries Association (CIA) has developed an EIL insurance program for gradual losses through a consortium of UK companies led by the subsidiary of a leading European reinsurer. Limits of coverage on a claims-made policy is $9.4 million in the aggregate. The CIA Environmental Liability Insurance Facility, or CELIF as it is referred to, covers only scheduled sites; risk assessments are required and the policy limit of indemnity ($9.4 million) represents the maximum payment for damages over a three year policy period. A single reinstatement of the limit is available for an additional premium.[30]

There are a number of key carriers currently providing or introducing new pollution insurance products into the UK marketplace. Noted insurers include Commercial Union P.L.C., Sun Alliance International, Ltd., Swiss Re (UK), Ltd., and Lloyds Syndicates. Other carriers are beginning to restrict pollution coverage on general liability policies in light of the United States' litigious environmental situation and recent developments in Britain against pollutants. The government is adopting the "polluter pays principle" according to the White Paper on the Environment and Proposed Environmental Protection Bill whose legislation introduces a system of integrated pollution control and pollution prevention utilizing source reduction and stiffer enforcement and penalties.[31]

The Association of British Insurers is currently tackling the environmental coverage issues because of the potential liability to industry carriers. This concern is a potential opportunity to A.I.U. (UK), Ltd., who plans to introduce a new EIL third party claims-made policy with $10 million limits in countries like the UK, Germany and France. Swiss Re, through Palatine Insurance Co., Ltd., continues their 15-year conservative ($9.4 million limits) underwriting of EIL in Europe and sees demand for this type of coverage rising in the 1990s.

Other insurance markets throughout Europe and, in particular, the European Community, provide pollution insurance coverage for both sudden and accidental and non-sudden and gradual coverages on an accommodation basis in general liability policies or through association pools.

### France

In France, sudden and accidental pollution is covered under most general liability policies. Policies are claims-made. There also exists pollution liability insurance coverage available through an association pool called Assurpol. Assurpol, formerly Garpol Pool, is a 1989 facility made up of 49 insurers and 14 reinsurers with pollution insurance limits of $23.83 million. This site specific coverage is provided for both sudden and nonsudden incidents. Assurpol coverage extends to French territories and on an accommodation basis for multinationals whose operations are in other EC countries.

### Italy

In Italy, sudden and accidental pollution incidents are excluded from coverage on the standard general liability policies; therefore, coverage (both sudden and gradual) is in greater demand and provided through the Pool Inquinamento. This facility offers limits up to $34.11 million of EIL insurance for bodily injury, third party property and business interruption claims. This facility is operated by the Italian Insurer's Association on a claims-made form. Seventy-six insurers make up this pool. Risk assessments are required prior to binding coverage.[32]

### The Netherlands

In The Netherlands the reinsurance facility known as the MAS Pool underwrites potential sudden and nonsudden pollution risks through an association of 80 Dutch carriers with 100 percent reinsurance to member companies. Limits of coverage are in excess of $2.7 million per incident.

### Canada

Finally in Canada there appears to be two markets that provide pollution liability insurance for industrial entities. The demand for EIL insurance is also weak in Canada and the buyers represent niche markets similar to those in the United States. Two of the more notable Canadian domiciled insurers are Ian Elliott, Ltd., and the Pollution Liability Association (PLA).

Ian Elliott, Ltd., is a Canadian insurance wholesaler that specializes in pollution liability insurance provided on a claim-made basis with a full retroactive liability cover per no prior knowledge of impairment. Policy limit is inclusive of cleanup costs and defense expenses. Limits of coverage are $2 million in the aggregate and $2 million per risk. Engineering risk assessments are required. Their portfolio of insureds includes manufacturers, chemical companies, resource companies, member states, institutions and waste management companies.

The other Canadian market has been PLA, a reinsurance pool with over 20 member companies that write limits of $1 million per incident and $2 million in the aggregate on a hybrid form that addresses only sudden and accidental pollution exposures.

### Other Countries

Other countries with strong environmental legislation and pollution insurance coverages offered to insureds include Denmark, Sweden, Spain, Portugal, Greece and Ireland. Denmark and Sweden rank among the worlds toughest countries on environmental pollution. In Sweden there do exist co-insurers and a reinsurance consortium who offer a special EIL insurance.

## Future Trends and Emerging Issues

The availability, adequacy and affordability of pollution insurance for both first party and third party coverages will become dependent upon industrial and manufacturing companies presenting insurers with risks that represent quantifiable exposures documented through risk assessment surveys, waste minimization audits and/or pollution prevention programs. Insurers will need to be able to measure the specific potential for loss exposure, since actuarial data is still inconsistent or lacking. The risk assessment or audit will provide the insurer with the appropriate number of exposure units in order to rate and rank the risks for purposes of underwriting (endorsing) and premium pricing.

Pollution insurers in the 1990s will require companies seeking pollution insurance to initiate integrated waste management programs. This approach ideally promotes premium reductions to insureds and leads to increases in insurer surplus from reduced claims and encourages stability in the casualty market for pollution type risks. In the short term, pollution insurance products and services continue to be developed and targeted at niche markets where account underwriting experience is available and where the product demand is driven by a strict liability scheme.

In 1991, one key niche market to emerge will be for lenders. Domestic carriers such as AIG (Commerce & Industry), and certain foreign insurers and brokers such as Willis Corroon will or have entered the market with a mortgage impairment liability-like product underwritten on a site-specific basis. AIG and a new facility, the Environmental Standard Group, will be offering first party coverages for lenders involved in real estate transactions. Currently two markets (ECS and First Environmental Review Insurance Co.) offer first party cleanup policies with the lender named as an additional insured.

With the reauthorization of Superfund, the casualty insurance capacity and market conditions may not improve for the next five years. Insurance buyers that cannot afford to or choose not to self-insure pollution risks (like many cleanup contractors, environmental consultants, real estate developers, and certain lenders) will be looking toward alternative risk financing mechanisms to share or transfer potential first and third party risks.

Government financial responsibility requirements such as those under RCRA for owners and operators of hazardous waste TSDFs and USTs will also expand to include solid nonhazardous waste facilities and aboveground storage tanks. These developments may create or expand the demand for pollution insurance.

At this time it appears that the availability of affordable and less restrictive pollution insurance may be determined primarily through court decisions arising out of continued litigation between policyholders and their primary and excess or umbrella property and casualty carriers. Unless there is resolution to this litigation, the reinsurers who are the backbone of such a market (and now also becoming litigants and participants in Superfund arbitration cases) will continue to stay away from reinsuring potential pollution risks. Risk managers need to support future Superfund risk financing alternatives, such as structured settlements using annuities to allocate funds for third party claims or cleanup costs, as well as support the proposals such as the AIG's National Environmental Trust Fund.[33] The AIG proposes to establish a $40 billion trust fund based on a two percent fee on all commercial and industrial property and casualty insurance premiums paid in the U.S.; such a fund would provide for the cleanup of approximately 1200 sites. Such proposals attempt to bring needed equity into the marketplace, as well as effectively spread the cost of Superfund cleanup.

The European casualty insurance market is cautiously monitoring the EC legislative proposals, directives, and regulations, which encourage strict liability standards as in "polluter pays principle." If the present availability of pollution liability insurance seen in general liability policies disappears, it will leave only a handful of specialty markets.

The 1990s will present corporate risk managers with shifting paradigms for incorporating environmental health and safety (EHS) issues into the present risk management (insurance and benefits) thinking. The EHS risk manager in the 1990s will adopt pollution prevention, information systems management and integrative waste management systems in order to reduce or eliminate potential loss exposures and liabilities and turn pollution prevention and control into insurable risks. Insurers, on the other hand, will look to pollution prevention and waste minimization as criteria for underwriting certain risks and for pricing premiums.

With emerging innovative technology satisfying regulatory requirements there will be an increased need for effective risk communication skills. These skills will become the focal point to reducing potential and real risk. Risk communication skills will be important in situations involving the transfer and retention of risk. It will be important in cases involving community relations for remedy selection at a Superfund site, or siting of a new TSDR facility in the face of public opposition, or making a presentation to a pollution liability insurer about how perceived pollution risks are being controlled or exposure prevented. Risk communications should become as important a tool as environmental compliance when assessing potential environmental and occupational loss exposure and liabilities. One of the corporate risk manager's more effective risk financing tools toward a balanced risk retention and high risk transfer program may be the ability to adequately communicate risk to insurers, government agencies, the community and his fellow employees.

Corporate management will continually be faced with striking a balance between production quotas and environmental protection. An environmental risk management and risk financing program prudently developed can turn risk management and risk financing control and loss prevention costs into production savings. Implementing pollution prevention and waste minimization programs; encouraging environmental compliance, self-audits and risk assessment surveys; creating accurate information management systems for inventory, reporting or notification will prevent the need for performing costly corrective measures or remedial actions to reduce and prevent potential pollution loss exposures from becoming liabilities. This balance between the careful retention and transfer of potential pollution risks is the cornerstone to protection of company assets and the key for acquiring available and affordable pollution insurance.

## About the Author

**Dean Jeffery Telego**, President, directs RTM corporate development and oversees company technical operations. RTM performs expert environmental risk management consulting services for industrial and financial services clients in the areas of government relations, regulatory and policy analysis, strategic planning, environmental auditing, risk assessment, Superfund technical assistance and communications. He has been in the environmental risk management field for 14 years. Mr. Telego received his formal education and training in human physiology and biophysics. He performed his graduate work at Georgetown University and undergraduate studies at Olivet College. He has published numerous technical papers on the pollution liability insurance marketplace and the role of environmental risk management and risk assessment. Mr. Telego is on the Board of Advisors for two Bureau of National Affairs publications, *The Toxics Law Reporter* and *Real Estate/Environmental Liability News,* and serves on the ASTM Subcommittee on Environmental Assessment in Commercial Real Estate Transactions.

1. William K. Reilly, "Aiming Before We Shoot: The 'Quiet Revolution' in Environmental Policy," National Press Club Speech, September 26, 1990, Washington, DC.

2. *Monoline policy* underwriting describes a separate line of insurance (pollutiom) versus multiple-line policies in which the underwriter handles numerous lines such as fire, inland marine and liability insurance (package policies).

3. William D. Fay, "Acid Rain Panel," speech at the Clean Air Conference, Inside Washington Publishers, September 18-19, 1990.

4. 21 *Environmental Reporter*, (BNA) p. 1370-71 (November 16, 1990). See also Chapter II, Clean Air Act--Separating the Old and the New, by Frank H. Hackmann.

5. John Quarles, "The Clean Air Act Amendments of 1990," Memorandum and speech at The Clean Air Conference of Inside Washington Publishers, September 18-19, 1990.

6. Inside EPA's *Superfund Report*, Volume IV, No. 14, July 4, 1990, p. 4, and Volume IV, No. 20, September 26, 1990.

7. Dean Jeffery Telego, "Inside Superfund," speech at "Inside Superfund: Strategies for Enforcement, Settlement and Claims Management", co-sponsored by Risk Management Technologies, Inc., and *Inside EPA Weekly Report*, October 23, 1990.

8. Thomas P. Grumbly, speech and reports by Clean Sites, Inc., "Improving Remedy Selection: An Explicit and Interactive Process," October 1990 at "Inside Superfund: Strategies for Enforcement, Settlement and Claims Management," co-sponsored by Risk Management Technologies, Inc., and *Inside EPA Weekly Report*, October 23-24, 1990.

9. 21 *Environmental Reporter*, p. 1355 (November 16, 1990).

10. Chapters IV, V and VI cover recent developments under RCRA and HSWA and the need to redefine solid wastes, measure the effects of the TC rule, land ban restrictions and corrective action on TSDFs and their SWMUs.

11. 40 C.F.R. 264.147.

12. Until 1986 *CGL* meant *Comprehensive* General Liability; after 1986 *CGL* stands for *Commercial* General Liability, which contains absolute exclusion of pollution coverage.

13. Dean Jeffery Telego, "Corporate Environmental Risk Management Strategies, The EIL Risk Assessment Process and Risk Financing Alternatives", Inside EPA and Risk Management Technologies Inc., Superfund Conference, September 23-24, 1988 and "Corporate Risk Management: Strategies for Indecent Pollution Exposures", Toxic Law Reporter, (BNA) pp. 116-127 (July 9, 1986). *See also*, Committee for Economic Development, *Who Should Be Liable? A Guide to Policy Dealing with Risk*, p. 155. "Tails on reinsurance are even longer than those on direct insurance because the large claims that penetrate the reinsurance limits of coverage tend to take long to settle. Reinsurers report that even excluding asbestos risks, they do not know as of as much as 75% if the losses that will arise from CGL reinsurance policy until the thirteenth year after the policy was in force. *See also New York Report*, 1977.

14. 40 C.F.R. 264.147 (a)(3), 264.147 (b)(3), 265.147 (a)(3), 265.147 (b)(3).

15. 40 C.F.R. Parts 280 and 281, Volume 55, Number 211, 46022, October 21, 1990.

16. *Guide to Liability Insurance,* "Pollution Insurance and Coverage," (Rough Notes, Indianapolis, Indiana: 1990) pp. 40-41.

17. *Ibid.*

18. Deborah Shalowitz, "EIL Market Flush with Tank Cover, but Little Demand," *Business Insurance,* October 8, 1990, p. 3.

19. *Ibid.*

20. Carolyn Aldred, "Pollution Crackdown in Europe," *Business Insurance,* October 8, 1990, pp. 31-36.

21. *Mealey's European Environmental Law Report,* pp. 12-15 (September 26, 1990).

22. Aldred, *Ibid.*

23. Peter Schroeder, "Managing Existing Hazardous Waste Facilities: Risk Assessment Issues," in *Integrating Insurance and Risk Management for Hazardous wastes,* edited by Howard Kunreuther and Rajeev Gowda, Kluwer Academic Publishers, London, Dordrecht and Boston: 1990, pp. 105-130.

24. Mealey's *Ibid.*

25. *Id.*

26. Shalowitz, *Ibid.*

27. Mealey's, *Id.*

28. Jan C. Bongaerts and R. Andreas Kraemer, "Liability Rules, Insurance and Reduction of Risk of Environmental Damages," *The Environmental Professional,* Volume 11, No. 3, 1989, pp. 209-219.

29. Carolyn Aldred, "Britain to Get Tough with Polluters," *Business Insurance,* October 15, 1990, p. 37.

30. Mealey's, *id.*

31. Carolyn Aldred, October 15, 1990, *supra.* at note 27.

32. Baruch Berliner and Jeurg Spuehler, "Insurance Issues Associated with Managing Existing Hazardous Waste Sites," in *Integrating Insurance and Risk Management for Hazardous Wastes,* edited by Howard Kunreuther and Rajeev Gowda, Kluwer Academic Publishers, London, Dordrecht and Boston: 1990, pp. 131-168.

33. Maurice R. Greenberg, "Financing the Cleanup of Hazardous Waste," The National Environmental Trust Fund, *Environmental Claims Journal,* Volume 1, No. 4, Summer 1989, Executive Enterprises, New York, pp. 421-429.

# XXIV

# An Integrated Risk Financing Approach to Remedial Action Contracting

*David J. Dybdahl, Jr.,CPCU & ARM,*
*Managing Director*
*Corroon & Black National Resource Division*
*Nashville, Tennessee*

Risk management issues become a significant barrier to entering the remedial action contracting industry. Not only is it difficult for contractors or engineers to enter into the field, it is difficult for insurers as well. The main problems are the infancy of the cleanup industry and the unique liability issues surrounding this work.

The cleanup of America has been projected to cost between $400 billion and $700 billion over the next 50 years. The magnitude of the revenues creates a powerful incentive to overcome the risk management problems associated with performing remedial contracting services. Hazardous materials contractors must depend on a multi-faceted risk management approach in order to handle the unique risks of environmental cleanups. Insurance cannot be relied on as an exclusive solution. The policies available today are significantly better than they were two years ago; however, most are still "claims-made" policy forms and only provide protection for a limited amount of time. To fill this gap in insurance protection, a hazardous materials contractor must depend on other forms of risk financing, for example; indemnification, holding harmless agreements or by self insurance.

This paper will illustrate some of the risk financing alternatives available in today's market place. The insurance marketplace for hazardous materials contractors has greatly improved during the past few years. Since April 1988, broader coverage is available at higher limits, from more sellers, and at reduced rates. Significant developments include:

- The availability of Contractors Pollution and General Liability coverages at Superfund sites in all 50 states;
- Limits of liability for Contractors Pollution liability insurance increasing from $1 million per occurrence and in the aggregate to $5 million per occurrence and in the aggregate ($10 million on a wrap-up project);
- Asbestos Abatement coverage on an occurrence basis;
- The development of Engineers Pollution Liability coverage;
- The availability of project wrap-up insurance programs.

Some of these new products took years of research and development to bring them to the marketplace. While the insurance marketplace is expanding, the traditional form of risk transfer for federal work, Federal Government Indemnification, is being severely restricted. In its original form, the EPA would indemnify its remedial action contractors for all liability arising out of their work and operations at a hazardous waste site up to the present limits of the Superfund trust fund. In 1986, under Section 119 of the SARA amendments, the scope of the indemnification was limited to apply only to pollution liability claims. After three years of research, the EPA released its proposed final guidance on indemnity. Among other things, EPA would like to restrict its indemnity to $50 million with a 10 year tail. This represents a significant shift in the original indemnification provisions which were basically unlimited as to time, place, and amount. The final terms of EPA indemnification will probably be released in the *Federal Register* in April, 1991. It is expected that the final terms of the indemnification will require commercial insurance on the primary levels. Hazardous materials contractors should be cognizant of both the expanding insurance market and the shrinking EPA role while formulating their overall risk management program.

This paper will outline the coverages necessary to build a meaningful insurance program for a hazardous materials contracting firm. The insurances as described within this paper are available in today's marketplace. The reader should be cautioned to pay particularly close attention to the date of its publication; the insurance market is expanding at an increasing rate, making most pictures of the insurance products available inaccurate within three weeks of publication date. The most rapidly expanding parts of this analysis are the available limits of liability coverage and the underwriting guidelines of the various markets that provide these coverages. However, the basic coverage parts in this analysis will remain unchanged for a longer period of time. The construction of Hazardous Material Contractors' insurance program is a very complex task. This situation is created by specialty underwriters that provide only pieces of the necessary coverage. Turf battles for the various insurance products, even within the same insurance company, create a situation where multiple insurance policies, each covering small pieces of the exposure must be purchased to complete the insurance coverage matrix. The resulting insurance program needs to be coordinated through a single broker, in order to successfully eliminate gaps or overlaps in coverage and premiums.

## Product Descriptions

The hazardous materials contractors insurance program for a firm providing design/build or single source environmental contracting, including asbestos abatement services, could include as many as eight basic insurance coverage parts. These policies are briefly summarized below. Each policy must be interfaced with other coverages to put the pieces of the insurance protection wall together. It is important to note that some of these policies are, in fact, duplications of policy forms, except that exclusions within one or the other makes the purchase of the second policy necessary. Particular attention must be paid to the rating basis on all policies in order to avoid duplicating premiums, although not necessarily coverage, between policies. The rates for some of these coverages may exceed the normal operating margins of a contracting firm, therefore, mistakes on the coordination of rates and revenue streams could potentially bankrupt a firm through audit premiums at the end of a policy period.

### Commercial General Liability Insurance

The General Liability Insurance policy is the litigation coverage purchased by all businesses. The policy is designed to provide insurance coverage for bodily injury, property damage, and defense arising out of the insured's premises, operations, products, and completed operations. In the absence of exclusions it could be argued that this would be the only liability insurance policy necessary to cover the vast majority of all firms. In general, these forms are standardized and the same form is purchased by firms ranging from flower shops to hazardous waste contractors. The General Liability policy is the equivalent to all risk protection subject to exclusions. The resulting gaps coverage created by these exclusions make it necessary to purchase other forms of liability insurance. Of significant importance for Hazardous Materials Contractors are the exclusions that eliminate coverage for claims arising out of pollution, claims arising from operations at a hazardous waste site, claims arising out of the maintenance, operation and use of an automobile, claims that arise out of injuries to the insured's employees, and claims that arise out of a professional error, act, or omission. To fill these gaps in coverage, the purchase of separate insurance coverages is necessary.

### Contractors Pollution Liability Insurance

The development of Contractors Pollution Liability (CPL) coverage was in response to the pollution exclusion on the General Liability Policy. A Contractors Pollution Liability policy has its roots in an Environmental Impairment Liability (EIL) policy. However, a CPL policy amends the coverage to more closely reflect the exposures of a contracting firm. Buyers should be aware that a standard EIL policy provides little or no insurance protection for a "contracting" exposure. A CPL policy is the stop-gap coverage for the General Liability exposure. Unlike the General Liability policy, it is not an "all risk" policy. It provides pollution liability coverage for bodily injury, property damage, defense costs, and clean-up cost for the contractor's described operations. Coverage can be purchased on either a blanket/reported sites or project specific basis.

### Architects & Engineers Professional
### Errors & Omissions Insurance

For design professionals the purchase of Errors & Omissions (E&O) coverage has historically been necessitated by a special exclusion endorsed onto the General Liability policy excluding claims from design errors. To fill this gap in coverage, the purchase of a professional E&O policy was necessary. The typical insuring agreement of these policies agrees to indemnify the insured for negligent acts, errors, or omissions arising out of the rendering of a described professional service. The majority of E&O policies on the market today contain an exclusion for claims arising out of a pollution incident. Some standard policies provide coverage for pollution by deleting the pollution exclusion in regards to the design of potable water systems or sewage treatment plants. It is also now possible to purchase E&O policies that provide coverage for pollution claims as part of the traditional errors and omissions coverage.

### Specialty Environmental Engineers Errors & Omissions Policy Forms

A number of new custom tailored Errors & Omissions policy forms have been introduced for firms that provide environmental remediation services. These policies usually start off with a traditional errors & omissions policy and by amending or deleting the pollution exclusion, and extend the professional liability coverage to claims arising out of a pollution incident.

### Asbestos Abatement Liability

The Asbestos Abatement Liability insurance policy has its roots in the General Liability insurance policy form. Most policies provide coverage for asbestos abatement operations by amending the pollution exclusion on a General Liability policy. Both the General Liability policy and Asbestos Abatement Liability policy use payroll and receipts as the rating basis to determine premium. Since these coverages are redundant for premium computation purposes, both carriers should be aware of the existence of the other policy and should issue endorsements that enable the insured to avoid paying double the necessary premium. Policy forms and insurer integrity vary a great deal within the Asbestos Abatement Liability insurance market. The advice of an expert broker is highly recommended on this line of coverage.

### Asbestos Consultants Errors & Omissions

This is a professional liability insurance policy that deletes or amends the pollution exclusion to the extent necessary to provide coverage for professional errors, acts or omissions arising out of the design of asbestos projects. Asbestos consultants E&O has the potential to be redundant to the engineers pollution liability coverage. It may also be unnecessary if the Engineers Pollution Liability policy or the standard Errors & Omissions policy has sufficiently broad wording so as not to exclude the asbestos hazard.

### Combined Policy Forms

Some underwriters are introducing specialty policy forms that combine pollution coverages with either Professional Liability or General Liability coverage. The principal advantage of these forms is cost: since all the coverages share one limit of liability, the underwriter has lower total exposed limits, and can charge a lower premium. A second advantage is that, in a claims situation, having a single carrier should eliminate the problem of disputes between coverage lines. The latter point is an important consideration when selecting a CPL or EPL carrier. Coverage disputes generally can be avoided if the policy providing the pollution coverage in the insurance program is written with the same underwriter that provides its "companion" coverage (e.g., General Liability/Contractors Pollution Liability or Professional E&O/Engineers Pollution Liability). A major disadvantage of combined forms is that they are exotic coverages that do not lend themselves to reinsurance or excess liability coverage. Therefore, the available limits of liability will remain relatively low, not only on the pollution coverage, but on the traditional General Liability and Professional Liability coverages as well. The second disadvantage to combined forms is that these are aggressive insurance products. They often require the buyer to disturb longstanding existing relationships with its incumbent underwriters or traditional insurance programs, only to lose the exotic combined coverage forms at the first signs of a hard insurance market — potentially leaving the buyer in a distressed situation to find a replacement traditional insurance program for a difficult class of business.

### Commercial Automobile Liability

The General Liability insurance policies and Professional Liability insurance policies exclude claims arising out of maintenance, use, or operation of a motor vehicle. The new standard Business Automobile Liability policy form excludes claims arising out of pollution. This can have a significant impact if the insured transports materials that could lead to an environmental claim. It is also important to note that the pollution exclusion in the policy overrides the coverage provided by the MCS-90 endorsement, which is required under the Motor Carrier Act. It has been estimated that, with the change in the standard Business Automobile Liability insurance policy effective in 1986, 50 percent of the hazardous materials transporters on the road do not have pollution coverage. Pollution coverage for upsets and overturns is available, but it must be requested by the insured and added by specific endorsement. Some underwriters will surcharge their premiums when adding pollution coverage to the Auto policy. The Automobile Liability insurance policy uses the number of vehicles as the rating basis, so its coordination with the other liability lines is not as critical from the standpoint of premiums overlapping.

### Worker's Compensation Insurance

This policy pays for claims arising out of injury, death or disability of employees, while performing within the scope of their employment, on a no-fault basis. Worker's Compensation policies do not contain a pollution exclusion. However, there are virtually no insurance carriers that will knowingly write Worker's Compensation coverage on their higher risk classes of hazardous materials contractors. This situation exists because of the lack of a hazardous materials contractors class code within the rating schemes for this coverage. Underwriters cannot charge a rate commensurate with the increased hazards associated with employees digging a ditch in "moonsuits" at a Superfund site, versus digging a ditch anywhere else. In the absence of a classification code, Worker's Compensation coverage placed in the states' assigned risk pools continues to be a bargain.

## Structuring the Program — An Art Form

Piecing together the coverages necessary to address the risk of the hazardous materials contracting firm can be an art form. Proper structuring of the insurance mechanics assures the client of insurance protection without gaps or overlaps in coverage and avoids stacking premiums for redundant coverages. As the engineering and contracting businesses throughout the country see the flow of money towards environmental cleanup, many of these firms are exploring the ramifications of entering this field. Usually, for the astute firms, the issue of liability and insurance becomes one of the more significant barriers to entry. The creation of a hazardous materials contracting subsidiary produces a vehicle that the insurance broker can use to structure an insurance program for the environmental contracting work. If done properly, this approach allows the insurance broker to structure completely separate insurance programs for the non-hazardous waste work and the hazardous materials work. The advantages of this approach are:

- It isolates the insurance programs;
- It may minimize insurance costs;
- There is possible protection under the corporate veil;
- It can create marketing advantages;
- It has proven to work.

The disadvantages include:

- Complexity: There may be up to 15 primary insurance; policies involved in a relatively simple insurance program;
- Administrative and accounting expenses;
- Possible gaps or over-laps in coverages and in premiums;
- It can create surety bonding problems;
- It can create marketing disadvantages.

An alternative approach to structuring the insurance program would be to combine the hazardous materials contracting exposures into a master insurance program. This may require shifting the master program into an insurer that has the ability to handle the environmental coverages. There is no concrete rule as to whether it is better to float a separate insurance program or combine the environmental exposures into a master program. Every firm and its business plan is unique, so guidance from an experienced insurance broker is the best way to evaluate which approach makes the most sense.

A separate issue when setting up a hazardous materials contractor's insurance program is whether to use blanket or project specific insurance coverage for the hazardous waste work. Under the blanket approach to insuring a firm, the firm obtains coverage for all of their described operations. Depending on the insurance policy being analyzed, the coverage can either be true blanket coverage or something fairly unique to remedial action contracting, blanket coverage for the described operations for specified sites named on the policy, which can provide some sort of automatic coverage for a period of time, pending the reporting to the insurance company of the specified site. The true blanket approach almost always produces the lowest rate for insurance, which is then applied against the total revenues of the named insured to arrive at the final premium. Still another option exists to address the insurance requirements of hazardous waste work. Corroon & Black has pioneered the project wrap-up approach to remedial action contracting work. Under this scenario, the general contractor provides the primary casualty insurance protection on the entire job for himself and the subcontractors.

The coverages that are involved usually include General Liability, Contractors Pollution Liability, Professional Errors & Omissions, and Engineers Pollution Liability. Where there is an asbestos exposure, Asbestos Abatement Liability and the Asbestos Consultants Errors & Omissions coverages must also be purchased. The wrap-up approach produces the following advantages:

- The insurance premiums are reimbursable as a line item for most government work.
- It eliminates minimum premium problems for subcontractors who would otherwise have to obtain a Hazardous Materials Contracting insurance program on their own.
- It may reduce remediation costs by expanding the universe of possible subcontractors to bid on work.
- This approach builds high insurance program aggregate limits of liability for contractors involved with many sites.
- The wrap-up insurance program will probably minimize total insurance costs on a particular project. Despite the advantages of using the wrap-up approach, it will only be useful to most firms on jobs exceeding $1 million in annual receipts. This is because all of the previously mentioned insurance policies have minimum premiums of at least $25,000, and there must be enough annual receipts associated with the job to absorb the minimum premium.

Firms doing a significant amount of hazardous materials contracting will probably find it useful to utilize both blanket and project specific insurance programs, depending on the situation. If the dual program approach is undertaken, the coordination of these policies becomes critical to avoid duplication of coverage and premiums. The scope of operations and services provided by a firm determines which insurance coverages are necessary. A specialty contractor providing only engineering services may need to purchase only General Liability, Professional Errors & Omissions with Pollution Liability, Automobile Liability, and Worker's Compensation coverages. At the other end of the spectrum, a firm providing design/build hazardous materials contracting services, including asbestos abatement, would have to purchase General Liability, Contractors Pollution Liability, Professional Errors & Omissions with Pollution Liability, Asbestos Abatement Liability, Asbestos Consultants Errors & Omissions, Automobile Liability and Worker's Compensation coverages. If a hazardous materials contracting firm is a subsidiary of a parent corporation whose insurance program was left intact, the insurance administrator for the entire program would be purchasing, in addition to the coverages provided on the hazardous materials contracting program, General Liability, Professional Liability, Automobile Liability, Worker's Compensation, and probably Umbrella Liability insurance policies.

## The EPA Connection

In order to attract contractors into the Superfund Program, the EPA offered indemnification for liability claims that arose out of the remedial action activities. The original EPA indemnification was quite broad covering "Liability" for bodily injury and property damage. Most of these original agreements did not restrict the terms of the indemnification to pollution liability claims.

Under Section 119 of the SARA Amendments to Superfund, the EPA is authorized to hold harmless and indemnify its response action contractors if they meet the requirements of that section. The indemnification under this section is limited to liabilities that result from a release of a hazardous substance or pollutant or contaminant if the release arises out of the response action activities. However, before a contractor is eligible to receive indemnity under Section 119 of SARA, he must have complied with the provisions of Section 119(c)(4), which mandates that RACS must meet the following requirements prior to receiving Federal Indemnification for potential pollution liability associated with Superfund response action activities:

- The RAC must make diligent efforts to obtain insurance coverage from non-Federal sources to cover pollution liability; and
- In the case of a RAC contract covering more than one facility, the RAC agrees to continue to make such diligent efforts each time the RAC begins work under the contract at a new facility.

Section 119 (c) (4) also requires that the following circumstances must exist before a RAC can receive Federal Indemification for potential pollution liability associated with Superfund response action activities:

- At the time the response action contract is entered into, insurance is not available, at a "fair and reasonable price," in sufficient quantity to offset potential RAC pollution liability risk;
- Adequate insurance to cover such liability is not generally available at the time the response action contract is entered into.

The "EPA Interim Guidance on Indemnification of Superfund Contractors," which was released on Oct. 6, 1987, goes into great detail as to exactly what a diligent effort to obtain insurance from non-federal sources entails. It includes the following:

- "The RAC must submit to EPA (or to the State Contracting Officer) written documentation addressing the additional efforts the RAC has made to secure pollution liability insurance coverage including:
  — Copies of applications submitted to three known underwriters of pollution liability insurance;
  — If pollution liability coverage was denied by an underwriter, a summary of the reasons why such a coverage was denied;
  — A status report of any pollution liability insurance obtained. The report would include:
    1) type of coverage;
    2) premium charge;
    3) limits of coverage;

4) deductible levels; and

5) any other major terms and conditions of the insurance coverage.

A copy of the actual policy and declaration page could be provided in lieu of a written status report:

- If pollution liability coverage was offered by an underwriter, but not accepted by the RAC, a report on the insurance offered (for example, the "status report" required above), and a summary of the reasons why such coverage was not accepted; and
- A status report concerning the alternative pollution liability risk transfer mechanisms the RAC has pursued other than commercial pollution liability insurance (e.g., risk retention groups, purchasing groups, association captives)."

The provisions of Section 119 are designed to force remedial action contractors to obtain insurance from non-federal sources. It is interesting to note that the EPA intends to make a determination at the time of the claim whether the contractor made a diligent effort to obtain insurance.

# Nuclear Materials
# Risk Management Considerations

Nuclear hazards are universally excluded in the General Liability, Contractors Pollution Liability, Architects & Engineers Errors and Omissions, Asbestos Abatement Liability policies. To address the nuclear exposure, risk managers need to differentiate between three broad types of work and clients:

- Low level nuclear work, private clients;
- Firms in the nuclear fuel cycle, private clients;
- Department of Defense and Department of Energy projects.

Low level nuclear hazards can be addressed within the context of the Contractors Pollution and Engineers Professional Liability policies. Although each policy contains an exclusion for nuclear materials, the exclusion can be overridden by adding a specific site and scope of work to the policies by endorsement. Firms engaged in the nuclear fuel cycle have access to the Nuclear Insurance Pools. The pools, led by the American Nuclear Insurers (ANI), provide coverage for Bodily Injury, Property Damage and Defense for liability arising from nuclear materials. Underwriting guidelines restrict the availability of coverage to firms that fall within the fuel cycle, beginning with fabricators and extending from reactors and by-products, to burial or disposal. Industrial and medical facilities are precluded from obtaining coverage in the pools and must rely on the traditional insurance market for coverage.

The nuclear pools actually insure the "facility" with a definition of named insured sufficiently broad to cover contractors working on the facility. Contractors working on these facilities do not purchase their own insurance to cover the nuclear hazard. Effective July 1, 1989, ANI provides $200 million of primary limits. Higher limits are provided under the Price-Anderson Act. Each reactor can be assessed $63 million for a nuclear damage claim, building total capacity to $7 billion under the program. Contractors working on government facilities have access to indemnification for nuclear hazards through Section 170, as amended by the Price-Anderson Act. The indemnification applies at the facility, during transportation, and to the materials handled. Current indemnification limits are $500 million. Although both the Department of Energy and the Department of Defense indemnify their contractors for nuclear and other extremely high hazard projects, both appear unwilling to provide any indemnity for remedial action projects. There even appears to be some unwillingness on the part of these agencies to cost-reimburse pollution liability insurance premiums. However, this problem can be overcome with the proper structuring of the insurance program. Since contractors working on nuclear facilities must provide their own traditional insurance programs for General Liability and Worker's Compensation, firms moving into nuclear cleanup area for the first time should consider the impacts that a "material change in the risk" will have on their overall insurance programs.

## Conculsion and Future Trends

Insurance for hazardous materials contractors is generally available in the marketplace today. The available limits of liability are increasing rapidly and rates continue to fall. The principal disadvantage of the coverages that are available today is the complexity of the insurance program that is created by the diversity of underwriters providing the

**An Integrated Risk Financing Approach
to Remedial Action Contracting**

various policy forms. A hazardous materials contractor's insurance program is extremely difficult to administer because of it's complexity; however, the fact that the various coverage forms are available to create a meaningful insurance program, should make it well worth the additional administrative burden. There are new packages available that should help to ease this burden. In order to help relieve some of that administrative burden, the contractor should be able to turn to his insurance broker to provide the support services.

The current hazardous materials contractors insurance marketplace is too complex to be practical. As underwriters gain more experience and historical loss data in underwriting this class of business, there will be a move towards packaging more of the coverages. This will produce a simplified insurance program for the environmental contracting industry. If the loss history of the hazardous materials contracting industry remains good, there will be an increase of capacity as the insurers writing this class of business are willing to commit more of their assets to there respective products. Perhaps the most significant future development affecting hazardous materials contractors will be the insurance industry's recognition that $100 billion of hazardous materials contracting market receipts really translates into $100 billion of additional revenue for their current book of engineers and contractors.

At this point, 80 percent of all the hazardous waste work done in the United States is insured by insurance companies that have home office underwriting guidelines that preclude them from writing this class of business. It will be interesting to watch as these insurance companies decide whether they should stay on accounts that do hazardous waste work, or if they are going to non-renew those accounts or cancel them. Significant barriers exist for insurance companies to enter the hazardous materials class of business. Most difficult is their ability to underwrite Environmental Impairment Liability coverage because in the effort to purge environmental risks from their books of business, the vast majority of insurance companies have purged themselves of any underwriting talent in the specialized area as well. Generally, it is difficult for an insurance company to issue liability insurance that excludes the essence of the insurance buyers risk; therefore, it is important for insurance companies to find a way to write pollution liability coverage on a hazardous materials exposure. The importance of EIL coverage, combined with the inability of most insurance companies to provide it, will dictate a cancellation

erage, combined with the inability of most insurance companies to provide it, will dictate a cancellation and non-renewal mode for the vast majority of insurance companies for the hazardous materials contracting firms they currently insure. In anticipation of this event, firms desiring to perform hazardous materials contracting services should proceed with lining up a fall-back-position insurance program designed to cover the environmental contracting business activities.

## About the Author

**David J. Dybdahl, Jr.**, CPCU & ARM, is Managing Director, Environment Risk Management Services, Corroon & Black National Resources Division, Nashville, Tennessee. He is an expert in designing and implementing risk management programs for clients having enviromentally related risks. These clients include contractors, engineers, manufacturers and public utilities for all lines of property and casualty insurance. In recognition, he was appointed by EPA to the Contractor Indemnification Technical Review Panel. He has published articles in several journals, including *Risk Management Magazine, Prima, Risk Management Today, Business Insurance, Civil Engineering,* and *Contractor Magazine.* He was graduated from the University of Wisconsin with an MBA in Finance, Risk Management and Insurance.

# XXV

# Risk Financing — A Case for Redomestication*

*Michael T. Rogers,*
*Vermont Insurance Management, Inc.*
*Montpelier, Vermont*
*and Jonathan Harkavy,*
*Vermont Insurance Management, Inc.*
*New York, New York*

It is now over four years since the Tax Reform Act of 1986 and the Risk Retention Act of 1986 seriously negated the advantages of offshore domiciled captive insurance companies. However, deciding on whether and how a captive should come back onshore has proved to be a difficult and complicated decision and one in which captives have received little help or encouragement from offshore captive managers and service providers. Although a considerable number of captives have weighed the advantages and disadvantages and come down in favor of moving to the comparatively safe harbor of a domestic domicile with favorable captive legislation, there is still a large majority who have adopted a "wait and see" attitude before making their decision. Still others have made the move onshore while retaining their offshore presence, a middle ground which, as we will see, may in the final analysis be the optimal solution.

In reviewing the merits of redomestication it is worth first reviewing the historical factors which likely resulted in the decision to go offshore and seeing if these factors still hold true today. The factors for single parent captives and group or association captives were not always the same and, where appropriate, these differences will be highlighted. Secondly, other factors which encourage redomestication will be reviewed and then, the alternative methodologies of physically moving from an offshore to an onshore domicile will be examined. Finally, we cover future trends.

# Historical Reasons
# for Choosing an Offshore Domicle

The factors can be categorized as insurance department regulation, infrastructure and income taxes, probably in that order of importance.

## Insurance Department Regulation

Insurance departments in the U.S. have a reputation for overburdensome regulation and bureaucratic red tape applied on a state-by-state basis. These departments have traditionally applied the same degree of regulation to a mono-line single parent captive, writing only parent company risks as they would for large multi-line commercial insurers. Faced with the prospect of unsympathetic state regulators trying to protect a public when there is no public to protect, companies wishing to set up captive insurance operations without incurring the wrath of state insurance departments had no choice until the early 1980s except to do so in the almost regulation-free environment. This they found in offshore locations.

Today the situation is fundamentally different. Several prominent insolvencies have made offshore locations, such as Bermuda and the Cayman Islands, re-think policy on regulation of captives. The emergence of well-run, liberal-thinking onshore domiciles with legislation sympathetic to captives, such as Vermont and Colorado and more recently Illinois and Hawaii, has created real alternatives to the offshore locations.

In Vermont, the leading onshore domicile, the attitude toward captives is that if it makes sense and is well conceived, adequately funded and soundly managed, then the captive will be welcome to transact business in the state. Vermont regulations were developed by risk managers for the benefit of risk managers and, recognizing the nature and purpose of captive insurance, apply appropriately different standards to regulation than the usual National Association of Insurance Commissioners (NAIC) rules. Rather than apply the NAIC ratios where they clearly are not appropriate, Vermont relies on the use of the feasibility study and open discussion with captive owners and managers to determine what is and what is not acceptable. The basic ground rules are dictated by statute but the majority of regulations are applied on a case-by-case basis. The open door policy of the regulators to sit down with captive owners, managers and lawyers to discuss issues before they arise results in effective communication, quick decisions and flexible regulations. Such advantages are particularly attractive to redomesticating captives used to dealing with the unapproachable finance ministries and infamously slow legal firms offshore.

With respect to regulation in other onshore domiciles, the jury is still out. Although Colorado was the first onshore captive domicile, the regulatory attitude toward captives has run hot and cold as Commissioners have come and gone. As a result of this unstable regulatory environment parent companies have been hesitant to form captives in Colorado and the number of captives remains stagnant at pre-1980 level.

In Illinois the situation is not dissimilar. Despite a well written law, Illinois' reputation for tough and inflexible regulation of traditional companies has undoubtedly caused concern amongst prospective captive owners irrespective of what assurances to the contrary they receive from the state.

Hawaii's law is a carbon copy of the Vermont legislation but with little regulatory presence to back it up. Hawaii is developing as a legitimate domestic domicile and will likely develop an important, if limited, role just as Cayman and Barbados have offshore.

Good regulation is infinitely better than no regulation or inadequate regulation. Many risk managers with captives in offshore domiciles would undoubtedly have preferred some guidance and input from regulators and managers before embarking on the disastrous ventures into third party business that led to serious losses for many captives and even insolvency for a few. Bermuda and other offshore domiciles have been slow to react to the changing nature of captives and interaction remains non-existent between captives and regulators. Furthermore, Bermuda continues to apply its out-dated solvency and liquidity ratios to captives, which have clearly not been effective in halting insolvencies in that domicile.

It should also be noted that there are neutral factors to both onshore and offshore domiciles, such as freedom to invest, recognition of reinsurance and exemption from guarantee funds, joint underwriting associations and assigned risk plans. Financial reporting is not onerous either offshore or in most onshore domiciles but association captives operating offshore must complete the dreaded "yellow peril" statutory NAIC blank while risk retention groups operating in Vermont currently are only required to complete the same "simplified annual statement" on a GAAP basis as do other single parent captives.

### Infrastructure

With its 30-year history as a captive domicile, Bermuda has created a strong infrastructure to service its captive insurance companies and this has been attractive to potential captive parents in domicile selection. The Bermuda insurance market presents an option to the domestic and London markets. The market, limited in development, caters to the financial reinsurers. The Bermuda risk exchange has been a non-starter. Many risk managers today may question whether the cost of doing business in Bermuda is justified compared with the level of service being provided.

In Vermont, 10 years after its landmark legislation was passed, the infrastructure is in place with all major captive management companies represented, several "Big 8" accounting firms resident in state and the legal and banking community in tune with the needs of the captive movement. Vermont State, is, perhaps, the only domicile worldwide to have a separate department with a dedicated full-time staff dealing exclusively with captive matters, funded by 7.5 percent of the annual premium tax. Vermont maintains stability of personnel in the management firms, the accounting firms and the insurance department and the support of the legislature who see captives as a non-polluting, job-creating industry that should be welcomed.

Domestic captive management firms with offshore captive experience and customized computer reports (available to clients just days after the close of a period) can be more cost effective than offshore facilities. Many offshore management companies have limited computerization of financial records. Effective April 1, 1990, Bermuda imposed a five percent payroll tax on its captive managers, a move that may result in higher managment fees, less service, or both.

Illinois and, to a lesser extent, Colorado also have strong infrastructures. Vermont has licensed five times more captives in 1989 than all other domestic domiciles. The smaller onshore domiciles will find their niche just as Cayman has in medical malpractice captives and Barbados in Canadian companies. Colorado and Illinois are attracting more than their share of local risks while Hawaii will likely grow to be a significant player for risks located west of the Rockies.

In terms of stability, the domestic domiciles may have an advantage over even the most politically stable offshore location. Redomesticated companies have found that the security of a U.S. based captive insurance company is more readily acceptable to reinsurance companies and third parties requiring certificates of insurance than the equivalent offshore captive.

Bermuda and other offshore domiciles appear to be temporary places of employment for expatriate account managers, auditors and other personnel. Communication with parent company officials can be frustrating especially where differences of interpretation arise between management companies and auditors. As captives become more complex, ease to communicate and access to a manager who is totally familiar with the captives' operations becomes vital. Running a captive offshore can be more expensive and inconvenient when compared to running the same operation onshore. Overall, management practices will be one of the key elements to the success of either an onshore or offshore captive facility.

A comparison of estimated costs and growth in the major onshore and offshore domiciles appears in Figure 1.

### Income and Excise Taxes

Contrary to popular belief, taxation, or the deferral thereof, was seldom the driving force behind the selection of an offshore domicile by parents or single parents, although, it was admittedly a more influential factor for group captives. It becomes a much more important subject in determining whether a captive should come back onshore because the Tax Reform Act of 1986 eliminated all tax deferral advantages for offshore single parent captives and all but eliminated them for group captives. Offshore captives are now taxed on imputed income in the same manner as U.S. domiciled captives and, hence, for all post 1986 income the tax treatment of U.S. domiciled and offshore domiciled captives is identical.

The Tax Reform Act of 1986 had the effect of ending Non Controlled Foreign Company (NCFC) status for U.S. shareholder group captives, eliminating the deferral of taxes and resulting in the current taxation of all Related Person Insurance Income (RPII). The tax issues have become so complex that many offshore group captives have retained tax counsel. While these tax opinions may still show an advantage in some situations, the advantage has been severely re-

Figure 1
Single Parent Captive Cost and Growth Estimates

| | Vermont | Bermuda | Barbados | Cayman | Colorado | Hawaii | Illinois | Tennessee |
|---|---|---|---|---|---|---|---|---|
| **Number of Captives** | | | | | | | | |
| Total | 175 | 1315 | 176 | 357 | 21 | 10 | 8 | 14 |
| 1989 Additions | 21 | 45 | 21 | 25 | 2 | 5 | 2 | 1 |
| 1989 Deletions | 4 | 68 | 3 | 30 | 1 | 0 | 0 | 0 |
| Net Growth | 17 | -23 | 18 | -5 | 1 | 5 | 2 | 1 |
| **Minimum Capital Onshore (offshore)** | | | | | | | | |
| Pure/(General) | $250,000 | 120,000 | 125,000 | 120,000 | 500,000 | 250,000 | 2,000,000 | 750,000 |
| Association/(Long term) | 750,000 | 250,000 | 125,000 | 240,000 | 750,000 | 750,000 | 2,000,000 | 1,000,000 |
| Industrial Insured, RRG/(Both) | 500,000 | 370,000 | 125,000 | 360,000 | 500,000 | 500,000 | 2,000,000 | 1,000,000 |
| **Regulatory** | | | | | | | | |
| Premium taxes/FET | 0.7%(1) | 4.0% | 4.0% | 4.0% | 1.0% | 0.25% (2) | 7.3%(3) | 1.0% |
| Annual fees | $300 | 2,900 - 9,000 | 2,500 | 5,487 | 300 | 300 | 0 | 100 |
| Application fees | 200 | 0 | 500 | 0 | 200 | 1,000 | 3,500 | 5,000 |
| Actuarial review | 1,200 | 0 | 0 | 0 | 0 | 0 | 0 | 500 |
| **Financial** | | | | | | | | |
| Management fees | $30,000 | 40,000 | 40,000 | 40,000 | 30,000 | 30,000 | 35,000 | 30,000 |
| Audit | 7,500 | 12,000 | 12,000 | 12,000 | 7,500 | 7,500 | 10,000 | 7,500 |
| Actuarial | 8,000 | 10,000 | 10,000 | 10,000 | 8,000 | 8,000 | 8,000 | 8,000 |
| Local legal | 1,500 | 5,000 | 5,000 | 5,000 | 1,500 | 1,500 | 10,000 | 1,500 |
| **Communications** | $ 500 | 2,500 | 2,500 | 2,500 | 400 | 2,000 | 750 | 500 |
| **Travel** | | | | | | | | |
| Airfare from East Coast | $ 250 | 375 | 800 | 650 | 600 | 1,500 | 600 | 650 |
| Accomodations/meals per day | 135(4) | 350 | 240 | 285 | 170 | 275 | 230(4) | 150 |

Notes:
(1) Reduces at $20m premium
(2) 0.7% on group captives
(3) Income taxes on Illinois Net Income
(4) If necessary

Environmental
Risk Management

duced and these opinions are open wide to different interpretation by the IRS. Many of the loopholes still existing today may be quickly closed by the IRS at the first opportunity.

Group captives are faced with an awkward situation with respect to the possible elections that can be made on their sub-part F income. If they decide not to elect to be taxed as a U.S. taxpayer then this results in additional sub-part F income taxes payable by the individual participants on income they may not receive. If they decide to elect, then the captive pays the tax and the captive may be drained of resources. The captive may have to post a letter of credit representing 10 percent of the prior year's gross premium as a security deposit. The tax paid by the captive may be higher than the combined tax paid by the individual members if the captive had not elected. The election is partially offset by a relief from federal excise tax and the 30 percent withholding tax on U.S. source investment income discussed below, and the availability of a three-year carry back of net operating losses, an advantage that is not lost on offshore group captives entering the fourth or fifth year of a claims-made program.

Apart from the decision on whether to elect or not to elect, there remains a bigger threat to group captives resulting from the Tax Reform Act of 1986: the danger of tax being assessed branch profits if the captive is held to be "engaged in a U.S. trade or business." Certain state insurance departments have also jumped on this bandwagon and threatened penalties or suits against representatives of groups who have claims-handling or policyholder services for the offshore captives located onshore.

Federal Excise Tax has been, in the past, an issue for group captives. Bermuda and Barbados domiciled captives recently lost their U.S. excise tax exemptions and this, together with the "Humana Decision" has made the federal excise issue a much more important consideration. The 0.7 percent and 0.25 percent premium tax (reducing at higher premium levels) for Vermont captives can be a big advantage over the 4 percent and 1 percent Federal Excise Tax payable on direct premiums and reinsurance premiums going offshore. Until the recent "Humana Decision," the disallowance of the deductibility of premiums paid by single parent captives resulted in their being treated as a non-insurance entity and, therefore, Federal Excise Tax was not an issue. However, for captives taking advantage of the "Humana Decision," which allowed deductibility of premiums for brother/sister companies of captives, the Federal Excise Tax question is now very relevant and even more so if the House Ways and Means Committee proposal to increase Federal Excise Tax on reinsurance premiums from one percent to four percent is passed. (Ed. Note: It did not.)

## Factors That Encourage Redomestication

With the apparent neutralization of historical advantages for setting up offshore captives there are several factors which encourage redomestication. These can be categorized as marketing and administration for group captives and other tax and regulatory issues for single parents.

### Marketing and Administration

Whether a group captive is formed as an offshore association captive or an offshore risk retention group, it has always been difficult to achieve and maintain the "critical mass" of insureds necessary to spread the risk, increase retentions and ensure survival. The soft market has severely hit membership of association and group captives as members are seduced by the short-run gains of low premiums and revert to traditional commercial insurance carriers. It has become increasingly difficult for groups to maintain mind and management offshore, raising once again the question of where the group is conducting business. Members and service providers of offshore group captives have had to prove to both state insurance departments and the IRS that the insureds came to the company rather than vice versa. Furthermore, the captive has had to try to overcome the perception to potential participants that a foreign domiciled insurer is less secure than a domestic captive. As a result, offshore group captives have not grown and their critical mass and very existence is constantly threatened.

The Risk Retention Act of 1986 has made many group captives abandon or consider abandoning their offshore domicile to take advantage of the marketing opportunities afforded by the exemption from federal security laws, state "blue sky" laws and many of the insurance restrictions preventing non-admitted insurers from doing business in other states. Once a risk retention group is licensed in its domicile state, brokers and agents can market the group without the added and increased cost of a fronting company. The elimination of the costs and problems of fronting, a role fewer admitted companies are willing to accept, allows the group captive much more flexibility in determining its coverage and policy form and allows the unbundling of the services included as part of the fronting package deal. For certain lines of business, fronting will still be needed but front companies tend to be much more receptive to a U.S. domiciled captive. The combination of marketing and cost advantages make onshore domiciles look very attractive for both new groups and offshore group captives alike, a fact reflected by the 67 risk retention groups already operating onshore despite a very soft insurance market.

### Other Tax and Regulatory Issues

Successful and mature single parent captives have generated substantial amounts of funds that they may wish to loan back to their parent companies, but several foreign domiciles have prohibited such loans or made them admissible only with special permission. For example, in Bermuda a loan to a parent does not qualify as an admissible asset for purposes of calculating the minimum liquidity ratio. Interest on such loans and U.S. equity investments is subject to a 30 percent withholding tax and this alone has been reason enough for some well-known single parent captives to redomesticate. Establishing a domestic captive eliminates the withholding tax problem and most regulators in onshore domiciles allow captives to make loans back to their parent companies.

In Vermont, another regulation which encourages redomestication is a "port of entry" rule, which allows captives moving to the state from offshore domiciles to do so without having to pay a one-time premium tax on their portfolio transfer.

## Methodologies of Redomestication

Once the decision has been made to redomesticate, actually bringing the company back onshore involves a lot more than packing up shop and taking the next plane out. The captive has to consider the effect of its move on the contractual arrangements it has and what to do with untaxed retained earnings accumulated before the 1986 Tax

Reform Act took effect. If the company has entered into third party reinsurance treaties or has a fronting arrangement with an admitted company, it is necessary to obtain permission from these parties to novate or alternatively try to commute the old agreements. Vermont has been sympathetic to offshore captives running off third-party business but Illinois specifically excludes redomesticating captives from bringing such business into the state.

The untaxed profits which offshore captives sheltered due to different definitions of Sub-part F income that existed prior to the 1986 Tax Reform Act are a major problem because of the so-called "toll charge" the owners or parent will likely incur when the captive is moved onshore. One way to bring a foreign domiciled captive onshore is to establish a new U.S. domiciled company to which all the assets and liabilities are transferred and then have the new company issue shares to the shareholders of the old company in exchange for the transfer of assets. The offshore company may then be wound up, run-off or left, as will be discussed below, as a going concern.

Another method of moving onshore is to use the shares of the offshore company as the principal asset to capitalize the domestic captive. In one situation, the offshore company paid a dividend to the parent which was passed through to the new company as the initial capital and later the parent contributed all the stock of the offshore captive as additional capital. The offshore captive could portfolio all or part of its loss reserves and unearned premiums to the new domestic captive and provide some relief to the "toll tax." In practice this has been one of the most common methods of redomestication primarily because of its simplicity and the fact that it avoids many of the jurisdictional headaches. The redomesticating company must satisfy the onshore regulators that it is matching its actuarial valued liabilities with corresponding hard assets. However this method should be as arms-length as possible as the IRS could question this as a vehicle to avoid paying tax.

Rather than setting up a new onshore company it is also possible to have the old offshore captive "continue" in the new domicile. Barbados, Turks and Caicos and the British Virgin Islands have passed special legislation to allow such continuation. On the other hand, if a company wishes to transfer out of Bermuda and "continue" it must do so by Private Act of the Legislature, which is not uncommon but can take up to six months. Continuation has the advantage of enabling the existing contractual obligations to continue without novation, but practice has shown that there must be corresponding legislation in the new domicile to make it work. While Colorado, Illinois and Delaware make reference to simplified redomestication rules in their legislation, there does not appear to be any offshore companies who have actually redomesticated using the mechanism.

Only one of the above methodologies address the "toll tax" problem; however, it should be remembered that the offshore captive has only "deferred" taxation on its untaxed accumulated retained earnings and that even under the old rules the profits will be taxed when ultimately remitted onshore.

Still it is possible to have it both ways. For single parent captives the offshore captive may be left to write foreign risks or run off the existing book of business while a new onshore captive is set up to write new U.S. sourced business. For groups, setting up an onshore Risk Retention Act captive and keeping the offshore captive to act as a reinsurer or direct writer of lines not allowed under the Risk Retention Act format can combine the advantages of both locations.

Developing loss reserves to cover pollution exposures is another issue and is addressed in the following section.

## Future Directions in Creative Risk Financing Programs for Potential Pollution Losses

Long term corporate incurred-but-not-reported (IBNR) liability exposures, have generally not been funded through the captive mechanism. Potential pollution exposures have been no exception. The likely primary reason for the under-utilization of captives as a risk funding mechanism for environmental impairment liability exposures is that Uncle Sam does not make it easy for captives to accumulate assets from which to fund these long-term IBNR losses. The government takes a significant tax bite from investment income earned by captive loss reserves; perhaps a greater bite, on a bottom-line percentage basis, than taxes paid by traditional carriers on their loss reserve investment income. Offshore captives fare little better than their U.S. counterparts, as investment income is imputed to the domestic parent, regardless of whether such income is repatriated onshore.

These hurdles imposed by the Internal Revenue Code must be overcome to maximize asset accumulation in the captive "war chest" from which future IBNR losses can be paid. One way of overcoming such obstacles is the use of corporately owned life insurance (COLI) as an investment instrument of choice for loss reserves held by the captive. It is extremely rare to hear COLI addressed in the context of captives. Any advantages offered by COLI as a funding investment are quickly eviscerated by the extremely high overhead and commission costs contained in the typical life insurance policy, which are often higher then 50 percent of the first year's premium. For COLI to be suitable as a funding mechanism, such overhead and commission costs must be cut to the marrow. This requires the active involvement of the life insurance carrier in the development of a product suitable for use by the captive to replace or enhance its existing loss reserves. Despite the legendary stodginess of the life insurance community, this can be accomplished.

Using my own experience as an example, by working with an A+ Bests' rated carrier, we were able to develop a policy which had a first-year cash surrender value in excess of the initial annual premium. As a loss funding mechanism such a product has significant advantages over taxable investments made by captives on loss reserves held for more than four years. Inside buildup of income earned by COLI policies is tax deferred, unlike taxable investments. Moreover, death benefits afforded by the COLI policy are received by the corporation tax free. Due to these tax advantages, a properly developed COLI product will outperform, on a guaranteed basis, a typically available taxable investment (for example, an 8 percent commercial paper offering) by more than 40 percent over a 20-year period.

In conclusion, most of the historical advantages of locating a captive offshore have either disappeared or been severely reduced while developments onshore more and more encourage the establishment of domestic captives. In the last three years the number of captives set up in Vermont has increased from 32 to 175 while the offshore domiciles have shown no growth. Some very well known parents have already analyzed the advantages and disadvantages and made the move to redomesticate their captives lock, stock and barrel. For others, who have not yet considered the move or are still holding a "wait and see" attitude, the combined advantages offered by operating captives in dual domiciles may yet be the optimal answer.

## About the Authors

**Michael T. Rogers** is Chief Operating Officer of Vermont Insurance Management, Inc., at their headquarters in Montperlier, Vermont. Prior to that her served as principal examiner for the Ontario Canada Department of Insurance and was audit manager for Deloitte, Haskins & Sells in both Toronto and Bermuda. He is chartered accountant educated in his native England and a member of the British, Canadian and Bermuda Institutes of Chartered Accountants.

**Jonathan Harkavy** is Vice President and General counsel for Vermont Insurance Management, Inc. and is located in New York City. For seven years he served as Chief Counsel for the Risk Insurance Management Society (RIMS) and prior to that was a legislative assistant to Congressman Raymond Lepered in Washington, D.C. He attended Penn State and Temple University School of Law. He is a member of the Washington, D.C. and Pennsylvania Bar and a member of the New York and American Bar Associations.

# XXVI     Future Environmental Energy Issues

*James B. Vasile, Partner
and Scott Slaughter, Esq.
Newman and Holtzinger
Washington, D.C.*

A number of environmental issues have been of great concern to the energy industry over the past few years. For example, PCBs continue to be a major problem for many natural gas pipelines and electric utilities. As another example, there still is no adequate means for disposing of radioactive waste. Future environmental developments are likely to pose new problems. The almost certain amendment of the Clean Air Act; probable amendment of federal laws to impose much more stringent requirements on the disposal of nonhazardous solid waste; and possible new legislative or international agreements related to "global warning" will or would have a great impact on the energy industry.

**PCBs**

### Regulatory Background

Polychlorinated Biphenyls (PCBs) are a major environmental problem for electric utilities — who may have used transformers, capacitors or other equipment containing PCBs — and for natural gas pipelines — who may have PCBs present in the pipeline either because they operated leaking compressors or other PCB-containing equipment, or because they are connected to other PCB-contaminated pipelines.[1]

Section 6(e) of the Toxic Substances Control Act (TSCA) prohibits the manufacture of PCBs, the processing and distribution of PCBs in commerce, and the use of PCBs after specified dates in the late 1970s, unless the PCBs are manufactured, processed, distributed, or used in a "totally enclosed manner."[2] EPA's rules, which are codified at 40 C.F.R. Part 761, define "totally enclosed manner" as "any manner that will ensure no exposure of human beings or the environment to any concentration of PCBs."[3] TSCA also authorizes EPA to grant exemptions for unenclosed PCB uses that the Agency finds "will not present an unreasonable risk of injury to health or the environment."[4]

EPA's TSCA rules constitute the primary federal regulatory scheme for PCBs. PCBs are not now subject to the hazardous waste requirements of the Federal Resource Conservation and Recovery Act (RCRA).[5] PCBs are, however, subject to the liability and reporting provisions of the Federal Comprehensive Environmental Response, Compensation, and Liability Act (CERCLA).[6] Thus, while the disposal of PCBs does not have to comply with RCRA, any actual or threatened release of PCBs from a facility can give rise to response (i.e., cleanup) cost liability under CERCLA.

TSCA contains a preemption provision that has created substantial confusion and uncertainty.[7] While there is no clear answer now as to whether this TSCA provision preempts state and local authority to regulate PCBs, EPA and at least three courts have concluded that state and local PCB disposal rules are not preempted so long as they are no less stringent than and do not interfere with EPA's PCB disposal rules.[8]

### Recent Developments

In the last few years, there have been several attempts to pass federal legislation which would impose RCRA-like requirements, including permits, on the transport and disposal of PCBs. So far, none of this legislation has been enacted.[9] Instead, Congress seems to be relying on new EPA rulemakings rather than new legislation to impose more stringent requirements on PCBs.

One of the most important of these new EPA PCB rules was published on December 21, 1989.[10] These new rules imposed requirements governing the transport, storage, and disposal of PCB waste that resemble the "cradle-to-grave" regulatory scheme for RCRA hazardous wastes. For example, a "generator of PCB waste" who transports or offers for transport such waste for commercial off-site storage or disposal must prepare a manifest to accompany the PCB waste from the point of generation to the point of disposal. The standard EPA RCRA manifest form is to be used for the manifesting of PCB waste unless state law requires use of a different state manifest. Certain states regulate PCBs as a hazardous waste and require appropriate management practices (i.e., New York).

On June 27, 1988, EPA published other new PCB rules governing exclusions, exemptions, and use authorizations.[11] These new rules amended the existing PCB rules in several respects, including the following:

- EPA allowed certain equipment and materials that had been adequately decontaminated to be used and distributed in commerce;
- EPA allowed waste oil containing less than 50 ppm PCBs to be used as a fuel in certain combustion units; and
- EPA excluded from the ban on processing, distribution in commerce and use, certain products containing less than 50 ppm PCBs that were "legally" manufactured, processed, distributed in commerce or used prior to October 1, 1984. [12]

Anyone dealing with equipment or property which might be contaminated with PCBs should also be aware of EPA's PCB spill Cleanup Policy.[13] This policy, which became effective on May 4, 1987, generally governs the cleanup of PCB-contaminated equipment and property.

In the spring of 1990, EPA announced a new PCB Penalty Policy. [14] EPA's policy explains that penalties for violations of the PCB rules will be based on a variety of factors, including "attitude." EPA explained that "[i]n assessing the violator's attitude, the Agency will look at the following factors: whether the violator is making good faith efforts to comply with the appropriate regulations; the promptness of the violator's corrective actions; and any actions taken to minimize harm to the environment caused by the violation."[15] EPA's Penalty Policy is intended to encourage voluntary disclosure of violations and voluntary corrective action by assessing much higher penalties on less cooperative parties. USEPA has been extremely active in enforcing both civil and criminal penalty provisions of TSCA with respect to violation of the PCB rules. For example, the Public Service Commission of Colorado, Inc., recently paid an $84,500 civil penalty for storage of improperly marked, leaking transformers.[16] In a recent criminal prosecution, five principals of the Martha C. Rose Chemicals Facility in Holden, Missouri, were indicted for illegal storage or disposal of over one million pounds of capacitor cores.

## Recent FERC Environmental Issues

Energy companies subject to Federal Energy Regulatory Commission (FERC) jurisdiction should be aware of several environmental issues which have recently arisen at FERC, some of which involve PCBs.

### PCB Testing Under FERC Environmental Assessment Requirements

FERC has required pipeline companies to test for PCB contamination as a prerequisite to the commission's approval of the construction or abandonment of a pipeline. The FERC's recent NEPA regulations require FERC staff to prepare an environmental assessment (EA) for construction and abandonment applications that includes an assessment of potential PCB contamination.[17] The FERC prepared several EAs in 1988.[18] When the FERC determines that pipes or compressors may be contaminated with PCBs, it can impose conditions to ensure that the pipeline will take steps to mitigate the problem.

### FERC Review of Environmental Expenditures

In order to pass through environmental costs to its customers, a FERC-regulated electric utility or gas pipeline will have to persuade FERC that those costs were prudently incurred. State-regulated utilities may also have to pass a similar prudence review before state commissions. As of the publication date for this book, FERC has not specifically addressed the issue of whether environmental cleanup costs (e.g., response costs incurred under CERCLA) should be considered prudent expenditures. Several gas pipeline cases involving PCB cleanup costs have not yet been decided. These cases may allow FERC the opportunity to address this issue.[19]

Electric utilities should also begin planning now as to how their companies will comply with what is likely to be a new and much more stringent Federal Clean Air Act, discussed at length in Chapter II. A new Clean Air Act is likely to force utilities to make complex, difficult decisions concerning issues such as fuel contracts, new pollution control equipment, and emission allowance purchases or sales. Careful planning and documentation of the decision-making process may be necessary to survive FERC or state utility commission prudence review if and when the utility tries to pass these compliance costs on to its customers.

## FERC Ruling On NEPA Applicability
## To Utility Merger Review

On May 5, 1989, FERC ruled that the National Environmental Policy Act of 1969 (NEPA) analysis was not required during FERC review of a proposed merger between Southern California Edison Company and San Diego Gas & Electric Company.[20] In its May 5 ruling, FERC explained that,

The approval of mergers under section 203 of the F[ederal] P[ower] A[ct] does not normally constitute a major federal action significantly affecting the environment. Such activity generally involves only a change in ownership or change in corporate structure. Therefore, mergers are categorically excluded from the requirement for [NEPA review].[21]

On October 27, 1989, FERC reversed its earlier ruling and ruled that NEPA analysis was required for this particular merger. FERC's reversal of its previous ruling was based on evidence presented by opponents of the proposed merger which claimed that the merger "could add hundreds of tons of additional air contaminants to the most polluted air in the Nation." It is clear from FERC's opinion that the current status of the air quality in Southern California played a major role in its decision to require NEPA review. Consequently, it is unclear whether NEPA analysis will be required during FERC review of utility mergers in other regions of the country.

The FERC has also ruled that when receiving applications for status as a qualifying cogeneration facility, FERC's "regulations do not contemplate, let alone expressly require, the preparation of an environmental document [i.e., an EA or EIS under NEPA] for a particular facility since QF certification only establishes eligibility for PURPA benefits; that is, the regulations do not contemplate preparation of an environmental document because neither the regulations nor an order granting certification authorizes construction or relieves a facility of any other requirements of local, state or federal law involving siting, construction, operation, licensing, or pollution abatement."

## More Stringent Requirements for Electric Utility Solid Waste Disposal

Coal and other wastes generated primarily from the combustion of coal and other fossil fuels are currently exempt from the hazardous waste requirements of the Federal Resource Conservation and Recovery Act (RCRA).[22] Pursuant to RCRA, EPA sent a report to Congress, "Waste from the Combustion of Coal by Electric Utility Power Plants," which recommended that this exemption be continued. There is, however, increasing concern over disposal of non-hazardous solid waste, such as the fly and bottom ash generated by fossil fuel powered electric power plants.

RCRA will probably be reauthorized and amended sometime in the next couple of years. All indications to date are that Congress will focus on the Act's solid waste provisions and will amend them to impose much more extensive requirements. For example, S.1113, entitled "Waste Minimization and Control Act of 1989," which was introduced by Senator Max Baucus in 1989, would amend RCRA by requiring states to issue permits for solid waste disposal and to develop regulatory plans that comply with certain minimum requirements. If a state fails to act, then EPA will administer the permits. Under the Baucus Bill, any new non-hazardous waste impoundment, land unit, or lateral expansion thereof must have a liner and groundwater monitoring system. Permits must also contain provisions specifying location standards; air and groundwater monitoring; financial responsibility; liners and a leachate collection system. Other potentially onerous conditions such as corrective action may also be required.

A similar bill introduced November 19, 1989, by Representative Thomas A. Luken would:

- require states to establish a permit program for all facilities treating, storing, transporting, or disposing of non-hazardous waste, including combustion wastes;
- require all new impoundments, all new land disposal units, and all lateral expansions of existing land disposal units to implement groundwater monitoring; and
- require EPA to promulgate regulations for industrial solid waste facilities that impose performance standards and monitoring requirements.

The EPA guidelines would be incorporated into the permits issued by the state. EPA could enforce compliance with the state permits, as could private citizens, under a citizen suit provision.

Electric utilities and other energy companies should also note that in 1988, under the current RCRA, EPA proposed rules applicable to municipal solid waste landfills.[23] While these proposals only cover municipal landfills, they will also be used to gather information on other solid waste facilities such as industrial landfills and surface impoundments (e.g., ash ponds). The proposed municipal rules impose rather stringent requirements on solid waste disposal. The final municipal rules, which are expected in the early fall of 1990, may provide some guidance on what energy companies can expect to face in regard to future regulation of their solid waste disposal units.

## Oil Spills

The federal law governing oil spills is Section 311 of the Clean Water Act.[24] Several states, including New Jersey, have enacted new legislation governing oil spill liability in the wake of the Exxon Valdez oil spill.[25] In June 1990, the Conference Committee on the federal legislation decided that the United States would not participate in the international accords, thereby preserving state authority to enact spill liability legislation.[26]

After a year of lively congressional debate in response to the Valdez oil spill disaster, Congress on August 18, 1990, enacted the Oil Pollution Act of 1990, Public Law 101-380. The statute may generally be described as a new Federal Superfund law applicable to petroleum discharges (otherwise excluded from the definition of hazardous substance under the Comprehensive Environmental Response Compensation and Liability Act).

The new law is applicable to owners and operators of vessels, onshore and off-shore facilities, pipelines and deep water ports. These parties are liable to Federal or State governments (or other persons acting consistently with the Federal National Contingency Plan) for costs associated with removal and remedial actions undertaken in response to the discharge or substantial threat of discharge of oil to navigable waters (as that term is broadly defined under the Clean Water Act). Liability for removal costs with respect to non-negligent discharges is capped at $10 million for tankers, $600 per gross ton for other vessels, $75 million for off-shore facilities and $350 million for on-shore facilities. Liability is unlimited in the event the discharge incident was caused by gross negligence, willful conduct, or violation of federal spill regulations. Further, no liability cap applies to governmental removal costs related to off-shore oil production or processing, vessels transporting oil from such production. Liability caps are also inapplicable if responsible parties fail to report a known release incident or to cooperate and provide assistance requested by responsible officials or comply with removal orders. The new legislation also requires that bulk oil cargo vessels entering services must have double hulls, and existing vessels must be upgraded or retired over periods ranging from five to 25 years.

# Nuclear Power Environmental Issues

The primary environmental issues currently facing the nuclear power industry are waste disposal; compliance with the recently promulgated National Emission Standards for Hazardous Air Pollutants (NESHAPs) for radionuclide emissions under the Clean Air Act; and the reporting of radionuclide releases under CERCLA.

### Low-Level Waste Disposal

In 1980, Congress passed the Low-Level Radioactive Waste Policy Act of 1980 (LLRWPA), which provided for state responsibility for the disposal of low-level waste by 1986.[27]  Although each state would be responsible for disposal of its own waste, the Act also provided for regional compacts, because the siting of disposal sites in all 50 states is economically and technically infeasible.  Non-compliance with the 1980 Act, due to technical and political problems, forced Congress to extend the Act's deadlines by amending it in 1985.[28]

Some progress has been made in establishment of compacts and generally the states are meeting the milestones under the LLRWPA. As of 1987, however, no new facilities had been sited.  Citizens in most areas that have come under consideration as potential sites have fought the facilities.  Nebraska citizens have challenged the constitutionality of portions of the LLRWPA. New York and Michigan are also challenging the law in court.  There is some question whether siting will actually occur soon, even with the penalties imposed by the LLRWPA.[29] One expert has stated that there is "no possibility of establishing the required new disposal sites by the 1993 deadline."[30]

The future of the LLRWPA currently rests in the courts. If the federal government is victorious, most states will eventually meet the law's guidelines, although not within the proposed time frame. Generators of waste can expect a sharp increase in disposal costs to result. If the Supreme Court eventually holds that the LLRWPA is unconstitutional, Congress will have to create a new federal scheme for the disposal of low-level waste since the three existing sites will eventually fill up.[31]

**High-Level Waste Disposal**

The Nuclear Waste Policy Act (NWPA) governs the disposal of high-level radioactive waste.[32] The NWPA establishes a national policy for the disposal of high-level waste in permanent deep facilities (repositories). The Department of Energy (DOE) became responsible in 1998 for accepting high-level waste from nuclear power plants. The siting of a repository has been delayed numerous times, and a repository is not expected to be completed until 2010, at the very earliest. To provide for storage in the interim, Congress amended the NWPA in 1987, to authorize the siting of a monitored retrievable storage facility (MRS) which would accept high-level waste for storage until the repository is completed. Since the MRS has also been delayed, the current practice of on-site storage remains the only method of storing high-level waste.

When the NWPA was amended in 1987, Congress decided that Yucca Mountain, Nevada would be the only site that would be tested and characterized as a possible repository. The State of Nevada is trying to block any testing at the site. The Governor of Nevada has stated that "Yucca Mountain is not going to be the site for the nuclear waste repository."[33] The State has refused to issue the environmental permits necessary for research and testing to begin. Nevada's legislature has also "disapproved" the siting of Yucca Mountain despite the fact the site has not yet been officially recommended.

The Department of Justice has sued Nevada in federal court over the legality of Nevada's "disapproval," and Nevada has also commenced litigation against the Department of Energy.[34] Nevada's legislature also passed a bill in 1989 which prohibits the storage of high-level waste within the state. If Nevada is successful in blocking further testing or development of the Yucca Mountain site, the prospects for a repository in the next two or three decades dim considerably.

The Office of Civilian Radioactive Waste Management predicts that a repository at Yucca Mountain would not be open to accept waste until 2010, at the earliest.[35] The prediction of a 2010 opening is admittedly optimistic. The necessary testing must first confirm that the site is suitable. Since the NWPA calls for acceptance of high-level waste by 1998, the DOE has turned its attention to MRS facilities.

Amendments to the NWPA call for the construction of at least one MRS facility.[36] Such a facility will provide long-term isolation of high-level waste, continuous monitoring, ready retrieval, and maintenance. The MRS program is subject to certain conditions including the following: the MRS may not be sited until the siting of a repository; the NRC may not license the MRS until the repository is licensed by the NRC; MRS construction must stop if repository construction stops; and limits are to be placed on both the amount of waste that the MRS can accept until the repository is open and on the total amount of waste that may be stored at the MRS.

Without a volunteer state, DOE predicts 2002 as the earliest possible opening date for an MRS facility. DOE has predicted that 27 plants would run out of on-site storage by 1998.[37] These facilities must increase on-site storage through the use of increased dry-storage and reracking, which will be costly. Utilities may have problems trying to pass these costs on to ratepayers. Some state regulators will not allow all these costs to be passed on since ratepayers already bear the MRS costs through the Interim Storage Fund fee.[38]

The Edison Electric Institute estimates that additional on-site storage will cost the industry $1.5 billion by 2010.[39] The American Committee on Radwaste Disposal (ACORD) has asked that some sort of funding mechanism be set up by the Department of Energy if it fails to accept fuel in 1998, as the NWPA requires.[40] ACORD also suggests that the DOE act more aggressively in implementing the NWPA, particularly by improving the staff and management working on the program.[41]

The implementation of the NWPA has been slowed, but the DOE appears to be making strides. The prospects for siting a

MRS and a repository are still tenuous, however, and the courts may have the final word. Meanwhile, nuclear facilities should expect that they will have to store high-level waste on-site at least through the year 2002.

## Mixed Waste Disposal

Mixed waste is a form of low-level radioactive waste consisting of "hazardous waste" regulated under RCRA[42] and radioactive waste regulated under the Atomic Energy Act (AEA).[43] Mixed waste constitutes less than 10% of all commercial low-level waste,[44] but its disposal is difficult. Through RCRA and the AEA, EPA and the NRC both govern the disposal of mixed waste.[45] This dual regulation creates a problem for generators of mixed waste because the two regimes are duplicative and inconsistent.

The Office of Technology Assessment prepared a report on mixed waste in 1989, concluding that "some specific regulations cannot be met, some regulations may be in conflict and inconsistent, and other regulations overlap and are duplicative."[46] Under the current dual scheme generators of mixed waste cannot ship mixed waste for storage or disposal since no commercially licensed facilities meet both EPA and NRC standards. The OTA Report found that mixed waste continues to be produced and stored despite the fact that storage is prohibited and no disposal facility has been developed.[47] The Edison Electric Institute has disputed these findings, claiming that OTA's report was oversimplified. EEI agrees, however, that EPA and NRC must devise a more efficient and tailored set of regulations.[48]

DOE recently opened the first mixed waste incinerator at the Idaho National Engineering Laboratory (for Department of Defense generated mixed waste). The EPA should approve commercial incinerators in the near future.[49] The nuclear industry expects that a commercial facility will be open by 1993. Currently, the greatest need in mixed waste disposal is for legislative reform or clarification so that generators and disposal facility operators know which provisions of RCRA will be enforced and which will be considered unnecessary. Recent Congressional attempts to clarify this matter have been unsuccessful.[50] The licensing of mixed waste incinerators is also crucial to solving this disposal problem.

Until legislative relief or further interpretation occurs, experts suggest the following steps: 1) segregate hazardous from radioactive waste when possible; 2) substitute non-hazardous materials for hazardous, when possible; 3) use processes which do not consume hazardous materials; 4) reclaim and recycle useable materials to avoid generating mixed waste; 5) process mixed waste to remove RCRA Subpart C hazardous characteristics; 6) avoid the need for a treatment permit by treating waste in an accumulation tank within generators' accumulation time; 7) dispose of waste under a Below Regulatory Concern rule, if possible; and 8) control admission of hazardous materials into the power block.[51]

## NESHAPS

In 1989 EPA, under the Clean Air Act,[52] promulgated National Emission Standards for Hazardous Air Pollutants (NESHAPs) for radionuclides emitted by NRC licensees (as well as other facilities).[53] Whether these NESHAPs will take effect is yet to be determined. The NESHAPs have been stayed pending judicial review and EPA reconsideration.[54] The new version of the Clean Air Act may also alter the regulation of radionuclides for NRC-licensed facilities[55] (see Chapter II, Hackmann). The necessity of EPA regulation of radionuclide releases has been questioned, because the NRC already regulates such releases.

The stayed NESHAPs do not require actual reductions in emissions levels, but they do increase monitoring and reporting duties for NRC licensees. The new requirements will cost utilities approximately $100 million.[56] These costs reflect additional training and monitoring necessary to comply with the NESHAPs.

The nuclear industry has challenged the NESHAPs, and EPA has stayed them for NRC licensed facilities pursuant to the Administrative Procedures Act.[57] The NESHAPs are undergoing both judicial review and EPA reconsideration during this stay. Judicial review has been held in abeyance pending the outcome of EPA's reconsideration. Meanwhile, Congress is considering changes to the Clean Air Act which would authorize EPA to use its discretion to determine if EPA regulation is necessary.

The Senate version of the Clean Air Act provides that EPA will not be required to set NESHAPs for NRC licensees if it finds that existing NRC regulations provide ample public protection. Under this bill, however, states would still be free to set standards for radio-nuclide emissions that are **more** stringent than the federal limits. Senator Simpson tried to attach an amendment to the Senate bill which would have eliminated all state, EPA, and local authority to control radionuclide emissions. The Senate defeated this amendment by a 61-36 vote.

No matter which version of the Clean Air Act becomes law, the individual states would have the ability to regulate radionuclide emissions. Industry supporters fear that states may effectively limit expansion of the nuclear industry by enacting their own "NESHAPs."[58]

Radionuclide emissions are currently regulated by only the NRC. The EPA regulations would increase costs to nuclear plants. EPA may conclude that dual regulation provides little benefit. If not, then plants must be prepared to implement the additional programs necessary to meet the requirements of the NESHAPs. In any case, states may also step into the radionuclide arena and impose other standards.

## RQ's of Radionuclides

The Comprehensive Environmental Response, Compensation, and Liability Act of 1980 (CERCLA),[59] requires persons in charge of facilities to report any release of hazardous substance that equals or exceeds a reportable quantity (RQ) to the National Response Center. The EPA has designated radionuclides a hazardous substance, and in 1989 EPA developed final rules for reportable quantities of radionuclides.[60]

The RQ rules require that owners of facilities report any release of a hazardous substance equal to or exceeding the reportable quantity set by the rules. Additionally, if a release has the potential to result in offsite exposure, state and local authorities may require notification.[61] The federal authorities evaluate the need for a response after a report is made. The government may also levy criminal and civil penalties as a result of a release. Under CERCLA there are a number of exemptions that affect the duty to report releases of radionuclides for nuclear facilities. Because of these exemptions the exact requirements of the RQ regulations are not clear.

The purpose of the rules is to alert the appropriate government officials to releases which may require action to protect the public health or the environment. Any report to the National Response Center triggers a governmental evaluation, but not every release will pose a threat that requires action. Since releases of radionuclides at nuclear facilities are also regulated by the NRC under the Atomic Energy Act, EPA has exempted certain releases from these regulations. The most important exemptions for the nuclear industry are the "federally permitted release" and the "nuclear incident" exemptions.

CERCLA provides an exemption to reporting for any release in compliance with a license, permit, regulation or order issued pursuant to the Atomic Energy Act ("federally permitted release"). A number of definitions exist for "federally permitted release".[62] Which one EPA will apply is not clear. CERCLA provides for eleven different types of federally permitted releases.[63] Not all the definitions would apply to all facilities. For nuclear licensees the important ones are the Technical Specifications contained in their licenses; the generic 10 C.F.R. Part 20 and Part 50 guidelines; and if the previously discussed stay is lifted, Clean Air Act NESHAPs for radionuclides.

The other exemption from CERCLA reporting is for a "nuclear incident." The definition of a nuclear incident comes from the Price-Andersen Act, and includes any occurrence causing bodily injury, sickness, death, loss of or damage to property, or loss of use of property, resulting from the radioactive, toxic, explosive, or other hazardous properties of source, special nuclear or byproduct material.[64] Any release from a nuclear incident subject to the NRC requirements with respect to the financial protection established under section 170 of the Atomic Energy Act is also excluded from reporting under CERCLA.[65] "Nuclear incident" is not the equivalent of standard "emergency classifications." Therefore, a utility may have to make a report even though it has declared an emergency. There is no quantitative standard for determining what is a "nuclear incident." Consequently, there is no simple rule to follow for determining whether a company need not report under CERCLA because of the "nuclear" incident exemption.

In sum, the nuclear industry should keep close watch over the future of the NESHAPs and ask the EPA for a clarification of the term "federally permitted release." Clarification is also needed on exactly what constitutes a nuclear incident. Until these questions are answered, facilities must use their best judgment and hope that they are acting in compliance with the regulations.

## Electric and Magnetic Fields (EMF)

One recent environmental issue which has caused substantial controversy and concern is whether there are any health risks from exposure to electric and magnetic fields (EMF). This issue is of particular concern to electric utilities because the EMF associated with high voltage transmission lines has been alleged to cause everything from cancer to headaches.[66] There is a great difference of opinion as to whether and to what extent EMF is a health hazard.[67] This uncertainty as to the risk, if any, from EMF has not deterred litigation over the issue.[68]

There have been several recent regulatory developments involving EMF. For example, the California Public Utilities Commission, in cooperation with the California Department of Health Services, has now completed a report which concludes that regulations to control EMF effects from electric utility operations would be,

> premature given current scientific understanding of this public health issue. Too little is known presently to be able to determine where or what rules would provide useful protection. Existing research data are not sufficient for adequate, accurate risk assessment. We do not know which components, if any, of electric power utility operations pose significant health hazards. Although biological effects are clearly established, the relationship of these effects to possible health risks is not yet established.[69]

As another example, the Colorado Public Utilities Commission ruled that Public Service of Colorado could upgrade an existing transmission line so long as Public Service complied with certain conditions designed to implement a policy of "prudent avoidance" of the unknown risk of potential harm from EMF. The Colorado PUC ruled that it would be imprudent to require Public Service to spend the $13,500,000 required to bury the power lines. It did, however, order Public Service to perform less expensive steps to reduce EMF exposure and risk. [70]

Electric utilities should also follow EPA's research on the potential carcinogenicity of electromagnetic fields. EPA's research and the Agency's reports on it may be an important factor in determining whether there will be federal regulation of EMF.[71]

## Acid Deposition

Both the House (H.R. 3030) and Senate (S. 1630) have passed bills that would amend the Clean Air Act to impose much more stringent limits on sulfur dioxide ($SO_2$) emissions. These bills' $SO_2$ provisions are in large part designed to address what many perceive to be an acid deposition problem. The House and Senate bills differ in several respects, and as of the date of this writing, final amendments to the Clean Air Act had not yet been enacted. Both the House and Senate bills, however, impose future caps on $SO_2$ emissions; both establish a system of $SO_2$ emission allowances for affected generating units; and both allow some form of emissions allowance trading. In all likelihood, the Clean Air Act will be amended in the near future to impose a regulatory scheme containing these elements in some form. (See Chapter II on the Clean Air Act as passed.)

Companies subject to what will probably be a new, complex, and much more stringent $SO_2$ emission control scheme will have to begin planning very soon as to how they will comply with it. Special attention should be paid to managing the company's quota of emissions allowances. For example, companies will have to decide whether to sell some of their allowances to other companies, or whether they should instead retain all of them for their own future use.

## Global Warming

Global warming is an alleged increase in the earth's temperature caused by an accumulation of atmospheric gases which prevents heat from escaping into space, creating a "greenhouse effect." These "greenhouse" gases include carbon dioxide ($CO_2$) from fossil fuel combustion and forest decay; chlorofluorocarbons (CFCs) used in refrigeration, air conditioning and as industrial solvents; methane; ozone; and nitrous oxide.[72] Carbon dioxide emissions, resulting mostly from the burning of fossil fuels, have been estimated to produce 50 percent of the alleged greenhouse effect; methane 20 percent; CFC 15 percent; nitrous oxides 10 percent; and ground-level ozone five percent.[73] Fossil-fuel fired electric power plants are a major source of $CO_2$ emissions in the United States.[74]

The global warming hypothesis suggests that a doubling of $CO_2$ levels in the next 50-to-100 years will increase global average temperatures by 1.5 to 4.5° centigrade, which would be warmer than at any time in human history, and that this increased temperature will set in motion major world-wide environmental, political, economic, and social changes.[75]

The controversy between legislators, scientists and environmentalists has focused not only on whether global warming actually exists, but on what remedies are appropriate if it does exist. Many advocate an immediate solution to the problem, claiming that awaiting scientific proof of global warming before taking any action would be "suicidal."[76] Others argue that there are currently too many questions about global warming to legislate regarding it. Instead, more research should be conducted to determine the magnitude of global warming effects, how severe the effects will be, and where the effects will be most felt before any remedial action is taken.[77] Advocates of further research are concerned that a hasty and inadequately considered course of action "may hinder rather than facilitate an effective response" to climate change, and may prove more expensive than necessary, thus creating economic and energy security risks.[78]

There are numerous bills pending in Congress which would require further study of global warming. These bills would establish and fund domestic and international research into global warming.[79] There are also several pending global warming bills which would require more than research. For example, one bill would require a 20 percent decrease in $CO_2$ emissions from 1988 levels by the year 2000.[80] Several bills would require state energy conservation plans.[81] Most of these bills encourage research into nuclear fission and nuclear fusion as a power source.

The pending bills which would amend the Clean Air Act also contain provisions related to global warming. For example, the House bill (H.R. 3030) contains provisions for the attainment and maintenance of national ambient air quality standards through clean fuel requirements, air pollution programs, emissions standards for motor vehicles, and hazardous air pollutant control.

The Senate bill (S. 1630) would amend the Clean Air Act to include a new title, "Stratospheric Ozone and Global Climate Protection."

This title's objectives are to significantly reduce the emission of pollutants caused by human activities and to promote rapid development and deployment of energy efficient alternatives to the use of CFCs and other manufactured substances which contribute to global warming.[82] It calls for a priority listing of the substances known or reasonably anticipated to cause or contribute significantly to atmospheric or climatic modification, and requires each person producing or importing such substances to report to the EPA, with subsequent phaseout of production or import, with an exception for medical and national security purposes. [83] It also calls for a national recycling and disposal program.[84]

States may also attempt to pass global warming legislation. For example, an initiative which would require a forty percent reduction in $CO_2$ emissions in California over the next 20 years has qualified for the November California ballot.[85] This state initiative, which has been nicknamed "Big Green," is far more stringent than any proposed federal global-warming legislation.

### The Effect of Global Warming on the Energy Industry

Electric utilities could be profoundly affected by the global warming debate:

> [I]f global warming is occurring, reliable electric generation will be imperative to help societies adapt. Electric utility companies will have to cope with changes in heating and cooling demand, the effects on facilities and equipment, demographic shifts, and possibly the need to reduce emissions through advanced technology, fuel switching, and/ or increased efficiency.

Much of the pending legislation promotes clean coal technology. Unfortunately, this technology currently cuts $CO_2$ emissions by no more than 10 percent.[86] In addition, $CO_2$ scrubbers could consume between 10 percent and 70 percent of a plant's electrical output.[87] Systems to capture $CO_2$ could increase the cost of producing electricity by 75 to 150 percent given the high cost of disposing of the gas.[88]

Natural gas has been advocated as a clean alternative to oil and coal for electric utilities, industrial boilers, and motor vehicles because it produces about half as much $CO_2$ as coal does.[89] However, a recent study claims that, despite lower levels of $CO_2$ emissions from burning methane (natural gas' primary molecular composition), it still is responsible for a "direct greenhouse effect" that is 30 times that of $CO_2$.[90] This study also claims that natural gas has an indirect effect based on its combination with other chemicals in the environment, making it an unsatisfactory choice over other fuels.

Some scientists and legislators argue that nuclear energy is the solution to the global warming problem. Much of the legislation currently pending supports further research in the field of thermonuclear fusion, as well as the development of fail-safe nuclear power plants. Others argue, however, that nuclear power has been largely abandoned by both industry and government.[91] Although nuclear power has reemerged in the past years as a major congressional issue, the impact of global warming legislation on the nuclear power industry cannot yet be determined.[92]

The most significant effect of the global warming issue has been to encourage research and development of renewable energy technology such as solar thermal power, hydropower and biomass technologies. The question, however, about these sources of energy is whether they can meet an increasing demand for energy.

In sum, at this point in time, there is no consensus as to whether there is a global warming problem. Assuming there is a problem, there is no consensus as to how to solve it. Given the great public concern over global warming and the amount of legislative activity in this area, however, energy companies should expect to be grappling with this issue for the foreseeable future.

## Future Trends

Prognosticating is always dangerous, but the most likely and significant environmental developments affecting the energy industry are amendments to the Clean Air Act; new and much more stringent federal standards for nonhazardous waste disposal; and possible global warming legislation. While new state laws and regulations are always a possibility, most of the activity in these areas will occur in Congress, or in the case of global warming, the State Department. Consequently, the energy industry, as usual, must keep a close eye on what happens in Washington, D.C.

## About the Authors

Jim Vasile is a partner in the firm of Newman & Holtzinger, P.C. He received a Bachelor of Arts Degree in Physics from Rutgers University in 1966 and the Degree of Doctor of Jurisprudence from Georgetown University in 1974. His practice involves the representation of clients in federal agency and court proceedings in connection with energy and environmental matters. His experience includes the representation of utilities before the Federal Energy Regulatory Commission in connection with hydroelectric projects. Mr. Vasile is also involved with the development of cogeneration and alternative energy projects. Mr. Vasile has participated in proceedings before the Environmental Protection Agency and the Nuclear Regulatory Commission involving environmental and public health and safety regulation of nuclear reactors and the development of natural resources.

Scott Slaughter is of counsel to Newman & Holtzinger and practices environmental law. He has a B.A. and M.A. from Harvard and a J.D. from Georgetown University.

## Endnotes

1. The Texas Eastern pipeline matter provided an example of how much of a headache PCBs can be for gas pipelines. *See generally United States v. Texas Eastern Transmission Corp.*, No. H-88-1917 (S.D. Tex. June 6, 1988) (Consent Decree) at 7-9, 10, 12. Texas Eastern has estimated that it will have to spend $400,000,000 to clean up PCB spills along its pipeline. Texas Eastern has also agreed to pay a $15,000,000 penalty for these spills.

2. 15 U.S.C. § 2605(e).

3. 40 C.F.R. § 761.3.

4. 15 U.S.C. § 2605(e)(2)(B). EPA has subsequently promulgated regulations allowing use of such PCB articles and items for the balance of their useful lives. 40 CFR, § 76C *et. seq.*

5. 42 U.S.C. §§ 6901, 6921 to 6936.

6. 42 U.S.C. § 9601 *et seq.*

Environmental
Risk Management

7. 15 U.S.C. § 2617(a)(2)(B).

8. *Potomac Elec. Power Co. v. Sachs*, 639 F. Supp. 856, 861 (D. Md.), *rev'd on other grounds*, 802 F.2d 1527 (4th Cir. 1986); *Chappell v. SCA Services, Inc.*, 540 F. Supp. 1087, 1089 (C.D. Ill. 1982); *People v. Todd Shipyards Corp.*, 192 Cal. App. 3d Supp. 30, 238 Cal. Rptr. 761 (Cal. App. Dep't. Super. Ct. 1987); 44 *Fed. Reg.* 31,514, 31,528 (1979); 43 *Fed. Reg.* 7150, 7153 (1978). Other courts have disagreed, holding that state and local PCB disposal rules are preempted by EPA's PCB rules. *See, e.g., Rollins Environmental Services, Inc. v. Parish of St. James*, 775 F.2d 627 (5th Cir. 1985). Minnesota recently enacted legislation banning land disposal of PCB-containing appliances. 41 (BNA), *Toxic Law Reporter*, 160 (July 1990).

9. *See, e.g.,* H.R. 3070 which was introduced by Rep. Synar (D. Okla.) in 1988. *See generally* Inside EPA Weekly Rep., Sept. 16, 1988, at 16.

10. 54 *Fed. Reg.* 52716.

11. 53 *Fed. Reg.* 24206.

12. 53 *Fed. Reg.* 24206 (June 27, 1988), (to be codified at 40 C.F.R. Part 761). U.S. EPA is currently considering a rulemaking which waives PCB disposal rules for high volume, low concentration wastes at Superfund sites, *see* 14 (BNA) *Chemical Regulation Register* 654 (July 27, 1990).

13. 40 C.F.R. Part 761, Subpart G.

14. Polychlorinated Biphenyls (PCB) Penalty Policy, "United States Environmental Protection Agency (April 9, 1990).

15. *Id.* at 17.

16. *See* USEPA Office of Toxic Substances *Chemicals-in-Progress Bulletin* (TSCA Bulletin) (March 1988).

17. 18 C.F.R. § 380.3, Appendix A; *Northeast U.S. Pipeline Projects*, 44 F.E.R.C. ¶ 61,148 (July 27, 1988).

18. *See Columbia Gas Trans. Corp.*, 44 F.E.R.C. (CCH) ¶ 62,337 (Sept. 28, 1988) (order granting certificate and approving abandonment); *Columbia Gas Trans. Corp.*, 44 F.E.R.C. (CCH) ¶ 61,388 (Sept. 16, 1988) (order granting certificate and approving abandonment); *William Nat. Gas. Co.*, 44 F.E.R.C. (CCH) ¶ 61,254 (Aug. 19, 1988) (order granting certificate and approving abandonment); *Penn East Gas Serv. Co. and Texas Eastern Trans. Corp.*, 44 F.E.R.C. (CCH) ¶ 61,152 (July 27, 1988) (order issuing certificates); *Algonquin Gas Trans. Co.*, 43 F.E.R.C. (CCH) ¶ 61,554 (June 29, 1988) (order granting certificate and approving abandonment).

19. *See, e.g., Texas Eastern Transmission Corporation*, 51 F.E.R.C. 61,384 (1990) (the issue of whether Texas Eastern's PCB remediation program costs were prudently incurred and can be recovered in its rates is set for a FERC hearing to commence in February 1991).

20. SOCAL-SDG&E I, 47 F.E.R.C. 61,196, 61,676 (1989).

21. SOCAL-SDG & E II, 49 F.E.R.C. 61,091 (1989).

22. 42 U.S.C. § 6921(b)(3)(A)(i).

23. 53 *Fed. Reg.* 33314 (Aug. 30, 1988).

24. 33 U.S.C. § 1321.

25. *See, e.g.*, 20 [BNA] Env't Rep. 672 (August 11, 1989).

26. *E.g.*, 21 [BNA] Env't Rep. 431 (July 6, 1990).

27. 42 U.S.C. § 2021b-2021d (1982). The LLRWP defines low level waste as that containing Class A, B, or C waste as defined by the NRC.

28. 42 U.S.C.A. §§ 2021b-2021i (West Supp. 1990); Berkowvitz, *Waste Wars: Did Congress "Nuke" State Sovereignty in the Low-Level Radioactive Waste Amendments Act of 1985?*, 11 Hav. Envtl. L. Rev. 437, 445 (1987).

29. *Colglazier & English, Low Level Waste: Can New Disposal Sites Be Found*, 53 Tenn. L. Rev. 621 (1986); Bord, "The Low-Level Waste Crisis: Is More Citizen Participation the Answer?," *Low-Level Radioactive Waste Regulation*, Ed. Michael Burns (1988).

30. Michael Burns, "Living the Past, Facing the Future," *Low-Level Radioactive Waste Regulation*, Ed. Michael Burns (1988).

31. The only three sites currently accepting civilian low level radioactive waste are Hanford, Washington; Beatty, Nevada; and Barnwell, South Carolina.

32. 42 U.S.C. §§ 10101-10226.

33. "High-Level Waste Management," *Nuclear News*, June, 1990, p. 110.

34. "DOE Sues Nevada for Blocking Mandated Studies," *Business Wire*, Jan. 25, 1990.

35. "Report to the Congress on Reassessment of the Civilian Radioactive Waste Management Program," U.S. Dept. of Energy (1989).

36. 42 U.S.C. § 10161 (1982).

37. "Watkins: 27 Nuclear Plants Face Waste Storage Crisis," UPI, March 3, 1990.

38. "Onsite Storage Funding Must be Set Up if DOE Can't Meet 1998 Date," *Nuclear Fuel*, Jan. 22, 1990, p. 8.

39. *Id.*

40. *Id.*

41. "On-Site Storage Funding Must be Set Up if DOE Can't Meet 1998 Date ACORD Says," *Nuclear Fuel*, Jan. 22, 1990.

42. 42 U.S.C. §§ 6901-6999.

43. 42 U.S.C. §§ 2011-2296.

44. "Partnership Under Pressure, Managing Commercial Low-Level Radioactive Waste," Office of Technology Assessment, November 1989 [hereinafter OTA Report].

45. Although there was some early confusion as to whether both RCRA and AEA applied, the EPA issued a notice in 1986 stating that the hazardous component of mixed waste was subject to RCRA. 51 *Fed. Reg.* 24,504 (1986).

46. *Id.*

47. "EEI Disputes OTA's Mixed Waste Report, Wants Dual Regulation Problems to End," *Public Utility,* Jan. 18, 1990, p. 11.

48. "EEI Disputes OTA's Mixed Waste Report, Wants Dual Regulation Problems to End," *Nuclear Fuel,* March 5, 1990, p. 11.

49. "The First Full-Scale Incineration of Nuclear and Non-Nuclear Mixed Waste," *Chementator,* March, 1989, p. 19.

50. "NRC Opposes Provisions in Waste Regulation Bills," *Inside N.R.C.,* Jan. 29, 1990, p. 17.

51. "The Management of Mixed Low Level Radioactive Waste in the Nuclear Power Industry," Nuclear Management and Resource Council, (1990) p. ES4-ES5; R.D. Baird *et al.,* "The Management of Mixed Low Level Radioactive Waste in the Nuclear Power Industry," *Waste Management,* (1989).

52. 42 U.S.C. 7401 *et seq.*

53. 54 *Fed. Reg.* 31,654 (1989) (to be codified at subpart I 40 C.F.R. part 61).

54. 55 *Fed. Reg.* 10,455 (1990).

55. S. 1630, 101st Cong., 2d Sess. (1990).

56. "Senate Endorses NRC Position on Dual Federal Regulation," *Inside N.R.C.,* April 9, 1990, p. 5.

57. 5 U.S.C. § 705 (1988).

58. "Senate Endorses NRC Position on Dual Federal Regulation," *Inside N.R.C.,* April 9, 1990, p. 5.

59. 42 U.S.C. §§ 9601 *et seq.*

60. 54 *Fed. Reg.* 22,524 (1989) (to be codified at 40 C.F.R. §§ 302.6(a) and 355.

61. 42 U.S.C.A. § 11004.

62. 42 U.S.C. § 9601 (101)(10)K & 103(a) (1982).

63. 42 U.S.C. § 9601 (10).

64. 42 U.S.C.A. § 2014(q) (West Supp. 1990).

65. 42 U.S.C.A. § 9601(22)(C) (West Supp. 1990).

66. *E.g.,* Brodeur, *Currents of Death: Power Lines, Computer Terminals, and the Attempt to Cover Up Their Threat to your Health* (Simon and Schuster, 1989).

67. *Compare id. with Harvard Medical School Health Letter* (March 1990).

68. *See e.g., Rausch v. The School Board of Palm Beach County,* Florida Circuit Court, Final Judgment, June 8, 1989, (Court refuses to order school closed because of proximity to transmission lines, but ordered school to ensure students stay a certain distance away from transmission lines); *Vandehe: Developers v. Public Service Commission of Wyoming,* (court upholds PSC's authorization and use of high voltage, overhead power lines).

69. "Potential Health Effects Of Electric Power Facilities," California Public Utilities Commission In Cooperation with California Department of Health Services (Sept. 15, 1989).

70. *In the Matter of Public Service Company of Colorado To Have Upgrades In Douglas County,* Docket No. 89A-028E (Dec. 20, 1989).

71. There are several other regulatory proceedings regarding EMF which electric utilities should follow. These proceedings include *In the Matter of the Application of Potomac Electric Power Company for a Certificate of Public Convenience and Necessity for the Construction of a 500-KV Overhead Transmission Line from the Brighton Substation in Montgomery County, To The Vicinity Of Baltimore Gas & Electric Company's High Ridge Substation in Howard County, Maryland,* Maryland Public Service Commission, Case No. 7004 (Dec. 21, 1989); *Hillsborough County, Florida v. Department of Environmental Regulation,* Division of Administrative Hearings, Case No. 90-0001R; and *Newport Electric Corporation v. Town of Jamestown Zoning Board of Review,* 106 PUR 4th 83 (1989).

72. *High Global Temperatures Indicate Trend, Not Chance Occurrence, NASA Official Says,* 19 [BNA] Env't Rep. 301 (July 1, 1988).

73. Yates, *Global Warming: A New Priority,* Public Utilities Fortnightly, Vol. 123, No. 3, p. 39 (Feb. 2, 1989).

74. *Witnesses Describe Range of Options to Slow Greenhouse Effect, Global Warming,* 19 [BNA] Env't Rep. 334 (July 8, 1988).

75. Yates, *Global Warming: A New Priority,* Public Utilities Fortnightly, Vol. 123, No. 3, p. 39 (Feb. 2, 1989).

76. *Waiting for Proof of Global Warming Would Be Suicidal, Former TVA Head Says,* 19 [BNA] Env't Rep. 1085 (Sept. 23, 1988).

77. *Id.*

78. *More Economic, Foreign Policy Analysis Needed to Address Climate Change, Group Says,* 20 [BNA] Env't Rep. 369 (Aug. 4, 1989).

79. *E.g.,* H.R. 2984, S. 169.

80. H.R. 1078.

81. *E.g.,* H.R. 1078, H.R. 3143, S. 324.

82. Sec. 502.

83. Secs. 504-508.

84. Sec. 509.

85. 21 [BNA] Env't Rep. 319 (June 8, 1990).

86. *U.S. Must Turn to Conservation, Natural Gas As Best Solution to Global Warming, Panel Says,* 20 [BNA] Env't Rep. 1629 (Jan. 19, 1990).

87. *Id.*

88. *Id.*

89. *"Clean" Natural Gas Could Increase Global Warming Problems, Professor Says,* 20 [BNA] Env't Rep. 1379 (Dec. 8, 1989).

90. *Id.*

91. *Id.*

92. *See The 100th Congress and Energy Legislation: A Final Appraisal,* Public Utilities Fortnightly, Vol 122, No. 12, p.28, (Dec. 8, 1988).

# XXVII

# Developments In Insurance Coverage For Environmental Losses — The Insurer's Perspective

*Timothy C. Russell, Partner*
*Sonnenschein, Nath and Rosenthal*
*Washington, D.C.*

Over the last several years manufacturers and other commercial and industrial enterprises have faced a spiraling threat of environmental liability. While the most publicized source of such liability has been the federal Comprehensive Environmental Response, Compensation and Liability Act, or CERCLA,[1] liability for past and present polluting activities may be imposed under state-law cognates of CERCLA, under other federal and state statutes, and under common law principles such as the doctrine of nuisance.[2] In addition, liability for pollution of the environment, or for personal injury caused by pollution, may be imposed in proceedings brought by federal, state or local environmental regulators, or by private firms or individuals.[3]

Not surprisingly, companies confronted with the specter of pollution-related liability have sought to shift the financial burden of pollution liability claims onto their property and casualty (i.e., comprehensive general liability) insurers.[4] The insurance companies, persuaded that in most instances their policies do not cover pollution liability, have resisted demands for coverage just as vigorously. The result has been an explosion of pollution coverage litigation in state and federal courts around the country; a profusion of pollution coverage commentary, much of it unabashedly advocative, in law reviews and other journals; and, increasingly, the recognition that the substantive and procedural issues raised by pollution coverage disputes implicate critical jurisprudential and "public policy" concerns.[5]

After the effective date of CERCLA in 1980, pollution coverage litigation began to move into high gear. One might reasonably have expected that ten years later a distinct pattern of judicial interpretation would have emerged, providing policyholders and insurers alike with a measure of predictability, and with a basis for informed settlement of pollution coverage disputes. Unfortunately, no consistent decisional pattern has developed, and courts have continued to diverge on many of the principal coverage issues. In addition, litigation over pollution coverage has increasingly become "fact-intensive," as courts have invited the litigants to explore the facts relating to polluting conduct and pollution conditions, and the parties' expectations and intent regarding the meaning of the insurance policies. These factors, in addition to confirming that pollution coverage litigation is likely to continue on a major scale for several years to come, have also underscored the need for policyholders and insurers to remain attuned to the substantive and procedural nuances that are emerging almost daily in the case law, and to refine and adjust their strategies accordingly.

The case law and related developments involving the principal coverage issues that have occupied the courts in pollution coverage controversies include the following:

- The interpretation and application of the standard "pollution exclusion" included in many general liability policies issued between 1970 and 1986;
- The question whether a particular pollution event or condition was "unexpected and unintended" by the policyholder, such that it constitutes a covered "accident" or "occurrence" within the meaning of the policies;
- Whether injunctive or "cost-recovery" cleanup remedies imposed under CERCLA constitute an insured claim seeking relief in the form of "damages" within the meaning of the policies;
- The "trigger of coverage" issue, which involves the question of which event (or events), from the initial discharge or release of pollutants until the discovery of the related pollution injury, activates the policy or policies then in force;
- Whether coverage for particular pollution claims is excluded by the so-called "owned property" exclusion contained in many general liability policies; and
- Whether a polluter's foreknowledge of a potential for pollution liability renders the pollution hazard uninsurable under after-acquired policies, as a "known loss" or "known risk."[6]

## The Coverage Issues

### The Pollution Exclusion

The "pollution exclusion" contained in many primary, umbrella and excess liability insurance policies written after 1970[7] has been a principal ground on which insurers have sought to disclaim or limit coverage for pollution liability claims. At the same time, and because of the potentially crippling financial impact of pollution liability, the community of commercial insureds has mounted a vigorous attack on the exclusion. The central focus of that attack has been on the "exception" to the exclusion, which preserves coverage where claims are based on polluting discharges that can be characterized as "sudden and accidental." In order to appreciate fully the interpretive problems that have arisen as the meaning of the exclusion has been litigated in the courts, a brief review of the history and background of the exclusion may be helpful.

The pollution exclusion provides that coverage that may otherwise exist under a general liability policy does not apply to claims based on:

> bodily injury or property damage resulting from the discharge, dispersal, release or escape of smoke, vapors, soot, fumes, acids, alkalis, toxic chemicals, liquids or gases, waste materials or other irritants, contaminants or pollutants into or upon land, the atmosphere or any water course or body of water; but this exclusion does not apply if such discharge, dispersal, release or escape is sudden and accidental.

The history of the exclusion confirms that the clause means just what it says, and was intended to exclude coverage for **all** pollution claims unless the **discharge** of pollutants (and not the resulting damage or injury) was both "sudden" — abrupt and confined to a brief period of time — and "accidental" — unforeseen and fortuitous. Until 1966, the insuring clause of the typical liability policy provided coverage for claims arising from "accidents," which had traditionally been understood to be non-recurrent, discrete and "noncontinuous" events limited as to time and place.[8] For an additional premium, an insured could purchase an endorsement providing so-called "occurrence" coverage applicable to claims based on a broader spectrum of events, including gradual or repeated causes characterized in the policies as "injurious exposure to conditions" (and, later, as "continuous or repeated exposure to conditions").[9]

In 1966, "occurrence" coverage became the standard basis of most general liability policies. Both the earlier "accident-based" policies and the new "occurrence-based" coverage comprehended and required fortuitous, unexpected events — in a word, "accidents" — as a predicate for coverage. However, the distinct notion of "suddenness" — non-recurrence and isolation to a limited time — that had been inherent in the classical meaning of the term *accident* was clearly **not** intended to restrict occurrence-based policies.[10]

As the insurance industry moved to the broader "occurrence" concept in the 1960s, the potential dimensions of environmental liability arising from non-sudden, "continuous or repeated" discharges, leaks or spills were not yet fully appreciated. A number of well-publicized pollution incidents in the late 1960s, however, caused concern that occurrence-based coverage, without any limitation to "sudden" causes, might be construed to extend to claims based upon repeated, ongoing industrial pollution discharges or gradual leaks or releases of pollutants that had been in progress for years before a policy was issued.[11] In response to these concerns, insurers revised the pollution exclusion to exclude **all** pollution coverage **except** with respect to claims arising from causative events that fit within the traditional, pre-1966 concept of "accident." That is, the general exclusion for pollution liability claims was expressly made subject to a narrow exception for claims resulting from polluting discharges that are **both** fortuitous, unexpected and unintended — "accidental" — **and** non-recurrent, abrupt and isolated in time, or truly "sudden."

Many of the early judicial interpretations of the pollution exclusion tended to ignore its literal terms and its obvious interplay with the "occurrence" clause, and paid little or no attention to the exclusion's history or purpose. Judicial rationales for disregarding the meaning and intent of the exclusion varied. Several courts disregarded the fact that the exclusion (including its exception for "sudden and accidental" events) focuses explicitly on the **discharge** of pollutants, rather than on the resulting pollution injury or damage. Courts also tended to conclude that the word "sudden" in fact was synonymous with "unexpected" or "unintended," and did not import any concept of abruptness or non-recurrence. The result of such reasoning was, in substance, that the pollution exclusion was construed to have no independent meaning or effect at all, and to be simply a "restatement" or reiteration of the "occurrence" clause and its limitation of coverage to claims based on injury or damage "neither expected nor intended from the standpoint of the insured."

The widely publicized decision in *Jackson Township Municipal Utilities Authority v. Hartford Accident & Indemnity Co.*[12] is a paradigm of this early "pro-policyholder" approach to the pollution exclusion. The *Jackson Township* court ignored the common-sensical distinction between "sudden" events and repeated or gradual events and, without any reference to the history of the exclusion, concluded that it was "ambiguous."[13] The court went on to overlook the fact that the exclusion, as well as the "sudden and accidental" exception, focuses explicitly and exclusively on the characteristics of the "discharge, dispersal, release or escape" of pollutants, and not on the resulting environmental damage. Accordingly, the *Jackson Township* court held the pollution exclusion,

> . . . can be interpreted as simply a restatement of the definition of "occurrence" — that is, that the [general liability] policy will cover claims where the injury was "neither expected nor intended." It is a reaffirmation of the principle that coverage will not be provided for intended results of intentional acts but will be provided for the unintended results of an intentional act.[14]

Similarly unsupported "reasoning," as well as a number of other rationales,[15] have led a substantial number of courts to conclude, as did the court in *Jackson Township*, that the pollution exclusion has no real meaning or effect, and is effectively a dead letter.[16] And despite the fact, as discussed below, that a majority of the recent decisions have tended to give the pollution exclusion a more straightforward reading and meaningful application, some courts continue to read it as nothing more than a "restatement" of the occurrence definition.[17]

Courts began in the mid-1980s to pay heed to the fact that the pollution exclusion, and particularly the exclusion's "sudden and accidental" exception, must be given a meaning independent of the policies' "occurrence" clause. Thus courts began regularly to acknowledge that (i) unlike the "occurrence" provision, the exclusion focuses entirely upon the nature of the polluting **discharge**, not the resulting environmental harm; (ii) the word "sudden" necessarily connotes a "temporal" element of abruptness and "non-recurrence;"

and (iii) therefore, the exclusion operates to exclude coverage for **all** pollution claims **unless** the polluting discharge was both "sudden" in this temporal sense, as well as fortuitous and unexpected and therefore "accidental." Such decisions had become so common by the end of the 1980s that several courts proclaimed the existence of "an emerging nationwide judicial consensus" that the exclusion was to be interpreted in this manner.[18]

Perhaps the clearest judicial explanation of the reasoning behind the courts' growing inclination to reject the argument that the pollution exclusion is nothing more than a "restatement" of the "occurrence" clause is that of the United States Court of Appeals for the Sixth Circuit in *United States Fidelity and Guaranty Co. v. Star Fire Coals, Inc.*:[19]

We have no difficulty reconciling the [exclusion with the "occurrence" provision]. We believe the "occurrence" definition results in a policy that provides coverage for continuous or repeated exposure to conditions causing damages in all cases except those involving pollution where coverage is limited to those situations where the **discharge** was "sudden and accidental." We fully agree with the conclusion that this "language is clear and plain, something only a lawyer's ingenuity could make ambiguous." *American Motorists Insurance Co. v. General Host Corp.*, 667 F.Supp. 1423 (D. Kan. 1987). . . .

We believe that the everyday meaning of the term "sudden" is exactly what this clause means. We do not believe that it is possible to define "sudden" without reference to a temporal element that joins together conceptually the immediate and the unexpected. It must also be emphasized that the focus of this "sudden and accidental" exception to the general pollution exclusion is on the nature of the discharge of the pollution itself, not on the nature of the damages caused.

We believe that the phrase "sudden and accidental" is not a synonym for "unexpected and unintended," and that it should not be defined by reference to whether the accident or damages were expected.

As is noted above, the approach to the pollution exclusion taken by the Sixth Circuit in *Star Fire Coals* probably reflects the current majority view on the issue.[20] Policyholders, however, have not abandoned their efforts to have the pollution exclusion construed out of existence. As it has become apparent that courts are increasingly inclined to adopt the insurers' reading of the exclusion, policyholders have responded by offering what they refer to as the "drafting history" of the exclusion in an effort to persuade courts that the insurance industry, in adopting the pollution exclusion in the early 1970s, actually intended that the exclusion would have no meaning or effect whatsoever. Consisting of selected statements culled from the files of various insurance rating organizations and other sources, the "drafting history" purportedly shows that industry members, acting with an absolute unity of intent, adopted the exclusion merely to "clarify" the "occurrence" clause. Thus, the policyholders urge, the exclusion itself was intended merely to underscore the notion that many pollution claims would fall outside the scope of coverage created by the "occurrence" provision.[21]

The "drafting history" argument is entirely unpersuasive, for a number of reasons. First, and as several courts have noted, the drafting documents simply do not show what the policyholders contend: under close scrutiny, the documents actually tend to support the insurers' reading of the pollution exclusion.[22] Moreover, policyholders generally have failed to lay the foundational predicates necessary for the use of the documents as "admissions" of contracting intent by any particular insurer.[23] In addition, of course, extrinsic evidence of contracting intent generally is admissible only if the contract is "ambiguous" on its face; decisions like *Star Fire Coals* typically find the pollution exclusion to be entirely unambiguous. And, finally, the "drafting history" argument is inherently implausible, resting as it does on the premise that the insurers debated and labored for months to draft a lengthy exclusion that they actually intended to have no effect or meaning at all.

Despite the emergence of something approaching a "trend" in favor of the insurers' interpretation of the pollution exclusion, some courts continue to adopt the policyholders' approach, and hold that the exclusion merely reiterates or "restates" the "occurrence" provision of the policies.[24] Other decisions, while adhering to the *Star Fire Coals* approach, have noted that any pollution coverage case may require a detailed evidentiary inquiry into the question whether particular discharges were truly "sudden."[25] Accordingly, pollution exclusion issues are likely to be contested vigorously in the courts for some time to come.[26]

### The "Occurrence" Issue

Although related in some respects to the analysis concerning the operation of the pollution exclusion, the question whether pollution of the environment constitutes an "occurrence" within the meaning of liability insurance policies rests on a fundamentally different inquiry. In policies that do not contain a pollution exclusion, the question whether there was an "occurrence" will often be a principal focus of the coverage determination.

Most standard general liability policies issued after 1966 provide that coverage exists for claims for "bodily injury" or "property damage" caused by an "occurrence." The policies define "occurrence," in substance, as,

> an accident, including injurious exposure to conditions [or, after 1973, "including continuous or repeated exposure to conditions"], which results in bodily injury or property damage  neither expected nor intended from the standpoint of the insured.[27]

As the language of the "occurrence" definition suggests, the focus of the clause is, at least in part, on the knowledge of the policyholder as to whether his activities were likely to create a pollution condition. Most courts thus require that, to constitute an "occurrence," there must have been an element of fortuity about the **results** of the insured's polluting conduct.[28] If the insured was aware of the likely consequences of his polluting conduct — or, in some jurisdictions, if such consequences were "highly expectable" — there can be no "occurrence."[29]

A number of courts considering the "occurrence" issue in the context of pollution coverage claims have held, explicitly or otherwise, that it is appropriate to apply something like an objective standard in determining whether a policyholder "expected or intended" to cause environmental pollution. That is, if a court (or a jury) can conclude from the facts that the pollution would have been "highly expectable", or would have appeared "substantially certain" to occur, to a person in the policyholder's position, there was no "occurrence" and thus no coverage. Cases adopting the objective approach to the "occurrence" issue tend to involve relatively sophisticated commercial policyholders, and/or lengthy courses of repeated or continuous polluting discharges that took place as a routine concomitant of the policyholder's everyday business operations.[30] Some cases have insisted that there is an "occurrence" unless it appears that the policyholder had something approaching an actual, subjective intention to cause environmental pollution.[31] Adoption of a subjective "expected or intended" standard, particularly if it is coupled with a requirement that the insured be shown to have had a "specific intent" to cause pollution, tends to extend pollution insurance coverage to the careless waste disposer who, even though he may not have acted with the purpose of polluting, almost certainly could have prevented pollution through the implementation of reasonable waste storage and disposal practices. Such a result is arguably at odds with the fundamental principle that liability insurance should only protect against "fortuitous," truly accidental losses.[32] In addition, such an interpretation of the "occurrence" clause, if applied over a significant number of cases, may diminish policyholders' incentives to avoid losses, thereby creating a pollution-related "moral hazard."[33] Whether an objective or subjective standard or some hybrid of the two is applied in interpreting the "occurrence" provision, the central inquiry in applying that provision will be on the policyholder's "state of mind" in connection with the handling, storage and disposal of waste materials or other pollutants. Accordingly, the "occurrence" determination is often likely to involve intensive factual inquiry into, and adjudication of, such questions as the "state of the art" regarding the hazardousness of particular wastes; the policyholder's own awareness of the hazardousness of its waste materials; decisions by the policyholder regarding methods of waste disposal; the policyholder's experience with workers compensation claims or compliance with local waste disposal regulations; and any other nucleus of facts from which an "expectation or intent" to pollute may be inferred.

### The "As Damages" Issue

The liability provisions of CERCLA provide that the government may, by injunction (or administrative order), force a person responsible for pollution to take measures to remedy the pollution condition.[34] In addition, the government, and in some instances private parties, may bring suit under CERCLA to recover costs actually incurred in responding to or remedying a pollution condition.[35] Finally, a separate provision of CERCLA authorizes suits by governmental authorities to recover "damages" for pollution-related injury to natural resources in which a government plaintiff has a proprietary or quasi-proprietary interest.[36]

Only this last "natural resources damages" provision of CERCLA allows for the recovery of amounts in the nature of compensation for injury to or destruction of the claimant's "property" — in other words, recovery of an award of "damages."[37] The other forms of relief authorized by CERCLA — injunctive cleanup orders and restitutional "cost-recovery" awards — clearly do **not** constitute "damages" in any accepted sense of that word.[38] At the same time, most liability insurance policies provide coverage only for "sums the insured shall become legally obligated to pay **as damages**," and for "suits against the insured seeking **damages**." Accordingly, most insurers contend that their liability policies do not provide coverage for the typical injunctive or cost-recovery cleanup suit, which seeks only equitable relief and does not seek an award of "damages" at all.[39]

A number of courts, acknowledging that CERCLA cleanup remedies cannot be characterized as "damage" awards, have carried established insurance jurisprudence[40] forward into the context of CERCLA claims, and have held that such cleanup remedies are not covered. One of the clearest of these "as damages" decisions is that of the United States Court of Appeals for the Fourth Circuit in *Maryland Casualty Co. v. Armco, Inc.*[41] In *Armco* the policyholder sought recovery under its general liability policies with respect to a cost-recovery action brought against it by the United States under § 107 (a) of CERCLA. The Fourth Circuit held that the relief authorized under that section was purely restitutional in nature, and could not be characterized as a covered award of "damages." In addition to relying on the plain language of the "as damages" limitation contained in the insurance policies, the Fourth Circuit offered a practical explanation of the reasons why liability coverage is limited to true "damages" awards:

> Insurance policies, probably for reasons of certainty and economy, traditionally reimburse only damages arising from actual, tangible injury. Insurers are very reluctant to cover what are essentially prophylactic measures, such as safety precautions, for the obvious reason that such expenditures are subject to the discretion of the insured, and are not connected with any harm to specific third parties. Insurers require certainty as to the extent of their liability and this certainty is set forth in the insurance policy. . . .

The less obvious, but perhaps more telling reason that the insurers are reluctant to cover avoidance costs is that insureds are far more likely to over-utilize safety measures where another party is paying the bill. Should policies be construed to cover some forms of harm-avoidance measures, courts would be faced with the very difficult problem of separating needed prophylactic measures from unnecessary or inefficient ones.

\* \* \* \* \*

From an insurer's perspective, investigative and remedial action taken by the government respecting potential environmental hazards constitutes a prophylactic measure. . . . [T]he government seeks to prevent or mitigate the occurrences or reoccurrences of hazardous contamination. This action is fundamentally prophylactic, and is not of the sort that [the insurer] contracted to cover.[42]

A number of decisions by federal and state courts around the country have come to the same conclusion as the *Armco* court. Under these decisions, **no** claim under CERCLA or a cognate state statute for injunctive relief, or for a "cost-recovery" award of cleanup or response costs, is a covered claim for "damages."[43]

Several courts confronting the "as damages" issue have overlooked the well-recognized substantive differences between a true "damages" award and injunctive or restitutional relief. In *Minnesota Mining and Manufacturing Co. v. The Travelers Indemnity Co.*,[44] for example, the court simply brushed aside what it chose to refer to as "antiquated distinctions between legal and equitable claims," and ruled, in effect, that **any** pollution claim which may require a policyholder to expend funds seeks relief in the form of "damages."[45] Other courts, purporting to adhere to the principle that policy provisions must be interpreted from the perspective of a "layman," have held, explicitly or otherwise, that the "lay" policyholder must be deemed not to comprehend the distinctions between "damages" and other forms of relief, and thus that the "as damages" limitation is effectively a nullity.[46] Increasingly, however, courts have held that while some forms of cleanup cost-recovery relief may be "damages," purely preventive relief, or injunctive cleanup relief that does not involve a monetary award to the claimant, cannot reasonably be deemed to constitute covered "damages."[47] Should this trend continue, future "as damages" controversies will not merely involve interpretation of policy language, but will entail closer scrutiny of the facts relating to the precise nature of particular pollution conditions, the nature of the response or remedial actions undertaken, and the nature of the relief sought from the policyholder. This factor will, in turn, require additional costly and time-consuming discovery in pollution coverage litigation.

### The "Trigger of Coverage" Issue

Pollution liability lawsuits and claims typically are based on allegations that the policyholder's (or its predecessors') waste generation or disposal activities have harmed or threaten to harm the environment by polluting surface water, groundwater or soil, by endangering animal or plant life, or by creating environmental conditions potentially hazardous to human health and the "public welfare."[48] To the extent that such pollution claims might be deemed to fall within the coverage afforded by a general liability policy, it would be under the coverage afforded for claims based on "property damage."[49] The question thus arises of **when** latent or long-developing "property damage" should be deemed to take place so as to "trigger," or activate, one or more liability policies in effect at that time.

The policy provisions relating to coverage for "property damage" claims, like those relating to "bodily injury" claims, typically require that the damages take place, or "result," during the policy period in order to trigger coverage.[50] Even in the context of claims for "latent" or "delayed manifestation" bodily injury, however, courts have adopted widely divergent theories as to when latent injury should be deemed to have occurred for purposes of triggering coverage. Some courts, for example, have held that bodily injury must be held to take place "continuously" at every instant from a liability claimant's first exposure to a hazardous substance until the discovery of the related disease.[51] Other courts have held that coverage is triggered only by the claimant's actual exposure to a deleterious substance,[52] while a number of decisions limit the triggering event to the "manifestation" or discovery of the injury or disease.[53] Finally, certain courts have rejected these "continuous trigger," "exposure" and "manifestation" theories, and have held, instead, that the language of the policies simply requires the existence of an "injury in fact" or "actual injury" during the policy period in order to trigger coverage.[54]

The many and varied types of environmental harm or "property damage " involved in a pollution liability case often cannot be analogized to "bodily injury." Despite this fact, a number of courts dealing with the trigger of coverage issue in the pollution context have looked uncritically to the bodily injury cases for guidance. Accordingly, a few courts have concluded, without substantial analysis, that pollution-related "property damage" must be deemed to take place at every instant from the first dumping of wastes at a site until the discovery of the pollution condition.[55] This "continuous trigger" view, reflexively applied, tends to overlook the fact that the precise pollution condition at which any particular cleanup or other environmental remedy is aimed may in fact **not** have taken place "continuously" at all — wastes may not have had any actual adverse impact upon the environment until years after their initial disposal, for example. This fact renders the "continuous trigger" approach inappropriate for across-the-board application to pollution liability claims.

Similarly, a small number of courts dealing with pollution coverage issues have appropriated what they understand to be the "exposure" approach to trigger of coverage that was developed in the bodily injury context.[56] Other courts, noting that "exposure" of the environment to pollutants, without more, does not necessarily give rise to a pollution condition that requires remediation, have held the triggering event to be the time when pollutants *actually* resulted in some material, adverse change in the environment.[57] This "actual injury" view, when applied to the facts regarding a particular polluted site, is likely to involve complicated and detailed evidentiary inquiry, based substantially on expert analysis and testimony, into the facts concerning the movement of pollutants in the environment, and the time at which the pollutants actually affected surface water, groundwater and other natural resources.

Finally, a number of courts have held that liability coverage for pollution claims is triggered, if at all, only at the time that the particular pollution condition is first discovered, or becomes "manifest."[58] The application of the "first discovery" principle in the pollution context is based, first, on the fact that a similar trigger principle has long been applied in cases involving "property damage" claims *not* based on pollution.[59] In addition, courts have noted that the cleanup claims for which liability coverage often is sought are predicated on the existence of a unitary, existing pollution condition, and have little to do with the manner in which pollutants were disposed of, or with the time or times at which the pollutants actually had an adverse impact on the environment. Finally, the "first discovery" principle also has the virtue of injecting some measure of certainty into the pollution coverage issue, and does not typically require resorting to complex and expensive expert testimony.

One additional and more narrow trigger of coverage problem also promises to continue to divide the courts, as the EPA and state governments increasingly pursue "damages" claims under CERCLA for injury to natural resources. In *Idaho v. Bunker Hill Co.*,[60] the court held that such damages are not recoverable with respect to any injury to natural resources that occurred prior to December 11, 1980, the effective date of CERCLA, and that natural resources "injury," as the term is used in CERCLA, is the equivalent of the "property damage" that would trigger coverage. Accordingly, the *Bunker Hill* court held, no liability insurance policy in effect prior to December 11, 1980 can be triggered with respect to a natural resources damages claim. In *In re Acushnet River & New Bedford Harbor Proceedings re Alleged PCB Pollution*,[61] however, the court held that the "damages" recoverable for pre-enactment injury to natural resources might have accrued **after** enactment of CERCLA. Therefore, the *Acushnet River* court held, the triggering "injury" or "property damage" on which a natural resources damages recovery is based may well have taken place before December 11, 1980, and insurance policies "on the risk" prior to enactment may be triggered by such pre-enactment phenomena.[62]

### The "Owned Property" Exclusion

For a defendant to incur cleanup liability under § 106(a) or § 107(a) of CERCLA, it is not necessary that pollutants from the defendant's facility have actually migrated "off site," or contaminated a third party's property: liability may result merely from a "threatened" release, and because of "imminent and substantial endangerment" to the environment. Accordingly, CERCLA cleanup liability may be imposed with respect to a pollution condition that is confined to the defendant's own property, or even with respect to pollutants stored on the defendant's property and not yet actually released into the environment.[63]

Liability insurance policies are plainly not intended to indemnify the policyholder for injury or damage to its *own* property; "first party" property damage coverage serves that function. Accordingly, many general liability policies explicitly exclude coverage for "property damage" claims based on damage to property owned, occupied, alienated or used by the policyholder, or that is in the policyholder's "care, custody or control." These exclusions are often referred to collectively, if imprecisely, as the "owned property" exclusion. Where a pollution liability claim is predicated exclusively or substantially on contamination of the policyholder's own property, the question thus may arise whether and to what extent the owned property exclusion bars coverage. Two principal issues have emerged in connection with the application of the owned property exclusion in the pollution context. The first is the question whether the exclusion applies where the remedial or cleanup work is necessary to prevent the migration of pollutants from the policyholder's property and onto the property of a third party. The second issue is whether a natural resource such as groundwater underlying the policyholder's site is "property" that is in the "care, custody or control" of the policyholder.

A number of courts that have considered the owned property exclusion have tended to ignore the apparent purpose of the exclusion and have held that it does **not** always exclude coverage with respect to remedial measures undertaken with respect to pollution confined to the policyholder's own premises. An instructive case is *Broadwell Realty Services, Inc. v. Fidelity & Casualty Co.*[64] In *Broadwell*, New Jersey environmental authorities advised the policyholder that gasoline had leaked from underground tanks on the policyholder's property onto adjacent land. The authorities ordered the policyholder to clean up the contamination on its **own** property in order to prevent further migration of hazardous substances onto the adjacent property; the work was performed **entirely** on the policyholder's property. The insurer, relying on the owned property exclusion, disclaimed coverage and argued that the intent of the policy was to provide coverage only with respect to "property damage" to the property of third parties. The court, however, after noting that the cleanup of the policyholder's property was "designed to prevent imminent and immediate danger to third parties" by virtue of ongoing offsite migration of pollutants, held that the exclusion did not apply to amounts incurred to affect such preventive measures, although it did apply "to remedies for damage confined to [the policyholder's] property."

The line drawn by the *Broadwell* court is difficult to apply: questions will arise in many cases whether cleanup measures were indeed preventive, and whether they were undertaken because of what is in fact "imminent and immediate endangerment" to a third party's property or to offsite natural resources.[65]

Other decisions appear to have diluted *Broadwell's* "imminent and immediate endangerment" standard. One court, for example, has held that costs incurred for arguably preventive cleanup measures on the policyholder's own property fall outside of the exclusion and are covered if there is a "demonstrated danger to the property of another."[66] The court did not clarify what burden the policyholder must meet in order to make such a "demonstration," and the very vagueness of this formulation may effectively negate the owned property exclusion altogether. Yet another court, seeking to draw a somewhat brighter line, has suggested that **all** cleanup activities undertaken on the policyholder's own site are subject to the exclusion, whether or not the cleanup is undertaken to prevent or mitigate a potential for offsite migration and contamination.[67]

Even where onsite pollutants pose no immediate threat to adjacent landowners' property, some courts have devised theories under which the owned property exclusion will not apply. For example, in *Polkow v. Citizens Insurance Company of America,*[68] the court held that adjacent landowners have a right to "reasonable use" of groundwater underlying a policyholder's property. Since, in the *Polkow* court's view, this right constitutes a "property" interest, groundwater on the policyholder's own land cannot be deemed to be "owned" by the policyholder, and claims based on contamination of such groundwater thus do not fall within the exclusion. This view, of course, overlooks the fact that the policyholder can readily be said to "control" the groundwater on its own land, and that such control triggers the application of the exclusion just as surely as ownership of property.

The *Polkow* court, as an alternative basis for avoiding the owned property exclusion, went one step further and suggested that **all** environmental cleanup claims can be characterized as "essentially for injury to the public interest in the well-being of the environment."[69] Under this view, no pollution cleanup claim can be deemed to be based on injury to the policyholder's "own" property, and the owned property exclusion is rendered meaningless in the pollution context.

## The "Known Loss" Issue

It is an essential principle of insurance law that a policyholder cannot obtain liability coverage for a loss that he knows, or is substantially certain, will take place. In his first treatise, Professor (now Judge) R. Keeton characterized the principle that such "known losses" are uninsurable as the "central idea that insurance concerns fortuitous losses only."[70] This limitation is inherent in "the very nature of insurance",[71] which involves the transfer from policyholder to insurer of a true "risk" of possible loss, not the transfer of the financial burden of loss that has already occurred or is substantially certain to occur, and the occurrence of which is already anticipated by the insured.

The rationale for this fundamental principle of insurability is not difficult to discern. The liability insurer accepts certain specified risks of possible future loss to many insureds. In return, the insurer receives premium payments from those insureds, with each payment amounting to substantially less than the total amount of coverage afforded. While the insurer expects that some percentage of the risks will result in actual losses, it also expects that other risks in the pool will not result in losses. Thus, the insurer is able to pay for those covered losses that do occur, and still make a profit. In short, "[i]nsurance is designed to spread the risk from a single individual or corporation to a large group of insureds."[72] The viability of this system of "risk transference" plainly depends upon the uncertainty of loss. If the insured is able to transfer responsibility for an already known or anticipated loss to the insurer, liability insurance is no longer economically viable — the insurer heads down the road toward insolvency, and that particular insured obtains a "free ride" on the coattails of the other premium-paying members of the risk pool, whose liability losses remain uncertain. No insurer can economically accept a small amount of money (the premium) in return for bearing certain liability for a much larger amount (the known loss), and hope to remain a viable "risk transference" pool.[73] As one commentator has put it, "[t]he insurance contract must. . .conform to the risk-shifting purpose of insurance. . . [C]ontracts which seek to cover losses already known by the insured . . .at the inception of the policy do not fulfill this purpose."[74]

The "known loss" doctrine has been applied in the pollution liability context, and courts have refused to find coverage obligations where, prior to the issuance of the policy, the policyholder had knowledge of the pollution condition and at least some reason to believe that the condition might give rise to a liability claim. For example, in *Central Quality Services Corp. v. Insurance Co. of North America*,[75] the policyholder was found to have been "well aware," prior to the time it purchased the policies in question, of perchloroethylene and trichloroethylene contamination at its site, and of leakage of these substances from its dry-cleaning operation. In addition, the policyholder had already been subject to liability claims based on the contamination. The court held, accordingly, that the policyholder "should have known there was a substantial probability of a loss before the policy period began," and that this constructive knowledge vitiated any insurance coverage.[76]

At least one court has shown a distinct reluctance to apply the "known loss" doctrine to vitiate liability coverage for pollution claims. In *City of Johnstown v. Bankers Standard Insurance Co.*,[77] the Second Circuit stated that, since insurance is purchased precisely to cover "risks, not certainties," the mere fact that a policyholder knows or should have known that it confronts a possible risk of environmental liability will not vitiate coverage. The evidence in the case did not show, however, that the policyholder knew or should have known that a pollution **loss** was substantially certain to occur; the "key, uncontested documents" relied on in the insurer's motion for summary judgment appear to have shown only that the policyholder was aware of the **possibility** of environmental liability.[78] Thus, while it does demonstrate the court's unwillingness to expand the "known loss" doctrine, *City of Johnstown* should not be read as having discarded the doctrine altogether.

As is the case with respect to the inquiry whether a policyholder "expected or intended" that its activities would cause pollution, the "known loss" issue often will involve intensive and detailed discovery and adjudication concerning the policyholder's "state of mind" regarding the hazardousness of its waste generation and disposal activities. However, while the "expected or intended" inquiry focuses on the policyholder's knowledge and awareness at the time of its polluting conduct, the "known loss" issue looks to the policyholder's state of mind as it existed immediately prior to the purchase of the insurance policy.

**Site-Specific Discovery**

It is generally to an insurer's advantage to place pollution coverage issues before a court in the context of a detailed factual record,
particularly where an underlying liability claim arises out of pollution at the policyholder's own manufacturing or waste disposal facility. Accordingly, in most cases it will be prudent for insurers to pursue intensive "site specific" discovery, utilizing traditional discovery
techniques to unearth facts relating to the policyholder's waste generation and disposal practices, its knowledge of the potential for or
actual existence of pollution injury, and its knowledge that liability
was likely to result.[79] Discovery in an environmental coverage action should also be used to develop a detailed and complete record
of the costs expended in the remedial actions against the insured.
This information can be crucial to such issues as which costs are allo-
cable to the cleanup of an insured's own property and which costs
were expended to clean up the property of third parties.[80] It is also
crucial to determine the date of the triggering event. Such information often has not been pleaded in the underlying liability complaint,
as it usually is immaterial to the plaintiff's cause of action, but it is
central to a determination of which policies, if any, are triggered by
the claim.

Discovery from other "potentially responsible parties" (PRPs)
should not be overlooked. Occasionally, in an attempt to clear itself,
a PRP will have developed inculpatory evidence against the other
PRPs allegedly involved in the matter. In matters which involve several PRPs, one or more may have developed information on their
own that may implicate the hazardous waste handling and disposal
practices of the policyholder seeking coverage under an insurer's
policies.

The formulation of discovery tactics should generally be an *ad hoc*
matter, tailored to the exigencies of a specific case. Policyholders are
increasingly seeking to deflect the attention of courts away from the
specific facts pertinent to each site-specific pollution liability claim.
One preferred policyholder tactic in this regard is to file an early motion for partial summary judgment, asking the court to declare "the

law" on the pollution coverage issues in the abstract, without reference to the facts. Accordingly, insurers are well advised to complete as much "informal" discovery and fact-marshalling as they can as early as possible, and to serve initial discovery requests promptly. It may be advisable, as well, to focus the initial discovery requests on factual matters pertaining to the sites and the insured's polluting conduct and knowledge of the potential for pollution injury, rather than to focus initially on "policy formation" issues. This may assist the insurers in persuading the court that resolution of the principal coverage issues should be deferred in order to allow the parties to marshal other pertinent facts.

There is a prevailing sense among insurers' counsel that it is not advisable to litigate most substantive pollution coverage issues in the context of a "duty to defend" dispute, because many states' laws do not permit wide-ranging consideration of facts in a "duty to defend" context. Accordingly, in certain instances, it may be advisable for primary carriers to agree to enter into an interim defense agreement with the policyholder, even where they otherwise might be inclined not to do so, to avoid an "abstract" decision on significant pollution coverage issues.

### Potential Fact Witnesses

Pre-discovery investigation is often helpful in identifying former employees of the policyholder and other potential third party witnesses who may have pertinent knowledge. The categories of former employees may include safety engineers, plant managers and other manufacturing personnel, persons formerly employed in the receiving and storage of industrial chemicals, custodial employees, production engineers, waste haulers and former executives. Counsel should assure themselves, of course, that interviews of former employees or other third parties conform to applicable ethical rules.

### Publicly Available Documents

In a given case, there may be numerous publicly available documents containing pertinent information concerning a policyholder's polluting conduct. These documents can and should be obtained without resort to formal discovery procedures; often

Freedom of Information Act (FOIA) requests or procedures under cognate state statutes can be utilized. Such documents may include the following:

**Public files of the United States Environmental Protection Agency, and/or of state and local environmental regulators.**

These files may contain a wealth of background information, including such documents as preliminary Remedial Investigation/Feasibility Studies (RI/FS), hydrogeological consultants' reports and other documents. A policyholder's National Pollution Discharge Elimination System (NPDES) permit or hazardous waste management Part B Permit file may also contain pertinent information. Other government data may also contain compliance and enforcement actions (Notices of Violation).

**Other state and federal regulatory agencies**

State "right-to-know" laws and implementing regulations also may provide "state of the art" information and information on industrial standards for handling of hazardous substances. OSHA regulations and guidelines may also provide this information, and records of a policyholder's OSHA citations or violations may contain information pertinent to a policyholder's conduct and knowledge. In a drinking water contamination case, the records of the county health department may also be instructive regarding the date of discovery of the pollution problem and early communications with the policyholder about the problem. Local sewerage authorities may also have pertinent information.

**Local newspaper archives**

Where a pollution problem has been relatively open and notorious, local news accounts will often contain a wealth of useful information relating to the policyholders' conduct and knowledge.

**Scientific and mercantile libraries**

It is often helpful to conduct a survey of scientific and mercantile literature to determine the "state of the art," at particular historical points, regarding knowledge of the hazardousness of particular chemicals used by the policyholders and the availability of various disposal techniques for the chemicals in question.

**Publicly available financial disclosure files**

Occasionally a policyholder's public filings with the Securities and Exchange Commission (SEC) will contain information pertinent to coverage issues, such as the fact that the insured was aware of potential liability relating to certain products. In addition, compilations of corporate financial and historical information such as *Moody's Industrial Manual* should be consulted.

### Court files in other litigations

Often a policyholder will have been involved in other litigation that has generated information useful in a pollution coverage case. Computerized legal searches, searches of workers compensation bureau files and other related inquiries may disclose such information.

### Discovery from the Policyholder

In any given pollution coverage case, there are any number of potentially fruitful avenues of inquiry in discovery, particularly with respect to the pollution exclusion issue, the "expected or intended" issue, and other coverage issues that may turn on the specific nature of the policyholder's polluting conduct. Among these areas of inquiry are the following:

- Is there any history of health-related complaints or claims by employees? Is there any history of workers compensation claims relating to exposure to chemicals?
- Is there any history of complaints or claims by neighboring landowners or residents?
- Did the policyholder's chemical suppliers provide warnings, i.e., Material Safety Data Sheets (MSDS), regarding toxicity, or instructions regarding safe methods of utilizing or disposing of chemical wastes?[81]
- Did the policyholder maintain waste discharge records, chemical usage or wastage records, or similar operating records?
- What experience or information did the policyholder have regarding the "useful life" of storage tanks, piping and other equipment?
- Did the policyholder expend any research and development monies with a view to finding substitutes for potentially hazardous chemicals used in its manufacturing process?
- What capital expenditures did the policyholder make with respect to chemical storage, use and/or disposal?
- Was the policyholder a participant in groups such as the Chemical Manufacturing Association (See Chapter XX by Ma-

son) or the Ad Hoc Committee on PCBs, whose activities dealt with environmental hazards and safety?

- Does the policyholder have a history of NPDES permit violations, local sewer or air-quality authority citations, or other pollution-related conduct?
- Did the policyholder seek to obtain Environmental Impairment Liability (EIL) insurance, or inquire of its brokers or others regarding the applicability of its general liability policies to pollution claims?

### Special Considerations in Multi-Site, Multi-Insurer Cases

In a multi-site, multi-insurer case, it is advisable to coordinate with other insurers' counsel to fashion a case management order that allows ample time for extensive site-specific discovery. It is also advisable to appoint a "discovery committee" of insurers' counsel to coordinate discovery efforts, identify likely sources of useful information, establish deposition schedules, interview potential third party witnesses, and prepare drafts of document production requests, interrogatories and requests for admission. The Discovery Committee should be separate from the Steering Committee, and should be small enough to be able to work efficiently yet large enough to be fairly representative of the interests of the insurer group.

A central document repository, financed by all of the insurers (pursuant to a cost-sharing agreement) and situated in a convenient location (usually at a law firm in the city where the case is pending) is advisable. Counsel for any insurer willing to share in the cost should have free access to the depository, and provisions should be made for the prompt copying of particular documents that counsel may request. The insurer group may wish to hire a "depository supervisor" or to share the cost of a paralegal from one of the insurers' counsels' firms who may act in that capacity. The discovery committee should assure that a document numbering and indexing system is devised early to allow for prompt and efficient retrieval of the documents. A depository for "hard copies" of documents is essential even if computerization and/or microfilming technologies are employed to allow each counsel more repaid access to particular documents.

### Discovery from the Insurer

#### "Drafting history" documents

As is discussed above, some policyholders, in their efforts to defeat the application of the pollution exclusion, have claimed that the so-called "drafting history" of the exclusion confirms that it was intended merely to "restate" the definition of "occurrence" contained in the policies. To bolster this argument policyholders have sought discovery of documents from the Insurance Services Office (ISO) that may repose in the insurers' files. A number of courts have rejected the "drafting history" argument.[82] Other courts have held that because the pollution exclusion is unambiguous, extrinsic evidence concerning the "drafting history" of the pollution exclusion is irrelevant and the insurer is not required to produce it. Arguments over the discoverability, relevancy and probativeness of "drafting history" will continue to occupy the courts.

#### Claim files of non-party insureds

Discovery into the claims files of other insureds is sometimes sought by the policyholder in an effort to establish "ambiguity" in the policy language. Obviously, such requests impinge upon the confidentiality of the insureds whose files are requested and, in appropriate circumstances, those insureds should be notified as they may want to seek a protective order. Some courts have flatly refused to compel production of such files, on the basis of irrelevancy.[83] Other courts have based their decisions to deny or substantially restrict "other insureds" discovery on burdensomeness.[84]

In *Independent Petrochemical Corp. v. Aetna casualty & Sur. Co.*,[85] the court limited the plaintiff's discovery to files pertaining to the same claim as involved in present suit and to claims paid to insureds for five years prior to plaintiff's claim. The court also required that the consent of third party policyholders be obtained before release of information, or that the information be released in such a way as would not identify their parties. In *Olin Corp. v. Insurance Co. of North America*,[86] a special master found that the discovery requested by Olin into INA's files on other insureds' delayed manifestation claims would be so "massive, with so little likelihood of any usable proof that it would represent an intolerable waste of the parties' recourses."

Application of work-product doctrine to claim department files

The question whether an insurer's claims file is entitled to work product protection has been litigated fairly intensively with a wide variety of results. The critical issue is whether the file was prepared in anticipation of litigation. Some courts have taken a dogmatic approach, determining that the complete file either was or was not prepared in anticipation of litigation. A number of courts have preferred instead to analyze the contents of such files. Two interesting cases illustrating this approach are *Pete Rinaldi's Fast Foods v. Great American Ins. Co.*,[87] and *Travelers Indem. Co. v. Allied-Signal, Inc.*[88] *Rinaldi's* was a "bad faith" suit resulting from the defendant insurance company's handling of a claim under a fidelity bond that arose from embezzlement by two employees. The defendant company reimbursed the plaintiff for one embezzlement, but refused to pay for the other. The plaintiff sought protection of both employees' claims files and all communications by or to the insurer with respect to the claims. The court held that the insured's claim file was not prepared in anticipation of litigation, emphasizing that the insured, rather than a third party claimant, made the claim. The court reasoned that an insurance company cannot sell a product offering protection and peace of mind, and then in good faith contend that it anticipated litigation with respect to every claim submitted. However, the court allowed that the part of the file which was prepared after a decision had been made with respect to the claim might be protected (except documents merely reporting prior investigations or evaluations), but the burden would be on the insurer to present objective facts with respect to each document demonstrating a resolve to litigate.

In *Allied-Signal* the court, ruling on the insured's motion to compel the production of documents and the insurer's objections thereto, found certain claim-department communications and memoranda to have been prepared and collected "in anticipation of litigation" and thus protected from discovery. Allied-Signal sought to obtain documents in the possession of a unit of Travelers' legal department formed specifically and exclusively to handle long-term industrial pollution claims. The court opined that the formation of the unit was prompted by the anticipation of coverage litigation and thus that its documents constitute protected work product. The court also ruled that Allied's assertion of "bad faith" could not be used as a means to obtain discovery which otherwise would be inappropriate.

# Future Trends in Environmental Coverage Law and Litigation

Despite at least ten full years of active litigation over environmental coverage, state and federal courts around the country continue to reach divergent conclusions regarding the principal coverage issues. Thus issues such as the interpretation of the pollution exclusion, the "as damages" question, and the trigger of coverage promise to occupy insurers, policyholders and the courts well into the 1990s.[89]

The unsettled state of environmental coverage law, and the absence of a clear decisional trend regarding most of the major coverage issues, are likely to have several significant effects. First, the contending parties are left with relatively little in the way of a reliable gauge of the "settlement value" of particular pollution coverage controversies. Consequently — and as experience to date has tended to confirm — efforts at settling major coverage disputes, whether undertaken before suit is brought or after, and with or without resort to mediation of other "alternate dispute resolution" mechanisms, are unlikely to be as productive as might be hoped.[90]

Another byproduct of divergent judicial treatment of the principal pollution coverage issues, and one that is already evident, is an elevated attention to choice-of-law questions. To the extent that courts continue to interpret and apply liability policies in radically different ways, the application of a particular state's substantive law to an environmental coverage issue may well preordain the manner in which a court will resolve that issue. Moreover, many states' choice-of-law rules dictate application of the substantive law of the state with the "most significant relationship" with, or the greatest "interest" in, the parties and/or the issues.[91] Imprecise standards such as these tend to leave the parties substantially uncertain over the outcome of the choice-of-law determination, and add to pollution coverage controversies yet another issue that may demand expensive and time-consuming discovery, motion practice and trial time. It is thus clear that the choice-of-law issue itself will increasingly become a critical threshold battleground in environmental coverage litigation.[92]

As the environmental coverage field continues to mature, another development that is becoming increasingly evident is the need for an intensely "fact specific" approach to many of the principal coverage issues. For example, in those jurisdictions in which the pollution exclusion is construed to impose on the insurer the burden of showing that the policyholder "expected or intended" to pollute (or where policies do not contain the exclusion), insurers have undertaken painstakingly detailed inquiries in the question of what the policyholder knew about the likelihood that its waste generation, handling and disposal activities might result in environmental pollution. Similar inquiries may be pertinent to "known loss" issues, as well as to the question whether a policyholder provided its insurers with timely notice of the facts that gave rise to a liability claim. In addition, the trigger of coverage issue is likely to require a detailed factual inquiry into such matters as when the policyholder discharged or disposed of pollutants, when the pollutants made their way into groundwater or otherwise had an impact upon natural resources, and when the pollution was first discovered. Discovery of evidence relating to those facts now consumes a substantial portion of the time devoted to pollution coverage litigation; numerous issues concerning what evidence is discoverable also increasingly occupy the parties and the courts.[93]

As is noted above, another phenomenon that has added to the time and cost consumed by pollution coverage litigation is the effort by policyholders to elicit and place before courts what is referred to as the "drafting history" of general liability policies, and particularly of the pollution exclusion.[94] In those jurisdictions where authoritative rulings have held the exclusion to be unambiguous, putative "extrinsic evidence" of a policy's purported meaning, whether in the form of so-called "drafting history" or something else, ordinarily will not be considered by the courts. In any jurisdiction in which the exclusion has not been conclusively interpreted, however, the "drafting history" battle promises to go on for some time.

All of these trends, taken together, leave little question that over the next several years environmental coverage litigation will grow even more complex and more expensive. This fact has already manifested itself in the last three years in the proliferation of "mega-cases" involving claims for coverage with respect to a policyholder's pollution liabilities at tens or even hundreds of sties, under hundreds of policies issued by numerous different insurers over a lengthy period. The stakes in such cases are so substantial — typically in the hundreds of millions of dollar — that the contending parties, insurers and policyholders alike, are unlikely soon to forsake litigation as the preferred method of resolving pollution coverage disputes. Nonetheless, environmental coverage cases may well begin to tax the time and resources of courts, as well as the financial resources of the litigants, to such a degree that a search for new and innovative methods of dispute resolution may become imperative.

## About the Author

Timothy C. Russell is a partner in the law firm of Sonnenschein Nath & Rosenthal in Washington, D.C. Mr. Russell practices in the areas of insurance and environmental law and litigation, and has represented insurers in a number of major pollution and "toxic tort" coverage controversies. He is a member of the Defense Research Institute, the Insurance Coverage Litigation Committee of the ABA's Litigation Section, and the American Law Institute's consultative group on complex litigation. Mr. Russell is a graduate of Dartmouth College and of the University of Pennsylvania Law School.

## Endnotes

1. 42 U.S.C. §§ 9601, *et seq.* (as amended).

2. *See, e.g., New Jersey Dep't of Envtl. Protection v. Ventron Corp.*, 468 A.2d 150 (N.J. 1983).

3. CERCLA, for example, authorizes cleanup "cost-recovery" actions against polluters by private parties as well as governmental authorities. While CERCLA does not authorize suits by private individuals alleging personal injury from pollution, any number of common law theories of liability are available. *See, e.g., Ayers v. Township of Jackson*, 461 A.2d 184 (N.J. Super. Law Div. 1983).

4. In a number of instances, large "Fortune 500" companies with pollution liability exposure at numerous sites around the country have sued all of their liability carriers (and in some instances their first-party property carriers as well) in a single case, seeking a declaration of coverage rights and obligations with respect to all of their pollution liabilities under hundreds of policies issued over a forty- or fifty-year period. *See e.g., Westinghouse Elec. Corp. v. Liberty Mut. Ins. Co.*, 559 A.2d 435 (N.J. Super. App. Div. 1989).

5. *See, e.g.,* K. Abraham, *Environmental Liability and the Limits of Insurance,* 88 Colum. L. Rev. 942 (1988) (discussing impact of pollution coverage cases on current cost and availability of pollution insurance); American Law Institute, *Complex Litigation Project,* Tent. Draft No. 1 (1989), at 17 (identifying pollution insurance coverage disputes as paradigms of modern "complex" litigation warranting new management and adjudicative techniques).

6. This chapter deals only with issues arising in connection with general liability and related umbrella and excess liability policies, and does not deal with pollution coverage issues that may arise under first-party property damage policies, or under "environmental impairment" liability or similar policies.

7. For the most part, the reported cases deal with the form of pollution exclusion developed by rating organizations such as the Mutual Insurance Rating Bureau in the early 1970s and included in the standard "ISO form" comprehensive general liability policy in 1973. *See generally* Note, *The Pollution Exclusion Clause Through the Looking Glass,* 74 Georgetown L. Rev. 1237, 1251-53 (1986). Certain insurers have used other forms of exclusion, which raise different interpretive issues. *See, e.g., Travelers Ins. Co. v. Waltham Indus. Laboratories, Corp.,* 883 F.2d 1092 (1st Cir. 1989). In addition, in 1986 a number of insurers began to use a new form of "absolute" pollution exclusion, which is discussed briefly at Note 26, *infra.*

8. *See, e.g, American Casualty Co. v. Minnesota Farm Bureau Service Co.,* 270 F.2d 686, 691 (8th Cir. 1959); *Massachusetts Turnpike Auth. v. Perini,* 208 N.E.2d 807, 813 (Mass. 1965).

9. *See* J. Hourihan, *Insurance Coverage for Environmental Damage Claims,* 15 Forum 551, 552-53 (1981); G. Bean, *The Accident Versus the Occurrence Concept,* 1959 Ins. L.J. 550, 551.

10. *See* J. Hourihan , *supra* Note 9, at 552-53; R. Keeton & A. Widiss, *Insurance Law* § 5.4(g), at 544 (1988).

11. Among the incidents often cited are the 1967 Torrey Canyon disaster, the oil spill in the Santa Barbara channel, and industrial mercury contamination in Minamata, Japan. *See generally* Kunzman, *The Insurer as Surrogate Regulator of the Hazardous Waste Industry: Solution or Perversion,* 20 Forum 469, 475 (1985); U.S. Dep't of the Treasury, *The Adequacy of Private Insurance Protection Under Section 107 of the Comprehensive Environmental Response, Compensation and Liability Act of 1980,* at 47 (U.S. Treasury Dep't 1983).

12. 451 A.2d 790 (N.J. Super. Law Div. 1982).

13. *Id.* at 992.

14. *Id.* at 994.

15. Some courts, for example, have purported to find the pollution exclusion "ambiguous" precisely <u>because</u> it excludes coverage for claims based on "continuous or repeated exposure to conditions," at the same time that the "occurrence" language in the policies' insuring clause creates coverage for such claims. *See, e.g., United States Fidelity & Guaranty Co. v. Thomas Solvent Co.,* 683 F.Supp 1139, 1159 (W.D. Mich. 1988). This argument, of course, overlooks the fact that an exclusion is exactly that — it "excludes" claims that, absent the exclusion, might otherwise fall within coverage. *See, e.g., Amer-*

*ican Motorists Ins. Co. v. General Host Corp.*, 667 F.Supp 1423, 1429 (D. Kan. 1987) ("[i]t is not a novel idea that broad exceptions to coverage can be made" by an exclusion). Still other courts have claimed to perceive in the exclusion an intention to deny coverage only to "active" or "actual" polluters, which phrases apparently refer to intentional polluters. *See, e.g., Niagara County v. Utica Mutual Insurance Co.*, 439 N.Y.S.2d 538 (App. Div. 1981), *aff'g* 427 N.Y.S.2d 171 (Sup. Ct. 1980).

16. *See, e.g, Avondale Industries, Inc. v. The Travelers Indemnity Co.*, 887 F.2d 1200 (2d Cir. 1989), *cert. denied*, 58 U.S.L.W. 3269 (1990); *New Castle County v. Hartford Accident & Indem. Co.*, 673 F.Supp 135 (D. Del. 1987); *Du-Wel Products, Inc. v. United States Fire Ins. Co.*, 565 A.2d 1113 (N.J. Super. App. Div. 1989); *Claussen v. Aetna Casualty & Surety Co.*, 380 S.E.2d 686 (Ga. 1989); *Kipin Industries, Inc. v. American Universal Ins. Co.*, 535 N.E.2d 334 (Ohio App. 1987); *United States Fidelity & Guaranty Co. v. Specialty Coatings Co.*, 535 N.E.2d 1071 (Ill. App. 1989); *Broderick Investment Co. v. Hartford Accident & Indem. Co.*, No. 86-Z-1033 (D. Colo. Oct. 4, 1989); *Jonesville Products Co. v. Transamerica Ins. Group*, 402 N.W.2d 46 (Mich. App. 1986).

17. *See Just v. Land Reclamation, Ltd.*, No. 88-1656 (Wis. Sup. Ct. June 19, 1990).

18. *Lower Paxon Twp. v. United States Fidelity & Guar. Corp.*, 557 A.2d 393, 398 (Pa. Super. 1989), *quoting Technicon Electronics Co. v. American Home Assur. Co.*, 533 N.Y.S.2d 91, 96 (App. Div. 1988), *aff'd*, 542 N.E.2d 1048 (N.Y. 1989).

19. 856 F.2d 31, 34 (6th Cir. 1988).

20. Other cases construing the exclusion in the same or a similar manner include *Lumbermens Mutual Cas. Co. v. Belleville Industries, Inc.*, No. S-5285 (Mass. Sup. Jud. Ct. June 14, 1990); *International Minerals & Chem. Corp. v. Liberty Mutual Ins. Co.*, 522 N.E.2d 758 (Ill. App. 1988); *Transamerica Ins. Co. v. Sunnes*, 711 P.2d 212 (Ore. App. 1985); *Powers Chemco, Inc. v. Federal Ins. Co.*, 548 N.E.2d 130 (N.Y. 1989); *Technicon Elec. Corp. v. American Home Assur. Co.*, 542 N.E.2d 1048 (N.Y. 1989); *Lower Paxon Twp. v. United States Fidelity & Guar. Co.*, 557 A.2d 393 (Pa. Super. 1989); *Centennial Ins. Co. v. Lumbermens Mut. Cas. Co.*, 677 F.Supp. 342 (E.D. Pa. 1977); *Borden, Inc. v. Affiliated FM Ins. Co.*, 865 F.2d 1267 (6th Cir.), *cert denied*, 110 S. Ct. 68 (1989); *Diamond Shamrock Chem. Co. v. Aetna Casualty & Sur. Co.*, No. C-3939-84 (N.J. Super. Ch. Div. Apr. 12, 1989); *Waste Mgt. of Carolinas, Inc. v. Peerless Ins. Co.*, 340 S.E.2d 374 (N.C. 1986); *Fireman's Fund Ins. Cos. v. Ex-Cell-O Corp.*, 702 F.Supp. 1317 (E.D. Mich. 1988); *State v. Amro Realty Corp.*, 697 F.Supp. 99 (N.D. N.Y. 1988); *Hayes v. Maryland Cas. Co.*, 688 F.Supp. 1513 (N.D. Fla. 1988); *Ray Industries, Inc. v. Liberty Mutual Ins. Co.*, 728 F.Supp. 1310 (E.D. Mich. 1989); and *In re Acushnet River & New Bedford Harbor: Proceedings re Alleged PCB Pollution*, 725 F.Supp. 1264 (D. Mass. 1989).

21. Space does not allow more than this brief sketch of the "drafting history" argument here. In fairness, the reader should consult a policyholder's brief, or one of the many articles by policyholder lawyers on the subject, to appreciate the argument fully. *See, e.g.*, Sayler & Zolensky, *Pollution Coverage and the Intent of the CGL Drafters: The Effect of Living Backwards*, Mealey's Litigation Reports (Insurance) (1986) at 4425.

22. *See, e.g., American Motorists Ins. Co. v. General Host Corp.*, 120 F.R.D. 129 (D. Kan. 1988). In a recent deposition, one of the insurance company executives who actually participated in drafting the exclusion testified that it was indeed intended to exclude from coverage all pollution claims except those based on truly "sudden" — abrupt and precipitous — discharges. *See* "Pollution Exclusion Dissected During Bruton Deposition," Mealey's Litigation Reports (Insurance) (Feb. 27, 1990) at 17.

23. There is nothing in the "drafting history" documents to indicate, for example, that the insurance rating organizations were authorized to bind a particular insurer by pronouncements concerning that insurer's specific contractual intent or understanding. The absence of such essential foundational proof has been noted by courts. *See, e.g., Lumbermens Mut. Cas. Co. v. Belleville Industries, Inc.* No. 84-2676-Y (D. Mass. Jan. 30, 1990) (bench ruling).

24. *See, e.g., Just v. Land Reclamation, Ltd.*, No. 88-1656 (Wis. Sup. Ct. June 19, 1990).

25. *See, e.g., Grant-Southern Iron & Metal Co. v. CNA Ins. Co.*, No. 88-1049 (6th Cir. June 18, 1990).

26. As is noted above, in 1986 a number of insurers began to include in their liability policies an "absolute" exclusion that does not provide coverage even for claims arising out of "sudden and accidental" events. Courts have tended to uphold the "absolute" exclusion in the face of challenges by policyholders. *See, e.g., Guilford Industries, Inc. v. Mutual Ins. Co.*, 688 F.Supp. 792 (D. Me. 1988), *aff'd*, 879 F.2d 853 (1st Cir. 1989).

27. "ISO form" general liability policies were amended in 1986 to include the "expected or intended" criterion in an exclusion rather than in the insuring clause itself.

28. As was discussed above, the pollution exclusion, unlike the "occurrence" clause, focuses on the nature of the causative pollution event — the discharge of pollutants — rather than on the result of that discharge.

29. It should be noted that the "occurrence" definition can be read to require a two-pronged analysis, that is, that the policyholder's conduct constituted an "accident" in and of itself, *and* that any resulting injury or damage was "neither expected nor intended." Some courts have applied such an analysis and, without considering whether the policyholder "expected or intended" to harm the environment, have found no "accident" where pollution resulted from routine, day-to-day business activities. *See, e.g., American States Ins. Co. v. Maryland Cas. Co.*, 587 F.Supp. 1549 (E.D. Mich. 1984). This appears to be the minority view, although some courts appear willing to allow an inference of expectation or intent concerning resulting injury from the fact of routine discharges of pollutants.

30. *See, e.g., James Graham Brown Foundation v. St. Paul Fire & Marine Ins. Co.*, No. 88-CA-2405-MR (Ky. Ct. App. Mar. 9, 1990) (pollution caused by normal plant operations over a period of years); *Shell Oil Co. v. Accident & Casualty Ins. Co. of Winterthur*, No. 278953 (Cal. Super. Ct. San Mateo City Oct. 6, 1988) (pollution by petrochemical company resulting from long series of discharges); *Diamond Shamrock Chem. Co. v. Aetna Casualty & Surety Co.*, No. C-3939-84 (N.J. Super. Ch. Div. Apr. 12, 1989) (claim for coverage based on years of systematic, knowing discharges of toxic chemicals); *City of Farragut v. Hartford Accident & Indemnity Co.*, 837 F.2d 480 (8th Cir. 1987) (deliberate pumping of raw sewage); *City of Carter Lake v. Aetna Casualty & Surety Co.*, 604 F.2d 1052 (8th Cr. 1979); *Fischer & Porter Co. v. Liberty Mutual Ins. Co.*, 656 F.Supp. 132 (E.D. Pa. 1986) (repeated dumping of toxic chemicals down drains known to lead directly to sewers).

31. *See, e.g., City of Johnstown v. Bankers Standard Insurance Co.*, 877 F.2d 1146 (2d Cir. 1989); *Pepper's Steel & Alloys, Inc. v. United States Fidelity & Guar. Co.*, 668 F.Supp. 1641 (S.D. Fla. 1987).

32.  *See* R. Keeton & A. Widiss, *Insurance Law* § 5.4(a), at 497 (1988).

33.  *See* K. Abraham, *Environmental Liability and the Limits of Insurance*, 88 Colum. L. Rev. 942, 946 (1988).

34.  *See* 42 U.S.C. § 9606(a).

35.  *See* 42 U.S.C. § 9607(a)(1)-(4)(A), (B), (D).

36.  *See* 42 U.S.C. § 9607(a)(1)-(4)(C).

37.  The distinctively compensatory, "substitutional" nature of an award of damages is well recognized. *See, e.g. Bowen v. Massachusetts*, 108 S. Ct. 2722, 2731-36 (1988); *United States v. Price*, 688 F.2d 204, 212 (3d Cir. 1982); 1 T. Sedgwick, *Damages* §§ 2, 30 (9th ed. 1912).

38.  *See, e.g., Dedham Water Co. v. Cumberland Farms Dairy*, 805 F.2d 1074 (1st Cir. 1986); *United States v. Dickerson*, 604 F.Supp. 448, 453 (D. Md. 1986).

39.  For similar reasons, insurers maintain that remedial costs incurred by a policyholder *before* any suit is brought, or environmental cleanup or preventative costs incurred voluntarily by a policyholder, cannot possibly constitute "damages."

40.  *See, e.g., Aetna Casualty & Surety Co. v. Hanna*, 224 F.2d 499, 503-04 (5th Cir. 1955); *Garden Sanctuary, Inc. v. Insurance Co. of North America*, 292 So.2d 75, 77 (Fla. App. 1977).

41.  822 F.2d 1348 (4th Cir. 1987), *cert. denied*, 484 U.S. 1008 (1988).

42.  822 F.2d at 1348, 1353-54.

43.  *See, e.g., Continental Ins. Co. v. Northeastern Pharmaceutical & Chem. Co.*, 842 F.2d 977 (8th Cir.) *(en banc), cert. denied*, 109 S. Ct. 66 (1988); *Lido Co. of New England, Inc. v. Fireman's Fund Ins. Co.*, No. 5447 (Maine S. Ct. May 3, 1990); *United States Fidelity & Guaranty Co. v. Morrison Grain Co.*, No. 86-1803-C (D. Kan. Mar. 21, 1990).

44.  No. 88-1931 (Minn. Sup. Ct. June 8, 1990); *see also C.D. Spangler Constr. Co. v. Industrial Crankshaft and Engineering Co.*, 388 S.E.2d 557 (N.C. 1990); *TBG, Inc. v. Commercial Union Insurance Co.*, No. 89-2374 (N.D. Cal. June 4, 1990); *Avondale Industries, Inc. v. Travelers Indemnity Co.*, 887 F.2d 1200 (2d Cir. 1989), *cert. denied*, 58 U.S.L.W. 3269 (1990).

45.  *Id.*, slip opinion at 8. Courts that have held that environmental cleanup costs do *not* constitute damages have noted the distinctive characteristics of an injunctive or restitutional award — its open-endedness, its "prophylactic" nature, and the fact that it is not limited by the market value of the claimant's property. *See, Maryland Casualty Co. v. Armco, Inc., supra* Note 41, 822 F.2d at 1348, 1353-54. The analysis undertaken by such courts thus does not rest at all on the simplistic "legal-equitable" distinction referred to by the *Minnesota Mining* court.

46.  *See, e.g., New Castle County v. Hartford Accident and Indemnity Co.*, 673 F.Supp. 1359, 1365 (D. Del. 1987)

47. *See, e.g., Boeing Co. v. Aetna Casualty & Surety Co.,* 784 P.2d 507 (Wash. 1990); *Aerojet-General Corp. v. Superior Court,* 209 Cal. App. 3d 973, *reprinted as modified,* 211 Cal. App. 3d 216 (1989); *Cooper Industries, Inc. v. American Mutual Liability Insurance Co.,* No. 864-00184 (Mo. Cir. Ct. Sept. 8, 1989); *Braswell v. Faircloth,* 387 S.E.2d 707 (S.C. App. 1989)

48. *See, e.g., United States v. Ottati & Goss, Inc.,* 630 F.Supp. 1361 (D. N.H. 1985).

49. Some courts have held, however, that a typical governmental pollution cleanup claim is not based on "property damage" at all, inasmuch as the government is not seeking compensation for injury to or loss of its own property. *See, e.g., Mraz v. Canadian Universal Ins. Co.,* 804 F.2d 1325 (4th Cir. 1986).

50. *See, e.g., American Home Products Corp. v. Liberty Mutual Ins. Co.,* 748 F.2d (2d Cir. 1984).

51. *See, e.g., Keene Corp. v. Insurance Co. of North America,* 667 F.2d 1034 (D.C. Cir. 1981), *cert. denied,* 455 U.S. 1007 (1982). The "continuous trigger " theory devised in *Keene* has not attracted a significant following, even in the context of asbestos-related bodily injury claims.

52. *See, e.g., Insurance Co. of North America v. Forty-Eight Insulations, Inc.,* 633 F.2d 1212 (6th Cir. 1980), *modified,* 657 F.2d 814, *cert. denied,* 454 U.S. 1009 (1981).

53. *See, also, Eagle-Picher Industries, Inc. v. Liberty Mutual Ins. Co.,* 682 F.2d 12 (1st Cir. 1982), *cert. denied,* 460 U.S. 1028 (1983)

54. *See, e.g, American Home Products Corp. v. Liberty Mutual Insurance Co.,* 748 F.2d 760 (2d Cir. 1984). It seems reasonably clear that the "injury in fact" approach, sensibly applied, only triggers coverage at the time of the *initial* injury, and that sequelae of that same injury do not trigger additional policies.

55. *See, e.g., Gottlieb v. Newark Ins. Co.,* No. A-2243-88T5 (N.J. Super. App. Div. Feb. 13, 1990); *Broderick Ins. Co. v. Hartford Accident & Indemnity Co.,* No. 86-2-1033 (D. Colo. Dec. 19, 1989).

56. *See, e.g., Fireman's Fund Insurance Co. v. Ex-Cell-O Corp.,* 662 F.Supp. 71 (E.D. Mich. 1987). A close reading of the principal "exposure" cases decided in the context of asbestos bodily injury cases suggests that exposure was adopted as the triggering event because of proof that asbestos-related bodily injury occurs at or very shortly after the time of exposure. *See, e.g., Insurance Company of North America v. Forty-Eight Insulations, Inc., supra* Note 52. Accordingly, it may be argued that the classical "exposure" theory is in fact an "injury in fact" or "actual injury" trigger approach.

57. *See, e.g., United States v. Conservation Chem. Co.,* 653 F.Supp. 152 (W.D. Mo. 1986); *Unigard Mut. Ins. Co. v. McCarty's, Inc.,* No. 83-1441 (D. Idaho, June 6, 1987).

58. *See, e.g., Mraz v. Canadian Universal Insurance Co.,* 804 F.2d 1235 (4th Cir. 1986); *American Motorists Ins. Co. v. Levolor Lorentzen, Ins.,* No. 88-1994 (D.N.J. Oct. 14, 1988); *Metal Bank of American v. Liberty Mutual Insurance Co.,* No. 861 (Pa. Court of Common Pleas, Phila. County Jan. 8, 1986), *aff'd on other grounds,* 520 A.2d 493 (Pa. Super. 1987).

59. *See, e.g., American Home Assurance Co. v. Libbey-Owens-Ford Co.*, 786 F.2d 22 (1st Cir. 1986); *Aetna Casualty & Surety Co. v. PPG Industries, Inc.*, 554 F.Supp. 290 (D. Ariz. 1983).

60. 647 F.Supp. 1064 (D. Idaho 1986).

61. 716 F.Supp. 676 (D. Mass. 1989).

62. *Id.* at 683 n.9.

63. *See, e.g., B.F. Goodrich Co. v. Murtha*, 697 F.Supp. 89, 96 (D. Conn. 1988) (§ 106(a) cleanup relief is available "even though the actual harm may not be realized for years").

64. 528 A.2d 76 (N.J. Super. App. Div. 1987).

65. As is noted above, CERCLA liability may be imposed because of merely "imminent" endangerment, and the statute does not, by its terms, require any "immediate" endangerment of public health or the environment. Thus, CERCLA's liability standard and the *Broadwell* standard are not necessarily coextensive. In *State v. Signo Trading Int'l, Inc.*, 562 A.2d 251 (N.J. Super. App. Div. 1989), the court held that since no prior offsite migration of pollutants had been proven, and there was no proof of an "immediate" danger of migration, the owned property exclusion applied. The trial court in *Signo* had found that there was a "risk" of damage to third parties, but this was held to be insufficient, without more, to meet the *Broadwell* standard.

66. *Allstate Insurance Co. v. Quinn Construction Co.*, 713 F.Supp. 35, 41 (D. Mass. 1989).

67. *See Sharon Steel Corp. v. Aetna Casualty & Surety Co.*, No. C-87-2306 (Salt Lake County Utah, July 20, 1988).
68. 447 N.W.2d 853 (Mich. App. 1989).

69. *Id.* at 857.

70. R. Keeton, *Insurance Law — Basic Text* § 5.4(c), at 297 (1971). The "known loss" or "fortuity" doctrine is sometimes referred to as the "known risk" principle. The "known risk" nomenclature may be misleading, since liability insurance is, after all, intended to cover "risks." Accordingly, "known loss" is a more apt phrase.

71. *Id.* § 5.4(a), at 288-89.

72. 1 R. Long, *Law of Liability Insurance* § 4A.02, at 4A-8; *see also Steere Tank Lines, Inc. v. United States*, 577 F.2d 279, 280 (5th Cir. 1978), *cert. denied*, 440 U.S. 996 (1979) ("[r]isk shifting or risk distribution is one of the requisites of a true insurance contract").

73. Assuming that an insurer were not bankrupted by having to pay losses resulting from known risks, one necessary effect of allowing an insured to collect for such losses would be the prospective inflation of premium rates applicable to other insureds who sought coverage for the risks. *See generally* G. Priest, *The Current Insurance Crisis and Modern Tort Law*, 96 Yale L.J. 1521, 1539-50 (1987).

74. 1 R. Long, *Law of Liability Insurance*, § 4A.01, at 4A-8. *See also Appalachian Insurance Co. v. Liberty Mutual Insurance Co.*, 676 F.2d 56, 63 (3d Cir. 1982) ("the purpose of insurance is to protect insureds against unknown risks").

75. No. 87-CV-74473-DT (E.D. Mich. Sept. 6, 1989).

76. *See also Township of Gloucester v. Maryland Casualty Co.*, 668 F.Supp. 394 (D.N.J. 1987) (knowledge of contamination two years prior to inception of policy vitiates coverage, since "[o]ne cannot obtain insurance for a risk that the insured knows already begun"); *New Castle County v. Hartford Accident and Indemnity Co.*, 685 F.Supp. 1321 (D. Del. 1988) (even though liability and loss were not a certainty, insured's knowledge of substantial probability that its landfill caused pollution vitiated coverage); *Advanced Micro Devices, Inc. v. Great American Surplus Lines Insurance Co.*, 199 Cal. App. 3d 791 (1988).

77. 877 F.2d 1146 (2d Cir. 1989).

78. *Id.* at 1151-52.

79. The wisdom of this approach is illustrated in the outcome of Diamond Shamrock Chems. Co. v. Aetna Casualty & Sur. Co., No. C-3939-84 (N.J. Super. Ct. Ch. Div. Apr. 12, 1989).

80. *See Sharon Steel Corp. v. Aetna Casualty & Sure. Co.*, Nos. C-87-2306, C-87-2311 (Utah Dist. Ct. Salt Lake C'ty July 20, 1988); *Broadwell Realty Servs., Inc. v. Fidelity & Casualty Co.*, 527 A.2d 76 (N.J. Super. App. Div. 1987).

81. For example, beginning in the early 1970s the major United States supplier of PCBs provided detailed information to its customers concerning the environmental hazards allegedly associated with PCBs, and generally required each customer to agree to indemnify the supplier against environmental liability resulting from PCB use.

82. *See, e.g., American Motorist Ins. Co. v. General Host Corp.*, 120 F.R.D. 129 (D. Kan. 1988). The ISO documents do contain much information which supports the insurers, and insureds may actually do themselves a disservice by bringing the "drafting history" into issue.

83. *See, e.g., Sylvester Bros. Dev. Co. v. Great Central Ins. Co.*, No. C2-88-2491 (Minn. Dist. Ct., Anoka C'ty Mar. 3, 1989).

84. *See, e.g., Carey-Canada, Inc. v. California Union Ins. Co.*, No. 83-1105 (D.C.C. May 24, 1986) (permitted only limited discovery in light of burden and likely minimal value); *National Union Fire Ins. Co. v. Stauffer Chem. Co.*, 588 A.2d 1091 (Del. Super. Ct. 1989) (insurers required to produce only "ten earliest and ten latest" claims and underwriting files relating to the insureds' account).

85. No. 83-3347 (D.D.C. Nov. 20, 1986).

86. No. 84-Civ. 1968 (LFM) (S.D.N.Y. July 10, 1986).

87. 123 F.R.D. 198 (M.D.N.C. 1988).

88. 718 F. supp. 1252 (D. Md. 1989).

89. For example, at the time of this writing, the standard "sudden and accidental" pollution exclusion has been interpreted authoritatively by the highest courts of only

five states: North Carolina, New York, Wisconsin, Massachusetts and Georgia. Two of those state courts, in Wisconsin and Georgia, have taken a distinctly "pro-policyholder" view of the exclusion. *See, Just v. Land Reclamation, Ltd., supra* Note 24; *Claussen v. Aetna Casualty & Surety Co., supra* Note 16. The other three have read the exclusion in the manner urged by insurers. *See, Technicon Electronics Co. v. American Home Assur. Co., supra* Note 18; *Waste Mgt. of Carolinas, Inc. v. Peerless Ins. Co., supra* Note 20; *Lumbermens Mutual Cas. Co. v. Belleville Industries, Inc., supra* Note 23.

90.   A number of other factors may contribute to the difficulty of settling pollution coverage cases. For example, policyholders frequently seek discovery of whether an insurer has compromised other, arguably similar coverage controversies, ostensibly in an effort to show that the insurer has in the past interpreted or applied its policies "inconsistently." An insurer that can anticipate that its settlement of even a relatively minor coverage controversy might later be offered as damaging "evidence against it will naturally be more hesitant to settle.

91.   *See, e.g., State Farm Mut. Auto. Ins. Co. v. Estate of Simmons*, 417 A.2d 488 (N.J. 1980) (New Jersey courts will apply law of place of contracting unless another state has "dominant" interest in application of its own law); *Auten v. Auten*, 124 N.E.2d 99 (N.Y. 1954) (law state with most significant "contacts" with an issue should be applied). Section 188 of the Second Restatement of Contracts lists five factors to be considered in determining the state with the "most significant relationship" to the issues and the parties, while § 193 of the Second Restatement, which is applicable in cases involving contracts of fire, casualty or liability insurance, suggests application of the law of the state that is the principal location of the "insured risk." At least one court has held that each particular polluted site is a separate "risk," and that a single liability policy must be interpreted under the laws of the several states in which such sites are located with respect to coverage claims involving those different sites. *See, Chesapeake Utilities Corp. v. American Home Assur. Co.*, 704 F.Supp 51 (D. Del. 1989).

92.   As is noted above, existing choice of law rules have led to the application of several different states' substantive laws in a coverage case involving numerous policies and numerous polluted sites. Despite the fact that this result conforms to established doctrine, one court, in an apparent effort to render such cases more "manageable'" has dictated that a *single* state's law should govern each policy of insurance, even where the policyholder seeks coverage with respect to pollution sites located in different states. *See, Westinghouse Elec. Corp. v. Liberty Mutual Ins. Co.*, 559 A.2d 435 (N.J. Super. App. Div. 1989).

93.   Among the discovery issues that insurers and policyholders regularly contest — and that courts have tended to resolve in divergent ways — are the "discoverability" of a policyholder's conduct at pollution sites or manufacturing facilities other than that involved in a particular case; the insurer's setting of reserves for a particular claim, and its reinsurance arrangements with respect to the claim; and the manner in which the insurer has handled arguably analogous claims submitted by other policyholders. Resolution of these issues typically consumes at least the first several months, or longer, of a major pollution coverage litigation. *See, In re Environmental Declaratory Judgment Actions*, UNN L 08573-89 (Super. Ct. Union Co. N.J.) (order regarding scope of permissible discovery, August 7, 1990).

94.   *See*, text accompanying Notes 21-23, *supra*.

# XXVIII Setting Priorities of Policyholder Procedural Issues

## John E. Heintz, Shareholder
## Popham, Haik, Schnobrich & Kaufman
## Washington, D.C.

The successful prosecution of a coverage action for hazardous waste cleanup claims begins with a careful selection of parties and forum. In many instances, a comprehensive action seeking coverage for all claims raising common issues against those carriers who might have to pay is the most effective and cost-efficient way of obtaining a consistent and complete resolution of coverage disputes. For reasons explained below, a policyholder's decision to file such an action should not be disturbed simply because the action involves out-of-state sites and evidence. If courts force policyholders to pursue litigation in each jurisdiction where a site is located on *forum non conveniens* grounds, policyholders will suffer substantial delays, greater costs and inconsistent and incomplete relief.

Thus, the favorable resolution of the basic party and forum issues — joinder, justiciability, removal and *forum non conveniens* and choice of law — in the early stages of litigation is of critical importance. These issues involve both objective and subjective considerations. From an objective viewpoint, the question is: "What is the most efficient way to litigate a particular dispute — in which jurisdiction and with which parties can the dispute be resolved most efficiently and effectively?" From a subjective viewpoint, the question essentially is: "Which forum will best serve the client's interests in the litigation?" Frequently, the hidden, unstated question boils down to: "Which forum is most likely to apply law favorable to the client?" While the courts are left to answer the objective questions, litigants' approaches to both the objective and the subjective questions will be guided by what serves their ultimate objective of winning. This discussion focuses on the more objective considerations, but the subjective considerations are, nonetheless, always present and cannot be ignored.

The initial litigation issues focus on the parties who should be joined in an action and where the action should be filed. In a simple action on an auto policy, the options are limited and the answers are relatively easy to develop. By contrast, in a typical environmental insurance case, there are a wide variety of possibilities and no clear answers.

To facilitate the discussion of those possibilities, we will consider a hypothetical policyholder. This policyholder is a manufacturing company with operations and facilities in ten states across the country. Over the last 40 years, these operations generated wastes that were shipped to 50 waste sites in 15 different states. During that 40-year period, our policyholder purchased primary comprehensive general liability (CGL) insurance from five different carriers. For the last 30 years, the policyholder obtained excess umbrella insurance from seven different carriers (including one of the primary carriers). Beginning in 1965, the company purchased upper-level excess insurance in increasing amounts from a total of 35 different carriers, including London market underwriters and companies.

At the present time, it is difficult to predict the company's potential liabilities with respect to government actions seeking clean up of the 50 waste sites and to related private party actions seeking damages on various theories. A few of the sites have already been resolved on a *de minimis* basis, and the company expects to resolve many of the other sites on a comparable basis. However, for at least ten of the sites, the company's potential liabilities are likely to be substantial. Under the best-case scenario, the policyholder's combined liabilities for all 50 sites would not exceed the combined aggregate limits of the primary policies issued by the five primary carriers. Under the worse-case scenario, the policyholder's liabilities would exceed the combined aggregate coverage available from all of the primary and umbrella policies issued to it over the last 40 years.

The policyholder has notified all of its primary and excess carriers of these claims and all carriers have issued general reservations of rights or disclaimers of coverage. At this time, the policyholder is paying its own defense costs and settlements. The policyholder has determined to file an action to obtain coverage because its ongoing defense costs and liabilities continue to mount. Who should the policyholder sue and where should it sue?

**Environmental
Risk Management**

### Joinder of Primary and Excess Carriers

The answer to the first question is straightforward. That is, for each waste site claim, the policyholder wants a declaration of coverage binding carriers who will be obligated to pay on that claim under one or more legal theories. If, for example, a claim **could** trigger each policy issued to the policyholder from 1950 to 1985 (as under a multiple trigger theory), the policyholder should join each carrier issuing a policy during that period in the same action.

In addition, the policyholder should consider joining all carriers who might be obligated to pay any amount of any claim. If it can be reasonably anticipated that the policyholder's aggregate liabilities for all claims will exceed the amount of coverage available at the primary level, the policyholder should, in most situations, join the first layer umbrella carriers in the action. If it can be reasonably anticipated that aggregate liabilities for all claims will reach upper levels of excess insurance, the policyholder should give serious consideration to joining those carriers as well.

With respect to each hazardous waste claim and to all claims combined, the main objective is to obtain consistent and complete relief in a way that maximizes coverage. The failure to join all carriers which might be obligated to pay on each particular claim, or the failure to join all carriers which might be required to pay on some claims presents the risk of inconsistent and incomplete relief.

### Risk of Non-Joinder

If all of the primary carriers whose policies might be implicated by the ABC dump site are **not** joined in the same action, the policyholder may end up with inconsistent relief that produces less coverage than would have been the case had all the carriers been joined in the same action. If there are separate actions and the carriers covering earlier years obtain a declaration that the discovery of contamination during the policy period triggers coverage, while the carriers covering later years obtain a declaration in a separate action that the disposal of waste during the policy period triggers coverage, the policyholder will be left with no coverage. Each case places the responsibility for coverage on the carriers joined in the other case. Had all the carriers been joined in one action, one interpretation would have applied to all of the policies, thereby providing coverage under one of the coverage theories.

If it can reasonably be anticipated that excess carriers will be required to pay on some claims, failing to join them in the same action with the primary carriers also presents the risk of inconsistent and incomplete relief. For example, if a primary policy is applied on a discovery trigger of coverage, but, in a separate action, the excess carrier successfully maintains that the underlying coverage should have applied on a disposal period basis and, therefore, should not have been exhausted, the policyholder will be left shouldering the gap created between the excess and primary policies. Clearly then, the only way to avoid this outcome is to join both the excess and primary carriers in the same case, thereby binding them to the same consistent resolution of coverage questions.

### Joinder Under the Federal Rules

The joinder of all carriers who might be obligated to pay on the same claim is unquestionably proper under the federal rules, as well as most state rules of civil procedure. Federal Rule 20(a) provides that:

> [A]ll parties. . .may be joined in one action as defendants if there is asserted against them jointly, severally, or in the alternative, any right to relief in respect of or arising out of the same transaction, occurrence, or series of transactions or occurrences and if any question of law or fact common to all defendants will arise in the action.[1]

Where more than one carrier may be obligated to pay the same claim, whether jointly, severally, or in the alternative, a policyholder's right to relief from any of those carriers arises out of the same occurrence. Moreover, the questions of law or fact concerning coverage for the particular claim will be largely, if not entirely, common to all defendants. In addition, "other insurance" clauses contained in most insurers' policies demonstrate the interdependence and interrelatedness of the various policies, and justify the joinder of all carriers who may potentially be liable for any portion of the policyholder's liability.

Rulings in numerous coverage actions demonstrate the appropriateness of joining all carriers who may have to pay in one action. In *Township of Gloucester v. Maryland Cas. Co.*,[2] a case involving insurance coverage for hazardous waste claims, the court held that three carriers that had provided coverage for only a portion of the period during which contamination took place were potentially liable for the full amount of indemnity provided by their respective policies, including cleanup costs. Another four carriers who did not argue this point were also held liable for the full amount of the policyholder's liabilities.

Similarly, in *Lac d'Amiante du Quebec. Ltee. v. Home Assurance Co.*,[3] the court held that three insurers covering the insured during different portions of the period in which continuous property damage caused by asbestos took place, were jointly and severally obligated to pay their policyholder's liabilities for such damage. 613 F. Supp. at 1559-61. Other courts have construed policies to require several carriers to respond to the same claim when injury or damage occurs over time.[4]

### Dismissal For Failure To Join

If the policyholder fails to join all carriers whose policies are likely to be implicated by the liabilities arising out of pending claims, one of the carriers that is joined in the action is likely to move to add one or more of the absent carriers. Of course, this would be of no tactical concern unless the action were commenced in federal court and the joinder of an absent carrier were to destroy diversity. This happened in a coverage case GAF filed against Insurance Company of North America (INA) and other carriers in the District Court for the District of Columbia in 1978. In that case, INA moved to dismiss the action for failure to join an indispensable, non-diverse, excess carrier. GAF ultimately dismissed its federal court action voluntarily and ended up in state court in California in an action joining all of its excess carriers.

In a recent case directly on point, a federal court dismissed a declaratory action brought by an insurance carrier for its failure to join other necessary and indispensable carriers that might be obligated to cover the same claim.[5] The court reasoned that:

> The absent insurers will have a strong interest in litigation over the [insurer's] duty to defend or indemnify... If the instant complaint is not dismissed, the prejudicial effect to [the policyholder] would be great.

The additional absent insurers would have destroyed diversity in the federal court action and the court ordered the matter to proceed in state court where all parties could be joined.[6]

There are cases, however, holding that other insurers are not necessary and indispensable parties. For example, in *National Sur. Corp. v. Sangamo Weston, Inc.*,[7] the court rejected the policyholder's assertion that joinder of two non-diverse carriers was required under Fed. R. Civ. P. 19. The policyholder attempted to defeat federal jurisdiction by claiming that the indispensability of the omitted carriers would compel dismissal of the case. The court held that the omitted carriers were not necessary or indispensable to the action since the present parties could obtain "complete relief" and "disposition of the action" would neither "impair the absent parties' interests" nor "subject a present party to inconsistent obligations".[8]

It is also possible that if high level excess carriers are included in a coverage action, they may seek to dismiss the action as to them for lack of a justifiable controversy. Carriers that have made such motions have typically argued that the policyholder had not yet exhausted its underlying insurance nor made an actual demand for coverage upon the excess carrier. Most courts, however, have concluded that where the combined damages sought in all underlying claims are of sufficient magnitude potentially to require coverage from an excess carrier, there is a justifiable controversy between the policyholder and the excess carrier sufficient to maintain a declaratory judgment action against the excess carrier.[9] For example, in *Aetna Casualty and Sur. Co. v. Morton Thiokol, Inc.*, the court observed that "the practical effect of letting [excess insurers] out of this case. . . would be to force the institution of new proceedings every time a new level of coverage [was] implicated."[10]

The fact that underlying limits have not been exhausted does not preclude proceeding against an excess carrier in a declaratory judgment action.[11] Indeed, excess insurers have, on occasion, asserted that they are proper parties to such actions.[12] Finally, the fact that many excess policies are following form policies means that a declaration interpreting the underlying coverage could have an impact on the excess carriers' rights.

### Ancillary Jurisdiction

A party faced with compulsory joinder might argue that adding a non-diverse party would not destroy diversity jurisdiction under the ancillary jurisdiction principles of Rule 13(h) of the Federal Rules of Civil Procedure. Rule 13(h) states that "persons other than those made parties to the original action may be made parties to a counter-claim or cross claim in accordance with the provisions of Rules 19 and 20," regarding joinder of parties. It would be improper, however, to use Rule 13(h) to circumvent the requirements of diversity jurisdiction. Rule 82 states that "these rules shall not be construed to extend or limit the jurisdiction of the United States District Courts or the venue of actions therein." *Owen Equip. & Erection Co. v. Kroger*.[13]

The Advisory Committee, in its notes on the 1966 amendment of Rule 13, stated that "the amendment of Rule 13(h). . .does not attempt to regulate Federal jurisdiction or venue." While the Advisory Committee did note the possible application of ancillary jurisdiction in certain circumstances, the Supreme Court subsequently made it clear that ancillary jurisdiction may not be used to create federal jurisdiction. In *Owen, supra*, the Court reversed a court of appeals' decision permitting assertion of a claim against a non-diverse third-party defendant pursuant to ancillary jurisdiction. The court held that "neither the convenience of litigants nor considerations of judicial economy can suffice to justify extension of the doctrine of ancillary jurisdiction to a plaintiff's cause of action against a citizen of the same state in a diversity case." Recent majority case law supports this position.[14] Most cases holding otherwise were decided before the Supreme Court case of *Owens*.[15]

The analysis is similar when a non-diverse party seeks to intervene. A party may intervene as of right under Rule 24(a) (2) of the Federal Rules of Civil Procedure if it has an interest in the action, disposition of the action may impair its ability to protect its interest, and that interest is not adequately represented by the existing parties. Permissive intervention is allowed when a party's claim and the main action have a question of law or fact in common.[16] Policyholders arguing that non-diverse insurers are indispensable need not acknowledge that such insurers may intervene as of right without regard to diversity jurisdiction requirements. A non-diverse party may normally intervene as of right without establishing independent jurisdictional grounds.[17] In contrast, a party seeking permissive intervention must establish independent jurisdictional grounds.[18]

Importantly, however, an indispensable party may not intervene as of right and overcome lack of diversity through ancillary jurisdiction.[19] Therefore, non-diverse insurers, if considered necessary and indispensable, cannot become parties to a federal suit based on diversity either through joinder or intervention because they cannot evade diversity jurisdiction requirements under the guise of ancillary jurisdiction.

### Joinder Of Claimants

A few jurisdictions, Pennsylvania being the most notable one, require that an underlying claimant is a necessary and indispensable party in a policyholder's suit for coverage against its carriers. *Vale Chem. Co. v. Hartford Accident and Indem. Co.*[20] This holding was based on the Pennsylvania Declaratory Judgment Act, which requires that:

> all persons shall be made parties who have or claim any interest which would be affected by the declaration, and no declaration shall prejudice the rights of persons not a party to the proceeding.[21]

The court concluded that all underlying claimants against the policyholder whose claims were the subject of the coverage dispute were parties whose joinder was required by the Declaratory Judgment Act. The irony is that the court vacated judgments in favor of coverage which in no way could have prejudiced the rights of claimants against the policyholder.[22]

For all concerned, the rule stated in *Vale* is not the majority rule. For example, in *Monsanto Co. v. Aetna Cas. & Sur. Co.*[23], the court denied the carriers' motion to dismiss, holding that joinder of the underlying claimants was not required. In making its decision, the court found that the claimants' interests were adequately represented by the policyholder and that the claimants were so numerous, joinder would be "obstructive and probably defeat the ends of justice."[24] This ruling makes great practical sense. So long as the coverage action could not jeopardize an underlying claimant's ability to recover the full extent of his judgment or settlement, the underlying claimant should not be considered a necessary or an indispensable party.

Obviously a dismissal for failure to join an underlying claimant can, in particular circumstances, serve the short-term tactical needs of either a policyholder or an insurer if it would result in a change of forum for the coverage dispute. However, in hazardous waste coverage litigation or other toxic tort coverage litigation involving hundreds, if not thousands, of claimants, it serves no purpose to burden the coverage litigation by requiring the joinder of the underlying claimants. Any short-term tactical advantage one might gain would be far outweighed by the addition of hundreds of claimants with objectives potentially adverse to carriers and policyholders alike.

## Forum Selection Issues

### Personal Jurisdiction

Once the threshold question of whom to sue has been decided, the question of where to sue must be addressed. The obvious first problem is whether the policyholder can obtain personal jurisdiction over each of the potential defendants. Typically, this should not be a problem with most insurance companies. All of the major carriers and most other carriers are licensed to do business and, in fact, do business in virtually every state. Thus, most carriers have sufficient continuous and substantial contacts with most jurisdictions to support the exercise of general jurisdiction.

Even where a carrier's contacts are not sufficiently continuous and substantial to support general jurisdiction, this may be overcome by a "consent-to-suit" clause in the policy. For example, the policies issued by London syndicates and companies often contain "consent-to-suit" clauses pursuant to which the carrier consents to jurisdiction in any court in the United States selected by the policyholder.

In a few instances, however, a small carrier that does business on a limited geographic basis may claim that it is not subject to personal jurisdiction in a particular state because it has no continuous or systematic contacts with that state. In that instance, a policyholder should be able to establish jurisdiction by demonstrating that the cause of action on the insurance contract arises out of the carrier's contact with the jurisdiction.

Consider, for example, a carrier that sold a policy to a chemical company that, at the time, had substantial operations or facilities in the forum state. Those facilities were covered under the policy against third-party bodily injury and property damage claims. If the claim for which the chemical company seeks coverage arose out of the operation of the facilities in the forum state, the carrier should be subject to personal jurisdiction in that state. Indeed, courts have even upheld the exercise of personal jurisdiction in circumstances involving far less contact with the state.

For example, in *Eli Lilly & Co. v. Home Ins. Co.*[25], the court found that a carrier that sold insurance to a manufacturer doing business on a nationwide basis would be subject to personal jurisdiction in forum where the manufacturer's product had been sold to consumers. The court concluded that the excess carriers in that action who disputed jurisdiction knew that Eli Lilly distributed products nationwide, that it was likely to be sued in any jurisdiction in the country, and that if it were sued, the carriers were likely to be impleaded.

In short, a carrier that contracts to provide insurance coverage to a policyholder doing business in numerous forums should anticipate being sued for coverage in all those forums.[26] If *Eli Lilly* is correct, as most practitioners believe to be the case, it would be the rare situation where a carrier was not subject to personal jurisdiction.

### Federal v. State Court

The next issue to be resolved is whether to proceed in state or federal court. Obviously, the question here is whether there is complete diversity of citizenship to support diversity jurisdiction in a federal court under 28 U.S.C. § 1332. If there is complete diversity, the action can be commenced in federal court or, if commenced in state court, can be removed to federal court under 28 U.S.C. § 1441(c). On a theoretical basis, the choice between state or federal court should not be outcome-determinative since a federal court is required to apply the same law as a state court in the same jurisdiction.[27] However, in practice, litigants frequently perceive substantive differences between state and federal courts in the application of state law, particularly when the law is unsettled and there are conflicting decisions.

### Removal

Even if there is not complete diversity of citizenship and the action is filed in state court, a diverse carrier may attempt to remove that part of the action concerning coverage under its policies to federal court under 28 U.S.C. § 1441(c), arguing that the policyholder's cause of action against each carrier is "separate and independent." This issue involves consideration of virtually the same considerations concerning the proper joinder of parties. Since more than one carrier may be obligated to defend and indemnify an insured with respect to a given claim, the policyholder's claims for coverage against each carrier are interrelated. As the court reasoned in *Sequa Corp. v. Aetna Cas. and Sur. Co.*,[28] "Fine distinctions between primary and excess carriers, or the times during which insurance policies were in effect, do not suffice to create a 'separate and independent' cause of action".[29]

### Forum Non Conveniens

Whether a suit proceeds in state or federal court, a plaintiff must be ready to address the issue of *forum non conveniens* early in the litigation. As a general proposition, a plaintiff's choice of forum will be upheld unless the defendant shows that the plaintiff's choice is "manifestly inappropriate."[30]

In determining whether a plaintiff's choice of forum is manifestly inappropriate, courts will evaluate such factors as:
- the relative ease of access to sources of proof;
- the availability of compulsory process for obtaining attendance of unwilling witnesses and the cost of obtaining the attendance of willing witnesses;
- the burden imposed on the courts and jurors;
- the need to apply non-forum law; and
- the availability of a more appropriate alternative forum.[31]

These considerations must be balanced by countervailing policy objectives of avoiding piecemeal litigation, avoiding inconsistent and conflicting determinations, avoiding wasteful duplication, and conserving judicial resources.

While these factors raise essentially objective considerations, parties frequently move to dismiss on *forum non conveniens* grounds, motivated more by perceived disadvantages in forum law than by considerations of convenience. In an action involving 12 to 45 carriers concerning coverage for more than 50 hazardous waste sites located in 15 states, there will be no one forum that will not cause some inconvenience to the parties, witnesses or the courts. The parties, their documents and their witnesses will be located in many states. In addition, non-party documents and witnesses, including those relevant to specific sites, also will be located in many states. This stems not only from the fact that the sites are located in many states, but from the fact that the parties are likely to be headquartered in numerous states across the country, including jurisdictions where no sites are located.

Under such circumstances, policyholders should be given substantial latitude in choosing a forum for several reasons. *First*, whether the policyholder is the plaintiff or the defendant in the action, the policyholder bears the initial burden of establishing that a claim is covered. If the policyholder would experience inconvenience however it proceeds due to the fact that it has claims pending against it in numerous jurisdictions, it should be given a fair degree of latitude in determining how best to pursue its coverage. *Second*, any *forum non conveniens* ruling should be aimed at protecting against delay in the resolution of coverage disputes. The status quo favors carriers because they are allowed to retain the money that might be due their policyholders pending the outcome of coverage disputes. Thus, any delay or inconvenience experienced in the litigation will generally serve to delay the day of reckoning for carriers. A policyholder is in the best position to determine what approach would best facilitate resolution of the dispute. *Third*, the general rule that close calls should be made in favor of the policyholder should apply with equal force here.

In *Union Carbide Corp. v. Aetna Cas. & Sur. Co.*,[32] the Supreme Court of Connecticut affirmed the dismissal of a single Connecticut coverage action, finding eight alternative site-specific forums more appropriate. The court, basing its decision on the doctrine of *forum non conveniens*, considered several factors in reaching its conclusion. The court found that none of the toxic waste sites were located in Connecticut; the plaintiffs and several carriers were content in having the litigation proceed in other jurisdictions; witnesses, local fact finders and documentary evidence would be more accessible in the states where the site was located; and a single action litigating all issues would place a substantial burden on the Connecticut court system.[33]

Clearly, the prospects of simultaneously litigating the same coverage issues in several parallel cases is daunting. In many cases, such an approach would be less convenient and far more costly for policyholders. It would require the policyholder to retain coverage counsel in every jurisdiction in which claims have arisen and to coordinate and manage parallel litigation proceeding simultaneously in numerous jurisdictions. Some policyholders may be situated to take on this burden and may indeed choose to do so by initiating several suits in various forums where sites are located. However, no policy-holder should be **forced** to carry this burden.

Indeed, in many cases, courts have held that a comprehensive approach is the most appropriate one. In *E.I. du Pont de Nemours & Co. v. Admiral Ins. Co.*,[34] the Delaware Superior Court upheld Dupont's choice of forum for a declaratory judgment action involving coverage for actions arising from contamination sites around the country. The court noted that "a great majority of courts presented with insurance coverage actions involving multiple sites and states have favored adjudicating these actions comprehensively."[35] The court went on to note that "In deciding whether to comprehensively adjudicate a case "the most significant factor — and ultimately the dispositive one — is the courts responsibility to discourage duplicative and piecemeal litigation."[36]

Similarly, in *Westinghouse Elec. Corp. v. Liberty Mut. Ins. Co.*,[37] the Appellate Court, reversing the trial court, ruled in favor of a single comprehensive coverage action. In holding that the doctrine of *forum non conveniens* was inapplicable, the Appellate Court expressly rejected the rationale that a single suit concerning all sites was "manifestly inappropriate" and that multiple adjudication throughout the country was more convenient. The court further found that the burden of handling the entire coverage dispute for all sites was not sufficient, in itself, to require dismissal of all out-of-state sites from the action. The court likewise reversed the holding in the companion case, *SCM Corp. v. Lumbermens Mut. Cas. Co.*,[38] in which the non-New Jersey sites had been dismissed.[39]

Other courts have handled such cases in a comprehensive manner when there were no motions to dismiss.[40] It is also worth noting that many insurance companies have commenced declaratory judgment actions which relate to numerous sites in various states.[41]

### The Recurring Coverage Issues and Choice of Forum

In the typical coverage action, issues common to all claims are likely to predominate. A review of recent coverage decisions reveals at least ten major issues that typically arise in coverage disputes. These are:
- the trigger and scope of coverage;
- the duty to defend;
- coverage for equitable relief claims;

- the definition of "property damage;"
- the meaning and application of the expected or intended language;
- the number of occurrences involved;
- the meaning and application of pollution exclusions;
- the meaning and application of owned-property exclusions;
- the fact and effect of an insured's non-disclosure of material risks in applying for insurance; and
- compliance with notice requirements.

The facts needed to resolve these and other coverage issues generally fall into three main categories:
- those pertaining to the intent and meaning of disputed policy provisions;
- those pertaining to the carriers' application of their policies to similar claims of other policyholders; and
- those pertaining to the specific claims for which the policyholder seeks coverage, including facts concerning the policyholder's operations and conduct relating to specific sites.

All of the major issues highlighted above would require an investigation of facts falling within the first two categories identified above. All of the issues would require a court to construe the policies for all claims before any application to specific claims would be possible: Many of these issues such as coverage for equitable relief claims, or the definition of property damage — would require little or no site-specific factual inquiry.

Resolution of such issues turns largely on facts concerning the placement of the insurance, the intent of the drafters of the standard language found in the policies, and the parties' processing and handling of claims. In many instances, the most important witnesses will be insurance company and industry witnesses. The same core body of facts would be at issue with respect to all sites. While some issues may involve site-specific factual inquiries, they too would involve consideration of the mutual intent, if any, of the parties and the intent of the drafters.

Requiring policyholders to pursue discovery of the same facts from the same documents and witnesses in numerous coverage cases pending in jurisdictions across the country would be more burdensome and expensive than doing so in one comprehensive action.

Similarly, it would be less convenient and more costly for many, if not most, witnesses, particularly those of the parties, who would be required to appear for deposition and, perhaps, for trial testimony to address repeatedly the same questions in many coverage cases rather than in one comprehensive action. The convenience of such witnesses would be best served by addressing coverage issues in a single, comprehensive fashion, even if this requires some of them to travel to a more distant forum. As several courts have observed, such inconvenience is to be expected by corporations doing business on a national basis. Moreover, such inconvenience is minimized by modern travel, videotape depositions and the like.[42]

Requiring coverage litigation to proceed in each jurisdiction in which sites are located or claims arise would certainly be more burdensome for courts across the country and for jurors. In the aggregate, fragmented coverage litigation would involve more courts, more jurors, and more court time than would be involved if coverage disputes concerning large numbers of virtually identical or similar claims were addressed in comprehensive actions. It is highly unlikely that the burden on any one court would be significantly less if it is allowed to address coverage only for claims arising within its jurisdiction. A case limited to forum sites would usually involve the same number of parties, the same number of legal issues and the same discovery of common factual issues as it would if sites from other jurisdictions were included.

On the other hand, it is quite likely that a court's burden would be increased by the need to coordinate the case before it with parallel litigation proceeding simultaneously in numerous other jurisdictions. As the parties simultaneously seek to conduct discovery on the same issues, the court would be required to resolve problems arising from, differences among the procedural and attorney/client privilege rules of various jurisdictions and conflicts in scheduling.

Significantly, what makes these cases large and seemingly difficult for courts to manage is not the numerous claims for which coverage is sought, but the number of parties. *In re Asbestos Insurance Cases*,[43] is often cited as a prime example of a "mega" case, a case so large, a special courtroom was required to accommodate all the lawyers for trial.[44] *In re Asbestos* is indeed a large case, but not because it addresses coverage for tens of thousands of asbestos-related bodily injury claims and for hundreds of asbestos-related property damage claims arising both in and outside of California. It is large because it involves five policyholders and 65 insurance companies. It is the number of parties, not the number of claims for which coverage is sought, that required an unusual amount of court involvement in structuring and controlling discovery and the construction of a special courtroom for trial. It is the number of parties and the scope of the common legal issues, not the number of underlying claims or the need for any claim-by-claim inquiry that has resulted in a lengthy trial. Indeed, none of the trial has been devoted to claim specific issues, and less than 15 percent of the trial has been devoted to issues concerning the generic nature of the underlying claims and the conduct of the policyholders that gave rise to such claims.

Similarly, *Shell Oil Co. v. Acc. and Cas. Ins. Co. of Winterthur*,[45] was an unusually large case despite the fact that it addresses coverage for only two hazardous waste sites, the Rocky Mountain Arsenal in Colorado and one California site. Like *In re Asbestos Insurance Coverage Cases*, the case was large because of the number of parties involved — over a hundred — not the number of underlying claims for which coverage is sought.

Thus, the assumption that a court's burden would be substantially reduced if it were relieved of the necessity of addressing claims arising outside its jurisdiction is unfounded. It would still have to address issues common to all claims. Moreover, the court's burden with respect to resolving those issues would be no less because it had fewer sites to address. In fact, it is quite possible that the burden on individual courts would be increased, rather than decreased, because policyholders would be forced to file coverage actions in every jurisdiction where it has sites.

Requiring policyholders to pursue coverage in the jurisdiction where a claim arises could seriously deter policyholders from pursuing the full extent of their contractual rights. The time, effort, and expense involved in filing separate coverage suits in every state in which an underlying hazardous waste or toxic tort claim has been made against a company may well exceed the possible benefit of doing so. In particular, this would be the case where individual claims in some jurisdictions are too small in value to warrant the cost of prosecuting a separate coverage action.

In addition, the fragmentation of coverage litigation would deter comprehensive settlements between policyholders and their carriers and would ultimately result in more litigation. Losing parties in one case may feel free to litigate the same coverage issues in other jurisdictions where other sites are located. As a result, either policyhold-ers or insurance companies would have less incentive to attempt to resolve their differences on a nationwide basis.

## Choice of Law

A court which denies a motion for *forum non conveniens* and there-by agrees to adjudicate an entire comprehensive coverage case in one proceeding must then concentrate on efficient resolution of the dispute. One of the central questions which must be addressed by the court is what state's substantive law will be applied. As case law regarding coverage questions has developed, and different judicial interpretations of identical coverage issues have emerged, choice of law has become an increasingly important issue. Efficient and effec-tive management of these cases requires that the court resolve the choice of law question relatively early in the proceedings and sug-gests that the court apply the same substantive law to all of the poli-cies.[46]

In determining what law to apply to a dispute, both state courts and federal courts sitting in diversity will apply the choice of law rules of the forum state.[47] State choice of law rules are far from con-sistent, but most take into account the *Restatement (Second) of Con-flicts of Law* (1971) (hereinafter *Restatement*) general considerations applicable to choice of law analysis which include: the interests of the various states in applying its law to the controversy, the interest in protecting the rational expectations of the parties, and the need for certainty, predictability and judicial economy.[48]

To best accommodate these general interests within the context of an insurance coverage case, courts have traditionally taken one of three approaches. Some courts have looked to a single factor such as where the policy was negotiated or signed (*lex loci contractus*) or to the principle location of the risk covered by the policy[49] and have routinely applied the law of the state or states which meets the sin-gle factor at issue.[50] The primary advantage of single-factored ap-proaches is their judicial economy. Under such approaches the choice of law inquiry is typically reduced to a factual determination of the state which relates to the single factor.

Other states, following **Restatement**, have chosen to apply a multi-factored test which takes into account a variety of contacts between various states and the dispute and eventually determines which state has the "most significant relationship" to the dispute.[51] The advantage of a multi-factored approach is that it considers the interests of the respective states in applying their own law to the controversy.

A third approach, which is probably the majority approach, is to consider both the single- and multi-factored approaches as potential ways of achieving the underlying objectives of *Restatement*.[52] The main advantage of this approach is the flexibility it gives courts to reject the application of either choice of law approach when application would conflict with the general objectives of choice of law determinations.

Such flexibility can be essential within the context of a large comprehensive coverage case where a mechanical application of either a single- or a multi-factored test will often conflict with the objectives of *Restatement* § 6 and may preclude efficient and effective resolution of these disputes. For example, if the court applies a single-factored approach such as *lex loci contractus* when the scores of policies were entered into with different carriers throughout the country, the court will be required to apply the substantive laws of multiple states to the same dispute. Under such an approach, the court would be required to conduct an analysis of the substantive law of each state in which a contract was formed and then apply these various bodies of law to scores of policies with identical standard form language in the context of similar if not identical factual situations. The burden such an approach would place on the judicial system is clear. It is also clear that such an approach is not necessary to meet the justified expectations of any of the parties. The carriers and policyholders involved in these suits are national or international corporations doing business in many if not every state in the country. The policies at issue may have been purchased and executed in many different states, but were intended to provide a consistent package of insurance against liability arising anywhere in the country based on standard form insuring language drafted by the insurance industry. Under these circumstances, a policyholder's right to coverage for identical claims under different policies should not depend on where the policy was entered into.

Courts faced with traditional choice of law approaches which would require the application of a large number of state's laws to an insurance coverage case may find it is wiser to forego application of the approach than to apply a multitude of conflicting state laws. This was the conclusion of the federal district court in *National Starch & Chem. Co. v. Great American Ins. Co.*[53] There the court considered the decision in *Leksi Inc. v. Fed. Ins. Co.*,[54] which instructed that the court apply the law of the state where the hazardous material ultimately comes to rest and causes contamination.. The court noted that in *Leksi* all of the waste sites were located in one state, while in *National Starch* there were waste sites located in twelve states. Thus, applying the *Leksi* test to the controversy would require the court to apply the laws of twelve states. The court refused to apply *Leksi* this way and held that the reasonable expectations of the parties was the controlling factor in interpreting insurance contracts, and application of twelve different bodies of law would run counter to their reasonable expectation that the policies would be interpreted uniformly regardless of where a claim arises.

A large majority of courts addressing comprehensive coverage cases have agreed that applying more than one state's law to the same dispute would run counter to the purpose of coordinating these hearings in one forum. In *In re Asbestos Insurance Coverage Cases*,[55] the court, in determining to apply forum law, stressed the importance of "arriving at a decision which will be universally applicable to the insurance policies at issue," particularly where "the large number and wide range of contracting parties and their activities make a single determination. . . of the place where[the contract] was made difficult, if not impossible."[56] Similarly, in *W.R. Grace & Co. v. Hartford Acc. and Indem. Co.*,[57] the Massachusetts Supreme Court stated that "to obtain uniform and practical coverage nationwide for a multi-state corporation such as Grace, it is desirable that the law of one state govern the interpretation of all Grace's comprehensive general liability insurance policies."[58]

A court, choosing to apply one state's law to all policies, must then determine which state's law should be applied. At this point the court may be inclined to apply the *Restatement* significant inter-

est test to determine whether to apply forum law or the law of another state.[59] The *Restatement* significant interest approach is a multi-factored one, requiring that the court address and "evaluate according to their relative importance," five types of contacts, namely:
- The place of contracting;
- The place of negotiation of the contract;
- The place of performance;
- The location or the subject matter of the contract; and
- The domicile, residence, nationality, place of incorporation, and place of business of the parties.

This test has been applied by a few courts addressing less complex environmental coverage claims. In *Marley-Wylain*,[60] for example, the court applied this test in a case involving one policyholder and seven carriers. The case concerned coverage for 19 suits in three states stemming from exposure to asbestos contained in the furnaces and boilers manufactured by the policyholder. Consideration of the five types of contacts indicated that thirteen states had some contact with the dispute; six states were implicated by more than one factor. The court then had to weigh the various state interests against one another "according to their relative importance." After a 20-page discussion, the court applied forum law because the policyholder's only manufacturing facility was located in the forum and "under the circumstances of (this) case, the location of the subject matter of the contract has dominant significance."[61] The chosen contact was the only factor which implicated the law of only one state.

Extrapolating from this case to a more comprehensive case involving scores of carriers and hundreds of policies, it is easy to see that application of a multi-factored test would be difficult if not impossible. Such an approach would require the parties to submit and the court to review an enormous file of information including: the history of the negotiation and signing of hundreds of policies; the risk which the parties agreed would be covered by the policies; and, the domicile, residence, nationality, place of incorporation, and place of business of the policyholder and the multitude of carriers involved in the suit. The result of this exercise will almost certainly be that a large number of states will have contact with the dispute but no one state will clearly have the 'most significant contact' with the dispute. In such a case, where the forum has significant contacts with the dispute, the court's choice of any law besides the forum's is likely to be seen as arbitrary and will almost inevitably result in appeals.

One alternative available to courts facing this difficult and inconclusive analysis is to apply forum law unless one of the parties can demonstrate that another forum has an overriding interest in applying its own law to the controversy which would be prejudiced by the application of forum law. Assuming that the forum state has sufficient contact with the dispute, as is typically the case, adopting this rule would greatly simplify the choice of law dimension of comprehensive coverage suits. Courts can simply apply forum law unless a party can convince the court that it is unfair to do so under the circumstances of the dispute. This approach would hurdle the false conflicts problem and avoid needless investigation into the interests of numerous states and their contacts with the parties where the application of forum law would not impair the public policy of the other states. It would also allow courts to apply familiar forum law in the majority of these cases where the forum has some interest in the case and no one other state has clearly a more substantial interest.

This has been the approach taken by courts in California. For example, in *In re Asbestos*,[62] the court applied forum law without a lengthy balancing of other states' interests, although Pennsylvania, Maryland, and England were also alleged as places of contracting and virtually every state had an interest in the underlying suits.[63] The court reasoned that "normally, even in cases involving foreign elements, the court should be expected, as a matter of course, to apply the decision found in the law of the forum."[64] The court could not perceive of "such an overriding interest on behalf of other states or governments" to warrant application of their law, and so applied forum law.[65]

The Ninth Circuit took a similar approach in *Industrial Indem. Ins. Co. v. United States*.[66] The court applied Idaho law (the law of the state where the lower court sat) to a case involving insured property located in six different states that was damaged when the Teton Dam collapsed. The court reasoned that "the contacts here were so diverse that choosing any other state's law would have to be random."[67]

As these and many other courts have recognized the comprehensive coverage cases involving contacts with a large number of states pose unique challenges to the judicial system which require innovative solutions. Choosing to apply one law to the entire dispute and applying forum law unless another state is shown to have a more substantial interest in the dispute may require that courts forego applying some of the more specific choice of law tests such as *lex loci contractus*, and the tests of *Restatement* §§ 188(2) and 193. Such an approach, however, may often be the only way the court can achieve the underlying objectives expressed in *Restatement* § 6, and can resolve the choice of law early and efficiently in the context of a comprehensive coverage suit.

## Certification to State Court

Even if an action ends up in federal court, obtaining a state court ruling on an important question of law in the case is still possible. A policyholder litigating in federal court may want to certify a specific question of law to the highest court of the state whose law controls the case. In arguing certification to the sitting federal court, a policyholder should argue that the relevant state law is unsettled, that the issue concerns a matter of important state policy, and that the state court is in the best position to rule on the issue. For example, some insureds have sought a state court ruling on whether funds spent on settlement and/or cleanup constitute damages. A recent example is *3M v. Travelers*,[68] in which 3M asked the federal court sitting in Minnesota to certify that precise question to the Minnesota Supreme Court. The carriers opposed certification, arguing that the Eighth Circuit had decided the issue in *Continental Ins. Co. v. Northeastern Pharmaceutical and Chem. Co. (NEPPACO)*. In *NEPPACO*,[69] the Eighth Circuit held that under Missouri law, cleanup costs do not constitute damages. The carriers in 3M argued that Minnesota and Missouri insurance law principles are substantially the same, and that because the Eighth Circuit had already ruled on the issue, certification was not necessary.

3M argued that the function of a federal court is not to choose the rule which it might follow were the question one of federal law, but rather to adopt the rule which it believes the state court would apply.[70] Since *NEPPACO* had been decided under Missouri law, not Minnesota law, and Minnesota courts had not addressed the issue, the need to make such a prediction would be obviated if the question were certified to the Minnesota Supreme Court, as the district court concluded.

## Environmental
## Risk Management

The Eleventh Circuit recently certified to the Georgia Supreme Court the issue of whether "the pollution exclusion bars coverage for polluting discharges which take place over an extended period."[71] The court certified the matter because it involved an "important issue of Georgia law. . .for which there is no clear precedent in the decisions of the courts of Georgia." Many other federal courts have also certified insurance issues to state courts.[72]

Certification can be an effective and efficient method by which litigants in federal court can narrow the issues and have state courts rule on state law issues.[73]

## Case Management Orders

A case management order (CMO) can be an effective litigation tool for policyholders facing numerous opposing parties. Three recent examples of CMO's entered in environmental insurance coverage actions are *Northrop Corp. v. Evanston Ins. Co.*,[74] *Monsanto Co., v. Aetna Cas. & Sur. Co.*,[75] and *North American Philips Corp. v. Aetna Cas. and Sur. Co.*[76] These CMO's address many of the issues that policyholders will confront.

First, a CMO can help streamline dealings with opposing counsel by requiring the carriers, among other things, to form a discovery, or steering committee to coordinate discovery. This reduces the cost of litigation and eases the burden of having to communicate with a potentially large number of parties on every issue. The insurers should also be required to file one common set of discovery orders and file additional discovery only as it is unique to that defendant. In addition, the parties should agree upon establishing a joint repository or one repository for the policyholder and one for all insurers, establishing procedures for the carriers to inspect and copy documents from a single master set of documents produced by the policyholder, procedures for each defendant to produce one master set of documents, procedures for prenumbering documents to identify the producing entity, and procedures for taking depositions, including advance notice of any documents to be used in a deposition.

A CMO can also set forth reasonable timetables for discovery which allow the policyholder to conduct discovery against the carriers and respond to the carriers' discovery in an effective and orderly fashion. The time necessary to respond to discovery will obviously vary depending upon the number of parties and sites involved in the claim, but a policyholder should insist on scheduling certain matters in phases. For instance, the policyholders should make sure that the CMO allows enough time for it to respond to all initial discovery before supplemental discovery is served. The order should also set out reasonable schedules for objecting to discovery and having meetings to resolve discovery disputes before filing discovery-related motions with the court. In addition, provisions can be made for appointing a master to resolve discovery disputes.

A policyholder faced with the short-term burden of responding to potentially voluminous discovery should also get the carrier to agree that depositions are not to be scheduled during the time given for responding to initial interrogatories and document requests. A deposition schedule will also prevent the insurers from burdening the policyholder by attempting to notice numerous depositions in a short period of time.

Similarly, the policyholder should insist that no dispositive motions may be filed until a substantial part of the discovery is concluded. It could prove burdensome for a policyholder to have to answer discovery and respond to a motion for summary judgment at the same time. The parties may also want to establish longer response times for partial summary judgment and summary judgment motions than for non-dispositive motions.

Scheduling dispositive motions after substantial discovery and many depositions have occurred has another advantage. Policyholders will frequently want to rely on evidence of the insurance industry's intent and/or practice to defeat motions for partial summary judgment or summary judgment concerning the meaning of certain policy terms. Effective scheduling in a CMO can give policyholders the opportunity to conduct thorough discovery on these issues before having to respond to such a dispositive motion.

Next, the carriers should not be allowed to cloak all communications among members of the defense committee and between themselves and non testimonial experts or consultants as privileged. It is perfectly reasonable for a policyholder to agree that any communication having a privilege does not automatically waive that privilege merely because it was exchanged among defense committee members. It is quite another thing, however, to agree that all communications become privileged merely because they are exchanged among defense committee members. A document otherwise not privileged does not gain privileged status merely because one defendant reveals it to another defendant.

The carriers will typically want the case management order to contain provisions for some sort of protective order to be submitted to the court. Policyholders, however, should not be too quick to agree to protective orders. It is advantageous for policyholders to have full disclosure of insurer documents concerning other policyholders in other cases.[77] Such information may reveal how insurers have handled similar claims and interpreted similar policy language in other cases.[78] By not having a protective order, a policyholder may help other policyholders and perhaps itself in future litigation.

The carriers, on the other hand, prefer to make it as difficult as possible for policyholders to get documents that have been helpful to policyholders in other cases. The insurers want each policyholder to start from scratch in discovering helpful documents.[79] A protective order helps insurers achieve that goal.

## Summary and Future Trends

A policyholder's decision to pursue coverage for all pending claims in a comprehensive action should not be disturbed under *forum non conveniens* doctrine simply because the action addresses out-of-state sites. Indeed, a comprehensive action serves important objectives of the doctrine in at least five ways:

- **First**, it ensures that a policyholder obtains consistent and complete relief. Parallel cases proceeding simultaneously risk the possibility that the policyholder will obtain inconsistent and incomplete relief. Inconsistent determinations result not only from different jurisdictions viewing the law differently, but also from the inability to bind all parties to a single approach, regardless of what that approach is.
- **Second**, a comprehensive action provides the policyholder the ability to control discovery in an orderly manner and to avoid duplication. A multi-state approach provides excessive opportunity to lawyers who want to use discovery as a litigating device to delay and obfuscate. In a comprehensive

case, a judge is more likely to focus on such conduct and to control discovery behavior strictly.

- **Third**, a comprehensive action eliminates the incentives to accelerate or delay proceedings on different issues in different jurisdictions. A multi-state approach multiplies the prospects for gamesmanship and posturing.
- **Fourth**, the cost of a comprehensive case is far less than the cost of 15 parallel cases, each of which would involve the same number of parties. The elimination of lawyers alone substantially reduces costs.
- **Fifth**, a comprehensive action enables a policyholder to obtain coverage for all claims, including those that would not be worth pursuing in a one-site, single coverage action.

The only potential disadvantage of a comprehensive action is size. One can sympathize with judges who face the prospect of devoting all or a substantial portion of their time over several years to a single case, as judges have done in such cases as *In re Asbestos Ins. Coverage* and *Shell Oil Co. v. Acc. and Cas. Ins. Co. of Winterthur*[80] Unfortunately, there is no real solution to this problem. Well thought out case management orders will address some of the problem, but breaking down coverage disputes into 15 parallel litigations spread throughout the country would not sufficiently reduce the size of any one case to warrant the added costs. What would be left to be resolved in any one action would still constitute a very large case. If every company in the country that faces hazardous waste claims in numerous jurisdictions is required to litigate coverage in each jurisdiction in which the company is involved, the courts would see a rash of coverage cases the likes of which have never been seen. The end result might be a lawyer's full employment and retirement program, but we will all be worse off for it.

## About the Author

John E. **Heintz** joined the Washington, D.C. office of Popham, Haik in 1986 after nine years with Covington & Burling. He is a shareholder in the Washington office and heads up the firm's rapidly growing insurance law practice. Mr. Heintz is a seasoned litigator with extensive experience in insurance coverage disputes and other complex, multi-party litigation. Mr. Heintz is responsible for four major pieces of litigation concerning insurance coverage for liabilities arising out of Superfund and private actions relating to contamination at numerous hazardous waste sites. He has also been instrumental in developing a nationwide *amicus* effort by policyholders in coverage cases across the country. Mr. Heintz received his B.A. from Cornell University (1970), his M.P.A. from Princeton University (1974), and his J.D. from New York University (1977).

## Endnotes

1.   New York, New Jersey and other jurisdictions have similar joinder rules. *See. e.g.,* *New Jersey Court Rules*, 1969 R. 4:29-a(a); *N.Y. Civ. Prac. L. & R.* 1002.

2.   668 F. Supp. 394 (D.N.J. 1987).

3.   613 F. Supp. 1549 (D.N.J. 1985).

4.   *See, e.g., Continental Ins. Co. v. Northwestern Pharmaceuticals and Chemical Co.* 811 F.2d 1180 (8th Cir. 1987), *rev'd on other grounds on reh'g* 842 F.2d 977 (8th Cir), *cert. denied, Missouri v. Continental Ins. Co.*, U.S., 109 S. Ct. 66 (1988) (carriers providing coverage during the period of disposal are obligated to cover a claim); *ACandS, Inc. v. Aetna Cas. and Sur. Co.*, 764 F.2d 968 (3d Cir. 1985); *Sandoz, Inc. v. Employer's Liab. Ass. Corp.*, 554 F. Supp. 257 (D.N.J. 1983); *Abex Corp. v. Maryland Cas. Co.*, 790 F.2d 119 (D.C. Cir. 1986); *Keene Corp. v. Ins. Co. of North America*, 667 F.2d 1034 (D.C. Cir. 1981), *cert. denied*, 455 U.S. 1007 (1982); *Ins. Co. of North America v. Forty-Eight Insulations. Inc.*, 633 F.2d 1212 (6th Cir. 1980), *clarified*, 657 F.2d 814 (6th Cir.), *cert. denied,* 454 U.S. 1109 (1981); *Techallo Co. v. Reliance Ins. Co.*, 338 Pa. Super. 1, 487 A.2d 820 (1984); *Dayton Indep. School Dist. v. National Gypsum Co.*, 682 F. Supp. 1403 (E.D. Tex. 1988); *United States Fidelity and Guar. Co. v. Thomas Solvent Co.*, 683 F. Supp. 1139 (W.D. Mich. 1988); *Air Products and Chemicals. Inc. v. Hartford Accident and Indem. Co.*, 707 F. Supp. 762 (E.D. Pa. 1989); *General Refractories Co. v. Travelers Ins. Co.*, No. 88-2250, (E.D. Pa. Feb. 28, 1989), *reported Mealey's Litigation Reports — Insurance* (March 28, 1989). *See also Developments in the Law. Toxic Waste Litigation*, 99 Harv. L. Rev. 1458, 1481-83 (1986) (concluding that the so-called "continuous trigger" rule is the appropriate standard for hazardous waste contamination cases because it promotes efficient risk reduction).

5.  *Travelers Indem. Co. v. Richard E. Ritchie*, No. 87-5036 (D.N.J. Feb. 16, 1988), *reported in Mealey's Litigation Reports - Insurance E* (March 9, 1988).

6.  *Evergreen Park Nursing & Convalescent Home. Inc., v. American Equitable Assurance Co.*, 417 F.2d 1113 (7th Cir. 1969) (dismissing action because two carriers not joined were indispensable); *cf. The Chesapeake & Ohio Railway Co. v. Certain Underwriters of Lloyd's London and London Market Insurance Co.*, 716 F. Supp. 27 (D.D.C. 1989) (requiring dismissal because of indispensability of absent subsidiary which was named in the insured's policies).

7.  C.A. 8:88-3437-17 (D.S.C. August 11, 1989), *reported Mealey's Litigation Reports - Insurance G* (August 22, 1989).

8.  *See also, Highlands Ins. Co. v. Celotex Corp.*, No. 89-2258 (D.D.C. Nov. 29, 1989) *reported in* Mealey's Litigation Reports - Insurance E (Dec. 27, 1989); *Special Jet Services v. Federal Ins. Co.*, 83 F.R.D. 596 (W.D.Pa. 1979); *Casualty Indem. Exch. v. Village of Crete*, 731 F.2d 457 (7th Cir. 1984); *Brinco Mining. Ltd. v. Federal Insur. Co.*, 552 F. Supp. 1233 (D.D.C. 1989); *Carey-Canada, Inc., v. California Ins. Co., et. al.*, 1984 Fire & Cas. (CCH) 65 (D.D.C. 1984); *Mutual Boiler and Mach. Ins. Co. v. Reynolds Mut. Co.*, 352 F.2d 520 (5th Cir. 1965).

9.  *The Firestone Tire & Rubber Co. v. AIU Insurance Co.*, No. CV-89-01-0158 (Ohio Ct. C.P., Summit Co. 1989), *reported in Mealey's Litigation Reports — Insurance* (August 22, 1989) (rejecting excess insurers' motion to dismiss because "potential to exhaust the policies is all that is needed and it appears that the potential does exist").

10.  No. C-3348-86E, slip op. at 3 (N.J. Super. Ch. Div. Aug. 27, 1987).

11.  *See North American Philips Corp. v. Aetna Cas. and Sur. Co.*, No. 88C-JA-155, (Del. Super. Ct., Aug. 21, 1989) *reported in Mealey's Litigation Reports D* (Sept. 12, 1989); *Carey-Canada. Inc. v. California Union Ins. Co.*, No. 83-1106, slip op. at 2 (LEXIS) (D.D.C. April 17, 1984); *Eli Lilly & Co. v. The Home Ins. Co.*, No. 82-0669, slip op. at 3-4 (D.D.C. Sept. 30, 1982).

12.  *Lumbermens Mut. Cas. Co. v. Connecticut Bank*, No. B-84-213, slip op. at 5 (D. Conn. Sept. 30, 1985), 806 F.2d 411 (2d Cir. 1986).

13.  437 U.S. 365, 370 (1978).

14.  *See Rheem Mfg. Co. v. Maryland Casualty Co.*, No. 87 Civ. 1923 (S.D.N.Y. Feb. 7, 1989) (declining to apply "creative option" offered by carrier to join non-diverse excess carriers under ancillary jurisdiction); *Birmingham Fire Ins. Co. v. Winegardner & Hammons. Inc.*, 714 F.2d 548, 553 (5th Cir. 1983) (court refused to invoke ancillary jurisdiction to permit policyholder to bring claim against non-diverse carriers in federal court); *Acton Co. of Massachusetts v. Bachman Foods, Inc.*, 668 F.2d 76 (1st Cir. 1982) (non-diverse party could not be added under ancillary jurisdiction as way to avoid destroying court's diversity jurisdiction).

15.  *See, e.g., H. L. Peterson Co., v. Applewhite*, 383 F.2d 430 (5th Cir. 1967); *Albright v. Gates*, 362 F.2d 928 (9th Cir. 1966); *United Artists Corp.. v. Masterpiece Prods., Inc.*, 221 F.2d 213 (2d Cir. 1955); *Dairyland Ins. Co.. v. Hawkins*, 292 F. Supp. 947 (D. Iowa 1958); *Dunbar & Sullivan Dredging Co., v. John R. Jurgensen Co.*, 44 F.R.D. 467 (D. Ohio 1967), *aff'd on other grounds*, 396 F.2d 152 (6th Cir. 1968).

16. Fed. R. Civ. P. 24 (b)(2).

17. *Hardy-Latham v. Wellons*, 415 F.2d 674 (4th Cir. 1968) ("if intervention is as of right, no independent jurisdictional basis need be established").

18. *Francis v. Chamber of Commerce of United States*, 481 F.2d 192 (4th Cir. 1973) (party seeking permissive intervention must generally establish independent jurisdictional grounds); *Butcher & Singer. Inc. v. Kellam*, 623 F. Supp. 418 (D.Del. 1985); *National Union Fire Ins. Co. of Pittsburgh v. Continental Illinois Corp.*, 113 F.R.D. 532 (N.D. Ill. 1986). *But see Telefast, Inc., v. VU-TV. Inc.*, 591 F. Supp. 1368, 1370, n.1 (D.N.J. 1984) (permissive intervention of non-diverse, non-indispensable party does not deprive court of jurisdiction).

19. *See, e.g., New York State Ass. for Retarded Children. Inc. v. Carey*, 438 F. Supp. 440 (E.D.N.Y. 1977) (only difference between intervention as of right and joinder is which party initiates the addition of the new party, and holding "no ancillary jurisdiction over an indispensable party because an indispensable party should have been a party from the beginning"); *Butcher & Singer, supra; Ins. Co. of North America v. Blindauers Sheet Metal and Heating Co.*, 61 F.R.D. 323 (E.D. Wisc. 1973); *Burger King Corp. v. American Nat'l Bank and Trust Co of Chicago* 119 F.R.D. 672 (N.D. Ill. 1988) (indispensable party may not intervene if non-diverse).

20. 512 Pa. 290, 516 A.2d 684 (1986).

21. 42 Pa. C.S. § 7540(a).

22. *Federal Kemper Ins. Co. v. Rauscher*, 807 F.2d 345 (3rd Cir. 1986); *Carlsson v. Penn. Gen. Ins. Co.*, 417 Pa. 356, 207 A.2d 759 (1965); *Township of Pleasant v. Erie Ins. Exchange*, 22 Pa. Commw. 307, 348 A.2d 477 (1975).

23. No. 88 C-JA-118 (Del. Super. Ct., New Castle County, May 22, 1989), *reported in Mealey's Litigation Reports - Insurance D* (June 13, 1989).

24. *See also W.R. Grace & Co. v. Admiral Ins. Co.*, No. 87-6624 slip op. at 4 (Mass. Super. Suffolk Cty. Nov. 25, 1987) ("The presence of the underlying claimants is not required or necessary. Moreover, requiring their presence is dilatory, and would produce no beneficial results."); *In re Asbestos Insurance Coverage Cases*, Judicial Council No. 1072 (Ca. Super.), (denying a motion to intervene filed by a group of asbestos tort claimants).

25. 794 F.2d 710 (D.C. Cir.), *cert. denied, Falcon Ins. Co. v. Eli Lilly Co.*, 479 U.S. 1060 (1987).

26. *Hirsch v. Blue Cross-Blue Shield of Kansas City*, 800 F.2d 1474 (9th Cir. 1986).

27. *Erie v. Tompkins*, 304 U.S. 64 (1938).

28. No. 89-234-JRR, slip op. at B5 (D.Del. Jan. 18, 1990) reported in Mealey's Litigation Reports — Insurance B (Jan. 30, 1990).

29. Slip op. at B5, *see also SCM Corp. v. Lumbermens Mut. Cas. Co.*, Nos. 86-4672, 86-4673, slip op.(D.N.J. Feb. 1, 1988) (Court remanded the case to state court ruling that a diverse carrier cannot properly remove part of such a coverage action to federal court,

leaving behind the coverage dispute affecting non-diverse carriers.) *But see Sangamo Weston, Inc. v. National Surety Corp.*, C.A. 6:89-642-17 (D.S.C. August 11, 1989), *reported in Mealey's Litigation Reports-Insurance G* (August 22, 1989) (retaining jurisdiction over removed state action after original ground for removal was eliminated and consolidating action with pending federal suit).

30. *See, e.g., Amercoat Corp. v. Reagent Chem. and Research. Inc.*, 108 N.J. Super. 331, 261 A.2d 380 (App. Div. 1970).

31. *See, e.g., Gulf Oil Corp. v. Gilbert*, 330 U.S. 501, 509 (1947); *Rheem Manufacturing Co. v. National Union Fire Insurance Co.*, No. 190849 (Ca. Super., Riverside Co., May 9, 1989), *reported in Mealey's Litigation Reports — Insurance I* (May 23, 1989); *Islamic Republic of Iran v. Pahlavi*, 62 N.Y. 2d 474, 478 N.Y.S. 2d 597, 467 N.E. 2d 245 (1984), *cert. denied*, 469 U.S. 1108 (1985); *Great N. Ry. Co. v. Superior Court*, 12 Cal. App. 3d 105, 90 Cal. Rptr. 461 (1970), *cert. denied, Curtin v. Superior Court of California*, 401 U.S. 1013 (1971).

32. 212 Conn. 31 (Conn. 1989).

33. *See also Avnet Inc. v. Aetna Cas. and Sur. Co.*, 554 N.Y.S 2d 134. App. Div. 1990) (Upholding as "not an improvident exercise of discretion" a lower court's *forum non conveniens* dismissal of claims relating to out of state sites.); *Texas Eastern Transmission Corp. v. Fidelity & Cas. Co. of New York*, No. WO30685-87 (N.J. Super. Ct. Law Div. March 17, 1988) (case involving contamination at 99 sites in 16 states dismissed on *forum non conveniens* grounds because only 3 sites in New Jersey and minimal contacts between New Jersey and litigation).

34. No. 89C-AU-99 (Del. Super. Ct. Nov. 12, 1989) *reported in Mealey's Litigation Reports — Insurance C* (Nov. 28, 1989).

35. Slip op. at 12.

36. Slip op. at 13, citing *Travelers Indem. Co. v. Monsanto Co.*, 692 F. Supp. 90, 92 (D. Conn. 1988).

37. 233 N.J. Super. 463, 559 A.2d 435 (App. Div. 1989), *motion to appeal denied* (N.J. July 14, 1989), *reported in Mealey's Litigation Reports — Insurance* (July 25, 1989).

38. No. L-96187-87, (N.J. Super. Law Div., Union City, May 25, 1988).

39. *Id.* at 450 n.4. *See also, Monsanto Co. v. Aetna Cas. & Sur. Co.*, 559 A. 2d 1301 (Del. Super. 1988) (holding that comprehensive approach would avoid inconsistent determinations and better serve judicial economy in case involving 37 defendants, 44 sites in 18 states); *American Mfg. Mut. Ins. Co. v. Superior Ct. of Cal.*, No. 5005572 (Cal. Super. Ct. Santa Clara County, (June 22, 1988), (California Supreme Court let stand California Superior Court decision denying insurer's motion to dismiss environmental insurance coverage action involving 174 insurers and 46 waste sites in 22 states.); *United Technologies Corp. v. Liberty Mutual Ins. Co.*, No. SJC-S-5228 (Mass. June 11, 1990) *reported in Insurance Industry Litigation Reporter* at 9340 (June 20, 1990) (Massachusetts Supreme Court vacates *forum non conveniens* dismissal of case involving 70 sites in 20 states); *North American Philips Corp. v. Aetna Cas. & Sur. Co.*, No. 88C-JA-155 (Del. Super. Ct. Oct. 21, 1988) (retaining jurisdiction over claim involving 16 sites in 14 states); *Peabody Int'l Corp. v. Commercial Union Ins. Co.*, No. C-242-87, (N.J. Super. Ct. Ch. Div. Dec. 9, 1987) (court adjourned *forum non conveniens* motion and opted to conduct test discov-

ery for 3 of 23 sites involved in case before deciding forum issues); *Allied Signal, Inc. v. Abeille-Paix Reassurance.*, No. MRSL-226-88 (N.J. Super Ct. August 25, 1988) (court retained jurisdiction over case involving 177 insurance companies, 239 sites, and 31 states to decide and limit certain issues and to possibly send portions of case into appropriate forums at later date).

40. *See, e.g., Detrex Chem. Ind. v. Employers Ins. of Wausau*, 681 F. Supp. 438 (N.D. Ohio 1987) (seven sites in four states); *Employers Ins. of Wausau v. McGray-Edison Co.*, No. K 86-48, (W.D. Mich. Aug. 8, 1987) *reprinted in Mealey's Litigation Reports (Insurance)* at 4,932 (Sept. 8, 1987) (5 sites in 4 states).

41. *See, e.g., Travelers Indem. Co. v. Monsanto Co.,* , No. H88-34-PCD (D. Conn., Jan. 19, 1988) (44 sites); *Travelers Indem. Co. v. Allied Signal, Inc.*, D. Md., No. JFM-88-99 (filed Jan. 14, 1988) (more than 85 sites); *Fid. and Cas. Co. of New York v. Texas Eastern Transmission Corp.*, No. CA3-87-2925-T (N.D. Tex., Dec. 11, 1987) (89 sites); *General Reinsurance Corp. v. CIBA-Geigy Corp.*, No. 87 Civ. 8304 (S.D.N.Y., Jan. 27, 1988) ("Large number" of sites); *Employers Ins. Co. of Wausau v. Xerox Corp.*, No. B87-625 (D. Conn., Sept. 14, 1987) (18 sites throughout United States and Canada); *Liberty Mut. Ins.Company v. Ins. Co.. of Ireland*, No. 87-1907 (W.D. Pa., Sept. 10, 1987); *Lumbermens Mut. Cas. Co. v. SCM Corp.*, No. 87-527 JJF (D. Del., Oct. 6, 1987) (32 sites); *Firemen's Fund Ins. Co. v. Ex-Cell-O Corp.*, 662 F. Supp. 71 (E.D. Mich., 1987) (22 sites in six states).

42. *Travelers Indem. Co. v. Monsanto Co.*, No. H-88-34 (AHN) (D. Conn. March 22, 1988).

43. Judicial Council No. 1072 (Ca. Super. Ct.).

44. *New York Times*, p. 23, col. 3, March 18, 1988.

45. No. 278953 (Ca. Super. Ct.).

46. Obviously, courts need not engage in this discussion if the policies include an effective choice of law designation.

47. *See Klaxon Co. v. Stentor Electric Mfg. Co.*, 313 U.S. 487 (1941).

48. *See Restatement* § 6.

49. *Restatement* § 193.

50. *See, e.g., Liberty Mut. Ins. Co. v. Triangle Indus. Inc.*, No. CC999 (W.Va. Feb. 19, 1990) *reported in Mealey's Insurance Litigation Reports — Insurance D* (March 13, 1990) (applying *lex loci contractus* to a case involving insurance purchased in New Jersey to cover waste generated in West Virginia and disposed of in Ohio).

51. *See Restatement* § 188, *Marley-Wylain Co. v. Liberty Mut. Ins. Co.*, S85-353, slip op. (N.D. Ind. June 1, 1989), *reported in Mealey's Litigation Reports — Insurance B* (June 27, 1989) (Rejecting single-factored tests and applying the multi-factored test set forth in *Restatement* § 188.)

52. *See Restatement* § 6, *Industrial Indem. Ins. Co. v. United States*, 757 F.2d 982 (9th Cir. 1985); *Compagnie des Bauxitis de Quince v. Argonaut-Midwest Ins. Co.*, 880 F.2d 685 (3d Cir. 1989).

53. No. 86 4481, slip op. (D.N.J. July 17, 1990) *reported in Mealey's Litigation Reports — Insurance K* (July 31, 1990).

54. No. 88-4123, slip op., (D.N.J., May 29, 1990), 1990 WL 71985.

55. Jud. Counsel Coord. precedings No. 1072 (Cal. Super. Jan 24, 1990), *reported in Mealey's Litigation Reports — Insurance* (Jan. 24, 1990) (Separate edition).

56. Slip op. at 9.

57. 407 Mass. 572, 555 N.E.2d 214 (1990).

58. *Id.* at 585, *see also Westinghouse Elec. Corp. v. Liberty Mut. Ins. Co.*, 233 N.J. Super. 463, 477 (App. Div. 1989) (policyholder was "entitled to a single consistent final resolution of the choice of law in a single comprehensive action which will bind [it] and all [its] insurers."); *Marley-Wylain Co. v. Liberty Mut. Ins. Co.*, No. S85-353, slip op. at 31 (N.D. Ind. June 1, 1989), *Reported in Mealey's Litigation Reports - Insurance B* (June 27, 1989) (application of one state's law to entire dispute is in accord with *Restatement* § 6 which "speaks of certainty, predictability and uniformity or result, and ease of determination and application of the law to be applied"); *Beckman Instruments v. International Ins. Co.*, No. CV 85 8382-MRP, slip op. at 8 (C.D. Cal. Jan. 27, 1988), *reported in Mealey's Litigation Reports — Insurance G* (Feb. 23, 1988) ("interests of justice are best served by resolving all issues in this case under the law of only one state") *But see Insurance Co. North America v. Forty-Eight Insulations*, 633 F.2d 112 (6th Cir. 1980)(court sitting in Michigan applied Illinois law to five contracts issued in Illinois and New Jersey law to one contract issued in New Jersey); *Chesapeake Utilities v. American Home Assurance Co.*, 704 F. Supp. 551 (D. Del. 1989)(court applied Delaware law to claim involving contamination at a Delaware plant and Maryland law to a claim involving contamination at a Maryland Plant.)

59. *Restatement* § 188(2).

60. *Marley-Wylain Co. v. Liberty Mut. Ins. Co.*, No. S85-353, slip op. at 31 (N.D. Ind. June 1, 1989), *Reported in Mealey's Litigation Reports — Insurance B* (June 27, 1989) (application of one state's law to entire dispute is in accord with *Restatement* § 6 which "speaks of certainty, predictability and uniformity or result, and ease of determination and application of the law to be applied").

61. Slip op. at 34.

62. *Supra.*

63. Slip op. at 10.

64. *Id.*

65. *Id. See also Beckman Instruments v. International Ins. Co.*, No. CV 85 8382-MRP, slip op. at 8 (C.D. Cal. Jan. 27, 1988), *reported in Mealey's Litigation Reports — Insurance G* (Feb. 23, 1988); *Strassberg v. New England Mutual Life Ins. Co.*, 575 F. 2d 1262 (9th Cir. 1978).

66. 757 F.2d 982 (9th Cir. 1985).

67. *Id.* at 986. *Cf. National Starch, supra,* slip op. at K-10 (court chooses forum law over other states in case involving 24 sites in 9 states arguing that "the liberal approach New Jersey courts have taken concerning insurance coverage in the area of environmental contamination should be taken into consideration.")

68. Case No. 3-87-140, (D. Minn., Jan. 30, 1987).

69. 842 F.2d 977 (8th Cir. 1988).

70. *Hatfield v. Bishop Clarkson Memorial Hosp.,* 701 F.2d 1266, 1267 (8th Cir. 1982).

71. *Claussen v. Aetna Cas. & Sur. Co.,* 865 F.2d 1217 (11th Cir., 1989).

72. *See, e.g. A.Y. McDonald Indus. v. Ins. Co. of North America,* No. C-88-1028 (N.D. Iowa, Nov. 9, 1989) *reported in Mealey's Litigation Reports — Insurance H* (Nov. 28, 1989) (Certification to Iowa Supreme Court on meaning of "damages."); *Liberty Mutual Ins. Co. v. Triangle Ind.,* No. CC999 (N.D.W. Va. July 12, 1989), *reported in Mealey's Litigation Reports — Insurance* (July 25, 1989) (certification to West Virginia Supreme Court concerning damages issue); *Eli Lilly & Co. v. Home Ins. Co.,* 764 F.2d 876 (D.C. Cir. 1985), *denied* 479 U.S. 1060 (1987) (certification to Indiana Supreme Court concerning meaning of "occurrence"; *Jackson v. Johns Manville Sales Corp.,* 750 F.2d 1314 (5th Cir. 1985) (certification to Mississippi Supreme Court concerning types of damages available for asbestos-related injuries); *Republic National Life Ins. Co. v. Taylor,* 752 F.2d 523 (11th Cir. 1985) (certification to Georgia Supreme Court regarding beneficiary designation when employer changes carriers or group life policy); *Meckert v. Transamerica Ins. Co.,* 742 F.2d 505 (9th Cir. 1984) (certification to Idaho Supreme Court regarding enforceability of "other owned vehicle" exclusion); *Allstate Ins. Co. v. Young,* 638 F.2d 31 (5th Cir. 1981) (certification to Georgia Supreme Court regarding proper notice to insurer); *Fiat Motors Co. v. Mayor & City Council of Wilmington,* 619 F. Supp. 29 (D. Del. 1985) (certification to Supreme Court of Delaware regarding whether purchase of liability insurance constitutes implied waiver of municipal tort immunity); *but see International Surplus Lines Ins. Co. v. Anderson Dev. Co.,* 432 Mich. 1239 (1989).(denying Sixth Circuit's request for certification concerning pollution exclusion question).

73. *Lehman Bros. v. Schein* 416 U.S. 386 (1974) (holding that certification "does. . .in the long run save time, energy and resources and helps build a cooperative judicial federalism"); *Higgins Ind. Inc. v. Fireman's Fund Ins Co.,* 730 F. Supp. 774 (E.D. Mich. 1989) (recognizing in a footnote of the decision "that the law should be settled by the Michigan Supreme Court." The court stated, "Interestingly, no one has suggested certification of the issue to that Court, and so we can look to more and more litigation with varying opinions, any one of which can ultimately be upheld.").

74. No. C-5661-29 (Calif. Super. Ct., Los Angeles, March 15, 1989).

75. No. 88 C-JA-118 (Del. Super. Ct, New Castle County, March 6, 1989), *reported in Mealey's Litigation Reports — Insurance* (April 11, 1989).

76. No. 88C-JA-155, (Del. Super. Ct., Mar. 1, 1990) *reported in Mealey's Litigation Reports — Insurance* (Mar. 27, 1990).

77. *See, e.g., Minnesota Mining & Mfg. co. v. Commercial Union Ins. Co.,* No. 87-1907 (D.N.J. July 10, 1989), reported in Mealey's Litigation Reports - Insurance G (August 8, 1989) (other insureds' claim files found relevant to policyholder's action against car-

riers); *but see, e.g., Shering Corp. v. Evanston Ins. Co.*, No. 9731-88 (N.J. Sup. Ct., Union Co. August 4, 1989), *reported in* Mealey's Litigation Reports-Insurance (August 22, 1989) (discovery request for other insureds' claim files held burdensome, inadmissible and unnecessary); *In re: Texas Eastern Transmission Corp., PCP Contamination Ins. Coverage Litig.*, No. MDL 764 (E.D. Pa. July 26, 1989), *reported in Mealey's Litigation Reports — Insurance J* (August 8, 1989) (refusing to order discovery of other policyholders' policies, interpretations or opinions).

78.  *See, e.g., Great Lakes Chem. Corp. v. Northwestern Nat'l Ins. Co. of Milwaukee*, No. 23C01-8711-CP-263 (Ind. Cir. Ct., Fountain Co. May, 1989), *reported in Mealey's Litigation Reports — Insurance* (May 23, 1989) (group of carriers successfully blocked discovery of insurance policy drafting history, other insureds' claim files and reinsurance and reserve information).

79.  *See, e.g. Imell Corp. v. Centennial Ins. Co.*, No. 887-739-WWE (D.Conn. February 15, 1989), *reported in Mealey's Litigation Reports — Insurance C* (April 25, 1989) (refusing to order production of claim files of any insured, other than plaintiff, which plaintiff's counsel represents.  Further, plaintiff's counsel precluded for five years after conclusion of action from representing any other policyholder in any dispute against the defendant-carrier which involves the subject of the claim files produced).

80.  No. 278953 (Ca. Super. Ct.).

# XXIX

# Developments in Criminal and Civil Enforcement Under OSHA

*Dennis J. Morikawa, Esq.*
*Morgan, Lewis & Bockius*
*Philadelphia, Pennsylvania*
*and Nancy L. Vary, Esq.*
*Morgan, Lewis & Bockius*
*New York, New York*

Enforcement initiatives by the Occupational Safety and Health Administration (OSHA) and the Environmental Protection Agency (EPA) under their respective statutes have historically been undertaken by each agency independent of the activities of the other. Recent developments suggest that, at least in areas of arguable jurisdictional overlap, risk managers can anticipate an increased level of inter-agency cooperation and coordination in future enforcement actions.

Illustrative of such cooperative efforts, the Hazardous Waste Incineration Task Force was formed in September 1990 by joint agreement between OSHA and EPA. The inter-agency cooperative agreement provided for the joint inspection of 30 hazardous waste incineration sites, focusing on compliance with OSHA's Hazardous Waste Operations and Emergency Response Standard and EPA's requirements under the Resource Conservation and Recovery Act (RCRA). Sites covered by this agreement included commercial incinerators, operating incinerators which had not yet been permitted, and incinerators treating Superfund wastes on Superfund sites. To ensure that neither agency's statutory mandate would be compromised by the joint inspection activity and that the employer would not be subjected to duplicative enforcement efforts by OSHA and EPA, differences in the agencies' enforcement policies and inspection procedures were resolved by the agreement. To accommodate these differences, the cooperation agreement expressly provided that the prohibition in the Occupational Safety and Health Act of 1970[1] (OSH Act) against giving advance notice of any inspection and OSHA's inspection procedures providing for opening and closing conferences and employee interviews would be followed by the task force.

This joint inspection activity evidences an increased level of inter-agency cooperation and signals a trend that is expected to continue in the 1990s. As increased inter-agency cooperation is encouraged, joint inspection activity is likely to become more commonplace. Thus, OSHA's enforcement policies, citation practices and inspection procedures can be expected to take on an increased significance for the environmental risk manager.

In the Fall of 1990, two significant changes took place which have the potential to substantially reshape Occupational Safety and Health Administration (OSHA) enforcement policies in the future. First, OSHA has now formally adopted an "Egregious" Citation Policy ("Egregious Policy") that provides for the proposed imposition of potentially enormous penalties against employers based on item-by-item citations for multiple violations of OSHA workplace safety and health standards.[2] Second, as a revenue-raising measure, the United States Congress has now amended the penalty provisions of the OSH Act to permit a sevenfold increase in such penalties and health standards and to require minimum penalties for certain violations.[3] In addition to these changes, legislative efforts to dramatically revise the OSH Act, which would include among other things a broadening of criminal provisions for violations of the Act, were begun in the 101st Congress, and it is likely that they will continue in the first session of the 102nd Congress.

Each of these developments has the potential to affect OSHA's relations with employers generally. In large measure, the extent to which they will do so depends on the enforcement strategy which OSHA elects to follow. This chapter focuses on the practical impact of each of these very recent developments in the context of OSHA's historical citation policy and practice.

## Citations: Classifications of Violation and Assessment of Civil Penalties

The Occupational Safety and Health Act of 1970[4] was enacted "to assure so far as possible every working man and woman in the Nation safe and healthful working conditions" through the promulgation of safety and health standards. The drafters of the Act conceived its purpose as remedial rather than punitive, and emphasized abatement of violations as the principal focus of that legislation. Consistent with that view and for the first two decades of its enforcement, the Act provided for the assessment of a range of civil penalties for violation up to a maximum penalty of $10,000. Now, however, the recent and dramatic increases in the permissible range of penalties along with OSHA's Egregious Policy have significantly increased the risk of economic loss that cited employers face as a result of OSHA inspections.

Generally, the nature of violations along with the range of permissible civil and criminal penalties for violations is defined by statute.[5] OSHA classifications, in descending order of magnitude, with accompanying civil penalties include the following:

- Willful, up to $70,000;
- Repeated, up to $70,000;
- Serious, up to $7,000;
- Other-than-serious, up to $7,000; and
- *De minimis*, at $0.[6]

### Willful Violations

Unlike other OSHA classifications, what constitutes a willful violation is not defined *per se*. However, the penalties that can be proposed against an employer for willful violations of OSHA standards or regulations are expressly provided in Section 17(a) of the Act, as amended.[7] Willful violations are, at least for penalty purposes, distinguished from all other classifications of violation. Employers who willfully violate OSHA standards or regulations are now subject to an assessment of civil penalty of not more than $70,000 but not less than $5,000 for each violation.

Notwithstanding the clearly defined penalty parameters in the Act, neither the Act and the regulations promulgated thereunder, nor

**Developments in Criminal and Civil Enforcement Under OSHA**

OSHA's Egregious Policy (discussed below), precisely defines "willfulness". Rather, this task has historically been left to the Courts. The Sixth Circuit, among others, has for example required only a showing of voluntary act taken with "intentional disregard" of or "plain indifference" to the Act.[8] Under this standard, no showing of venal motive or bad intent is required and a willful violation may be established if OSHA proves that a violation occurred, and the violation was committed voluntarily with intentional disregard or plain indifference to the Act.

The Occupational Safety and Health Review Commission ("Review Commission") has generally employed an objective test to determine whether an employer has acted willfully or in good faith.[9] For example, the employer's conduct has been held to lack the element of intentional disregard or plain indifference (i.e., willfulness) where an employer knows of a violative condition and takes steps to rectify the situation, even if such steps are not totally complete or effective.[10] An employer's knowledge of a standard and a subsequent violation of that standard does not necessarily establish a willful violation; rather the burden remains on OSHA to prove each and every instance of violation.[11] The Review Commission has specifically recognized that an employer may in good faith dispute the existence of a violation, and that such a good faith opinion may negate a charge of willfulness.[12] Implicitly the Review Commission has, in at least one recent case, recognized reliance on advice of counsel as one factor mitigating in favor of finding "good faith" conduct.[13]

On the other hand, the consideration of an employer's good faith non-compliance with the Act has been held not inconsistent with a finding of willfulness.[14] At least one court has held that, notwithstanding the employer's arguably good faith belief that its policy conformed to the Act's requirements, the employer's announcement that it would not comply with the Court's interpretation constituted voluntary and intentional disregard, and thus a willful violation.[15]

Although there appears to be no legal requirement that a willful violation also be a serious one, willful violations often seem to accompany acts or omissions resulting in actual or potential death or serious injury. In OSHA's new penalty scheme, the initial classification of violation takes on an increased importance in view of the substantially increased statutory minimum and maximum penalties. That classification also dictates whether the employer will be subject to OSHA's new Egregious Policy discussed below.

## Repeated Violations

Repeated violations are those recurring violations of an already cited practice. Generally, a repeated violation may be found only if a Final Order has previously issued by the Review Commission or the employer has executed a settlement agreement containing an admission of such violation.[16] In at least one jurisdiction, however, a repeated violation may only be found where an employer has on at least two prior occasions violated the same OSHA standard or regulation and has deliberately flaunted the Act.[17] As with willful violations, repeated violations now subject the employer under Section 17(a) of the Act, as amended, to a civil penalty of up to $70,000 but not less than $5,000 per instance of violation.

## Serious Violations

Serious violations are found where ". . .there is a substantial probability that death or serious physical harm could result from a condition which exists, or from one or more practices, means, methods, operations, or processes which have been adopted or are in use, in such place of employment unless the employer did not, and would not with the exercise of reasonable diligence, know of the presence of the violation".[18] Section 17(b) of the Act, as amended, mandates the assessment of a civil penalty of up to $7,000 per violation for each serious violation.[19]

## Other Than Serious Violations

Non-serious or other-than-serious violations, on the other hand, include any violations not specifically found to be willful, repeated or serious. In essence, violations are presumed to be non-serious unless the elements of a serious violation are proved.[20] Section 17(c) of the Act, as amended, provides for the discretionary assessment of a civil penalty of up to $7,000 per violation for each other-than-serious violation. In the recordkeeping context, non-serious violations have been found by the Review Commission for failure to report employee fatalities and failure to report restricted work days on the OSHA 200 Log.[21]

### De Minimis Violations

*De minimis* violations are those which cannot reasonably be said to affect the health and safety of employees. Generally, no penalty is assessed for these violations.

OSHA has, in the past, demonstrated some degree of flexibility in the assessment of penalties for violating its regulations.[22] Factors which may be considered in the determination of magnitude and the assessment of civil penalty are statutorily defined and include the employer's size, the seriousness of the violation, the employer's good faith and prior history of violation. In the context of OSHA's Egregious Policy, these factors can be expected to have little, if any, impact in mitigating the size of penalties proposed against employers.

## OSHA's Egregious Policy

On October 1, 1990, OSHA issued Instruction CPL 2.80 that formally established procedures for identifying and handling "egregious" cases. In essence, this instruction formalized an enforcement policy which has been employed by OSHA for the past few years in an increasing number of cases. Indeed, in 1986, OSHA issued its first egregious citation with proposed penalties totalling more than $1 million dollars against Union Carbide Corporation following an inspection at its Institute, West Virginia chemical plant. That citation signaled a fundamental shift in OSHA's enforcement strategy.

Since that time, employers in increasing numbers have received egregious citations. Proposed penalties for egregious violations have ranged from approximately $40,000 to $7.3 million. These large aggregate penalties, which have now been institutionalized in OSHA's Egregious Policy, have thus been an integral part of OSHA's overall compliance initiative for some time.

Unlike the penalty provisions discussed above, whether or not to amend the Act to provide for an "egregious" classification has never been the subject of Congressional legislation. Significantly, the issue of whether OSHA's Egregious Policy, which includes the assessment of penalties on an item-by-item basis, is consistent with the policy and provisions of the Act or could only be adopted by resort to the rulemaking procedures of the Administrative Procedures Act is currently on review before the Review Commission.[23]

Historically, OSHA has grouped or combined related or similar violations for penalty purposes. This approach resulted in the assessment of a single penalty for the grouped violations. In egregious cases, OSHA considers a violation to be so flagrant that it considers each instance of non-compliance as a separate violation for which a separate penalty is proposed rather than grouping similar violations and proposing a single aggregate penalty.[24] Under this violation-by-violation or instance-by-instance assessment, penalties are significantly increased inasmuch as the penalties permissible under the Act are now multiplied by the number of instances of violation. As a result, in egregious cases, it is not uncommon for companies to receive citations which run into millions of dollars.

What constitutes an "egregious" case has not been precisely defined by the Act, by regulations promulgated thereunder or by OSHA's instruction. It is clear, however, that egregious cases are willful cases. Under OSHA's CPL 2.80, the classification of a violation as willful is a necessary predicate to the application of its Egregious Policy.[25] Although the instruction seeks to objectively define what constitutes a willful violation, there appears to be sufficient ambiguity to suggest that whether an employer's conduct is or is not willful will be the subject of continued litigation.

CPL 2.80 mandates that a willful classification is to be assigned when the employer is found in violation of an OSHA requirement:

(a) Of which she/he has actual knowledge at the time of the violation. Such knowledge may be demonstrated through previous citation history, accident exposure, widely publicized agency enforcement, direct evidence of specific recognized job site hazards or other appropriate factors; and

(b) Intentionally, through conscious, voluntary action or inaction, having made no reasonable effort to eliminate the known violation.[26]

What constitutes "other appropriate factors" under subparagraph (a) or a "reasonable effort to eliminate [a] known violation" under subparagraph (b) is not defined. This will no doubt be the subject of continued debate.

Even where willful violations are found, OSHA's Egregious Policy would not necessarily apply. Before subjecting the employer to an egregious citation, OSHA's CPL 2.80 requires that at least one other of the following six factors be present:

- A worker fatality, worksite catastrophe or large number of injuries or illnesses resulting from the violations;
- Persistently high worker injury or illness rates resulting from the violations;
- An extensive company history of prior violations;
- An employer's intentional disregard of its health and safety responsibilities;
- Clear bad faith on the employer's part; or
- Commission of a large number of violations significantly undermining the company's safety and health program.[27]

As with the willful classification itself, concepts such as whether an employer's conduct constituted "clear bad faith" or whether the number of violations was so large that it "undermined significantly" the effectiveness of the employer's safety and health program will almost certainly become the subject of future litigation.

To date, OSHA's Egregious Policy has been applied perhaps most frequently in the context of recordkeeping. Through the promulgation of CPL 2.80, OSHA has announced that records inspection activity and assessments of large penalty dollars for alleged recordkeeping violations, alone or in tandem with assessments for safety and health violations, will continue.

As part of a national emphasis program launched by OSHA in late 1986, highly visible employers in certain high hazard industries, including meatpacking, were selected for inspection and subjected to the imposition of substantial penalties for alleged "willful" recordkeeping violations. OSHA's aggressive citation of certain employers in certain industries for recordkeeping violations was premised largely on the notion that targeting the most visible employers in a particular industry or state would have a "trickle down" effect on other employers within that same industry, as well as on employers generally, not only with respect to correction of records but also on underlying safety and health issues.

On a more practical level, OSHA's concentration on recordkeeping cases has proven to be a successful strategy indeed. From a litigation perspective, the records themselves have often proved to be the most damaging evidence against employers since they were prepared by the employers and often conflicted with other employer records of injuries that were compiled for purposes of insurance and risk assessment.

The prime focus of OSHA's recent enforcement efforts appears to have shifted somewhat toward more fundamental safety and health issues, such as protections against bloodborne pathogens, hazard communication and ergonomics. OSHA has now launched a "national emphasis program" to identify employees at ergonomic risk and to protect them from the hazards of repeated stress. To date, OSHA's efforts have met with some measure of initial success.

As part of its recent ergonomics offensive, OSHA has targeted highly visible employers in certain high risk industries for inspection. In 1989, OSHA expended enormous effort in attempting to prevent ergonomic-related illnesses in the red meatpacking industry. As with recordkeeping, it is clear from CPL 2.80 that OSHA will continue to focus substantial resources to scrutinize ergonomic conditions in the workplace.

In terms of its overall enforcement strategy, OSHA's ergonomics emphasis program is consistent with its current strategy of imposing substantial penalties on large, highly visible corporations in an effort to obtain corporate-wide settlements. The theory behind this strategy appears to be that the work practices, job design, and physical plant or work station layouts employed by such employers may expose their workers to repeated tissue stress, thereby posing a potentially serious health risk. To date, OSHA's focus has largely been on the initial identification, elimination and/or modification of occupational conditions having the potential to cause various cumulative trauma disorders (CTD), such as carpal tunnel syndrome. Although its strongest enforcement efforts have been in the meatpacking, poultry and food processing industries, OSHA has also shown an active interest in such other diverse industries as grocery stores, apparel, and automotive manufacturing.

OSHA's ergonomics initiative is only a very recent one and has met with early success in negotiating pre-litigation corporate-wide settlements. To date, specific OSHA regulations defining an employer's obligations with respect to ergonomics have not been promulgated. Rather, the only guidance that OSHA has thus far made available to employers is found in the ergonomic guidelines issued for meatpacking plants.[28]

Among currently unanswered questions that remain to be addressed are whether in the ergonomics context medical screening for the susceptibility to CTD runs afoul of handicap discrimination laws, whether causal relationships exist between specific jobs and CTD injuries, and whether OSHA may require an employer to significantly increase its workforce or slow production if effective engineering controls to reduce ergonomic hazards cannot be developed. To date, there is no settled case law with respect to ergonomics. The relative merits of particular legal defenses and abatement methods, which may in fact be available to cited employers in this area have not yet been fully tested.[29] Until such time as they are, the law in this area can be expected to remain uncertain. In view of that, OSHA's aggressive enforcement action in the area of ergonomics is likely to remain particularly troublesome for employers.

The nature and scope of OSHA inspection activity to date and comments rendered by OSHA officials in a variety of forums suggest that the enforcement effort aimed at the meatpacking industry is only a precursor of what is to come in the 1990s. Notwithstanding the lack of medical certainty concerning the causes and treatment of ergonomic-related diseases, OSHA can be expected to continue to aggressively cite employers for ergonomic violations. As Assistant Secretary of Labor for OSHA, Gerard Scannell has recently been quoted as saying, "If there was a marquee over my office door, it would say Coming Attractions — Ergonomics."[30]

In terms of future initiatives, an increasing focus by National Institute of Occupational Safety and Health (NIOSH) on potential hazards to video display terminal users and state initiatives to require related ergonomic controls suggests the potential for increased OSHA activity. Significant studies have recently been undertaken or completed in the newspaper and telecommunication industries to determine the effects on clerical workers of lighting, furniture, work station design and keyboard. Recent legislative efforts to regulate video display terminal (VDT) use in New York have been overturned by the Courts, which stated that the subject was a proper one for state or federal regulation.[31] For these reasons, future initiatives by OSHA that would affect a far broader range of employers than we have seen to date are not unlikely.

## Corporate-Wide Settlement Agreements

Both in policy and practice, the Department of Labor has linked its Egregious Policy with corporate-wide settlements. The Department of Labor has indicated that it favors the assessment of item-by-item penalties because they ultimately lead to corporate-wide settlements. Indeed, it has been estimated that nearly two-thirds of the nearly 100 egregious citations issued by OSHA since Union Carbide Corporation was first cited under the policy in 1986 were settled "often with committments for corporate-wide abatement of hazard."[32]

As with its Egregious Policy, it is expected that the agency will issue a directive detailing corporate-wide settlements. In the interim, OSHA can be expected to continue to seek corporate-wide settlements in appropriate cases. Typically, these settlements involve corporate-wide agreements whereby the company agrees to correct the violations OSHA cited both at the location where the violations occurred, and in the company's other facilities as well. In many instances, employers have agreed to implement company-wide changes, often costing as much, if not more, than the penalties proposed in the original citation. How and to what extent OSHA will be able to effectively monitor these geographically vast agreements remains to be seen.

From OSHA's perspective, corporate-wide agreements have become an increasingly important part of its overall enforcement strategy. Indeed, it has been estimated that, with the resources available to it in terms of manpower and budget, OSHA can inspect only about two percent of the nearly six million workplaces covered by the OSH Act.[33] Given these limitations and ongoing budgetary pressures, OSHA's ability to exact changes in multiple workplaces through inspection at a single location permits it to substantially expand the level of its enforcement activity beyond that which its staffing would otherwise permit.

To date, OSHA has been particularly successful in reaching corporate-wide settlements with respect to both recordkeeping and ergonomic citations. As discussed above, both of these areas have within the last few years been the subject of national emphasis programs and significant enforcement initiatives.

In many respects, large recordkeeping citations in particular have lent themselves to corporate-wide agreements. In the recordkeeping context, the same records (e.g., OSHA 200 logs) are maintained at each location, and recording practices in one plant often reflect those policies and procedures which have been put in place at a corporate level or at least have analogs throughout the company. Thus, in circumstances where corporate-wide recording policies and operational similarities exist, corporations cited in one location for recordkeeping deficiencies are almost certainly at risk of similar if not increased citations in other locations.

As part of its overall compliance strategy, an employer may address its OSHA obligations on a plant-by-plant basis or on a more comprehensive basis. By agreeing to correct on a company-wide basis violations before OSHA inspects and cites other locations, an employer may avoid concurrent or consecutive inspection activity at those other locations. From a cost-benefit standpoint, companies can sometimes effectively foreclose OSHA's further inspection and citation efforts and potentially larger penalties by agreeing in the first instance to a corporate-wide abatement plan covering all its facilities. In return for these lower penalties, OSHA secures a committment from the employer for an increased abatement effort.

As discussed above, many of the ergonomics cases have already been subject to the increased penalties of OSHA's Egregious Policy and corporate-wide settlements have been negotiated involving employers who were cited. These agreements have typically required the employer not only to abate alleged violations but also to implement training and medical programs for their employees.

As with corporate settlements which have been negotiated in other contexts, these agreements have generally required the self-assessment or self-audit by the employer of its safety and health program and practices and the development of an operational plan to correct the deficiencies discovered by that audit. As demonstrated, for example, by OSHA's recent citations and proposed penalties of $7.3 million issued against USX Corporation, such audits once undertaken may serve to significantly increase an employer's potential liability should it fail to correct violations which its audit reveals. From a litigation perspective, the employer's audit can sometimes prove to be the most damaging evidence against it. From an inspection and penalty perspective, it provides OSHA with a roadmap to monitor the employer's subsequent abatement efforts and documentation to support citation on an instance-by-instance basis where the employer fails to make such efforts. As recent citations against USX Corporation and other companies suggest, once deficiencies are identified, the employer must take adequate steps to correct them or face potentially substantial OSHA liability for the failure to do so.

## Criminal Sanctions

Historically, enforcement of the Act has been viewed almost exclusively as a civil matter. Indeed, Section 17 of the Act permits criminal proceedings to be instituted against employers under only very narrowly circumscribed situations. Unless an employee death results from the employer's conduct or the employer knowingly falsifies records required to be filed or maintained under the Act, enforcement remains a strictly civil matter.[34] Assuming such conduct, criminal proceedings brought under the Act do not rise to the level of a felony prosecution; rather criminal offenses under the Act constitute misdemeanors.

Under the OSH Act, an employer who willfully violates any standard, rule or order, and thereby causes the death of an employee, may be fined up to $10,000 and imprisoned for no more than six months.[35] A second conviction carries with it a maximum penalty of $20,000 and one year in jail. Pursuant to the 1984 Comprehensive Crime Control Act and Criminal Fine Collection Act, any misdemeanor which results in a death is punishable by a fine of $250,000 for individuals and $500,000 for corporations.[36] The U.S. Department of Justice has confirmed that these penalties apply to OSHA violations.[37]

Historically, OSHA has relied on civil rather than criminal penalties to enforce the mandates of the Act. Unlike the commitment the government has shown in prosecuting environmental polluters, criminal prosecutions under the Act have to date been rare. In stark contrast to the level of criminal enforcement activity under federal environmental laws, OSHA has referred 58 employee death cases to the Department of Justice for criminal prosecution during the first 19 years of the Act.[38] During the first 18 years of the Act, the Department of Justice chose to criminally prosecute only 14 of the 42 employee death cases which OSHA referred to it, resulting in 10 convictions.[39] Since the Act was passed in 1970 only one person has been sent to prison as a result of federal prosecution under the Act.

In large measure, differences in criminal enforcement activity under OSHA and EPA can be attributed not only to key distinctions between the criminal provisions of the underlying statutes but also of the enforcement mechanisms which have grown up around them. Unlike EPA's program for criminal environmental enforcement, OSHA has no dedicated prosecutorial resources, no special criminal investigators authorized as federal law enforcement officers, nor a complement of FBI agents assigned to investigate alleged criminal violations.

A significantly more vigorous level of criminal safety prosecutions, both under state occupational safety and health laws and general criminal statutes, has been seen at the state level.[40] Pursuant to Section 18 of the OSH Act, individual states may opt to establish and enforce their own occupational safety and health standards, subject to approval by federal OSHA.[41] At present, twenty-three states have OSHA-approved state plans ("state plan"), and their respective state agencies enforce workplace safety and health standards established pursuant to those plans. Generally, violators of state plan standards are subject to prosecution only under that state's safety laws and general criminal statutes. In the remaining twenty-seven states, where federal OSHA has retained responsibility for enforcement of the occupational safety and health standards which have been promulgated under the Act, the extent to which violators of safety standards may be amenable to prosecution not only at the federal level but also at the state or local level is less clear.

In a number of non-state plan jurisdictions, state court convictions have been challenged on the grounds that state or local prosecutions for workplace injuries or fatalities are pre-empted by Section 18 of the OSH Act. Recently, at least two courts have held that, where federal OSHA governs workplace safety and health standards, state laws which pertain to those occupational safety and health issues addressed by OSHA's standards are pre-empted.[42] However, courts which have considered the issue of whether criminal safety prosecutions under state criminal laws in non-state plan states are pre-empted by the Act have reached differing conclusions.[43] In upholding the state's right to criminally prosecute safety violators, both New York and Illinois courts, for example, have held that state causes of action exist independently of OSH Act violations.[44] Courts in other jurisdictions, for example Texas, have rejected this view and concluded that state safety prosecutions are pre-empted by the Act.[45]

Recent events suggest that the U.S. Department of Labor may seek not only increased civil penalties, but may also seek increased criminal prosecutions in the future. For example, it recently obtained its first OSHA-related jail sentence when the president of a South Dakota plumbing company pled guilty to willfully violating OSHA's trenching standards.[46] Two workers had been killed when the trench involved had collapsed. In a second successful prosecution, the president of a utility company has pleaded guilty to a criminal charge of willfully failing to comply with OSHA's trenching standards.[47] He has agreed to pay a $2,500 civil fine and has received probation and a four month suspended jail sentence from the U.S. District Court for the District of Kansas.[48]

## OSHA Inspections

Employers now face substantially expanded liabilities resulting from OSHA inspections and subsequent citations. In this context, employers' OSHA rights and responsibilities take on an increased importance and must be reexamined in light of the new enforcement scheme. Recent comments by OSHA Administrator Scannell suggest that these newly increased penalties and minimum penalties will lead to an increase in the number of employer-contested citations.[50] Similarly, employers may want to consider whether, as predicted by many experts, warrant rights are to be executed in increasing numbers.

Under Section 8 of the OSH Act,[51] representatives of the Secretary of Labor may inspect and investigate any place of employment in order to determine whether the employer has complied with safety and health standards established pursuant to the Act. The sole statutory limitation upon the Secretary's right to conduct inspections is to inspect only at reasonable times, within reasonable limits and in a reasonable manner.

The permissible scope of an OSHA inspection is dictated to some extent by its initial categorization. OSHA has developed four categories for the initiation of inspections which meet the requirement of demonstrating a rational basis (i.e., probable cause) for the selection of an employer for inspection:[52]

- Imminent danger inspections;
- Fatality-catastrophe investigations;
- Complaint inspections; and
- General schedule (programmed) inspections.[53]

OSHA will generally conduct inspections of any facility based on an employee complaint of a violation threatening physical harm or information regarding a fatality, catastrophe or imminent danger. If OSHA determines from the complaint that a violation threatening physical harm or imminent danger does not exist, no inspection will be conducted. Although OSHA is required to furnish the employer with a copy of the complaint at the time of the inspection, the identity of the complaining employee is protected under the OSH Act and will not be disclosed.

Employers selected for general schedule or "programmed" safety inspections are those in high risk industries randomly chosen on the basis of industry and company lost work day injury rates. Irrespective of the employer's lost workday injury rate, OSHA may undertake a safety inspection where, for example, the Compliance Safety and Health Officer (CSHO) observes a serious hazard or imminent danger in the workplace or where the CSHO notes an unusual number or type of injury within a single time period, area, or operation. Industries identified as using hazardous substances are selected for programmed health inspections according to the number of employees potentially exposed to these substances and the severity of the potential adverse health effects resulting from exposure to these substances.

### The Permissible Scope of the Inspection

The scope of an OSHA inspection is limited by consent, warrant or statute. As discussed above, the statutory limit is one of reasonableness. The limitations placed on the scope of inspections conducted pursuant to warrants or with the consent of the employer are more closely defined. Generally speaking, however, inspections other than those arising from the programmed establishment list may be limited to the specific site which gave rise to the inspection.

## Consensual Inspections

When faced with a request for inspection, the employer may either consent to the inspection, or request that OSHA obtain a search warrant prior to entering the facility. Although an employer is free to consent to an OSHA inspection at any time and for any reason, the entire facility need not be open for scrutiny under such circumstances. Rather, employers may restrict the scope of their consent to those particular areas giving rise to the inspection request. For example, if an inspection is based upon an employee complaint of inadequate machine guarding, an employer may permit a safety inspection of that machine, while not agreeing to allow either a general safety or health inspection.

If an employer appropriately restricts the scope of his consent, inspection beyond that scope will be considered involuntary, and provide grounds for vacating a subsequent citation.[54] Consensual inspections have, for example, been deemed to be involuntary where an employer is misled by representations of OSHA officials. In one such instance, an employer's consent was found to be involuntary and the resultant citations were vacated where he was led to believe no penalties would be assessed.[55] In another, a compliance officer was found to have coerced an employer's consent by stating that he would guarantee finding a violation if he were forced to obtain an inspection warrant.[56]

Although the scope of the consent may be limited, under the "plain view" exception to the warrant requirements, violations which OSHA observes while in an area for which consent has been given may nevertheless be the subject of a citation. Similarly, a citation based upon observations from open terrain, rather than private premises, will be upheld, irrespective of the existence of consent or a warrant.[57] For example, a CSHO may observe violations of a scaffolding regulation while standing in a park across from a building under construction or renovation and subsequently cite the employer. Where there is a multiemployer site, it is also possible that the consent of either the owner of the site, or of any one employer on site, may be effective to permit a full-scale inspection.

### Inspections by Warrant

Under the United States Supreme Court decision in *Marshall v. Barlow's, Inc.*,[58] an employer has a Constitutional right to demand that OSHA obtain an inspection warrant prior to entering its premises. Such warrant must be based upon "probable cause," i.e., a reasonable basis for selection of the workplace. If an employee demands a warrant and OSHA fails to obtain one, or the warrant is subsequently found not to be based upon probable cause, employers need not permit an inspection, and any citations based upon an invalid warrant will be vacated.

Some courts have concluded that an application for a warrant based upon an employee complaint will be considered probable cause for an inspection limited to the violations which form the subject of the complaint.[59] Other jurisdictions nonetheless permit a complete "wall-to-wall" inspection based upon a single employee complaint.[60]

The application for a warrant must specify the reason for the requested inspection and the activities that OSHA intends to perform during the course of the inspection. If the inspection is conducted pursuant to a warrant, the warrant should also detail the reasonable investigative techniques permitted to be used by the CSHO. Under certain circumstances, and in certain jurisdictions, OSHA must secure an administrative subpoena to review records maintained by the employer.[61] Again, the subpoena must describe with adequate specificity the records that are to be inspected.[62]

Under OSHA regulations, a warrant may be obtained *ex parte*, i.e., without employer participation.[63] Even where an *ex parte* warrant is issued, the employer may, under appropriate circumstances, challenge its propriety by refusing to permit the inspection to go forward and contesting the warrant in federal district court either by moving to quash the warrant or defending against a motion for civil contempt filed by OSHA. Alternatively, the employer may permit the inspection to go forward and contest the validity of the warrant in the context of proceedings before the Occupational Safety and Health Review Commission.[64]

The legal requirement of "probable cause", will vary depending upon the nature of the inspection. Thus, employers should carefully review the warrant secured by OSHA to determine whether it complies with that requirement. Evidence obtained in an inspection conducted in violation of the warrant requirements may be excluded from consideration by the Commission and the courts.[65] Thus, the employer should ensure that the scope of the inspection set forth in the warrant is appropriately limited, and that the warrant states the information relevant to the inspection in sufficient detail to permit a determination of probable cause.

### Employer Rights and Responsibilities During an Inspection

Once an OSHA Compliance Officer or Industrial Hygienist has entered the premises to conduct an inspection, by consent or pursuant to warrant, the employer should ensure that proper administrative procedures are followed and that his rights under the Act are preserved. As a general rule, the employer must supply only that information which is required to be maintained or provided under the Act and accompanying regulations. Other statements made or records submitted by the employer or his representative to OSHA may be utilized against it in subsequent proceedings.

### Opening Conference

The OSHA Compliance Safety and Health Officer must hold an opening conference with the employer and employee representatives. After presenting his credentials, the CSHO is required to state the basis and scope of the inspection, and to supply the employer a copy of the warrant and/or employee complaint, where applicable. Given the extent of potential liability under OSHA's new enforcement scheme and particularly in accidental death cases, employers may wish to consider raising with the CSHO at this juncture the issue of whether this is an egregious case inspection or a potential criminal investigation. If the potential for criminal prosecution exists, consideration should be given at the outset to the need to retain criminal counsel to assure that individual employee rights and constitutional protections are not compromised during the course of OSHA's inspection.

At this time, the CSHO may request other information, concerning for example the nature of the employer's operations, and may also seek to examine safety and health records maintained by the employer (e.g., OSHA Form 200). It has been recognized that the disclosure of individual employee records implicates employee privacy interests.[66] Thus, some employers take the position that such records should not be disclosed absent adequate safeguards, such as those in an administrative subpoena that also specifies the need for such records.

Section 15 of the Act does provide for protection against unauthorized disclosure of "confidential information-trade secrets" or other proprietary information. To preserve those protections, however, the employer must inform the CSHO of all areas which contain trade secret information. Subsequently, any such information gathered by OSHA will be labeled as "confidential-trade secret" to prevent the unauthorized disclosure of such proprietary information. Disclosure of these documents will generally be restricted to OSHA officers and employees. However, if relevant, the same information may be required to be produced in judicial or administrative proceedings.

### Conduct of Inspection

Both employer and employee representatives (e.g., shop stewards) have "walkaround" rights to accompany the CSHO during his inspections, although employees need not be paid for this time. If the employer is not permitted to accompany the CSHO, and the employer is prejudiced as a result, any citations resulting from the inspection should be vacated.

During the walkaround, the employer is permitted to perform the same investigative activities undertaken by the CSHO. This may include conducting both air and personal monitoring, taking photographs, and noting the type of measuring instruments and procedures utilized by the CSHO. Such information may be used in later litigation proceedings, both as evidence at hearings and in settlement discussions.

The Compliance Officer may interview employees to the extent that such discussions do not interfere with the performance of work. These interviews may be held privately, without the presence of an employer representative,[67] and OSHA officials need not reveal the identity of the employee(s) interviewed. The employer may, however, legitimately restrict these interviews to the employees' nonworking time on or off company property. Employees should be instructed that they are free to speak with the Compliance Officer during their nonworking time or, alternatively, that they may decline to speak with the CSHO, if they so desire.

## Closing Conference

After the inspection, the CSHO will conduct a closing conference with the employer and employee representatives. During this conference, the Compliance Officer will advise the employer of any violations and explain and provide copies of the regulations allegedly violated. In addition, the CSHO should provide an explanation of all abatement requirements, including suggested methods and time periods to accomplish abatement. Employer statements made at the closing conference could be considered admissions of violations, thereby limiting its right to later contest a citation. Unless the statements are made and agreed to as non-admissions of liability, they will be admissible against the employer in later proceedings.

## Informal Conference

The purpose of this conference is to discuss issues raised by the citation, such as the existence of a hazard, the size of proposed penalties, and abatement requirements in order to amicably resolve the dispute. As is the case throughout the inspection process, employer statements made at this juncture could be considered admissions of violations and liability. To facilitate resolution and yet preserve its rights, the employer should seek the agreement of all parties at the conference that any statements made will not constitute admissions of liability. Rather, any such statements are made in the context and for the purpose of discussing settlement.

The Area Director has authority to modify penalties, abatement dates and characterizations of violations in a Settlement Agreement executed by OSHA, the employer and an employee representative.

If no settlement can be reached, the employer may file a notice of contest within fifteen working days of the receipt of the citation, thereby commencing the administrative litigation process. Alternatively, the employer may file a Petition for Modification of Abatement (PMA) by the end of the working day following the abatement date specified in the citation. To receive an extension, the employer must show good faith effort to comply with the Standard allegedly violated, including interim steps taken to protect employees, and specify reasons why additional time is necessary. If unopposed, this Petition will be decided by the Area Director; if opposed, the Petition will be decided by the Review Commission.

Recent developments in OSHA's civil and criminal enforcement strategies suggest an increasing awareness of and concentration on workplace safety and health issues not only by the agency but by Congress as well. The new penalty structure, efforts to broaden the scope of criminal liability under the Act which were begun in the 101st Congress and are expected to continue in the 102nd Congress, and increased inter-agency cooperation and coordination in investigating workplace safety and health hazards suggest the possibility of significantly increased enforcement activity in the future. Thus, risk managers can no longer monitor or manage OSHA issues in isolation but rather must factor them into their overall risk management strategy.

## Future Trends and Legislative Initiatives in Criminal Sanctions

On February 21, 1990, Senator Howard Metzenbaum (D-Ohio) introduced S. 2154, the "OSHA Criminal Penalty Reform Act." Concurrently in the House, Representative Tom Lantos (D-California) introduced the companion bill, H.R. 4050. These bills were referred to the Senate's Committee on Labor and Human Resources and the House Committee on Education and Labor, respectively. Although the Senate Labor Committee approved a compromise version of that bill, the 101st Congress failed to act on it this session.

Among its key provisions were:

- An increase in the maximum jail sentence for a willful violation of the Act resulting in an employee death from six months to ten years for a first offense, and from one year to 20 years for a second conviction;
- The establishment of criminal liability for willful violations of the Act resulting in serious bodily injury to any employee, with maximum jail sentences of up to five years for a first offense and up to ten years for a second offense; and
- An increase in the maximum civil fines which may be assessed to $250,000 for individuals and $500,000 for corporations.

In addition, the legislation as originally proposed would have extended both civil and criminal liability to any director, officer, or agent of an employer who "willfully authorizes, orders, acquiesces, or carries out a violation, failure, or refusal to comply with safety and health standards."[49] It would not, however, have pre-empted state criminal prosecutions.

Although this legislation was not enacted in the 101st Congress, it is likely that efforts to expand criminal liability under the OSH Act will be made in the next Congress. Irrespective of the expansion of criminal liability under the Act, the adoption of a substantially more aggressive citation policy by OSHA coupled with the recently enacted sevenfold increase in maximum penalties permissible under the Act would almost certainly create a more adversarial environment between employers and the Agency. In a more adversarial posture, contest rates would be expected to rise as will the number of cases which are litigated. If, in addition, legislation similar to S. 2154 is enacted, it has the potential to significantly alter the OSH Act's enforcement scheme.

## About the Authors

**Dennis J. Morikawa** is a partner in the Philadelphia office of Morgan, Lewis & Bockius where his practice is concentrated in the area of labor relations law. He represents management in such areas as employment discrimination and wrongful discharge litigation and matters before the Occupational Safety and Health Administration. He is Management Co-Chair of the American Bar Association Committee on Occupational Safety and Health Law. He is co-author of the book entitled *Employee Dismissal Law: Forms and Procedures* (Wiley 1986) and its Supplements.

**Nancy L. Vary** is an associate in the New York office of Morgan, Lewis & Bockius where she specializes in labor and employment law, representing management in such areas as employment discrimination, wrongful discharge and matters arising under the Occupational Safety and Health Act. She currently serves as a member of the American Bar Association Committee on Occupational Safety and Health Law.

# Endnotes

1. 29 U.S.C. § 651 *et seq.*

2. *See,* OSHA Instruction CPL 2.80 (October 1, 1990).

3. Omnibus Budget Reconciliation Act of 1990, Section 3101, Public Law 101-508.

4. 29 U.S.C. § 651(b). *See also* Chapter XII by M. Duvall.

5. Under the provisions of both the Act and the United States Criminal Code criminal sanctions including fines and/or imprisonment could be imposed under appropriate circumstances.

6. Section 17(d) of the Act also provides for penalties of up to $7,000 per day for each day that the employer has failed to abate a prior violation. 29 U.S.C. § 666(d). The Act does not, however, expressly provide for *de minimis* classifications. OSHA has in the past cited employers for technical violations of the Act but, recognizing their effect on employee safety and health, assessed no penalty.

7. 29 U.S.C. § 666(a).

8. *Empire-Detroit Steel v. OSHRC,* 579 F.2d 378 (6th Cir. 1978); *Donovan v. Capital City Excavating Co.,* 712 F.2d 1008 (6th Cir. 1983).

9. *See, for example, S. Zara & Sons Contracting Co.,* 10 BNA OSHC 1334, 1982 OSHD (CCH) ¶ 25,892 (Rev. Commn. 1982), *petition for review denied,* 697 F.2d 297 (2d Cir. 1982); *Lukens Steel Co.,* 10 BNA OSHC 1115, 1981 OSHD 25,742 (Rev. Commn. 1981); *Wright & Lopez, Inc.,* 10 BNA OSHC 1108, 1981 OSHD(CCH) ¶ 25,728 (Rev. Commn. 1981).

10. *Mobil Oil Corp.,* 11 BNA OSHC 1700, 1983 OSHD 26,699 (Rev. Commn. 1983).

11. *See Stone & Webster Engineering Corp.,* 8 BNA OSHC 1753, 1980 OSHD(CCH) ¶ 24,646 (1980), *petition for review withdrawn,* No. 80-1605 (1st Cir. 1980) (employer merely showed poor judgment); *General Electric Co., Inc.,* 5 OSHC 1448, 1977 OSHD (CCH) ¶ 21,853 (Rev. Commn. 1977), *reversed,* 6 BNA OSHC 1868, 583 F.2d 61 (2d Cir. 1978) (good faith misinterpretation of standard cannot constitute willful failure to comply).

12. *C.N. Flagg & Co., Inc. d/b/a Northeastern Contracting Co.,* 2 BNA OSHC 1539, 1974-75 OSHD(CCH) ¶ 19,251 (Rev. Commn. 1975).

13. *Keco Indust., Inc.,* 13 BNA OSHC 1161 (Rev. Commn. 1987).

14. *See S. Zara & Sons Contracting Co., supra; C.N. Flagg & Co., supra.*

15. *RSR Corp. v. Brock,* 764 F.2d 355 (5th Cir.), *reh'g den.,* 773 F.2d 1236 (1985).

16. *See* Sections 10(c) through 12 of the Act for enforcement and review procedures relative to Review Commission Final Orders. 29 U.S.C. § 659 *et seq.*

17. *See, for example, Bethlehem Steel Corp. v. OSHRC,* 540 F.2d 157 (3rd Cir. 1976).

18. Section 17(k), 29 U.S.C. § 666(k).

19. *Logan County Farm Enterprise, Inc.*, 7 BNA OSHC 1275, 1979 OSHD(CCH) ¶ 23,425 (Rev. Commn. 1979).

20. *See, for example, Crescent Wharf & Warehouse Co.*, 2 OSHRC 1318, 1 BNA OSHC 1219, 1971-73 OSHD(CCH) ¶ 15,687 (Rev. Commn. 1973); *Owens-Corning Fiberglass Corp. v. Donovan*, 659 F.2d 1285 (5th Cir. 1981).

21. *See, Hurd Printing & Decorating Co., Inc.*, 10 BNA OSHC 1670, 1982 OSHD (CCH) ¶ 26,047 (Rev. Commn. 1982) (no penalty assessed for employer's failure to report to OSHA employee's job-related death within 48 hour period); *J. R. Simplot Co.*, 13 BNA OSHC 1313 (Rev. Commn. J. 1987) (reporting violation cannot be classified as *de minimis* but constitutes a non-serious violation for which no penalty assessed).

22. *Stowe Canoe Co., Inc.*, 4 BNA OSHC 1012, 1975-76 OSHD(CCH) ¶ 20,509 (Rev. Commn. 1974).

23. *Secretary of Labor v. Sanders Lead Co.*, OSHRC Docket No. 87-0260.

24. This citation and penalty assessment practice has also resulted in the somewhat anomalous situation whereby OSHA is now required to prove each and every item of violation. Similarly, it provides the employer the opportunity to defend against each and every instance of violation cited.

25. *See* CPL 2.80 H.2.

26. CPL 2.80 H.2.b(1).

27. CPL 2.80 H.2.b(2)-(b)(7).

28. *See*, Ergonomics Program Management Guidelines for Meatpacking Plants (OSHA Publication 3123).

29. Unlike recordkeeping, there is no specific regulation or series of regulations which regulate the ergonomics of the workplace. Rather, OSHA has cited employers under the OSH Act's § 5(a)(1), or General Duty Clause, for exposing employees to the hazard of cumulative trauma disorder.

30. 19 OSHR (BNA) (A Special Report) No. 31 at 1357 (January 10, 1990).

31. *ILC Data Device Corp. v. County of Suffolk*, NY Sup. Ct. Suffolk Cty, No. 88-12149 (12/27/89).

32. 20 OSHR (BNA) (Current Reports) No. 19, at 829-30 (October 10, 1990).

33. *Id.*

34. The Act also permits criminal proceedings against government employees who provide employers with advance notice of inspection. 29 U.S.C. § 666(f).

35. 29 U.S.C. § 666(e) (1985).

36. 18 U.S.C. § 3571 (1985).

37. 17 OSHR (BNA) (Current Reports) No. 12, at 483-84 (Aug. 19, 1987).

38. S. Rep. No. 409, 101st Cong., 2d Sess. 23 (1990).

39. H. R. Rep. No. 1051, 100th Cong., 2d Sess. 4 (1988).

40. California, for example, has recently enacted the California Criminal Liability Act (AB 2249) which, effective January 1991, will permit the criminal prosecution of corporations and business managers who knowingly conceal serious workplace dangers from their employees or from Cal/OSHA. Corporations convicted under this law will be subject to fines up to $1 million, and individual business managers will face fines up to $25,000 and up to three years imprisonment.

41. Section 18 of the OSH Act provides:
(a) Nothing in this Act shall prevent any State agency or court from asserting jurisdiction under State law over any occupational safety or health issue with respect to which no standard is in effect under section 6.

(b) Any State which, at any time, desires to assume responsibility for development and enforcement therein of occupational safety and health standards relating to any occupational safety and health issue with respect to which a Federal standard has been promulgated under section 6 shall submit a State plan for the development of such standards and their enforcement.

29 U.S.C. § 667.

42. See, New Jersey Chamber of Commerce v. Hughey, 774 F.2d 587, 592 (3rd Cir. 1985); Environmental Encapsulating Corp. v. City of New York, 855 F.2d 48, 57 (2d Cir. 1988).

43. See, for example, People v. Hegedus, 432 Mich. 598, 443 N.W.2d 127 (Mich. 1989) (no preemption); Illinois v. Chicago Magnet Wire Corp., 126 Ill.2d 356, 128 Ill. Dec. 517, 534 N.E.2d 962, cert. denied sub nom., Asta v. Illinois, 110 S.Ct. 52 (1989) (no preeemption); Wisconsin ex rel. Cornellier v. Black, 144 Wis.2d 745, 425 N.W.2d 21 (Wis. Ct. App.), review denied, 430 N.W.2d 351 (Wis. 1988) (no preemption); People v. Pymm (No. 189) (N.Y. October 16, 1990) (no preemption). Cf., Sabine Consolidated Inc. v. Texas, 756 S.W.2d 865 (Tex. Ct. App. 1988) (preemption); Colorado v. Kelran Construction Inc., 13 OSHC 1898 (Colo. D. Ct. 1988) (preemption).

44. Id.

45. See endnote 43, supra.

46. Daily Labor Report (BNA) at A-10 (Sept. 20, 1989).

47. Employment Safety and Health Guide (CCH) No. 976, at 2 (Jan. 23, 1990).

48. U.S. v. Chism, No. 90-10012-01 (DC Kan. 1990).

49. S. 2154, as introduced by Sen. Metzenbaum.

50. Daily Labor Report (BNA) at A-4 (October 11, 1990).

51. 29 U.S.C. § 657.

52. *Marshall v. Barlow's, Inc.*, 436 U.S. 307 (1978).

53. OSHA also conducts follow-up inspections subsequent to the issuance of citations to insure abatement of violations.

54. *Ennis Automotive, Inc.*, 10 BNA OSHC 1672, 1982 OSHD(CCH) ¶ 26,301 (Rev. Commn. J. 1982).

55. *Bowman Handles, Inc.*, 10 BNA OSHC 1454, 1982 OSHD(CCH) ¶ 25,949 (Rev. Commn. J. 1982).

56. *Ennis Automotive, Inc., supra.*

57. *Donovan v. A.A. Beiro Construction Co., Inc.*, 746 F.2d 894 (D.C. Cir. 1984).

58. 436 U.S. 307 (1978).

59. *See, for example, Donovan v. Sarasota Concrete Co.*, 693 F.2d 1061 (11th Cir. 1982).

60. *See, for example, In re Establishment Inspection of Cerro Copper Products Co.*, 752 F.2d 280 (7th Cir. 1985).

61. *See, for example, In re Establishment Inspection of Kulp Foundry, Inc.*, 691 F.2d 1125 (3d Cir. 1982).

62. *Donovan v. Fall River Foundry Co., Inc.*, 712 F.2d 1103 (7th Cir. 1983).

63. 29 C.F.R. § 1903.4 (1981); *Rockford Drop Forge Co. v. Donovan*, 672 F.2d 626 (7th Cir. 1982); *Donovan v. Blue Ridge Pressure Castings*, 543 F. Supp. 53 (M.D. Pa. 1981).

64. *See, for example, Rockford Drop Forge Co. v. Donovan, supra.* At least one jurisdiction has held that a warrant may be contested in federal court even subsequent to inspection. *Weyerhauser Co. v. Marshall*, 592 F.2d 373 (7th Cir. 1979). *Gooch Mill & Elevator Co. v. Donovan*, 10 BNA OSHC 2206, 1982 OSHD(CCH) ¶ 26,328 (W.D. Mo. 1982). In general, however, once an inspection has occurred, an employer must exhaust administrative remedies before the OSHA Review Commission prior to challenging the validity of a warrant in federal court. *Robert K. Bell Enter., Inc. v. Donovan*, 710 F.2d 673, 11 BNA OSHC 1583 (10th Cir. 1983), *cert. denied*, 464 U.S. 1041 (1984); *In re Establishment Inspection of the Metal Bank of America, Inc.*, 700 F.2d 910 (3d Cir. 1983).

65. *Babcock & Wilcox Co. v. Marshall*, 610 F.2d 1128 (3d Cir. 1979); *Savina Home Indus., Inc. v. Secretary of Labor*, 594 F.2d 1358 (10th Cir. 1979); *Donovan v. Sarasota Concrete Co.*, 693 F.2d 1061 (11th Cir. 1982); *Carl M. Geupel Const. Co.*, 10 BNA OSHC 2097, 1982 OSHD(CCH) ¶ 26,309 (Rev. Commn. 1982).

66. *See, for example, In re Establishment Inspection of Kulp Foundry, Inc., supra; United States v. Westinghouse Elect. Corp.*, 638 F.2d 570, 580-81 (3d Cir. 1980).

67. *In re Establishment Inspection of Keokuk Steel Casting Co.*, 638 F.2d 42 (8th Cir. 1981); *Donovan v. Metal Bank of America, Inc.*, 516 F. Supp. 674 (E.D. Pa. 1981).

Environmental
Risk Management

# XXX

# Developments in Criminal and Civil Enforcement Under Key Environmental Statutes

### Kenneth A. Reich, Esq.*
### Widett, Slater & Goldman, P.C.
### Boston, Massachusetts

The past 20 years since the first Earth Day have witnessed an explosion in civil and criminal enforcement in the environmental area at both the federal and state levels. This explosion was caused by the enactment of significant federal and state environmental protection statutes, the establishment of the United States Environmental Protection Agency (EPA) and parallel state agencies, the increasing sophistication of governmental law enforcement agencies in this new field and the demands of the public for stricter enforcement of environmental laws and regulations. Other important factors are citizens suits which have been very effective in uncovering violations and enforcing the laws where the government has been reluctant or too busy to address the particular violations. While the vagaries of funding and politics have resulted in temporary slowdowns in enforcement, for the most part the trend has been steadily upward. This is reflected in larger enforcement staffs at the United States Department of Justice, the EPA, and in the states, more criminal prosecutions, larger civil and criminal fines, and increasing frequency of offenders going to jail.

*The author acknowledges with great appreciation the valuable asistance of Meredith A. Helmer, a law clerk with Widett, Slater & Goldman, P.C.

## Overview of Key Federal Statues
## and Recent Developments

There are a host of federal statutes which regulate in the environmental field. A discussion of all of them, and their myriad state counterparts, is beyond the scope of this chapter. The chapter also does not discuss other non-environmental statutes, e.g., 18 U.S.C. § 1001 (false statements), which the government uses to prosecute environmental crimes. Instead, the chapter will summarize the civil and criminal enforcement provisions of the key federal environmental statutes which have formed the core of the federal government's enforcement efforts over the last five years or more.[1]

Next, the chapter will discuss important recent judicial decisions and developments under these key statutes. While the chapter does not discuss environmental agency administrative actions, it should be recognized that they constitute the majority of enforcement activities under these statutes.[2] The focus is on those decisions under each statute which reflect the direction of federal enforcement and the courts' interpretation of the limits on that enforcement effort.

# Comprehensive Environmental Response,
# Compensation & Liability Act (CERCLA)

### The Statute

The Comprehensive Environmental Response, Compensation and Liability Act, (CERCLA,[3] or Superfund) first enacted in 1980, gives the federal government two principal, powerful weapons for enforcement. First, the government may maintain an action for injunctive relief under Section 106 to abate conditions which pose an "imminent and substantial endangerment" to health, welfare or the environment by reason of a release or threatened release of a hazardous substance. The same section provides for penalties of up to $25,000 per day, enforceable in district court, for willful violation of or failure to comply with a compliance order "without sufficient cause."[4]

Second, the government may institute a cost recovery action under Section 107[5] against certain enumerated owners/operators, past and present, generators and transporters. This second weapon is subject to very limited defenses, e.g., an act of God, act of war, act or omission of third parties other than employees, agents or persons contractually connected to the defendant (and providing the defendant establishes he exercised due care and took precautions against foreseeable acts or omissions of such third parties), or a combination of these defenses.[6] "Innocent landowners" are provided with a limited defense to liability under the SARA amendments.[7] (See Chapter X, Heymann.) The liability is for all costs or response, damages to natural resources and related transactional costs (e.g., studies, enforcement costs), subject to certain very generous limitations on liability (e.g., for "sites," response costs plus $50 million in damages).

A person who refuses to comply without sufficient cause with an enforcement order under Sections 104 or 106 can also be liable for treble damages.[8]

CERCLA, unlike the other key environmental statutes discussed, does not have any general criminal provisions. However, a key provision penalizes failures to report releases of reportable quantities of hazardous substances or false reporting, by imprisonment for three years (five years for second offenders) and by fines in accordance with applicable provisions of the federal criminal code.[9]

Like many of the federal environmental statutes, CERCLA has a citizens suit provision.[10] That section permits citizens suits against any person, including the government, alleged to be in violation of any standard, regulation, condition, requirement or order under CERCLA or against the federal government for failure to perform a non-discretionary duty. There is the usual 60-day-notice provision. The court may award appropriate relief, including an injunction, penalties, and costs and attorneys fees to the "prevailing or the substantially prevailing party."

A separate citizen provision allows an award of up to $10,000 to any individual providing information leading to a conviction for failure to report a hazardous substance release.[11]

### Developments

CERCLA has spawned an immense amount of litigation, both public and private, in the ten years since it was enacted. By now most of the principal issues regarding the constitutionality and breadth of the statute have been settled and new, subsidiary issues are being resolved.

While the case law and the SARA amendments in 1986 have largely put to rest questions such as whether there is a private right to contribution under CERCLA and whether the standard of liability is strict, joint and several, the past several years have seen some significant decisions in such areas as the scope of the government's enforcement authority, the limitations of joint and several liability, the extent of secondary liability of parents, successors, lenders, trustees and the liability of "arrangers."

In a series of recent cases, the First Circuit Court of Appeals has grappled with a number of hotly debated issues under CERCLA. In *O'Neal v. Picillo*,[12] the court rejected arguments by non-settling, *de minimis* parties that imposition of joint and several liability for the balance of past costs owed to the state for cleanup of a site and for future costs was unconstitutional or fundamentally unfair even though defendants could end up owing far in excess of their proportionate share. The court examined the plain language of the statute and concluded that Congress meant to impose such liability, despite the harshness of the result, where the harm was indivisible. It also noted the availability of a contribution action to the defendants to seek to minimize their liability.

In *United States of America v. Cannons Engineering Corp., et al.,*[13] the same court in a sweeping decision upheld the broad discretion of the government to settle CERCLA cases in the face of substantial challenges to the fairness of a settlement. In that case some 671 parties — owners/operators, generators and transporters — were notified by EPA, the states of New Hampshire and Massachusetts of their potential liability for cleanup of four separate sites in the two states.

The government divided the parties into a large "*de minimis*" class and a much smaller non-*de minimis* class for purposes of settlement discussions. It entered into separate settlements with most of the members of each class of potentially responsible parties ("PRPs"), some of which were embodied in administrative consent orders and the rest of which were embodied in judicial consent decrees.

The Court of Appeals considered an appeal by several non-settlors from the order of the district judge approving the consent decree settlements. The non-settlors challenged all aspects of the fairness and reasonableness of the decrees. Their principal complaint was that in offering them a *de minimis* buyout, the government did not inform them that if they rejected it they would be ineligible to settle on the same basis as the non-*de minimis* parties. (Some of the *de minimis* parties were actually quite large generators and claimed that they faced substantially more liability than the major generators because of the differences between the two settlement terms). The Court of Appeals rejected this challenge and found not only that the government had acted in good faith but that "[a]s a matter of law, we do not believe that Congress meant to handcuff government negotiators in CERCLA cases by insisting that the EPA allow polluters to pick and choose which settlements they might prefer to join. As a matter of equity, we think that if appellants were misled at all, it was by their own wishful thinking."[14] The court proceeded to uphold the substantive fairness of the settlement as well and established the broad discretion of the government in negotiating and settling these cases.

Specifically, the court approved of EPA's tactic of upping the ante on settlement by imposing an escalating penalty (equal to a multiple of its liability) on late settlors.[15] As in *Picillo*, the court also upheld the validity of the imposition of disproportionate liability on non-settlors.[16] The court held, in sum, that EPA had very broad power and discretion in the CERCLA settlement process, subject only to the constraints that it not mislead the parties, discriminate unfairly or engage in deceptive practices. This is not much of a constraint.

Finally, in *United States v. Ottati & Goss, Inc.*,[17] the court reviewed a remedy/damages determination of the district court in one of the longest CERCLA trials to date. It affirmed the bulk of the district court's judgement, but reversed and remanded with respect to several issues. The first issue was whether the volatile organic (VOC) cleanup was adequate; the court ordered the district court to direct additional remedial work on the basis of evidence that the VOC's had not been cleaned up to the district court's standard.

The second issue was whether the district court should have disallowed EPA some $337,000 of indirect costs as a sanction for its alleged misconduct. The court of Appeals remanded for further fact finding on this issue. Most importantly, the court found that in a Section 106(a) case for injunctive relief, a district court was not bound to adopt the government's preferred remedy unless it found it arbitrary and capricious, but was free to exercise its equitable power to order any appropriate remedy. This ruling appears to be inconsistent with the statute, as amended by SARA.[18] The court indicated that the arbitrary and capricious deference standard only applied in the context of the enforcement of an EPA cleanup order or in a suit for cost recovery.[19]

The government's increasingly aggressive attempt to bring a wider range of parties under the CERCLA umbrella has largely been supported by the courts in recent decisions. In *United States v. Aceto Agric. Chem. Corp.*[20] the Eighth Circuit Court of Appeals found that chemical companies who contracted with pesticide formulators to produce pesticides could be liable for "arranging" for the disposal of hazardous substances in these circumstances. The companies' retaining title to the chemicals and inadvertent disposal, through leaks, spills, production of unusable batches and other waste production, was an inherent part of the formulation process. The court also held that defendants could be liable for having "contributed to" the disposal of waste under RCRA.

In *Smith Land & Improvement Corp. v. The Celotex Corp.*[21] the Third Circuit Court of Appeals applied a federal rule of decision and held a successor corporation liable for its predecessors' waste disposal practices. While this is a straight forward application of traditional corporate law, EPA in a published policy would go farther and subject corporations that purchased assets of another liable simply by reason of their continuation of the same business.[22] This policy also takes a broad view of parental liability. Recently the Fifth Circuit appeared to have put the brakes on this trend in refusing to pierce the corporate veil to hold the parent liable without specific congressional directive. In *Joslyn Mfg. Co. v. T.L. James & Co., Inc.,*[23] the Court of Appeals held: "Significantly, CERCLA does not define 'owners or operators' as including the parent company of offending wholly-owned subsidiaries. Nor does the legislative history indicate that Congress intended to alter so substantially a basic tenet of corporate law."[24] The court also held on the facts that there was no evidence that the subsidiary was used as a "sham," a "bogus shell" to avoid liability. But see *U.S. v. Kayser-Roth Corp.*[25] where a Rhode Island district court had no problem in piercing the corporate veil where the parent "exhibited overwhelming persuasive control" over the subsidiary. The court also held the parent liable as an "operator" without veil piercing.

However, in a recent decision, the Eleventh Circuit Court of Appeals sent shivers down the spines of lenders when it held in the case of *U.S. v. Fleet Factors Corp.*[26] that a lender could be liable under CERCLA "if its involvement with the management of the facility is sufficiently broad to support the inference that it could affect hazardous waste disposal decisions if it so chose."[27]  The court refused to dismiss the government's claim against the lender even though the lender had not foreclosed on the property and had not involved itself in the day-to-day operation of the facility. The court appears to have created a third category of liability between owner and operator.

This whole area of "secondary liability" is still in considerable flux as the courts struggle with the question of how far to cast the CERCLA net. The EPA recently announced that it will be reviewing this entire issue to determine if its policies or rules and regulations need to be changed.[28] The EPA also came out with a 1989 policy on "innocent landowners" but the policy unfortunately does not settle any of the hard questions concerning the scope of this statutory defense.[29]

In *U.S. v. Vineland Chemical Company, Inc.*[30] a district court in New Jersey upheld the government's broad authority under section 3008 to issue compliance orders and to collect penalties for violation. It fined a non-complying company $1.2 million for its failure to comply with an EPA administrative order.

In *U.S. v. Bogas,*[31] a defendant convicted of failing to report a release of a hazardous substance and making of a false statement in connection with illegal disposal of 55-gallon paint drums at the Cleveland airport was the first person reported to be sentenced under the new federal Sentencing Guidelines.[32] He was sentenced to four years of probation and 1,000 hours of community service. The court considered the enhancement and downgrading provisions under the Guidelines and refused any enhancement for environmental contamination due to lack of evidence.

# Clean Water Act

## The Statute

The Clean Water Act provides the standard menu of civil and criminal enforcement. It also now provides EPA with the authority to seek administrative penalties as a result of the 1987 amendments.

# Developments in Criminal and Civil Enforcement under Key Environmental Statutes

The principal enforcement provisions are contained in Section 309 of the act. Under Section 309,[33] EPA may issue administrative enforcement orders or can seek judicial enforcement for violations of the act or permits issued pursuant to the act. The act authorizes the court to assess civil penalties of up to $25,000 per day of violation and to award appropriate relief.

The criminal penalties are more complex and depend on the types of violations. Negligent violations of the act or of permits issued under the act and negligent discharges into a sewer system, which the person knew or reasonably should have known could cause personal injury or property damage or which causes a sewage treatment works to violate its own permit, are punishable by fines of $2500 - $25,000 per day of violation, or imprisonment for not more than one year, or both. Second offenders are punishable by fines of up to $50,000 per day of violation or imprisonment of up to two years, or both.[34]

The 1987 amendments added a category of knowing violations, which are felonies. Knowing violations are punishable by fines of $5000 - $50,000 per day, or three years imprisonment, or both. Second offenders are punishable by fines of up to $100,000 per day or imprisonment of up to six years, or both.[35]

The 1987 amendments also added the category of knowing endangerment, similar to the 1984 amendments to RCRA. This section provides that any person who knowingly violates the act or a permit issued pursuant to the act who "knows at that time that he thereby places another person in imminent danger of death or serious bodily injury" shall be subject to a fine of up to $250,000 or imprisonment for up to 15 years, or both. For organizations, the fine is up to $1,000,000. The punishment is doubled for second offenders.[36]

Finally, the act punishes knowing false statements and knowing tampering with monitoring devices, with fines of up to $10,000 or imprisonment of up to two years, or both. Second offenders can receive double these maximum penalties.[37]

The 1987 amendments also added a new section which gives EPA administrative penalty authority. Section 309(g) provides EPA with the authority to assess two classes of penalties.[38] Class I penalties may not exceed $10,000 per violation, or $25,000 in the aggregate. The person receiving the notice of penalty is entitled to an informal hearing not subject to the formal administrative procedures under the Administrative Procedure Act (APA). For the more serious Class II penalties, the maximum penalty that may be assessed is $10,000 per day of violation with a total maximum of $125,000. Recipients of such penalty assessments are entitled to a formal, APA-type administrative hearing on the record. The section provides a right of appeal but the penalty order shall not be set aside unless it is unsupported by substantial evidence in the record or assessment is an abuse of discretion. With certain limitations, enforcement and payment of a penalty under this section is a shield against civil judicial penalty enforcement, including citizens suits, for the same violations.[39]

Another section of the act provides criminal penalties of up to $10,000 or imprisonment of up to one year, or both, for failure to promptly notify of spills of oil or hazardous substances (regulated under the Clean Water Act)[40] into the waters of the United States.

For releases of oil or hazardous substances from vessels or facilities, there are separate penalties under Section 311 as well as a provision for cost recovery.[41] This is the precursor to CERCLA. The Coast Guard may administratively assess penalties for such releases of up to $5000 per violation. EPA also can seek penalties from the courts of up to $50,000 per violation, except for wilful violations where the penalty is up to $250,000. In cases of releases or threatened releases into the waters of the United States, which pose an imminent and substantial threat to health or welfare, the government can seek appropriate relief in the courts. As in CERCLA, subject to certain limitations and narrow defenses, the government can recover its cleanup costs against responsible parties, under Section 311(f). These costs include the costs of restoration or replacement of natural resources.[42]

The Clean Water Act also has a citizens suit provision, in Section 505. This Section provides that a citizen can sue the government or any party alleged to be in violation of effluent standards, limitations or orders under the Act or against the government for failure to perform a non-discretionary duty. As in CERCLA, the court may award appropriate relief, including penalties, as well as costs and attorneys fees to the prevailing or substantially prevailing party. There is a 60-day-notice period.[43]

### Developments

One of the most significant recent developments is the 1987 amendments to the Clean Water Act allowing for the administrative assessment of civil penalties. The EPA is beginning to aggressively use its new enforcement tool as reflected in the statistics for administrative actions initiated by the EPA for the fiscal year 1989. In that year there were a combined total of 2,146 administrative actions initiated under the Clean Water Act and Safe Drinking Water Act, up from 1,345 in fiscal year 1988.[44]

EPA's civil and criminal enforcement efforts under the Clean Water Act also reflect increasing aggressiveness. Civil referrals to the Department of Justice from EPA increased from 37 in FY 1981, the beginning of the short-lived Gorsuch era, to 123 in FY 1988 and 94 in FY 89.

In June of 1990, EPA announced a consent decree settlement with a Michigan paper company and its parent for the largest civil penalty ever assessed against private companies under the Clean Water Act: $2.1 million. The companies also agreed to settle criminal charges and to pay $100,000 in criminal penalties. The violations were for exceedances of their NPDES discharge permit limit for pretreatment violations.[45]

In May of 1990, the United States obtained its first conviction under the new "knowing endangerment" provision of the Clean Water Act against a Massachusetts metal plater.[46]

There were several recent precedent-setting decisions under the Clean Water Act. In the case of *Gwaltney of Smithfield v. Chesapeake Bay Found.*,[47] a citizens suit against a Virginia meatpacker for violations of its NPDES discharge permit, the Supreme Court held that in a citizens suit under the act there must be an allegation of "continuous or intermittent violations" to sustain the action against the polluter. The court held that the language in the citizens suit provision[48] permitting citizens suits against persons "alleged to be in violation of [effluent standards or orders]" does not allow for suits for wholly past violations. The court held, however, that if there was a good faith allegation of a continuous violation, the suit could stand. The Fourth Circuit Court of Appeals, on remand, interpreted the court's holding to mean that if there were ongoing violations when the suit was brought (not when it was tried), the suit could go forward.[49] The case recently settled with a payment of a civil

penalty of $289,922, based on the calculation of "continuing viola-
tions" and payment of $300,000 in attorneys fees.[50]   This holding
was followed by the Eleventh Circuit Court of Appeals in *Atlantic
States Legal Found., Inc v. Tyson Foods, Inc.*,[51] a citizens suit against a
poultry processing plant for violation of its NPDES permit.

In another important case, *Tull v. U.S.*,[52] the Supreme Court held
that a defendant in a civil enforcement case alleging illegal discharges into wetlands under Section 404 of the Act was entitled to a jury
trial on all issues, even though the government was seeking both
civil penalties and injunctive relief.  The court held that this jury
trial right was guaranteed by the Seventh Amendment to the Constitution since the case was similar to an action for debt.  The court
also held that the actual assessment of a particular penalty was up
to the judge, not the jury to decide.[53]  It remains to be seen whether
this decision will have ramifications for civil enforcement under the
other key federal environmental statutes. [54]

In a case analogous to the pre-enforcement review cases under
CERCLA, the Seventh Circuit in *Hoffman Group v. EPA*[55] was confronted with the issue whether a recipient of an EPA administrative
order requiring it to cease and desist from filling wetlands, to re-
store the wetlands and to pay an administrative penalty, was entitled to judicial review of the compliance order.  The court held, by
analogy to cases under CERCLA and the Clean Air Act, that there
was no right to pre-enforcement review.  Rather, the defendant
must await civil enforcement of the compliance order and must exercise its appeal rights as to the administrative penalties.  This was
the first judicial interpretation of the new administrative penalty
provisions of the Clean Water Act.

The court's ruling provides EPA with broad latitude to proceed
administratively to assess penalties without judicial interference.
Interestingly, the court did not seem troubled by the Scylla and Cha-
rybdis choice facing the target of an administrative compliance order who is subject to civil penalties of $25,000 per day for violations
of the order but must await an enforcement action to challenge it
and raise its good faith defenses.  Unlike the analogous provision of
CERCLA, Section 309(d) of the Clean Water Act does not provide a
defense based on "sufficient cause" or wilfulness.  It remains to be
seen whether the courts will provide a judicial gloss on this section,
although the 1987 Amendments also enumerated a number of factors which a court must consider in determining the amount of the

penalty, including good faith efforts to comply, which may as a practical matter afford the non-complying defendant with some measure of relief.[56]

# Resource Conservation and Recovery Act

### The Statute

RCRA is largely a regulatory statute. It provides the framework for enforcement of detailed regulations under 40 CFR sections 260 *et seq.* and state-approved programs with respect to the handling, storage transportation, treatment and disposal of hazardous wastes. Unlike CERCLA, RCRA does not have a cost expenditure/recovery mechanism but achieves its results through enforcement against owners/operators and "contributors."

The principal civil judicial remedy under RCRA is Section 7003[57] which authorizes suit when the "past or present handling, storage, treatment, transportation or disposal of any solid waste or hazardous waste may present an imminent and substantial endangerment to health or the environment." Suit may be brought against any person. . . who has contributed or who is contributing to such handling, etc., to order appropriate relief.[58] The 1984 Amendments to RCRA added *past* handling, etc., and *past* contribution to make it clear that RCRA addressed both present and *past* generators and others. It also confirmed that responsible parties under RCRA were the same as those under CERCLA by adding express language defining liable parties.[59]

In addition to Section 7003, RCRA provides the government with the authority to issue a compliance order, assess a civil penalty of up to $25,000 per day or to seek judicial relief for violations of the statute under Section 3008.[60] Section 3008(h), added by the 1984 Amendments, authorizes corrective action orders, provides penalties of up to $25,000 per day for violations, and provides for judicial enforcement and relief. Under Section 3008(g) a court may assess penalties of up to $25,000 per day for violations of the statute.

RCRA also provides a battery of criminal penalties for violations of the statute under Section 3008(d).[61] The criminal penalties were significantly increased as a result of the 1984 Amendments. For knowing violations of the following, the maximum fine is $50,000 per day of violation and/or the imprisonment set forth below: transport hazardous waste to an unpermitted facility;[62] treat, store or dispose of hazardous waste without a permit or in knowing violation of any material condition of a permit or of interim status;[63] material omission or false material statement in documents required to be filed or maintained under RCRA; generate, store, treat, transport, dispose, export, or otherwise handle hazardous waste or used oil and destroy, alter, conceal or fail to file required records, documents;[64] transport without a manifest hazardous waste or used oil;[65] export hazardous waste without consent of a receiving country or in violation of an applicable international agreement;[66] transport, treat, store, dispose of or otherwise handle used oil in violation of applicable permit or regulations.[67] For the same violations, the maximum term of imprisonment is five years for violations of the first two categories and two years for the others. For second offenders, the maximum penalties are doubled.

A special category of enhanced punishment is reserved for offenders who knowingly transport, treat, dispose, store or export hazardous or used oil in violation of the above provisions who "knows at that time that he thereby places another person in imminent danger of death or serious bodily injury."[68] The penalties for this offense are a maximum fine of $250,000, imprisonment of 15 years, or both. Organizations are subject to maximum fines of $1,000,000. The relevant terms are defined in the statute.[69]

As do the other key federal environmental statutes, RCRA has a citizens suit provision.[70] Section 7002 of RCRA provides for citizens suits against (a) any person alleged to be in violation of a permit, standard, regulation, condition, requirement, prohibition or order or (b) against past or present generators, transporters, owners or operators of facilities who have or are contributing to handling, storage, treatment, transportation or disposal of solid or hazardous waste which may present an imminent and substantial endangerment to health or the environment or (c) against EPA for failure to perform a nondiscretionary duty.[71] There is a 60-day-notice requirement for actions under subcategories (a) and (c) above, except for actions alleging violation of any hazardous waste regulations or requirements. There is a 90-day-notice requirement for the second category of actions except for allegations of violations of the hazardous waste regulations. Also, such activities cannot be commenced if EPA or the state is already prosecuting an action, or, in the case of an endangerment allegation, if EPA or the state is prosecuting an action under the endangerment provisions of RCRA or CERCLA, is engaging in a cleanup of the site, or a responsible party is under an order to conduct and is conducting a cleanup.[72]

## Developments

As with CERCLA, many of the fundamental issues regarding the scope of the enforcement provisions under RCRA are well settled. Recent cases have addressed other important issues under the statute.

In *U.S. v. Aceto Agric. Chem. Corp.*[73] discussed above, the Eighth Circuit Court of Appeals held that pesticide companies who arranged with formulators to produce their pesticides could be liable for having "contributed to" the disposal of hazardous waste at the site in an action brought under Section 7003. The court held that it could find no basis for distinguishing between the phrase "arranging for" under CERCLA and "contributing to" under RCRA for purposes of the case and the defendants were thus liable under both statutes.[74]

In *National Standard Company v. Adamkus*[75] the Seventh Circuit Court of Appeals held that EPA has broad discretion to inspect a facility. The absence of proof of presence of hazardous wastes or releases was not a bar to this inspection authority.

In two cases, two separate circuits split on the issue whether the "knowing" requirement under the RCRA provision, making it a crime to knowingly treat, store or dispose of hazardous waste without a permit, meant that the government had to prove the defendants knew of the absence of a permit.[76]

In *U.S. v. Hoflin*,[77] the Ninth Circuit Court of Appeals held that the government did not have this burden and that proof the defendant knew the waste was hazardous and that he knowingly treated, stored or disposed of it was sufficient. The court relied on its plain reading of the statute which requires that handling of hazardous waste in violation of a permit be "knowing", but not so for handling without a permit.[78] It also held that its reading of the statute was consistent with the broad purposes of RCRA to protect the public health and environment from clandestine dumping.[79]

The *Hoflin* Court expressly disagreed with the Third Circuit's decision in *U.S. v. Johnson and Towers, Inc.*[80] In that case the court held that a knowledge element must be read into Section 3008(d)(2)(a) because "[i]t is unlikely that Congress could have intended to subject to criminal prosecution those persons who acted when no permit had been obtained irrespective of their knowledge (under Section A), but not those persons who acted in violation of the terms of a permit unless that action was knowing (subsection (B)."[81]

The "knowing endangerment" provision of RCRA was upheld by the Tenth Circuit Court of Appeals in reviewing the first conviction under that section. In *U.S. v. Protex Industries, Inc.,* [82] the court affirmed the conviction of a drum recycling company whose employees were placed at risk of solvent poisoning and showed evidence of acute health effects. It rejected in strong language the defendant's argument that the statute as applied was unconstitutionally vague because the alleged health effects — enhanced risk of developing cancer in the future and impairment of mental faculties — did not constitute "serious bodily injury." "Appellant's position demonstrates a callousness toward the severe physical effect the prolonged exposure to toxic chemicals may cause or has caused to the three former employees."[83]

In *U.S. v. Dee, Lentz and Gepp*[84] three federal employees were sentenced to three years probation and 1,000 hours community service on their conviction for knowing violations of hazardous waste requirements at the U.S. Army's Aberdeen Proving Grounds facility. This was the first such prosecution of federal employees for environmental violations which occurred in the course of their official duties.

## The Former Clean Air Act

### The Statute

The former Clean Air Act (1977 - 1990), like RCRA, provides the skeleton on which hangs a very complex set of regulations as described in Chapter II, on the new Clean Air Act. Both Clean Air Acts are quite complex and confusing and regulate or will regulate a myriad of stationary sources, mobile sources, sources in "clean air" areas and the like. The rest of this chapter describes enforcement applied under the Act in effect from 1977 to 1990.

Under Section 113(a) of the former Act,[85] EPA is empowered to issue administrative orders against those persons who violate the applicable provisions of a state implementation plan and to bring civil actions. However, such orders and actions can only be brought if the violations continue for more than 30 days after the date of EPA's notice of violation. The EPA is also empowered under the former Act to issue compliance orders and file civil actions for violations of new source performance standards, regulations of hazardous emissions, regulations of energy-related authorities and violations under EPA's inspection authority, without the 30 day wait.[86] Under Section 113 (b)[87] the EPA "shall" in the case of a major stationary source and may in the case of other sources, file a civil action for injunctive relief and recover civil penalties of up to $15,000 per day of violation for failure to comply with administrative orders under that subsection and for other specifically enumerated causes. This subsection also authorizes recovery of Section 120 administrative non-compliance penalties. In awarding penalties, the court is to take into account certain factors, including the size of the business, economic impact and seriousness of the violation.[88] The former Clean Air Act does not give EPA the authority to assess penalties administratively, (except for the Section 120 non-compliance penalties.)

There are also separate penalties for violation of the mobile source provisions dealing with tampering with pollution control devices, sale of vehicles without appropriate pollution control devices, and other similar provisions. The penalties are $2500-$10,000.[89]

The former Clean Air Act also provides in Section 113(c)[90] for criminal penalties for knowingly violating an applicable implementation plan more than 30 days after notice, knowing violations of orders, knowing violation of new source performance standards, hazardous emission regulations, and other enumerated violations. The penalties are a fine of not more than $25,000 per day of violation, imprisonment for not more than one year, or both. Second offenders are subject to double these penalties. The penalties for knowingly making false statements or for tampering with monitoring devices is a fine of not more than $10,000 or imprisonment of not more than six months, or both.

Section 304 of the former Clean Air Act[91] provides for citizens suits against the United States and other persons alleged to be in violation of emission standards, limits or a federal or state order, against EPA for failure to perform a non-discretionary duty, or against a person in violation of a permit or who proposes to construct or constructs a new or modified major source without a permit.[92] There are the usual

60-day-notice requirements except for actions for violations of orders or for violations of national emission standards for hazardous air pollutants.[93] Unlike the other citizens suit provisions, the former Clean Air Act does not allow for recovery of civil penalties.

## Developments

Civil actions under the Clean Air Act continue to make up a significant segment of the federal government's enforcement effort. They have represented from 25 percent to 40 percent of the civil referrals from EPA to the Department of Justice in the years 1985 - 1989.

The Supreme Court on June 14, 1990, decided a major enforcement issue under the act. The issue is the enforceability of a federally approved state implementation plan pending EPA's inaction on a state's proposed revision of the plan. In *General Motors Corp. v. United States*[94] the Supreme Court resolved a split among the First, and Fifth D.C. Circuits on this issue and the related issue of whether EPA was required to rule finally on a proposed implementation plan revision within the four month deadline for original implementation plans. The case involved GM's automobile assembly plant in Framingham, Massachusetts. The federally approved state implementation plan required GM to meet certain volatility limits in its paint by December 31, 1985. The state proposed a revision to EPA which would have allowed GM until August, 1987 to meet the deadline, which it would have done by shutting the old facility and building a new, cleaner facility. GM constructed the new facility and closed the old facility, but the EPA did not finally reject the implementation plan revision until well afterward, more than two and one-half years after submittal by the state. The United States sued GM for violations of the original, unrevised implementation plan. The district court dismissed the suit on the basis of a Fifth Circuit decision, *American Cyanamid Co. v. U.S. Environmental Protection Agency*,[95] which held in similar circumstances that once the initial four month review period had passed EPA was barred from collecting penalties for violations of the existing implementation plan until it ruled on the proposed revision. The Court of Appeals agreed that there was a four-month review period but held that EPA was not barred from suing GM and that the period and reasonableness of EPA delay could be considered in deciding whether to assess penalties, and in what amount.[96]

The Supreme Court held, in reversing the First Circuit Court of Appeals, and most of the other courts of appeals which had considered the issue, that there was no four month deadline in the Clean Air Act for EPA to rule on implementation plan revisions.[97] The court also held that there was no bar to enforcement whether or not EPA's delay was unreasonable. The court cited a long line of authority for the proposition that an applicable approved implementation plan is the law until it is revised.[98] The court concluded that since the statute contained no bar provision, the court should not infer one.[99] The source's remedies were to seek a mandamus to force the agency to act (good luck!) or a request to the district court for reduction or elimination of penalties during any period of unreasonable delay.[100]

The Third Circuit Court of Appeals, in an earlier case, also upheld the principle that a source must comply with existing legal requirements until they are revised. In *U.S. v. Wheeling Pittsburgh Steel Corp.*,[101] the court reversed a district court's order unilaterally amending a consent decree to provide a steel company additional time to comply with certain requirements to install pollution control equipment. The court held that the plain language of the provision of the Clean Air Act regulating the steel industry[102] severely curtailed the court's equitable discretion to extend the statutory compliance deadlines.[103] The court also held that under the consent decree and the Act, a pending "bubble" application did not relieve the steel company of its obligation to comply with the existing emission limitations. The court finally held that the automatic stay provisions of the Bankruptcy Code do not apply when the government is seeking to enforce its police powers and that economic infeasibility is not a defense to enforcement.[104]

In addition to these judicial developments, there were several recent substantial consent decrees under the Clean Air Act. For instance, in *U.S. v. Volkswagen of America* , Volkswagen agreed to pay a civil penalty of $600,000 for various violations and not to reopen its Pennsylvania plant without being in compliance with applicable law.[105] In *U.S. v. AVCO Corp.*, the defendant entered into a consent decree which provided for payment of a civil penalty of $333,000 for VOC violations at its Tennessee plant coating operations. In a subsequent decree the company agreed to pay additional penalties of $167,000.[106] In *U.S. v. J. Pizzuto Company, Inc. and Reynolds Metals Company*, the parties agreed to pay a civil penalty of $105,000 for asbestos violations.[107]  P.W. Stephens Contractors, Inc. agreed to pay a civil penalty of $125,000 for late notices of asbestos renovation and/ or demolition operations.[108]  There were also significant cases filed (and settled) under the mobile source program against refiners, automobile manufacturers, and gasoline distributors.[109]

## Future Developments

As the following statistics indicate, environmental enforcement has dramatically increased over the last 5 - 10 years at both the federal and state level.  The Environmental Enforcement Section of the newly renamed Environmental and Natural Resources Division (formerly the Land and Natural Resources Division) has a current staff of approximately 130 attorneys, four times its staff in 1985.[110]  There is a separate Environmental Crimes Section of approximately 23 prosecutors who work in conjunction with the U.S. Attorneys offices to prosecute environmental crimes.[111]

In FY 1989 there were a total of 101 indictments, 107 pleas and convictions, a total of nearly $13 million in fines imposed and jail sentences of 53 years.[112]  In the same year, EPA imposed over $35 million in civil penalties (civil and administrative), the second highest total in its history.[113]

In FY 1988 EPA referred 372 civil cases to the Department of Justice for filing in court.  It referred 364 cases in FY 1989.  The number of civil referrals in FY 1978 was 262 and in FY 1979 was 242.  In FY 1981 and 1982 it dropped to 118 and 112 respectively.[114]  Thus there has been a dramatic increase in judicial enforcement over the last 10 years.  Administrative actions have nearly quadrupled in the same time period.[115]

As the following table reflects, the mix of cases has radically changed over the past 10 years in the direction of hazardous waste enforcement.  Hazardous waste cases referred in FY 1981, the first year after the passage of CERCLA, were only 14, 12 percent of the total cases referred.  Air cases totalled 66, or 56 percent of the total. By FY 1989, however, hazardous waste referrals totalled 143, or 38 percent of the total, while air cases were 25 percent of the total and water cases about the same.

## Table 1
### EPA Civil Referrals to the Department of Justice
### FY1972-FY1989

| | FY72 | FY73 | FY74 | FY75 | FY76 | FY77 | FY78 | FY79 | FY80 |
|---|---|---|---|---|---|---|---|---|---|
| Air | 0 | 4 | 3 | 5 | 15 | 50 | 123 | 149 | 100 |
| Water | 1 | 0 | 0 | 20 | 67 | 93 | 137 | 81 | 56 |
| Hazardous Waste | 0 | 0 | 0 | 0 | 0 | 0 | 2 | 9 | 53 |
| Toxics/Pesticides | 0 | 0 | 0 | 0 | 0 | 0 | 0 | 3 | 1 |
| | | | | | | | | | |
| Totals | 1 | 4 | 3 | 25 | 82 | 143 | 26 | 242 | 210 |

| | FY81 | FY82 | FY83 | FY84 | FY85 | FY86 | FY87 | FY88 | FY89 |
|---|---|---|---|---|---|---|---|---|---|
| Air | 66 | 36 | 69 | 82 | 116 | 115 | 122 | 86 | 92 |
| Water | 37 | 45 | 56 | 95 | 93 | 119 | 92 | 123 | 94 |
| Hazardous Waste | 14 | 29 | 33 | 60 | 48 | 84 | 77 | 143 | 169 |
| Toxics/Pesticides | 1 | 2 | 7 | 14 | 19 | 24 | 13 | 20 | 9 |
| | | | | | | | | | |
| Totals | 118 | 112 | 165 | 251 | 276 | 342 | 304 | 372 | 364 |

*Source: EPA 1989 Enforcement Accomplishments Report.*

---

In FY 1989 the states referred over 700 civil cases to states' attorneys general for enforcement and issued over 12,000 administrative actions to violators. [116] The states also significantly stepped up their criminal enforcement efforts. [117]

It is possible to predict some trends for the future. With a significant amendment of the Clean Air Act expected to be signed into law shortly, there will be increased criminal enforcement and fines under that act as prosecutors are given new weapons and more stringent penalties in their arsenal. There will be increasing use of the administrative penalty provisions of the Clean Water Act, RCRA and CERCLA to achieve enforcement goals in a more efficient and cost-effective manner than pursuing civil litigation. However, EPA will continue to seek recovery of its remedial and removal costs under CERCLA and will be vigilant about pursuing non-settlors for unreimbursed amounts under the joint and liability doctrine. Once the RCRA corrective action rules are promulgated, EPA will have another set of regulations to enforce to achieve site cleanups and there will be increasing reliance on corrective action orders as well as judicial enforcement of them. Multi-media or cross-media investigations and enforcement will be stressed in the 1990s as the government moves away from single-media cases and takes a broader view of the problem.[118] Moreover, the states will continue to aggressively pursue environmental enforcement and in some cases will be more aggressive than the federal government, especially with respect to federal facilities.

New statutes and regulations are being passed yearly and the public's demand for increased regulation and enforcement of environmental laws will, if anything, increase. Offenses that may in the past have been handled civilly will be prosecuted criminally and convicted defendants who formerly may have received a fine and suspended sentence will be joining other white collar criminals in prison. In short, while the government will always be short-staffed and under-funded, enforcement, at least against those companies and individuals who know better, will continue to be a priority. Those who violate the laws will be at increased risk. To quote James Strock, EPA's current Assistant Administrator for Enforcement, "For those who stumble off the road of responsible environmental citizenship, the message from EPA enforcement should be clear: The bear is hungry."[119]

## About the Author

**Kenneth A. Reich** is head of the Environmental Law Practice Area with Widett, Slater & Goldman, P.C. in Boston, Massachusetts. From 1979 to 1986 he served as a trial attorney and Assistant Chief of the Environmental Enforcement Section, Land and Natural Resources Division, of the United States Department of Justice in Washington, D.C. Mr. Reich received a J.D. degree, *cum laude,* from Harvard Law School in 1972 and a B.A. degree from Cornell University in 1968. Mr. Reich is presently chairman of the Clean Air Committee of the Boston Bar Association and a member of the Boston Bar Ad Hoc Committee on the Massachusetts Contingency Plan. He is admitted to the bars of Georgia, Maryland, the District of Columbia and Massachusetts.

## Developments in Criminal and Civil Enforcement under Key Environmental Statutes

# Endnotes

1. Other important statutes include the Toxic Substances Control Act, 15 U.S.C. § 2601 *et seq.* and especially the PCB regulations at 40 C.F.R. Part 761, the Safe Drinking Water Act, 42 U.S.C. § 300(f) *et seq.*, and the Federal Insecticide, Fungicide, and Rodenticide Act, 7 U.S.C. § 136 *et seq.* (*See* Chapter VIII, by S.R. Heymann)

2. *Enforcement Accomplishments Report: FY 1989*, USEPA Pub. 20E-2001 (February 1990). The chapter also does not discuss judicial settlements or consent decrees, although most cases are resolved by settlement.

3. 42 U.S.C. § 9601 *et seq.* (as amended).

4. 42 U.S.C. § 9601(b)(1). This section was amended by the SARA amendments in 1986 to increase the penalty for violations of orders to $45,000 from $5000 per day and to provide a defense to enforcement, based on "sufficient cause." The amended section also sets out a procedure for reimbursement of response costs where the person had a good faith defense to liability or where it can demonstrate that the government's remedy was arbitrary and capricious or otherwise not in accordance with law. 42 U.S.C. § 9606(b)(2).

5. 42 U.S.C. § 9607(a).

6. 42 U.S.C. § 9607(b).

7. New Section 101(35), 42 U.S.C. §§ 9601(35), added by the SARA amendments, establishes the circumstances under which "innocent landowners" can avoid liability, despite their contractual relationship to the prior owner. Basically the would be "innocent landowner" must show (a) that in purchasing the property it conducted "all appropriate inquiry" and did not know customary practice" into the prior ownership and uses of the property, (b) that the hazardous substances were disposed of prior to its ownership, (c) that it exercised due care with respect to the hazardous substances. This section also provides a defense to the government if it acquired property involuntarily or through eminent domain and to landowners who inherited the property. EPA has issued guidance on this subject but the guidance answers none of the hard issues raised by the amendment. *See, Guidance on Landowner Liability Under Section 107(a)(1) of CERCLA, De Minimis Settlements Under Section 122(g)(1)(B) of CERCLA, and Settlement with Prospective Purchasers of Contaminated Property*, June 6, 1989. These issues will have to be addressed by the courts or by further amendment to CERCLA.

8. 42 U.S.C. § 9607(c)(3).

9. 42 U.S.C. § 9603(b).

10. 42 U.S.C. § 9659.

11. 42 U. S. C. § 9609(d) and *See* 53 *Fed. Reg.* 16086 (May 5, 1988).

12. 883 F.2d 176 (1st Cir. 1989), *cert. denied*, 110 U.S. 115 (1990).

13. 899 F.2d 79 (1st Cir. 1990).

14. *Id.* at 87.

15. *Id.* at 89.

16. *Id.* at 91-92.

17. 900 F.2d 429 (1st Cir. 1990).

# Environmental
# Risk Management

18. 42 U.S.C. § 6913(j) states that "in any judicial action judicial review of any issues concerning the adequacy of any response action taken or ordered by the President shall be limited to the administrative record."

19. *Ottati & Goss, Inc.*, 900 F.2d at 434, 435.

20. 872 F.2d 1373 (8th Cir. 1989).

21. 851 F.2d 86 (3rd Cir. 1988), *cert. denied*, 109 U.S. 837 (1989).

22. Memorandum, Courtney Price, Assistant Administrator for Enforcement and Compliance Monitoring dated June 3, 1984, "Liability or Corporate Shareholders and Successor Corporations for Abandoned Sites Under the Comprehensive Environmental Response, Compensation and Liability Act (CERCLA)."

23. 893 F.2d. 80 (5th Cir. 1990).

24. *Id.* at 82.

25. 724 F. Supp. 15 (D.R.I. 1989), *aff'd* 910 F.2d. 24 (1st Cir. 1990).

26. 901 F.2d. 1550 (11th Cir. 1990).

27. *Id.* at 1558.

28. *See* remarks of William Reilly, EPA Administrator, summarized in the Toxics Law Reporter of June 27, 1990 at 139 (". . . to involve innocent bystanders and lenders in these liability cases is not what we really intended.")

29. *See* Endnote 8.

30. 692 F. Supp. 415 (D.N.J. 1988); *see* 21 Env't Rep. (BNA) 162 (May 11, 1990) (penalty assessed April 30, 1990).

31. 731 F. Supp. 242 (N.D. Ohio 1990).

32. These Guidelines have been heavily criticized as requiring mandatory minimum and maximum environmental penalties in violation of the factors set forth in the environmental statutes and for other inconsistencies with the congressional scheme. *See, e.g.,* B. Sharp and L. Shen, "The (Mis)Application of Sentencing Guidelines to Environmental Crimes", 5 Toxics Law Rep. 189 (July 11, 1990); *see also* J. Starr and T. Kelly, Jr., "Environmental Crimes and the Sentencing Guidelines — The Time has Come . . . and it is Hard Time", 20 Envtl. L. Rep. (Envtl. L. Inst.) 10096 (March 1990).

33. 33 U.S.C. § 1319.

34. 33 U.S.C. § 1319(c).

35. 33 U.S.C. § 1319(c)(2).

36. 33 U.S.C. § 1319(c)(3). This section defines "serious bodily injury" and the conditions for determining if a person knew his conduct placed another person in imminent danger of death or serious bodily injury.

37. 33 U.S.C. § 1319(c)(4).

38. 33 U.S.C. § 1319(g).

39. 33 U.S.C. § 1319(g)(6).

40. Section 311(b)(5), 33 U.S.C. § 1321(b)(5).

41. 33 U.S.C. § 1321.

42. 33 U.S.C. § 1321(f)(4).

43. 33 U.S.C. § 1365.

44. EPA, FY 1989 Enforcement Accomplishments Report, Table 2 in "EPA's Environmental Enforcement in the 1990s", James M. Strock, 20 Envtl. L. Rep. (Envtl. L. Inst.) 10327, Table 1 (August 1990).

45. 21 Env't Rep. (BNA) 421 (June 29, 1990).

46. *U.S. v. Borjohn*, No. 89-259 (D. Mass. May 23, 1990). Sentencing on Nov. 7, 1990: two years probation and $50,000 fine; execution of sentence stayed pending appeal.

47. 484 U.S. 49 (1987).

48. 33 U.S.C. § 1365(a)(1).

49. *Chesapeake Bay Found. v. Gwaltney of Smithfield*, 890 F.2d 690 (4th Cir. 1989).

50. 21 Env't Rep. (BNA) 418, 419 (June 29, 1990).

51. 897 F.2d 1128 (11th Cir. 1990).

52. 481 U.S. 412 (1987).

53. *Id.* at 426, 427.

54. *See, e.g., In Re Acushnet River and New Bedford Harbor: Proceedings re Alleged PCP Pollution*, 712 F. Supp. 994 (D. Mass. 1989), where Judge Young held there was a right to a jury trial under CERCLA in a case seeking recovery of damages to natural resources.

55. 902 F.2d 567 (7th Cir. 1990).

56. Amended Section 309(d), 33 U.S.C. § 1319(d), provides as follows: "In determining the amount of a civil penalty the court shall consider the seriousness of the violation or violations, the economic benefit (if any) resulting from the violation, any history of such violations, any good-faith efforts to comply with the applicable requirements, the economic impact of the penalty on the violator, and such other matters as justice may require."

57. 42 U.S.C. § 6973.

58. 42 U.S.C. § 6973(a).

59. "The Administrator may bring suit on behalf of the United States . . . against any person (including any past or present generator, past or present transporter, or past or present owner or operator of a treatment, storage, or disposal facility)." 42 U.S.C. § 6973(a).

60. 42 U.S.C. § 6298(a).

61. 42 U.S.C. § 6928(d).

62. 42 U.S.C. § 6928(d)(1).

63. 42 U.S.C. § 6928(d)(2).

64. 42 U.S.C. § 6928(d)(4).

65. 42 U.S.C. § 6928(d)(5).

66. 42 U.S.C. § 6928(d)(6).

67. 42 U.S.C. § 6928(d)(7).

68. 42 U.S.C. § 6928(3).

69. 42 U.S.C. § 6928(f).

70. 42 U.S.C. § 6972.

71. 42 U.S.C. § 6972(a).

72. 42 U.S.C. § 6972(b),(c).

73. 872 F.2d 1373 (8th Cir. 1989).

74. *Id.* at 1384.

75. 881 F.2d 352 (7th Cir. 1989).

76. 42 U.S.C. § 6928(d)(2)(A).

77. 880 F.2d 1033 (9th Cir. 1989), *cert. denied*, 110 S. Ct. 1143 (1990).

78. Compare 42 U.S.C § 6928(d)(2)(B) with § 6928 (d)(2)(A).

79. *Hoflin*, 880 F.2d at 1038,1039.

80. 741 F.2d 662 (3rd Cir. 1984).

81. *Id.* at 668.

82. 874 F.2d 740 (10th Cir. 1989).

83. *Id.* at 743.

84. No. ___ (D.Md. May 10, 1989), *cited in* Enforcement Accomplishments Report: FY 1989, USEPA Pub. 20E-2001 (February 1990).

85. 42 U.S.C. § 7413(a).

86. 42 U.S.C. § 7413(a)(3).

87. 42 U.S.C. § 7413(b).

88. 42 U.S.C. § 7413(b).

89. Both the House and Senate-passed versions of the Clean Air Act reauthorization provide for administrative penalties.

90. 42 U.S.C. § 7524.

91. 42 U.S.C. § 7413(c).

92. 42 U.S.C. § 7604.

93. 42 U.S.C. § 7604(a).

94. 42 U.S.C. § 7604(b).

## Developments in Criminal and Civil Enforcement under Key Environmental Statutes

95. 110 S. Ct. 2528 (1990).

96. 810 F.2d 493 (5th Cir. 1987).

97. *U.S. v. General Motors Corp.*, 876 F.2d 1060 (1st Cir. 1989).

98. The Court interpreted Section 110(a)(3), 42 U.S.C. § 7410(a)(3), which requires EPA to approve a revision which meets the requirements of Section 110(a)(2), regarding original implementation plans, as incorporating only the **substantive**, not the **procedural** elements of Section 110(a)(2). *General Motors Corp. v. U.S.*, 110 S. Ct. at 2532.

99. *E.g., Train v. Natural Resources Defense Council, Inc.*, 421 U.S. 60 (1975).

100. *General Motors Corp. v. U.S.*, 110 S. Ct. at 2534.

101. *Id.* at 2534, n.4.

102. 818 F.2d 1077 (3rd Cir. 1987).

103. 42 U.S.C. § 7413(e)(9).

104. *U.S. v. Wheeling Pittsburgh Steel Corp.*, 818 F.2d at 1082, 1083.

105. *Id.* at 1087-1088.

106. Enforcement Accomplishments Report: FY 1989, USEPA Pub. 20E-2001 at p. 23, (February 1990).

107. *Id.* at 21.

108. *Id.* at 22.

109. *Id.* at 23.

110. *Id.* at 23, 24.

111. "Environmental Quality," The Twentieth Annual Report of the Council on Environmental Quality together with The President's Me ssage to Congress, at p. 172 (1990).

112. *Id.* at 173.

113. *Id.* at 174, Table 5-9.

114. Overview of EPA Federal Penalty Practices: FY 1989, USEPA Pub. 20E-2001 (February 1990).

115. 20 Envtl. L. Rep. (Envtl. L. Inst.) 10327, Table 2 (August 1990), *reprinted from* Enforcement Accomplishments Report: FY 1989, USEPA Pub. 20E-2001 (February 1990).

116. *Id.* Table 1.

117. *Id.* at 19.

118. *See* cases discussed in "Current Trends in the Prosecution of Environmental Offenses," Paul Nittoly, 5 Toxics L. Rep. (BNA) 161 (July 4, 1990).

119. *See generally,* "EPA's Environmental Enforcement in the 1990's" James M. Strock, 20 Envtl. L. Rep. (Envtl. L. Inst.) 10237 (August 1990).

# Appendix A

## Environmental Law Acronyms*

### Acronyms for Selected Environmental Statutes

AHERA    Asbestos Hazard Emergency Response Act of 1986 (see TSCA)

APA    Acid Precipitation Act of 1980 (42 U.S.C. §§ 8901 to 8912)

APA    Administrative Procedure Act (5 U.S.C. §§ 551 to 559, 701 to 703)

CAA    Clean Air Act (42 U.S.C. §§ 7401 to 7626)

CERCLA    Comprehensive Environmental Response, Compensation, and Liability Act of 1980 (42 U.S.C. §§ 9601 to 9675)

CWA    Clean Water Act (see FWPCA)

CZMA    Coastal Zone Management Act of 1972 (16 U.S.C. §§ 1451 to 1464)

EPCRA    Emergency Planning and Community Right-to-Know Act (42 U.S.C. §§ 11001 to 11050)

ESA    Endangered Species Act (15 U.S.C. §§ 1531 to 1544)

FDCA    Food, Drug and Cosmetic Act (21 U.S.C. § 321 *et. seq.*)

FIFRA    Federal Insecticide, Fungicide, and Rodenticide Act (7 U.S.C. §§ 136 to 136y)

FOIA    Freedom of Information Act (see APA)

---

* Reprinted with permission from the Morgan, Lewis & Bockius, *1990 Environmental Desk Book with revision by RTM Communications, Inc.*

FWPCA    Federal Water Pollution Control Act (33 U.S.C. §§ 1251 to 1387)

HMTA    Hazardous Materials Transportation Act (49 U.S.C. §§ 1801 to 1813)

HSWA    Hazardous and Solid Waste Amendments of 1984 (see RCRA)

LLRWPA    Low-Level Radioactive Waste Policy Act (42 U.S.C. §§ 2021b to 2021j)

MPRSA    Marine Protection, Research, and Sanctuaries Act of 1972 (16 U.S.C. §§ 1431 to 1445; 33 U.S.C. §§ 1401 to 1445)

NEPA    National Environmental Policy Act of 1969 (42 U.S.C. §§ 4321 to 4347)

NWPA    Nuclear Waste Policy Act of 1982 (42 U.S.C. §§ 10101 to 10270)

OSHA    Occupational Safety and Health Act of 1970 (29 U.S.C. §§ 651 to 678)

PHSA    Public Health Service Act (see SDWA)

RCRA    Resource Conservation and Recovery Act (42 U.S.C. §§ 6901 to 6992)

SARA    Superfund Amendments and Reauthorization Act of 1986 (see CERCLA and EPCRA)

SDWA    Safe Drinking Water Act (42 U.S.C. §§ 300f to 300j-26)

SMCRA    Surface Mining Control and Reclamation Act of 1977 (30 U.S.C. §§ 1201 to 1328)

SWDA    Solid Waste Disposal Act (see RCRA)

TSCA    Toxic Substances Control Act (15 U.S.C. §§ 2601 to 2671)

WQA    Water Quality Act of 1987 (see FWPCA)

**Acronyms Under Selected Environmental Laws**

**RCRA**

| | |
|---|---|
| BDAT | Best Demonstrated Available Technology |
| BPATT | Best Practicable Available Treatment Technology |
| DAF | Dilution/Attenuation Factors |
| HOC | Halogenated Organic Compounds |
| MSW | Municipal Solid Waste |
| MSWLF | Municipal Solid Waste Landfill Facility |
| MTR | Minimum Technology Requirement |
| OSW | Office of Solid Waste |
| OSWER | Office of Solid Waste and Emergency Response |
| OE | Office of Enforcement |
| SWMU | Solid Waste Management Units |
| TCLP | Toxicity Characteristic Leaching Procedure |
| TSD | Treatment, Storage and Disposal |
| UST | Underground Storage Tank |

**CERCLA, SARA, EPCRA**

| | |
|---|---|
| ARAR | Applicable or Relevant and Appropriate Requirements |
| CERCLIS | Comprehensive Environmental Response, Compensation, and Liability Information System |

| EA | Endangerment Assessment |
| EHS | Extremely Hazardous Substance |
| FS | Feasibility Study |
| HRS | Hazard Ranking System |
| LEPC | Local Emergency Planning Committee |
| MSDS | Material Safety Data Sheet |
| NBAR | Nonbinding Preliminary Allocation of Responsibility |
| NCP | National Contingency Plan |
| NPL | National Priorities List |
| NRC | National Response Center |
| OERR | Office of Emergency and Remedial Response |
| PHE | Public Health Evaluation |
| PRP | Potentially Responsible Party |
| QA/QC | Quality Assurance/Quality Control |
| RA | Remedial Action |
| RD | Remedial Design |
| RI | Remedial Investigation |
| ROD | Record of Decision |
| RQ | Reportable Quantity |
| SERC | State Emergency Response Commission |
| UST | Underground Storage Tank |

**CWA, FWPCA, SDWA**

BAT          Best Available Technology

BCT          Best Conventional Technology

BOD        Biochemical Oxygen Demand

BPCTCA    Best Practical Control Technology Currently Available

BPT          Best Practicable Technology

CAPA       Critical Aquifer Protection Area

COD        Chemical Oxygen Demand

CWT        Centralized Waste Treatment

DO           Dissolved Oxygen

DMR        Discharge Monitoring Report

ITR           Innovative Technology Requirement

MCL        Maximum Contaminant Level

MCLG      Maximum Contaminant Level Goal

MEP        Maximum Extent Practicable

NPDES     National Pollution Discharge Elimination System

NPDWS    National Primary Drinking Water Standards

NRC        National Response Center

NRT         National Response Team

POTW      Publicly Owned Treatment Works

| | |
|---|---|
| SMCL | Secondary MCL |
| SOCMI | Synthetic Organic Chemical Manufacturing Industry |
| SPCC | Spill Prevention Control and Countermeasure |
| SWTCP | Surface Water Toxic Controls Program |
| TSS | Total Suspended Solids |
| UIC | Underground Injection Control |
| WET | Whole Effluent Toxicity Limits |
| WQMP | Water Quality Management Plan |

**CAA**

| | |
|---|---|
| BACT | Best Available Control Technology |
| CO | Carbon Monoxide |
| ERC | Emission Reduction Credits |
| ESP | Electrostatic Precipitation |
| FBC | Fluidized Bed Combustion |
| FGD | Flue Gas Desulfurization |
| GEP | Good Engineering Practice |
| HC | Hydrocarbons |
| LAER | Lowest Achievable Emission Rate |
| MACT | Maximum Available Control Technology |
| NAAQS | National Ambient Air Quality Standards |
| NESHAP | National Emissions Standard for Hazardous Air Pollutants |
| $NO_x$ | Nitrogen Oxide |

| | |
|---|---|
| NSPS | New Source Performance Standards |
| PSD | Prevention of Significant Deterioration |
| RACT | Reasonably Available Control Technology |
| RAM | Real-Time Air-Quality Simulation Model |
| RVP | Reid Vapor Pressure |
| SIP | State Implementation Plan |
| $SO_2$ | Sulfur Dioxide |
| TSP | Total Suspended Particulates |
| VMT | Vehicle Miles Traveled |
| VOC | Volatile Organic Compound |

**TSCA**

| | |
|---|---|
| PMN | Pre-Manufacturing Notices |
| SNUR | Significant New Use Rule |
| TME | Test Marketing Exemption |

**FIFRA**

| | |
|---|---|
| IPM | Integrated Pest Management |
| RPAR | Rebuttable Presumption Against Registration |

**NEPA**

| | |
|---|---|
| DEIS | Draft Environmental Impact Statement |
| EIS | Environmental Impact Statement |
| FEIS | Final Environmental Impact Statement |

**OSHA**

| | |
|---|---|
| PEL | Permissible Exposure Limit |
| STEL | Short-Term Exposure Limit |

**PHSA**

| | |
|---|---|
| NTP | National Toxicology Program |

**Miscellaneous**

| | |
|---|---|
| ACO | Administrative Consent Order |
| AO | Administrative Order |
| ALJ | Administrative Law Judge |
| ATSDR | Agency for Toxic Substances & Disease Registry |
| CD | Consent Decree |
| CEQ | Council on Environmental Quality |
| CO | Consent Order |
| GAO | Government Accounting Office |
| IG | Inspector General |
| NOAA | National Oceanic and Atmospheric Administration |
| NOV | Notice of Violation |
| OTA | Office of Technology Assessment |
| PCB | Polychlorinated Biphenyl |
| SAB | Science Advisory Board |
| UAO | Unilateral Administrative Order |

# Appendix B

## Where To Find Selected Federal Environmental Regulations

### RCRA Hazardous Waste Management Regulations

| | |
|---|---|
| General-Definitions and Delisting Procedures | 40 CRF Part 260 |
| Identification and Listing of Hazardous Waste-Definition of Solid/Hazardous Waste; Recycling; Small Quantity Generators | 40 CFR Part 261 |
| Generator Standards | 40 CFR Part 262 |
| Transporter Standards | 40 CFR Part 263 |
| Final Permit Standards for Treatment, Storage, and Disposal Facilities | 40 CFR Part 264 |
| Interim Status Standards for Treatment, Storage, and Disposal Facilities | 40 CFR Part 265 |
| Recyclable Material Standards; Used Oil/Waste Combustion; Batteries | 40 CFR Part 266 |
| Land Disposal Restrictions | 40 CFR Part 268 |
| Permit Issuance Procedures | 40 CFR Part 270 |
| State Programs | 40 CFR Part 271-272 |
| Underground Storage Tanks | 40 CFR Part 280-281 |
| Standards for the Tracking and Management of Medical Waste | 40 CFR Part 253 |

**Superfund**

| | |
|---|---|
| National Contingency Plan | 40 CFR Part 300 |
| National Priorities List | 40 CFR Part 300 |
| Spill Reporting - Reportable Quantities | 40 CFR Part 302 and 355 |
| Citizen Rewards for Information on Superfund Criminal Violations | 40 CFR Part 303 |
| Arbitration Procedures for Small Superfund Cost Recovery Claims | 40 CFR Part 304 |
| Reimbursement to Local Governments for Emergency Response to Hazardous Substance Releases | 40 CFR Part 310 |
| Natural Resource Damage Assessments (Department of Interior) | 43 CFR Part 11 |

**Emergency Planning And Community Right-to-know**

| | |
|---|---|
| Trade SecrecyClaims and Disclosure to Health Professionals | 40 CFR Part 350 |
| Emergency Planning and Notification Procedures — Spill Reproting | 40 CFR Part 302 and 355 |
| Hazardous Chemical Reproting (MSDS) | 40 CFR Part 370 |
| Toxic Chemical Release Reporting (Form R) | 40 CFR Part 372 |

**Clean Air Act**

| | |
|---|---|
| National Ambient Air Quality Standards (NAAQS) | 40 CFR Part 50 |
| State Implementation Plan Requirements (SIP; PSD) | 40 CFR Parts 51-52 |

| | |
|---|---|
| Ambient Air Monitoring Reference and Equivalent Methods | 40 CFR Part 53 |
| Citizen Suit Notification | 40 CFR Part 54 |
| Regional Consistency | 40 CFR Part 56 |
| Ambient Air Quality Surveillance | 40 CFR Part 58 |
| Performance Standards dor New Stationary Sources | 40 CFR Part 60 |
| National Emission Standards for Hazardousz Air Pollutants (NESHAPs) | 40 CFR Part 61 |
| Delayed Compliance Orders | 40 CFR Part 65 |
| Noncompliance Penalties | 40 CFR Parts 66-67 |
| Clean Air Act Exemptions | 40 CFR Part 69 |
| | Freedom of Information Act |
| | EPA Procedures 40 CFR Part 2 |

## Environmental Impact Statements, Coastal Zone Management Act, and Endangered Species Act

| | |
|---|---|
| Environmental Impact Statements Council on Environmental Quality Regulations | 40 CFR Parts 1500-1508 |
| Coastal Zone Management Act - NOAA Regulations | 15 CFR Parts 921-933 |
| Joint Agency Endangered Species Regulations | 50 CFR Parts 17,401-453 |

### Safe Drinking Water Act

| | |
|---|---|
| Drinking Water Standards (MCL and MCLG) | 40 CFR Parts 141-143 |
| National Secondary Drinking Water Regulations | 40 CFR Part 143 |
| Underground Injection Control Programs | 40 CFR Parts 144-148 |

### Clean Water Act

| | |
|---|---|
| Discharge of Oil and SPCC Plans | 40 CFR Parts 109-112 |
| State Certification of Activities Requiring a Federal License or Permit | 40 CFR Part 121 |
| NPDES Permit Program | 40 CFR Part 122 |
| State SPDES Permit Program Requirements | 40 CFR Part 123 |
| Permit Decisionmaking Procedures | 40 CFR Part 124 |
| NPDES Criteria and Standards | 40 CFR Part 125 |
| Water Quality Planning and Management | 40 CFR Part 130 |
| Procedures for Improving State Water Quality Standards | 40 CFR Part 131 |
| Secondary Treatment Regulations | 40 CFR Part 133 |
| Test Procedure Guidelines for Pollutant Analysis | 40 CFR Part 136 |
| Lists of Conventional and Toxic Pollutants; pH Limits | 40 CFR Part 401 |
| Pretreatment Regulations | 40 CFR Part 403 |
| Effluent Limitation Guidelines and Performance Standards; Pretreatment Standards | 40 CFR Parts 405-471 |

## Ocean Dumping

Ocean Dumping                                    40 CFR Parts 220-229

## Wetland Regulations

### EPA

Section 401(b) Guidelines                        40 CFR Part 230

Section 404(c) Veto Procedures                   40 CFR Part 231

Section 404 Program Definitions; Exempt
Activities                                       40 CFR Part 232

State 404 Programs                               40 CFR Part 233

### Army Corps of Engineers

General Policies                                 33 CFR Part 320

Dam Permits                                      33 CFR Part 321

Permits for Work Affecting Navigable Waters      33 CFR Part 322

Permits for Discharges of Dredged or
Fill Material                                    33 CFR Part 323

Permits for Ocean Dumping of
Dredged Material                                 33 CFR Part 324

Permit Processing                                33 CFR Part 325

Enforcement, Supervisions and Inspection         33 CFR Part 326

Public Hearings                                  33 CFR Part 327

Definition of Navigable Waters of
the United States                                33 CFR Part 329

Nationwide Permits                               33 CFR Part 330

# Index of Key Words and Phrases

# S